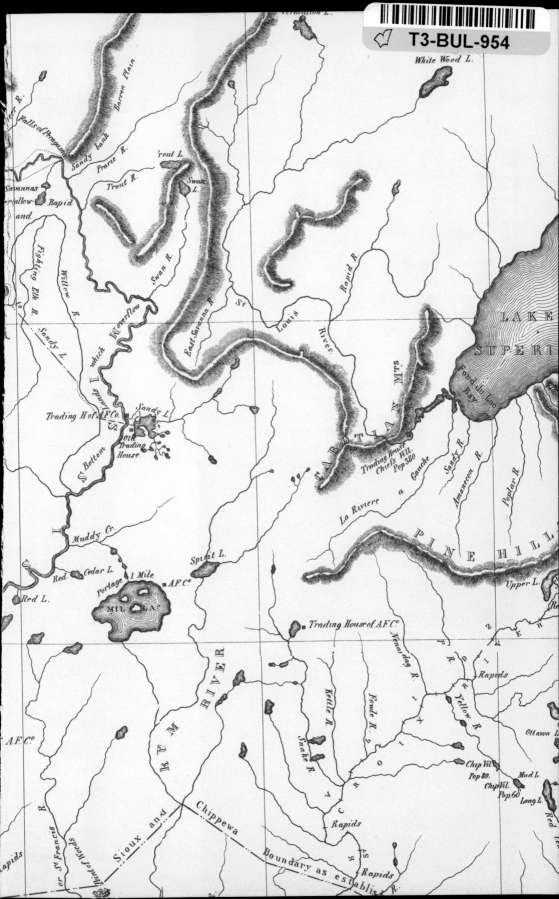

White Wood L.

Vermillion L.

Falls of Pewgamaw

Sandy bank

Barren Plain

Prarie R.

'rout L.

Trout R.

Swan L.

Savannas

allow-

and

Rapid

Fighting Elk R.

Willow R.

Sandy L.

Sandy bank

Swan R.

which Overflow

East Savanna R.

St Louis River

Rapid R.

LAKE SUPERI

Fond du lac Bay

Trading H of A.F.Co.

Sandy L.

Old Trading House

S. Bottom

CABO THAN MTS

Trading House Chiefs Vill. Pop 380

La Riviere a Gauche

Sandy R.

Amanecon R.

Poplar R.

Muddy Cr.

Red Cedar L.

1 Mile

Portage

Spirit L.

A.F.C°

PINE HILL

Upper L.

Red L.

MIL LA.

Trading House of A.F.C°

Nemadeg R.

KUM RIVER

Kettle R.

Fowle R.

Snake R.

Yellow R.

Ottawa L

A.F.C°

Chip Vil. Pop 80.

Mud L.

Chip Vil. Pop 60

Long L.

or St Francis Ry

Lake of Woods

Sioux and Chippewa

Boundary as establis

Rapids

Rapids

Rapids

SCHOOLCRAFT'S EXPEDITION TO LAKE ITASCA

The Discovery of the Source of the Mississippi

SCHOOLCRAFT'S EXPEDITION TO LAKE ITASCA

The Discovery of the Source of the Mississippi

Edited by

PHILIP P. MASON

MICHIGAN STATE UNIVERSITY PRESS

1958

Dedicated
to the memory of the late
MENTOR L. WILLIAMS
out of respect for his work on Henry Rowe Schoolcraft.
Before his untimely death in 1956, Professor Williams
edited *Schoolcraft's Narrative Journal of Travels* and
Schoolcraft's Indian Legends.

PREFACE

HENRY ROWE SCHOOLCRAFT was one of the most remarkable men of the nineteenth century. He won acclaim as a writer, scientist, authority on the North American Indian, and poet. His books on exploration and travel in the Old Northwest were widely read by his contemporaries and gave him an international reputation. In recent years there has been a reawakening of interest in this man and his writings. Consequently all the numerous books he wrote are collectors' items.

Schoolcraft's *Narrative of an Expedition Through the Upper Mississippi to Itasca Lake,* the subject of this edition, was published in 1834 by Harper & Brothers. It was reissued in 1855 as a part of Schoolcraft's *Summary Narrative of an Exploratory Expedition to the Sources of the Mississippi River in 1820: Resumed and completed by the discovery of its Origin in Itasca Lake in 1832.* To the earlier volume, Schoolcraft added an extensive appendix, including many of the official letters and reports relating to the original expedition. Some of these, such as Schoolcraft's "Lectures on the Chippewa Substantive," and his essay, "Vocabulary of Words and Phrases in the Chippewa Language," have little to do with the 1832 expedition. They were obviously added to lengthen his book. His "Remarks on the Lead Mine Country on the Upper Mississippi" were also included. These articles and lists of shells, plants, and minerals observed and collected by the expedition are omitted from the present edition, as well as Schoolcraft's official report of the expedition to Elbert Herring, Director of the Office of Indian Affairs, dated December 3, 1832; this lengthy report is a summary of the *Narrative,* and does not contain enough new information to warrant its publication.

In this edition, the editor has included in the "Appendices" additional correspondence and reports which did not appear in Schoolcraft's edition. Letters written by Dr. Douglass Houghton, the Reverend Mr. William T. Boutwell, and Lieutenant James Allen, describing the journey, are appended to the main text, as are the various newspaper accounts of the expedition. Also included are the daily journals of Allen, Houghton, and Boutwell. Lieutenant Allen's journal was printed by the federal government shortly after the expedition, but the complete diaries of Houghton and Boutwell appear for the first time in this book. It is possible that George Johnston, the interpreter, and other members of the military escort kept diaries, but they have not been discovered. Although the various journals and reports are to some degree repetitious, there is enough different information in each to warrant including them in full.

Whenever possible, the editor has retained the original text, although in some cases the punctuation has been changed slightly and obvious typographical errors have been corrected. One of the problems of editing Schoolcraft's *Narrative* is the frequent misspelling of Indian names. In numerous cases the names are spelled in different ways not only in the same chapter, but even in the same paragraph. When there were differences in the spelling of places in the other diarists' writing, the editor has interposed the generally accepted spelling in brackets. Modern geographical names have been inserted in brackets wherever a reader might fail to identify them.

The map used as end papers in this volume has been adapted from Lt. James Allen's original manuscript map filed in the National Archives.

Notes appear at the end of each of the journals. The diarist's initials are added in brackets to distinguish original footnotes from those of the editor.

Many persons have helped with this book. I am particularly indebted to Dr. F. Clever Bald of the University of Michigan, who offered many suggestions, and who stimulated my original interest in the history of Michigan. I am grateful also to Mr. George Wiskemann of Lansing, who made available to me many of his rare Schoolcraft books; to Mr. R. D. Burroughs and Miss Helen Martin of the Michigan Conservation Department, who gave many helpful suggestions about Dr. Douglass Houghton; to Miss Geneva Kebler and Mrs. Elizabeth Rademacher of the Archives of the Michigan Historical Commission; to Mrs. Esther Loughin of the Michigan Section; and to Mr. Francis X. Scannell, Director of Readers Services of the Michigan State Library.

I take this opportunity to thank Dr. Amy McPherson and Mr. Robert Land of the Manuscripts Division of the Library of Congress; Dr. Oliver Holmes and Mr. Victor Gondas of the National Archives; Mr. Russell Fridley, Director of the Minnesota Historical Society; Mr. Howard Peckham and Mr. William Ewing of the William L. Clements Library of the University of Michigan; Miss Dorothy Martin, curator of manuscripts at the Burton Historical Collection of the Detroit Public Library; and Mrs. Carroll Paul and her able staff of the Marquette County Historical Society.

PHILIP P. MASON

March 24, 1958
DETROIT, MICHIGAN

CONTENTS

EDITOR'S INTRODUCTION

IN A DENSE FOREST in northern Minnesota, nestled in a range of hills known to generations of fur traders as the *hauteurs des terres* or "height of land," lies a placid lake. It is shaped like an inverted letter "V" and made up of two arms, each about eight miles long. A small wooded island, the only one in the lake, lies in the upper part. Several rivulets empty into the lake at the south, and at the opposite shore a small river, several yards wide and about a foot deep, serves as the lake's outlet.

As this river winds its way northwest and then northeast, other streams flow into it; gradually, it increases in size and speed. Finally, its channel veers to the south and before it reaches the Gulf of Mexico it is 2,350 miles in length. This river, of course, is the Mississippi, and the picturesque lake which is its source, Itasca.

From the time the white man first set foot in America, explorers were attracted to this mighty river. Its lower course was discovered by Hernando de Soto in 1541. Over a century later, in 1673, Louis Joliet and Father Jacques Marquette examined the upper Mississippi as far south as the Arkansas River. Robert Cavelier de LaSalle completed the exploration to its mouth in 1682.

No attempt was made to locate the source of the Mississippi until Thomas Jefferson became president in 1801. The famous Virginian had always been interested in the great unchartered West, and even before he was elected chief executive he had encouraged many exploring expeditions to the area. In 1804 he sent William Clark and Meriwether Lewis to explore the Missouri River and to find a route to the Pacific Ocean. The following year he ordered the exploration of the headwaters of the Mississippi River. A young army officer, Lieutenant Zebulon M. Pike, was selected to lead the expedition. Receiving his orders in August, 1805, Pike was to "proceed up the Mississippi with all possible diligence" and "to ascend the main branch to its source." He was directed to record his topographical observations of the explored area, to examine the condition of the Indians, and to select sites for military posts.

It was late in the season for such an expedition, but Pike set out from St. Louis on August 9, 1805, in a seventy-foot keelboat, with twenty soldiers. Unfavorable weather forced the party to abandon their plans to complete the trip before the freezing of the river. After building a winter fort on the west bank of the Mississippi, near what is now Little Falls, Minnesota, Pike waited until the river had frozen sufficiently and then started out by sled with a small detachment. The party reached the Northwest Fur Company's post at Sandy Lake on January 8, 1806, and after a twelve-day rest they set out for the fur post at Leech Lake. The frigid

ix

Minnesota winter failed to discourage Pike and his men, and on the evening of February 1, 1806, they arrived, half-frozen, at Leech Lake. Pike described this body of water as the "main source of the Mississippi." Before returning to Sandy Lake he traveled to Upper Red Cedar Lake, which he claimed was the "upper source" of the river.

The War of 1812 interrupted plans to follow up Pike's discoveries, and it was 1820 before another attempt was made to explore the headwaters of the Mississippi. In that year Lewis Cass, the territorial governor of Michigan, led a thirty-eight man expedition along the southern shore of Lake Superior and into the wilderness of Minnesota and Wisconsin. On July 21, 1820, the party reached Upper Red Cedar Lake, the spot which Pike had reached fourteen years earlier. In honor of their leader, the men agreed to change the lake's name to Cassina, which has since been shortened to Cass.

Some historians have maintained that Cass, like Lieutenant Pike, believed that Upper Red Cedar, or Cass Lake, was the "true source" of the Mississippi. It has also been stated that Henry Rowe Schoolcraft, a member of the expedition, who wrote the semiofficial account of the trip, was obliged to support this claim "out of deference to his chief . . ." Furthermore, the inference is made that Schoolcraft and other members of the party "duped" Cass into thinking that he had made a great discovery.

Although this story of intrigue makes interesting reading, the facts do not support it. The diaries and papers of members of the expedition give indisputable evidence that the men knew that Cass Lake was not the true source. David Bates Douglass, the topographer, noted that the Mississippi emptied into the west side of Cass Lake and "took its rise in a small lake called Lac la Biche . . ." This is supported by James Duane Doty, the official journalist, who wrote that "they did not go to the extreme source of the river, only to red cedar Lake . . ." Furthermore, there is conclusive evidence from Cass's reports that he knew that Cass Lake was not the true source.

The confusion is undoubtedly due to Schoolcraft's contradictory account of the episode. On the one hand, he referred to Upper Red Cedar Lake as the "origin" of the Mississippi, and claimed that he was the only person living to "have visited both the mouth and sources of this celebrated stream." On the other hand, he went on to acknowledge "Lac la Beesh" as the "true source," and explained that the low level of the river forced the party to abandon its search for this lake. Moreover, twelve years later, in the *Narrative* of his 1832 expedition Schoolcraft reported that Cass had let the rest of the party decide whether they should continue to Lac la Biche.

How does one explain these obvious contradictions? Was Schoolcraft unaware of his conflicting statements? Perhaps he made them to justify the title of his book, *Narrative Journal of Travels Through the Northwestern Regions of the United States . . . to the Sources of the Mississippi River . . . in the Year 1820.* Or perhaps he was trying to dramatize what proved to be a relatively uneventful expedition.

Schoolcraft's *Narrative Journal of Travels* was hardly off the press when another explorer arrived in Minnesota to search for the source of the

Mississippi. He was Giacomo Constantino Beltrami, an Italian, who had dreams of making for himself a place in history as a great explorer. Soon after his arrival in the United States in 1823 he hurried via the Ohio and Mississippi rivers to Fort Snelling. There he joined Major Stephen Long, who was leading an exploring party to Canada's Lake Winnipeg area. At Pembina, Beltrami left Major Long and started out on his own to find the source. After a hazardous trip, during which he was deserted by his Chippewa guides and left stranded in unknown country, he landed at a heart-shaped lake located between Red and Cass lakes. Naming it Julia, he announced to the world that the true source of the Mississippi had at last been found. Two volumes, written by this romantic Italian to describe his expedition, failed to convince the American people of the authenticity of his discovery, nor did he succeed in discouraging others from seeking the source.

The honor of discovering the actual source goes to Henry Rowe Schoolcraft, who, from the time he left New York State in 1817 at the age of twenty-four, played an important role in the development of the Old Northwest. Receiving some notice after the publication of his book on a journey to the lead mines of Missouri, Schoolcraft was invited to join the Cass expedition of 1820 as mineralogist. The friendships he made on this trip and the public attention he received for his *Narrative Journal of Travels,* the semiofficial account of the journey, gave great impetus to his career. With the help of Lewis Cass he was appointed in 1822 as Indian agent in charge of the tribes of the Lake Superior region, with headquarters at Sault Ste. Marie.

In 1823 he married Jane Johnston, the charming, well-educated daughter of John Johnston, a prominent fur trader of Sault Ste. Marie. Jane's mother was Ozhaw-Guscoday-Wayquay, or "Woman of the Green Prairie," daughter of the powerful Indian chief, Waub Ojeeg, of Chequamegon Bay. After an education abroad, Jane returned to Sault Ste. Marie to live with her parents and Indian relatives. It was here in 1820 that she met Schoolcraft. Soon thereafter she and her family used their influence with the Indians to avert battle between the Cass party and Chippewa tribesmen. Her knowledge of Indian customs, legends, and the language, as well as the contacts she maintained through her mother's relatives, proved to be of inestimable value to her husband in later years. Without such help it is doubtful that Schoolcraft could have become a recognized authority on the Chippewa Indians.

In addition to his work as Indian agent, Schoolcraft participated actively in the affairs of the Territory of Michigan. He served in the Territorial Legislature from 1828 to 1832, and was a leader in the educational and cultural life of the territory. He helped found the State Historical Society of Michigan in 1828, the Michigan Territorial Library in 1828, and the Algic Research Society in 1832.

A deeply religious man, he actively supported the temperance movement, and as Indian agent vigorously enforced the federal laws prohibiting the sale of liquor to Indians. With the assistance of his wife and her fam-

ily, in 1822, Schoolcraft began to collect data on Indian history and customs, and soon built up an archive of Indian lore. It was this material that
he later used as the source for his volumes on the American Indian, including *Algic Researches,* which inspired Longfellow to write his epic poem,
Hiawatha.

Despite his widespread activities, Schoolcraft was keenly interested in
the exploration of the Northwest Territory. He welcomed opportunities to
visit Indian tribes along Lake Superior and to attend treaty meetings at
Prairie du Chien and Butte des Morts, Wisconsin, in 1825 and 1827, respectively, and at Fond du Lac, Minnesota, in 1826. On these trips he
made careful notes about villages, ceremonies, trails, picture writing, and
other aspects of Indian life. Foremost in his mind, however, was his desire
to search the headwaters of the Mississippi for the source of this river. Not
only would such a discovery give him great prestige as an explorer, but it
would serve as an excellent basis for another travel narrative.

But how could such an expedition be justified? The Indian Agency had
a limited operating budget; and, furthermore, the summer season, the
busiest time for the Sault Ste. Marie Indian Agency, was the only time
during which an extended expedition would be feasible. Finally, in August,
1830, Schoolcraft got the chance he had been awaiting. The War Department directed Governor Cass to request Schoolcraft to proceed into "Chippewa country to endeavor to put an end to the hostilities between the
Chippewas and Sioux."

The conflict between the Sioux and the Chippewa tribes in the Minnesota-Wisconsin area dated back to the seventeenth century when the
Chippewa were driven westward into Sioux country by the Iroquois of the
New York State area. Although no match for the more powerful Iroquois,
the Chippewa, armed with steel knives and the white man's musket, easily
took over the territory of the Sioux, whose culture was still at the Stone Age
level. The struggle continued between the two nations for control of the
rich hunting grounds of Minnesota and Wisconsin. Full-scale battles were
fought at Mille Lacs, Point Prescott, Sandy Lake, Crow Wing River, Elk
River, the Falls of St. Croix, and at numerous other places in the following
two centuries.

Raids of small proportions went on constantly between the two tribes.
Once an Indian had been killed, it was the duty of his family and tribe to
avenge his death by taking the life and scalp of an enemy. Since both the
Sioux and the Chippewa held the same view, the result was frequent and
deadly forays. Furthermore, taking the scalp of an enemy was a means of
gaining prestige in both tribes, and so there was an added incentive to kill
each other. Each tribe blamed the other for the encounters. The Chippewa
asserted that their warfare was one of self-defense, necessary to maintain
their territorial rights. The Sioux, on the other hand, maintained that the
Chippewa were intruders and must be driven out. Although it was evident
to both groups that the constant raids and counterraids were useless, the
traditional enmity between the tribes was so strong that the leaders were
unable to restrain their warriors even if they had wanted to.

At first, the federal government was not concerned about this warfare. The only Americans involved were fur traders, who were safe if they avoided the battle zone between the tribes. However, when settlers began to pour into the Ohio Valley and westward into Wisconsin and Minnesota in the early nineteenth century, government officials became alarmed for their safety. Not only was there a real threat of Indian attack on the settlements, but intertribal conflicts might set the frontier afire.

Both the Sioux and Chippewa signed peace treaties, pledging their recognition of the President of the United States. To protect the settlers and to quell intertribal warfare, the federal government built and manned forts at strategic locations in the West. Important among these were Fort Howard at Green Bay, Fort Crawford at Prairie du Chien, Fort Dearborn at Chicago, and Fort Snelling at the junction of the Mississippi and Minnesota rivers. Special government agents at such forts regulated the fur trade and protected the Indians from ruthless practices of white traders.

In August, 1825, the federal government took further action to end the hostilities between the Sioux and the Chippewa when it called a grand conference at Prairie du Chien, Wisconsin, to establish a boundary line between the tribes. Over a thousand tribal chiefs, representing the Sioux, Chippewa, Potawatomi, Winnebago, Sak and Fox, and Iowa tribes, attended. Major Lawrence Taliaferro, the Indian agent at Fort Snelling, arrived with 385 Sioux and Chippewa from his district, and Schoolcraft came with a flotilla of 150 Chippewa and an escort of sixty soldiers from Sault Ste. Marie. Chippewa chiefs from Fond du Lac, Mille Lacs, Leech Lake, Cass Lake, and Red Lake also attended. The federal government was represented by Lewis Cass of Michigan and William Clark of Missouri, both holding the title of Superintendent of Indian Affairs by virtue of their positions as territorial governors.

After several days of negotiation, accompanied by considerable pomp and ceremony by the Indians, a treaty was drawn up and signed. Involving no cession of land, it merely established a boundary line between the Sioux and Chippewa. The line stretched in a southeasterly direction from the junction of Goose Creek, a North Dakota stream, and Red River, crossing the Mississippi River between present-day St. Cloud and Sauk Rapids and the St. Croix River below Taylor Falls; it continued eastward to the Chippewa River below Eau Claire, Wisconsin, thence eastward to the Black River. Both the Sioux and the Chippewa solemnly promised not to cross the line except on peaceful missions.

In 1826 government officials held another meeting with the northern Chippewa at Fond du Lac, Minnesota, to explain the earlier treaty. Some concessions were made to the Indians in return for their promise that the boundary line would be respected. The following year still another meeting was held at Butte des Morts, Wisconsin, and the boundary line separating the Chippewa, Menominees, and Winnebagos was adjusted.

In spite of the sanguine reports of the American commissioners, these treaties failed to curb hostilities. The boundary was clear on paper, but it was not surveyed nor marked, and it immediately became the cause of controversy. Indian hunting parties came into contact with each other; blood was spilled, and the frontier was afire again. During the summer of 1826 a group of Chippewa on their way to visit the Indian agent at Fort Snelling was ambushed by some Sioux on the eastern shore of the Mississippi almost opposite the fort. "Men, women, and children were indiscriminately butchered," quoted Henry H. Snelling, who viewed the massacre from the walls of the fort.

In May, 1827, another group of Chippewa visited Fort Snelling and, as a precautionary measure, encamped near the walls of the fort. These Indians were promised protection as long as they remained there, but precautions seemed unnecessary after a peaceful visit to the Chippewa camp by a group of Sioux. After dark, however, the Sioux returned and attacked the unsuspecting Chippewa, killing two and wounding many others. Although the murderers were captured by troops from the fort and turned over to the Chippewa for punishment, the incident only served to stir up animosity on both sides.

By 1830 tension between the two tribes had risen to such a point that the Department of War decided action must be taken immediately to stop the useless slaughter. As noted earlier, Schoolcraft was directed to meet the Chippewa chiefs and warn them to stop hostilities. He was further advised to impress upon them that now that the Sioux were free from "pressure in other quarters," they could "direct their combined forces against them." Receiving the directive too late in 1830 to proceed, Schoolcraft and his small party, including Dr. Douglass Houghton as physician and George Johnston as interpreter, set out in June, 1831. Visiting Indian tribes in Michigan, Wisconsin, and northern Illinois, the party returned to Sault Ste. Marie on September 4, 1831, after traveling an estimated 2,300 miles in seventy-two days.

In his report to the Office of Indian Affairs, Schoolcraft showed considerable restraint in evaluating the success of the trip. He asserted that the "spirit of predatory warfare" among the Chippewa had been "checked and allayed" and he stated that his mission had restored peace during the "present fall and ensuing winter and will leave to each party the unrestricted chase of their lands." He called upon the Secretary of War to adjust the boundary line between the Sioux and Chippewa so that both sides would know its exact location. He also recommended that a military post on the Red Cedar River be constructed and that an investigation be made into the detrimental influence of British traders upon the Indians.

When no response to his suggestion was received, Schoolcraft took the initiative, and on February 13, 1832, he wrote to Elbert Herring, chief of the Office of Indian Affairs, and recommended an expedition to visit the Chippewa tribes of the northern Minnesota region. In justification, he called attention to the disastrous effects that the intertribal conflict was having upon the Indians and their village life. Since the expedition into Wisconsin in 1831 had been "efficacious in checking this spirit of predatory warfare, and impressing upon their minds the true character of our government, its benevolent intentions towards them, and its watchfulness, power, and resources," would it not be proper, Schoolcraft argued, to send a "similar mission to the tribes of the Upper Mississippi?" Furthermore, he noted with alarm the undesirable influence of agents of the Hudson's Bay Company over the Indian population. "Merely to visit the Indian and American traders at their posts, will be to encourage and to sustain them." With this letter, he submitted a detailed estimate of expenditures for such a trip. He suggested that an engineer be sent along to make a map of the area visited and proposed that a missionary of the American Board of Foreign Missions go for the purpose of "evangelical observation." Nothing in his letter indicated an intent to explore the Mississippi River to its actual source.

Schoolcraft evidently believed his recommendations would be acted upon favorably, for within two weeks he had invited the Reverend Mr. William T. Boutwell, a Presbyterian missionary, to accompany him on the proposed expedition, and had requested the American Board of Foreign Missions to approve his choice. Furthermore, a letter from Schoolcraft to Lewis Cass on February 24, 1832, makes it clear that Cass, the new Secretary of War under President Andrew Jackson, had already given his approval of the expedition. Thus, Schoolcraft's request to the Indian Office, which was then in the War Department, was simply a formality.

On May 3, 1832, Schoolcraft received official authorization for the expedition from the Office of Indian Affairs. It is interesting to notice how the scope of the expedition was enlarged. The main purpose was, of course, to curb hostilities between the Sioux and Chippewa. "It is no less the dictate of humanity than of policy," the orders stated, "to repress this feeling [of hostility] and to establish permanent peace among these tribes." Schoolcraft was instructed to investigate the condition of the fur trade in the area and to determine whether the laws and regulations governing the trade were adequate. Statistical facts about the Indians were to be compiled showing "the numbers, situations, disposition and prospects . . ." Finally, the Indian agent was directed to vaccinate the Indians for smallpox under an act which had just passed Congress. The orders designated a budget of $3,200 for the expedition. Although this sum was later cut to $2,500 and then to $2,200 by the War Department, Schoolcraft's records show that he was reimbursed for the total sum actually spent on the trip, $3,166.45.

The selection of personnel was Schoolcraft's foremost problem. He offered the position of physician to Dr. Douglass Houghton, who had served as surgeon and naturalist on the expedition of the previous summer. This was a wise choice, for Houghton was competent in the fields of geology, botany, and natural history, as well as medicine; thus, Schoolcraft knew that vaccinating the Indians would not be Houghton's only contribution to the success of the expedition.

This remarkable man, who was later to play a leading role in the development of Michigan and its resources, had first come to Michigan in the fall of 1830 to deliver a series of lectures on chemistry and natural history to the culture-starved people of Detroit. Although he was only twenty-one years old at that time, he was already a professor at the Rensselaer Poly-

technic Institute in New York. His stimulating series of lectures in Detroit
had won him an enviable reputation, and he had been urged to stay on in
the rapidly expanding frontier city. It was there that he had met Schoolcraft, who had come to the then capital city of Michigan to attend the
legislative session. In the spring of 1831 Schoolcraft had invited him to go
on the expedition of that year as surgeon and naturalist, and he had
eagerly accepted. During the trip Houghton found time to take careful
notes on the mineral resources of the area and to collect samples of rocks
and plants. His findings had been sent to eastern scientists, and had received widespread public attention.

Eager to continue his research in natural history of the West, Houghton,
during the summer of 1832, had applied for a position as surgeon and
naturalist for another exploring expedition, to be directed by Lucius Lyon,
a government surveyor. The party was to explore the Mississippi River
below the Falls of St. Anthony and the Missouri River as far as Council
Bluffs. Houghton had altered these plans, however, when he received an
invitation from Schoolcraft in April, 1832. Another opportunity had also
opened for Houghton that spring; a medical practice in Fredonia, New
York. Considering such a practice a "dog's life," he had declined the offer,
accepting that of Schoolcraft, writing, "They can but little realize the pleasure of a mental feast upon the hidden treasures of nature."

Lieutenant James Allen of the Fifth United States Infantry was selected
to direct the ten-man military escort. Although his orders came from the
commandant of Fort Brady at Sault Ste. Marie, it was Schoolcraft who had
recommended him. Allen had been sent to this post after his graduation
from West Point in 1825, and it was there that he had met the Indian
agent. Aware of the officer's ability in map-making, Schoolcraft felt Allen
would be ideal for the job. In addition to map-making for the expedition,
Lieutenant Allen was ordered to keep a daily journal, which was to be
transmitted to the War Department on his return. He was to take note of
the "manners and customs of the various Indian tribes," to observe their
strength in numbers, their attitude toward the United States, and the influence of foreign traders. Also to be covered in his report was a description
of the "nature of the soil, the geology, mineralogy, and natural history"
and availability of "game and fishes." The soldiers who volunteered for the
trip were promised extra pay for fatigue duty.

The fourth "gentleman" member of the expedition was the Reverend
William Thurston Boutwell, who joined the group on the personal invitation of Schoolcraft rather than as a result of an official directive from the
Office of Indian Affairs. Schoolcraft believed with great conviction that the
introduction of Christianity among the Indian tribes of the northern Minnesota region was necessary to improve their "moral and political" position.
"Unless the Indian mind can be purified by gospel truth, and cleansed from
the besetting sin of a belief in magic and from idolatry and spirit worship,"
he stated, "all attempts in the way of agriculture, schooling, and the mechanic arts are liable to miscarry and produce no permanent good." The
trip would give the missionary an opportunity to meet the principal chiefs

of the region and to determine the feasibility of establishing church schools and missions among them.

Boutwell had come to Mackinac Island in August, 1831, after his graduation from the Andover Theological Seminary. With two classmates, Frederick Ayer and Sherman Hall, he had vowed to enter the missionary field among the Chippewa Indians, and the three men had offered their services to the American Board of Foreign Missions, an organization representing the Presbyterian, Congregationalist, and Dutch Reformed denominations. Eager to expand its work in the Lake Superior area, the Board had accepted their applications and had sent them to Mackinac Island. There they were separated. Hall and Ayer had moved on to La Pointe in Chequamegon Bay to establish a mission and church school, and Boutwell had remained to study the Chippewa language and to assist in the Mackinac Island Mission. In the fall of 1831 Boutwell had accepted Schoolcraft's invitation to continue his language study at Sault Ste. Marie, and it was there that the two men had developed their close friendship.

Schoolcraft's obvious choice for the position of Indian interpreter and baggage master was his brother-in-law, George Johnston of Sault Ste. Marie. He had served in this capacity on many other exploring expeditions, including, as already noted, the one led by Schoolcraft in the summer of 1831. A half-Indian, Johnston could speak numerous Indian dialects fluently, as well as French and English. Furthermore, through his long years of experience in the fur trade he had acquired intimate knowledge of the interior.

Born in 1796, the second son of John Johnston, George had been educated at Montreal. Returning to the Sault, he had taken an active part in family business affairs. During the War of 1812 he had fought on the British side, an act which later caused bitter recriminations against him by the Americans. He had met Henry Schoolcraft in 1822, and the following year their friendship had been cemented by his oldest sister's marriage to the Indian agent. On Schoolcraft's recommendation George was offered several government positions. In 1826 he was appointed subagent at La Pointe, and after this agency was abandoned, he was employed in various capacities at Sault Ste. Marie. He often accompanied Schoolcraft on trips and handled many of the Indian agent's private business affairs.

The reader may wonder why Schoolcraft in his *Narrative of an Expedition to Itasca Lake* never identified George Johnston as his wife's younger brother, nor did he indicate that Waub Ojeeg, whom he mentioned frequently in the *Narrative,* was the grandfather of George and Jane Johnston. The answer is not clear. It is possible that Schoolcraft was reluctant to publicize that fact that he was married to a half-breed woman. If this were the reason, his attitude must have later changed, for in his *Personal Memoirs of Residence of Thirty Years with Indian Tribes on the American Frontier,* published in 1851, Schoolcraft wrote at some length and with obvious pride about his relationship to the Johnston family. Perhaps a more logical explanation of his failure to note his relationship to the inter-

preter in his *Narrative* of the 1832 expedition was the attack on Schoolcraft then for staffing his Indian agency with relatives.

In addition to the five "gentlemen" of the expedition, as Schoolcraft
referred to them, and the ten soldiers of the military escort, twenty boatmen or engagés were hired for the trip. Most of them were French, some
were half-breeds, and a few were full-blooded Chippewa Indians. Among
the group were: Charles Macier, Joseph Chevalier, Etienne St. Martin,
Baptiste Nawdewance, Joseph Lerose, Antoine McGulpen, Joseph and
Louis Picquette, John Burns, Kanosh LeBlanc, Louis Lameronde, Michael
Boyer, Joseph LeLonde, and Waubonoquet, familiar names on the roles
of the American Fur Company. The more experienced boatmen received
one dollar per day, and the others twenty dollars a month in addition, of
course, to their daily provisions.

The selection of personnel was only a part of the job of planning for
the expedition. Transportation had to be arranged to carry the thirty-five
man party on a journey of several thousand miles. Schoolcraft purchased
three canoes, ranging in price from fifteen dollars for an Indian canoe to
thirty dollars for the Northwest type, and for thirty-five dollars he hired a
large Mackinaw boat to carry the party from Sault Ste. Marie to Fond du
Lac. Another large Mackinaw boat and several canoes belonging to the
Indian Agency completed the expedition's needs for water travel.

Other items that Schoolcraft purchased were: tents, oil cloths, portage
collars, mess baskets, cooking and eating utensils, and burlap and "Russia"
sheeting for bags. Forty kegs were obtained for the pork and beef, and
canisters, firkins, and other containers for the rest of the provisions. For
the repair of canoes, a large supply of gum, red lead, and paint was secured.

The biggest and most difficult item to estimate was the food supply. Not
only would the party be gone from two to three months, but there would be
constant demands for food by the Indians whom they met and visited. On
the other hand, care had to be taken not to overload with provisions since
they had to be carried over many miles of portages and might unnecessarily delay the party. Of the $600 appropriated for provisions, Schoolcraft
spent $580.89. Included in his purchases were: 25 barrels of flour, 10 bar-
rels of mess pork, 132 pounds of ham, 103 pounds of dry loaf, 50 pounds
of butter, 57 pounds of rice, 25 pounds of crackers, 30 pounds of coffee,
200 pounds of sugar, 87 pounds of mess beef, and 12 pounds of hyson tea.
In addition to these bulky items, Schoolcraft stocked small amounts of
molasses, ginger, preserves, lemon syrup, beans, peas, and corn meal.

Almost as bulky and equally as essential as the provisions were the
presents for the Indians. The tribes had become so accustomed to receiving
gifts from visiting government agents that it is doubtful whether Schoolcraft could have secured audiences for his speeches without them. With
$700 appropriated for this purpose, Schoolcraft bought large quantities of
blankets, colored cloth, mirrors, combs, ribbon, and sewing utensils. Gunpowder, steel, fishhooks, axes, and 350 pounds of sweet-scented Virginia
tobacco, the most important item of all, rounded out the list of presents.

A supply of liquor was one notable omission on the list of provisions.

It was the usual custom on such expeditions to carry a stock of whisky or rum to treat the men after a fatiguing day or on special occasions. It was not uncommon for members of such a party, including the voyageurs or boatmen, to take along a personal supply for their own use. However, at Schoolcraft's order, no liquor except four gallons of wine was taken on the trip. As a strong advocate of temperance, the Indian agent was convinced that the liquor was not essential to the success of such an expedition. Another reflection of his strict religious beliefs was Schoolcraft's decision that the party would not travel on the Sabbath.

On receiving his orders, Schoolcraft wrote to Lewis Cass, "If I do not see the 'veritable source' of the Mississippi, this time, it will not be from a want of the intention." Leaving Sault Ste. Marie on June 7, 1832, the party skirted the southern shore of Lake Superior, and at Fond du Lac, now within the limits of Duluth, Minnesota, made preparations for the long, arduous inland journey ahead. Lac la Biche was the real destination, but all the while the members carried out the purposes for which the expedition had been commissioned.

When the party arrived at Lac la Biche, on July 13, Lieutenant Allen wrote in his journal, "There can be no doubt but that this is the *true source and fountain of the longest and largest branch of the Mississippi*." Houghton factually and unenthusiastically commented, "We arrived at the lake at about one o'clock P.M. and having coasted through it & made some examinations of our sole object, of visiting [the source of the] Mississippi was accomplished and at half after four we commenced descending the outlet of the lake, . . ." No notice whatever is given by Boutwell in his journal that the party arrived at the source of the Mississippi, other than the party raised a flag on the island in the lake. Only Schoolcraft recaptured the dramatic moment of discovery when he wrote, ". . . we followed our guide down the sides of the last elevation, with the expectation of momentarily reaching the goal of our journey. What had been long sought, at last appeared suddenly. On turning out of a thicket, into a small weedy opening, the cheering sight of a transparent body of water burst upon our view. It was Itasca Lake—the source of the Mississippi."

Despite the momentous occasion, Schoolcraft was anxious to return immediately to Cass Lake. He had orders to carry out and did not want to be criticized for an unauthorized excursion, regardless of its historic importance. Within four hours after arriving at Itasca, the party was again on the Mississippi.

One of the curious enigmas of the expedition is the naming of Lake Itasca. For many years it had been known to the fur traders as Lac la Biche or Elk Lake, because of the likeness of its shape to the head of that animal. To the Indians it was "Omushkos"—the Chippewa name for elk. Schoolcraft, not satisfied with these names, renamed it Itasca. The origin of the name was in doubt for many years and has been the source of much controversy.

Schoolcraft did not explain the origin of the name in his *Narrative* of the 1832 expedition. Furthermore, the name does not appear in any other journal: Allen refers to the lake as "Lac la Biche," Houghton, as "Elk Lake," and Boutwell as "Omushkos." Did Schoolcraft neglect to inform his colleagues of the new name he was giving the lake? Above all, Lieutenant Allen should have been told, since he was making a detailed map of the journey; yet his map shows the lake as "La Biche."

The word, "Itasca," unquestionably was taken from the Latin words, "veritas caput." According to Boutwell, during the early part of their trip, Schoolcraft asked him the Latin term for "true source." Boutwell replied, "veritas caput." Schoolcraft took the *last* syllable of "veritas" and the *first* of "caput," making "Itasca." Although Schoolcraft never gave credit to the missionary for his contribution, he did admit publicly that the name had been formed from these Latin words. This account appeared in the issue of August 22, 1832, of the *Galenian* of Galena, Illinois, the *Detroit Journal and Michigan Advertiser* of September 26, 1832, and the *Democratic Free Press and Michigan Intelligencer* of October 25, 1832.

Despite this admission, Schoolcraft later suggested a different origin of the name. In his *Summary Narrative* published in 1855, he wrote: "I enquired of Oza Windib the Indian name of the lake; he replied *Omushkos,* which is the Chippewa for Elk. Having previously got an inkling of some of their mythological and necromantic notions of the origin and mutations of the country, which permitted the use of a female name for it, I denominated it ITASCA." He went further and took the pen of the poet to write:

> Within a beauteous basin, fair outspread
> Hesperian woodlands of the western sky,
> As if, in Indian myths, a truth there could be read,
> And these were tears, indeed, by fair Itasca shed.

What he meant by this explanation is not entirely clear. Mary Eastman, the author—wife of Schoolcraft's friend, Seth Eastman—wrote in 1853 in her *American Aboriginal Portfolio* that Schoolcraft had told her that Itasca was the name of an Indian maiden who was borne to the underworld by an evil spirit. Her tears for her lost lover formed the eternal springs which welled up to form Lake Itasca and the Mississippi River. This poetic story found wide credence.

The question was finally cleared up in 1872 when Boutwell explained the origin of the name in a letter to the St. Paul *Daily Pioneer* of June 16, 1872. This account was later substantiated by Jacob V. Brower, first commissioner of Itasca State Park, who visited Boutwell shortly before the latter's death in 1890.

It is difficult, if not impossible, to explain the inconsistency in Schoolcraft's writings. That he took the name from the Latin words "veritas caput" is well-documented, even by his own admissions. That he later inferred that it was from an Indian legend is also a matter of record. Perhaps he came to believe that the Indian myth was more poetic and altered the historical truth to support it. At any rate, it does indicate that one must read Schoolcraft with caution.

On August 14, 1832, Schoolcraft arrived at the Sault after completing a 2,800-mile journey. He reported no serious injuries or mishaps, except for the incident involving the separation of the military escort. Schoolcraft announced to his superiors that the trip had been a success. Promises from some Chippewa bands to stop hostilities against the Sioux had been secured, and several thousand Indians had been vaccinated against smallpox. Finally, although Schoolcraft did not elaborate on the subject in this report to the Indian Office, the ultimate source of the great Mississippi had been discovered at long last.

With over one hundred and twenty-five years elapsed since this historic expedition, an objective evaluation of the trip can now be made. What were its accomplishments and its failures? What was the value of the information obtained regarding the land, the fur trade, and the Indians and their problems? Which of Schoolcraft's recommendations were acted upon and what immediate effect did the expedition have upon government policy? Finally, what is the historic importance of the trip and of the journals left by the leaders of the expedition?

The official aim of the expedition, of course, was to curb fighting between Chippewa and Sioux bands of the upper Mississippi Valley. The Indian Office did not expect a permanent peace to result, but it hoped that the frequency of the raids and battles might be diminished. That Schoolcraft attempted to accomplish this objective is indisputable. However, he was not deceived by the assurances of the Chippewa chiefs. In his final report to the Director of the Office of Indian Affairs, Schoolcraft warned that the federal government must make "continued efforts" to check the hostility of the Sioux and Chippewa. Moreover, he notified his superiors that serious trouble would begin once the white settlers pushed into the area. "Causes are in silent but active operation," he cautioned, "which will bring the Indians into contact with our frontier settlements and renew . . . the necessity of resorting to arms to quell or pacify them."

Schoolcraft made several specific recommendations to ease the growing tension among the Indian tribes. He urged that the boundary line of the Treaty of 1825 be surveyed and marked so that the Indians would know the limits of their territory. Under no circumstances should the War Department reduce the number of troops on the frontier; in fact, new forts should be built at other strategic points. He proposed further that the introduction of "Christianity, schools and agriculture will do much to meliorate their condition and subdue their animosities." Finally, Schoolcraft recommended that deputations of Indians be sent to Washington to visit government officials and that other exploratory trips into Minnesota should be sponsored by the Office of Indian Affairs.

Many of Schoolcraft's recommendations were acted upon by the federal government. The boundary line was surveyed in 1835, prominent Indian leaders were invited to Washington, additional forts were built, and the War Department encouraged the introduction of missions among the Sioux and Chippewa. Furthermore, subsequent treaties provided for specialists to teach the Indians the art of farming.

Despite the efforts of the War Department and the promises of the Sioux and Chippewa to preserve peace, fighting and bloodshed continued. With a few months after Schoolcraft's expedition, a raiding party of Sandy Lake Chippewa led by Soangikumig swept down upon a sleeping Sioux village and killed or wounded sixty inhabitants. In retaliation, a revenge-thirsty party of one hundred Sioux warriors attacked Chippewa villages at Mille Lacs and on the Snake River. Even the survey of the boundary failed to curb the warfare, for the Indians pulled the stakes as fast as they were driven, and threatened the lives of the government surveyors. Indeed, the battles increased in intensity until the government forcibly removed the Sioux from Minnesota in 1862.

The vaccination of Indians against smallpox was another primary aim of the Schoolcraft expedition, and this effort was particularly successful. Over two thousand Indians were vaccinated, and in practically every case the treatment was received "with cheerfulness and apparent gratitude." In fact, observed Houghton, "When objections were made to vaccination, they were not usually made because the Indian doubted the protective power of the disease, but because he supposed that the remedy must nearly equal the disease which it was intended to counteract." Although he did not have the opportunity to test the results of all of the vaccinations, those cases which were checked were seventy-five percent effective. The surgeon left lancets and vaccine matter with numerous chiefs to follow up his work when it might be needed. The statistical data Houghton gathered on Indians was an important by-product of the trip. A census of each band was taken and information compiled relating to the history of the disease among the Indians. Houghton's final report was a useful monograph on the history of smallpox among the Chippewa, and led to continued government efforts to vaccinate Indians against smallpox.

Few expeditions have surpassed the one of 1832 for the amount of information collected on the social life and customs of the American Indian. Boutwell, Houghton, and Allen, kept daily journals of the trip and made extensive reports to their superiors, in addition to those made by Schoolcraft. Although observations of the men varied according to their experience and personal interests, taken together they give a candid and extremely valuable picture of the life of these Indians in the early nineteenth century. Moreover, many of these reports were made public by the federal government or by Schoolcraft in his famous *Narrative*. As noted in the Preface, the journals of Houghton and Boutwell, however, have never previously been printed in full.

All four journalists left vivid descriptions of the numerous Indian villages which they visited. Schoolcraft kept accurate statistics on the number of families by district and their breakdown by sex and age. Lieutenant Allen was also concerned with vital statistics of the bands, particularly their military strength and attitude of the tribes toward the United States government. Boutwell was mainly interested in the salvation of the Indians and the prospects of introducing missions among them.

The various tribal customs and ceremonies were of particular interest to the members of the expedition. At Cass Lake they witnessed the famous Chippewa "scalp dance," a public ceremony held to celebrate a victory over the Sioux. The use of herbs and other methods of treating the sick were observed, as were Indian burial ceremonies and other tribal customs. Boutwell criticized Indian spirit worship, but his words were mild compared to his expression of disgust with Indian habits of eating, "All get around the kettle, or soup dish, and each uses his finger or the whole hand even . . ." He could endure the sight of naked children, "but to see a squaw lick a kettle cover, both in diameter and circumference" revolted him. What is even more remarkable, in view of his delicate and cultivated tastes, is the fact that he later chose life among these savages to that of the refinements of civilized society.

Another subject of interest to the expedition was the influence of agents of the Hudson's Bay Company in United States territory. American fur traders had complained bitterly about the competition from British agents, particularly after the supplying of "ardent spirits" to Indians by American fur traders was restricted. The Secretary of War directed Schoolcraft and Allen to investigate these complaints. In carrying out these orders, they interrogated clerks of the American Fur Company, and half-breeds and Indians who lived near the border. Although no direct evidence was found to prove that Hudson's Bay Company agents traded on American soil, it was discovered that they had considerable influence. They offered liquor, medals, and other inducements to American Indians who would bring their furs to Canadian posts, and in some cases these agents would furnish Indians with goods to trade with Indians living in the United States.

Schoolcraft was interested also in the conditions of the American fur trade within the limits of his agency and reported his findings to the War Department. He listed, for example, the location of the various interior posts, the number of clerks and traders attached to each, the names of the chief agents, and the dollar value of annual fur export. From these reports on the fur trade which were appended to Schoolcraft's *Narrative of an Expedition to Itasca Lake,* one can get a vivid picture of the declining years of this famous industry.

It was the discovery of the true source of the Mississippi, rather than the storehouse of information on Indian conditions and the fur trade, which captured the popular imagination of the American public and gave Henry Rowe Schoolcraft his place among explorers. Newspapers carried accounts of the exploit and some, like the New York *American* and the *Detroit Journal and Michigan Advertiser,* ran excerpts from the journals of the members of the expedition. In 1834 Harper & Brothers gave the American public the complete account of the expedition in *Narrative of an Expedition Through the Upper Mississippi to Itasca Lake, the Actual Source of This River . . .*

Another important contribution of the Schoolcraft expedition to the geographical knowledge of the West was the detailed map of the Minnesota area made by Lieutenant Allen. In spite of the crude instruments he used, the young officer did a remarkable job of drawing the map with great care. This map greatly increased the information about the vast Minnesota wilderness, and was described as the "first topographical and hydrological delineation of the source of the Mississippi." Allen's notes on the topography, geology, climate, and soil of the area were also of great importance. Descriptions of important landmarks and features, such as the Grand and Knife portages, the Falls of St. Anthony, the Dalles of the St. Croix, and the famous Copper Rock on the Ontonagon River, which he presented in great detail, increased the public knowledge of the unexplored West.

Considerable information on the natural history of the explored area was also made available to the public by Schoolcraft, Allen, and Houghton. The various forms of wild life were described and classified and, as in the case of similar expeditions, samples of shells, minerals, and plants were collected and sent to scientists at eastern universities for further examination. Numerous articles were written about their findings; and a "List of Shells Collected by Mr. Schoolcraft, in the Western and Northwestern Territory," by the country's leading conchologist, William Cooper, appeared in the appendix to Schoolcraft's *Narrative,* as did Schoolcraft's "Localities of Minerals Observed in the Northwest in 1831 and 1832," and Houghton's "Localities of Plants Collected in the Northwestern Expeditions of 1831 and 1832." The hundreds of plants which Houghton collected on the expedition were sent to Professor John Torrey of New York University, the country's leading botanist, who credited the surgeon with several outstanding discoveries.

The copper deposits in the Lake Superior region caught the interest of Houghton, and on the expeditions of 1831 and 1832 he investigated the Keweenaw Peninsula and the Ontonagon region. In fact, in 1831 and on the return leg of the journey from La Pointe in August, 1832, he made special trips up the Ontonagon River to examine the famed Copper Rock. His report on the subject to the Secretary of War, which was printed in the appendix to Schoolcraft's *Narrative,* described in detail the attempts to mine copper in the Ontonagon region and the reasons for failure. Houghton reported on the existence of large formations of copper on the Keweenaw Peninsula, but cautioned that accurate estimates of the amount of such ore "can be determined only by minute and laborious examination." After his appointment as state geologist in 1837 he continued his explorations of the Keweenaw area, and it was his report in 1841 that started the first great mining rush the country ever witnessed, despite his warning that no quick fortunes were to be made.

One of the most lasting contributions of the expedition of 1832 was the naming of various places in Minnesota. Proceeding west from Cass Lake, the following bodies of water still bear the names given by Schoolcraft and his colleagues in 1832: Allen's Bay, Lakes Andrusia, Irving, Marquette, Plantagenette, and most famous of all, Itasca. As noted earlier, the island in the famous lake was called Schoolcraft, and later the east fork of the Mississippi River below Lake Bemidji was referred to as the Schoolcraft or Yellow Head Branch. Many names were given on the return journey from Cass Lake, including Moss and Shiba lakes in what is now Cass County,

and Lake of the Mountain, Lake of the Island, and Johnston and Boutwell
lakes on the Crow River chain. Peace Rock on the Mississippi was also
named by Schoolcraft for its proximity to the boundary line established by
the Treaty of Prairie du Chien. Although some of these names fell into
disuse in the decades which followed, most are still used on maps of
Minnesota.

An important by-product of the expedition was the introduction of
Protestant missions in the interior. Boutwell sent detailed reports to the
American Board of Foreign Missions regarding the great opportunities for
missionary work among the Chippewa and, as a result, the Board increased
its work in the area. With the approval of his superiors, Boutwell remained
at La Pointe to help his friends, Sherman Hall and Frederick Ayer, instead
of returning with Schoolcraft to Sault Ste. Marie. During the summer of
1833 he went to Leech Lake and there established a mission among the
warlike Pillager tribe. He remaided there for four years, working under
extremely adverse conditions, until the Board transferred him to Lake
Pokegama to continue his missionary work. Hall and Ayer soon followed
him into the interior, and the Board sent others to assist in the work.

The Schoolcraft expedition to Lake Itasca did not end the search for
the source of the Mississippi River. On the contrary, explorers, adven-
turers, and others in search of personal fame flocked to the area during
the following decades, some intent on adding to the geographical knowledge of the region, and others hoping to discredit the findings of Schoolcraft.

Four years after Schoolcraft announced the geographical significance of
Lake Itasca, a scientist-astronomer, Joseph Nicollet, studied in detail the
topography of Itasca Basin. With accurate astronomical instruments, he
fixed the latitude, longitude, and height above sea level of the lake. By
careful examination he located five small creeks flowing into Itasca from
the surrounding hills. The largest of these, which he called "truly the
infant Mississippi," he traced to several small lakelets. Nicollet did not
challenge Schoolcraft's earlier claim; in fact, he credited the expedition of
1832 for the significant finding upon which he merely enlarged. An excellent map of the area and his survey report show the valuable contribution
Nicollet made to the geographical knowledge of the Lake Itasca region.

Not until 1881 was the "true source" of the Mississippi challenged. In
that year an ex-captain in the Civil War, Willard Glazier, visited Lake
Itasca to survey the area. Although there less than a day, he found an
inlet on the west arm of the lake which he believed to be the true source
of the Mississippi. The unquestionable fact that the inlet in Schoolcraft's
and Nicollet's day was an actual part of the lake did not sway Glazier's
judgment. He called the inlet Lake Glazier, and publicly announced that
he had at last discovered the actual source of the greatest river in the
United States. Not content with a mere announcement of his discovery,
Glazier published several books supporting his claim, which in content so
closely resembled Schoolcraft's 1832 *Narrative* that charges of plagiarism
were leveled against him. Moreover, he and a number of his friends car-

ried on an impressive publicity campaign in behalf of his alleged discovery.

Many interested individuals doubted Glazier's claim, and a spirited controversy ensued. In 1886 a party sent by a New York publisher to reconnoiter Lake Itasca and its basin corroborated the report of Joseph Nicollet. The Minnesota Historical Society also took an interest in the controversy, and immediately repudiated Glazier's story. The Society's position was supported by Jacob V. Brower, who made exhaustive surveys of the lake area in 1888 and 1889. Brower's report, which was published by the Minnesota Historical Society as Volume VII of its *Collections,* showed conclusively that Nicollet's discovery of the "infant Mississippi" was correct, and that Glazier's claims were not only incorrect but fraudulent.

This controversy had another important result in addition to disproving the findings of Glazier. Brower's report drew public attention to the geographical and historical importance of the Itasca Lake area and firmly established Henry Rowe Schoolcraft as the discoverer of the main source of the Mississippi. In 1891 the state of Minnesota formally recognized the public interest in the much-explored and discussed spot when it established the Itasca Lake State Park for future generations to enjoy.

SCHOOLCRAFT'S
NARRATIVE OF AN EXPEDITION
THROUGH THE UPPER MISSISSIPPI,
TO ITASCA LAKE

TO
Gen. HUGH BRADY,
OF THE UNITED STATES ARMY

SIR:

In prefixing your name to this volume, I am reminded that, while indulging the gratification of personal friendship, I am addressing a soldier, who early entered the field of western warfare under the veteran Wayne; and who, for a period of upwards of forty years, during the changing circumstances of war and of peace, has even been found faithfully, bravely, and honorably serving his country.

With sentiments of respect,
HENRY ROWE SCHOOLCRAFT

CHAPTER I

Introductory observations on the sources of the Mississippi.—Pike's expedition in 1805, for exploring its course, and ascertaining its origin.— The expedition of Gov. Cass, directed to the same objects, in 1820.—Its extent, termination, and results.—Renewed efforts to ascend to its source, by the author, in 1831.—Diverted to the unexplored country lying in the area between Lake Superior and the Upper Mississippi, south of St. Anthony's Falls.—Summary of the route.—The St. Croix and Chippewa Rivers.—Massacre of the Monomonees at Prairie du Chien, in 1831.— Mine country.—Return to the Straits of St. Mary.

AMERICAN GEOGRAPHY may be said to have had three important problems to solve, in modern times. The first and second of these, related to the source of the Missouri, and to the course and termination of the Columbia. Both, were substantially resolved by the expedition of Lewis and Clark, under the administration of Mr. Jefferson. It is to be borne in mind, however, that but one of the three forks, up to which the Missouri was traced, has been explored, that its two northwestern branches have not been ascended, and that, consequently, we do not actually know, which of its primary tributaries is the longest, or brings down the greatest volume of water.

The true source of the Mississippi, which forms the third topic of inquiry, was brought into discussion at the same period. And immediately after the acquisition of Louisiana, the American government sent an officer, with a suitable body of men, to determine it. Lieut. Pike, who was selected for this service (who, nine years afterwards lost his life as a general in the service, at the taking of York) did not, however, set out early enough in the season (1805) to accomplish the object.[1] After the selection and purchase of the site, on which the fort [Snelling] near the Falls of St. Anthony, is now situated, he encountered delays in ascending the rapids characteristic of that part of the Mississippi. Winter overtook him before reaching the junction of the De Corbeau [Crow Wing]. He prepared for its severities by erecting a block house, for the security of his provisions and men.[2] He then proceeded with a small detachment, on snow shoes to Sandy Lake, and Leech Lake; two points of central influence, which were then occupied by the North West Fur Company. As the partners of this company consisted of foreigners, and their operations were continued after the legal transfer of the country to the American government, Lieut. Pike would have been justified in making a seizure of the valuable furs then in their possession. He did not, however, adopt this course, and exhibited a magnanimity in relation to it, which is in ac-

3

cordance with his subsequent acts of disinterested intrepidity. He collected
the geographical data, which are embodied in his published map and
journal, and returned from his wintry station, on the opening of navigation in the spring.

No further effort was made to explore the sources of the Mississippi, for
several years. In 1820, Gov. Cass, then administering the government of
Michigan Territory and exercising jurisdiction over Indian affairs, obtained
the sanction of the general government to visit the region.[3] He left Detroit,
with a party of thirty-eight men, including the gentlemen composing his
suit, during the latter part of May. He was supplied for a journey of four
months. After traversing the coasts of Lake Huron, and visiting Michilimackinac, he proceeded north-west-ward, by ascending the primitive summit at the Falls of St. Mary, went through the extended and picturesque
basin of Lake Superior, and first struck the waters of the Upper Mississippi at Sandy Lake. To this point he was accompanied by the military
escort, and by the train of larger canoes employed to transport stores and
baggage. But the fatigues which the men had undergone in crossing portages, added to the low state of the water, induced him to form a permanent
encampment at this place. And he proceeded with a select party, in canoes
to explore the Mississippi.

It was the middle of July when the expedition reached Sandy Lake, and
the difficulty of subsisting so large a party in so remote a position, with the
constant claims of suffering and hungry tribes, who presented themselves at
every point, began to be severely felt. The exploring party, which was now
organized, went out, under a sense of these circumstances, and with a feeling of the responsibility pressing upon the claims of the expedition in other
quarters, which limited the time applicable to the ascent. They entered the
Mississippi on the 17th of the month, and found a strong current, with alluvial banks, and a vegetation indicative of a fertile soil. For the distance of
about one hundred and fifty miles, above this point, the party found no
diminution in the average strength of the current, which was frequently
accelerated by rapids. The latter then assumed a more formidable aspect
for ten or a dozen miles, at the end of which they were terminated by the
falls of Peckágama [Pokegama]. At this cataract, the river, which below has
its course through alluvial banks, densely wooded, is compressed between
rocks of granulated quartz, over which it rushes with a velocity, which
would seem to threaten destruction to any species of craft that should attempt the descent. It became necessary, at this point, to transport the canoes
and baggage from two to three hundred yards over land.

On reaching the Peckágama summit, the channel of the Mississippi was
found to flow more directly from the west, with a comparatively sluggish
current. But the most distinctive trait of this part of the river was found to
consist of a series of extensive savannahs, through which the river displays
itself in the most elaborate windings. The junction of the Leech Lake
branch takes place at this plateau, at the computed distance of fifty-five
miles above the falls. After passing this point, the course of the river is
again, generally, from the north-west, about forty-five miles to Lake Winni-

pec [Winnibigoshish], a handsome body of clear water, estimated to be ten miles broad. The course of the ascent is then west, for about fifty miles, at which distance the river is found expanded into a more considerable lake, presenting an area of limpid water of, perhaps, 120 square miles. This sheet, which has subsequently been found to be the largest expansion of the Mississippi, is since denominated Cass Lake.[4] It was the highest point reached. The party entered it on the 21st of July. The question of pursuing the stream further, was then submitted by Gov. Cass, to the gentlemen composing his party. Anxious as all were to see the actual source of so celebrated a stream, their wishes were controlled by circumstances. Inconveniences had been felt from leaving the supplies at so considerable a distance below, and as the waters were found to be low, and the preparations inadequate for a journey of indefinite extent, a decisive opinion was expressed in favor of a return from this point. This decision was immediately carried into effect.[5]

From the best information that could be obtained, the Mississippi was represented to have its origin in a lake called *La Biche*,[6] supposed to be sixty miles distant, in a north-west direction. Upon this estimate, the length of the river was computed to be 3038 miles, and by a series of approximate estimates, its altitude placed at 1330 feet above the Atlantic.[7] Numerous rapids and lakes were, however, stated to exist in this remote part of the stream, and a degree of vagueness and uncertainty exhibited in relation to it, which evinced, that the traders, who were relied on for information, either, had seldom frequented it, or preserved an indefinite recollection of its geographical features.

Such was the state of public information on this point in 1820. A veil of obscurity was still cast about the actual source of the Mississippi, which there was no further attempt to remove for ten or eleven years. In 1830, the writer of these sheets was directed to proceed into the Chippewa country, north-west of Lake Superior, in the execution of duties connected with Indian affairs. But the instructions were received so late in the season, that their execution became impracticable until the next year. In the mean time, means for more extensive observation were provided, a physician and botanist engaged, and a small detachment of troops, under the command of a subaltern, ordered to form a part of the expedition.

This expedition numbering twenty-seven persons, exclusive of guides and Indian auxiliaries, employed on the portages, left St. Mary's at the foot of Lake Superior, late in June 1831. After entering, and coursing around the shores of Lake Superior to Lapointe, it was found, from every representation, that the low state of the water on the Upper Mississippi, would render it difficult, if not impracticable, to reach the bands at its sources, during the drought of summer. Public reasons were, at the same time, urgent for visiting the interior bands, located between the groupe of islands at the head of Lake Superior, and the Mississippi—where a useless and harrassing conflict was kept up between the Sioux and Chippewa nations.

The expedition returned eight miles on its track, and entered the mouth

of Mushkigo, or Mauvais [Bad] river of Lake Superior. This stream, which
carries down the waters of an extensive slope of highlands, is embarrassed
with permanent rafts of flood wood, and with numerous rapids, presenting
an arduous ascent. The axe, the canoe-pole, and the carrying-strap were
alternately employed in the ascent, and they were employed under the influence of the midsummer's heat, and the annoyance of the hordes of
smaller insects, who are on the wing, in this secluded valley, during the
greater part of the twenty-four hours. This stream was ascended one hundred and four miles, to the portage. The goods and canoes were then carried
8¾ miles, across highlands, to a lake called Kaginógumoc [Owen], or the
Longwater; and thence by four separate portages, and three intervening
lakes, to the Namakágon river. The latter was descended one hundred and
sixty-one miles, to its junction with the St. Croix, of which it is the right
fork, and the channel of the latter pursued to Yellow River. From this
point, where a public council was convened, the expedition re-ascended the
Namakágon to the portage into *lac Courtoriélle* [Court Oreilles],[8] or
Ottawa Lake. This portage consists of a carrying place of three miles and
a lake, then another carrying place of 750 yards and a lake, from the latter
of which there is a navigable outlet into the Ottawa for canoes.

Ottawa Lake is a sheet of water about twelve miles long, having an outlet into the Chippewa river of the Upper Mississippi. In order, however, to
visit certain hostile bands, a portage was made from this outlet (after following it down about half a day's journey,) of 3½ miles, into lac Chetac,
the principal source of Red Cedar river. The latter was then pursued,
through four principal expansions, called Wigwas, Warpool, Red Cedar
and Rice Lakes, to its falls. A short portage over horizontal sand-rock,
interrupts the navigation, after which there is a series of rapids, extending
about 24 miles. Deep and strong water was then found to its junction with
the Chippewa river, which it enters at the estimated distance of 40 miles
from the confluence of the latter with the Mississippi, (on its eastern bank.)

The entire line of country travelled by this interior route was 643 miles.
The Mushkigo, the St. Croix, and the Chippewa, were the rivers, which by
their common origin and interlocking on the summit lands, afforded this
communication. Many bands of Indians were visited in their fastnesses,
where they had hitherto supposed themselves out of the reach of observation. Councils were held at various points, and presents distributed. And the
pauses afforded by these assemblages, and by the necessary delays of over-
land transportation, furnished opportunities for preserving notes on the
manner of living, among those bands, and their population, traditions and
resources, as well as the geographical features and the natural history of
the country. On entering the Mississippi, the truth of the information, derived on Lake Superior, respecting its depressed state, was verified. Extensive portions of its outer channel and bars were found exposed and dry.
The party encamped on a sand bar formed by the junction of the Chippewa, which is usually several feet under water.

From the mouth of the Chippewa, the expedition descended the Mississippi to Galena, in Illinois. While at Prairie du Chien, the murder of twenty-

six Monomonee men, women, and children, by a war party of the Sacs and Foxes, which had transpired a few days previous, was the subject of exciting interest.[9] It was narrated with all its atrocious circumstances. A flag waved over the common grave of the slain, and several of the wounded Monomonees, who had escaped the massacre, were examined and conversed with. This affray unparalleled for its boldness and turpitude, having occurred in the village of Prairie du Chien, in the hearing of its inhabitants, and in sight of the fort, was made the subject of demand by the government for the surrendry of the murderers, and produced the concentration of troops on that frontier, which eventuated in the Indian War of 1832. Some excitement was also felt at Galena, and its vicinity, in consequence of the menacing attitude which the Sacs and Foxes had recently assumed, in the vicinity of Rock Island, and a general mistrust felt of their sincerity in the treaty concluded with the United States a short time previous.

At Galena, the exploring party separated, part returning in canoes up the Wisconsin, and part crossing the mine country, over the branches of the Pekatolika [Pecatonica], and by the way of the Blue Mounds, to fort Winnebago [at Portage]. From this point, Fox River was descended to Green Bay, and the route of the lake coast pursued northward to the straits, and to the Sault of St. Mary.

A narrative of this expedition, embracing its principal incidents, and observations on the productions of the country, is in preparation for publication by one of the gentlemen of the party.[10] In the mean time, the official report transmitted to Government, and submitted to Congress by the War Department, together with remarks in a series of letters on the mine country, are subjoined in the appendix [A] to this volume.[11]

CHAPTER II

Farther observations on the exploration of the Upper Mississippi, and the discovery of its source.—An expedition authorised by the United States government, in 1832.—Its organization, objects, and route.—Leaves St. Mary, and proceeds through Lake Superior.—Sketch of this lake.— Notice of the murder of Brunet, by an Indian, in 1831.—Mission at La Pointe, or Chegoimegon [Chequamegon].—The importance of this point in Indian history.—Mongozid, Wahbojeeg. Meet Ozawindib, at the Brule.—Route to Sandy Lake, on the Upper Mississippi.—Portages on the St. Louis.—The Savanne portage—Sandy Lake.—Assassination of Mr. Kay.

EARLY IN 1832, the plan of visiting the source of the Mississippi, was resumed. And a memoir for its execution, accompanied by estimates, forwarded to the Department of War, which received the sanction of the Hon. L. Cass, then placed at the head of that department.[12] An expedition was accordingly organized, consisting of thirty persons, including an officer of the army, detached, with ten men, for topographical duty, a surgeon and geologist, an interpreter of the language, and a missionary to the north-western Indians, who was invited to accompany the exploring party. This expedition was based on a renewal of the effort to effect a permanent peace with the two principal Indian nations, who inhabit that region, and whose continued feuds, not only weaken and harrass each other, but embarrass the trade, interrupt the execution of the intercourse laws, and involve the lives and property of the frontier inhabitants. Additional weight was given to these considerations, by the unquiet state of the Indians on the Upper Mississippi, which broke out in open hostility during the year. These reasons were connected with the supervision of the trade, the acquisition of statistical facts, and the carrying into effect an act of Congress of that year, for extending the benefits of vaccination to the Indian tribes. To which end it was enjoined "to proceed to the country on the heads of the Mississippi, and to visit as many Indians in that, and the intermediate region, as circumstances would permit."

This expedition, to the account of which the present volume is devoted, left St. Mary's on the 7th of June, 1832. As the route through Lake Superior, and thence north-west, on the waters of the Upper Mississippi, to Cass Lake, has been described in a "Narrative Journal of Travels in the Northwest," of 1820,[13] heretofore published by the author, no details of the geography of the country then passed over and described, or of the ordinary incidents of a journey through this portion of the country, will be given. A brief sketch, however, of the general route, will serve to refresh the memory

8

of readers whose attention has been before called to the subject, and cannot but prove acceptable to all, who feel an interest in the development of its natural features and character.

The village of the Sault of St. Mary's is situated on the communication which connects Lake Huron with Lake Superior, fifteen miles below the foot of the latter. A strong and continued rapid, over shelving sand rock, interrupts the navigation for vessels. The water has been computed to sink its level, twenty-two feet ten inches, at this place. A portage exceeding half a mile, enables boats to proceed beyond. The river above has a brisk current, which is imperceptibly lost on entering between the two prominent capes, which form the opening into Lake Superior.

This lake, which is called Igomi, Chigomi, and Gitchigomi, by the Indians, as the term is more or less abbreviated, is remarkable for its extent, its depth, and the purity of its waters. It lies in a bason of trap rocks, with alternations of the granite and sand stone series. No variety of calcareous rock is present, and its waters are consequently free from impregnations from this source. As it is the largest and the purest of the series of lakes it is also the highest in position; its altitude being computed at 640 [602] feet above the Atlantic. Its banks are diversified with mural precipices, with extensive deposits of marine sand, and with beds of mixed detritus. Its immedate margin is loaded with primitive boulders and pebble-stones, alternating with shores of yellow and of iron sand. Several bold mountains of primitive construction stand near the central parts of its south shores, which are in striking contrast with the ruin-like, walled masses, of horizontal structure, which characterize other parts. Among the detritus of its shores are still occasionally found masses of native copper, which are now referred to the trap formation.

Of a body of water so irregular in its shape and imperfectly defined, it may be vague to speak of its superficial area, but this may be assumed to cover 30,000 square miles. It embraces numerous islands, the largest of which are Grand, Royal, and Magdalen [Madeline] islands. It has several noble harbors, bays and inlets, and receives numerous rivers. It abounds with fish, the most noted of which are white-fish, sturgeon, and salmon-trout. But by far the most valuable product of its present commerce, is its furs and peltries. The Indian population of its immediate shores is not great. Exclusive of bands located on the heads of its rivers, it does not exceed 1006 souls, to which may be added 436 for the American side of the St. Mary's river. Their trade is conducted by 15 clerks, licensed by the Indian department, employing 70 boatmen, interpreters and runners. Recently a mission has been established on Magdalen Island (*La Pointe* of the traders,) by the American Board of Foreign Missions, and the gospel began to be preached to the natives.[14] The estimated population which, in a comprehensive view, should be added for the south shores, extending to the borders of the Winnebago and Monomonee lands, and running west, to the Sioux line,[15] is, for the northern curve of Green Bay, 210; heads of the Monomonee and Wisconsin rivers, 342; the Chippewa river and its tributaries, 1376; the St. Croix and its tributaries, 895; Grand Portage, and Rainy

Lake, 476; to which latter may perhaps be added, 249, making, with the former estimates, 5000 souls.

In travelling through this lake, in boats or canoes, the shores are followed round. The distance from Point Iroquois to the entrance of the St. Louis river of Fond du Lac is estimated at 490 miles, exclusive of the journey around the peninsula of Keweena, which is ninety miles more. The general course is nearly due west, in consequence of which, the climate is deemed to be decidedly more favorable to agriculture at its head than at its outlet. Traders, who course round the peninsula in boats, take, on an average, twenty-six days in the voyage. Fifteen were employed on the present expedition. Indians were met at various points, and wherever it was practicable, they were vaccinated. The surgeon employed on that service reported 699 vaccinations on the voyage through the lake, and experienced no difficulty in getting them to submit to the process.

At the mouth of the Ontonagon, where the party arrived on the 19th of June, a band of Indians was encamped on its way out, from Ottawa lake. Mozojeed, their chief, confirmed a report of the murder of an *engagé*, or under clerk, named Brunet, by a Chippewa, named Waba Annimikee, or the White Thunder. He said that he had concurred with the traders in apprehending the Indian, and bringing him out to be delivered up to the Indian agent. But that he had effected his escape on the Mauvais Portage. He promised to exert himself to re-apprehend him, the following year. And he rigidly performed his promise. In July, 1833, the White Thunder was delivered by Mozojeed and his followers, to the civil authorities. He was tried for the murder at the U. S. circuit court holden at Michilimackinac, in that month. Counsel being assigned to defend him, every advantage was secured to him that the laws provide. His own confessions were proved, to substantiate the murder, and on these he was convicted.

He made no defence whatever on the trial, silently submitting to the determinations of his counsel. When judgment had been pronounced, he arose, and, through an interpreter, stated to the judge the reasons which had actuated him. He observed, that after aiding Brunet, on a certain occasion, in carrying his goods to the banks of a river, he had taken a canoe bound there, (being his *own* canoe) to cross the stream. For this Brunet threatened him, and *shook a tomahawk over his head*. On another occasion, having sold Brunet a shaved deer-skin, he asked him (as is customary after getting payment) for tobacco; but he replied abusively, that he did not give tobacco to *such scaly dogs*. Not long afterwards, being engaged in playing at the Indian game of bowl, Brunet took him by the hair, *on the crown of his head,* and shook him. Finally, on the morning of the day of the murder, Brunet had struck him on the chin, with violence. This, together with the other indignities, took place in the presence of the Indians, in whose eyes he was, consequently, disgraced. In the afternoon of that day, Brunet went back from the lake on which they were encamped, into the forest to procure some birch bark for making flambeaux for fishing. The White Thunder secretly followed him. He observed him tie up a roll of bark, put it across his shoulders, and commence his return. He soon crossed a log which lay in his path. The Indian quickly followed him, mounting the same log, and, from this elevation, raised his gun and deliberately shot him in the back. He fell dead.

At *La Pointe,* the party were introduced to Mr. and Mrs. Hall, missionaries, who, with Mr. Ayer, had proceeded to this place, in 1831, to establish a mission among the Chippewas.[16] Mrs. Hall had presented to her husband a daughter during their residence, which is believed to be the first child of white parents, both by father and mother, ever born within the precincts of this lake. The mission had encountered no unforeseen obstacles in its first efforts. It has since been enlarged in its means and the number of its laborers, and promises to exert a happy influence in the region.[17]

It is interesting to observe the dawning of the gospel at a spot, which has been long noted as the scene of Indian trade, and the rallying point of Indian war parties. It is at this place, the Chegoimegon of early writers, that tradition places the ancient council fire of the Chippewa nation. And here resided the presiding chief, called Mudjikiwis, or Waishki, who exercised the sovereign power over a rude confederation of local tribes, whose dissolution, or separation into independent fragments, may be traced to the right of each chieftain of declaring a negative to any decision, and silently withdrawing his aid, for the time being. Personal influence and authority may be supposed to have counteracted this defect, while the tribe was small, as tradition represents it to have been when it first migrated from *the east,* to this lake; but its increase and spread over the adjacent country, would naturally destroy so feeble a tie of political power, and must soon have left each local band as it now remains, independent and sovereign in its acts. Yet the voice of tradition refers to this era of the reign of the Mudjikiwis as one of comparative splendor. Although republican in all that is left of their institutions, the succession of the Mudjikiwis is said to have been hereditary among the Chippewas, and the descendants of this magistrate, who yet exist at Chegoimegon, evince a pride of ancestry which we should only look for, among feudal or despotic nations. The last person who may be said to have exercised this office was Mongozid, (or Mamongazida,) who was in high favor with the French. He is represented to have visited Quebec in the time of Montcalm, and to have been an actor in the final battle in which that distinguished commander fell. His son Wahbojeeg, or the White Fisher, succeeded him as the ruling chieftain of the band, and eminently distinguished himself as a war leader. He died in 1793, after having been greatly instrumental in driving his cousins-german, the Foxes, from the Chippewa country. The present chieftain, Chi Waishki, alias Pizhickee, or the Buffalo, is the representative of this line. He said to the Indian Agent, who, by direction of the commissioners at the treaty of Fond du Lac, in 1826, invested him with a silver medal, "What need I of this! It is known whence I am descended."[18]

But there is no space for these reminiscences. Many scattered parties of Chippewas were encountered east of this point, interspersed with the loaded boats of the traders, bringing out their annual returns. Some of the parties were bound to the British post of Penetanguishine [on Georgian Bay, Ontario], others, to St. Mary's or Michilimackinac. Chi Waishki, the chief above alluded to, was met at Keweena, on his way to visit the Agency. He expressed his regret that the agent would not be there, evinced a strong interest in the object of the expedition, and presented a peace-pipe, as the evidence of his friendship. At the mouth of the river Brule, a small party of the Chippewas was encountered, from the sources of the Mississippi. It turned out to be the family of Ozawindib, one of the principal Chippewas, from Cass Lake. He was persuaded to return, and proved himself to be a trusty and experienced guide through the most remote and difficult parts of the route.

The expedition entered the mouth of the St. Louis river on the 23d of June. The ascent of this stream is attended with separate portages of nine, and of three miles.[19] There is, finally, a portage of six miles across a sandy tract, which separates the Lake Superior from the Mississippi waters, making 18 miles of land carriage. The other portions of the route consist of rapid water, much of which is shallow and interspersed with sharp rocks, requiring both strength and dexterity in the men to manage the canoes, and to repair them when injured. A part of the summit portage, immediately after quitting the Savanne river, consists of bog, the sod of which being cut through, it becomes necessary to wade in a pathway of mud and water, portions of which, are mid-thigh deep. The entire distance from Lake Superior to the Mississippi, estimating from water to water, is 150 miles. The expedition spent about ten days on this part of the route, and reached the trading house of Mr. [William] Aitkin, on the banks of the Mississippi, on the 3rd of July.[20] It remained there, until the evening of the 4th, giving Lieut. Allen, who was in command of the troops, an opportunity to fire a salute in honor of the day, to the no small gratification of the Indians, who, being apprized of the occasion, thronged the banks of the river to witness the ceremony.

Sandy Lake has been a post of importance in the fur trade from the earliest French times, being one of the central seats of Indian power on the Upper Mississippi. An assassination occurred here in 1785, which affords a striking illustration of the evils of using ardent spirits in the Indian country. Mr. Kay, the victim of Indian resentment on this occasion, was a gentleman of Montreal, who had come out with an adventure of Indian goods, into this region. After passing the winter on the waters of the Mississippi, he awaited the assembling of his clerks at this place, and employed himself in closing the spring business with the Indians, preparatory to his return to Michilimackinac. On the 2nd of May, he was informed of the near arrival of one of his clerks, and prepared to go and meet him. The sequel is given in a translation of the words of an eye witness, whose manuscript account is before the author.[21]

"Mr. Kay said that he would himself go, although somewhat fatigued by the continual running of the Indians, the night previous. On parting he told me to draw some rum, of which he took a stout drink. And as he knew there was no rum at the post of Pine River, when he left Mr. Harris, he thought a dram would be pleasing to him also; for which reason he told me to fill one of the flagons of his liquor case, to take with him. And he gave me orders to give the Indians no drink during his absence, which was difficult, because they were already tipsey.

"The Indians had given me the name of The Writer, which they are accustomed to do to all whom they observe writing. As soon as Mr. Kay had gone, I did not want for visits, his *savagesse* remaining in the tent with me. A great many Indians came in; among the number was Katawabida and Mongozid, who said to me, "Writer, give us rum!" I told them that I could not—that I was not master. They tormented me a long time. Mongozid threw to me a pair of *metasses,* which he had got on credit, and had not paid for, (for he was a poor paymaster,) demanding rum for them. I told him, no! He then talked with Mr. Kay's woman, who was tired of them, as well as myself. She begged me to give them a little, after which they went out of the tent.

"Within an hour after *Le Barrique Eau* arrived, and told me that Mr. Harris and Mr. Pinot had actually arrived at the fish-dam. The Indians, one and all, set up a shout of joy, and ran to the beach to receive them. They did not however, meet with a very good reception, the flagon Mr. Kay had taken with him having intoxicated the whole party. They debarked, and while Mr. Harris was getting his tent pitched, Mr. Kay entered mine and took a glass in my presence. Mr. Harris was quite noisy. To complete the scene, the ferocity of *Cul Blanc* [22] (an Indian unfriendly to Mr. K.) had returned. He had persuaded *Le Cousin* to stab Mr. Kay, in the course of the winter, saying to him, that he had not courage enough himself to do it. The other gloried in being equal to the commission of a crime, which he had promised to perpetrate when they came together.

"The Cul Blanc was sitting, with many others, on a hillock, before the fire, smoking, directly before Mr. Kay's tent. Le Cousin got up and went towards the tent, at the entrance of which he met Mr. Kay. Mr. Kay's bed was placed across, opposite the pole supporting the tail-piece of his tent. The barrel of rum was behind the bed, in the bottom of the tent. Mr. Kay saw him coming, as he was going to take a seat beside me on the bed. At this moment Le Cousin entered. He tendered his hand, and asked for rum. Mr. Kay, who did not like the man, answered, "No! You do not pay your credits! You shall have none! Go out, immediately!" With this, he took him by the arm, and conducted him out of the tent. On turning round to re-enter, the Indian, who was armed with a knife, which he had concealed under a *mantelet de calmande,* gave him a stab in the back of the neck. He then retired towards the camp fire, which was surrounded by a great many Indians and our men. I got up immediately, hearing the scream of his wife, whom I perceived in front of me. "Have you been stabbed?" I inquired of Mr. Kay. "Yes!" he replied, "but he shall pay for it." So saying he put his hand in the mess-basket and drew out a large, pointed table knife, with which he sallied furiously from the tent, without my being able to stop him. The Indians seeing the knife in his hand, asked the cause of it. He said that Le Cousin had stabbed him, and that he was in search of him to kill him.

But Le Cousin had taken refuge in his own lodge which was near our camp. Mr. Kay went towards the lodge. We ran after him to prevent some fatal accident. The tumult was, by this time, very great. Great numbers were collected from all sides, and all, both French and Indians, bereft of their reason, for it was in the midst of a general carouse. In a moment, every one seized his arms, and there was a motley display of knives, guns, axes, cudgels, war-clubs, lances, &c. I found myself greatly at a non-plus, for I had not before witnessed such a scene. I saw so many preparations that I judged we should have a serious time.

"Mr. Kay pursued Le Cousin, but before he could reach him, the passage to his lodge was blocked up by the crowd. Le Cousin's mother asked him what he wanted. "Englishman!" said she, "do you come to kill me?" She made her way among the crowd, armed with a small knife, and reached the spot where Mr. Kay was standing, without any one's observing the knife, for she came in an humble attitude imploring Mr. Kay for the life of her son. In a moment, Mr. Kay cried out, in a loud voice, "I am killed," and he fell. We entered, and found that she had struck him in the side, making an incision of more than three inches. We now took him to his tent, bathed in his blood. We laid him on his bed, which in a moment, was soaking with his blood.

"At this moment his friend *Le Petit Mort,* (Jeebyains) who had been tipsey and gone to sleep, started up. He ran to Mr. Kay's tent, where the first object he saw, was his friend pale and quivering. He went and embraced him amidst a flood of tears, saying, "My friend, you are dead, but I survive to revenge you." In contemplating a calico nightgown which Mr. Kay had on when he was wounded, and which was all bloody, he could no longer restrain his anger. He took up the knife which Mr. Kay had, at the time he was wounded, and which had been brought back by his wife, who was present. He sallied out of the tent to seek revenge, not of Le Cousin,— who was the instrument, but not the author of the murder—but of Cul Blanc, who was sitting before the fire, smoking his pipe. He seized him by the scalp-lock, drew his body back with one hand, exclaiming, "Die, thou dog!" with the other hand, he plunged a knife into his breast, Cul Blanc begging all the while for mercy.

"This scene of carnage put a stop to the drinking. The women spilled out all the rum, of which there was still no small quantity in the different lodges. The stab Cul Blanc had received did not prove mortal, notwithstanding the ghastliness of the wound, the knife having passed out through the flesh without penetrating any vital part. But the blood issued copiously and disfigured his wife, who carried him off, trailing his blood through the camp.

"This tragedy being finished, Le Petit Mort re-entered the tent. He told his wife, who followed him, to go and search for certain roots, which he chewed and formed into a cataplasm for the wound, after having applied his mouth to it, and sucked out the extravasated blood, an operation that caused Mr. Kay great pain. He enjoyed a little ease during the remainder of the night and following day. Le Petit Mort passed the night opposite to his bed. The next day he took off the compress, and replaced it by another, after having once more sucked out the blood and cleaned the wound. The patient became so exhausted by this dressing, that for the space of half an hour he lost all recollection. When he regained his senses he felt easier, and asked for the Bras Casse, (the chief of the band,) who had not yet heard what had happened, for the Indians had been occupied in drinking, and he had been getting ready to depart, having only delayed a little, to give some game to the Frenchmen. He came to the field of these atrocities, entered Mr. Kay's tent, and gave him his hand, saying, "My friend, your misfortune has given me much pain. If I had been here, it would not have taken place. One thing, however, consoles me. It is, that I had not gone off; you may depend on my best efforts to restore you." Mr. Kay accepted his offer, having confidence in him, and in his skill in the medical art, in which he was very expert. He resolved to take him along with him on his route to Mackinac, to take care of him.

"On the third of May, the Bras Casse took him in hand, and began to apply his medicines, which were found to be efficacious. After letting him repose a little, he told him he would cure him, but in order to do this he must consent to bridle his appetites. He must abstain from the use of pepper and salt in his food; he must guard against drinking, *de ne point toucher des femmes*. The next day Mr. Kay was a little better. He sent for M. Harris and myself to come to his tent, to receive his orders. He said to us: "Gentlemen, you see my situation. I do not know whether God will spare my life or not. I have determined to leave you, and at all hazards to set out for Mackinac with seven men, accompanied by the Bras Casse and his wife, to take care of me on the road. Assort the remainder of the goods, and ascend to Leech Lake, and wait there for the return of the Pillagers, who are out on the prairies. In short, complete the inland trade. Mr. Pinot is too feeble an opponent to do you much injury. I confide in the capacity of you both." A few moments afterwards Mr. Harris went out, when he said to me particularly, taking hold of my hands—"My dear friend, you understand the language of the Chippewas. Mr. Harris would go with me, but he must accompany you. He is a good trader, but he has, like myself and others, a strong passion for drinking, which takes away his judgment. On these occasions, advise him. I will myself speak to him before my departure. Prepare every thing to facilitate our passage over the portages and along the lake. I shall set out to-morrow. I find myself better every day."

"I left him with his physician, and went to distribute the provisions and and lading for two inland canoes, one for Mr. Kay, and one for the four men who were to take the furs from Pine river, consisting of 19 packs of 80 lbs. each, and four packs of deer skins, to serve as seats for Mr. Kay's men. The next day Mr. Kay was a little better, which diffused pleasure among us all. I constructed a litter *(un broncard)* for two men to carry him over the portages, and he set out the same day, being the 5th of May, about two o'clock, in the afternoon. Mr. Pinot also departed the same day. Bras Casse and his wife departed about sun set."

The sequel of this tale is briefly told. Mr. Kay reached Mackinac, where

Capt. [Daniel] Robinson [Robertson], then in command, had a second operation performed on him by the post surgeon. He afterwards closed his business, and went to Montreal. A supuration of his wound, however, took place at the Lake of Two Mountains, which terminated his life on the 26th of August, 1785, three months and twenty-four days after receiving the wound.

CHAPTER III

General arrangements for the route of the expedition on the waters of the Upper Mississippi.—The width of this stream at Sandy Lake ascertained.—Notices of the ascent from that point by the Falls of Peckagama and Lake Winnipec, to Cass Lake.—Attack of a party of Mandans on the Chippewas at Pembina.—The route of the Bogottowa Lake.—Encamped at Winnipec House.—Inquiries respecting the opposition trade, and the traffic in ardent spirits.—Reach Cass Lake.—The width of the Mississippi, at its outlet.—Encamped on an island in this lake.—Yellow Head's town; its population and hunting grounds.—Remarks on the Fur Trade.—North West, Hudson's Bay, and American Fur Companies.—Lord Selkirk's triumph.—Murder of Owen Keveny.

AT SANDY LAKE the expedition made its general arrangements for the route. Most of the Indians at that post being absent, with their principal Chief [Grosse Gueule or Big Mouth], on the plains near the junction of the Des Corbeau, it was determined to assemble them at that point, so as to meet the expedition on its return down the Mississippi, and to deposit at Sandy Lake House, the presents intended for distribution to this band, together with the supplies required for the home route. These were placed in charge of a trusty person, with directions to proceed down the river with them, to the Isle Des Corbeau, in season to meet the party at that place on the 24th July. Relieved of this portion of the burthen of transportation, it was then settled that the expedition should go up the Mississippi, through all its windings, to Cass Lake; there make a final deposit of the remainder of its heavy baggage, and fit out a select exploring party, in light canoes, to ascend to its actual source. This point fixed, the party would again descend to Cass Lake, thence, across the interior, by a route, represented to be practicable, to Leech Lake, and from the latter, strike southwestwardly, falling on a series of portages and lakes leading to the head of the great Des Corbeau, or Crow Wing River. This river it was proposed to follow down its entire length, to its entrance into the Mississippi, the point fixed on, for assembling the Sandy Lake, Pine River, and Mille Lac Indians.

In conformity with these arrangements, the party left Sandy Lake House, on the afternoon of the 4th of July, having previously ascertained the width of the Mississippi, at that place, to be 331 feet. The evening of this day and the two following days, were employed in reaching the vicinity of the Peckagama Falls,[23] against a brisk current, with occasional rapids. They made a portage on the 7th over the Granular Quartz ridge, producing the Falls, and encamped the same evening at Point aux Chenes,[24] in the savannahs above. The next day, being the Sabbath, was passed at that point. While

17

there, a French *engagé* arrived from Leech Lake, being on his way to Sandy Lake. Advantage was taken of this opportunity, to send directions for the hastening the meeting of the Indians at *Isle Des Corbeau* [Crow Island], by the space of two days, as the waters were found even more favorable, than had been anticipated.

This man, whose name was La Plante, confirmed reports which had been current at Fond du Lac and at Sandy Lake, of the going out of a strong war party of the Leech Lake Indians against the Sioux. But he added, that the party, which had been headed by the popular Chief, Aishkibugikozh, or the Geulle [Gueule] Platte [Plat],[25] had returned, bringing, as a trophy of their victory, three Sioux scalps. He also reported the attack of a hostile party of Indians, supposed to be Sioux, on the outskirts of the Pembina [North Dakota] settlement, where they scalped a girl, in open day, but were pursued by a party of Chippewas, overtaken in the act of crossing a stream, and lost several men. It was found, by subsequent information, of an authentic character, that the attacking party, on this occasion, were Mandans, and that it consisted of forty men. They crossed the river Pembina, at the point of its junction with Red River, on a raft, went down the latter about four miles, and concealed themselves in the vicinity of a trading house, at which there were several lodges of Chippewas. After waiting a definite time, and finding no opportunity to effect their purpose, they resolved to return to the raft at the crossing of the river, leaving a select party to make a sally upon the Chippewas. This party met the girl, tore off her scalp in haste, and fled to rejoin their companions at the raft. But as the girl was not killed, the alarm was immediately given. Nine Chippewas started in the pursuit. They overtook and fired upon the Mandans, killing one man, and driving them into their main party. The latter, in the mean time, had tied their guns together and laid them on the raft, preparatory to crossing. Being suddenly roused by the warwhoop, in their midst, and without arms, they plunged into the Pembina, and swam across. During this effort, they were fired upon by their pursuers, who killed two more of their number. One of these succeeded in gaining the opposite bank, and was carried a short distance by his companions before he expired. His body was left. The remainder of the party pursued their flight. But they were without the means of subsistence, for they had lost their arms. A new calamity overtook them. The Sioux (who were also their enemies, as well as the enemies of the Chippewas,) fell upon them, and, in their defenceless state, killed thirty-six men. The survivor reached his people on the Missouri to narrate the disaster.

The expedition pursued its way on the 9th. The ascent of this part of the river, being through a series of savannahs, the guides availed themselves of an intimate knowledge of the country, and the high state of the water, to avoid numerous curves, which would have consumed much time in coursing around, and led the way through extensive fields of reeds and grass, assuming the character of semi-lakes. Not far above Oak Point, a side route was taken, through a lake called the Bogottowa, or *Lac a le Crosse* [Ball Club Lake[26]]. This lake, which is a clear and pleasant sheet of water of some ten miles in extent, receives a small but narrow creek at its head, noted for its helices, which is ascended to a small lake terminating a few hundred yards east of the Little Winnipec Lake [Winnibigoshish] of the Mississippi. The portage is through a fine forest. By taking this route the circuitous south bend of the Mississippi, at the entrance of the Leech Lake branch, was avoided, and the better part of a day's travel saved. Day light was still undiminished, when the party reached the minor trading post of Winnipec House,[27] where they encamped.

The following queries were put to the Clerk[28] in charge of this post, respecting the opposition trade, and the traffic in ardent spirits.[29]

1st. Do the Hudson's Bay Clerks cross the American lines from the post of Rainy Lake, for the purposes of trade? Ans. No. They furnish goods to Indians who go trading into the American Territories.

2d. Do the Partners, or Clerks of the Hudson's Bay Company, present flags and medals to Indians? Ans. Yes.

3d. Do they give such flags and medals to Indians living within the American lines? Ans. No. I have heard that they took away an American flag given to an Indian on the United States' borders of Rainy Lake, tore it, and burnt it, and gave him a British flag instead.

4th. Was the Hudson's Bay Company's post on Rainy Lake, supplied with ardent spirits last season? (i. e. 1831 and 1832.) Ans. It was. They had about sixty kegs of highwines, which were shewn to some of our Indians, who went there, and Mr. Cameron, the person in charge of the post, said to them, that although their streams were high, from the melting of the snows, they should swim as high with liquor if the Indians required it.

5th. What is the usual strength of the highwines? Ans. One keg is reduced to four.

6th. Have the Indians sent on *derwin* by the Hudson's Bay Company, approached near to your post? Ans. They have come very near—having been on the Turtle Portage, with goods.

7th. Did they bring liquor thus far? Ans. No. The liquor is kept at Rainy Lake, to induce the Indians to visit that place with their furs.

8th. Did the disposition made of the liquor, which the Secretary of War permitted the principal Factor of the Fond du Lac Department, to take in last year, (1831,) embrace the post of Winnipec? Ans. It did not. It was kept chiefly at Rainy Lake, and on the lines, to be used in the opposition trade.

Another trader, inquired of, in the country below, observed that five Chiefs had been invested with medals and flags, by the British trader at *Lac le Pluie* [Rainy Lake].

The party traversed Lake Winnipec on the morning of the 10th, and entered and passed up the sand-hill bordered valley of the Mississippi, to Cass Lake, the entrance to which they reached about one o'clock, being eleven days earlier in the season than this lake had been visited by the light canoes of Gov. Cass, twelve years previous. The outlet of this lake, was ascertained to be 172 feet in width, with an estimated depth of eight feet;

being over half the width of the river, immediately *below* the inlet of the Sandy Lake branch.

At this point, being the *ultima Thule* of previous discovery, our narrative may assume a more personal character. The day was characterised by the striking warmth of the month of July in this latitude. The fore part of it had been spent in a diligent ascent of the Mississippi from Lake Winnipec; and the party reached the point of entrance, with a feeling of gratification, arising from the accomplishment of one of its objects. We halted a few moments, to allow the hindmost canoes to come up, so as to enter the Lake together. Oza Windib, or the Yellow Head, our Chippewa guide, had preceded the party a little, as he often did, to get the first glance of little bays and inlets, where water fowl are usually found. He had put his canoe ashore behind a small point, where he met a party of the Cass Lake band. Of this he kept us ignorant till turning the same point, that he might surprise us with an unexpected salute. The Indians then approached in their canoes in a body, with a welcome, which could hardly have been more cordial, had we been old friends. They represented their residence to be on a large island, bearing southwest from the entrance. And for this island we set forward, with every appliance. The Indians accompanied us, imparting a spirit of emulation to the men, by shouts and firing. In making this traverse, we left the mouth of Turtle river, (the spot of Gov. Cass' landing in 1820,) on our right, and did not come near enough to the shore, distinctly to recognise its features. We were upwards of an hour in reaching the island, which is called Grand Island, or Colcaspi [Star Island[30]]. On approaching it, a number of Indians were observed, running across an elevation, and pointing, with wild gestures, to a bay beyond. It was the best place of landing. They were assiduous in directing the men to the spot. They ranged themselves along the shore, fired a salute, and then came eagerly to the water's edge, giving each one a hand, as he alighted from the canoe. He, who has formed his estimate of an Indian from the reading of books, in which he is depicted as cruel and morose, without any insight into his social character, need only to be ushered into a scene like this, to be convinced that he has contemplated an overshadowed picture. We found these Indians to be frank, cheerful, and confiding.

On ascending the elevation before referred to, it was found to be the site of an abandoned village, now covered partially with corn-fields, and overgrown, in other parts, with sumac and other shrubbery. The cutting down too much of the forest, and the consequent exposure to winds, had probably been their reason for removing the village to a more southerly and sheltered part of the island. An Indian town, all America over, is nothing but an assemblage of wigwams, built, exclusively to suit the particular convenience of the occupant, without right angled streets, for which (as they have no carts or waggons) they have no occasion, and they get thereby the additional advantage of having no clouds of dust blown up from the denuded surface. There is (as we should say) a public *square,* or rather, an open grassy spot, where councils and dances are held, and the ceremonies of the wabeno and medicine society performed. Hillocks and elevated grounds are selected for erecting their lodges on; and clumps of small trees and shrubs are sought. Large trees are avoided, for the simple reason, that they often loose a limb during windy weather, and are liable to be blown down by tempests. But the whole circular opening, constituting a town plat, is surrounded with forest, to shelter them, in summer and winter. Gardens are variously located, and generally without fences, as there are no domesticated cattle. Such, at least, was the town of Oza Windib, situated nearly a mile from the spot of our landing, to which he was welcomed, on his return, by groups of men, women, and children. The total population, as counted during our stay, was 157, and it does not, probably, at any time, exceed 200 or 250. They rely, in the main, on hunting for a subsistence, deriving considerable aid, as the season shifts, from fishing, the gathering of wild rice, and the products of small fields of corn and potatoes, cultivated by the women. We were assured that the corn crop was always relied on, and that seed corn is preserved from year to year, and has not been known to fail. About sixty miles northwest, at Red Lake, corn is stated by the traders, to be a profitable crop, and it is among the singularities of the fur trade, that this article has, within a few of the last years, been furnished in considerable quantity, from that lake, to the posts on the Upper Mississippi, and even as far east as Fond du Lac.

The hunting grounds of Yellow Head's band, embrace the extreme sources of the Mississippi, and his village is the last fixed location in the ascent. Part of them go to Lac Travers [Bemidji], and encamp there, for the purpose of making the winter hunt. And from this point, they ascend southerly, which carries them still further into the red deer and stag and hind country of (the absolute head of the Mississippi,) Itasca Lake. The furs and skins collected are exchanged for goods with traders, who visit them annually in the fall, and remain during the winter. These goods are brought in canoes from Michilimackinac, an estimated distance, as travelled, of 1120 miles. Of this distance there are only 18¾ miles land carriage, separated into five portages, at distant points.

We may observe in this singular facility of internal water communication, one of the primary reasons of the heads of the Mississippi, being supplied with Indian goods at first from Montreal, and afterwards from New-York. Not only were these facilities early found to exist, but it was the track of interior discovery, while the Mississippi itself opposed an obstacle to the trade, by its difficult navigation, and the unhealthiness of the climate of its lower lattitudes. Political considerations, also, entered into the earlier arrangements. Indeed, whoever is curious to examine into this matter, will find the history of the fur trade in north-western America, to be intimately blended with the civil history of the country, for about two hundred and fifty years after its discovery. Dating this discovery from the arrival of Ja[c]ques Cartier in the gulf of St. Lawrence, in 1534, (the first well settled era,) the traffic then commenced with the natives, and, soon assuming an engrossing character, may be traced through various modifications, up to the surrender of the lake posts to the American government in 1796. This momentous interval of two hundred and sixty-two years is fraught with incidents of a deeply interesting character, which it will be sufficient here, to allude to. Through every change of things the fur trade continued to be, not only cherished, but formed one of the cardinal interests in the policy of the government which France and Great Britain successively exercised over this portion of North America. Under the French government the system was intimately connected with military and with missionary efforts, in a manner which was peculiar to that government. Licenses to trade were granted by the governor general to superannuated officers, and other servants of the crown, by whom they were sold out to enterprising individuals. These persons went inland to exchange their goods for furs, and first drew upon themselves the epithet of *Couriers du Bois*. Great irregularities, however, existed. Civil and ecclesiastic power were alternately exerted to restrain them. And an order to prohibit the traffic in the article of brandy was issued by one of the French governors.

Under English rule, local agents were authorised, in the name of the king, to oversee Indian affairs, grant licences, and exercise a general supervision over the trade. Serious difficulties arose in acquiring the confidence of the northern Indians after the fall of Quebec [in 1759]. But, after an interruption of four or five years, (say from '59 to '64,) including the period of Pontiac's war, the trade gradually resumed its healthful action.[31] French enterprise had spread it through the region of Lake Superior and the Upper Mississippi, to the banks of the Saskatchawine. Scottish intrepidity carried it to the mouths of the Mackenzie, and the Columbia.

The date of American authority in the lake country may be placed in 1796. It was, however, but feebly felt in its influence on the north-west fur trade, for several years. Congress first legislated on the subject in 1802, but four years afterwards Lieut. Pike, on reaching the Upper Mississippi, found it in the exclusive possession of the North West Company. The Indians were then as much attached to the English, as they had been to the French, in 1759. It cost the British crown the expenses of a war to gain this ascendancy, and the Americans were not permitted to succeed them, as the sovereign power over Indian territory, at a less hazard. The war of 1812 found all the northern tribes confederated with the English. Tecumseh had risen to re-act the part which Pontiac had failed to accomplish, fifty-two years before, namely, driving back the infringing power. This happened, in 1759 [1763], to be Great Britain; but in 1812, it was the United States. With less sterling capacity to organise and command, however, than his great predecessor had, and with the powerful resources of England to back him, he utterly failed. It was not till after this failure, and the re-establishment of American garrisons at Detroit and Michilimackinac, that the Jeffersonian Indian code of 1802,[32] began to be put into effect in the north-west. In 1816, a law was passed by Congress to exclude foreigners from the trade. In 1819 St. Peter's was established. In 1820, Gov. Cass personally visited the tribes, and in 1822, a military post [Fort Brady] was advanced to St. Mary's Falls, the most northern point occupied by the United States army.

Although the North West Company had [been] now transferred to an American company, organised by Mr. Astor [in 1808], all their posts south and west of the lines of demarkation, they maintained, however, an active trade along the lines, and waged one of the most spirited and hard contested oppositions against the Hudson's Bay Company, which has ever characterised a commercial rivalry. Lord Selkirk had now placed himself at the head of the Hudson's Bay Company, and staked his character and resources on the maintenance of its territorial and commercial rights. It is no part of our object to go into details. Let it suffice, that he took Fort William on the 13th of August, 1816, carried his power over the region of Red river, where he planted a colony, and, after losing the lives of several of his most zealous agents and officers, (including the governor of his colony,) finally triumphed in asserting the rights of the Hudson's Bay Company, and quieted, by an amalgamation of stocks, the claims of his intrepid rivals.[33]

One of the most painful atrocities which arose, in the course of this rivalry, was the murder of Owen Keveny. As the facts were subsequently detailed in a court of justice, they may be succinctly narrated. Mr. Keveny, a gentleman in the service of the Hudson's Bay Company, was taken prisoner by the North West Company, in the summer of 1816; and ordered to be sent out from Red river to Montreal. On ascending the river Winnipec, (northwest of the Lake of the Woods,) he was finally put in charge of a couple of *engagés,* named Faye and La Pointe, in a canoe, with an Indian guide, called Joseph, Son-of-the-White-Patridge, with directions to take him to Rainy Lake. By these he was landed on an island below the Dalles, where they slept. Next morning Keveny complained of being ill, and asked Faye to bring him some warm water. The latter, on coming to the beach, found that La Pointe, and the Indian, had put out into the stream. On being called, they came ashore and took in Faye, and all then went down the river together, abandoning Keveny on the island. A few days afterwards one of the *engagés* in the canoe, quarrelled with the Indian, and the latter left them. They then turned about and began to ascend the river, but, having lost their guide, could not find their way, and soon encamped on a small island, resolved to wait till some canoe should pass. Four or five days had elapsed, when their expectations were answered, by the arrival of a light canoe, with two partners of the North West Company, and Charles de Reinhard, a clerk, and a *Boisbrulè,* named Mainville, besides the Indian, Joseph, Son-of-the-White-Patridge, who had fled from Faye and La Pointe, below. After a short halt, during which Mr. M'Lellan, (a partner of the North West Company,) beat the two men with a canoepole, all embarked for Rainy Lake. The same day they met other canoes, from which they learned, that Keveny, whose life had been threatened by de Reinhard and others, had left the island, where he was first abandoned, and gone up the river five or six leagues, to another island situated above the Dalles. He was now the subject of engrossing interest and conversation. On reaching this, they found Keveny, as expected. Mr. Grant, one of the partners, landed, with others, and shook hands with him. They then embarked, leaving de Reinhard, Mainville, and Joseph, Son-of-the-White-Patridge, on the island with Keveny. After going two or three leagues further up the river, they encamped. Some time after landing, the report of a gun was heard in the direction they came from. In half an hour's time, a canoe came from the same direction, having in it de Reinhard, Mainville, and Joseph, Son-of-the-White-Patridge. It had much blood in it, together with the trunks, and clothes worn by Keveny, but Keveny himself was not there. On examining the coat, there was perceived to be a ball hole, and an incision, in different parts of it. Keveny's trunks were then landed, unlocked, and a division made of his clothes, linen, and other effects. De Reinhard wiped the blood from his sword, declaring in the hearing of the men, as if glorying in the perpetration of the act, that he had killed him, and was entitled to the best apparel, which he accordingly appropriated to himself. Mainville took the perforated coat.

The facts of this foul deed appeared to be these. Keveny, with the three persons left with him, by the Northwest partners, embarked in a small Indian canoe, to ascend the river. He complained of being unwell, and was landed at a certain spot. De Reinhard, Mainville, and Joseph waited at the beach. De Reinhard stood near the canoe as Keveny re-embarked, and suddenly drawing a short sword, thrust it into his body. Keveny doubled down under the blow, but being a tall and powerful man, (although weakened by disease,) he recovered himself, seized the blade of the sword, and would have wrenched it away and overpowered the assassin, had he not called to Mainville to fire. The latter obeyed. The ball passed through Keveny's neck, and he instantly fell. It does not seem that the Indian participated in the act. The body was stripped and left on shore, unburied. Two years after (i.e. 1818,) de Reinhard, who had, it seems, been a subaltern officer in one of the disbanded foreign regiments, was tried for the murder at Quebec, proved guilty, (by his own confessions to the men at the encampment,) and sentenced to the gallows. Mainville escaped.

CHAPTER IV

Brief detail of transactions at Cass Lake.—A select exploring party is organised here, for ascending to the actual source of the Mississippi.—Council with the Indians.—Speech of Oza Windib.—The Indians furnish canoes and guides.—Arrangement of the party.—Notice of a Warrior's widow.—Scalp dance.—Facts respecting foreign interference in the trade of the Upper Mississippi.—The question of the use of ardent spirits in the trade.—Act of Congress of 1832, prohibiting it.—Departure of the exploring party.—Ascent to Pamitchi Gumaug, or Lac Travers.—Its elevation and size.—A Shingaba Wossin.—Image worship.—Bay.—Ultimate forks of the Mississippi.—Ascend the east fork.—Lake Marquette.—Lake La Salle.—Kubbakunna Lake.—Notices of the Natural History.

HAVING DETERMINED TO ORGANISE a select party at this lake, to explore the source of the river, measures were immediately taken to effect it. A council of the Indians was assembled, and the object declared to them. They were requested to delineate maps of the country, and to furnish the requisite number of hunting canoes and guides. Oza Windib, said, "My father, the country you are going to see, is my hunting ground. I have travelled with you many days.[34] I shall go with you farther. I will myself furnish the maps you have requested, and will guide you onward. There are many rapids in the way, but the waters are favorable. I shall consult with my band about the canoes, and see who will step forward to furnish them. My own canoe shall be one of the number."

Before night the maps were completed, and five different individuals, including Oza Windib, brought each a canoe of the proper size and laid it down. Two young men expressed their willingness to go, as additional guides. Seven engagés and a cook, were added to this number, making, with Lieut. J. Allen, (who declared he could push his men no farther, Doct. Douglass Houghton, the Reverend Wm. T. Boutwell, Mr. George Johnston, and myself,) sixteen persons. These, with their travelling beds, were distributed among five canoes, with provisions for ten days, a tent and poles, oil cloth, mess basket, tea-kettle, flag and staff, a medicine chest, some instruments, an herbarium, fowling pieces, and a few Indian presents. The detachment of infantry was left in their encampment on the island, under the command of their non-commissioned officer. The remainder of the party, with the baggage and travelling equipment, was placed in charge of Mr. Le Default, a clerk of one of the upper posts of trade [Red Lake], who was attached to the expedition from Fond du Lac, and obligingly undertook the acquisition of certain points of information, during the contemplated absence.

25

While these arrangements were in process, a mixed group of men, women, and children, from the Indian village, thronged our encampment. Among them I observed the widow of a Chippewa warrior, who had been killed some three or four weeks previous, in the foray of the Leech Lake war party, in the Sioux country. She was accompanied by her children and appeared dejected. I asked one of the Indians the place of her residence. He replied, here; that her husband had been a brave warrior, and went, on the call of the Leech Lake chief, with a number of volunteers, to join the party. I asked him, of what number the party consisted? He replied, about one hundred. Who had led them? The Gueule Platte. Where they had met the enemy? South of the head of Leaf river. What had been the result of the action? They were victorious, having taken three scalps on the field, and lost but one, being the husband of the widow referred to. The action had however, been at long shots, with frequent changes of position, and the enemy had finally fled to a village for reinforcement. The Chippewas took this opportunity to retreat, and, after consultation, returned, bringing back the three scalps, as memorials of their prowess. These trophies had, we learned, been exhibited in the customary dances at Leech Lake, after which one of them was forwarded to Oza Windib's band, to undergo a like ceremony. And it was finally presented to the widow.

It was now exhibited by the young men, in her behalf, for a purpose which was certainly new to me. Although I knew that this people were ingenious in converting most circumstances, connected with both fortune and misfortune, into a means of soliciting alms, I had never before seen the scalp of an enemy employed as a means of levying contributions. Such, however, was the purpose for which it was now brought forward. It was exhibited with all the circumstances of barbarian triumph. Shouts and dancing, intermingled with the sounds of the rattle, and Indian drum, form the conspicuous traits of such a scene. Short harangues, terminated by a general shout, fill up the pauses of the dance, and at this moment the drums cease. It was an outcry of this kind that first drew my attention to a neighboring eminence. I observed some of the simple bark enclosures, which mark the locality of a Chippewa burial ground. Near them, was erected a sort of triumphal arch, consisting of bent and tied saplings, from the arc formed by which, depended an object, which was said to be the remains of decaying scalps. Around this, was gathered a crowd of dancers, moving in a circle. The fresh scalp was suspended from a rod. Every time it waved, a new impulse seemed to be given to the shouting. The widow and her children were present. And the whole group of spectators, Canadians as well as Indians, appeared to regard the ceremony with an absorbing interest. In the brief pause, which separated each dance, presents were thrown in. And all that was given was deemed the property of the widow. This was the scalp dance.

Other incidents of the sojourn of the expedition on this island will be mentioned on the return of the party to it. A few may be added here.

Representations having been made to the Department, on the subject of foreign interference in the trade of the Upper Mississippi, a number of queries were addressed to an American trader, well acquainted with its geography and resources. I inquired of him, whether the American traders on that border, were strenuously opposed in their trade by the inhabitants of the Red river colony, or by the partners and clerks of the Hudson's Bay Company. He replied that the inhabitants of Pembina were in the habit of making temporary voyages of trade to Voleuse, or Thief river, south of the parallel of forty-nine degrees, but that they had not built or made a permanent stand there. He said, that the open nature of the country about the Red river settlement, gave great facilities for making short excursions into the Indian country, on horseback and in carts. But he did not know any place to which permanent outfits had been sent, except the river Souris, west of Red river. He believed that this traffic was carried on, exclusively, by the inhabitants of the colony and not by the Hudson's Bay Company.

I asked him whether the Indians of the Lake of the Woods visited the post of Red lake, and whether our traders were annoyed in their trade in that quarter by the servants of the Hudson's Bay Company. He replied, that the Lac du Bois Indians came across to Red Lake ordinarily; that it is a three days' journey; but that no annoyance is experienced in the trade of that part from the Hudson's Bay factors. He was of opinion that they do not send outfits into any part of the territory south or west of the national boundary, beginning at *Portage des Rats* on the Lake of the Woods.

A quite different aspect was put upon the temper of this opposition by the Principal of this department of trade, who was met below. He complained of the influence which the Hudson's Bay Company exert across the lines, and the moral character of the means which were resorted to, to induce the American Indians to go to their posts. He said that in 1831, (I think) one of his petty clerks had been induced to abscond with his outfit, and had been well received by one of the partners of the Hudson's Bay Company. On inquiry, I found this clerk to be Mainville, one of the murderers of Keveny. He said that high wines was the great power of the supremacy of the Hudson's Bay Company on the lines, and brought forward the usual arguments of those persons, who either deem ardent spirits essential to the success of the trade, or justify its temporary use on the principle of expediency.

It may here, in brief, be observed, that all such arguments plausible as they may appear, are founded on a false principle. They assume the existence of an evil, which is alleged to be so fixed, that it is better to tolerate it, than to run the risk of uprooting it; as if it were better to submit to a disease, than to attempt its cure, by a removal of its causes. No trader, will however, deny the existence of the *evil,* as an abstract question. Neither is it denied, that ardent spirits is a tax upon the trade, in the exact ratio of its entire cost, doubled, and trebled, and quadrupled, as this cost is by the expense of interior transportation. But the question is, "Who shall begin to give up its use?" This is a question internally, between trader and trader, externally, between company and company. As such it has been bandied between New-York and London, the seats of commercial power. But neither side has felt the requisite degree of confidence, to risk the experiment of a voluntary arrangement for its entire exclusion *from the lines.*[35]

Congress has terminated this question, so far as it respects American citizens, by an act of the 9th of July, of the present year,[36] (1832,) which contains this provision: "That no ardent spirits shall be hereafter introduced, under any pretence, into the Indian country." The enforcement of this act, has been rigidly enjoined, and it is in the process of successful execution. Posterity will probably regard this measure as reflecting more honor upon our national legislation, than if we had decreed a hundred monuments to fallen greatness.

But we are writing a homily, where we intended to offer a few hints, and must hie to the labor of the journey before us. Every arrangement being completed on the evening of the 10th, we embarked, at the island, at three o'clock the next morning. Our course lay westward, through a strait, formed by the approach of a part of the island, to a part of the main shore. We then passed two islands, called Garden and Elm islands. The morning was too hazy to give us any extensive prospect of the lake, or its shores. We had been a little more than an hour in motion, when we found ourselves nearing the western head of the lake, and the men soon shoved our canoes upon a sandy beach, with the exclamation of *un portage*. We found this portage to extend about fifty yards, over a plain of sand, bearing pine, and terminating on the banks of a small lake. Through this lake the Mississippi has its course, and the two lakes are connected by a circuitous channel, which might, perhaps, have occupied a half, or three quarters of an hour, to ascend. The lake [Andrusia[37]], for which we heard no name, is several miles in extent. We passed it transversely, and entered the channel of the river on its western border. It presents a still current, with an edging of savannah, which, at no great distance above, is again expanded around the margin of another lake, called Tascodiac [Wolf[38]]. Hills of sand, covered with yellow pines, here present themselves, and the river exhibits for several miles above, either a sand bank, or a savannah border. Time is the only measure of distance, which we had the means of referring to. About eight o'clock, rapid water was encountered, and at this point, which may be fifteen miles above Cass Lake, the meadow lands cease. Boulders, of a primitive character, are found on the rapids. The rapids are such, in their force and inequality of depth, as to require the men frequently to wade, and pull up the canoes. There are, say, ten of these principal rapids,[39] in the ensuing twenty or twenty-five miles, at which distance, we reach the most northern point of the Mississippi, which is marked by the fine expanse of the Pamitchi Gumaug, or Lac Travers.[40] This lake may be fifty feet above the level of Cass Lake. It is about 12 miles long, from north to south, and six or seven broad, with elevated shores, presenting to the eye a beautiful vista of hard wood groves.

We landed a few moments, on the right hand shore in entering it, to examine an object, which the men had been conversing of on the way, namely, a Shingaba Wossin.[41] It proved to be a boulder of gneiss rock, water worn, so as to present the figure of a rude shaft, with an entablature, but not exceeding in weight, the maximum of a man's strength. One of the canoe-men lifted it. It had been set up, on its base, and was decorated with a ring of red paint. The name may be freely translated Image Stone, and has no reference to the composition of the mass, any farther than that the name is usually found to be applied to rocks of the primitive kind, both from the liability of this class of rocks to assume these forms, and from their hardness, which has enabled them to endure the power of attrition. Offerings are usually left at such rude altars, and they afford, perhaps, the nearest approach to idol worship, in its grosser forms, which an examination of our Indian customs present. The soil, at this spot, appeared to be rather rich, bearing a growth of elm, soft maple and white ash.

We were an hour in crossing the lake southwestwardly, and were impressed with the extent and beauty of the prospect. On gaining the opposite shore, we found the Mississippi flowing with a brisk and deep current into it, and exhibiting a width of, perhaps one hundred and fifty feet. In landing, a few moments, at this point, we found the beach strewed with small shells, both uniones, and helices. A log house, used as a winter trading camp, stood a few hundred yards northwardly. And this may be referred to, as the most advanced trading location on the main waters of this river.

Lac Travers is separated by a short channel, from a bay or lake [Irving[42]] of moderate dimensions, which is, from its proximity, considered a part of the main lake, although the current of the separating channel, indicates the latter to be rather a *river* than a strait. It will be convenient to refer to it, as it is from this point that the Mississippi, which has now been pursued to its utmost northing, is ascended directly south. About four miles above this bay, the Mississippi has its ultimate forks, being formed of an east [Schoolcraft River[43]] and west branch, of which the west branch is decidedly the largest, and considerably the longest. Reasons indicated by our guide, induced him to conduct us up the east branch, which we soon found expanded into a small lake, denoted Marquette, and not far above, into another, denoted La Salle.[44] We were twenty-four minutes in passing through the last, and on leaving it, found the stream strikingly diminished in volume, with a limited depth, and a vegetation of a more decidedly alpine character. About four miles above the latter, the stream expands into a lake some six or seven miles in length, and about half that distance in width. This lake, which is called Kubbakunna, The Rest in the Path [Plantagenette[45]], presented a pleasing aspect, after the sombre vegetation, we had passed below. Rushes, however, were abundant toward its head, and we found the ground too low and wet for encamping. After ascending the river, for a distance, we put ashore for the night, at a point of woods extending into the marsh-land, constituting the river margin. The soil at this place, appeared to be of the most frigid character. A carpet of moss covered it, which the foot sank deep into, at every step. The growth was exclusively small grey pine, with numerous dead branches below, and strikingly festooned with flowing moss. Nearer the margin of the river, alder, tamarack, and willow occupied the soil. As night approached it commenced raining, which served to add to the natural gloom of the spot.

Notices of the natural history of the country, during this day's journey are meagre. The principal growth of forest trees, out of the immediate valley, is pine. The plants appear to present little variety, and consist of species peculiar to moist, cold, or elevated situations. Water fowl are abundant, and were frequently shot. Among the number brought in from the different canoes, in the evenings, were the duck and mallard, wood-duck, and saw-bill. One of the latter species, had a unio firmly attached to its lower mandible, having been in the act of opening it when shot.

CHAPTER V

Ascent of the east fork of the Mississippi, from Kubbakunna Lake to the Naiwa rapids.—Its productions.—Indians kill a deer; their mode of dissecting it.—Reach the foot of Naiwa rapids.—The Naiwa portage.— Copper-head snake.—Zoned agate.—Journey from thence to Ossowa Lake, the source of this branch of the Mississippi.—Mistake in the latitude.—Portage from the east to the west branch.—Hauteur des Terres— the height of land between the Hudson's Bay and Gulf of Mexico waters. —Geographical notices of its extent.—Its natural productions.—Its geology.—Arrival at Itasca Lake.

WE RESUMED the ascent at five o'clock in the morning, (12th.) The course of this branch of the river, above the Kubbakunna Lake, resembles a thread wound across a savannah valley. A species of coarse marsh-land grass covers the valley. Clumps of willow fringe this stream. Rushes and Indian reed are gathered in spots most favorable to their growth. The eye searches in vain, for much novelty in the vegetation. Wherever the stream touches the solid land, grey pine, and tamarack are conspicuous, and clumps of alder here take the place of willow. Moss attaches itself to almost every thing. And there is a degree of dampness and obscurity in the forest, which is almost peculiar to the region. Water fowl seem alone to exult in their seclusion, and evince the infrequency of intrusion by flying a short distance, and frequently alighting within gun-shot.

After we had gone on a little more than an hour, the Indian in the bow of the forward canoe, fired at, and killed a deer. We all landed to look at the animal. Although fairly shot through the fore part of the body, it ran several hundred yards before it fell. The Indian traced it by its blood, and found it quite dead. He brought it to the banks of the river, before skinning it. We stood in astonishment at the dexterity with which this operation was performed. In a very few minutes it was disrobed of its skin, quartered and dissected. The owner presented me the quarters. He gave the *moze* to our guide. This term comprehends all parts of the carcass except the four quarters, head and entrails. Nothing was, however, thrown away; and we had occasion, at night to observe, that the aid of fire enables them, with very little of the culinary art, to despatch those parts of the animal, which, it might be inferred, were most in need of preparation. Signs of this animal were frequently seen, and had the objects of the journey permitted delay, it might have been often killed.

Our progress through the savannahs was rendered more unpleasant than it would otherwise have been, by frequent showers of rain, which gave, as is usual, a peculiar activity and virulence to the musquito. When the usual

31

hour of landing for breakfast had arrived, the banks were too marshy to admit of it, and we went on until a quarter past twelve. We then again renewed a labor with little variety of incident.

At half past five we came to an elevated sand-hill on the right shore, covered with yellow pine, and presenting a naked face towards the river. As one of the canoes required mending, I directed the men to land at this spot, for that purpose. Oza Windib, who was a little in the rear, at the moment, said, on coming up, that we were within a few hundred yards of the junction of the Naiwa, the principal tributary of this fork; that a series of rapids commenced at that point, which would render it necessary to make a portage the whole extent of them, and that it was better to commence the portage at this place, as the river so ran, that we might go directly back through the forest, and strike its channel. He said that the Naiwa, which came in on the left, was a stream of considerable length, and originated in a lake [George] which was infested by copper-head snakes, to which its name has reference. I observed that the soil at this place was of a diluvian character, and embraced pebbles, and small boulders of syenite, trap rock, and quartz, and other debris of primitive and secondary rocks. One of the party picked up a well characterised piece of zoned agate.

While the mending of the canoes was in progress, the baggage was put in portable order, and as soon as all was ready, the men moved on with the canoes and effects, which were so arranged that all could be carried at one load, and it did not require them to go back. This was a point originally kept in view, in the curtailment of the baggage at the island, and it was an object of the highest importance to the speed and success of the trip. Each canoe and its apparatus, with some of the lighter pieces was carried by one man. The guide led off the men, with no slight burden on his own shoulders, first scrambling up the sandy acclivity, and then striking through a growth of scrub oak and pines. The showers of the morning had so thoroughly wet the grass and shrubbery, that a few moments walking through it, was sufficient completely to saturate both pantaloons and stockings. I walked out a few hundred yards from the trail, towards the left which brought me into the curve of the river, in view of the rapids. There appeared to be a series of small rapids, with intervening shallows. The noise of falling water and the white wreaths of foam, induced me to think there might be distinct falls, but I could discern nothing entitled to the name. The average descent of the river, at this series of rapids, appeared to be, however, considerable, and might perhaps be estimated at forty-eight feet. I rejoined the party at the spot they had selected for their first pause, somewhat to their relief, probably, as guns had been fired by them, under the belief of my having missed the way. We first came in sight of the river again, on the brow of an elevated sand-hill, precipitous towards the water. The guide halted to inquire whether it would not be preferable to encamp at this spot, as we should suffer less from insects than if we encamped in the valley of the river, at the termination of the portage. As the day light was not gone, and some distance still remained, I deemed it better to go on, that we might have nothing to do in the morning, but to put our canoes in the water. On reaching the bank of the stream, we found its current placid, and our guide informed us that we had now surmounted the last rapids.

A fog prevented our embarking until five o'clock in the morning, (13th) and it was then impossible to discern objects at a distance. We found the channel above the Naiwa, diminished to a clever brook, more decidedly marshy in the character of its shores, but not presenting in its plants or trees, any thing particularly to distinguish it from the contiguous lower parts of the stream. The water is still and pond-like. It presents some small areas of wild rice. It appears to be a favorite resort for the duck and teal, who frequently rose up before us, and were aroused again and again by our progress. An hour and a half diligently employed, brought us to the foot of Ossowa [Assawa[46]] Lake. We halted a moment to survey it. It exhibits a broad border of aquatic plants, with somewhat blackish waters. Perch abound in it. It is the recipient of two brooks, and may be regarded as the source of this fork of the Mississippi. We were precisely twenty minutes in passing through it. We entered one of the brooks, the most southerly in position. It possessed no current and was filled with broad leaved plants, and a kind of yellow pond-lily. We appeared to be involved in a morass, where it seemed equally impracticable to make the land, or proceed far by water. In this we were not mistaken; Oza Windib soon pushed his canoe into the weeds and exclaimed, *Oma, mikunna,* (here is the portage.) A man who is called on for the first time, to debark, in such a place, will look about him to discover some dry spot to put his feet upon. No such spot however existed here. We stepped into rather warm pond water, with a miry bottom. After wading a hundred yards, or more, the soil became firm, and we soon began to ascend a slight elevation, where the growth partakes more of the character of a forest. Traces of a path appeared here, and we suddenly entered an opening affording an eligible spot for landing. Here our baggage was prepared for the portage. The carbonaceous remains of former fires, the bones of birds, and scattered camp poles, proved it to be a spot which had previously been occupied by the Indians. The prevailing growth at this place is spruce, white cedar, tamarack and grey pine. We here breakfasted.

Having followed out this branch of the Mississippi to its source, it may be observed, that its existence, as a separate river, has hitherto been unknown in our geography. None of the maps indicate the ultimate separation of the Mississippi, above Cass Lake, into two forks. Little surprise should therefore be manifested that the latitude of the head of this stream, is found to be incorrect. It was not however to be expected that the inaccuracy should be so great as to place the actual source, an entire degree south of the supposed point. Such however is the conclusion established by present observations.

The portage from the east to the west branch of the river is estimated to be six miles. Beginning in a marsh, it soon rises into a little elevation of white cedar wood, then plunges into the intricacies of a swamp matted with fallen trees, obscured with moss. From this, the path emerges upon dry ground. It soon ascends an elevation of oceanic sand, having boulders, and bearing pines. There is then another descent, and another elevation. In short, the traveller now finds himself crossing a series of deluvial sand ridges, which form the height of land between the Mississippi Valley and Red River. This ridge is locally denominated Hauteur des Terres where it is crossed in passing from Lac Plaie to Ottertail Lake, from which point it proceeds northward, separating the tributaries of the River des Corbeau from those of Red River. It finally subtends both branches of the Mississippi, putting out a spur between the east and west fork, which intersects the portage, crosses the west or Itascan fork about the point of the Kakábikonce, or Little Rock Falls, and joining the main ridge, passes northeastwardly of Lac Travers and Turtle Lake, and is again encountered in the noted portage path from Turtle Lake to Red Lake. It is, in fine, the table land between the waters of Hudson's Bay and the Mexican Gulf. It also gives rise to the remotest tributaries of the river St. Louis, which, through Lake Superior and its connecting chain, may be considered as furnishing the head waters of the St. Lawrence. This table land, is probably, the highest in Northwestern America, in this longitude.

In crossing this highland, our Indian guide, Oza Windib, led the way, carrying one of the canoes, as his portion of the burden. The others followed, some bearing canoes, and others baggage. The whole party were arranged in Indian file, and marched rapidly a distance—then put down their burthens a few moments, and again pressed forward. Each of these stops is called a *posè* by the voyageurs, and is denominated Opugidjiwunon, or a place of putting down the burthen, by the Indians. Thirteen of these rests, are deemed the length of the portage. The path is rather blind, and requires the precision of an Indian eye to detect it. Even the guide was sometimes at a loss, and went forward to explore. We passed a small lake occupying a vale, about midway of the portage, in canoes. The route beyond it, was more obstructed with underbrush. To avoid this, we waded through the margins of a couple of ponds, near which we observed old camp poles, indicating former journies by the Indians.

The weather was warm and not favorable to much activity in bird or beast. We saw one or two species of the falco, and the common pigeon, which extends its migrations over the continent. Tracks of deer were numerous, but travelling without the precaution required in hunting, we had no opportunity of seeing this animal on the high grounds. It was observed in the valleys of the river, on both branches. Ripe strawberries were brought to me, by the men, at one of the resting places. I observed a very diminutive species of the raspberry, with fruit, on the moist grounds. Botanists would probably deem the plants few, and destitute of much interest. Parasitic moss is very common to the forest trees, and it communicates a peculiar aspect to the grey pine, which is the prevailing growth on all the elevations.

To the geologist, the scene is one of interest. The boulders of granite, and other primitive strata, occurring on the surface, remind him of the original position of these masses, in the system of nature and indicate revolutions affecting the earth's surface, which have widely changed both the position and form of these solid materials. When the soil itself is examined, it adds further evidences of such changes. We may refer its sand to consolidated strata of this mineral which have been broken down by oceanic action, and distributed in the remarkable ridges and elevations, which now characterise the face of the country. In whatever light the subject is viewed, it seems difficult to resist the conclusion, that water has been the cause, under providence, in effecting these changes, and that the highest grounds in this region, have been subjected to the peculiar influence which this element alone exerts in the work of attrition and deposition of strata, solid or diluvial. It might be interesting to inquire, in what manner this agent of change was withdrawn, and whether a current was created toward either of the cardinal points. It would aid this inquiry to observe, in which direction the debris and soils were deposited in the heaviest masses? How far granite boulders had been carried from their beds? And whether wood, bones, and other organic remains had been subjected to like removals? We think these accumulations are abundantly witnessed in casting the eye down the Mississippi valley, with a measured decrease in the size and weight of the pulverised masses, in proceeding from the head to the mouth of this river. It is thus evident, that the heaviest boulders are found on its upper branches, while they become rare in its central plains, and disappear altogether, long before its entrance into the deltas at its mouth. And this remark may be coupled with the accounts given by travellers of the bleak, and denuded, and sterile character of the northern rock formations.

But we have no leisure to devote to this investigation, and must proceed with the narrative that is before us. Every step we made in treading these sandy elevations, seemed to increase the ardor with which we were carried forward. The desire of reaching the actual source of a stream so celebrated as the Mississippi—a stream which La Salle had reached the mouth of, a century and a half (lacking a year) before, was perhaps predominant; and we followed our guide down the sides of the last elevation, with the expectation of momentarily reaching the goal of our journey. What had been long sought, at last appeared suddenly. On turning out of a thicket, into a small weedy opening, the cheering sight of a transparent body of water burst upon our view. It was Itasca Lake—the source of the Mississippi.

CHAPTER VI

Outlines of Itasca Lake.—Its scenery and productions.—Forest trees, deer, fish, shells.—Width of its outlet.—Altitude above the ocean.—Length of the Mississippi.—Its course above Cass Lake.—Its origin south of latitude 47 deg. 16 minutes.—General observations on the Mississippi.— Erect a flag on the island in Itasca Lake.—Commence the descent of the West, or Itascan branch of the Mississippi.—Character of its channel.— Rapids and plateaux.—Falls of Kakabikons.—Portage.—Encamp at Pine Banks.

ITASCA LAKE, the *Lac la Biche* of the French, is, in every respect, a beautiful sheet of water, seven or eight miles in extent, lying among hills of diluvial formation, surmounted with pines, which fringe the distant horizon, and form an agreeable contrast with the greener foliage of its immediate shores.[47] Its greatest length, is from south-east to north-west, with a southern prolongation, or bay, which receives a brook. The waters are transparent and bright, and reflect a foliage produced by the elm, lynn, maple, and cherry, together with other species more abundant in northern latitudes. The lake itself is of irregular form. It has a single island [Schoolcraft[48]], upon which we landed, after an hour's paddling from the spot of our arrival and embarkation. We found here, the forest trees above named growing promiscuously with the betula and spruce. The bones of fish and of tortoise, found at the locality of former Indian camp fires, indicate the existence of these species in the lake. We observed a deer, standing in the margin of the lake. And, here, as well as throughout the lakes of the region, found the duck, teal and loon, in possession of their favorite seclusions. Innumerable shells, (a species of small helix,) were driven up on the head of the island. Other parts of the lake yield small species of the unio, which were found strewing the bed of the outlet. And it may here be remarked, that this shell exists, in the largest and heaviest species heretofore known, in the lower parts of this stream—the Mississippi having its origin here.

The outlet of Itasca Lake, is perhaps ten to twelve feet broad, with an apparent depth of twelve to eighteen inches. The discharge of water appears to be copious, compared to its inlet. Springs may, however, produce accessions which are not visible, and this is probable both from the geological character of the country, and the transparency and coolness of the water.

The height of this lake, above the sea, is an object of geographical interest, which, in the absence of actual survey, it may subserve the purposes of useful inquiry, to estimate. From notes taken on the ascent, it cannot be short of one hundred and sixty feet above Cass Lake. Adding the estimate of 1330 feet, submitted in 1820, as the elevation of that lake, the

36

Mississippi may be considered to originate at an altitude of 1490, say 1500 feet, above the Atlantic. Its length, assuming former data as the basis, and computing it, through the Itascan, or west fork, may be placed at 3160 miles, one hundred and eighty-two of which, comprises an estimate of its length above Cass Lake.[49] Its general course, in *ascending,* above the latter point, is north of west, as far as Lac Travers. Then south to its primary forks which is continued, following up the east fork to Kubbakunna Lake, and for some distance further. It then varies a short distance, north and northwest, then southwest and south, and finally southwest, to its main source in Ossowa Lake. The portage thence to Itasca Lake is west southwest. Both these lakes appear to rise in springs, on the height of land. They are separated by about six miles of country. Their latitude, we had no means of accurately determining. From daily notes of the courses and distances, kept by Lieut. J. Allen, as indicated by a compass and watch, their position is, however, shown to be *southwest,* and not, as heretofore supposed, *northwest,* of Cass Lake. They are, in fact, a little south of west from Leech Lake, which is placed, on our best maps, in forty-seven degrees sixteen minutes. The highest northing attained by the Mississippi, is on the great diluvial plateau, containing the contiguous waters of Lakes La Salle, Marquette and Travers, which cannot vary more than a few minutes, from forty-eight degrees. These facts will explain the error of the elder geographical writers, who supposed that the parallel of forty-nine degrees would intersect the Mississippi. Its origin in the remote and unfrequented area of country between Leech Lake and Red river, probably an entire degree of latitude south of Turtle Lake, which still figures on some of our maps as its *source,* throws both the forks of this stream out of the usual route of the fur trade, and furnishes, perhaps the best reason why its actual sources have remained so long enveloped in obscurity.

The Mississippi river traverses more degrees of latitude than any other river in America, and the remark might, perhaps, be extended to the habitable globe. The extremes of its changes in climate and vegetable productions, are, consequently, very great. It occupies more than three thousand miles of the distance between the arctic circle and the equator. Long as it is, however, it has a tributary longer than itself, (the Missouri.) Like the Niger, its mouth was discovered by expeditions down its current, but unlike that stream, which has so long held the geographical world in suspense, its sources have been also sought from its central parts. Its entire course is, at length, known. And we may now appeal with full certainty to the Balize [Louisiana] and to Itasca Lake, as its most extreme points. At the latter, it is a placid basin of transparent spring water. At the former, it is as turbid as earth in suspension can make it, and carries a forest of floating trees on its bosom. Below the junction of its primary forks, it expands at very unequal distances, into eight sheets of clear water, each of which has features worthy of admiration. Four of these, Lac Travers, Cass Lake, Winnepec, and Lake Pepin, are lakes of handsome magnitude, and striking scenery. The number of its tributaries of the first, and the second and the third class, is so large, that it would furnish a labor of some research, to determine it. The Missouri, the Ohio, and the Arkansas are of the noblest class. Whoever has stood at the junction of these streams, as the writer has done, must have been impressed with an idea of magnitude and power, which words are incapable of conveying. The broadest parts of its channel lie in the central portions of its valley. Its depth is great in all its lower parts, and increases as it flows on to the Gulf, and its general descent and velocity are such as to appear very striking characteristics.[50] Noble views arrest the eye of the observer, in every part of its diversified course. Originating in a heavy and extensive bed of diluvial soil, superimposed upon primitive strata, it soon wears its channel down to the latter, and after running over them for several hundred miles, plunges at length, at the Falls of St. Anthony, over the carboniferous limestone formation, which is so prevalent and so valuable for its mineral deposits, below that point. This is finally succeeded by diluvial and alluvial banks, the latter of which are semi-annually enriched by fresh deposits, and exhibit a delta as broad and as exuberant as the Nile. Like the latter, it has its cataracts in the Falls of St. Anthony and Pukaigama [Pokegama], and in numerous lesser leaps and cascades, where its current is tossed into foam and threatens destruction to the navigation. Such are its physical traits, and there is enough in their character, magnitude, and variety to lead our contemplations irresistibly "through nature up to nature's God."

Having gratified our curiosity in Itasca Lake, we prepared to leave the island, but did not feel inclined to quit the scene without leaving some memorial, however frail, of our visit. The men were directed to fell a few trees at the head of the island, thereby creating an area, for the purpose of erecting a flag staff. This was braced by forked stakes, and a small flag hoisted to its place. Taking specimens of the forest growth of the island, of a size suitable for walking canes, and adding its few species to our collections of plants and conchology, we embarked on our descent. The flag which we had erected continued to be in sight for a time, and was finally shut out from our view by a curve of the lake. We found this curve drawn out in such a manner as to form, with the opposite shore, the channel of the outlet. We soon felt our motion accelerated by a current, and began to glide, with velocity, down a clear stream with a sandy and pebbly bottom, strewed with shells and overhung by foliage. Ten feet would, in most places, reach from bank to bank, and the depth would probably average over a foot. The water was not, however, equally distributed. A strong and winding channel made it a labor of active watchfulness for the canoemen, to keep our frail vessels from being dashed against boulders, or torn in pieces by fallen timber or overhanging trees. Chopping with the axe was frequently necessary to clear the passage, and no small labor was imposed by getting through the drift wood, piled up at almost every sudden bend. We were almost imperceptibly drawn into a series of rapids and petty falls where the stream was more compressed, and the water deepened; but the danger rendered tenfold greater by boulders of blackened rocks, and furious jets of the stream. We were rather hurled than paddled through these rapid passes, which increased in frequency and fury as we advanced. After being driven down about twelve miles of this species of navigation, during which the turns are very abrupt, the river displays itself, so to say, in a savannah valley, where the channel is wider and deeper, but equally, or more circuitous, and bordered with sedge and aquatic plants. This forms the first plateau. It extends eight or nine miles. The river then narrows and enters another defile, beset with an almost continued series of rapids. The sensation, in going down these, where the channel is free from stones, can be compared to nothing so aptly, as the emotion which every one has felt as the enterprise of youth has buoyed him up, in directing his tiny sled down a snow covered declivity. The brevity of the emotion takes away nothing from the truth of the comparison. The frow[n?]ing rock, often rears its dark head to dispute the passage, and calls for the exertion of every muscle, in the canoemen, to avoid, by dexterity of movement, a violent contact. Often it became necessary for them to step into the channel, and lead down the canoes, where the violence of the eddies made it impracticable otherwise to guide them. At a place called Kakábikonce, or the Little-rock falls, we made a short portage. Two of the canoes, however, made the descent, but not without imminent peril, and a delay eventually greater, than if they had been carried across the portage. We descended this second series of rapids a distance of about nine miles, and encamped, at a late hour, on a high fine bank, having come altogether about thirty-two miles below Itasca Lake. Wearied with the continued exertion, the frequent wettings, and the constant anxiety, sleep soon overshadowed the whole party, "with his downy pinions."

CHAPTER VII

Continuation of the descent.—Velocity of the rapids.—One of the canoes is upset, and its contents carried over the falls.—Notices of the vegetation and zoology.—Fork-tailed hawk.—A novel species of lizard.—The Yellow Head's failure in hunting.—Instinct of the saw-billed duck in preserving its young.—The river continues to exhibit a succession of rapids and plateaux, during its passage through the alpine region.— Purity and frequency of springs on its banks.—Influx of the Cano and Piniddiwin rivers.—Notice of an inroad and murder committed by the Sioux in former years.—A night descent.—Some of its incidents.— Reach the junction of the east and west forks.—Return to Cass Lake.— Observance of the Sabbath.—Missionary field of labor in the northwest. —Superstitions and idolatry of the Indians.—Their name for the Deity. —Its probable derivation.

WE WERE IN MOTION AGAIN a little before five o'clock, in the morning, (14th.) The rapids continued. The branches of large trees often hung so near to the water, that if we were not in peril of being entangled, like the jewish rebel king, we were in a more continual danger of having every movable article swept from the canoes. An accident occurred to one of the canoes, about six o'clock in the morning, which might have had a fatal termination. My men had paused a few moments at the head of a formidable rapid, to determine the best place of going down it. Lieut. Allen, who, with his canoe, was behind at the moment, soon came up. His bowsman caught hold of my canoe to check his own velocity. It produced that effect, but the stern of his canoe swung across the stream, so that the steersman caught hold of a branch to prevent its being carried broadside over the rapid. Being thus rendered tense between bank and bank, the velocity of the water poured over the gunnel, and it was instantly reversed, with all its contents. This whole occurrence could not have occupied half a minute. It was impossible to render assistance, and Mr. Allen was hardly conscious of the matter, till he found himself in the stream. With no little exertion, he recovered himself, so as to be able to keep his feet, against the pressure of the current. The water was breast high. The canoe-compass was irrecoverably lost. He fetched up his fowling piece himself. Other articles went over the falls.

The character of the stream made this part of our route a most rapid one. Willing or unwilling we were hurried on. But we had every reason to desire rapidity. Less time was given to the examination of objects than might otherwise have been devoted. Yet I am not aware that any important object was neglected. Where there is much sameness in natural features, frequent

40

landings are unnecessary, and whoever has devoted his time in going thus far up the Mississippi will have made himself so familiar with its plants, soil and productions, that "he who runs may read." The pine, in its varieties, is the prevailing tree; and whenever we get out of the narrow alluvions of the valley, arenaceous plains appear. Among the plants that border the river, the wild rose, which is so conspicuous on all the streams northwest of Lake Superior, is very often seen. The salix, so common to the lower Mississippi, and so uniformly infested with musquittoes, presents itself on the first plateau, and is afterwards one of the constant shrubs on the savannahs.

The Indian reed first shews itself distinctly about the mouth of the Piniddiwin [Little Mississippi], and is here associated with wild rice. The stag and hind appear to be the species of deer, which were most frequently seen, and were several times fired at by the party, along this branch of the river. We also observed the *falco furcatus,* or swallow tailed hawk, a species not heretofore, thought to inhabit the continent, so far north. A small animal of the amphibious kind was here brought to our notice, under the name of *Ocaut Ekinabic,* or legged snake, a species of lizzard, striped blue, black, and white, with a disproportionate length of tail. It is thus readily distinguished from ordinary species. Its most striking peculiarity of habit is its extreme activity and swiftness of motion.

The Yellow Head landed, during the morning, to fire at a deer, which was seen grazing on a meadow, at some distance. He approached cautiously, but was unsuccessful in the shot he fired. What most excited our surprise, was the rapidity with which he reloaded and fired again, before the deer had got without the range of his shot. This was effected without the use of wadding to separate the powder from the ball. It did not, however, arrest the deer, who pursued his flight. The Indian returned to his canoe with a look of marked disappointment. Frequent opportunity was given in the course of the day, for firing at the various species of water fowl which resort to this stream. The saw-billed duck,[51] which is a common species, has an art of protecting its young, which we had frequent opportunities of observing. When the mother is surprised with a brood, she affects to have a wing broken, and flaps awkwardly on the water, as if unable to rise. By thus attracting notice to herself, the young, who are unable, at this season, to fly, have an opportunity to screen themselves: and the mother then boldly rises from the stream, and puts an end to the pursuit.

The river continues to descend in steps. The second series of rapids was followed by a second level, or plateau, in which the channel assumes a width nearly, or quite, double to that which it presents on the rapids. On this level, the Cano [LaSalle[52]] river comes in, as a tributary on the right shore. The volume of water is perceptibly increased by it. This plateau may extend nine miles. It is succeeded by rapids of a milder character, below which the river again displays itself in savannahs, with a comparatively wide, winding channel. These are finally terminated by short and easy rapids, which bring the river out of what, we may designate as its alpine passes. We landed for the purpose of breakfast, on an open pine bank, (left shore,) near the termination of the third plateau. Several beautifully clear and cool springs were observed running from its base into the river. It requires, indeed, but a bare recollection of observed facts, to make it evident that the waters of both branches of the Mississippi, have their origin in springs of bright and pure water. It may be farther observed, that although the Upper Mississippi receives a number of colored tributaries, all its larger rivers are pure, and it is itself essentially a clear stream, when not in flood, as far as its junction with the Missouri.

At four o'clock, we came to the junction of the Piniddiwin,[53] a tributary from the left, having its origin in a lake, and entering the Mississippi amidst an extensive marsh of rice, reeds, and rushes, which give it rather the appearance of a marsh than a lake. It is, however, called *Lac la Folle* [Monomin]. This spot was estimated to be one hundred and four miles below Itasca Lake. The name of the river employed above, is an abbreviation of the phrase *Tah-pinuniddewin,* the place of violent deaths, in allusion to an inroad and murder committed at this place, in former times, by the Sioux. A party of this tribe had previously entrenched themselves on the river above, at a spot which concealed their position and gave them command of the river channel. After waiting here for a time, without success, they proceeded lower, and discovered a Chippewa lodge, not far below the entrance of this river. It was cautiously approached, assaulted, and all its inmates killed, without distinction of age or sex. This event happened at an early period. No persons are now living who were contemporary with the victims. And it may be regarded as one of the occurrences which marked the Chippewa conquest of this portion of the country.

About eighteen miles below the junction of the Piniddiwin, we debarked for the purpose of cooking supper, and preparing our canoes for a night descent, as the channel of the river was now sufficiently broad, deep, and equable to justify it. An *Ocaut Ekinabic* was killed at this place. Lieut. Allen, wishing day light, to finish tracing the river to its junction with the east fork, encamped here. By the time we were ready to embark, clouds had overcast the moon, which afforded a clear light before. But we trusted to our experienced guide, on a part of the river familiar to him, and we had no cause to repent of our confidence. Several shots were fired during the night at deer, standing in the edge of the water. The men landed at one spot, and pursued an animal, supposed to have been wounded. We found ourselves at the junction, about half past one o'clock in the morning, (15th.) Having given notices of our ascent of the river thus far, it is unnecessary to add to them. We were borne along with the double force of current and paddles, and with no care of topographical observation to delay our progress. The night air became very damp and chilly. To defend ourselves from it, we disposed of our travelling cloaks and blankets in the best manner possible. Neither sleep nor rest were, however, truly attainable, in a confined position where there was not room enough to extend the body, and every limb was so hampered as to make it impracticable to afford the relief of a change of position. Day light broke upon us in our descent from Lac Travers, and we reached our permanent encampment on the island in Cass Lake, at nine o'clock in the morning. We had been eleven hours and a half in our canoes. Mr. Allen did not rejoin us till four o'clock in the afternoon.

The day being the Sabbath, the Reverend Mr. Boutwell, devoted a part of it, as he had done on the previous Sabbaths of our route, in giving religious instruction. As three of the soldiers of the party were christians, and two of our canoemen could sing Indian hymns; singing, both in English and in Indian, became practicable. Mr. Johnston's readiness in scripture translation, put it in the power of Mr. B. to address them on the leading doctrines of the gospel. With what effects these exhortations were listened to, on this, or on other occasions, cannot be fully stated. Strict attention appeared to be paid by the Indians, during these little forest meetings, which were generally held under some spreading tree, or on the grassy area of some sheltered glade, contiguous to the camp. Incredulity and bold cavilings were more observable, I think, at the most remote points of our route; and most interest manifested in the subject in the villages situated nearest the frontier posts. Whatever were the results, it is to be hoped that no circumstances will prevent Mr. B. from communicating his observations to the christian public, at an early period.

The field for missionary labor, in all the region northwest of St. Mary's and Michilimackinac, is certainly a very extensive and important one. And the incitements to its occupancy, at the present era, may be said to be decidedly greater, than they have been at any time, since the discovery of the country. No very strong barriers appear to stand in the way of the introduction of christianity among the northern tribes. Their institutions, moral and political, are so fragile, as to be ready to tumble on the application of the slightest power. They are not worshippers of the sun, or the moon. They have no list of imaginary gods, of the horrid character, which belong to the idolatrous nations of Asia and Africa. A Hindoo worshipper would hardly be able to impose his tale of multiform incarnations, and transmigratory existence, upon their belief. And a votary of Juggernaut, would verily be looked on by them as little better than a mad man. It is not, however, to be inferred that because these gross forms of idolatry do not exist, they have no idolatry at all. Their *medicinism* is nothing more nor less than a species of idolatry. They impute supernatural powers to certain material substances, which are preserved and guarded with religious care. These objects, which are often taken from the mineral kingdom, are carried about in sacks, and are appealed to under every form of solemnity, to perform cures, and to grant deliverances, which would require a miracle. Their lesser *monedos,* of which the number is endless, are expected to operate through these idol-medicines. And although they do not bow down to them, nor appear to place an implicit confidence in them, they remain in a state of mental alarm, which often impels them to resort to their influence. Nothing is more common, however, on conversing with them, than to find individuals, who are ready to acknowledge, the insufficiency of these means, and who appear to be prepared to abandon them, and embrace the doctrine of the Savior, the moment the fear of popular opinion among *their own people* can be removed. No dead man has been deified by them, and they have not a name or word in their language, so far as known, which represents a god, but that of "Monedo." This word, I am inclined to think, is itself, a derivative from one of the forms of the active verb, Momo, to take. But, like other Chippewa verbs, it is so buried and clogged with adjuncts, in the nature of prefix and suffix, that it might often require a Champollion to decipher it. And here, it may be observed, that Indian verbs, have not only the active and passive forms, but these forms are indicated by separate words. Thus, momo, verb active to take. Odápin, verb passive, to take. Each verb has the animate and inanimate forms. As most verbs are transitives, and their simplest forms indicate the third person singular of the imperative mood, the following conjugations of the verb, to take, result:

Momih, verb active, animate, take him.
Momon, verb active, inanimate, take it.
Odápin, verb passive, animate, take him.
Odapinun, verb passive, inanimate, take it.

CHAPTER VIII

*Council with the Chippewas at Cass Lake.—Speeches of Oza Windib,
Neezh Openais, and Wai Wain Jeegun.—Distribution of presents.—Geo-
graphical and Geological notices of Cass Lake.—Colcaspi Isle. Allen's
Bay.—Pike's Bay.—Heights and distances.—Tributary of Turtle River.
—Turtle Lake.—Portage from Cass Lake to Leech Lake.—Hieroglyphic
marks.—Moss Lake.—Reach Lake Shiba.—The source of the River
Shiba flowing into Leech Lake.—Traverse Leech Lake at night, and
encamp at Guelle Plat's village.—Received by the Indians with respect.
—Description of Leech Lake.—Its population and principal Chiefs.—
Warlike character of the Pillagers.—Efforts made by them to defend
the Chippewa frontiers.—Their warfare defensive.*

HEALTH, AND A PEACEABLE INTERCOURSE with the natives, had, under
Providence, preserved our party at the island in Cass Lake, and we rejoined
them in their encampment, with mutual pleasure. The day following our
arrival, being Monday, was devoted to the formalities of a council with the
Indians. I stated to them the objects of my visit to the region, so far as
these related to them—the desire felt by the Government for their welfare,
and its anxiety to cultivate their friendship—and endeavored to impress
upon their minds, the importance of terminating their warfare with their
hereditary enemies, the Sioux.

Oza Windib spoke in reply. Thanks, he said, were all they had to offer
me, and through me, to the Great Chief of America, for the charitable feelings which had led to my visit, and the good counsels he had received. He
should remember these counsels. They would be kept in his heart. He
would endeavor to act by them. And although not himself a Chief, or the
son of a Chief, he would exert the influence he possessed, to induce his
people to live in peace, and to listen to the voice of counsel. He rejoiced to
see the American flag displayed at this remote point, and should the master
of life preserve him till another year, it was his fixed purpose to visit the
Agency at Michilimackinac.

The son of Neezh Openais, or the Twin Birds, followed him. He said
his father had received his medal from the American Chief, (the present
Secretary of War, Hon. Lewis Cass,) who had visited, this lake, thirteen
summers before. His father was now at Red Lake, but in going there, he
had carried with him his friendship for the American Government, and
he had directed him to express it to me, and to unite in the promotion of
any good measure proposed. He assented to the sentiments uttered by Oza
Windib. He approved of the advice. He would act by it. He thanked me,

45

as being the bearer of it, and he looked to me to direct the Chippewas in their affairs, and to make them prosper.

A deputy from the band at Red Lake, then delivered a peace pipe, with its garnished stem, decked with feathers, from Wai Wain Jeegun, a War Chief of that lake. He had sent it, it was declared, as a token of his friendship—his remembrance of the power that permitted traders to come into their country to supply them with goods, and his hope and expectation, that his remote position, and limited authority, might not operate, to render his present unwelcome. It had been prepared by his own hand. Although he had wielded the war club, it was in self defence, and to prevent others from saying he is a coward. The peace pipe he offered, he smoked, however, with his heart.

The distribution of presents to the promiscuous assembly of men, women, and children, the payment of those who had furnished canoes, and the rewarding of the guides, closed the business of the council. I invested Oza Windib with a flag and the President's medal, delivered a flag into the hands of Neezh Openais, for his father, and sent a message, with an acknowledgment and presents, to Wai Wain Jeegun. These things dispatched, we prepared to embark for the portage to Leech Lake. But previous to quitting this lake, it may be proper to subjoin a few particulars respecting it, which, from a desire to gain a more perfect knowledge of it, were omitted, on first entering it.

Cass Lake occupies a position on the American continent, and particularly in relation to the Upper Mississippi, which makes it desirable to acquire more accurate details and observations than it fell to our lot to be enabled to make. But in the absence of such data, such facts as our means permitted may be substituted. We were impressed with its extent, the picturesque character of its islands, and the diversified appearance of its very irregular woodland shores. Its geological features are similar to those of Leech Lake and Lake Winnipec, being a basin of deluvial formation, spotted with islands, occupying a position on the great marine sand district of the Upper Mississippi. This district abounds in pure springs, and is so impervious in its lower strata, that it has probably retained to the present day, more water in the character of lakes, large and small, than any other part of the world. The greatest expanse of the lake appears to lie in the direction from north to south. Its length is from northeast to southwest. From the time consumed in passing through it, it cannot fall short of sixteen miles. It has four islands, the largest of which Colcaspi or Grand Island, which is itself of a most striking shape, occupying a large area in its centre and presenting its green forests of elm and oak in striking contrast with the bright expanse of waters. Allen's[54] Bay is, properly the head of this lake, receiving the Mississippi from the west. Nothing, however, in the mere figure of the lake, is so characteristic as the noble bay which puts out from its southern shore, presenting an expanse of clear and deep water which we were an hour, with every exertion, in crossing transversely. This bay was visited on the ice by the late General Pike, in his search of the sources of the Mississippi in the winter of 1806, and it may be appropriately named after a man, who, both as a traveller and a soldier, has so fair a claim to rememberance.

Cass Lake has been estimated to be within a few miles of 3,000 from the Gulf of Mexico, and to lie at an elevation of 1,330 feet above that point of the Atlantic waters; its distance northwest of Sandy Lake, is about two hundred and seventy miles, and of Fond du Lac, four hundred and twenty miles. Estimates make it one hundred and eighty-two miles below the true source of the Mississippi in Itasca Lake, and sixty south of Red Lake. It receives Turtle River on its northern shore. This river is ascended through eleven small lakes, a distance of about thirty-eight to forty miles to its origin in Turtle Lake, once deemed to be the source of the Mississippi.[55] There is a portage from the lake, for light packages of goods, across the summit level of the Mississippi valley into Red Lake, and the fertile valley of Red river. The latter embraces the settlements planted by the Earl of Selkirk, the inhabitants of which maintained their existence for several years against the strenuous opposition of the North West Company, and they appear now to be in a state of comparative prosperity under the direction of a local governor, council, and clergy.

The portage from Pike's Bay, (where we arrived at twelve o'clock in the morning, after a two hours's journey from the island,) commences on the edge of an open pine forest, interspersed with shrub oak. The path is deeply worn, and looks as if it might have been used by the Indians, for centuries. It lies across a plain presenting the usual aridity of similar formations, and exhibiting the usual growth of underbrush and shrubbery. I observed the alum root, harebell and sweet fern scattered through the more prevalent growth of wortle berry, L. latifolia, &c. Markings and hieroglyphic characters were pointed out to us on the pines, some of which were said to be so ancient as to have been made by the people who occupied the country before the Ojibwais. Of the truth of this assertion there did not appear to be any certain means of judging. A blaze on the pinus resinosa, if made upon a matured tree, may be considered as comparatively permanent, from the fact that the outer bark is not apt to close over it, while the gum that exudes over the wounded surface has some of the properties of a varnish. How long the rude drawings of birds and animals made with charcoal would thus be preserved is mere matter of conjecture, and must depend upon observations which we had no means of making.

A portage of nine hundred and fifty yards brought us to the banks of a small lake, called Moss Lake, which we were but a short time in crossing. The water being clear, large masses appeared to rise from the bottom, which had very much the aspect of boulders. On reaching down, however, the men brought up on their paddles, a species of moss of a coarse fibrous character. And this moss seemed to be quite a characteristic trait of the lake. There is a slight relief, to both mind and body, in these changes from land to water transportation, even where the distance is very short; and the men resume their labor, in carrying, with greater alacrity. We found it so on the present occasion. No change however appeared in the general character of the country. We crossed a bog of perhaps fifty or sixty yards in extent,

where the water appeared to have some motion towards the left. All the
rest of the way consists of an unvaried sand plain, which is sometimes
brushy, but generally open, presenting facilities for travelling. A walk of
four thousand and one hundred yards, or about two and a half miles
brought us out to the edge of Lake Shiba,[56] a body of clear water, of moderate dimensions, which has its outlet into an arm of Leech Lake. There is
a portage path from its southern side which the Indians use when they are
passing with light canoes.

The day was well nigh spent, by the time the men brought up all the
baggage to the banks of this lake. And the fatigue of the route itself might
have justified our encamping. But whoever has a definite point to reach in
a given time, will find that the loss of a single hour, or half hour of an
evening's journey, on sundry days, will soon combine to waste an entire
day, which may be the exact time necessary to accomplish the route. Besides, when the question of going on is at a spot where a *land* is to be exchanged for a *water* journey, there is a sensible relief to the men, in the
position of sitting and being freed from the pressure of the head-strap, or
apicun, by which they carry. And north-men thus embarked, in a state of
fatigue, will soon resume their strength and gaiety. I felt this, on the present
occasion, and directed them not to lose a moment in getting afloat. We
crossed the lake, with but little effort, and entered its thread-like outlet, so
tangled and wound about, in a shaking savannah, covered with sedge, that
every point of the compass seemed to be alternately pursued. In this maze
it was joined, from the right by a tributary of its own size, very welcome
for its accession of waters, but not aiding to straighten the channel. Another tributary flows in directly opposite the Indian portage before referred
to. This tributary appears to be the outlet of a contiguous, narrow and long
lake [Steamboat], which can be, in part observed. The channel is suddenly
enlarged by it, and it is soon after still further swelled by a similar inlet.
Both these inlets are referred to by the Indians, by the phrase, "Kapucka
Sagitowag." The stream is so enlarged by them, as not only to assume the
character of a river [Steamboat], but it is a river of handsome magnitude,
broad and deep but without strong current. Its shores assume a low and
marshy character, and they are fringed with extensive fields of wild rice.
Amidst these, the river opens into an arm of Leech Lake. The last glimpses
of day light here left us. We pursued our way by moonlight for a time. The
sky was overcast before we effected our first traverse. Sometime previous
to landing it became quite dark. Even with the knowledge of an Indian
guide, it was necessary to fire guns, to ascertain the position of the principal
village. It was ten o'clock, on our landing, and it was an hour later before
the military canoes came up. Salutes were separately fired by the Indians
through the top openings of their lodges. In the morning, (17th,) a more
formal salute was given. Fresh fish and wortle-berries were brought in:
and an invitation to breakfast sent from the presiding chief.

Leech Lake is one of the most irregular shaped bodies of water that can
be conceived of.[57] It is neither characteristically long, spherical, or broad,
but rather a combination of curves, in the shape of points, peninsulas, and

bays, of which nothing short of a map can convey an accurate idea. The Indians, whom I requested to draw a sketch of it, began by tracing an oblong as large as half a sheet of foolscap would admit of. They filled it up by projecting points inwardly, or extended it by tracing bays outwardly. Ten islands were drawn in different parts of it, and seven rivers and creeks made to enter it. Its outlet is called by them the great river, and is towards the northeast. The lake cannot be less than twenty miles across the extreme points of the waters. Its principal peninsula resembles in shape the letter T. Ottertail Point is a part of its northern shore. Its waters are deep and clear in all its central parts, and yield the whitefish and other species. Its numerous and extensive bays abound in wild rice, and attract in the proper season, a great variety of water fowl. The pelican, swan, brant, and cormorant are the largest of the species that annually visit it. Its shores yield the deer and bear. Beavers were formerly abundant, but they have, in a great measure, disappeared. The muskrat and marten are now the principal items of its fine furs.

My intercourse with the Indians at this lake occupied the day after my arrival. The population was reported at eight hundred and thirty-two souls. Seven eights of this number are of the band called Mukkundwais, or Pillagers, a term derived from occurrences in their early history.[58] The remainder are locally denominated the Bear Island Indians. The principal chiefs are Aish Kibug Ikozh, or The Gueula Plat, and [Nesia] The Elder Brother, and Chianoquot [or Big Cloud]. This band appear[s] to have separated themselves from the other Chippewas, at an early day, and to have taken upon themselves the duty which Reuben, Gad, and Manasseh assumed, when they crossed the Jordan. They have "passed armed before their brethren," in their march westward. Their geographical position is one, which imposes upon them the defence of this portion of the Chippewa frontier. And it is a defence in which they have distinguished themselves as brave and active warriors. Many acts of intrepidity are related of them which would be recorded, with admiration had white men been the actors. Perfectly versed in the arts of the forest, they have enjoyed the advantage of concealment in the progress of a war, which has been directed against the Sioux, a powerful assemblage of tribes, who live essentially in plains, but who aim to make up the disadvantage of this exposure, by moving habitually in larger bodies. It seems, however, indisputable, that, with fewer numbers, the Chippewas have not hesitated to fall upon their enemies, and have routed them, and driven them before them, with a valor and resolution, which in any period of written warfare, would have been stamped as heroic. It is not easy, on the part of government, to repress the feelings of hostility, which have so long existed, and to convince them, that they have lived into an age when milder maxims furnish the basis of wise action. Pacific counsels fall with little power upon a people situated so remotely from every good influence, and who cannot perceive in the restless spirit of their enemies, any safeguard for the continuance of a peace, however formally it may have been concluded. This fact was adverted to by one of their chiefs, who observed that they were compelled to fight in self defence. Although the Sioux had made a solemn peace with them at Tipi-sagi in 1825,[59] they were attacked by them that very year, and had almost yearly since, sustained insidious or open attacks. He said, "his own son, his only son," was among the number, who had been basely killed, without an opportunity to defend himself.

CHAPTER IX

Transactions at Leech Lake.—Notice of the Pillager band.—Their chief, Aish Kibug Ekozh, or the Flat Mouth.—He invites the agent and his interpreter to breakfast.—His address on concluding it.—Vaccination of the Indians.—A deputation from the Rainy Lake band is received, and a flag presented to their leader, The Hole in the Sky.—Council with the Pillagers.—Speech of Aish Kibug Ekozh, in which he makes an allusion to Gen. Pike.—He descants on the Sioux war, the Indian trade, and the interdiction of ardent spirits.—Personal notices of this chief.

THE DOMESTIC MANNERS and habits of a people, whose position is so adverse to improvement, could hardly be expected to present any thing strikingly different, from other erratic bands of the northwest. There is indeed a remarkable conformity in the external habits of all our northern Indians. The necessity of changing their camps often, to procure game or fish, the want of domesticated animals, the general dependence on wild rice, and the custom of journeying in canoes, has produced a general uniformity of life. And it is emphatically a life of want and vicissitude. There is a perpetual change between action and inanity, in the mind, which is a striking peculiarity of the savage state. And there is such a general want of forecast, that most of their misfortunes and hardships, in war and peace, come unexpectedly. None of the tribes who inhabit this quarter, can be said to have, thus far, derived any peculiarities from civilized instruction. The only marked alteration which their state of society has undergone appears to be referable to the era of the introduction of the fur trade, when they were made acquainted with, and adopted the use of, iron, gunpowder, and woollens. This implied a considerable change of habits, and of the mode of subsistence; and may be considered as having paved the way for further changes in the mode of living and dress. But it brought with it the onorous evil of intemperance, and it left the mental habits essentially unchanged. All that related to a system of dances, sacrifices, and ceremonies, which stood in the place of religion, still occupies that position, presenting a subject which is deemed the peculiar labor of evangelists and teachers. Missionaries have been slow to avail themselves of this field of labor, and it should not excite surprise, that the people themselves are, to so great a degree, *mentally* the same in 1832, that they were on the arrival of the French in the St. Lawrence in 1532 [1534].

"Unknown the measured joys of peaceful art,
"Love, hatred, pity, storm, by turns, the heart,
"And all the evils of the savage state,
"Arise from false conceits of being great."

51

Partial exceptions in the acquisition of civil information are to be found; and the incident I am about to relate, is the more remarkable as connected with the history of a chief, who has passed his life in so very unfrequented a part of the continent, with only the advantages of occasional short visits to the posts of St. Mary's, St. Peter's and Michilimackinac. Aish Kibug Ekozh, or the Guelle Plat, is the ruler of the Pillager band, exercising the authority of both a civil and war chief. And he is endowed with talents which certainly entitle him to this distinction. Complying with European customs, he directed his young men to fire a salute on the morning of my arrival. Soon after he sent one of his officials to invite me to breakfast. I accepted the invitation. But not knowing how the meal could be suitably got along with, without bread, I took the precaution to send up a tin dish of pilot bread. I went to his residence at the proper time, accompanied by Mr. Johnston. I found him living in a comfortable log building of two rooms, well floored, and roofed, with a couple of small glass windows. A mat was spread upon the centre of the floor, which contained the breakfast. Other mats were spread around it, to sit on. We followed his example in sitting down after the eastern manner. There was no other person admitted to the meal but his wife, who sat near him, and poured out the tea, but ate or drank nothing herself. Tea cups, and tea spoons, plates, knives and forks, of plain manufacture, were carefully arranged, and the number corresponding exactly with the expected guests. A white fish, cut up and boiled in good taste, occupied a dish in the centre, from which he helped us. A salt cellar, in which pepper and salt were mixed in unequal proportions, allowed each the privilege of seasoning his fish with both or neither. Our tea was sweetened with the native sugar, and the dish of hard bread seemed to have been precisely wanted to make out the repast. It needed but the imploring of a blessing, to render it essentially a christian meal.

This chief brought me a letter from the interior some years ago, at St. Mary's, in which he is spoken of as "the most respectable man in the Chippewa country." And if the term was applied to his mental qualities, and the power of drawing just conclusions from known premises, and the effects which these have had on his standing and influence with his own band, it is not misapplied. Shrewdness and quickness most of the chiefs possess, but there is more of the character of common sense and practical reflection, in the Gueule Plat's remarks, than, with a very extensive acquaintance, I recollect to have noticed in most of the chiefs now living, of this tribe.[60] He is both a warrior and a counsellor, and these distinctions he holds, not from any hereditary right, for he is a self-made man, but from the force of his own character. I found him ready to converse on the topics of most interest to him. And the sentiments he uttered on the Sioux war, the fur trade, and the location of trading posts and agencies, were such as would occur to a mind which had possessed itself of facts, and was capable of reasoning from them. His manners were grave and dignified, and his oratory such as to render him popular with his tribe.

During the repast, the room became filled with Indians, apparently the relatives and intimate friends of the chief, who seated themselves orderly

and silently around the room. When we arose, the chief assumed the ora-
torical attitude, and addressed himself to me.

He expressed his regret that I had not been able to visit them the year
before, when I was expected.[61] He hoped I had now come, as I came by
surprise, to remain some days with them. He said, they lived at a remote
point, and were involved in wars with their neighbors, and wished my advice. They were not insensible to advice, nor incapable of following it.
They were anxious for counsel, and desirous of living at peace, and of
keeping the advice which had heretofore been given them. They had been
told to sit still on their lands, but their enemies would not permit them to
sit still. They were compelled to get up, and fight in self defence. The Sioux
continued to kill their hunters. They had killed his son, during the last visit
he had made to my office. They had never ceased to make inroads. And he
believed there were white men among them, who stirred them up to go to
war against the Chippewas. He named one person particularly.

It was necessary, he continued, to take some decisive steps to put a stop
to these inroads. This was the reason why he had led out the war party,
which had recently returned. This was the reason why I saw the stains of
blood before me.

He alluded, in the last expression, to the flags, war clubs, and medals,
which decorated one end of the room, all of which had vermilion smeared
over them to represent blood. I replied, that I would assemble the Indians
at a general council, at my camp, as soon as preparations could be made;
that notice would be given them by the firing of the military, and that I
should then lay before them the advice I came to deliver from their Great
Father, the President, and offer, at the same time, my own counsel, on the
subjects he had spoken of.

During the day constant accessions were made to the number of Indians,
from neighboring places. And before the hour of the council arrived, there
could have been but little short of a thousand souls present. Most of the
warriors carried their arms, and were painted and drest in their gayest
manner. And they walked through the village with a bold and free air, in
striking contrast with the subdued and cringing aspect, which is sometimes
witnessed in the vicinity of the posts and settlements. Many applications
were made for the extraction of decayed teeth, and for blood letting, the
latter of which appears to be a favorite remedy among the northern Indians.
Most of the time of the surgeon, (Dr. Houghton,) was however employed
in the application of the vaccine virus, which constituted one of the primary
objects of the visit. Among the number vaccinated by him, one was past
the age of eighty, several between sixty and eighty, and a large number
under the age of ten. Little difficulty was found in getting them to submit
to the process, and wherever there was hesitancy or refusal, it seemed to
arise from a distrust of the protective power of the disease. None had been
previously vaccinated. Of the younger classes, it was remarked here, as at
other places, that the boys evinced no fear on the display of the lancet, but
nearly every female child, either came with reluctance and entreaty of the
parents, or was absolutely obliged to be held, during the process. The rav-

ages made by the small pox in this quarter, about the year 1782, were remembered with the distinctness of recent tradition, and had its effects in
preparing their minds, generally, not only to receive the vaccine virus, but
in imparting a solicitude that all might be included, so as to ensure them
from the recurrence of a pestilence, which they regard with horror. Their
name for this disease, of Ma Mukkizziwin, suggests the disfiguration of the
flesh and skin produced by it.[62]

Among the number of Indians who arrived here, during the day, were a
party of nine Rainy Lake Indians under the leadership of a man named
Wai Wizhzhi Geezhig, or The Hole in the Sky. He represented himself and
party as part of a small band residing at Springing-bow-string Lake, in the
middle grounds between Lake Winnipec and Rainy Lake. He said, they
had heard of my passing the post of Winnipec, with an intention of returning through Leech Lake. This was the cause of his visit. They lived off from
the great lake, and seldom saw Americans. He came to express his good
will, hoping to be remembered, as he now saw his father, among his children, &c. I presented him, publicly, with my own hand, with a flag, and
directed to be laid before him an amount of presents, committing to him,
at the same time, a short address to be delivered to the American portion
of the Rainy Lake Indians.

The hour for the council having arrived, and the Mukkundwa [is], or
Pillagers, being present with their chiefs and warriors, women and children,
I caused the presents intended for this band, to be displayed in bulk, on
blankets spread on the grass, in front of my tent. I called their attention to
the subjects named in my instructions, the desire of the government for the
restoration of peace, and its paternal character, feelings, and wishes in relation, particularly, to them—reminded them of their solemn treaty of peace
and limits with the Sioux, at Prairie du Chien in 1825, enforcing the advantages of it, in its bearings on their hunting, trade, and well being. The
presents were then delivered to the chiefs, as an earnest of good will and
sincerity on the part of the government, and were by them directed to be
immediately divided and distributed.

Aish Kibug Ikozh, or the Guelle Plat, was their speaker in reply. He
called the attention of the warriors to his words. He thanked me for the
presents, which reminded him, in amount, of the times when the British
held possession in that quarter. He pointed across an arm of the lake, in
front, to the position formerly occupied by the North West Company's fort.
He said many winters had now passed since the Americans first sent one
of their chiefs to that post, (alluding to the visit of Pike.) He remembered
that visit. I had now come, it appeared, to remind them that the American
flag was flying in the land, and to offer them counsels of peace. He thanked
me for them. He had hoped that I was to spend more time with them, that
they might consult on a reply, but as they must speak on the instant, (orders had been given for embarking that evening) they would not loose the
opportunity of declaring their sentiments.

He had before heard the Americans say, peace, peace! But he thought
their advice resembled a rushing wind. It was strong and went soon. It did

not abide long enough to choke up the road. At the treaty of Tipisagi, it had been promised that the aggressors should be punished; but that very year they were attacked by the Sioux; and almost yearly since, some of their nation had been killed. They had even been fired on by the Sioux, under the walls of the fort at Ishki Buggi Seebi [St. Peter's], and four of their number had been killed. He had, himself, been present. He here asked one of his subordinates for a bundle of sticks, which he handed to me saying, it is the number of the Leech Lake Chippewas who have been killed by the Sioux, since they signed the treaty of Tipisagi. The number was forty-three.

He then lifted up four silver medals, attached by a string of wampum, and smeared with vermilion. Take notice, he said, they are bloody. I wish you to wipe off the blood. I am unable to do it. I find myself irretrievably involved in a war with the Sioux. I believe it has been intended by the creator that we should be at war with this people. I am not satisfied with the result of the last war party. My warriors are not satisfied. They are brave men. It is to them I owe success, and not to myself. Both they, and I, have heretofore looked for help where we did not find it. (He alluded to the American government.) We are determined to revenge ourselves. If the United States does not aid us, I have it in mind to apply for aid else-where. (He alluded to the British government.) My warriors are in a rest-less state. I have sent my pipe and invitations to my friends around, to con-tinue the war. Circumstances control me. I cannot avoid it. My feelings are enlisted deeply in the contest. When the enemy killed my son, I resolved never to lay down the war club. I have sought death in battle but have not met it. All I now can say is this, that perhaps I shall not lead out the next war party.

Other parts of his speech on the war are omitted. This is, however, the thread, although a broken thread of his argument, omitting frequent and glowing appeals to his warriors, who expressed their approbation at every pause.

He proceeded to accuse persons on the waters of the Upper Mississippi, of giving advice to the Sioux to go to war against the Chippewas. He said it was the interest of persons in the trade to induce the Sioux to extend their hunting grounds across the boundary lines. He evinced a familiarity with persons and places. He boldly accused, not only traders, but even some persons holding offices under government, of participating in this course of mal-advice.[63]

He complained of the traders. He criticised their conduct with severity. He declared their prices to be exorbitant, and said they were so intent on getting furs, that they did not deem it necessary to use much formality in their dealings. He complained of the exclusion of ardent spirits, but at the same time admitted, that formerly it was brought in to buy up their wild rice—a practice which left them at the beginning of cold weather, in a desti-tute situation.

Much of the sentiment of this address appeared to be uttered for popular effect. There was a marked difference between the tone of his private conversation, and his public address, of which more will appear in the sequel. Such parts of it, as required it, were replied to, and the simple truths, political and moral, dictating the visit to them, brought clearly before their minds, so as to leave definite impressions.

So far as related to the traders withdrawing the article of whiskey from the trade, I felt it due to say, that no hard feelings should be entertained towards them. That it was excluded by the Indian Office. They should, therefore, in justice, blame me or blame the government, but not the traders. I was satisfied, I added, that the use of whiskey was very hurtful to them, in every situation of life, and felt determined to employ every means which the control of the agency of the northwest gave me, to exclude the article wholly, and rigidly from the Chippewas, and to set the mark of disapprobation upon every trader who should make the attempt to introduce it.

It was near the hour of sunset when the council closed. Minor duties employed some time after. And while these were in the progress of execution, the Gueule Plat, who had been the principal actor during the day, gave us occasion to observe, that if he had studied effect in speaking, he was also a judge of propriety in dress. At a dinner to which I invited him, at my tent, and also during the public council following it, he appeared in his native costume. But after the close of the council and before we embarked, he came down to the lake shore, to bid us fare well, dressed in a blue military frock coat, with red collar and cuffs, with white underclothes, a linen ruffled shirt, shoes and stockings, and a neat citizen's hat. To have uttered his speeches in this foreign costume, might have been associated in the minds of his people, with the idea of servility; but he was willing afterwards to let us observe, by assuming it, that he knew we would consider it a mark of respect.

This chief appears to be turned of sixty. In stature he is about five feet nine or ten inches, erect and stout, somewhat inclined to corpulency. He is a native of this lake, of the *totem*[64] of the Owásissi, a kind of fish. He observed at my table, at St. Mary's, four years ago, that he had been twenty five times on war parties, either as leader or follower, and had escaped without a wound. He was once surrounded by a party of Sioux, with only three companions. They cut their way out killing two men. He was early drawn into intercourse with the British at Fort William, on Lake Superior, where he received his first medal. This medal was taken from him by Lieut. Pike, in 1806. I renewed it, by the largest class of solid silver medals, July 19th, 1828.

Reciprocating the customary compliment in parting, we embarked and encamped on a contiguous part of the coast, where we could procure fire wood, and be sure of making an early start on the morrow.

CHAPTER X

Observations on the Leech Lake Chippewas.—Data respecting the former state of the fur trade.—Their turbulent character.—Assassination of Relle by Puganoc.—Causes of the emigration of the Northwestern Indians.—The unsatisfactory character of their traditions.—Their language.—Brief synopsis of its grammatical structure.

LEECH LAKE has been one of the principal posts of trade in the northwest since the region was first laid open to the enterprise of the fur trade, and it has probably yielded more wealth in furs and skins, than one of the richest mines of silver would have produced. European goods were extremely high at the period referred to, at the same time, that furs were abundant, and the ability of the Indians to pay, consequently, ample. The standard of value and computation in this trade, is an abminikwa, or prime beaver, called *plus* by the French. A plus, tradition states, was given for as much vermilion as would cover the point of a case knife, and the same price was paid respectively for four charges of powder, or four charges of shot, or fifteen balls, or two branches of wampum. It is related that an outfit of six bales of goods, worth, say $2000, brought from Athabasca,[65] ninety-six packs of beaver, each of which would weigh ninety pounds, at a time when prime beaver was worth four dollars per pound. A fine gun, worth ten guineas, was sold to a chief at one of the northern posts, for one hundred and twenty pounds of beaver, say four hundred and eighty dollars. The post of the Pic,[66] alone, is said to have yielded one hundred packs of beaver, during a single season. From the MSS. of M. Perrault,[67] now before us, referred to in a previous part of our narrative, the rates at which furs were reduced to the plus, at this lake, in 1784, were the following. A bear was estimated to be one plus, an otter, three martens, a lynx, fifteen muskrats, respectively, one plus. A buffalo robe, two plus. A keg of mixed rum, which was then the kind of spirits used in the trade, was sold at thirty plus, and the Indians, when they commenced trading, first put out the furs they intended as pay for their liquor.

The Leech Lake Indians were then stated to be numerous, although, in common with other northern bands, they had also suffered from the general ravages of the small pox, in this region, two years previous. They were, however, then, as now, deemed a turbulent band, and such was the fear of giving additional excitement to their passions, that the liquor which was sold to them, was put in *cache* at the entrance of the river, that it might not be delivered to them, until the traders had finished their traffic, (which on that occasion, occupied but a *single* day,) and embarked on their return for Michilimackinac. Besides the original robbery of a principal

trader, which drew upon them the name of Pillagers, their intercourse
with the traders has been of a character to require perpetual caution to
avoid the recurrence of serious difficulties. It is but two years ago that they
confined a trader to his lodge, and threatened him, in such a manner, that
he was happy to escape from the country with his life, and has not since
returned to it.

During the winter of 1821-22, a man named [Constant] Relle, who was
employed at Leech Lake, to collect credits, as it is termed, entered the
lodge of a hunter named Puganoc i. e. Nutwood, and without much ceremony, obtained the Indian's furs. He had as he conceived, got consent
which the Indian afterwards withdrew. Relle, however, whose business it
was to collect furs for his employer, and who had, from long usage, become expert in that employment, did not pay that deference to the Indian's wishes, which he probably would have done, could we suppose that
he considered them to indicate any more, than a mere reluctance to part
with the furs. On this point we are without particular information. Be this
as it may, Relle took up the furs, and proceeded homewards. Puganoc followed him but without any demonstrations of anger. It might be supposed
that he intended in[to] make a friendly visit to the post, for the purpose of
further trading, and Relle evidently so considered the circumstance of his
accompanying him, for he was wholly unsuspicious of latent revenge. Silent as this passion was kept, it burned, however, in the Indian's breast,
and, in crossing a lake, on the ice, the Indian treading in the hindmost step,
(a practice in walking with snow shoes,) he suddenly discharged his piece.
The ball entered his victim's back below the shoulders. He fell dead.
Puganoc then drew his knife, cut off two of the voyageur's fingers, to make
it appear that he had been struggling with an adversary, then threw down
the knife on the snow, and returned with a report that the man had been
killed by the Sioux.

It may be interesting to notice the fate of Puganoc. Attempts for his
surrender to the civil authorities were made, but without success. Meantime he was regarded as having forfeited his life by a young Chippewa of
his own band, a relative, perhaps, of the deceased voyageur's Indian wife.
While assembled to amuse themselves by firing at a mark, this young man,
as it became his turn to fire, saw Puganoc lifting the cloth door of his tent,
and wheeling half a circle in his aim, fired his ball through the neck of the
assassin, and killed him on the spot.

Pride, and the desire of personal distinction, as in other tribes which
have not the light of christianity to guide them, may be considered as
lying at the foundation of the Indian character. For there are no tribes so
poor and remote as not to have pride. And this passion seems always to be
coupled with a desire of applause, and with the wish on the part of its
possessors to be thought better than they real[l]y are. We have found pride
in the remotest Indian lodge we ever visited, and have hardly ever engaged in ten minutes conversation with a northern Indian, without discovering it not only to exist, but, where there was moral energy at all, as
constituting the primary motive to action. It has always been found, how-

ever, unaccompanied by one of its most constant concomitants, in civilised life—namely, the desire of wealth.

The workings of this principle may, indeed, be looked upon as the chief motive of Indian emigration, and as causing tribe to secede from tribe, and leading to that multiplication of petty nations, each with some peculiarities of language, which marks the face of the northern regions. Did we possess any thing like a clear and connected tradition of these migrations, even for a few hundred years, we should perhaps have cause to blush that so many blunders had been committed in assigning so many primitive stocks, when, in fact, there is great reason to believe, that the primitive stocks are few.

Tradition does not reach far, where there is neither pen nor pencil to perpetuate the memory of events. People who are constantly and habitually concerned, how they shall subsist, and what they shall wear, will soon forget, in the realities before them, occurrences which can no longer produce fear or excite hope. And were it otherwise,—were they as prone to reflect as they are to act, the very misery in which they live, would take away the pleasure of historical reminiscence. Oral history is very uncertain at best. Every repetition varies the language at least, and it must be a very stoical people, indeed, who, in repeating their own story, do not add to the coloring, if not the number of circumstances, which serve to give pleasure or to flatter pride. Unfortunately such appears to have been the state of the northwestern Indians, as far as we know any thing of them, that they could not, in strict truth, repeat very little of their history, without giving pain, or exciting feelings, often of pity, and often of humiliation. The few favorable points would naturally grow by the process of repetition, out of all proportion. And fiction would often be called on, to supply lapses. Hence it is, perhaps, that in looking over our printed materials for Indian history, we are so apt to find that every tribe arrogates to itself the honor of being original, great, brave, magnanimous, above its neighbors. Indeed we regard all unrecorded Indian tradition, referring to events beyond the close of the sixteenth century, as entitled to no confidence.

The names the Indians bestowed upon themselves, contain no clue to their early history. They were, for the most part purely accidental, as they are at this day. They do not refer to their origin. They do not in some cases, even signify their peculiarities. This is, we think, emphatically true of the various tribes of Algonquins. To part of the people composing this stock, who were settled in a country abounding in lakes and streams, they gave the local name of Nipissings, i. e. People of the Place of Waters. Part, who lived on the north shore of the Gulf of St. Lawrence, subsisting on fish, they called Popinoshees, alluding to a kind of fish. Those who dwelt in swampy grounds, (as between that point and Lake Superior,) were called Mushkeegos, from the name for swamp. Those who lived in plains, southwest of Lake Michigan, Muscotins, from plain. Others having a peculiarity of intonation, were called Ojibwas, or Chippewas; a band who lit up a council fire for themselves, Pottawattamies; another band, given to trading, Ottawas; another who inflicted cruelties in their northern wars,

Kenistonos; another who lived inland, Nopimings. Others might be added to the list. These were all identical people; but not one of the name referred to their origin. The French, on their arrival increased the confusion, by bestowing a new name upon each, rendering the thread of history more entangled, and utterly confounding all attempts to trace their affiliation by etymology. They called the first band whom they found speaking this language, on the St. Lawrence, Algonquins, probably because they subsisted on the oga. This term has become generic. But there is no light thrown by it on the history of the race. Nay, there is not a particle of proof that the Indians had bestowed it upon themselves, or that it was not given like all their other appellations, as a mere *nom de guerre*. No wonder should therefore be expressed that classifications founded on etymological proofs should have been found defective.

But we shall not pursue the subject. The Leech Lake Indians, like others of the stock, derive their distinctive appellation from a mere accident. They are not, however, separated by any distinctive feature, from the rest of the more favorably located Chippewas. Their prominent manners and customs, ceremonies and opinions, are the same. They migrated by the same track, adopted the same means of living, sought the attainment of the same general objects, and speak the same language. There are minor peculiarities of speech in most of the bands of this nation, separated by a few hundred miles. But they consist mostly in accent, with some interchanges of the labial and liquid consonants. The vowel sounds are identical. Whatever remarks could be made, therefore, on the principles of the language, would be equally applicable to the current language of other Chippewa bands.

This language covers an extensive area in the west, and the north-west. It is emphatically the *court language* of the Indians, being the medium of communication, in all general councils. Its copiousness and freedom from the barbarities which disfigure many of the native languages, were remarked at an early day, and have led to its being more studied and spoken, than perhaps any other native American language. The regret has been expressed, that where so many good points exist, there should be found any defects to mar them. In its grammatical structure, it exhibits some peculiarities, which do not, perhaps, admit of being strictly classed with other transpositive languages, although it has most features in coincidence with them. Originally, simple in its character, and consisting of scarcely any distinctions of speech, beyond the verb and substantive, and the pronominal and other primary particles, the tendency of usage and invention has been, to increase the length of words by combination, rendering them formidable to the eye, and pompous to the ear. These combinations assume almost every shape, in which words can be made to coalesce. And the primitives when thus united, are still further compounded by inflections for time and person, for number and quality, and sometimes to indicate other circumstances, as if it were the chief scope of the speaker to concentrate all the offices of speech in a single word, or a single expression. But in this process of accretion, as might be expected, clearness and simplicity are often sacrificed to sound, and the distinctions of person, and number, and tense, are not, perhaps, always accurately preserved. So many letters, and even whole syllables, are also dropped, to effect the purposes of a harmonious coalescence, agreeably to the Indian ear, that it becomes extremely difficult to trace analogies, and one of the usual helps to comparison, is thus withdrawn. Number is entirely wanting in the third person of the declension of their pronouns and nouns, and in the conjugation of their verbs. Nor is there any distinction to mark the sex of the third person, although the first and second persons, are uniformly and scrupulously thus marked. He and she, him and her, are expressed by the same word, or the same pronominal sign. Although there is a positive and a conditional future, in the conjugation of their verbs, the compound tenses are generally thought to be defective.

Notwithstanding these deficiences, the language admits of many fine turns of expression, and pointed terms of irony, and in its general simplicity, and nervous brevity, will admit of a comparison with some terms of scripture phraseology. Among its grammatical forms, there are several, which exhibit beautiful and succinct modes of conveying thought. All its active verbs can be multiplied as often as there are distinct objects of their action, and they are conjugated both negatively, as well as positively. Substantives admit of adjective terminations, and adjectives of substantive terminations. Both can be turned into verbs, and both are endowed with number. Pronouns are inflected for time, and in this shape, supply the want of our auxiliary verbs. The verb, to be, may be said to characterize this language, as differing from some of the Indian languages, although its use is restricted, and there is no declarative existence indicated in the ordinary conjugation of verbs. As all nouns assume verbal terminations, they undergo all the modifications of other verbs. Possession is indicated by an inflection analogous to, but differing from case. Locality, diminution, and derogation, may be, either separately, or all together, denoted by inflections of the noun. Particles are very copiously used. And this part of speech is very important, making the use of words definite or exact, which without these adjuncts, would often lack both coherence and exactitude. Adverbs are liberally employed, and by their help, the degrees of comparison are formed. There is but one degree of comparison formed by an inflection of the substantive. There is a numerous list of prepositions, which are not, however, disjunctively used, but always as the prefixed syllable or syllables, to substantives. Conjunctions, of which the language has a number, are not thus restricted, and cannot thus be used. The most important distinction, however, which belongs to the language, and that which most rigidly pervades its forms, is the separation of words into two classes, distinguished as *animate* and *inanimate,* or personal and impersonal, carrying also, the idea of noble and ignoble. This principle, merges the ordinary distinctions of gender, and imparts a two-fold character to the verb, substantive, and adjective, and consequently creates the necessity of double conjugations and declensions. This results from the transitive character of the whole language, and its habitual application to material objects. The verb which would be used to imply vision, is made to indicate the presence or absence of vitality, creating the distinction of the *animate* and *inanimate* forms. The same principle interdicts the promiscuous use of adjectives. A strong man and a strong house require different modifications of the word strong. All its concords are directed to the upholding of this rule. This novel and curious principle appears to lie at the foundation of the syntax, and imparts to the language its most marked characteristic feature. Whatever modifications other rules require, they all coincide in this. It is a point which every good speaker pays attention to. And as the rule may be arbitrarily employed, it enables him to invest the whole inanimate creation with life, and thus to throw a charm over the most barren waste; an advantage which is very freely resorted to, in their oral tales and mythological fables.

In contemplating such a language, it is impossible to avoid the observation of many beauties and many defects. But its beauties do not appear to be of a character to entitle them to the enthusiastic encomiums which have been bestowed upon some of our Indian languages; nor do its defects and barbarisms merit the depreciating terms which have been applied to others. Truth, in this, as in many other metaphisical investigations, will be found to lie in a mean. If there are forms and expressions suited to call forth the applause of the speculative philologist, there are also many features for him to rectify or condemn. Like the character of the people by whom it is spoken, its principles are perpetually verging to extremes. There is either a redundancy of forms creating distinctions, not, in all cases, of very obvious utility, or an absolute want of them. And the inquirer is often led to wonder, how a people who require the nice distinctions in the one case, should be able to dispense with distinctions altogether in the other.

From this vacillation between barbarism and refinement, poverty and redundance, a method strictly philosophical or purely accidental, there might be reason to infer that the people themselves, by whom the language is spoken, were formerly in a more advanced and cultivated state. And that a language once copious and exact, partaking of the fortunes of the people, degenerated further and further into barbarism and confusion, as one tribe after another separated from the parent stock. Change of accent would alone produce a great diversity of sound. Accident would give some generic peculiarities: and that permutation of the consonants, which we see among the Algonquin bands, would, in the end, leave little besides the vowel sounds, and the interchangeable consonants, to identify tribes long separated by time and by distance, without means of intercommunication, without letters, and without arts. If compared by these principles there is reason to believe, philologists would find the primitive languages of America extremely few, and their grammatical principles, either identical or partaking largely of the same features. And to this result, the tendency of inquiry on this side the Atlantic is slowly verging, however it may contravene the theories of learned and ingenious philologists in Europe. The inquiry is fraught with deep interest to the philosophical mind; and it offers a field for intellectual achievement, which it may be hoped will not be left uncultivated by the pens of piety, philosophy, or genius.

CHAPTER XI

Encampment on a peninsula in Leech Lake.—Departure for the portage to the source of the De Corbeau river.—Traverse a bay.—Commencement of the portage.—The mode of passing it.—First portage to Warpool Lake.—Pass successively Little Long Lake, the Four Lakes, Lake of the Mountain, Lake of the Island, and encamp at the Kagi Nogumaug or Long Water, the source of the De Corbeau.—Are visited by the Chief of the Pillagers, who performs a journey for that purpose.—Recognize in his attendant the murderer of Gov. Semple.—Narrative of facts leading to this event.—Commence the descent of the river De Corbeau, passing successively the Long Water, Little Vermillion, Birch Ple, Boutwell's Vieu, Desert, Summit, Longrice, Allen's, Johnston's, and Leelina Lakes.—Junction of the Shell River fork.—Encamp in a storm.

ON LEAVING the Gueule Plat's village, the Surgeon and Interpreter, with Lieut. Allen's command, were left behind to complete the vaccination of the Indians, while the rest of the party went forward a couple of leagues, to form the night's encampment. It was after seven o'clock before they came up, and we waited some time after supper, which is generally a late meal in voyaging, for the arrival of the Indian guides, who had been promised to conduct us next day, to the landing of the portage to the river De Corbeau. Morning, however, came without them, and we embarked, (18th,) and proceeded towards the southern shore of the lake, under the hope of being able to find the portage, from the descriptions which had been given of it. Our course lay, for a distance, along the peninsula, on which we had encamped. Its trending too far to the east induced us to hold a southerly course across a spacious bay. On gaining its centre, doubts arose, as to the proper course. A separation of the party was made. Part of the canoes took a south, and part, a south-east course, having agreed to concentrate on the firing of a gun, a signal which was eventually given, by the southern canoes under Mr. Johnston and Lieut. Allen. They had discovered a path, having every appearance of a portage, being in the required direction. Examination served to confirm this opinion. The baggage was immediately landed, the loose articles put in a portable shape, and the order of march on a portage, taken up. For this purpose, every article of the outfit, is originally put up in the most compact and convenient form, not exceeding ninety pounds weight. Pork is packed in kegs, flour in sail cloth bags, groceries in wooden or tin canisters, goods in corded bales. These are carried on the back, by a strong strap of leather passed around the forehead, and tied by its tapering ends, to the bag, or other article, forming the first, or lower piece. This is swung over the shoulders, and

63

other pieces laid on, to the number of two, or sometimes three, according to the carrier's strength. He then bends strongly forward, and proceeds at a half trot. He goes on the length of a *pause,* say half a mile, where the burden is put down, the strap untied, and the carrier, after a few moments rest, briskly returns, for another load. This process is continued till all the goods, are brought up to the first *pause.* The canoe and its apparatus are then brought up, when the men commence making the second *pause,* and this order is repeated at every *pause.* This is a severe labor, and re-quires able bodied men, well practiced. And where the ground is low or swampy and often travelled, it soon becomes a perfect bed of mire.

The present portage, however, was found to lie across a pine plain, of-fering a clean beach of sand to debark on, and a dry smooth path to travel. A portage of 1,078 yards, brought us to the banks of a small lake [May[68]], after crossing which we came to the entrance of a small clear brook, having not over two or three inches depth of water, spread over a bed of yellow sand. It seemed impossible to ascend it, especially with the larger canoe, but by the men's first carrying the lading, by widening the channel in cutting down the banks with paddles, and then by walking in the stream and lifting the canoe by its gunnels, they succeeded in getting it up to another lake, called Little Long Lake. We were twenty-four minutes in crossing this latter lake, and found its inlet to be connected with four other small lakes of a pondy character, redolent with nymphae odorata, through which we successively passed, and debarked at the head of the last lake on a shaking bog, being the commencement of portage *Ple.* This portage is quite short and dry, lies over a hill-prairie, and terminates on the banks of a transparent, bowl-shaped lake, with elevated shores, where we made our breakfast, at twelve o'clock. This lake, which we may refer to as the Lake of the Mountains, notwithstanding the liveliness and purity of its waters, has no visible outlet, a characteristic of which it partakes in common with a very great number of the small lakes of this quarter, which may be supposed to lie in aluminous strata. Next, in the order of travel-ling south of it, is the Mountain Portage, appropriately so called. Its ex-tent is nine hundred and ten yards. The elevation is considerable, but no rock strata appear in situ. The soil is diluvial, with boulders. The growth, yellow pine, with small maples and underbrush. It terminates on the Lake of the Island. There is then a portage of two pauses, or 1,960 yards into another lake, quite pond-like, where it is first entered, but assuming a clear and bright surface after turning a prominent point. There is then a further portage of one pause, a part of it, through a morass, but terminating on highlands, surrounding the head and shores of a handsome and compara-tively extensive sheet of water called Kagi Nogumaug, or The Long Water [Eleventh Lake[69]], where we encamped for the night. This day's journey was a hard and fatiguing one, to the men. The Gueule Plat, who with one of the minor chiefs from Leech Lake, overtook us on the banks of the Lake of the Island, expressed his surprise that, with all our baggage and heavy canoes, we had pushed on so far. It was, however, a definite point in the journey. We were now on the source of the Kagági, or De

Corbeau river. To have stopped short of it, would have seriously broken in on the labors of the following day; and the knowledge that the series of portages terminated there, and the downward passage commenced, buoyed up the men to make exertions. The day was particularly severe upon the soldiers, who were less accustomed to this species of fatigue. Never were the shadows of night more grateful to men, who had employed the morning, and the noon, and the evening of the day, in hard labor. We had now reached the *fourth* source of the primary rivers of the Mississippi, and all heading on the elevation of the Hauteur des Terres, within a circle of perhaps seventy miles. These sources are Itasca Lake, its primary, Ossowa, east fork, Shiba Lake and river, source of Leech Lake, and the present source, The Long Water, being the source of the De Corbeau, or Crow-wing river.

Gueule Plat, with his Indian secretary, so to call him, or Mishinowa, and their families, came and encamped with us.The chief said that he had many things to speak of, for which he had found no time during my visit. I invited him to sup with the party. Conversation on various topics ensued, and the hour of midnight imperceptibly arrived, before he thought of retiring to his own lodge. I was rather confirmed in the favorable opinions I have before expressed of him, and particularly in the ordinary, sober routine of his reflections, and the habitual, easy manner, which he evinced of arriving at correct conclusions. I could not say as much for his companion and pipelighter, Maji Gabowi, a very tall, gaunt, and savage looking warrior, who appeared to be made up, body and mind, of sensualities. And although he appeared to be quiet and passive, and uttered not a single expression that implied passion or vindiction, I could not divest my mind of the recollection that I was in company with the murderer of Gov. Semple. Whoever has given much attention to northwestern affairs will recollect that this event occurred in the fierce strife carried on between the North West and Hudson's Bay Company. And that, in the desperate struggles which these corporations made for the possession of the fur trade, the Indians often became the dupes of whichever party appeared, at the moment, to possess the power of influencing them. The event referred to took place near the close of a long struggle in which the spirit of opposition had reached its acme, in which company was furiously arrayed against company, charter against charter, and agent against agent. A period, at which, like the increasing energies of two powerful bodies moving towards each other, they were destined to come into violent contact, and the destruction of one, or both, seemed inevitable. The dispute respecting territory which imbittered the strife, appeared to be carried on, not so much from political ambition or the intrinsic value of the soil, as to decide which party should have the exclusive right of gleaning from the lodges of the unfortunate natives, the only commodity worth disputing for—their furs and peltries. A question, in which the Indians, in reality, had no other interest, but that which a serf may be supposed to feel on an exchange of masters, in which he has neither the right to choose nor the power to reject. Whichever party prevailed, they were sure to loose or gain nothing, if they kept aloof

from the contest, or if they had any hopes from its effects upon their condition, they arose more from a prolongation, than a termination of the
rivalry, as they were sure to fare better, both "in script and store," so
long as they possessed the option of rival markets.

Semple had accepted a governorship, which the late John Johnston,[70]
Esq. had the forecast to refuse. He appeared to be a man zealously devoted
to the objects of the company (the Hudson's Bay) whose interests were
committed to him. But he does not appear clearly to have perceived the
great difference which circumstances had interposed between a magistracy
in an English or Scottish county, and the naked solitudes of Red River. He
sallied forth himself, with a considerable retinue, to read the riot act, to a
disorderly and threatening assembly of all kinds of a northwest population,
on the plains. The agents and factors of the North West Fur Company, were
accused of being at the bottom of this uproar, and it is certain that some of
their servants were engaged, either as actors or abettors. It is among the
facts recorded in a court of justice, that when certain of the clerks or partners of the North West Company heard of the tragic result of this sally,
they shouted for joy.[71]

While the act was in the process of being read, one of the rioters fired his
piece. This was taken as a signal. A promiscuous and scattering firing commenced. Semple was one of the first who received a wound. He was shot in
the thigh, and fell from his horse. He was unable to sit up. At this moment
a rush was made by the Indians in the North West interest, and a total and
most disastrous route of the Hudson's Bay party ensued. Panic, in its wild-
est forms, seized upon Semple's men. He was himself one of the first victims
despatched. Maji Gabowi, (one of our guests this evening) coming up,
struck his tomahawk in his head. He was then scalped.

We embarked at sunrise, on the 19th, bidding adieu to the Leech Lake
chief and his companion, who returned from this point, after having requested, and received a lancet, with directions from Dr. Houghton, for
vaccinating such of his people as had not been present on the 17th. We
were forty minutes in passing the Kagi Nogumaug, which is a handsome
sheet of pure water presenting a succession of sylvan scenery. Its outlet is
a narrow brook overhung with alders. It may average a width of six feet,
but the bends are so extremely abrupt, and the channel so narrowed with
brushwood, that it became necessary to dig down the acute points, and to
use the axe in cutting away branches, to veer about a canoe thirty-two feet
in length. We were just half an hour in clearing this passage, when the
stream opened into another lake, denominated on our travelling map, Little
Vermillion [Tenth] Lake. The growth on the banks of this lake is birch and
aspen, with pines in the distance. We were twenty minutes in passing it. The
outlet is full doubled in width, and free from the embarrassments encountered above. Tamarack is a frequent tree on the shores, and the pond lilly,
flag and Indian reed, appear in the stream. This outlet is followed about
eight miles, where it expands into a small lake, called Birch [Ninth] Lake,
which we were only thirteen minutes in passing. Its outlet exhibits a pebbly
bottom, interspersed with boulders, which produce so much inequality in

the depth, that the men were obliged often to wade. Not more than seven or eight minutes were thus occupied, in the course of which we passed through a broken fish-dam, when we entered another expanse called *Lac Ple* [Eighth].

Lac Ple[72] is about three and a half, or four miles long. Vegetation here appears to show a more southerly character. Part of its shores are prairie, interspersed with small pines. It is particularly deserving of notice, as being the point, from which a series of portages is made to Ottertail Lake. A map of these furnished by the traders, who often use this route, exhibits the following features. First, a portage of four pauses, to Island Lake, then a portage of one pause, into a small lake, which has an outlet, through another small lake into Lake Lagard, having a transverse position. Thence half a pause, into a small lake, a pause and a half into another small lake, and thence four pauses into Migiskun Aiaub, or Fish-line Lake. Thence one pause into Pine Lake, and five into a small river which falls into Scalp Lake. The latter has an outlet which expands into three lakes, at nearly equal distances apart, and is finally received by Lac Terrehaut, on the Height of Land. The outlet of the latter is twice expanded into the form of a Lake, the last of which is, from its peculiarities called the Two Lakes, and is finally discharged west of the Height of Land, into Ottertail Lake. I had designed to come down this route, or down Leaf river, had circumstances favored my going into Red river, from the sources of the Mississippi. But these sources were found so much further south, than it had been supposed, and so considerably removed from any practicable route into Red river that I found it would be a consumption of time altogether disproportionate to the anticipated results; and it was, therefore, given up.

On going out of Lac Ple, the channel exhibits numerous fresh water shells driven up against the shore, or lodged against inequalities in the bottom.[73] And these productions are afterwards seen in all the subsequent outlets which connect the numerous lakes of this river. But little variety was, however, noticed among the species, although greater attention than we could bestow, might elicit new characteristics. Generally, they were small, or middle sized, often decorticated and broken. Soon after entering this channel, one of my men fired at, and brought down, a fork-tailed hawk, a species which had before been noticed on the wing, but we had now an opportunity of closer scrutiny. We did not observe any characteristics in which it differed from the described species. And if we except the numerous species of duck, the Colomba migratoris, catbird, and some other land species almost equally common, this constitutes the substance of our observations on the birds of this river. We saw the deer, of which there are apparently two species. And we had frequent occasion to observe the antlers and bones of these animals around deserted camps, evincing their abundance in this part of the country.

We had been three fourths of an hour in descending this outlet, when we entered a lake called Boutwell [Ossowa or Seventh], with banks of rather sombre vegetation, which we were nineteen minutes in passing. Its outlet, of a spreading, sandy, shelly character, is about a mile and a half in extent, at which distance it expands into Lac Vieux Desert, or the Lake of the Old Wintering Ground, where we halted long enough to prepare breakfast. This lake we were twenty-six minutes in passing through. Its outlet is about two miles long, where it again expands into a lake of about two and a quarter miles extent, which may, from its position, be denominated Summit Lake. The course, which, from the Kagi Nogumaug, is thus far generally southwest, here suddenly veers to the east and northeast, and after a striking circuit, comes round to the southeast, and eventually again to the southwest, before its junction with Shell River. And the stream which thus far seems to have its course on a level or summit, is here deflected into a valley, and is beset with rapids, and by the flood wood lodged upon its banks, and their partial denudation, puts on the appearance of a stream which must sometimes assume the fury of a torrent. It probably, at such times, is a turbid stream, but was now clear with a gravely bottom. We were hurried along through this channel for the space of two hours and fifteen minutes, when it expanded into Longrice [Fourth or Miller] Lake. We were thirty-five minutes in passing this lake. Shortly below it, the channel expands again into a lake, which from Lieut. Allen's exploring it, we called Allen's [Third or Swift] Lake. It is probably the largest of the series below the Kagi Nogumaug. It receives a tributary from the northwest, which was visited by Lieut. Allen.

The atmosphere had for some time admonished us of a storm, and it broke upon us, on entering this lake. Dark clouds rolled over each other, until the light of day was sensibly and suddenly obscured. We have seldom known an equal quantity of the electric fluid discharged in so short a space of time, or with the incessant repetition of an electric light, so subtil and painful to be endured. The rain fell in a heavy and continued torrent, and it began with gusts of wind which threw the canoe-men into alarm. They veered the canoe for the nearest shore, but before reaching it, the tempest settled, and the rain fell less violently. We therefore, continued our way without landing, and passed out of the lake. A short channel, on the banks of which the elm and oak appeared conspicuously, terminated in a moderate sized lake [Second] of handsomely elevated hard wood and pine shores, for which, as our maps afforded neither Indian nor French name, we made use of the circumstance of Mr. Johnston's landing to fire at a deer, to name it after him. On going out of this lake, we had our attention excited by an unextinguished fire, on the banks of the outlet. But no person appeared, nor was there any canoe ashore, nor lodge-poles, which there would have been, in the case of a travelling Chippewa family. These evidences were deemed conclusive by the canoe-men, of the presence of Sioux, who, it is supposed, perceiving the character of the party, had concealed themselves. And the circumstance was suited to alarm a class of men, who, being of the Gallic-Chippewa race, retain very strong attachments to the Chippewas, and have imbibed with very little abatement, all the prejudices which this people feel for a powerful hereditary enemy.

An hour's voyage from this spot brought us to the entrance and merely to the entrance of the eleventh, and last lake of the series called Kaichibo

Sagitowa [First or Sibley], or the Lake which the River passes through one End of, or Lake Leelina.[74] Not many miles below this point, the river forms its first forks, by the junction of Shell river, a considerable stream of nearly equal size with itself. Below this point, there is always water enough, although the channel exhibits numerous rapids, and is often spread over a wide bed, giving rise to shallows. We descended about fourteen miles below the junction, and encamped. It was after eight o'clock when we put ashore. The rain had fallen, with steadiness for some hours previous. And the flashes of lightning, which lit up the sombre channel of the stream, excited a feeling of no very pleasant kind. We landed wet, cold and cheerless. The rain continued to fall. But the cheerfulness and activity of our canoe-men did not desert them. They searched among the prostrate vegetation, to discover dry fibres, or the unwetted parts that could be pulled from the nether rind of fallen trees. They ignited the mass with spunk, and soon sent up the gladdening flames of an ample camp fire. To pitch the tent, arrange its interior furniture, and place the heavy baggage under oil-cloths, secure from rain, or night dews, is the work of a few moments with these people—and he who would travel fast over an intricate interior route and be well served on the way, should not fail to prepare himself with a canoe *allêge* and a crew of *voyagèurs*. They will not only go, when they are bid to go, but they will go unmurmuringly. And after submitting to severe labor, both of the night and day, on land and water, they are not only ready for further efforts, but will make them under the enlivening influence of a song.

CHAPTER XII

Further descent of the De Corbeau.—Remarks on its general course and character.—Junction of Leaf and Long Prairie Rivers.—The latter pursued by the Pillagers in their wars against the Sessitons and Yanktons.—Cause of the appellation of Mukkundwa.—Their robbery of Berti, and assertion of a belligerent principle.—Forest trees of the De Corbeau.—Monotony of its scenery.—Meeting with a Chippewa hunter. Arrival at the mouth of the river, and entrance of the Mississippi.—Concourse of Indians assembled at that point.—Council with them.—Sketch of the speeches of Grosse Gueule, Soangikumig, and White Fisher.—Arrival of the Pierced Prairie.—First intelligence of the breaking out of the Sauc War.—Close of the Narrative.—Notice of the effects of the disuse of ardent spirits by the men, and the observance of the Sabbath.

THE ENSUING PORTION of our voyage down this stream, occupied a day and a half, during which we probably descended a hundred and twenty miles. Its general course, from the forks, is south-east. It is swelled by two principal tributaries from the west, called Leaf and Long Prairie rivers, each of which brings in an ample volume, and both bear the impress of draining an extensive area. On the other bank, it is joined by the Kioshk, or Gull River, a stream of inferior size. Lesser streams or creeks, were noticed at several points, on either shore, by which the mass of water is considerably augmented. Altogether it is a stream of noble size, and is driven on through a diluvial formation, with a velocity indicating no small ratio of descent. There is no part of it which can be called still water; much of it is rapid. For about seventy miles below the junction of Shell River, there is a regular series of distinct rapids, in each of which, the descent is several feet, and it requires dexterity to avoid running against the boulders, or "lost rocks," which shew themselves above the water. Below the junction of Leaf River, this characteristic becomes less noticeable, and it disappears entirely, below the entrance of the Long Prairie branch. Its banks are elevated, presenting to the eye, a succession of pine forests, on the one hand, and an alluvial bend, bearing elms and soft maple, on the other. There is a small willow island about eighteen miles below the junction of Shell river, and several small elm islands in its central parts; but nothing at all comparable, in size, soil and timber, with the large and noted island, called *Isle De Corbeau*,[75] which marks its junction with the Mississippi.

Long Prairie River is the avenue through which the Chippewas ascend, in their war excursions against the Sessitons and Yanktons. And many tales are related of mishaps and adventures on this stream, and the plains contiguous to it. Some of these it may be supposed, are *tales* merely. Others

70

are the events of Indian history. But truth and fiction appear to be so blended in the accounts, that the separation of the one, from the other, must be often difficult, if not impossible. The recent war party, of which we saw one of the trophies, while encamped on the island of Colcaspi, went up this river in canoes. They encountered the Sioux, as they affirm, coming out against them. A fight ensued in the prairies, and was continued with changes of position throughout the day. Three Sioux and one Chippewa fell. The Sioux withdrew to a more remote position near their village. And the Chippewas returned to exult over the scalps of their enemy, and to meditate another blow. We saw several traces of this war party in our descent of the De Corbeau, in their places of hasty encampment, and also in remains of very small fires, tracks in landing on an open sand bank, and abandoned canoes, stranded and partly sunk, on the shores.

This war, between the Chippewas and Sioux, appears to be of ancient origin. It is at least coeval with the discovery of the country. Although the Chippewas are confessedly conquerors of the country they possess on this border, the conquests are of remote date. For the French, in exploring northward, found them already seated here. The part the Leech Lake Indians have played in this war, has rendered them conspicuous in their nation, and as before indicated, led to the appellation of Mukkundwais, or Pillagers, by which they are distinctively known. The circumstances which imposed upon them this name are these.

Tradition asserts that in the interval which happened between the first attack on the French power in Canada, and the final acknowledgement of English supremacy, great irregularities existed in the fur trade in this quarter. The French were loved by the Indians, and naturally retained their influence to the last. And when the English entered the field of the trade, they were essentially dependent upon French clerks, and wholly so, on French or Canadian boatmen. During this era, a Mr. Berti entered the country, with a large assortment of goods. He took his station at the mouth of the De Corbeau, where he carried on a lucrative trade with the Chippewas. He had, however, more goods than these had furs to purchase, and among them, guns and ammunition, which he very well knew would find a ready sale among the Sioux. But, the Leech Lake Indians, forbid his going into the Sioux country, alleging that the Sioux were their enemies, and that the putting of guns and powder in their hands, would be to join their cause. Mr. Berti did not probably consider these declarations as absolutely final, for he proceeded towards the mouth of the Long Prairie River, in order to go to the Sioux. The result, however, was most disasterous to him. This band arrested his progress, and with arms in their hands, robbed him of all his goods without discrimination, but spared his own life and the lives of his men, who were suffered to go back, with their private effects. Mr. Berti was probably overwhelmed by this misfortune, for he never returned from the country, but soon after this event, died a natural death, and was buried in the region about Sandy Lake.

The forest of this fork of the Mississippi, abounds in almost every variety of the pine family. We observed the sugar maple less frequently on our whole route, than would be inferred from the knowledge, that this tree is spread over the sources of the Mississippi, and flourishes, even in its most northern latitudes; and that the sugar made from it, is relied on by the Indians, as one of the regular of the minor means of their subsistence. This may be accounted for, perhaps satisfactorily, from knowing that river alluvions, and low grounds generally, are unfavorable to its growth. Its true position is the uplands, to which the Indians are known to resort, in the season of sugar making. Other species of the maple, frequently exhibited their soft foliage, over the stream, together with the elm, and the ash, and some varieties of the oak. Pine is, however, by far the most abundant and valuable timber tree, disclosed along the immediate banks of this river, and it affords a repository of this species, which will be much resorted to, when the agricultural plains above the falls of St. Anthony, shall team with their destined population.[76]

The mere exhibition of woods and waters, however inspiring in their effects, is not sufficient to keep the attention from flagging, if there be no striking succession of variety in their character. It seems not less a physical, than a moral truth, that "uniformity will tire, though it be uniformity of excellence." The eye is perpetually searching for something new, and however it may have been with other explorers, I think we may venture to say, that with us, novelty has been a far more constant or immediate passion than utility. The "lightning splintered" pine, which raises its dead arms, amid the living foliage, is suited to call forth a remark. The waterfowl with a tuft, or the shell with a deep cicatrice or a pearly interior, gives occasion for interrupting the silence, that plainer species would have left unbroken. And it is this search for something distinctive or peculiar, that gives an edge to the zeal of discovery.

On the third day of our voyage down this river, towards noon the monotony of its incidents, was relieved by descrying an Indian canoe, ascending the channel before us. A simultaneous yell of recognition, both from it, and from our men, shewed the accuracy, with which each could identify, on a first glance, and at a distance, the approach of friends, for it proved to be a Chippewa with his family. Our flag-staff was instantly placed in its socket, in the stern of the canoe, and the distance between us and them, made to appear less, under the influence of *un chanson du voyegeur*. The Indian, who, on reaching him, seemed pleased, informed us that we were at no great distance from the mouth of the river, where the Sandy Lake and Mille Lac bands were assembled, awaiting our arrival. And that the count, by which they were assured of the day appointed for meeting them, would be finished with the setting of this day's sun. We had pushed forward to attain the object, and were highly gratified, that it had pleased a favoring Providence, to enable us to keep our word, with them. Every face in this canoe, appeared to wear a smile, and the *maja! maja!* which the owner of it uttered on parting, conveyed with a truth, which could hardly be mistaken, the equivalent English sentiment of "God speed you!"

The remainder of the distance was easily despatched. We reached the parting of the channels, which encloses the large island of *De Corbeau,* about twelve o'clock. On issuing out of the upper channel, and entering the broad current of the majestic Mississippi, we beheld the opposite shore lined with Indian lodges, with the American flag conspicuously displayed. The Indians commenced firing a salute the instant we hove in sight, and continued it, with yells of joy, to the moment of our landing. A throng then crowded the banks, among whom I recognized the two principal chiefs, who, with their retinue, evinced, both by word and act, the gratification they felt; not only at the meeting, but the punctuality with which it had been observed. We were gratified on being told, within a few hours of our arrival, that our canoe, with the goods and supplies from Sandy Lake, was in sight; and soon found the event verified, in the safe arrival of the men, and the landing of the packages.

Being thus enabled to proceed with the council, it was determined immediately to assemble the Indians, and state to them, in a more full and formal manner than had been done at Sandy Lake, the objects of the visit. On closing the address, the presents and provisions designed for these bands, were issued to them. Kwiwizainsish, or the Grosse Gueule, Soangikumig, or the Strong [Echoing] Ground, White Fisher, and the son of Pugusainjigun, were the principal speakers in reply. The peculiarities in the speech of each, may be averted to.

The Grosse Gueule, observed, that, as the line was a question between the Chippewas and Sioux, a firm peace could never exist, until the line was surveyed and marked, so that each party could see where it ran. This was wanted in the section of country, immediately west of them. The Sioux, were in the habit of trespassing on it. And when their own hunters went out, in the pursuit of game, they did not like to stop short of the game, and they saw no marked line to stop them. He said that it had been promised at the treaty at Prairie du Chien, that the line should be run, and he wished me to convey his words on the subject, to the President. He was in favor of peace now as he had been, when he had met the Government in council at Tipisagi, and at Fond du Lac.

Soangikumig,[77] said, through his brother, that he had taken a part in defending the lines. He hoped that they might be made plain, so that each party could see them. As it was, a perpetual pretence was given, for crossing the path, (or lines.) It must be expected that the peace would often be broken, when it could be, so easily.

Wabojeeg [or Waub Ojeeg], or the White Fisher, stated that he had given his influence to peace counsels. He had been present at the treaty of Fond du Lac. The Sandy Lake Indians had been lately reproached, as it were, for their pacific character, by hearing the Leech Lake war party passing so near to them. (This party went up Long Prairie River.) He hoped the same advice given to Chippewas, would be given to Sioux. If the Sioux would not *come* over the lines, they, (the Chippewas,) would not *go* over them. He thought the lines might have been differently run. Their hunters always came out of Sauc river, which had been given up to the Sioux. But as they had been agreed to, by their old Chiefs, who were now gone, (he

referred particularly to the late Kadawabida, and Babisikundadi,) it would
be best to let them remain.

Nittum Egabowa, or the Front Standing Man, confined his speech to
personal topics. He said the medal he wore, and by virtue of which, he
claimed the Chieftainship, had been presented to his deceased father, at
the treaty of Prairie du Chien. He presented a pipe.

Ascertaining the trading house of a Mr. [Benjamin F.] Baker to be near
our encampment, after closing the council, we embarked and descended the
Mississippi about eighteen miles to *Prairie Piercee*.[78] Intelligence had
reached this place a few days before, by way of St. Peter's, of open hostilities among the Saucs and Foxes, and we here saw a western paper, giving
an account of an action with the militia on River Rock, the murder of
[Felix Delassus] St. Vrain, the agent for these tribes, and other particulars
indicating the frontier to be irretrievably plunged into an Indian war.

At this point, (i.e. the mouth of the De Corbeau) a remote point in our
northwestern geography, the route intersects that of the expedition to the
sources of the Mississippi, under the direction of the present Secretary of
War, Gov. Cass, in 1820. And in order that no part of the present volume
may be considered as going over grounds preoccupied by the details embraced in our "Narrative Journal of Travels," the account of the present
expedition is here terminated.

In submitting it to the public, it is conceived suitable to remark, that it
has been accomplished, from beginning to end, without the use of so much
as a drop of ardent spirits, of any kind, either by the men upon whom the
fatigues of the labor fell, or by the gentlemen who composed the exploring
party. This fact itself might be deemed an empty annunciation, were it not
in my power to add the gratifying result, that no dimunition of the strength
or capacity of the men to perform their labor has been, at any time experienced; nor has any sickness at all supervened. At no stage of the journey, have the men, who were originally engaged with a distinct understanding on this point, asked for or required any liquor, or evinced any
murmuring that it had been excluded from the supplies. But even, where
the labor was most severe, on portages, in morasses, or in crossing highlands, they have evinced a readiness, a cheerfulness, and an ability for
sustaining continued fatigue, which has often been the subject of remark
and commendation by the party. Often when the day's work was done,
when they had labored hard at the paddle or carrying-strap, and sometimes
when even a portion of the night had been added to it, they showed a joyful
spirit in the encampment. And they frequently went to gather wood, after
such fatigues, for supplying the night fires, with the boatman's song.

Another fact, may, with equal pleasure, be recorded, and it seems intimately connected, in its influence with the preceeding. No Sabbath day was
employed in travelling. It was laid down as a principle, to rest on that day,
and wherever it overtook us, whether on the land, or on the water, the
men knew that their labor would cease, and that the day would be given
them for rest. Such of them as felt the inclination, had the further privilege
of hearing a portion of the scriptures read, or expounded, or uniting in other

devotional rites. There were but a few hours of a single morning and a few hours of a single evening, of separate Sabbaths, at distant points, which were necessarily employed in reaching particular places. And the use of these appeared to be unavoidable under the particular circumstances of our local position. It may, perhaps, be thought, that the giving up of one seventh part of the whole time, employed on a public expedition in a very remote region, and with many men to subsist, must have, in this ratio, increased the time devoted to the route. But the result was far otherwise. The time devoted to recruit the men, not only gave the surgeon of the party an opportunity to heal up the bruises and chafings they complained of, but it replenished them with strength; they commenced the week's labor with renewed zest, and this zest was, in a measure, kept up by the reflection, that the ensuing Sabbath would be a day of rest. It was found by computing the whole route, and comparing the time employed, with that which had been devoted on similar routes, in this part of the world, that an equal space had been gone over, in less time, than it had ever been known to be performed, by loaded canoes, or (as the fact is) by light canoes, before. And the whole expedition, its incidents and results, have been of a character furnishing strong reasons for uniting in ascriptions of praise to the Eternal Power, who hath been our shield from "the pestilence that walketh in darkness, and from the destruction that wasteth at noon-day."

EXPLORATORY TRIP
THROUGH THE
ST. CROIX AND BURNTWOOD
(OR BRULÉ) RIVERS

CHAPTER I

Interval of the banks of the Mississippi, between the mouths of the River De Corbeau and St. Croix, adverted to.—Plains above St. Anthony's Falls, agricultural.—Fact respecting the recession of the bison.—Geological change in the character of the Mississippi, in crossing 45 deg. parrallel.—Fort Snelling.—Council—Reach the mouth of the St. Croix. —Picturesque character of St. Croix Lake. Traits of its natural history. —Encamp near a diminutive kind of barrows.—"Standing Cedars."—An Indian trader.—Green-stone rock.—Falls of the St. Croix.—Traditionary account of an ancient Indian battle, fought at these falls by the Chippewas, Saucs, Foxes, and Sioux.—Wahb Ojeeg [or Waub Ojeeg].

THAT PORTION of the Upper Mississippi, lying between the junction of the De Corbeau and St. Anthony's Falls, presents to the eye a succession of prairie and forest land, which has the characteristics of a valuable agricultural country. It is difficult in passing it, to resist the idea, that it will, at some future day, sustain a dense population. It is so elevated above the bed of the Mississippi, as to be out of the reach of its periodical floods. The banks are rendered permanent by resting upon a basis of fixed rocks, (the primitive,) which appear in the channel of the river. The soil is arable upland, apparently light, but of that ferruginous character, which has turned out so durable and fertile in Michigan. Like the prairies of the latter, the plough might be set in motion, without the labor of clearing and grubbing, and a farm reclaimed with no additional labor but that of fencing. Wood is often wanting on the immediate margin of the river. It is not always so; and when thus wanting, forests may be observed on the hilly grounds, at a distance. Wild hay might be cut in any quantity. It is among the facts which mark the natural history of the region, that the buffalo, or more strictly speaking, the bison, which fed on these plains, in 1820, has not appeared here since. The Virginia deer and the elk are, however, still abundant. The absence of lime stone will probably prove the most formidable bar to its settlement. Nothing of this kind is found except in its southern borders. There appears to be no formations of rock elevated above the soil, but the limited district called the *Pètites Roches*. And the strata here are exclusively referrable to the primitive series.

The entrances of a small river called Nokassippi, about two hundred miles above St. Anthony's Falls, may be considered as the termination of this tract. Above this point, although the Mississippi has some rich alluvions, as at the mouth of Sandy Lake River, its vegetation assumes generally an alpine character, and a large portion of the wide area of its valley, is traversed by pine ridges, with innumerable intervening lakes, and extensive tracts of, what the natives denominate, mushkeegs.

On crossing through the forty-fifth parrallel of latitude, the Mississippi exhibits a change in the materials of its banks preparatory to its entering the limestone region. This is first rendered strikingly visible on the rapids immediately above the Falls of St. Anthony. The fall itself is an imposing exhibition of geological scenery. The river here sinks its level about forty feet, in the distance of, say 1,500 yards.[79] Sixteen feet of this has been estimated to consist of a perpendicular fall, reaching, with irregularities from shore to shore. Debris is accumulated in rude masses below, and the rapids are filled with fallen or rolled rocks which impart a character of wildness to the scene. We made a portage of 1,250 yards, having descended nearer to the brink of the fall than is common. Fort Snelling is situated at the estimate distance of nine miles below the falls, at the junction with the river St. Peter's [Minnesota]. It occupies a commanding position, and exercises it may be inferred, an important influence over the contiguous Indian tribes, and the Indian trade. We reached this post on the 24th of July. Capt. [William R.] Jouett, the commanding officer, promptly afforded every facility for communicating the object of the visit to the Sioux, and requesting their concurrence, which was promised by the chiefs, in a council convened at the Agency House. We refer to the subjoined report for its results. No recent details of the progress of the Sauc war had been received. Having accomplished the object we proceeded down the Mississippi, and reached the mouth of the St. Croix, at three o'clock in the afternoon of the 26th, five days before the decisive action of Gen. Atkinson with the combined Saucs and Foxes below.

The River St. Croix has one peculiarity, to distinguish it from all other American rivers. It has its source and its termination in a lake, and each of these bears the same name with itself. The lake at its mouth is not less than thirty miles in length, and is, probably, no where, much over a mile wide. Its banks are high and afford a series of picturesque views, which keep the eye constantly on the stretch. The country is an upland prairie, interspersed with groves and majestic eminences. The waters are beautifully transparent, and the margin exhibits a pebbly beach, so cleanly washed, that it would scarcely afford earth enough to stain the fairest shoe. If "Loch Katrine" [Scotland[80]] presents a more attractive outline of sylvan coast, it must be beautiful indeed. We went up it, turning point after point, with the pleasure that novelty imparts, aided by the chanting of our canoe-men. We were in hourly expectation of reaching its head for our night encampment; but we saw the sun set, casting its golden hues and its deep shadows over the water, and going down in a gorgeous ampitheatre of fleecy clouds. The moon almost imperceptibly shone out, to supply its place, creating a scene of moonlight stillness, which was suited to fix a living impression of

> "The silence that is in the starry sky,
> "The sleep that is among the lonely hills."

Nothing could present a greater contrast, to the noisy scene of horses and horsemen, war and bloodshed, which, we were then unconscious, was about being acted, so near to us. We allude to the pursuit and destruction of the Black Hawk's army.

We encamped at a late hour, near a lofty eminence, which exhibited on its summit, a number of small mounds or barrows strongly relieved by the moonlight, which shone across the eminence, and left us in the shade. We resumed our way again, before the hour of five in the morning, (27th) and were still something more than two hours in reaching the head of the lake. In going out of this beautiful sheet of water, we would revert to some traits in its natural productions which serve to distinguish it, as well as its prominent scenery, although there are none equally distinctive. The great carboniferous limestone formation,[81] which fills the Mississippi valley, also reaches here, although there is now reason to believe that it reaches but little farther north. Its vegetation has little that is peculiar. The red cedar is found, hanging from some of its craggy shores on the lower part. Some fresh water shells, generally thin and small, with primary and lateral teeth wanting, characterize the sandy portions of its shore. There are some willow islands at the point where the River St. Croix enters it. And this point of the ingress of a large stream, presents the characteristics of what have been, not inaptly, called *drowned lands,* i.e. land bearing trees permanently standing in the water.

The St. Croix above this point exhibits the appearance of a wide, deep, ample river, with prominent banks, and forests of hard wood, and pine species. Its islands consist of rich alluvions, heavily timbered and subject to inundations. About two o'clock we passed the "Standing Cedars,"[82] a point called so, in the treaty of limits between the Sioux and Chippewa tribes, and described in the inexact phraseology of the Indians, to be "about a day's paddle, in a canoe, above the lake." Howbeit, we were but a few minutes over nine hours, in performing the distance, with a strong crew of engagès, however, in light canoes, and with every appliance in pushing forward.

As evening approached, we encountered a man descending the river, having four canoes in company, with several Frenchmen and their Indian families. It turned out to be a Mr. [Joseph R.] B[rown?] who had been engaged in trade, in the Chippewa country.[83] We examined his papers to determine whether he had been legally licensed, and caused a search of his canoes in quest of whiskey. None of this article, or strong drink of any kind was discovered. Little doubt had been felt, from information, which was not, however proved, of his having used this article in the course of his trade; whether with or without permission, could not be determined. We revoked his license for the unexpired part of the time specified in it, and permitted him to proceed out of the country, with the canoes and the very trifling property which he possessed, which seemed, indeed, to be essential to the mere subsistence of the numerous persons with him.

The narrowing of the valley, and increased rapidity of the current, had, for some time, admonished us of our approach to the falls. About six o'clock we entered through a defile, formed by perpendicular walls of rock on either shore.[84] Its seamed and mossy surface did not permit us to determine its character, without getting a fresh fracture. It proved to be greenstone. We were in the midst of a formation of this rock, and for two hours, urged our way up rapids and swift channels, made by the broken and angular character of this stratum. We reached the foot of the falls, and encamped there at eight o'clock in the evening.

The word "falls," as applied here, is but another name for impracticable rapids. The river tears its way through a vast bed of greenstone, whose black and square masses, stand on either side, and in the bed of the stream. Common quartz, imperfectly chrystalized, is seen in the mass, and is the sole mineral apparent, although a more attentive search may disclose others. A portage of four hundred yards is made to avoid the falls. But there is still a series of rapids, extending, with short interruptions, several miles above.

The physical character of this spot is such as to arrest a passing attention; but it is inferior to the moral interest arising out of it. It is the battle ground of Wahb Ojeeg, a celebrated Chippewa war chief of the last century, and testifies to an event in Indian tradition, which is not so remote as to be added to the events of the oblivious years of their residence upon this continent. We have neither time nor space to enter into details of this kind, and can merely advert to the incident we have named. Like most of the incidents of Indian warfare in the region, it is connected with the restless spirit, erratic adventure, and ambitious daring of the tribes who are, this season, (1832,) arrayed in hostility to the settlements on the Wisconsin. It is one of the links of the curious chain of history, of the Sauc and Fox tribes, who have fought their way from the St. Lawrence, thus far across the continent, and been successively embroiled, with each of the white powers, and, perhaps with some exceptions, with each of the Indian tribes of the north. They appear, by their language and traditions, to be Algonquins, and may be traced, as a starting point, to the north shores of Lake Ontario. They appear to have been driven thence for perfidy. They attacked the fort of Detroit, unsuccessfully. They lived long at, and gave name to Sagana[w]. They went to the Fox River of Green Bay which is named after them, and here embroiled themselves with the Monomonees, the Chippewas and the French. They were finally driven thence by force of arms. They fled to the Wisconsin where Carver speaks of their villages in 1766,[85] thence to their recent residence on Rock River, and by the last tragic act in their history, are confined to a limit commencing west of the Mississippi. We speak of the Saucs and Foxes as connected, in the gauntlet-like warfare they have maintained, for they appear to have been intimate allies from the earliest times. The Indian name of the one tribe signifies, Those who went out of the land, (Osaukee,) and the other, Redearths, (Miskwakee,) known by the *nom de guerre,* of Foxes.

While resident at Green Bay, they occupied also Lac du Flambeau, and extended themselves to Lake Superior, and southwest of its shores, to the Sauc and Little Sauc Rivers, above the Falls of St. Anthony. While thus located, they appear to have fallen out with the Chippewas, their cousins-german, and leagued with the Sioux, whom they have, of late, so strenuously fought. With the aid of the latter, at first covertly given, they maintained the possession of the rice lakes and midland hunting grounds. But they were finally overthrown in a general defeat, at these falls, by the combined Chippewa bands of Lake Superior. The latter came down the St. Croix, by its Namakagon branch. They were led by Wahb Ojeeg. Their spies reached the falls without having encountered an enemy, but they unexpectedly found the Foxes, (whom they call Ootaigahmees,) with their allies, encamped at the other end of the portage. A partial action ensued. It was rendered general by the arrival of the whole Chippewa force. It was a fierce and bloody action. The Foxes made a resolute stand. But they were overpowered and fled. And they have not since re-appeared in the region. Among the slain several Sioux were found, and this is said to be the first actual testimony of the Sioux being leagued with them, in the war against the Chippewas. But this assertion is hardly reconcileable with the date of the war in other places.

Wahb Ojeeg, or the White Fisher, who is noticed as the leader on this occasion, is said to have led out seven other expeditions against the Foxes and Sioux. He died at Chegoimegon, in Lake Superior, in 1793.

CHAPTER II

Ascent of the St. Croix above the falls.—Direct the burning of illegal trading houses.—Snake River.—Its chief, Pezhicki [Pizhickee].—Notices of Snake River.—Its population and trade.—A foreign trading company formerly located here.—Effects upon the Indian intercourse of the present day.—Anecdote of the former mode of using rum and tobacco.—Kettle Rapids.—Shell River.—A hunting party of Chippewa boys.—Pokanokuning, or Yellow River.—Its population and trade.—Notices of its natural history.—Shells.—Prairie squirrel.—Widow of a murdered Indian, called the Little Frenchman, declines having her son put to school.—Reach the forks of the St. Croix.—Notice of the Namakágon Branch.—The chief, Kabamappa.—Women's Portage.—The Sturgeon Dam.—Kabamappa's village.—Upper St. Croix Lake.

WE PURSUED OUR WAY as early on the morning (28th) as the clearing up of the fog would permit. Soon after reaching the head of the series of rapids, we observed a couple of buildings of logs, upon the left shore, and landed to examine them. They proved to be deserted cabins which had been occupied by traders, with their doors open, and containing nothing of value. As these had been erected contrary to decisions of the Indian office, made under the law of Congress regulating trading posts, and at a point where the Sioux and Chippewas are thus improperly brought into contact, we directed them to be burned.[86] The remainder of the day was diligently employed in the ascent. The following day, being the Sabbath, was devoted to rest. The water in the river appeared to be very low, and was momently falling. We removed our place of encampment in the evening, about ten miles. A Chippewa whom we met with his family, in a canoe, informed us that Snake River was *baishoo,* a term denoting near at hand.

The next morning, (30th,) after about three hours paddling, we reached the mouth of the Kinábic, or Snake River. We found Pezhicki, (or the Buffalo,) the principal chief of that place, and his band, encamped on the small peninsula which is formed by the junction. They fired a salute, and crowded down to the shore, to welcome us. This chief was one of a delegation who visited Washington, some years ago. He came back with a profusion of ornaments, and a sword and tassels. These were of no real utility, and have long since disappeared. The visit had the effect to shew him the strength and resources of the Americans. With little force of character, he has been pacific, so far at least, as relates to white men. He was present at the treaties of Prairie du Chien, and Fond du Lac. He is not the war chief of the Snake River band. We know not, that he encountered in his journey, any teacher or preacher to inform him that there was a savior.

Official business occupied a part of the morning. We found not the slightest evidence of any participation, or disposition to participate, in the hostile schemes of the Saucs and Foxes. Pezhicki approved of the requests made by the Chippewas of the Upper Mississippi, for having their lines surveyed, and united strongly in the measure. He said that the Sioux had manifested a disposition to claim the country above the Standing Cedars, and that they had, and still continued to trespass on it. He said, that they had this season, crossed through the Chippewa hunting grounds on the St. Croix to go against the band at Rice Lake on the Red Cedar Fork of the Chippewa River. He cheerfully promised to assist the military canoes, in their ascent and immediately sent three young men for that purpose.[87]

Snake River is an important tributary of the St. Croix. It constitutes an established post of trade, for which licences are granted by the Indian department. Its Indian population is reported at three hundred and one souls. Persons of the mixed cast, thirty-eight. This river is connected, by an easy portage, with Rum River, a route much used by Indians going to the Mille Lac and Sandy Lake borders. Masses of native copper have been brought out of its bed by the Indians, who report the existence of further indications of its presence. The North West Company formerly held a post on this river [at Pokegama Lake], and it remained for several years, a central place of trade for the Indians of the lower St. Croix. The influence of this company over the Indians was every where visible, and so far as this influence was connected with political feelings, it was, as a matter of course, exerted in favor of the British government. As not more than twenty years have elapsed, since the authority of the American government began at all to be exercised in this quarter, and a much shorter period must be assigned for any active influence from its posts and agencies, it should not excite surprise that the elder Indians should, as they do, feel an attachment for that government. Nor is it strange, that ambitious and designing men among them, should occasionally form combinations for open resistance, of the character of that which has recently been witnessed among the Saucs and Foxes. Time, and judicious counsels, will afford the surest corrective.

In looking back to the condition of the trade, as it existed here, fifty years ago, some striking changes have supervened. A Mr. Harris, who is still living at the age of about eighty-four, informed me, that about the close of the American war, when he first came to this river, rum was an article in high request among the Indians. When they had purchased a keg of it, it was customary to pour it out into a large kettle and place it over a fire. A hand of tobacco was then put in. After being heated and stirred about for a time, the mixture was drank.

The distance from Snake River to Yellow River is about thirty-five miles. We employed the 30th, from about eleven in the morning till eight at night, and the 31st until eight o'clock in the morning, in performing this distance. The water was very low, and it frequently required the men to get out and wade. The Kettle Rapids, nine miles in extent, are, however, the most formidable obstacle. The St. Croix receives, in this distance, the Akeek or Kettle River, from the left, and the Aissippi, or Shell River [Clam], from the right. The latter takes its rise in a lake [Clam], which is noted for the number and large size of its fresh water shells. Hence its name. We met a number of Indians, on this day's journey who evinced a friendly feeling. We encamped at eight o'clock, with a party of Indian boys, who had come down the river hunting. They were rejoiced on seeing us approach, and spent much of their ammunition in saluting us, which a colder feeling of foresight, might have induced them to reserve for the chase. And they offered us some of the scanty products of their evening's labour, thus evincing the truth of the remark,

> "Yet is he free; a morsel though his fare,
> "That morsel will he, unrepining, share;
> "A kind companion, and a liberal friend,
> "Not prone to hoard, nor cautious to expend,
> "Thence, often poor; but not that craven kind,
> "The low-born meanness of a stingy mind."

One of the canoemen lacerated his foot on the angular masses of greenstone, which form a shore of angular pebbles, near Snake River. And this rock appeared again distinctly, in place, on the Kettle rapids. Masses of it, were frequently seen in the bed of the river and incumbering its shores, below that point. They were observed to decrease in size and frequency above these rapids, from which it may be inferred, that the rapids themselves are situated near the limits of the formation.

At Yellow River, we found a considerable assembly of Indians, who, as they saw our approach for some distance, ranged themselves along the shore, and fired a formal salute. I had visited this place, the same month and nearly the same day, in 1831, and then entered the mouth of the river to form my encampment. But on attempting again to reach the same spot, the water was found so low, that it was impracticable, and I came to the landing in front of a naked eminence, which, the Indians call Pokonokun-ing, or Place of the Hip Bone,[88] a term by which the river itself is (by them) designated.

This river is a post of trade, containing a population estimated at three hundred and eighty-two souls. The lands are fertile, and afford in connection with Ottawa [Court Oreilles] Lake, and the adjacent country, a good location for a mission and school. The river originates near the head of Long River of the Red Cedar Fork of the Chippewa, to which there is a canoe portage. It expands at unequal distances, beginning at its source, into Lac Vaseux [Spooner Lake], Rice Lake, and Yellow Lake. Wild rice is one of its productions, and is among the means of subsistence on which the natives rely. Its natural history is further deserving of remark, as yielding abundantly, univalve shells of a fine size. The purple winged unio is found in abundance; and the natives make use of this species, for spoons, by rubbing off the alatae and rounding the margin—a process by which they are rendered of no value as specimens of the species. The copperhead snake is said to exist in the waters of this river. Its banks afford much of the open grounds which are favorable to the thirteen striped, or prairie squirrel, (S. tredecem, of Mitchill.) The Indians exhibited to me the skin of this little animal, which is peculiarly marked with alternations of stripes and spots.

We observed among the group of Indians at this place, the widow and children of Waimit-Egozhains, a Chippewa, having an admixture of white blood, who, with three others, was murdered by the Sioux while descending the lower part of the St. Croix, in a canoe, in the fall of 1830. We directed the interpreter to say to her, that as providence had removed her natural protector, and her means of subsistence must be small, the elder of her boys, who was present, would be taken and sent to school, and also taught the arts of an industrious life, if she would direct him to embark in one of our canoes. She appeared to be pleased but at the same time embarrassed. She consulted with a brother who was one of the Indians present, and then replied that the boy was not altogether useless in aiding her to get a support, as he could fish and kill patridges. She did not feel willing thus suddenly to part with him, but observed that she would send him out in the spring.

We were five hours and a half in going from Yellow River to the Forks of the St. Croix. The distance is probably not over thirteen miles. These data will show how slowly we proceeded, with every exertion, against the obstacles of a very low state of water. And at this spot we knew that we were to lose, at least, one half of the entire volume. The loss is indeed greater, for the Namakágon, or right hand fork, which we were here to leave, is decidedly the largest of the two.

The Namakágon Branch has its rise in a lake, which the Indians call Mattedhair [Namekagon] Lake, very near the source of the Mushkee or Mauvais River of Lake Superior. Neither of these streams can, however, be ascended to their sources. There is a portage across the intervening grounds, interspersed with small lakes which is practicable for canoes and packages of goods, carried after the northwest manner. The Namakágon has another portage, at a lower point to Ottawa Lake, the source of one of the navigable branches of the Chippewa River. This river, after running about one hundred and seventy miles, joins the northwest branch at the Forks of the St. Croix, and from this point, the joint volume, increased by a number of tributaries is carried on, to swell the mass of the Mississippi.

We found the chief Kabamappa, with others, encamped at the Forks. They evinced the same feeling of welcome, and pleasure we had met from the Chippewas on the lower part of the stream. Kabamappa said that nothing had been very recently heard from the direction of Lac du Flambeau and the borders of the Sauc disturbances. He readily communicated many facts respecting the existing difficulties, and the means taken to enlist the Indians in a general war. He said that the confederacy, as it is, had been reported to consist of nine tribes, whom he named.[89] With respect to a permanent peace with the Sioux, he cordially approved it. He had, he observed, given much of his thoughts and his time to that object, and particularly so since our previous visit. It was, primarily, through the influence of this chief that a general peace-council had been held by the Sioux and Chippewas, during the fall of 1831, on Snake River.

As to the state of the water his expression was, "iscutta! iscutta!" indicating an exhausted state. He added, that though we had encountered difficulties on the stream below, they would be multiplied on the branch we were about to ascend. Even within sight of his lodge, he pointed to shallows, where it would be impossible to ascend without wading in the stream and carrying all the baggage. The river, he said, was uncommonly low for the season, and was daily getting lower. Under these circumstances, we had no time to lose. We employed the remainder of the day in going about seven miles, and encamped after dark at a place called the Women's Portage. Just before encamping, and when we were seeking a spot along the thick brushy shore, to debark at, Kabamappa suddenly appeared standing on the bow of his canoe, and pointing onwards, guided us to the spot of our encampment. Daylight had completely disappeared and it was barely possible, in a dark atmosphere, to discern contiguous objects. As the tall and gaunt form of the chief glided by, with his spear-pole elevated in the direction we were to go, it might have needed but little power of the imagination, to transform him into a spirit of supernatural power. Owing to the darkness we found it difficult to procure fire-wood for the night. It was sought with torches. The chief joined us at our evening meal. We were pleased with his urbanity.

A fog detained us at our encampment until after daylight, (1st Aug.) We were enabled to proceed at five o'clock. Our first labor was the ascent of a rapid, our *second,* our *third,* and our *fourth* labors were also rapids. In short, rapid succeeded to rapid, and with such short intervals, that it would be impracticable from any notes preserved of the route, to speak of this part of the stream, in any other light than as a continued series of rapids. We often thought ourselves above them but we as often found, in the language of our canoemen, *"encore un."* About two o'clock in the afternoon we came to still waters with sedgy shores, and at seven in the evening reached and landed at Kabamappa's village [Whitefish Lake]. The distance may be twenty-five miles above the Women's Portage. We encamped there.

The village is situated on a part of the river called Namai Kowagon, or Sturgeon Dam. It occupies an eligible prairie bank, and exhibits in the style of the lodges and gardens, considerable industry and regard to comfort. It would seem to be no difficult effort to induce Indians, who had proceeded thus far in fixed industry, to labor on their lands more extensively and effectually. The lodges represent, on the ground plan, oblongs enclosed with strong elm bark, sustained on a frame work of saplings, tied on posts firmly set in the ground. They have a moveable piece or door, at each end, and an opening in the centre of the lodge, in the place of a chimney. Corn and potatoe fields, covered the surrounding grounds. The corn was in tassel, but the wilting of its blades, indicated, that they had been touched by a slight frost. Its effects were particularly apparent in some vines near one of the lodges. Although the lodges had been carefully closed, the chief said

during his absence, a wolf had broken into his lodge and committed depredations. He observed, in speaking of game, that the red deer was found on
the adjoining plains. In order to hunt the moose an animal formerly abundant in the region, he observed that it was necessary to go to one of the
remote forks of the Burntwood or Brulè River. He represented the population of his village at eighty-eight souls, of whom twenty-eight were men.
This estimate was understood to include the minor chief Blackbird and his
followers, who are sometimes referred to as a distinct band. We asked the
chief, while sitting at the camp-fire in the evening, whether he did not feel
tired, having observed that during the day, he had alone, with the aid only
of his wife, poled up his canoe and managed to keep ahead, so as to guide,
our canoe with seven men. He was evidently fatigued, but replied, smiling,
no.

We parted with this chief, who has become respectable for his influence
in this part of the country, at four o'clock on the next morning, (2d.) We
had now got above all the strong rapids, and attained very nearly the height
of land. The river, above this point, receives the Clearwater [Eau Claire]
and Buffalo [Ox] Rivers, as tributaries on the right bank. It is finally traced
to Lake St. Croix, a handsome sheet of clear water, about six miles long.
This lake has an island[90] which is the site of a small village. Its head is perhaps ten or eleven leagues distant from the Namai Kowagon.

CHAPTER III

Character of the St. Croix.—Its productiveness in wild rice.—Population and trade.—Condition of the Indians, and their prospect.—Portage to the Burntwood.—Marine sand formation.—Bass lake.—Character of the Burntwood river.—Arrival at its discharge into Fond du Lac of Lake Superior.—Indian friends.—Close of the Narrative.—Brief general remarks on the condition of the Chippewas.—Traits of character and government.—The institution of the Totem.—Tale of the origin of White Fish.

ON ENTERING lake St. Croix we were favored with a fair wind, and made use of our sails in passing it. As we approached its head, we found the swell formidable, but were able, nevertheless, to keep the lake. We debarked, on a marshy margin at its head, being the commencement of the portage to the Brulé. As the river St. Croix has its origin here, a few general remarks on its geographical features, may be subjoined.—This stream is an important tributary to the Upper Mississippi, originating on elevated grounds, and consequently, having a rapid mean descent. Although not remarkable for its length, its waters spread in a lateral line, an unusual distance. It has many tributaries, connecting it, on the north, with Rum river, on the south, with Chippewa river, and towards the east with the Mauvais and the Brulé rivers of Lake Superior. The main channel may be estimated, by its windings, at two hundred miles. The length of its Namakagon fork is estimated to be one hundred and seventy miles, while that of its northern branch does not probably exceed sixty-five miles. Both branches, together with its lower tributaries, and their numerous lakes, yield the northern rice plant. The abundance of the plant, has led to the local term of the Folle Avoine country, a name by which it is particularly known in the transactions of the Fur Trade.

It has a comparatively mild climate, and rich soil, and in addition to the small fur bearing animals, on the sale of which the Indians rely for their woollens, arms, and ammunition; it affords the spontaneous means of subsistence, more fully, perhaps, than most other parts of the northwest regions. Its present aggregate population has been estimated the present year, at eight hundred and ninety-five, say nine hundred souls, numbering those only who are permanently located in its valley.—What quantity of furs and peltries is annually got from it, and what amount of Indian goods are required to pay for them, are questions which might be ascertained, with general accuracy, by consulting official records. But it is sufficient for the purposes of moral enquiry, to remark, that both the supplies and the returns, are less than they were in former years, and that there is a declension in the trade, which must at length produce a migration of the Indians, or induce them to become agriculturists. The fate that has overtaken other tribes, enjoying a more southerly position, must inevitably overtake these bands. And the period will probably arrive earlier, than it might be anticipated. They occupy a portion of the Mississippi valley, which is adapted for agriculture. Many parts of it, possess a rich soil, and are well timbered. Other portions are prairie land, suited for pasturage. Its most arid tracts abound in pine, and there is hardly a stream, of its many tributaries which does not afford numerous eligible seats for saw and grist mills. Hunting seems the only occupation, which cannot be a permanent one. But,

> "While thus the chase declines, and herds depart,
> And heaven in prospect, dooms his favorite art,
> No care of lands or flocks prepares his mind,
> To mend his fortunes, and to save his kind."

The portage from the St. Croix to the Burntwood, begins at the head of (the Upper) lake St. Croix. It lies over an elevated sandy pine ridge, which divides the two streams. The distance which the canoes and packages require to be carried is 3,350 yards, or nearly two miles. On the left hand, in carrying from the St. Croix, there is a deep tamerac valley, which is said to afford the head springs of both streams. On the right, is seen, at some distance, a small lake, which is stated to yield the black bass, and to have no outlet. Its existence in a sand formation, indicates perhaps, coral rag, hardpan, or some firmer material below. This sand is apparently of marine deposition, and agrees, in this respect, with the extensive formations at the sources of the Mississippi.

The goods after being carried this distance, are put down, on the banks of a sandy bottomed brook of very clear cold water, overhung with alders. Any other person, but one who had become familiar with northwest portages, would be apt to say, on being ushered to this secluded spot, "well, this is certainly an eligible spot to quench one's thirst at, but as for embarking on this rill, with a canoe and baggage, the thing seems to be preposterous." And so it certainly appeared, on our arrival.—There was not an average depth of water of more than two to four inches. But by going some distance below, and damming the stream, it rose in a short time, high enough to float a canoe, with a part of its lading. The men walking in the stream, then led the canoes, cutting away the brush to veer them, and carrying such parts of the lading as could not, from time to time, be embarked. We did not begin the descent, till six o'clock, in the evening, and went about a mile during the first hour and a half. It then became so dark, that it was necessary to encamp. And to encamp in such a place, seemed impossible. We could not, however, hesitate. There was no alternative, we could neither advance nor recede, and we were surrounded with a shaking bog. We slept on a kind of bog, which the men, call *tetes des femmes*. Some rain fell during the night, but we were happily relieved from the fear of inundation, by the showers passing off. The next morning brought with it, a resumption of the toil of the evening. The canoes were sent on entirely empty. All the baggage was carried about a mile, at which distance the stream is perhaps doubled in width, and more than doubled in depth. The next mile rendering the going quite easy. At this point, say three miles from the portage, we embarked all our baggage, and after this, found no want of water, till we came to the rapids. These commence about twenty-four miles below the portage, and they extend with intervals of smooth water, "few and far between," to within three or four miles of the point of the entrance of the river, into Lake Superior. The entire length of this river may be estimated at one hundred miles, more than eighty miles of this distance consists of rapids. It has been said that there are two hundred and forty distinct rapids. At most of these, there is several feet fall. At some of them eight to ten feet. Four of them require portages of short extent. Six or seven hundred feet would not appear to be an extravagant estimate for the entire fall. The river itself is a perfect torrent; often on looking down its channel, there are wreaths of foam constituting a brilliant vista, overhung with foliage. It would never be used at all, for the purposes of the trade, were it not, that there is much water on the rapids, so that experienced men can conduct loaded canoes both up and down them. The river might appropriately be called Rapid, or Mad River, or almost any thing else, but by its popular name of *Brulé*. This is, in fact, rather a departure, than a derivative from the Indian, Wisákoda, i.e. burnt-pines, or burnt-wood, in allusion to a signal destruction of its pine forests, by fire. We were two days, and part of an evening, in effecting the descent, and regained our outward track, at the point of its discharge into the Fond du Lac of lake Superior. We reached this point on the fourth of August, late at night, having gone later than usual, from the fact of finding ourselves below the rapids, and consequently knowing that we must be near the lake. Our first certain indication of our proximity to it, was, however, given by hearing the monotonous thump of an Indian drum. We soon after came in sight of camp fires, with Indian forms passing before them.—And we found ourselves, on landing, in the midst of former Indian acquaintances. Among them were Mongozid (Loon's Foot,) the second Chief of Fond du Lac, and Chamees, (Pouncing Hawk,) a young man who had first recommended himself to notice in 1820, by guiding a part of Governor Cass' expedition above the Knife Portage, and who evinced the same disposition, during the forepart of the present summer, by acting as a guide to the party, between Fond du Lac and Sandy Lake. We were pleased on observing the military boat, used by Lieutenant Allen on the lake, safely moored, with its sails and tackle, within the mouth of the river, having been brought down, agreeably to promise, by Mongozid, who had faithfully remained in charge of it.

The day following, being the Sabbath, was spent at this place. And the narrative of our route from the Mississippi may here be appropriately closed. Some remarks arising from observations on the condition of the Indians, among whom we have passed, it may be proper to add; but from the little leisure we can command, they are necessarily few and brief.

The Chippewas are spread over a very large area in the north, divided into local bands, and separated by extensive tracts which are, in great part, sterile. They are not fixed in their habitations at any point, during the whole of the year, being compelled to go in search of the game, fish, and other spontaneous productions, on which they depend. The space which each band periodically traverses, in this effort, is extensive, and subjects them to casualties, which they would otherwise escape. Their condition is still further imbittered by hostilities with the Sioux tribes, who occupy the whole line of their western frontier. They cover the entire northwestern angle of the United States, extending down the Mississippi valley on both banks, as low as the Wadub, being the first stream above Sac river. At this point their territorial line crosses from the west to the east banks of the Mississippi, pursuing a southerly course, at the distance of about forty miles from it, until it intersects the lands of the Winnebagoes, north of the Wisconsin. This portion of the territory affords decidedly the largest and best body of farming lands in their possession, and will, probably, hereafter yield them, either by the proceeds of its sale, or cultivation, a more sure reliance at a period when the land becomes divested of game. The climate of this area is comparatively mild, and the Indians who inhabit it, notwithstanding their partial losses from wars, have evidently increased in population. They might be concentrated here, could the agricultural be substituted for the hunter life—a result which may be expected to follow, but cannot in any reasonable estimate be expected to precede, their conversion to christianity.

This tribe offers no prominent obstacles to the introduction of the gospel. We have before adverted to the slender frame work of their native religion, which seems to be made up, primarily of certain superstitious ceremonies, winding themselves about the subject of medicine. It appears to occupy that void in the barbaric mind, which the soothsayers and magii of other lands, pressed forward, in the absence of revelation, to fill. But we do not know that the ritual has any striking features in common. The principal obstacle which missionaries will have to contend with is a want of the knowledge of their language. And to surmount this is a labor which they cannot too early begin nor too zealously persevere in. The language itself, as we have before indicated, presents a copious vocabulary, and is capable of being made the medium of religious instruction. It has some defects which will require to be supplied, and some redundancies which will demand curtailment, when it comes to be written. But they offer very slight obstacles to oral communication. It is obviously better suited to convey narrative than disquisitive matter. And has been so long applied to corporeal objects, that it requires caution and a familiar knowledge of its idioms, in the conveyance of intellectual and still more of spiritual conceptions.

In mere externals, the Chippewas are not essentially different from other tribes of the Algonquin stock in the western country. And the points in which a difference holds may be supposed to have been, for the most part, the effects of a more ungenial climate. They are, to a less extent than most of the tribes, cultivators of the soil, and more exclusively hunters and warriors. Living in a portion of the continent, remarkable for the number of its large and small lakes, they find a common resource in fish, and along with this, enjoy the advantage of reaping the wild rice.

Their government has been deemed a paradox, at the same time exercising, and too feeble to exercise power. But it is not more paradoxical than all patriarchial governments, which have their tie in filial affection, and owe their weakness to versatility of opinion. War and other public calamities bring them together, while prosperity drives them apart. They rally on public danger, with wonderful facility, and they disperse with equal quickness. All their efforts are of the partizan, popular kind. And if these do not succeed they are dispirited. There is nothing in their institutions and resources suited for long continued, steady exertion.

The most striking trait in their moral history is the institution of the Totem—a sign manual, by which the affiliation of families is traced, agreeing, more exactly, perhaps, than has been supposed, with the armorial bearings of the feudal ages. And this institution is kept up, with a feeling of importance, which it is difficult to account for. An Indian, as is well known, will tell his specific name with great reluctance, but his generic or family name—in other words, his *Totem,* he will declare without hesitation, and with an evident feeling of pride.

None of our tribes have proceeded farther than the first rude steps in hieroglyphic writing. And it is a practice in which the Chippewas are peculiarly expert. No part of their country can be visited without bringing this trait into prominent notice. Every path has its blazed and figured trees, conveying intelligence to all who pass, for all can read and understand these signs. They are taught to the young as carefully as our alphabet, with the distinction, however, that hieroglyphic writing, is the prerogative of the males. These devices are often traced on sheets of birch bark attached to poles. They are traced on war-clubs, on canoe paddles, bows or gun stocks. They are often drawn on skins, particularly those used as back dresses, by warriors. They have also other hieroglyphic modes of communicating information, by poles with knots of grass attached to them, or rings of paint, and often by antlers, or animals' heads suspended by the banks of rivers.

The following tale is added as an example of the kind of imaginative lore indicated by it.

ORIGIN OF THE WHITE-FISH.

In ancient times when the Indians were better than they now are, when their laws were enforced by the chiefs, and when every crime was promptly punished, there lived a noted hunter and a just man, at a remote point on the north shore of Lake Superior. He had a wife and two sons, who were usually left in the lodge, while he went out in quest of the animals upon whose flesh they subsisted. As game was then abundant, his exertions were well rewarded, and he lived in the enjoyment of every blessing. But there was at this time a venom preparing for his heart, which was not the less poisonous, because it was for a time kept in secret. His two little sons had observed the visits of a neighboring hunter, during the absence of their father, and they ventured to remonstrate with their mother on the propriety of receiving clandestine visits, but she was in no temper to be reasoned with. She rebuked them sharply, and finally, on their intimation of disclosing the secret, threatened to kill them if they made any disclosure. They were frightened into silence. But observing the continuance of an improper intercourse, kept up by stealth as it were, they resolved at last to disclose the whole matter to their father. The result was such as might be anticipated. The father being satisfied with the infidelity of his wife, took up a war club at a moment when he was not perceived, and with a single blow despatched the object of his jealousy. He then buried her under the ashes of his fire, took down his lodge, and removed to a distant position.

But the spirit of the woman haunted the children who were now grown up to the estate of young men. She appeared to them in the shadows of evening. She terrified them in dreams. She harrassed their imaginations wherever they went, so that their life was a life of perpetual terrors. They resolved to leave the country, and commenced a journey of many days towards the south. They at length came to the Poiwateeg falls. (St. Mary's.) But they had no sooner come in sight of these falls, than they beheld the skull of the woman (their mother) rolling along the beach after them. They were in the utmost fear, and knew not what to do, to elude her, when one of them observed a large crane sitting on a rock in the rapids. They called out to the bird. "See, Grandfather, we are persecuted by a spirit. Come and take us across the falls so that we may escape her."

This crane was a bird of extraordinary size and great age. And when first descried by the two sons, sat in a state of stupor, in the midst of the most violent eddies of the foaming water. When he heard himself addressed, he stretched forth his neck, with great deliberation, and then raising himself on his wings flew across to their assistance. "Be careful" said the crane, "that you do not touch the back part of my head. It is sore, and should you press against it, I shall not be able to avoid throwing you both into the rapids." They were, however, attentive on this point, and were both safely landed on the south side of the river. The crane then resumed its former position in the rapids.

But the skull now cried out. "Come Grandfather and carry me over, for I have lost my children, and am sorely distressed." The aged bird flew to her assistance, but carefully repeated his injunction, that she must by no means touch the back part of his head, which had been hurt, and was not yet healed. She promised to obey, but she soon felt a curiosity to know, where the head of her carrier had been hurt, and how so aged a bird could have acquired such a bad wound. She thought it strange, and before they were half way over the rapids, could not resist the inclination she felt to touch the affected part. Instantly the crane threw her into the rapids. The skull floated down from rock to rock, striking violently against their hard edges, until it was battered to fragments, and the sons were thus happily and effectually relieved from their tormentor. But the brains of the woman, when the skull was dashed against the rocks, fell into the water, in the form of small white roes, which soon assumed the shape of a novel kind of fish, possessing a whiteness of color peculiar to itself; and these rapids have ever since been well stocked with this new and delicious species of fish.

The sons meantime took up their permanent abode at these Falls, becoming the progenitors of the present tribe, and in gratitude to their deliverer adopted the Crane[91] as their Totem.

NOTES

1. For an account of Lt. Zebulon Pike's 1805 expedition see: Henry Whiting, "Life of Zebulon M. Pike," in Sparks, *Library of American Biography,* XV (Boston, 1845), pp. 217-314; William J. Backes, "General Zebulon M. Pike, Somerset-Born," *Somerset County* [New Jersey] *Historical Quarterly,* VIII (Oct., 1919), pp. 241 and 251; William W. Folwell, *History of Minnesota,* I, (St. Paul, 1921), pp. 91-101; and Pike, *An Account of Expeditions to the Sources of the Mississippi . . . during the Years 1805, 1806 and 1807* (Philadelphia, 1810).

2. Lt. Pike's blockhouse was located a short distance south of Painted Rock Falls, now known as Little Falls. It was still standing in 1820 when the Cass expedition passed the spot. Mentor Williams, *Schoolcraft's Narrative Journal of Travels* (East Lansing, 1953), p. 188.

3. A number of accounts of the Cass expedition have been published. Henry R. Schoolcraft wrote the first in 1821 under the title, *Narrative Journal of Travels through the Northwestern Regions of the United States Extending from Detroit through the Great Chain of American Lakes to the Sources of the Mississippi River . . . in the Year 1820* (Albany, 1821). This was edited by Mentor Williams and published by Michigan State University Press in 1953. Included in the appendix of this monumental work by the late Professor Williams are the journals and letters of David B. Douglass, James Duane Doty, Charles C. Trowbridge, and Lewis Cass.

4. Originally known as Upper Red Cedar Lake, Schoolcraft named it Cass or Cassina Lake in 1820 to distinguish it from Red Cedar Lake located 250 miles downstream. Williams, *Schoolcraft's Narrative Journal of Travels,* p. 168.

5. Many questions have been raised about this decision. If Schoolcraft knew of the existence of Lake La Biche in 1820, as his journal indicates (p. 254), why did he refer to Cass Lake as the true source of the Mississippi? What prompted him to claim in 1820 that he was the only man to have visited both the source and the mouth of the Mississippi? Some writers have maintained that Schoolcraft did not want to disagree with Governor Cass, who thought the true source of the Mississippi was Cass Lake. This explanation is neither supported by Schoolcraft's lack of modesty nor his journal entry of July 21, 1820: "Finding it impracticable to proceed at this season of the year, in canoes to lake La Beesh an immediate return was here determined upon. . . ." It is possible that Schoolcraft made such claims for Cass Lake to support the title of his book, *Narrative Journal of Travels . . . to the Sources of the Mississippi River.*

6. Lake "La Biche" or "Beesh," also known as Elk Lake, from the Chippewa word, "Omushkos," is southwest of Bemidji. Schoolcraft changed its name to Itasca from parts of the Latin words, *veritas caput,* meaning true source. Although Schoolcraft later implied that the word, "Itasca," was taken from Indian mythology, the facts indisputably support the Latin derivation. Since 1891 the celebrated source of the Mississippi has been a part of Itasca State Park. See J. V. Brower, *Itasca State Park,* in *Minnesota Historical Collections,* XI (1904).

7. The actual elevation of Cass Lake above sea level is 1,300 feet. Schoolcraft's error stemmed from his miscalculation of the elevation of Lake Superior, which he thought was 640 feet above the Atlantic. It is actually 602.22 feet above sea level.

8. Lac Court Oreilles, or "Short Ears," was named for the Ottawa Indians, who once frequented the area on hunting expeditions. The name originated, not from the practice of clipping their ears, but because the Ottawa, unlike many tribes who distended their ear lobes by ornaments, let them keep their natural shape. The lake, located in Sawyer County, Wisconsin, is now a Chippewa Indian Reservation.

9. An account of this incident is found in the correspondence files of the Office of Indian Affairs, Record Group No. 75, National Archives. See also Schoolcraft, *Personal Memoirs of a Residence of Thirty Years with the Indian Tribes on the American Frontiers* (Philadelphia, 1851), pp. 392-93 (hereafter cited as *Thirty Years with Indian Tribes*).

10. Accompanying Schoolcraft on the 1831 expedition were Douglass Houghton and Melancthon L. Woolsey, plus a small detachment of soldiers under the command of Lt. Robert E. Clary, and numerous voyageurs. Douglass Houghton was to have furnished a narrative and map of the expedition, and Schoolcraft was to have supplied a preface, an account of the Iowa mine country, and an official report on geology, botany, mineralogy, and conchology. Both Schoolcraft and Houghton prepared part of the proposed book, but they decided to defer publication to include results of the 1832 expedition. Henry R. Schoolcraft to John Torrey, Sault Ste. Marie, June 2, 1832, Appendix A.

11. Schoolcraft's official account of the 1831 expedition is in *House Executive Documents,* No. 152, 22d Cong., 1 Sess., Vol. IV. See also Schoolcraft's *Thirty Years with Indian Tribes,* pp. 363-96.

12. See: Henry R. Schoolcraft to Elbert Herring, Office of Indian Affairs, Feb. 13, 1832, Appendix A.

13. See note 3.

14. The mission was established in 1831 by the Reverend Sherman Hall and his wife. Frederick Ayer and the Reverend William T. Boutwell later joined Hall and formed the first Protestant church in Wisconsin. For an account of the mission at La Pointe see: Hamilton N. Ross, *The Apostle Islands,* 1951; John N. Davidson, "Missions of Chequamagon Bay," *Wisconsin Historical Collections,* XII (1892), pp. 434-52; Lyman Draper, "The Story of Chequamegon," *Wisconsin Historical Collections,* XIII (1895), pp. 397-425; Stephen Riggs, "Protestant Missions in the Northwest," *Minnesota Historical Collections,* VI (1894), pp. 117-25; and Edward D. Neill, "Memoirs of William T. Boutwell," *Macalester College Contributions,* Second Series, No. 1.

15. Schoolcraft referred to the boundary line separating the Sioux and Chippewa tribes established at the Treaty of Prairie du Chien in 1825. It stretched in a southeast direction from a point on the Red River of the North to a point on the St. Croix, eight miles south of Osceola, Wisconsin. The line was not surveyed until 1835, and even then it served little purpose since the Indians pulled up the stakes as fast as they were driven. C. J. Kappler, Indian Affairs, *Laws and Treaties,* II, pp. 251-52, and William W. Folwell, *History of Minnesota* (St. Paul, 1921), I, p. 147.

16. Sherman Hall, Frederick Ayer, and William T. Boutwell were classmates at Andover Theological Seminary in the late 1820's. Hall was the first

to volunteer for missionary work with the Ojibway Indians of the Lake Superior region and later his two friends, Ayer and Boutwell, followed suit. In 1831 the three men arrived at Mackinac Island, then a center of missionary activities, and began their newly chosen career. Ayer went to La Pointe the same year to open a mission school, and in 1831 he was joined by the Reverend and Mrs. Hall. Boutwell remained on Mackinac Island to study the Ojibway language until 1832, when he joined Schoolcraft's expedition. He rejoined his friends at La Pointe in the fall of 1832, but later journeyed to the interior to establish a mission at Leech Lake. These missionaries played an important part in the development of Minnesota.

17. Schoolcraft's optimism relating to the work of the mission was not shared by Lt. James Allen. Indeed, the army officer believed that both the missions at La Pointe and Mackinac Island were "unproductive" and he questioned the propriety of sustaining them at such great expense "until more successful methods can be adopted by both to accomplish the benevolent designs of those contributing to their support. . . ." See Allen Journal, Entry of June 21, 1832, Appendix C.

18. Schoolcraft was apparently reluctant to mention his family ties with these men. Waub Ojeeg was a grandfather of Schoolcraft's wife, Jane, and Chi Waishki was her uncle. It is of interest to note, also, that Schoolcraft never mentions in the journal the fact that George Johnston, the interpreter, was his brother-in-law.

19. For a detailed account of the Grand Portage on the St. Louis River and the other portage between this river and Sandy Lake, see the journal of James Allen, Appendix C.

20. William Alexander Aitken, a Scotsman, was in charge of the Fond du Lac department of the American Fur Company. It was Aitken who convinced the missionary, Frederick Ayer, to open a school at Sandy Lake in 1833 for the children of the fur traders and voyageurs. Aitken was important enough in Minnesota's history to have a county and town named after him. G. L. Nute, *Voyageurs Highway* (St. Paul, 1947), p. 45.

21. Relation des traverses et des aventures d'un Marchand Voyageur dans les territoires Sauvages de l'Amérique Septentrionale, parti de Montreal, le 28 de Mai, 1783. Par Jean Baptiste Pérault. [H.R.S.]

22. Wabidea. [H.R.S.]

23. The Pokegama Falls are located about three miles above Grand Rapids, Minnesota.

24. Point aux Chenes was located a short distance south of the present town of Deer River.

25. Schoolcraft is inconsistent in his spelling of this chief's name.

26. This lake was so named by the Indians because its form suggested a lacrosse racket. It is now called Ball Club Lake.

27. The Winnipec House was located on the northern end of the lake at the mouth of the Turtle Portage River.

28. The clerk was probably Jean Bt. Belonger, although it may have been Alfred Aitkin, son of William A., the famous fur trader mentioned in the *Narrative*. Alfred was killed at Cass Lake in 1836 by an Indian who became enraged because Aitken had stolen his wife and refused to return her. The Indian was brought to trial and acquitted. W. H. C. Folsom, *Fifty Years in the Northwest* (1888), p. 483, and Edward D. Neill, *History of the Upper Mississippi Valley* (Minneapolis, 1881), pp. 190-91.

29. One of the avowed aims of the expedition was to determine the influence of British fur traders on the American side of the boundary. See Appendix A.

30. Colcaspi was an anagram composed of the names of Schoolcraft, Cass, and Pike, the geographical discoverers, in reverse order, of the region. Schoolcraft, *Summary Narrative* (Philadelphia, 1855), p. 227. It is now called Star Island. According to Allen's original map, the party encamped on the point of the northeast side of the island.

31. The English took over control of French North America in 1760, although the war in Europe continued until 1763 when the Treaty of Paris was signed. Several months later, in October, the English government announced the Proclamation of 1763, which established regulations for trade with the Indians.

32. The 1802 code gave the president authority to restrict the sale of liquor to Indians. *U.S. Statutes at Large,* 7th Cong., 1 Sess., Chap. 13, Sect. 21, Vol. II, p. 146. The passage of the law in 1816 forbidding foreigners from engaging in the fur trade on American soil gave the American Fur Company control over the fur trade of Minnesota.

33. For an account of the Lord Selkirk settlement and the tragic death of Governor Robert Semple see: Chester Martin, *Lord Selkirk's Work in Canada* (Oxford Historical and Literary Studies, Vol. 7, Oxford, 1916); Alexander Ross, *Red River Settlement* (London, 1856); and Folwell, *History of Minnesota,* I, pp. 213-17.

34. He had returned with the expedition from Lake Superior. [H.R.S.]

35. It is believed that the American Fur Company did, however, submit such a proposition to the directors of the Hudson's Bay Company in London, which was not acceded to by the latter. [H.R.S.]

36. *U.S. Statutes at Large,* 22d Cong., 1 Sess., Vol. IV, p. 564.

37. Schoolcraft gave this lake the name "Andrusia" in honor of President Andrew Jackson. It still bears that name. Schoolcraft, *Summary Narrative,* p. 228.

38. Or Pami-tascodiac. [H.R.S.] It is now called Wolf Lake.

39. These rapids were called the Metoswa Rapids from the Indian numeral for ten. Schoolcraft, *Summary Narrative,* p. 229.

40. Schoolcraft later varied the Indian spelling slightly—Pemidjegumaug. (Schoolcraft, *Summary Narrative,* p. 229.) Because there were others named "Lac Traverse" in North America, Schoolcraft called it Queen Anne's Lake, a name which was never accepted. The Indian name, "Bemidji," is now used.

41. A similar image stone was found on an island in Thunder Bay, Lake Huron, by the Cass expedition in 1820. Williams, *Schoolcraft's Narrative,* p. 75.

42. Schoolcraft named this lake in honor of Washington Irving.

43. Schoolcraft called the east fork the Plantagenian Branch. It was later named the Schoolcraft River, and has sometimes been referred to as the Yellow Head River, for the Indian guide who led the party to Lake Itasca.

44. There is actually only one lake, now called Marquette, although it is nearly divided into two by a strait.

45. Schoolcraft named this lake "Plantagenet," for the line of English kings who reigned from 1134 to 1397.

46. On the map in Schoolcraft's *Narrative* (1834), this lake is spelled Usawa. In his *Summary Narrative* (1855), p. 239, he used the name, Assawa or "Perch Lake."

47. For photographs of Lake Itasca, see: Jacob V. Brower, *Itasca State Park, An Illustrated History, Minnesota Historical Collections,* XI (1904).

48. This island was named Schoolcraft by Lt. Allen.

49. There is considerable controversy as to the actual elevation of Lake Itasca and the distance of the lake from the Gulf of Mexico. The figures accepted by the Mississippi River Commission are: elevation of Lake Itasca, 1,466 feet; length of Mississippi to Lake Itasca, 2,350 miles.

50. From the data, above given, the descent of the Mississippi will average a fraction over five inches, per mile, a result not essentially different from that furnished by the data, which I submitted in my Narrative Journal in 1820, but which was differently stated from haste and inadvertence. For a prompt notice of the error, I feel indebted to Hamilton Fulton, Esqr., who, soon after the appearance of the work, wrote to my publishers, on the subject. [H.R.S.]

51. Onzig, of the Chippewas. [H.R.S.]

52. In his *Summary Narrative* (1855), p. 248, Schoolcraft named it Chemaun or Ocano. The former word is Chippewa for a birch canoe, and the latter is from the French *aux canots,* of canoes. On his map in the same edition, Schoolcraft called it "DeWitt Clinton's River." In 1881 the stream was named LaSalle by the adventurer, Willard Glazier, and in 1892 it was named Andrus Creek by J. V. Brower for the treasurer of the Minnesota Fish and Game Commission. LaSalle is the name popularly used today. Warren Upham, *Minnesota Geographic Names, Minnesota Historical Collections,* XVII (1920), p. 134.

53. In his *Summary Narrative* (1855), p. 248, Schoolcraft notes that it was called the "Peneddewin or Carnage River." He named the river DeSoto and the lake from which it originated Monomina, from the Chippewa *Monomenauing*—a place of wild rice. It now bears the name Monomin.

54. So called in honor of Lieut. James Allen, U.S.A., who, on his return down the Mississippi, was the first to explore it. [H.R.S.]

55. A few years ago, a Mr. Beltrami, returning from the settlement of Pembina, by the usual route of the traders from Red Lake to Turtle Lake, published at New Orleans, a small 12mo volume under the title of "La découverte des sources du Mississippi, et de la Riviere Sanglante," a work which has since been expanded into two heavy 8vo volumes by the London press. [H.R.S.]

56. Composed of the initials of the names of the gentlemen of the party. [H.R.S.] Schoolcraft, Houghton, Johnston, Boutwell, and Allen were members of the party. Schoolcraft does not explain the letter "i" in the Lake's name, but perhaps it represented Johnston.

57. A detailed map of Leech Lake drawn from notes made by Lt. Allen may be found in the 1834 edition of Schoolcraft's *Narrative,* p. 76, and also in his *Summary Narrative* (1855), p. 259.

58. The Pillagers received their name from an incident which occurred in 1767 or 1768, while they were encamped on the Crow Wing River, preparing for a special ceremonial rite. A group of white traders arrived at their camp, laden with merchandise, but refused to trade with the Indians until their leader had recovered from his illness. Anxious to trade their furs for the colorful cloth, one of the Indians boldly tore off a sample for a breechcloth and told the trader that he had beaver skins in his lodge to repay him. Others followed suit, and soon bedlam prevailed. Liquor was discovered among the traders' goods and confiscated. The white traders fled the scene in fear for their lives. Although the Indians later went to Mackinac to make amends for their actions, the name, "Pillagers," stuck. William W. Warren, "History of the Ojibways, Based upon Traditions and Oral Statements," *Minnesota Historical Collections,* V(1885), pp. 256-60, and Upham, *Minnesota Geographic Names, Minnesota Historical Collections,* XVII (1920), p. 91.

59. The Treaty of Tipisagi, or Prairie du Chien, dealt mainly with the establishment of a boundary between the Sioux and the Chippewas in an attempt to stop the long-time feud between these two tribes. General William Clark of St. Louis and Governor Lewis Cass of Michigan Territory represented the national government, and over one thousand tribal chiefs attended on behalf of the Sioux, Chippewa, Potawatomi, Winnebago, Saks and Foxes, and Iowa tribes. The treaty was unique in that it did not involve a cession of land. Although both tribes promised not to cross the boundary line, except on peaceful missions, bloody warfare continued until the Sioux were removed in 1862. C. J. Kappler, *Indian Affairs, Laws and Treaties* (Washington, D.C., 1904), II, 250-55.

60. Among the dead, Wahb Ojeeg, Cadiwabida, or the Bréche, Chingaba Wossin, and Mozobodo, are the Chippewa patriarchs of modern days. [H.R.S.]

61. It has been stated in the "Preliminary Observations," that it became impracticable to visit these bands, during the expedition of 1831. [H.R.S.]

62. For a historical account of smallpox epidemics, see the report of Dr. Douglass Houghton to Schoolcraft, Sept. 21, 1832, Appendix D.

63. Although Schoolcraft did not mention him by name, he is obviously referring to Major Lawrence Taliaferro, Indian agent at St. Peters. The Reverend Boutwell substantiates this in his journal when he reports that the chief openly accused Taliaferro. When the Major read Schoolcraft's *Narrative* in 1834 he was enraged by Schoolcraft's inference and accused Schoolcraft of falsifying Flat Mouth's words. As the Minnesota historian, William Folwell, pointed out, however, relations between Schoolcraft and Taliaferro had been very poor since the Treaty of Prairie du Chien. *History of Minnesota,* Vol. I, p. 115n.

64. Family mark, or coat of arms—a kind of sirname. [H.R.S.]

65. A fur-trading center in northwestern Canada, hundreds of miles west of Grand Portage, the fur-shipping port of northern Lake Superior. Because of the difficulty of bringing out the furs from this post to Grand Portage and returning before the rivers froze, a special depot, the Athabasca House, was built at Rainy Lake to shorten the journey of Athabasca traders. See: Grace L. Nute, *Voyageurs Highway* (St. Paul, 1947), p. 8, and *Voyageur* (New York, 1931), p. 64-65.

66. The Pic Post was on the northern shore of Lake Superior.

67. This manuscript was prepared, at Schoolcraft's request, by Jean Baptiste Pérault, a veteran fur trader. It was written in 1830 when Pérault was seventy —apparently from his diaries. The original manuscript is in the Schoolcraft Collection at the Library of Congress. It was edited and published in the *Michigan Pioneer and Historical Collections,* Vol. 37 (1909-10), pp. 508-619, "Narrative of the Travels and Adventures of a Merchant Voyageur in the Savage Territories of Northern America Leaving Montreal the 28th of May, 1783 (to 1820)."

68. This lake, as Schoolcraft noted on his map, was called Warpool. It was named by the Chippewa, who there began war expeditions against the Sioux. It was later changed to Frances Lake and finally to Lake May. Upham, *Minnesota Geographic Names, Minnesota Historical Collections* XVII (1920), p. 98.

69. Starting with the Long Water, Schoolcraft passed through eleven lakes on his journey down the Crow Wing River. In descending order they were: the Little Vermillion, Birch, Lac Plé, Ossowa, Lac Vieux Desert, Summitt,

Long Rice, Allen's, Johnston's, and Lake Kaichibo Sagitawa. Two of them, Allen's and Johnston's lakes, were named for members of the expedition; and a third, Ossowa, was named Boutwell by Schoolcraft. These original names were later replaced by numbers by the early settlers and lumbermen, starting with the lowest as First Lake, and going up to the Eleventh, Long Water. *Ibid.* (1920) pp. 245-46.

70. John Johnston was born at Craignear, Grant's Causeway, Ireland, in 1763, the son of a wealthy nobleman. After receiving an excellent education, he came to Canada in 1792 and entered the fur trade. He was stationed at La Pointe in Chequamegon Bay, and while there met and married "Ozhaw-Guscoday-Wayquay," the "Woman of the Green Prairie" [Susan], the daughter of the Chippewa Chieftan, Waub Ojeeg. In 1794 Johnston moved his headquarters to Sault Ste. Marie, where his residence became the center of civilized society. He had a fine library in his home, and most of the important travelers and explorers visited him on their way West. His children were well educated; one, George (1796-1861) became Schoolcraft's interpreter on the 1832 expedition, and Jane became Schoolcraft's wife. See Alice Clapp, "George Johnston, Indian Interpreter," *Michigan History,* XXXIII (Autumn, 1939), pp. 350-66; and "Fur Trade in the Upper Lakes," *Wisconsin Historical Collections,* XIX (1910), p. 361.

71. Report of the proceedings connected with the disputes between the Earl of Selkirk and the North West Company, at the assizes held at York in Upper Canada, Oct. 1818. Montreal. 8vo. 564 p. [H.R.S.]

72. Lac Plé or Pele was so named because it was partly bordered by a prairie. Upham, *Minnesota Geographic Names, Minnesota Historical Collections,* XVII (1920), p. 246.

73. Genera Unio, Anadonta, Alasmadonta. [H.R.S.]

74. In his *Summary Narrative* (1855), p. 265, Schoolcraft stated that he named this lake "Douglass" for his friend, Prof. David B. Douglass, who was on the Cass expedition in 1820.

75. According to Upham, Crow Island was later called McArthur after an early settler of the area. *Minnesota Geographic Names, Minnesota Historical Collections* XVII (1920), p. 163.

76. Schoolcraft, the prognosticator, is at his best here, in predicting that the area above the falls, "shall team with their destined population." The Twin Cities, Elk River, St. Cloud, Little Falls, and Brainerd have become important urban centers in Minnesota. Indeed, according to the 1950 federal census the twin cities of St. Paul and Minneapolis contributed almost one third of the total Minnesota population.

77. This Chief attacked a Sioux war party, which imprudently ventured in the vicinity, in the fall of this year, (1832,) and achieved a victory, in which he killed forty persons, and lost not a single man. [H.R.S.]

78. There is some disagreement as to the exact location of the Baker Trading Post. Boutwell (Appendix E) and Schoolcraft stated in their journals that it was eighteen miles below the mouth of the Crow Wing River. Lt. Allen (Appendix C) reported that it was ten miles below, and Douglass Houghton (Appendix D) wrote that it took from six to eight P.M. to make the trip. Dr. Nute, however, wrote that it was located two miles below the mouth of the Crow Wing River. "Minnesota Fur-Trading Posts," *Minnesota History,* XI (Dec., 1930), p. 373.

79. The total descent of the river at these falls, including the rapids above

and below them is stated in my "Narrative Journal of Travels to the Sources of the Mississippi," at 65 feet, an estimate which it is believed may exceed the actual aggregate descent, and certainly does so, in the hasty estimate which is given of the perpendicular fall. [H.R.S.]

80. A lake in Perth County, Scotland, made famous by Sir Walter Scott in "The Lady of the Lake."

81. I am not certain that I fully comprehend the brevity of Mr. Eaton's division of this formation of the English geologists; but if I do so, he deduces from it, or from its equivalent in American geology, 1. Second graywake, 2. Calciferous sandrock, 3. Silicious limerock, 4. Metalliferous limerock. [H.R.S.]

82. Standing Cedars is located at Cedar Bend, about a half mile southwest of the northeast corner of Washington County, Minnesota. This line was established in the Treaty of Prairie du Chien in 1825.

83. Schoolcraft is referring to Joseph Renshaw Brown, one of Minnesota's prominent pioneers. This is substantiated by Lt. Allen's entry of July 28, 1832, which indicates that on the evening of the 27th he met "a trader, Mr. Brown of the American Fur Company," who informed Allen that Schoolcraft was "seven or eight miles ahead."

Brown, born in 1805, came to Minnesota at the age of fourteen as a drummer boy in the army. After leaving the army in 1825, he engaged in Indian trade, lumbering, and other business in the St. Croix River area and in other parts of Minnesota. He served as secretary of the territorial council of Minnesota and held other posts in state government. Brown County, Minnesota, is named after him.

84. This area of the river near present-day Taylor's Falls, Minnesota, was called by the French "the Dalles of the St. Croix," because of its rock-walled gorges. Wisconsin and Minnesota now maintain an interstate park here. See Upham, *Minnesota Geographic Names, Minnesota Historical Collections,* XVII (1920), pp. 110-12.

85. *Travels of Jonathan Carver through the Interior Parts of North America in the Years 1766, 1767 and 1768* (London, 1778), pp. 46-51.

86. W. H. C. Folsom examined these ruins in 1851 and found the remains of the foundations of nine houses. Over some, trees "two feet in diameter were growing." He believed that they were remnants of an old mid-eighteenth century fur-trading post. *Fifty Years in the Northwest,* pp. 302-303.

87. This incident was part of a bitter controversy between Schoolcraft and Lt. Allen. Schoolcraft, as did Houghton (see entry of July 30, Appendix D), expected the Indians to guide Allen and the military escort to the portage between Upper Lake St. Croix and the Brule River. Lt. Allen reported that the Indians would go only as far as their village, "as this was as far as Schoolcraft had asked them to go." See entries in Allen Journal of July 30, 1832, Appendix C.

88. Alluding to a mound on an eminence at the mouth of the river. [H.R.S.]

89. See letter from Schoolcraft to Governor George Porter, Aug. 15, 1832, Appendix B.

90. This island has been the scene of a subsequent murder, in which an Indian was excited to kill his father-in-law. [H.R.S.]

91. The Crane is the totem of the reigning chiefs of the band of Sault Ste. Marie. [H.R.S.]

APPENDICES

APPENDIX A

*Letters and Reports Relating to the Organization
of Expeditions in 1831 and 1832
to the Northwestern Region of the United States*

THIS SERIES of letters pertain to expeditions in Indian Country in 1831 and 1832. In 1831 Henry Rowe Schoolcraft, the leader of these expeditions, was forced to abandon his plan to visit Indian tribes in the Upper Mississippi River region and instead, traveled into Wisconsin to contact tribes living along the St. Croix, Red Cedar, and Chippewa rivers. The account of this trip along with documents bearing upon the plans for the 1832 expedition are printed in this appendix.

1. Lewis Cass to Henry Rowe Schoolcraft, August 9, 1830. Schoolcraft Papers, Library of Congress.

2. Henry Rowe Schoolcraft to the Chippewa chiefs, October 1, 1830. Schoolcraft Papers, Library of Congress.

3. Lewis Cass to Charles C. Trowbridge, April 21, 1831. Trowbridge Papers, Burton Historical Collection of The Detroit Public Library.

4. Alexander Macomb to Commanding Officer at Sault Ste. Marie, April 23, 1831. Enclosure: Lewis Cass to Sec. of War Eaton, Washington, April 19, 1831. *Territorial Papers of the United States—Michigan,* compiled by Clarence Edwin Carter (Washington, 1945), Vol. XII, pp. 281-82. Hereafter referred to as *Territorial Papers.*

5. Samuel S. Hamilton to Henry Rowe Schoolcraft, April 25, 1831. Schoolcraft Papers, Library of Congress.

6. Henry Rowe Schoolcraft to Lewis Cass, June 28, 1831. *Territorial Papers,* Vol. XII, pp. 304-305.

7. Henry Rowe Schoolcraft to Lawrence Taliaferro, August 1, 1831. Schoolcraft Papers, Library of Congress.

8. Report of Expedition of 1831, Henry Rowe Schoolcraft to Elbert Herring, September 21, 1831. *Narrative of an Expedition Through the Upper Mississippi to Itasca Lake* (New York, 1834), pp. 265-85. Hereafter referred to as *Narrative to Itasca.*

9. Henry Rowe Schoolcraft to George B. Porter, October 1, 1831. Schoolcraft Papers, Library of Congress.

10. Henry Rowe Schoolcraft to Elbert Herring, February 13, 1832. Schoolcraft Papers, Library of Congress.

11. The Reverend William Thurston Boutwell to Henry Rowe Schoolcraft, February 21, 1832. Schoolcraft Papers, Library of Congress.

12. William M. Ferry to Henry Rowe Schoolcraft, February 21, 1832. Schoolcraft Papers, Library of Congress.

13. Henry Rowe Schoolcraft to Lewis Cass, February 24, 1832. Cass Papers, William L. Clements Library, University of Michigan.

14. Henry Rowe Schoolcraft to the Reverend David Greene, February 25, 1832. Schoolcraft Papers, Library of Congress.

15. Lewis Cass to Henry Rowe Schoolcraft, March 28, 1832. Schoolcraft Papers, Library of Congress.

16. The Reverend David Greene to Henry Rowe Schoolcraft, April 12, 1832. Schoolcraft Papers, Library of Congress.

17. Elbert Herring to Henry Rowe Schoolcraft, May 3, 1832. *Territorial Papers,* Vol XII, pp. 473-74.

18. Lewis Cass to Henry Rowe Schoolcraft, May 4, 1832. Schoolcraft Papers, Library of Congress.

19. Alexander Macomb to De Lafayette Wilcox, May 9, 1832. *Executive Documents,* 23d Cong., 1 Sess., Doc. No. 323, pp. 1-2.

20. Elbert Herring to Henry Rowe Schoolcraft, May 17, 1832. *Territorial Papers,* Vol. XII, p. 481.

21. Elbert Herring and William Ward to Henry Rowe Schoolcraft, May 21, 1832. *Territorial Papers,* Vol. XII, pp. 481-82.

22. Lewis Cass to Henry Rowe Schoolcraft, May 22, 1832. Schoolcraft Papers, Library of Congress.

23. Henry Rowe Schoolcraft to George Johnston, May 29, 1832. Johnston Papers, Burton Historical Collection.

24. Henry Rowe Schoolcraft to John Torrey, June 2, 1832. Torrey Papers, New York Botanical Garden.

25. Special Order No. 2 by De Lafayette Wilcox, June 6, 1832. *Executive Documents,* 23d Cong., 1 Sess., Doc. No. 323, p. 2.

1. Lewis Cass to Henry Rowe Schoolcraft.

DETROIT, August 9, 1830

SIR:

I have been directed by the War Department to request you to proceed into the Chippewa country, to endeavor to put an end to the hostilities between the Chippewas and Sioux. The general route must be left to your discretion. Whether it will be necessary for you to go beyond Fond du Lac, you can best determine on your arrival there. From the limited means applicable to this object, I am apprehensive that your journey cannot be extended beyond that place. But in that event, it will be necessary to summon some of the principal Mississippi Chiefs to meet you, as without their concurrences no durable pacification can be effected.

Your object will be to impress upon them, the necessity of terminating their hostilities with the Sioux. And the considerations connected with the subject are so familiar to you, that I need not dwell upon them. You are perfectly acquainted with their useless and harrowing contests, and the miseries these have inflicted, and yet threaten to inflict upon them. But it will be well to state to them the result of the recent council at Prairie du Chien [in 1825], that they may know what has been done by the other Indians, and that the Sioux now freed from the pressure in other quarters, can direct their whole force against them.

In addition to the other considerations you may wage, I enclose a speech to be delivered to them, which you will please to accompany with a proper belt: I think it will be best for them to send a message to the Sioux without delay, stating their determination to refrain from hostilities in conformity with the wish of their great father the President, and their adhesion to the treaty of Prairie du Chien. This message should be sent while you are with them, and I recommend that one from you be likewise sent to the Sioux, explanatory of the matter.

You will proceed to the execution of this duty without delay, if the season be not too far advanced when you receive this letter. But I am apprehensive it will not reach you in season. Should it be so, you will please send a message to the chiefs stating your intention to visit them next summer, and recommending them to sit still until you can see them. It may have the effect of keeping them quiet. If, however, you cannot proceed this fall, it is probable that circumstances may require some change in these instructions before the next season, and your arrangements must therefore depend upon such as may be hereafter given.

Very respectfully, &c.

LEW. CASS.

2. Henry Rowe Schoolcraft to the Chippewa chiefs.

INDIAN AGENCY, SAULT STE. MARIE, October 1st, 1830

MY CHILDREN,

Your great Father at Washington has heard of the war between the Sioux & yourselves. He had given orders that a stop should be put to it, *this year,* and had directed an officer to proceed to your country to remind you of the mutual folly of continuing hostilities. But this order came too late to the Sault for the officer to go Inland. He will enter the Chippewa country *next spring.* In the mean time your father advises you to be still. Listen to his words, and when you have occasion to speak, he will listen to you.

This much I have been commanded to say to you each & all.

Your friend

HENRY R. SCHOOLCRAFT

[This message was sent to a number of Chippewa chiefs after Schoolcraft decided that it was too late in the year to follow Cass's orders to proceed into Chippewa country.]

3. Lewis Cass to Charles C. Trowbridge.

WASHINGTON, April 21, 1831

DEAR TROWBRIDGE,

I have arranged Schoolcraft's expedition, and I write to you upon the subject, as he intended to leave some of the details with you, should he have left Detroit, before the information could reach him. He is allowed, in addition to his $500 on hand,

$300 for contingencies
300 in addition to the usual allowance to his agency for presents.
100 on acct. of provisions
100		Interpreter.

And a canoe with soldiers will accompany him. So that on the whole he will be well fixed. The official letter to him will be prepared in a day or two. I wrote him a short note yesterday, but it was before the final arrangements were made. Should a vessel be upon the point of leaving Detroit, let him know the result by it. I shall write him again in a few days. . . .

[The rest of the letter relates to affairs of the Bank of Michigan, of which Trowbridge was Cashier.]

Ever Yours

LEW CASS.

[This letter was printed in the *Burton Historical Collection Leaflets,* Vol. III (November, 1924), pp. 29-30.]

4. Alexander Macomb to the Commanding Officer at Sault Ste. Marie.

HEADQUARTERS OF THE ARMY, WASHINGTON April 23d. 1831.
SIR: I transmit to you herewith a copy of a letter which has been submitted by Governor Cass to the Secretary of War, on the subject of an expedition to be undertaken by Mr. Schoolcraft and which has met the approbation of the Secretary and been duly sanctioned by him.

You will therefore detach an officer and ten or twelve men as proposed, to make part of the expedition. The officer will be directed to keep a Journal of the proceedings of the expedition, making all observations that may be important, and describing the country through which the expedition may pass, deliniating topographically the route and several points of importance, ascertaining the names and character of the various Indian tribes, their numbers, strength in warriors, conditions, mode of living, of obtaining subsistence, whether at peace with their neighbors, or engaged in war with any other tribes, places of resort for foreign supplies, how supplied and by whom:—To note the nature of the soil, the geology, mineralogy, natural History, remarking particularly on the game and fishes, as to quantity, quality and facility of procuring them. The officer will transmit his report to Head Quarters for the information of the General-in-Chief and to be laid before the Secretary of War. The Officer will be considered as on topographical duty, during the period he may be absent from the Post, and employed on the expedition, and the men will be allowed the extra allowance accorded to soldiers on fatigue duty. The Officer will report to Mr. Schoolcraft and take his directions.

I am Sir, Yours respectfully.

ALEX. MACOMB
Maj. Genl. Comdg. the Army

[Enclosure of a Copy of the Letter from Gov. Cass to the Secretary of War, transmitted with the above.]

WASHINGTON, April 19th, 1831
To the Hon. Jno. H. Eaton.
SIR: I had the honor in my Letter to the Dept. of the 4 Jany last to submit my views of the propriety of directing Mr. Schoolcraft to proceed into the Lake Superior and Mississippi Country, of the objects to be obtained by him, and of the route to be taken. I beg leave again to call the subject to your attention, and to suggest the following arrangement.
First. That 300$ from the contingencies be allowed to him in addition to the sum of 500$ already received by him for this object.
Second. That 300$ be added to the usual allowance to his agency for presents.
Third. That 100$ be allowed on account of Interpreter. [At this point another copy reads: "Third. That 100$ be allowed on account of provisions, and 150$ on account of Interpreter."] These sums include the whole ex-

pense. I would also suggest the expediency of directing the Commanding Officer at the Sault de St. Marie, to detach an Officer with ten or twelve men in a boat or canoe, to form part of the expedition. They would add much to the effect of the movement.

Very Respectfully I have the honor to be Yr. Ob. Servt.

LEWIS CASS.

Approved J. H. E.

[Gov. Cass's letter to Eaton is printed in *Territorial Papers,* Vol. XII, p. 282. The original is in Record Group No. 75, Office of Indian Affairs, National Archives.]

5. Samuel S. Hamilton to Henry Rowe Schoolcraft.

DEPARTMENT OF WAR, OFFICE OF INDIAN AFFAIRS, 25th April, 1831
SIR:

Since writing the letter to you of the 5th instant, Gov. Cass has arrived here, and submitted to the Secretary of War his views, as to the propriety of directing you to proceed into Lake Superior and the Mississippi country, &c. These views have been approved, and I am accordingly directed to instruct you to proceed as soon as your arrangements can be made for the purpose, on the proposed expedition. The objects to be accomplished are so well known, and have also been so fully explained in the letter of Gov. Cass to you of the 9th of August last, that it is deemed unnecessary to give you any further instructions on the subject.

Orders will be issued through the proper department, to the Commanding Officer at the Sault Ste. Marie for a detachment of the troops, to form a part of the proposed expedition.

Very respectfully, &c.

SAMUEL S. HAMILTON

[On April 5 Hamilton ordered Cass to delay the Schoolcraft expedition. A duplicate of this letter, which was sent to Schoolcraft, is apparently the one referred to above. See *Territorial Papers,* Vol. XII, p. 275.]

6. Henry Rowe Schoolcraft to Lewis Cass.

VERMILLION BAY, LAKE SUPERIOR
June 28th, 1831

DEAR SIR,

I heard of your transfer from Detroit to Washington on the eve of my setting out from St. Mary's. And it is only necessary to say that there is no political event which could have given me as high a gratification. Report has also vaguely spoken of your successor in Michigan, but I shall not hear of the definite arrangement until I strike the settlements on Green Bay.

All has thus far gone well with my little expedition. My arrangements are calculated neatly to the appropriation. I have two canoes, besides a canoe of Indians to go as far as may be necessary, & to be replaced by others from village to village. Lt. [Robert] Clary is with me, with ten soldiers in a barge provisioned for 2 months. And he has four Canadians to bring back his barge from the head of the Lake, where it will be necessary to exchange his mode of conveyance.

Our route will be up the Brule & from the country of the St. Croix, by a line diagonally drawn to Green Bay, probably to the head of Wolf River. This will carry me through the populous parts of the Chippewa country on the war grounds between them & the Sioux, & on the frontier between them & the Winnebagoes, Menomonies & Wabunockies [Wabanakies]. And by expresses I can make arrangements to assemble them all, men women & children, at three important points, viz Yellow River, Lac Courtoreille [Court Oreilles] & Lac du Flambeau.

I shall address you from Green Bay, & should be happy to get a line from you there.

With my respects to Mrs. Cass & the family, I am dear Sir with sincere regard Yours.

HENRY R. SCHOOLCRAFT

[Schoolcraft was referring to Cass's appointment as Secretary of War. Although he was not appointed until July, rumor of the appointment had reached the West earlier.]

7. Henry Rowe Schoolcraft to Lawrence Taliaferro, Indian Agent at St. Peters.

YELLOW RIVER, Aug. 1, 1831

SIR:

It is in accordance with the instructions under which I am acting, to solicit your co-operation in keeping the Sioux and Chippewas at peace, and to induce them to adhere, in good faith, to the articles of the treaty of Prairie du Chien. Blind to their true interests, these tribes continue a warfare as hopeless in its termination as it is inglorious in its results. Notwithstanding every pains which has been taken by the government to convince them of the erroneous policy of such a contest, and to inspire in them fidelity to their public treaties with each other, restless and ambitious young men, on either side, continue to lead war-parties into the territories of the other, and to waylay the unsuspecting. I am satisfied that the authority of the chiefs is not always sufficient to restrain the incursions of these young warriors, who are led on by the thirst of fame, and stimulated by hereditary animosity. Such a course is not surprising among savages. But it is the dictate of humanity to restrain this false ardor, and to make use of every practicable means to put a stop to scenes at which the heart sickens. It is but recently that a Mr. Cadotte, a young half-breed of the Sault Ste. Marie, another young man of mixed blood, called the Little Frenchman, living as an

Indian, and two Chippewas, one a female, travelling down the St. Croix in a canoe, were fired upon from an ambush by the Sioux, and killed. And this injury still remains unredressed.

The Chippewas complain of this mode of warfare, which it would be an idle affectation to designate by any other term than murder. They say the Sioux are indeed ready to smoke the pipe of peace with them, and never fail to do so when it is presented to them; but that a confidence, on their part, in these smoking councils, is paid with the loss of lives.

I have despatched a message to the Sioux chief, Petite Corbeau [Little Crow], and another to Wabisha, reminding them of their treaty engagements with the Chippewas, and of the recent violation of them above referred to, and requesting them to use their influence efficaciously to terminate further inroads. These messages are accompanied by others from Shakoba and from Kabamappa, Chippewa chiefs on the St. Croix and Snake Rivers.

I am, sir,
Very respectfully,
Your obedient servant,
H. R. SCHOOLCRAFT

8. Report of Expedition of 1831.
   Henry Rowe Schoolcraft to Elbert Herring.

SAULT STE. MARIE, Sept. 21, 1831

SIR,

In compliance with instructions to endeavour to terminate the hostilities between the Chippewas and Sioux, I proceeded into the Chippewa country with thirteen men in two canoes, having the necessary provisions and presents for the Indians, an interpreter [George Johnston], a physician [Douglass Houghton] to attend the sick, and a person in charge of the provisions and other public property [Melancthon Woolsey]. The commanding officer of Fort Brady furnished me with an escort of ten soldiers, under the command of a lieutenant [Robert Clary]; and I took with me a few Chippewas, in a canoe provided with oars, to convey a part of the provisions. A flag was procured for each canoe. I joined the expedition at the head of the portage, at this place, on the 25th of June; and, after visiting the Chippewa villages in the belt of country between Lake Superior and the Mississippi, in latitudes 44° to 70°, returned on the 4th of September, having been absent seventy-two days, and travelled a line of country estimated to be two thousand three hundred and eight miles. I have now the honor to report to you the route pursued, the means employed to accomplish the object, and such further measures as appear to me to be necessary to give effect to what has been done, and to ensure a lasting peace between the two tribes.

Reasons existed for not extending the visit to the Chippewa bands on the extreme Upper Mississippi, on Red Lake, and Red River, and the river De Corbeau. After entering Lake Superior, and traversing its southern shores to Point Chegoimegon [Chequamegon] and the adjacent cluster of [Apostle] islands, I ascended the Mauvaise [Bad] River to a portage of 8¾ miles into the Kaginogumac or Long Water [Owen] Lake. This lake is about eight miles long, and of very irregular width. Thence, by a portage of 280 yards, into Turtle Lake; thence, by a portage of 1,075 yards, into Clary's Lake, so called [for Lt. Robert Clary]; thence, by a portage of 425 yards, into Lake Polyganum; and thence, by a portage of 1,050 yards, into the Namakagon River, a branch of the river St. Croix of the Upper Mississippi. The distance from Lake Superior to this spot is, by estimation, 124 miles.

We descended the Namakagon to the Pukwaewa, a rice lake, and a Chippewa village of eight permanent lodges, containing a population of 53 persons, under a local chief called Odabossa. We found here gardens of corn, potatoes, and pumpkins, in a very neat state of cultivation. The low state of the water, and the consequent difficulty of the navigation, induced me to leave the provisions and stores at this place, in charge of Mr. Woolsey, with directions to proceed (with part of the men, and the aid of the Indians) to *Lac Courtorielle* or Ottowa Lake, and there await my arrival. I then descended the Namakagon in a light canoe, to its discharge into the St. Croix, and down the latter to Yellow River, the site of a trading-post and an Indian village, where I had, by runners, appointed a council. In this trip I was accompanied by Mr. [George] Johns[t]on, sub-agent, acting as interpreter, and by Dr. Houghton, adjunct professor of the Rensselaer [Polytechnic Institute] school. We reached Yellow River on the 1st of August, and found the Indians assembled. After terminating the business of the council (of which I shall presently mention the results), I reascended the St. Croix and the Namakagon to the portage which intervenes between the latter and Lac Courtorielle. The first of the series of carrying-places is about three miles in length, and terminates at the Lake of the Isles *(Lac des Isles)*; after crossing which, a portage of 750 yards leads to *Lac du Gres*. This lake has a navigable outlet into Ottowa Lake, where I rejoined the advanced party (including Lieutenant Clary's detachment) on the 5th of August.

Ottowa Lake is a considerable expanse of water, being about twelve miles long, with irregular but elevated shores. A populous Chippewa village and a trading-post are located at its outlet, and a numerous Indian population subsists in the vicinity. It is situated in a district of country which abounds in rice lakes, has a proportion of prairie or burnt land, caused by the ravages of fire, and, in addition to the small fur-bearing animals, has several of the deer species. It occupies, geographically, a central situation, being intermediate, and commanding the communications between the St. Croix and Chippewa Rivers, and between Lake Superior and the Upper Mississippi. It is on the great slope of land descending towards the latter, enjoys a climate of comparative mildness, and yields, with fewer and shorter intervals of extreme want, the means of subsistence to a population which is still essentially erratic. These remarks apply, with some modifications, to the entire range of country (within the latitudes mentioned) situated west and south of the high lands circumscribing the waters of Lake Superior. The outlet of this lake (Ottowa) is a fork of Chippewa River, called Ottowa River.

I had intended to proceed from this lake, either by following down the Ottowa branch to its junction with the main Chippewa, and then ascending the latter into *Lac du Flambeau,* or by descending the Ottowa branch only to its junction with the North-West fork, called the Ochasowa River; and, ascending the latter to a portage of sixty *pauses,* into the Chippewa River. By the latter route time and distance would have been saved, and I should, in either way, have been enabled to proceed from *Lac du Flambeau* to Green Bay by an easy communication into the Upper Ouisconsin [Wisconsin], and from the latter into the Menomonie River, or by Plover Portage into Wolf River. This was the route I had designed to go on quitting Lake Superior; but, on consulting my Indian maps, and obtaining at Ottowa Lake the best and most recent information of the distance and the actual state of the water, I found neither of the foregoing routes practicable, without extending my time so far as to exhaust my supplies. I was finally determined to relinquish the *Lac du Flambeau* route, by learning that the Indians of that place had dispersed, and by knowing that a considerable delay would be caused by reassembling them.

The homeward route by the Mississippi was now the most eligible, particularly as it would carry me through a portion of country occupied by the Chippewas, in a state of hostility with the Sioux, and cross the disputed line at the mill. Two routes, to arrive at the Mississippi, were before me—either to follow down the outlet of Ottowa Lake to its junction with the Chippewa, and ascend the latter to its mouth, or to quit the Ottowa Lake branch at an intermediate point, and, after ascending a small and very serpentine tributary, to cross a portage of 6,000 yards into Lake Chetac. I pursued the latter route.

Lake Chetac is a sheet of water about six miles in length, and it has several islands, on one of which is a small Chippewa village and a trading-post. This lake is the main source of Red Cedar River (called sometimes the *Folle Avoine* [wild rice country]), a branch of the Chippewa River. It receives a brook at its head from the direction of the portage, which admits empty canoes to be conveyed down it two *pauses,* but is then obstructed with logs. It is connected by a shallow outlet with Weegwos Lake, a small expanse which we crossed with paddles in twenty-five minutes. The passage from the latter is so shallow, that a portage of 1,295 yards is made into Balsam of Fir or *Sapin* Lake. The baggage is carried this distance, but the canoes are brought through the stream. Sapin Lake is also small; we were thirty minutes in crossing it. Below this point, the river again expands into a beautiful sheet of water, called Red Cedar Lake, which we were an hour in passing; and afterward into *Bois Francois,* or Rice Lake. At the latter place, at the distance of perhaps sixty miles from its head, I found the last fixed village of Chippewas on this stream, although the hunting camps, and other signs of temporary occupation, were more numerous below than on any other part of the stream. This may be attributed to the abundance of the

Virginia deer in that vicinity, many of which we saw, and of the elk and moose, whose tracks were fresh and numerous in the sands of the shore. Wild rice is found in all the lakes. Game, of every species common to the latitude, is plentiful. The prairie country extends itself into the vicinity of Rice Lake; and for more than a day's march before reaching the mouth of the river, the whole face of the country puts on a sylvan character, as beautiful to the eye as it is fertile in soil, and spontaneously productive of the the means of subsistence. A country more valuable to a population having the habits of our North-Western Indians, could hardly be conceived of; and it is therefore cause of less surprise that its possession should have been so long an object of contention between the Chippewas and Sioux.

About sixty miles below Rice Lake commences a series of rapids, which extend, with short intervals, 24 miles. The remainder of the distance, to the junction of this stream with the Chippewa, consists of deep and strong water. The junction itself is characterized by commanding and elevated grounds, and a noble expanse of waters. And the Chippewa River, from this spot to its entrance into the Mississippi, has a depth and volume, and a prominence of scenery, which mark it to be inferior to none, and superior to most of the larger tributaries of the Upper Mississippi. Before its junction, it is separated into several mouths, from the principal of which the observer can look into Lake Pepin. Steamboats could probably ascend to the falls.

The whole distance travelled, from the shores of Lake Superior to the mouth of the Chippewa, is, by estimation, 643 miles, of which 138 should be deducted for the trip to Yellow River, leaving the direct practicable route 505 miles. The length of the Mauvaise to the portage is 104; of the Namakagon, from the portage, 161; of the Red Cedar, 170; of the Chippewa, from the entrance of the latter, 40. Our means of estimating distances was by time, corrected by reference to the rapidity of water and strength of wind, compared with our known velocity of travelling in calm weather on the lakes. These estimates were made and put down every evening, and considerable confidence is felt in them. The courses were accurately kept by a canoe compass. I illustrate my report of this part of the route by a map protracted by Dr. Houghton. On this map our places of encampment, the sites and population of the principal Indian villages, the trading-posts, and the boundary lines between the Sioux and Chippewa, are indicated. And I refer you to it for several details which are omitted in this report.[1]

The present state of the controversy between the Sioux and the Chippewas will be best inferred from the facts that follow. In stating them, I have deemed it essential to preserve the order of my conferences with the Indians, and to confine myself, almost wholly, to results.

Along the borders of Lake Superior, comparatively little alarm was felt from the hostile relation with the Sioux. But I found them well informed of the state of the difficulties, and the result of the several war-parties that had been sent out the last year. A system of information and advice is con-

stantly kept up by runners; and there is no movement meditated on the
Sioux borders, which is not known and canvassed by the lake bands.

They sent warriors to the scene of conflict last year, in consequence of
the murder committed by the Sioux on the St. Croix.[2] Their sufferings from
hunger during the winter, and the existence of disease at Torch Lake (Lac
du Flambeau), and some other places, together with the entire failure of the
rice crop, had produced effects, which were depicted by them and by the
traders in striking colours. They made these sufferings the basis of frequent
and urgent requests for provisions. This theme was strenuously dwelt upon.
Whatever other gifts they asked for, they never omitted the gift of food.
They made it their first, their second, and their third request.

At Chegoimegon, on Lake Superior (or La Pointe, emphatically so
called), I held my first and stated council with the Indians. This is the
ancient seat of the Chippewa power in this quarter. It is a central and commanding point, with respect to the country lying north, and west, and south
of it. It appears to be the focus from which, as radii from a centre, the
ancient population emigrated; and the interior bands consequently look
back to it with something of the feelings of parental relation. News from
the frontiers flies back to it with a celerity which is peculiar to the Indian
mode of express. I found here, as I had expected, the fullest and most recent information from the lines. Mozojeed, the principal man at Ottawa
Lake, had recently visited them for the purpose of consultation; but returned on the alarm of an attack upon his village.

The Indians listened with attention to the message transmitted to them
from the President, and to the statements with which it was enforced. Pez-
hickee [or "The Buffalo"], the venerable and respected chief of the place,
was their speaker in reply. He lamented the war, and admitted the folly of
keeping it up; but it was carried on by the Chippewas in self-defence, and
by volunteer parties of young men, acting without the sanction of the old
chiefs. He thought the same remark due to the elder Sioux chiefs, who
probably did not sanction the crossing of the lines, but could not restrain
their young men. He lived, he said, in an isolated situation, did not mingle
in the interior broils, and did not deem himself responsible for acts done
out of his own village, and certainly not for the acts of the villages of Torch
Lake, Ottowa Lake, and the St. Croix. He had uniformly advised his people to sit still and remain at peace, and he believed that none of his young
men had joined the war-parties of last year. The government, he said,
should have his hearty co-operation in restoring peace. He referred to the
sub-agency established here in 1826, spoke of its benefits, and wished to
know why the agent had been withdrawn, and whether he would be instructed to return? In the course of his reply, he said, that formerly, when
the Indians lived under the British government, they were usually told
what to do, and in very distinct terms. But they were now at a loss. From
what had been said and done at the treaty of Fond du Lac, he expected the
care and protection of the American government, and that they would advance towards, instead of (as in the case of the sub-agency) withdrawing

from them. He was rather at a loss for our views respecting the Chippewas, and he wished much for my advice in their affairs.

I thought it requisite to make a distinct reply to this point. I told him that when they lived under the British government, they were justified in shaping their course according to the advice they received; but that, on the transfer of the country, their allegiance was transferred with it. And when our government hoisted its flag at Mackinac (1796), it expected from the Indians living within our boundaries the respect due to it; and it acknowledged, at the same time, the reciprocal obligations of care and protection. That it always aimed to fulfill these obligations, of which facts within his own knowledge and memory would afford ample proofs. I referred him to the several efforts the government had made to establish a lasting peace between the Chippewas and Sioux; for which purpose the President had sent one of his principal men (alluding to Gov. Cass), in 1820, who had visited their most extreme north-western villages, and induced themselves and the Sioux to smoke the pipe of peace together at St. Peters. In accordance with these views, and acting on the information then acquired, the President had established an agency for their tribe at Sault Ste. Marie, in 1822. That, in 1825, he had assembled at Prairie du Chien all the tribes who were at variance on the Upper Mississippi, and persuaded them to make peace, and, as one of the best means of ensuring its permanency, had fixed the boundaries of their lands. Seeing that the Chippewas and Sioux still continued a harassing and useless contest, he had sent me to remind them of this peace and these boundaries, which, I added, you, Perikee [Pizhickee], yourself agreed to, and signed, in my presence. I come to bring you back to the terms of this treaty. Are not these proofs of his care and attention? Are not these clear indications of his views respecting the Chippewas? The chief was evidently affected by this recital. The truth appeared to strike him forcibly; and he said, in a short reply, that he was now *advised*; that he would hereafter feel himself to be advised, &c. He made some remarks on the establishment of a mission school, &c., which, being irrelevant, are omitted. He presented a pipe, with an ornamented stem, as a token of his friendship, and his desire of peace.

I requested him to furnish messengers to take belts of wampum and tobacco, with three separate messages, viz. to Yellow River, to Ottowa Lake, and to Lac du Flambeau, or Torch Lake; and also, as the water was low, to aid me in the ascent of the Mauvaise River, and to supply guides for each of the military canoes, as the soldiers would here leave their barge, and were unacquainted with the difficulties of the ascent. He accordingly sent his oldest son (Che-che-gwy-ung) and another person, with the messages, by a direct trail, leading into the St. Croix country. He also furnished several young Chippewas to aid us on the Mauvaise, and to carry baggage on the long portage into the first intermediate lake west of that stream.

After the distribution of presents, I left Chegoimegon on the 18th July. The first party of Indians met at the Namakagon, belonging to a Chippewa village called Pukwaewa, having, as its geographical centre and trading-

post, Ottowa Lake. As I had directed part of the expedition to precede me
there, during my journey to Yellow River, I requested these Indians to
meet me at Ottowa Lake, and assist in conveying the stores and provisions
to that place—a service which they cheerfully performed. On ascending
the lower part of the Namakagon, I learned that my messenger from Lake
Superior had passed, and on reaching Yellow River, I found the Indians
assembled and waiting. They were encamped on an elevated ridge, called
Pekogunagun [Pokonokuning], or the Hip Bone, and fired a salute from its
summit. Several of the neighbouring Indians came in after my arrival.
Others, with their chiefs, were hourly expected. I did not deem it necessary
for all to come in, but proceeded to lay before them the objects of my visit,
and to solicit their co-operation in an attempt to make a permanent peace
with the Sioux, whose borders we then were near. Kabamappa, the principal chief, not being a speaker, responded to my statements and recommendations through another person (Sha-ne-wa-gwun-ai-be). He said that
the Sioux were of bad faith; that they never refused to smoke the pipe of
peace with them, and they never failed to violate the promise of peace thus
solemnly made. He referred to an attack they made last year on a band of
Chippewas and half-breeds, and the murder of four persons. Perpetual vig-
ilance was required to meet these inroads. Yet he could assert, fearlessly,
that no Chippewa war-party from the St. Croix had crossed the Sioux line
for years; that the murder he had mentioned was committed within the
Chippewa lines; and although it was said at the treaty of Prairie du Chien
that the first aggressor of territorial rights should be punished, neither punishment was inflicted by the government, nor had any atonement or apology
thus far been made for this act by the Sioux. He said his influence had been
exerted in favour of peace; that he had uniformly advised both chiefs and
warriors to this effect; and he stood ready now to do whatever it was reasonable he should do on the subject.

I told him it was not a question of recrimination that was before us. It
was not even necessary to go into the inquiry of who had spilt the first
blood since the treaty of Prairie du Chien. The treaty had been violated.
The lines had been crossed. Murders had been committed by the Chippewas
and by the Sioux. These murders had reached the ears of the President, and
he was resolved to put a stop to them. I did not doubt but that the advice of
the old chiefs, on each side, had been pacific. I did not doubt but that his
course had been *particularly* so. But rash young men, of each party, had
raised the war-club; and when they could not go openly, they went secretly.
A stop must be put to this course, and it was necessary the first movement
should be made *somewhere*. It was proper it should be made here, and be
made at this time. Nothing could be lost by it; much might be gained; and
if a negotiation was opened with the Sioux chiefs while I remained, I would
second it by sending an explanatory message to the chiefs and to their
agent. I recommend that Kabamappa and Shakoba, the war-chief of
Snake River, should send wampum and tobacco to the Petite Corbeau and
to Wabisha [Wabasha], the leading Sioux chiefs on the Mississippi, inviting them to renew the league of friendship, and protesting their own sin-

cerity in the offer. I concluded, by presenting him with a flag, tobacco, wampum, and ribands, to be used in the negotiation. After a consultation, he said he would not only send the messages, but, as he now had the protection of a flag, he would himself go with the chief Shakoba to the Petite Corbeau's village. I accompanied these renewed offers of peace with explanatory messages, in my own name, to Petite Corbeau and to Wabisha, and a letter to Mr. [Lawrence] Taliaferro, the Indian agent at St. Peter's, informing him of these steps, and soliciting his co-operation. A copy of this letter is hereunto annexed.[3] I closed the council by the distribution of presents; after which the Indians called my attention to the conduct of their trader, &c.

Information was given me immediately after my arrival at Yellow River, that Neenaba, a popular war-leader from the Red Cedar fork of Chippewa River, had very recently danced the war-dance with thirty men at Rice Lake of Yellow River, and that his object was to enlist the young men of that place in a war-party against the Sioux. I also learned that my message for Ottowa Lake had been promptly transmitted through Neenaba, whom I was now anxious to see. I lost not an hour in reascending the St. Croix and the Namakagon. I purchased two additional canoes of the Indians, and distributed my men in them, to lighten the draught of water, and facilitate the ascent; and, by pushing early and late, we reached Ottowa Lake on the fifth day in the morning. Neenaba had, however, delivered his message, and departed. I was received in a very friendly welcome manner, by Mozojeed, of the band of Ottowa Lake; Wabezhais, of the Red Devil's band of the South Pukwaewa; and Odabossa, of the Upper Namakagon. After passing the usual formalities, I prepared to meet them in council the same day, and communicate to them the objects of my mission.

In the course of the conference at this place, I obtained the particulars of a dispute which had arisen between the Chippewas of this quarter, which now added to their alarm, as they feared the latter would act in coincidence with their ancient enemies, the Sioux. The reports of this disturbance had reached me at the Sault, and they continued, with some variations, until my arrival here. The following are the material facts in relation to this new cause of disquietude: In the summer of 1827, Okunzhewug, an old woman, the wife of Kishkemun, the principal chief of Torch Lake, a man superannuated and blind, attended the treaty of Butte des Morts, bearing her husband's medal. She was treated with the respect due to the character she represented, and ample presents were directed to be given to her; among other things a handsome hat. The latter article had been requested of her by a young Menomonie, and refused. It is thought a general feeling of jealousy was excited by her good reception. A number of the Menomonies went on her return route as far as the Clover Portage, where she was last seen. Having never returned to her village, the Chippewas attributed her death to the Menomonies. Her husband died soon after; but she had numerous and influential relatives to avenge her real or supposed murder. This is the account delivered by the Chippewas, and it is cor[r]oborated by reports from the traders of that section of the country. Her singular disappearance and secret death at the Clover Portage, is undisputed; and whether caused or not by any agency of the Menomonies, the belief of such agency, and that of the most direct kind, is fixed in the minds of the Chippewas, and has furnished the basis of their subsequent acts in relation to the Menomonie hunting-parties who have visited the lower part of Chippewa River. Two women belonging to one of these parties were killed by a Chippewa war-party traversing that part of the country the ensuing year. The act was disclaimed by them as not being intentional, and it was declared they supposed the women to be Sioux.[4] On a close inquiry, however, I found the persons who committed this act were relatives of Okunzewug, which renders it probable that the murder was intentionally perpetrated. This act further widened the breach between the two hitherto fraternal tribes; and the Chippewas of this quarter began to regard the Menomonie hunting-parties, who entered the mouth of the Chippewa River, as intruders on their lands. Among a people whose means of verbal information is speedy, and whose natural sense of right and wrong is acute, the more than usual friendship and apparent alliance which have taken place between the Menomonies and Sioux, in the contest between the Sacs and Foxes, and the murder by them jointly of the Fox chief White Skin and his companions at a smoking council, in 1830, have operated to increase the feeling of distrust; so much so, that it was openly reported at Chegoimegon, at Yellow River, and Ottowa Lake, that the Menomonies had formed a league with the Sioux against the Chippewas also, and they were fearful of an attack from them. A circumstance that had given point to this fear, and made it a subject of absorbing interest, when I arrived at Ottowa Lake, was the recent murder of a Menomonie chief by a Chippewa of that quarter, and the demand of satisfaction which had been made (it was sometimes said) by the Indian agent at Prairie du Chien, and sometimes by the commanding officer, with a threat to march troops into the country. This demand, I afterward learned from the Indians at Rice Lake, and from a conversation with General [Joseph M.] Street, the agent at Prairie du Chien, had not been made, either by himself or by the commanding officer; and the report had probably arisen from a conversation held by a subaltern officer in command of a wood or timber-party near the mouth of the Chippewa River, with some Chippewas who were casually met. Its effects, however, were to alarm them, and to lead them to desire a reconciliation with the Menomonies. I requested them to lose no time in sending tobacco to the Menomonies, and adjusting this difference. Mozojeed observed that the murder of the Menomonie had been committed by a person *non compos,* and he deplored the folly of it, and disclaimed all agency in it for himself and his band. The murderer, I believe, belonged to his band; he desired a reconciliation. He also said the measures adopted at Yellow River, to bring about a firm peace with the Sioux, had his fullest approbation, and that nothing on his part should be wanting to promote a result in every view so wise and so advantageous to the Indians. In this sentiment, Wabezhais and Odabossa, who made distinct speeches, also concurred. They confirmed their words by pipes, and all the assembly made an audible assent. I invested Mozojeed with a flag and a medal, that he might exert the influence he has acquired among the Indians beneficially for them and for us, and that his hands might thus be officially strengthened to accomplish the work of pacification. I then distributed presents to the chiefs, warriors, women, and children, in the order of their being seated, and immediately embarked, leaving them under a lively and enlivened sense of the good-will and friendship of the American government, on this first official visit to them, and with a sincere disposition, so far as could be judged, to act in obedience to its expressed and known wishes.

The Indians at Torch Lake being dispersed, and my message to them not having been delivered, from this uncertainty of their location, I should have found reasons for not proceeding in that direction, independent of the actual and known difficulties of the route at that time. I was still apprehensive that my appearance had not wholly disconcerted the war-party of Neenaba, and lost no time in proceeding to his village on the Red Cedar fork. We found the village at Lake Chetac, which in 1824 was 217 strong, almost totally deserted, and the trading-house burnt. Scattering Indians were found along the river. The mutual fear of interruption was such that Mr. B[enjamin] Cadotte, sen.[ior], the trader at Ottowa Lake, thought it advisable to follow in our train for the purpose of collecting his credits at Rice Lake.

While at breakfast on the banks of Sapin Lake, a returning war-party entered the opposite side of it: they were evidently surprised, and they stopped. After reconnoitering us, they were encouraged to advance, at first warily, and afterward with confidence. There were eight canoes, with two men in each; each man had a gun, war-club, knife, and ammunition bag: there was nothing else except the apparatus for managing the canoe. They were all young men, and belonged to the vicinity of Ottowa Lake. Their unexpected appearance at this place gave me the first information that the war-party at Neenaba had been broken up. They reported that some of their number had been near the mill, and that they had discovered signs of the Sioux being out in the moose having been driven up, &c. In a short conference, I recited to them the purpose of the council at Ottowa Lake, and referred them to their chiefs for particulars, enjoining their acquiescence in the proposed measures.

I found at Rice Lake a band of Chippewas, most of them young men, having a prompt and martial air, encamped in a very compact form, and prepared, at a moment's notice, for action. They saluted our advance with a smartness and precision of firing that would have done honour to drilled troops. Neenaba was absent on a hunting-party; but one of the elder men pointed out a suitable place for my encampment, as I intended here to put new bottoms to my bark canoes. He arrived in the evening, and visited my camp with forty-two men. This visit was one of ceremony merely; as it was late, I deferred any thing further until the following day. I remained at this place part of the 7th, the 8th, and until 3 o'clock on the 9th of August. And the following facts present the result of several conferences with this distinguished young man, whose influence is entirely of his own creation, and whose endowments, personal and mental, had not been misrepresented by the Indians on my route, who uniformly spoke of him in favourable terms. He is located at the most advanced point towards the Sioux borders, and, although not in the line of ancient chiefs, upon him rests essentially the conduct of affairs in this quarter. I therefore deemed it important to acquire his confidence and secure his influence, and held frequent conversations with him. His manner was frank and bold, equally free from servility and repulsiveness. I drew his attention to several subjects. I asked him whether the sawmill on the lower part of the Red Cedar was located on Chippewa lands? He said, Yes. Whether it was built with the consent of the Chippewas? He said, No; it had been built, as it were, by stealth. I asked him if any thing had been subsequently given them in acknowledgement of their right to the soil? He said, No; that the only acknowledgement was their getting tobacco to smoke when they visited the mill: that the Sioux claimed it to be on their side of the line, but the Chippewas contended that their line ran to a certain bluff and brook below the mill. I asked him to draw a map of the lower part of Chippewa River, with all its branches, showing the exact lines as fixed by the treaty at Prairie du Chien, and as understood by them. I requested him to state the facts respecting the murder of the Menomonie, and the causes that led to it; and whether he or any of his band received any message from the agent or commanding officer at Prairie du Chien, demanding the surrender of the murderer? To the latter inquiry he answered promptly, No. He gave in his actual population at 142; but it is evident that a very considerable additional population, particularly in men, resort there for the purpose of hunting a part of the year.

The day after my arrival, I prepared for and summoned the Indians to a council, with the usual formalities. I opened it by announcing the objects of my visit. Neenaba and his followers listened to the terms of the message, the means I had adopted to enforce it, and, finally, to the request of cooperation on the part of himself and band, with strict attention. He confined his reply to an expression of thanks; allusions to the peculiarity of his situation on an exposed frontier; and general sentiments of friendship. He appeared to be mentally embarrassed by my request to drop the war-club on the successful use of which he had relied for his popularity, and whatever of real power he possessed. He often referred to his young men, over whom he claimed no superiority, and who appeared to be ardently attached to him. I urged the principal topic upon his attention, presenting it in several lights. I finally conferred on him, personally, a medal and flag, and directed the presents intended for his band to be laid, in gross, before him.

After a pause, Neenaba got up, and spoke to the question, connecting it with obvious considerations, of which mutual rights, personal safety, and the obligation to protect the women and children, formed the basis. The latter duty was not a slight one. Last year the Sioux had killed a chief on the opposite shore of the lake, and, at the same time, decoyed two children, who were in a canoe, among the rice, and killed and beheaded them. He said, in allusion to the medal and flag, that these marks of honour were not necessary to secure his attention to any requests made by the American government. And after resuming his seat awhile (during which he over-heard some remarks not pleasing to him, from an Indian on the opposite side of the ring), he finally got up and declined receiving them until they were eventually pressed upon him by the young warriors. Every thing appeared to proceed with great harmony, and the presents were quickly distributed by one of his men. It was not, however, until the next day, when my canoes were already put in the water, that he came with his entire party, to make his final reply, and to present the peace-pipe. He had thrown the flag over one arm, and held the war-club perpendicular in the other hand. He said, that although he accepted the one, he did not drop the other; he held fast to both. When he looked at the one, he should revert to the counsels with which it had been given, and he should aim to act upon those counsels; but he also deemed it necessary to hold fast the war-club; it was, however, with a determination to use it in defence, and not in attack. He had reflected upon the advice sent to the Chippewas by the President, and particularly that part of it which counselled them to sit still upon their lands; but while they sat still, they also wished to be certain that their enemies would sit still. And the pipe he was now about to offer, he offered with a request that it might be sent to the President, asking him to use his power to prevent the Sioux from crossing the lines. The pipe was then lit, handed round, the ashes knocked out, and a formal presentation of it made. This ceremony being ended, I shook hands with them, and immediately embarked.

On the second day afterward, I reached the sawmill, the subject of such frequent allusion, and landed there at 7 o'clock in the morning. I found a Mr. Wallace in charge, who was employed, with ten men, in building a new dam on a brook of the Red Cedar, the freshet of last spring having carried away the former one. I inquired of him where the line between the Sioux and Chippewas crossed. He replied that the line crossed above the mill, he did not precisely know the place; adding, however, in the course of conversation, that he believed the land in this vicinity originally belonged to the Chippewas. He said it was seven years since any Sioux had visited the mill; and that the latter was owned by persons at Prairie du Chien.

The rapids of the Red Cedar River extend (according to the estimates contained in my notes) about twenty-four miles. They commence a few miles below the junction of Meadow River, and terminate about two miles below the mills. This extension of falling water, referred to in the treaty as a fixed point, has led to the existing uncertainty. The country itself is of a highly valuable character for its soil, its game, its wild rice, and its wood. We found the butter-nut among those species which are locally included under the name of *Bois franc* by the traders. The land can, hereafter, be easily brought into cultivation, as it is interspersed with prairie; and its fine mill privileges will add to its value. Indeed, one mile square is intrinsically worth one hundred miles square of Chippewa country, in some other places.

The present sawmills (there are two) are situated 65 miles from the banks of the Mississippi. They are owned exclusively by private citizens, and employed for their sole benefit. The boards are formed into rafts: and these rafts are afterward attached together, and floated down the Mississippi to St. Louis, where they command a good price. The business is understood to be a profitable one. For the privilege, no equivalent has been paid either to the Indians or to the United States. The first mill was built several years ago, and before the conclusion of the treaty of Prairie du Chien, fixing boundaries to the lands. A permit was given for building, either verbal or written, as I have been informed, by a former commanding officer at Prairie du Chien. I make these statements in reference to a letter I have received from the Department since my return, but which is dated June 27th, containing a complaint of one of the owners of the mill, that the Chippewas had threatened to burn it, and requesting me to take the necessary precautionary measures. I heard nothing of such a threat, but believe that the respect which the Chippewas have professed, through me, for the American government, and the influence of my visit among them, will prevent a resort to any measures of violence; and that they will wait the peaceable adjustment of the line on the rapids. I will add, that *wherever* that line may be determined, in a reasonable probability, to fall, the mill itself cannot be supplied with logs for any length of time, if *it is now so supplied,* without cutting them on Chippewa lands, and rafting them down the Red Cedar. Many of the logs heretofore sawed at this mill, have been rafted, *up stream,* to the mill. And I understood from the person in charge of it, that he was now anxious to ascertain new sites for chopping; that his expectations were directed up the stream, but that his actual knowledge of the country, in that direction, did not embrace a circumference of more than five miles.[5]

The line between the Chippewa and Sioux, as drawn on the MS. map of Neenaba, strikes the rapids on Red Cedar River at a brook and bluff a short distance below the mill. It proceeds thence, across the point of land between that branch of the main Chippewa, to an island in the latter; and thence, up stream, to the mouth of Clearwater River, as called for by the treaty, and from this point to the bluffs of the Mississippi valley (where it corners on Winnebago land), on Black River, and not to the *"mouth"* of Black River, as erroneously inserted in the 5th article of the treaty; the Chippewas never having advanced any claims to the lands at the mouth of Black River. This map, being drawn by a Chippewa of sense, influence, and respectability, and exact copy of it is herewith forwarded for the use of the Department, as embracing the opinions of the Chippewas on this point. The lines and geographical marks were drawn on paper by Neenaba himself, and the names translated and written down by Mr. Johnston.

It is obvious that the adjustment of this line must precede a permanent peace on this part of the frontiers. The number of Chippewas particularly interested in it is, from my notes, 2,102; to which, 911 may be added for certain bands on Lake Superior. It embraces 27 villages, and the most influential civil and war chiefs of the region. The population is enterprising and warlike. They have the means of subsistence in *comparative* abundance. They are increasing in numbers. They command a ready access to the Mississippi by water, and a ready return from it by land. Habits of association have taught them to look upon this stream as the theatre of war. Their young men are carried into it as the natural and almost only means of distinction. And it is in coincidence with all observation, to say that they are now, as they were in the days of Captain [Jonathan] Carver, the terror of the east bank of this river, between the St. Croix and Chippewa Rivers. No other tribe has now, or has had, within the memory of man, a village or permanent possession on this part of the shore. It is landed on in fear. It is often passed by other nations by stealth, and at night. Such is not an exaggerated picture. And with a knowledge of their geographical advantages, and numbers, and distribution, on the tributary streams, slight causes, it may be imagined, will often excite the young and thoughtless portion of them to raise the war-club, to chant the war-song, and follow the war-path.

To remove these causes, to teach them the folly of such a contest, to remind them of the treaty stipulations and promises solemnly made to the government and to the Sioux, and to induce them to renew those promises, and to act on fixed principles of political faith, were the primary objects committed to me; and they were certainly objects of exalted attainment, according as well with the character of the government as with the spirit and moral and intellectual tone of the age. To these objects I have faithfully, as I believe, devoted the means at my command. And the Chippewas cannot, hereafter, err on the subject of their hostilities with Sioux, without knowing that the error is disapproved by the American government, and that a continuance in it will be visited upon them in measures of severity.

Without indulging the expectation that my influence on the tour will have the effect to put an end to the spirit of predatory warfare, it may be asserted that this spirit has been checked and allayed; and that a state of feeling and reflection has been produced by it, which cannot fail to be beneficial to our relations with them, and to their relations with each other. The messages sent to the Sioux chiefs, may be anticipated to have resulted in restoring a perfect peace during the present fall and ensuing winter, and will thus leave to each party the undisturbed chase of their lands. The meditated blow of Steenaba [Neenaba] was turned aside, and his war-party arrested and dispersed at the moment it was ready to proceed. Every argument was used to show them the folly and the insecurity of a continuance of the war. And the whole tenor and effect of my visit has been to inform and reform these remote bands. It has destroyed the charm of their seclusion. It has taught them that their conduct is under the supervision of the American government; that they depend on its care and protection; that no other government has power to regulate trade and send traders among them; finally, that an adherence to foreign counsels, and to antipacific maxims, can be visited upon them in measures of coercion. That their country, hitherto deemed nearly inaccessible, can be penetrated and traversed by men and troops, with baggage and provisions, even in midsummer, when the waters are lowest; and that, in proportion as they comply with political maxims, as benevolent as they are just, will they live at peace with their enemies, and have the means of subsistence for an increased population among themselves. The conduct of the traders in this quarter, and the influence they have exerted, both moral and political, cannot here be entered upon, and must be left to some other occasion, together with statistical details and other branches of information not arising from particular instructions.

It may be said that the Indians upon the St. Croix and Chippewa Rivers, and their numerous branches, have been drawn into a close intercourse with government. But it will be obvious that a perseverance in the system of official advice and restraints, is essential to give permanence to the effects already produced, and to secure a firm and lasting peace between them and the Sioux. To this end the settlement of the line upon the Red Cedar fork is an object which claims the attention of the Department; and would justify, in my opinion, the calling together the parties interested, at some convenient spot near the junction of the Red Cedar River with the Chippewa. Indeed, the handsome elevation, and the commanding geographical advantages of this spot, render it one which, I think, might be advantageously occupied as a military post. Such an occupancy would have the effect to keep the parties at peace, and the point of land, on which the work is proposed to be erected, might be purchased from the Sioux, together with such part of the disputed lands near the mills as might be deemed necessary to quiet the title of the Chippewas. By acquiring this portion of country for the purposes of military occupancy, the United States would be justified in punishing any murders committed upon it; and I am fully convinced, that no measure which could, at this time, be adopted, would so certainly conduce to a permanent peace between the tribes. I therefore beg leave, through you, to submit these subjects to the consideration of the honorable the Secretary of War, with every distrust in my own powers of observation, and with a very full confidence in his.

I have the honor to be, sir,

Very respectfully, your obedient servant,

H. R. SCHOOLCRAFT

NOTES

1. This map was not published with the report of the Expedition of 1831 in Schoolcraft's *Narrative of an Expedition* (New York, 1832).

2. The Sioux ambushed and murdered a Mr. Cadotte, a half-breed from Sault Ste. Marie, another half-breed called the "Little Frenchman," and two Chippewa.

3. The letter from Schoolcraft to Taliaferro is reprinted in Appendix A, No. 7.

4. Schoolcraft annexed the reply of Mozobodo in relation to the murder of the Menomonie woman:

"My father at the Sault Ste. Marie: I have not forgot what was told me at Prairie du Chien, Fond du Lac, and Butte des Morts. I have kept always what you told me until the last summer. My young men were foolish, and went to war.

My father: The war-club was sent to them from Lac Chetac twice, before they accepted it. They did not go to war of their own accord. I did all I could to prevent them.

My father: They did not kill our friends intentionally. They supposed them to be their enemies, and killed them accidentally.

My father: This pipe I send to you in token of peace. My young men will hereafter keep quiet.

My father: I hope you will not take our traders away from us. If you do, our little children will suffer; and not only they, but all of us.

Mozobodo."

Lac du Flambeau, May 28, 1831.
Interpreted by Charles H. Oaks.

5. For information relating to the construction of sawmills on the Chippewa River and its tributaries see *Territorial Papers,* Vol. XI, pp. 1048-49 and 1072; Vol. XII, pp. 107 and 341-42.

9. Henry Rowe Schoolcraft to George B. Porter, Governor of Michigan, and Superintendent of Indian Affairs.

[Letter Transmitting Report of Expedition.]

SAULT STE. MARIE, October 1, 1831

SIR,

I have now the honor, through your intervention, to forward to the Department my report of the late tour through the Huron Territory. It has not been possible to prepare the map referred to in season to accompany the report, but it will be forwarded as soon as it can be completed. In the mean time, I send a sketch of portions of the country intermediate between Lake Superior and the Mississippi, from which you will be enabled to trace my particular route, and the location of the principal streams, lakes, and villages. The imperfect state of public information respecting the geography of this region, and the numerous errors which still continue to characterize our maps, render something of this kind essential.

With the limited means assigned for the accomplishment of the object, it became necessary that every moment of time should be used in pushing forward. This will account for the great space travelled in a comparatively short time. I am of the opinion, however, that little or nothing has been lost from the efficacy of the movement by its celerity. Lakes, rivers, and villages succeeded each other, with short intervals. But, in ascending each river, in crossing each lake and portage, the object of the expedition was definitely impressed upon the natives who witnessed our progress; and it was acquiesced in by the chiefs and warriors, at the several councils which I held with them. For a general detail of these councils, the report may be consulted.

It will be perceived that new topics for discussion arose from a recent misunderstanding between the Chippewas and Menomonies; and from the uncertainty as to the spot where the boundary line between the Chippewas and Sioux strikes the falls on the Red Cedar fork, agreeably to a just construction of the treaty of Prairie du Chien of 1825. With respect to the first, I am of opinion that time will only serve to increase the difficulty of restoring a perfect understanding.

The line on the Red Cedar is important, as opposing an obstacle to a firm peace between the Sioux and Chippewas; and I doubt whether any steps could be taken by the government to induce them to live peaceably near each other, with so little cost of time and money as the taking post, with a small military force, on the frontier in dispute, at some suitable point between Prairie du Chien and St. Peters. With this impression, I have brought the subject to the consideration of the secretary of War; and I shall be gratified, if, on a review of it, you shall concur in opinion with,

Sir, very respectfully,
Your obedient servant,
H. R. SCHOOLCRAFT

10. Henry Rowe Schoolcraft to Elbert Herring.

SAULT STE. MARIE, February, 13, 1832

SIR,

Events growing out of the political condition of the Indian tribes on the head-waters of the Mississippi, call for the continued interposition of the friendly influence of the government on that remote part of our north-western frontier. It has been long known that desperate and deep-rooted feuds continue to harass the tribes whose local position brings them into frequent contact. These contests operate to divert their attention from hunting, and to abstract their minds from objects essential to their well-being. They embarrass every effort to better their condition. They repel the advance of teachers. They deaden the effect of counsel. And by keeping the Indian mind in a state of perpetual alarm, destroy its capacities of healthful action. Every year is giving new proofs of the inveteracy of their hatred for each other, and the deteriorating effects of cultivating, as they do, the passion for warlike achievement. It is destructive to the industry of the young, and paralyzing to the counsels of the old.

The effect of the expedition ordered by the government last year, into the country of the Chippewas, is believed to have been efficacious in check-ing this spirit of predatory warfare, and impressing upon their minds the true character of our government, its benevolent intentions towards them, and its watchfulness, power, and resources. It was not practicable, how-ever, to go over the whole area proposed to be visited, the effect of the expedition having been directed exclusively to the bands located south of the latitude of St. Anthony's Falls. It is believed that a similar mission to the tribes of the Upper Mississippi, living north of that point in our geog-raphy, would result in effects equally useful to them and to the govern-ment. And I therefore submit to the Department the propriety of authorizing it.

Additional weight is given to the reasons applicable to this subject, by the increased hazards at which the trade of our citizens is conducted in that quarter, and the influence they have to contend with, from the proximity of a foreign and a rival frontier. The agents of the Hudson's Bay Company are wakeful and active opponents, and there is reason to believe that the measure of control which they exercise over the Indian population, is irrespective of an imaginary territorial line. At any rate, our traders complain loudly of infractions and losses from this source. Merely to visit the Indians and the traders at their posts, will be to encourage and to sustain them.

It is proposed to perform the journey in a single canoe, manned by *engages,* accompanied with an escort of soldiers, and with such auxiliary aid from the native population as may be necessary. It would give additional utility to the effort, if the Engineer Department should judge proper to subjoin an officer to take observations for latitude, and to collect the materials for a correct map. The moral condition of the native population is such as to render it an interesting field for evangelical observation, and I propose to offer to a clergyman in the service of the A.[merican] B.[oard of] F.[oreign] Missions, now on the frontier, the opportunity of exploring it.

The route from the head of Lake Superior will extend, through the River St. Louis and its connecting waters, to the Mississippi at Sandy Lake, and by the way of Leech Lake to the sources of the Mississippi. From the point where navigation is checked a portage is proposed to be made into Red Lake (a remote tributary of Hudson's Bay). And the route by Ottertail Lake, and the river De Corbeau, will be pursued so as to re-enter the Mississippi at the confluence of the latter. Thence by the Falls of St. Anthony to St. Peters, and through the St. Croix, the Chippewa, or the Wisconsin, to the lakes. Circumstances may require changes in this programme.

The extent of the country to be traversed requires an early departure from this place, and the toil of interior transportation makes it desirable that as little baggage, and as few men, should be taken, as may suffice for the certain accomplishment of the object. Under this view of the subject, I have prepared a detailed estimate of expenditures, on an economical scale, which is herewith submitted.

I have the honour, &c.

HENRY R. SCHOOLCRAFT

11. The Reverend William T. Boutwell to Henry Rowe Schoolcraft.

MACKINAW, Feb. 21, 1832

MY DEAR CHRISTIAN BROTHER;

Your kind & [illegible word] favour of the 14 & 15th which came safe to hand last Eve. shall be acknowledged not only with sincere thankfulness to you, but with devout gratitude to God. To say your kind & gracious proposition to me, was like a cup of cold water to the thirsty soul, is saying but a *part,* a *small* part too, of what I felt. Through you, My Brother,

God seems now to be opening & preparing the way for me to meet the wishes of the A. Board & to accomplish one of the prominent & leading objects contained in their instructions.

Not only do I heartily enter into all your sentiments relating to the necessity & importance of the object, but am happy to assure you that Br. F[erry] fully appreciates them & accords with us. But I exceedingly request to say that I am obliged from existing circumstances, to say, my answer at present cannot be decisive. And for the following reasons.

After Br. Fs. return from the Grand Traverse, & during my stay at the Saut, he wrote the Board respecting the wishes of the Band at the Traverse & the door which Providence had there opened for Missionary labours.

He suggested the propriety of my going to the Traverse rather than that Mr. F. & myself should both go into the interior. He has yet recd. no return, & advises me to write & apprise the Board of your kind offer. This I shall do by the next express & trust I shall be able to get a return in season to accompany you unless this Board now abandon one of the principal & leading objects contained in our instructions viz. that of a moral survey of the whole Chip[pewa] field.

I feel as deeply as Br. F. *can,* & no deeper than you *will,* the importance of occupying the field at the T[raverse] when you come to learn the state of things there, & the management of the Catholics, provided circumstances in the spring are such as when he last saw the Chief of that band. Br. F. will give you them.

All that I dare now say, (& that may be too flattering to me & encouraging to you), is, that I think the chances as one to five, that I may accompany you. This is just as the case now stands in my mind. How important the Board will deem it to establish a mission at the T. for the benefit of one band only, compared with kindling a light that may shine through all the Chip. country, I know not. Besides, if they deem it important & it is found practical in the spring to commence operations at the T. I trust they may find a man to supply that exigency. I refer to a young man now in the Theo. Sem. at Andover, who expressed to Br. [Sherman] H[all] & myself that he would follow us next Spring, in case the Board would send.

As you say, "if I did not think it *almost* certain that you would go with me I would write Mr. [David] Greene." I will say even more, if I did not think it quite certain, that I should accompany you, I would not fail of having you write.

Your proposition not only covers the leading feature in the instructions of the Board to Br. H. & myself, but it even more than covers it, since it gives us the means of collecting both the general & particular information they wish & that free from expense to them or ourselves.

I shall not fail to write the Board by the next Express & give them an extract of your letter. But should you find time to give them an idea of the facilities & advantages which you possess & could put directly into my hand of seeing, conversing with & learning the views & feelings of the principal Indians relative to the grand object of the A[merican] B[oard]— advantages which you possess over any other person—and facilities of accomplishing in three or four months, what, to an individual travelling alone, might & probably would be the labour of as many years—if you find time & it would not be taxing you too much, this, I am sure would give them a view of the subject, which I fear may not have its due weight.

If you should write—Superscribe, Rev. David Greene, Cor. Sec. of the Amer. B. C. F. Missions—Boston . . .

I shall give you a line by the Ex[press] which we trust will bring us intelligence from the Board, touching the subject of the Traverse. Though I cannot help feeling the deepest interest in prosecuting the object specified in our instructions, yet, he that loves God, will go *where* & do *what* God makes known to him as duty. This is the Christians highest priviledge, to this may God give me grace to aspire.

Thanks, my Brother, express but the smallest sum of what I send with this, to *one*, to *all*, of whose undeserved kindness, God gave me so richly to share—but to *one*, who has now laid me under the strongest possible moral obligation & which none but God can help me repay. My kindest regards to Mrs. S. Much love to my little Jane and Johnston. How often do I think of them & of you all! Much love & many thanks to Br. P[orter] for his kind letter.

My kindest regards & best wishes to Mrs. J[ohnston]. & *all* her kind family.

Ever & truly yours in Christian love,
W. T. BOUTWELL

12. William M. Ferry to Henry Rowe Schoolcraft.

MACKINAW, Feby. 21st. 1832

VERY DEAR SIR,

The intel[l]igence we have received by your letters, Mr. Boutwell, & of the Lords doings among you as a people at the Saut, has rejoiced our hearts much. Surely it is with you a time of the right hand of the Most High. And my earnest prayer is that there may yet be many made to bow & sing of Redeeming love.

Your letter to Mr. Boutwell proposing that he should accompany you in your intended tour next Summer, opens the prospect of an excellent op[p]ortunity for him to acquire information concerning the Indian Country, Interests &c. and I think it will be most desirable for him to accompany you, provided he should not be directed by the Board to occupy Missionary station designed to be formed at Grand-Traverse a place 90 or 100 miles from this, on the Eastern shore of Lake Michigan. The Chief of that band has become somewhat interested in feeling to have Missionaries come among his people, & some belonging to his band have in their visits to Mackinaw last summer, Shown much interest & feeling in listening to Instruction. In 2 cases there was hopeful evidence of conversion. This band of Indians are Chippeways & have refused any aid or connection with the Catholics. I wrote to the Board late in the fall giving a statement relative to that Band & my views of what would be desirable to have done in their behalf. What will be the measures adopted by the Board in relation to the subject I do not know. Possibly they may direct Mr. Boutwell, with some one or two more members of our family, to go there. Should the Board settle upon this plan then I think it would be improper for Mr. B. to accept your kind offer. But otherwise, I should think it altogether best for him to accompany you. As there will be time to confer with the Board Mr. Boutwell has concluded to write them; & there is no doubt on [in] my mind but that the Board will approve in case they do not send him to Grand-Traverse.

Please remember me affectionately to Mr. [Jeremiah] Porter, with my best desires that the Lord may be with him—stand by him,—Strengthen & comfort him;—with many souls as his hire.

Present my cordial respects to Mrs. S.—Mr. [John] Hulbert & family with Mr. [Abel] Binghams family & believe me, dear sir, ever yours in the bonds of Christ.

WM. M. FERRY

13. Henry Rowe Schoolcraft to Lewis Cass

SAULT STE. MARIE, Feb. 24, 1832

DEAR SIR,

Our last express brought me your letter of the 11th. December. With it, I received one from Mr. Lewis announcing the settlement of my accounts up to the 30th September, including the allowance you mention for extra services. The latter is quite satisfactory. Indeed, the whole settlement, so far as I can judge of it, without having any statement for the year 1830, appears to be more satisfactory in its adjustment, than any previous one for some time.

While relieved from the necessity of a visit to Washington, I gladly embrace the proposal to go to the heads of the Mississippi, to carry into effect the plan of last year. I have prepared a letter and estimates which will be submitted to you. And adopted the necessary measures here, to secure supplies for the voyage. I am in hopes that the best results will flow from it. At any rate, I shall address myself to the task with zeal and diligence, and endeavour to go over as much ground, and acquire as much information, aside from the main object, as is possible. If I do not see the "veritable source" of the Mississippi, this time, it will not be from a want of the intention. But much will depend upon the amount you assign for the object. When you cast your eye over my estimates, you may, at first, think them high. But when it is reflected, that about double the time will be consumed, and that less than double the amount expended last year, is asked for, you will see that my data, with every economy, will run up the sum of contingencies. I beg you rather to exceed, than diminish my estimates. At least, grant me all that you can, and I will make it go as far, and accomplish as much as possible. I have invited Dr. Houghton to accompany me, and should he be commissioned as an assistant surgeon, he would, I think, be glad of permission, to go on this expedition, before reporting for duty at any of the posts. Every thing depends upon an early start, and I trust you will let me have my instructions, and transmit the funds to Trowbridge, as early as possible. Lt. Allen of Ohio, & now on furlough, would, I think, deem it a privilege to go in command of the soldiers. He is competent to perform topographical duty, and may, under the prospect of a modification of that corps, apply to be put on topographical duty. It is desirable that he should be furnished with a sextant.

I have remarked, with pleasure, the expressions of your letter approbating my reports, and saying that they "will be sent to Congress." And also the warm renewal of your friendship, in another part of the letter. While such expressions are gratifying to my heart, I trust there is nothing said which will have a tendency to inflate me, or induce me to alter the sober estimate, which cool reason and reflection dictate. I think there is less danger of this now, than formerly, as the slow but sure advance of years, has somewhat calmed my hopes, and the folly of such a course, is among the things which I daily pray to be delivered from.

The allusion to Tanner, I have made the subject of a separate letter and statement, which will put you in possession of all the facts necessary to a decision. I also forward the original letters forming the basis of my claim for services as translator.

Those whom you have remembered, desire most kindly to reciprocate the remembrance. Mrs. S. writes with me, in making our respects to Elizabeth and Mary.

With sincerity, I am dear Sir
Your friend & servant.
HENRY R. SCHOOLCRAFT

[This letter reflects the great interest of Schoolcraft in discovering the source of the Mississippi. Although the ostensible purpose of the trip was to visit Indian tribes in the Interior and to quell the warfare between the Sioux and the Chippewa, it is obvious that Schoolcraft was primarily interested in locating the "veritable source" of the Mississippi. For obvious reasons this objective was not publicized. The Office of Indian Affairs would undoubtedly have been criticized for using its funds for an exploring expedition.]

14. Henry Rowe Schoolcraft to the Reverend David Greene, Corresponding Secretary, American Board of Foreign Missions.

SAULT STE. MARIE, February 25th, 1832

SIR,

Objects connected with the political condition of the Chippewas inhabiting the upper Mississippi, have induced the Dept. of War to notify me that it is deemed important I should visit these bands, during the ensuing season.

The opportunity will be favourable for inquiring into their moral, as well as political necessities. And the region is, on several accounts, a very attractive field for evangelical observation. Having been informed that the American Board have directed their attention to this hitherto neglected quarter, and that it is in accordance with their wishes to procure authentic information respecting it, I have invited the Rev'd Mr. Boutwell to accompany me, feeling personally, a deep interest in the success of their efforts to better the condition of the Chippewa nation.

Placed by the government as an Agent to this people, their advancement in the scale of moral & accountable beings, is to me, an object of high importance, and I know not what could have so direct an influence in raising them to the dignity of life, as the introduction of Christianity. I am quite satisfied that their *political,* must result from their *moral* motivation. And that all our attempts in the way of agriculture, schooling & the mechanic arts, are liable to miscarry & produce no permanent good, unless their Indian mind can be purified by gospel truth, & cleansed from the besetting sin of a belief in magic, & from idolatry and spirit-worship.

Mr. Boutwell spent a part of the present Winter in this place in the acquisition of the Chippewa language. But I did not then know of the proposed expedition. Since his return to Mackina[c], a proposal to establish a Mission at Grand Traverse, on Lake Michigan, has been submitted to his consideration. Whatever may be the decision of the Amer. Board respecting it, I hope it may not operate to prevent his going with me to the heads of the Mississippi. It would afford me much pleasure to introduce him to the principal Chiefs & men in that quarter—to aid him in obtaining a correct knowledge of the local position, & population of the Indian towns—the means of access to them—the acquisition of their language, and any other objects which the Board may deem it proper, preparitory to their main design, to commit to him.

With high respect, I am Revd Sir,

Your Obedient Servant
HENRY R. SCHOOLCRAFT

15. Lewis Cass to Henry Rowe Schoolcraft.

WASHINGTON, March 28, 1832

DEAR SIR,

I wrote you about the beginning of the present session of Congress, informing you that again your accounts were all settled to September, and but one small voucher suspended; which would pass on explanation. There was also allowed you the sum of five dollars per day, while upon your expedition. The service for translations was not acted on, because the letters, referred to in yours, could not be found. Be good enough to send them, and I think there will be no difficulty in the case. This will terminate, and I hope satisfactorily, all your pecuniary affairs with the government.

I requested you to send me a *project* of an expedition in the Sioux and Chippewa Countries above the head of the Mississippi and west. I think it very important you should carry into effect our original wishes in visiting them, and endeavouring to check their natural inclination to hostilities. Reports from various quarters of the Indian Country lead to the belief, that the Indians are in an unsettled state and that prudence requires we should advise and restrain them. I think one more tour would be very useful in this respect, and would complete our knowledge of the geography of that region. I shall wait a few days in the hope that possibly my letter may have only been delayed; and not lost; and that it may yet reach you; and that, I shall receive a project in time to issue instructions to go up by the first vessel, and I write now, unofficially, to let you know my intentions, lest possibly a vessel might depart from Detroit, earlier that I anticipated. . . .

[Cass advises Schoolcraft of his plan to consolidate the Indian agencies at Sault Ste. Marie and Mackinac Island and place Schoolcraft in charge.]

I have nothing special to say to you. Things go on here, as usual. I lead a life of great labour; still on the whole my health has improved, and the incubus of dyspepsia is leaving me.

But in health or not my feelings toward yourself and family are and will be the same; and I beg you to present to them, and accept for yourself, the assurance of my best regards and friendship.

I am My dear Sir
Truly yours
LEW CASS

16. David Greene to Henry Rowe Schoolcraft.

MISSIONARY ROOMS, BOSTON, April 12, 1832

DEAR SIR,

In reply to your esteemed favor of February 25, received on the 6th instant, I am instructed by the Prudential Committee to communicate to you the following resolution, adopted by them at their meeting yesterday.

"Resolved,

that the thanks of the Committee be expressed to H. R. Schoolcraft, Esqr., U. S. agent for Indian Affairs at Sault Ste. Marie, for his kind & generous proposal & that he be informed that they shall instruct Mr. Boutwell to avail himself of the advantages thus afforded for accomplishing one of the important objects of his mission."

The Committee wish me also to express to you the satisfaction they have, in learning that your views, respecting the importance of making known the great truths of the gospel to the Indians as the basis on which to build their improvement in all respects, accord so perfectly with their own. It is our earnest desire that our missionaries may act wisely in all their labors for the benefit of the Indians, and that all the measures which may be adopted by them, or by others, who seek to promote the present

& future welfare of this unhappy & long abused people, may be under the divine guidance and crowned with great success.

Any facilities which you may now or hereafter be able to afford our missionaries in obtaining information & in the promotion of their labors, or any suggestions which you make on the subject of our missions in the Northwest, will be gratefully received and acknowledged by our Committee.

With Sentiments of high respect.

I am, Sir, yours very truly,

DAVID GREENE

17. Elbert Herring to Henry Rowe Schoolcraft.

DEPARTMENT OF WAR
OFFICE INDIAN AFFAIRS, May 3, 1832

SIR,

Your letter of February 13th has been received, and its general views are approved. The Secretary of War deems it important that you should proceed to the country upon the heads of the Mississippi, and visit as many of the Indians in that, and the intermediate region, as circumstances will permit. Reports have reached the Department from various quarters, that the Indians upon our frontiers are in an unquiet state, and that there is a prospect of extensive hostilities among themselves. It is no less the dictate of humanity than of policy, to repress this feeling, and to establish permanent peace among these tribes. It is also important to inspect the condition of the trade in that remote country, and the conduct of the traders. To ascertain whether the laws and regulations are complied with, and to suggest such alterations as may be required. And generally to inquire into the numbers, situations, dispositions, and prospects of the Indians, and to report all the statistical facts you can procure, and which will be useful to the government in its operations, or to the community in the investigation of these subjects.

In addition to these objects, you will direct your attention to the vaccination of the Indians. An act for that purpose has passed Congress, and you are authorized to take a surgeon with you. The compensation fixed by law is six dollars per day, but this includes all the expenses. As the surgeon with you must necessarily be transported and subsisted at the public expense, the whole sum of six dollars per day will be allowed for this service, but of that sum only three dollars per day will be paid to the surgeon, and the residue will be applied to the expenses of the expedition.

Vaccine matter, prepared and put up by the surgeon-general, is herewith transmitted to you; and you will, upon your whole route, explain to the Indians the advantages of vaccination, and endeavour to persuade them to submit to the process. You will keep and report an account of the number, ages, sex, tribe, and local situation of the Indians who may be vaccinated, and also of the prevalence, from time to time, of the small-pox among them, and of its effects as far as these can be ascertained.

The following sums will be allowed for the expenses of the expedition.

Provisions	. . . . $ 600.	Iron, Steel &c	. . . . . .	100.
Presents	. . . . 700.	Expense of Vaccination		600.
Interpreters	. . . . 300.	Contingencies	. . . .	900.

$3,200.

These are all the sums, which in the present state of the funds of the department can be allowed for these objects, and you will please to be careful, that they are not exceeded. The appropriation bills have not yet passed; but as soon as they do, the amount above stated shall be remitted to you.

Very respectfully, Your obt Servt

ELBERT HERRING

[For other material relating to the smallpox epidemics among the Indians and the use of vaccination in checking it, see *Territorial Papers,* Vol. XII, p. 474, n. 17.]

18. Lewis Cass to Henry Rowe Schoolcraft.

WASHINGTON, May 4, 1832

DEAR SIR;

The official letter to you on the subject of your expedition will go today. It has been this long delayed, on account of the delay in the appropriation bills. These have not yet passed, but they are in such a state and the session is so far advanced that they must soon pass. The moment we receive them, the necessary funds shall be remitted. We have allowed you all it was possible, and you must on no account exceed the sum, as the pressure upon our funds is very great.

Whether you can be permitted to go or not must depend upon your own views of the situation of your agency, and of the calls upon your care and attention. If affairs can be so placed, that you can leave your agency without injury to the publick, and I presume they can, I wish you by all means to go.

Being much hurried, I must conclude with my respects to your family and my regard to yourself.

Truly your friend

LEW CASS

19. Alexander Macomb to Captain De Lafayette Wilcox.

HEAD QUARTERS OF THE ARMY
WASHINGTON, May 9, 1832

SIR:

I have been informed that Mr. Schoolcraft intends making an expedition into the Indian country, under the authority of the War Department.

You will detail an officer and ten or twelve men, to make a part of that expedition. The officer will be directed to keep a journal of the expedition; to describe the country through which it may pass; to delineate, topographically, the route and several points of importance; to ascertain the manners and characters of the various Indian tribes, their numbers strength in warriors, condition, mode of living, of obtaining subsistence, whether at peace with their neighbors or not, their places of resort for foreign supplies, how supplied, and by whom. He will also be directed to note the nature of the soil; the geology, mineralogy, and natural history; he will remark upon the game and fishes, as to quantity, quality, and facilities of procuring them.

The officer will transmit his report to Head Quarters, for the information of the General in chief, and to be laid before the Secretary of War. He will be considered as on topographical duty during the time he may be absent from his post, and engaged in the expedition. The men will have the extra allowances accorded to soldiers on fatigue duty. The officer will report to Mr. Schoolcraft, and take his directions.

> I am, sir, with respect,
> Your obedient servant,
> A. MACOMB
> *Major General Commanding the Army*

20. Elbert Herring to Henry Rowe Schoolcraft.

DEPARTMENT OF WAR, OFFICE INDIAN AFFAIRS, May 17, 1832

SIR,

The Secretary of War has this day issued a requisition in favor of the Cashier of the Bank of Michigan at Detroit for $2,500, being $700 less than the sum proposed in the letter to you of the 3rd inst. to be remitted; there being no funds under the head of appropriation for Presents; which sum he is requested to deposit in that Bank to your credit and subject to your order.

Very respectfully Your Obt. Srt.

> ELBERT HERRING

21. Elbert Herring and William Ward to Henry Rowe Schoolcraft.

DEPARTMENT OF WAR, OFFICE INDIAN AFFAIRS, May 21, 1832

SIR,

Since the letter of the 17th ins. was written, the Comptroller has reported, that there are no funds to pay Interpreters. The requisition in favor of Mr. Trowbridge will, therefore, be for the sum of Twenty two hundred dollars only.

When the Appropriations for this year are made, the balance of the amount at first applied to the purposes of your contemplated tour, will be remitted to Detroit, Subject to your order.

I am Sir, Very respectfully Your obt. Svt.

ELBERT HERRING

22. Lewis Cass to Henry Rowe Schoolcraft.

WASHINGTON, May 22, 1832

DEAR SIR,

It has been impossible before now to make you a remission of funds, and they cannot yet all be sent for your expedition. Our annual appropriation bill has not passed, and when it will, I am sure I can't tell. So you must get along, as well as you can. I trust however, that the amount now sent will be sufficient to enable you to start your expedition. The residue promised to you, as well as the funds for your ordinary expenditures shall be sent, as soon as the appropriation is made.

I have not time to tell you more, and I know you will attribute it to the unceasing pressure upon me, which I am afraid is breaking me down, but whether or not,

I am ever your friend

LEW CASS

23. Henry Rowe Schoolcraft to George Johnston.

[SAULT STE. MARIE, May 29, 1832]

DEAR SIR,

I omitted to request you to get a new mess basket for the Expd. from Mr. Sibley. And a canoe & also a boat oil cloth. I shall send Mr. Chapman's new boat with stores to Fond du Lac. Bring a bill.

If there is *one two* or *three good* canoemen at Mackinac who will work for $20 a month & no whiskey bring them along.

Leave the little canoe, & bring over William's, which was left by Chapman.

truly yours,

H. R. SCHOOLCRAFT

24. Henry Rowe Schoolcraft to John Torrey.

SAULT STE. MARIE, June 2nd.1832

MY DEAR SIR,

Your letter of February did not reach me until rising [?] of three months after date. This prevented me from writing in favour of your friend Dr. [Dwight] Harris as early as it might have been wished. I have addressed to Gov. Cass a letter, of which I annex a copy; And shall also mention the subject in a private letter, which will be forwarded by the mail that takes this.

I hope the plants collected by Dr. Houghton last summer have been placed in your hands for examination ere this. And shall feel gratified to send you duplicates of any that may be collected on the exploration of the present year. But on this subject, I am under anxiety on account of the non-arrival of the Dr. He wrote to me that he would certainly come, and that he had notified you of this determination. I am now within a few days of starting, & no physician—no one to make observations on the natural history of the country, and, no one to vaccinate the Indians—the latter being a special object of my instructions. I trust Houghton is on his way, and will make his appearance within a few days.

The shells collected last year are numerous & interesting, illustrating the conchology of a very large, and some of it, and unexplored part of the N. W. territory. I will have them packed, labeled, & directed to Mr. [William] Cooper, for the purpose of examination & description.

My minerals & geological specimens have lain in the same room with the shells since last fall. The winter was severe, and we were much engrossed with other subjects, so that I did not find a single day to devote to them. I'm now so much engaged in duties connected with the public service, that I must postpone all attempts to dress & label, such as can be recognized. I will however direct some masses of the serpentine rock with magnesia to be boxed up & sent to you, with a specimen of the lake Superior copper for your lectures, and some other things, which may interest you. I propose also to send you three or four specimens in zoology, which you will please accept.

I have nothing, of recent date, requiring crystallographical examination & measurement. Hitherto, the prim, rocks of the n. w. have yielded very little of interest in a crystallized form, and have been found very barren of imbedded minerals of any kind. The locality of serpentine, near "Granite Point" is likely to prove the most interesting mass. The copper, agates, etc. are connected with newer formations.

You ask, who is to write the account of the Expedition (last year's) as you infer from my allusion to an "Appendix" that such an account is to appear. This subject was discussed here last season, & before Houghton went away, it was arranged that a publication should be made. In the programme that was drawn up, the Dr. was to furnish a narrative of the Expd. with a map, to which I was to contribute a preface & an account of the Iowa mine country (between Galena & Fort Winnebago). The Appendix to consist of my official Report, the Drs. Report on the subject of Copper, and separate Papers on geology, botany, mineralogy, & conchology. Also, on the grammatical structure of the Indian languages and a lexicon of the Chippewa. Part of this, has been written. Until I see the Dr. I cannot speak with any certainty as to the prospect of publication; but suppose, that the work will (as a necessary consequence of recent arrangements) be deferred to embrace the results of this year's explorations. It is very desirable to me, that, if such a work appears, as much of your labours & those of Mr. Cooper, in the examination of specimens transmitted, as possible, should be incorporated in the appendix. Perhaps, important modifications of our original ideas, on the subject, may be judged expedient.

Yours, with regard
HENRY R. SCHOOLCRAFT

[This letter was in response to Torrey's letter of February 4, 1832. Schoolcraft and Houghton sent Torrey samples of the plants, minerals, and shells which they collected on their expeditions.]

25. Special Order No. 2.

HEAD QUARTERS, FORT BRADY,
June 6, 1832

In obedience to general order, dated 9th May, 1832, Lieutenant Allen, Corporal Wibru, of K, Privates Briscoe, Beemis, Burke, Dutton, Ingram, and Riley, of B, Privates Copp, Lentz, and Wade, of K companies, are detailed to accompany Mr. Schoolcraft on his expedition into the Indian country. Lieutenant Allen will be furnished with a copy of the order, by which he will be governed.

The acting assistant quartermaster will furnish a boat to transport the party.

D. WILCOX,
Captain 5th Regiment commanding.
J. ALLEN,
Lieut. and P. Adj't.

APPENDIX B

Reports and Letters of Henry Rowe Schoolcraft
On the Expedition of 1832

SCHOOLCRAFT made a number of separate reports to governmental officials in addition to his official Journal of the expedition. In many respects, these reports contain more historical information than the Journal itself, which is limited primarily to day-to-day entries. The condition and population of Indian tribes, the conflict between the Sioux and the Chippewa, the Black Hawk War, and the fur trade are subjects covered in these communications. Also included in the Appendix is a selection of letters written by Schoolcraft during or immediately after the trip. Many of these items were printed in the *Narrative to Itasca;* others have been taken from the Schoolcraft Papers in the Library of Congress.

1. Henry Rowe Schoolcraft to Jane Johnston Schoolcraft, June 15, 1832. Schoolcraft Papers, Library of Congress.

2. Henry Rowe Schoolcraft to Joseph M. Street, July 25, 1832. *Narrative to Itasca,* pp. 261-62.

3. Henry Rowe Schoolcraft to Elbert Herring, August 15, 1832. *Narrative to Itasca,* p. 213.

4. Henry Rowe Schoolcraft to George B. Porter, August 15, 1832. *Narrative to Itasca,* pp. 214-16.

5. Henry Rowe Schoolcraft to Elbert Herring, September 1, 1832. *Summary Narrative of an Exploratory Expedition to the Sources of the Mississippi River . . .* (Philadelphia, 1855), pp. 573-74. Hereafter referred to as *Summary Narrative.*

6. John Torrey to Henry Rowe Schoolcraft, October 5, 1832. Schoolcraft Papers, Library of Congress.

7. Henry Rowe Schoolcraft to Elbert Herring, November 21, 1832. *Narrative to Itasca,* pp. 217-27.

1. Henry Rowe Schoolcraft to Jane Johnston Schoolcraft.

L'ANSE, June 15, 1832

MY DEAREST JANE,

While the boats are going round the Peninsula of Kewywenon [Kewee-naw], I have gone down the Bay, to vaccinate the Indians. Many of the interior Indians were found here, & nearly two hundred have submitted to the process.

We have experienced the kindest hospitality from Mr. [William] Holliday & family. Little Jane & her mother have both been re-vaccinated. I am very anxious to know how my own little Jane & her brother, and *thee,* my dearest, are doing under the effects of the vaccine virus. Write to me, if it is possible. And tell me all you think a husband & father would like to hear.

Ever truly

HENRY R. SCHOOLCRAFT

[The Schoolcraft Collection in the Library of Congress contains many letters between Schoolcraft and his wife. As the granddaughter of a powerful Chippewa Chief, Jane had great insight into Indian life and customs. Her letters to her husband and her brother, George Johnston, reveal much about Upper Peninsula life in the early nineteenth century.]

2. Henry Rowe Schoolcraft to Joseph M. Street, Indian Agent at Prairie du Chien.

ST. PETERS, July 25, 1832

SIR,

I arrived at this place yesterday from the sources of the Mississippi, having visited the Chippewa bands and trading-posts in that quarter. Much complaint is made respecting the conduct of the persons licensed by you last year, who located themselves at the Granite Rocks, and on the St. Croix. No doubt can exist that each of them took in, and used in their trade, a considerable quantity of whiskey. And I am now enabled to say, that they each located themselves at points within the limits of my agency, where there are no trading-posts established. My lowest trading-post on the Mississippi, is the Pierced Prairie, eighteen miles below the mouth of the De Corbeau. It embraces one mile square, upon which traders are required to be located. On the St. Croix, the posts established and confirmed by the Department are Snake River and Yellow River, and embrace each, as the permanent place of location, one mile square. I report these facts for your information, and not to enable you to grant licenses for these posts, as the instructions of the Department give to each agent the exclusive control of the subject of granting licenses for the respective agencies.

Much solicitude is felt by me to exclude ardent spirits wholly from the Chippewas and Ottowas, the latter of whom have, by a recent order, been placed under my charge. I am fully satisfied that ardent spirits are not necessary to the successful prosecution of the trade, that they are deeply pernicious to the Indians, and that both their use and abuse is derogatory to the character of a wise and sober government. Their exclusion in every shape, and every quantity, is an object of primary moment; and it is an object which I feel it a duty to persevere in the attainment of, however traders may bluster. I feel a reasonable confidence in stating, that no whiskey has been used in my agency during the last two years, except the limited quantity taken by special permission of the Secretary of War, for the trade of the Hudson's Bay lines; and saving also the quantity clandestinely introduced from Prairie du Chien and St. Peters.

I know, sir, that an appeal to you on this subject cannot be lost, and that your feelings and judgment fully approve of temperance measures. But it requires active, persevering, unyielding efforts. And in all such efforts, judiciously urged, I am satisfied that the government will sustain the agents in a dignified discharge of their duties. Let us proceed in the accomplishment of this object with firmness, and with a determination never to relinquish it, until ardent spirits are entirely excluded from the Indian country.

I am sir,
Very respectfully,
Your obedient servant,
HENRY R. SCHOOLCRAFT

P.S. Capt. Jouett, commanding at this post, has recently seized sixteen kegs of high-wines. His prompt, decisive, and correct conduct in this, and other transactions relating to Indian affairs, merit the approbation of government.

The Petite Corbeau has requested that no trader may be located at the mouth of the St. Croix.

3. Henry Rowe Schoolcraft to Elbert Herring.
   Preliminary Report of Expedition

SAULT STE. MARIE, August 15th, 1832

SIR:

I hasten to inform you that I yesterday returned from my expedition to the northwest. On reaching the Mississippi I found the state of the water favorable for ascending. No difficulty was experienced in reaching the highest point, to which this stream has hitherto been explored. At this point, I procured canoes of the smallest class, and ascended, with Indian guides, to its actual source in Itasca Lake.

Upwards of two thousand Chippewas have been met in council, in their villages, or in detached parties on the way. At every point, vaccinations have been made, under the authority of the act of the last session of Congress. No opportunity has been omitted to enforce the objects of the instructions respecting their hostilities with each other, and to point out and make clear to their comprehension, their true relation to the United States.

The efforts made to procure the assent of the Chippewas to the advice given them on this head, were stated to the Sioux in a council to which I invited them at the Agency of St. Peter's.

The acquisition of data respecting the trade and population, and the geographical distribution of the bands, has been, with other details, resulting from my instructions, at all times, kept in view. I shall devote the earliest attention I can spare from the accumulated duties of the office, in drawing up a detailed report.

I am, Sir,
very respectfully,
your ob. serv't,
HENRY R. SCHOOLCRAFT

4. Henry Rowe Schoolcraft to George B. Porter.
   Report on the Black Hawk War.

SAULT STE. MARIE, August 15, 1832
SIR:

I have the honor to inform you that I returned from my visit to the Chippewa bands on the Upper Mississippi, yesterday evening. The state of feeling among them, partakes of the excitement growing out of a knowledge of the disturbances existing near their southern boundary. But their friendly position with respect to the United States, is not altered by events, thus far. Such of them as had received invitations to join in the Sauc league, have refused their assent. And notwithstanding the complacency with which some of the bands regard the hostile efforts of a people, with whom they are connected by the ties of language, and the decided preference others feel, and have expressed, for the counsels and government of Great Britain, as exercised in the Canadas, I feel a confidence in pronouncing the nation, as a whole, uncommitted in any negociations with the hostile Indians, and satisfied to remain in their present pacific attitude. Several of their most influential chiefs are quite decided in this policy, and would view it as foolish and desperate in the extreme, to entertain propositions to give aid to the enemy.

The only portion of them, of whom there were reasons to apprehend hostilities, are the villages of Torch Lake [Lac du Flambeau], comprising the Chippewa population on the heads of the Wisconsin, Ontonagon, and Chippewa rivers. These bands murdered four of our citizens at Lake Pepin, in the spring of 1824. Several of the persons implicated were imprisoned at Mackinac, whence they escaped. And it has not been practicable to carry into effect the measures of punishment, which were determined on. Their position, on the head waters of remote streams, is an almost inaccessible one, and the offence has ceased to be the subject of any further efforts by the Department. They have never, however, been relieved from the fears entertained on this account, and these fears have confined them very much to their particular villages and hunting grounds.

A war message was transmitted to the Torch Lake (or du Flambeau) Indians by the Black Hawk, or his counsellors, in 1830. This message was repeated in 1831, and again in 1832. They were reminded by it, of their affinity by blood, their ancient alliance, and their being arrayed as common enemies of the Sioux. It was addressed to the whole Chippewa nation, and they were invited to take up arms. It is not known that this message has been accepted. The recent death of Mozobodo, their first chief, and a man of understanding, has diminished my confidence in his band. It has been stated to me, very lately, by neighboring chiefs, that the Lac du Flambeau Indians were not in alliance with the malcontent tribes. That section of country has not been within the track of my recent journey. I have seen and conversed with some of the Indians, including one of the minor chiefs. Little, or no definite information has, however, been obtained.

I feel convinced that should the Black Hawk pursue his fight thither, he would, from obvious circumstances, be received with, at least, negative friendship. He would be allowed to recruit his followers and succor himself upon their hunting grounds towards the Mississippi borders, where there is a comparative abundance of deer and elk. And it is not improbable that some of the young men would follow his fortunes. I think, however, the policy of Black Hawk has been to bend his course westward after passing the Wisconsin, with the view of crossing the Mississippi, at some point where this stream is wide and shallow, (say between the Painted Rock and Lake Pepin,) and withdrawing to the plains of the Des Moines, where he has resources.

I have found the Chippewas, generally, not inclined to be communicative on the subject of the disturbances. But in cases where information has been obtained, it evinces a full knowledge of passing events. Kabamappa, a decidedly friendly and respectable chief of the St. Croix, informed me that the league consisted originally of nine tribes. I requested him to name them. He commenced by mentioning Saucs, Foxes, and Iowas, and added cautiously, and with a pause that allowed him to double down a finger at each count, Kickapoos, Flatheads, Earthlodges, Pottawattomies, Winnebagoes, and after some inquiry of the interpreter, Osages. Another Indian met on Lake Superior, said that the hostile Indians claimed to have killed 200 persons, since the war commenced.

Evidence has been furnished to me, that the Saucs who appear to be the principals, have taken much pains to form a league against the government, —that several tribes have assented to it, who have not boldly joined his standard, and that information favorable to their success, has been rapidly spread by them, among the northern Indians. This information they are prone to credit. Even the Sioux, whom I met in council at St. Peter's, on the 25th of July, have been accused of being lukewarm in the contest, and rather favoring, than opposed to their active enemies. This, the Petite Corbeau, their venerable chief, pointedly denied. He said the insinuation was untrue—that the Sioux, who went to the theatre of the war, had not returned from friendly feelings to the Saucs; and that they stood ready to go again, if officially called on.

The British band of Chippewas near this place were formally invited to unite in the war. A painted war club and pipe accompanied the message. It was transmitted by the Saucs, and given, by one of their emissaries to one of the northern Chippewas at Penetanguishine. It was received here (St. Mary's) by the Little Pine, (alias Lavoire Bart) a chief who co-operated with Tecumseh, in the late war, by leading a party of warriors from this quarter. He determined not to accept it, and communicated the fact to me in January last. He said the message was very equivocal. It invited him to aid them in fighting their enemies. He said he did not know whether the Sioux or Americans were intended.

Visits from the Indians within our lines to the British posts in Upper Canada, continue to be made. The Ottawas of L'arbre Croche, and the British band of the Chippewas of Lapointe, Lake Superior, have made their usual journey to Penetanguishine, during the present season. More than the ordinary numbers from this vicinity, have joined them.

I have the honor to be, Sir,

very respectfully,

your ob't servant,

HENRY R. SCHOOLCRAFT,

U.S. Indian Agent

5. Henry Rowe Schoolcraft to Elbert Herring.
   *Official Report of the Exploratory Expedition to the Actual Source of
   the Mississippi River in 1832.*

SAULT STE. MARIE, Sept. 1, 1832

SIR:

I had the honor to inform you, on the 15th ultimo, of my return from the sources of the Mississippi, and that I should communicate the details of my observations to you as soon as they could be prepared.

On reaching the remotest point visited heretofore by official authority, I found that the waters on that summit were favorable to my tracing this river to its utmost sources. This point having been left undetermined by prior expeditions, I determined to avail myself of the occasion to take Indian guides, with light canoes, and, after encamping my heavy force, to make the ascent. It was represented to be practicable in five days. I accomplished it, by great diligence, in three. The distance is 158 miles above Cass Lake. There are many sharp rapids, which made the trial severe. The river expands into numerous lakes.

After passing about forty miles north [west?] of [Upper] Red Cedar Lake, during which we ascended a summit, I entered a fine large lake, which, to avoid repetitions in our geographical names, I called Queen Anne's Lake [Bemidji]. From this point the ascent of the Mississippi was due south; and it was finally found to have its origin in a handsome lake, of some seven miles in extent, on the height of land to which I gave the name of Itasca.

This lake lies in latitude 47° 13′ 25″. It lies at an altitude of 1,575 feet, by the barometer, above the Gulf of Mexico. It affords me satisfaction to say, that, by this discovery, the geographical point of the origin of this river is definitely fixed. Materials for maps and plans of the entire route have been carefully collected by Lieut. James Allen, of the U. S. Army, who accompanied me, with a small detachment of infantry, as high as Cass Lake; and, having encamped them at that point, with my extra men, he proceeded with me to Itasca Lake. The distance which is thus added to the Mississippi, agreeably to him, is 164 miles, making its entire length, by the most authentic estimates, to be 3,200 [2,350] miles. In this distance there are numerous and arduous rapids, in which the total amount of ascent to be overcome is 173 feet.

Councils were held with the Indians at Fond du Lac, at Sandy Lake, Cass Lake, at the mouth of the Great De Corbeau River [Crow Wing], &c.

In returning, I visited the military bands at Leech Lake; passing from thence to its source, and descending the whole length of the Crow-wing River, and thence to St. Anthony's Falls, I assembled the Sioux at the agency of St. Peter's, and at the Little Crow's [Petite Corbeau] village. The Chippewas of the St. Croix and Broule [Brule] Rivers were particularly visited. Many thousands of the Chippewa and Sioux nations were seen and counselled with, including their most distinguished chiefs and warriors. Everywhere they disclaimed a connection with Black Hawk and his schemes. I left the Mississippi, about forty miles above the point where, in a few days, the Sauk chief was finally captured and his forces overthrown; and, reaching the waters of Lake Superior, at the mouth of the Brule, returned from that point to the agency at Sault de Ste. Marie.

The flag of the Union has secured respect from the tribes at every point; and I feel confident in declaring the Chippewas and Sioux, as tribes, unconnected with the Black Hawk movement.

I am, sir, very respectfully,

Your obedient servant,

HENRY R. SCHOOLCRAFT,

U. S. Ind. Agent

6. John Torrey to Henry Rowe Schoolcraft.

NEW YORK, October 5th, 1832

MY DEAR SIR,

I rejoice to learn that you have returned in safety from your fatiguing & perilous journey to the northwest. D[r.] Houghton wrote me a letter, which I received a few days ago, Dated Sault de Ste. Marie, stating the general results of the expedition, but I have read with great satisfaction the account which was published in the Detroit Journal of Sept. 26th. [See Appendix F, No. 4] A kind Providence has preserved you during another absence, & I hope He will cause the results of your labours to prove a blessing to our red brethren, as well as to the United States at large.

Dr. H[oughton] had not yet arranged his Collections, but he expected to have them in order before many days, & he promised me a sight of them as well as a portion of the duplicates. He has flattered me with the prospect of his spending the next winter in New York, as it is his desire to improve himself in practical anatomy & some other Departments of Medical Science. It will be a good opportunity for him to consult our libraries, for the purpose [of] determining all the doubtful objects in Natural History which he has collected. You must send all your queer & doubtful things by him. Dr. H. sent me some of the more interesting plants which he brought with him last year but he said that the best part of your collections were destroyed by getting wet.

By all means send Mr. [William] Cooper your shells—He will return safely & promptly all that you wish to keep. He knows more about freshwater shells than any other Naturalist in New York. By the way, have you seen Mr. Lea's splendid monograph (with colored plates) of Unios, in the Transactions of the American Philosophical Society?

Don't forget to let me have a piece of Native Copper, & a specimen of the Serpentine containing Magnesia.

Are we to have a NARRATIVE of the two expeditions in print? I hope you will consent to publish & let us have an appendix containing descriptions of the objects in Natl. Histy. I will aid Dr. H. all in my power, or will write the Botanical appendix if he prefers it but I would on no account deprive him of the honor he has acquired with so much labour & at so much risk.

I am much obliged to you for writing to Gov. Cass in behalf of my friend Dr. Harris, who, I believe has received his appointment.

It would afford me much pleasure to have you make us a visit this fall. My house must be your home when you are in New York. I have plenty of room, & you will have a hearty welcome. Let it be this season, for I expect to sail for Europe early next Spring—to be absent till the following October.

You have heard perhaps, something about the New University of the *City* of N. York, which was planned about two years ago. It went into operation a few days ago, under the most favorable prospects. The Council have given me a place in it (Prof. Chem. Bot. & Mineralogy) the duties of which I can discharge in addition to those which I attend to in the Medical College, as the latter occupies me only four months in the year.

If you see my friend Whipple, tell him his letter has been recd. & that it shall be answered soon—that we have thus far been mercifully preserved from the dreadful Cholera, & that Mrs. T. is to sail shortly for Europe with her uncle, to remain in Ireland till next spring when I hope to join her.

Believe me, My Dear Sir,
Yours truly
JOHN TORREY

7. Henry Rowe Schoolcraft to Elbert Herring.
Statistical Report on Indian Population and the Fur Trade.
SAULT STE. MARIE, November 21, 1832
SIR:
In obedience to such parts of the instructions of the third of May last directing me to proceed to the country on the heads of the Mississippi, as

relates to the Indian population, and to the condition of the fur trade, I
have the honor herewith to enclose a series of statistical tables which exhibit the geographical distribution of the lands, the name of each village
or permanent encampment, its course and distance from the seat of the
agency, the number of men, women and children, expressed in separate
columns, the number of the mixed blood population, and the total population of districts. Also, the names and position of the trading posts established under the act of Congress of May 26th, 1824, the number and
names of the clerks, and the number of interpreters and boatmen employed
in the trade under licences from the Indian office, the amount of goods
bonded for, agreeably to duplicates of the invoices on file, together with an
estimate of the capital vested in boats and provisions, or paid out in men's
wages, and an estimate of the returns in furs and peltries, based on the
outfits of 1832.

An examination of these tables will shew, that the entire Indian, mixed
and trader population, embraced within the consolidated agency of St.
Mary's and Michilimackinac, is 14,279, of which number 12,467 are
Chippewas and Ottawas, 1553 persons of the mixed blood, and 259 persons of every description engaged in the fur trade. That this population is
distributed in 89 principal villages, or fixed encampments, extending by
the route of Lakes Huron and Superior, through the region of the Upper
Mississippi, to Pembina on Red River. That 302 of the whole number live
in temporary encampments, or rather, migrate, along the bleak shores of
Lake Huron west of the 2nd, or Boundary Line Detour; 436 occupy the
American side of the straits and river St. Mary's; 1006 are located on the
southern shores of Lake Superior between the Sault of St. Mary's and
Fond du Lac, 1855 on the extreme Upper Mississippi, between Little Soc
River, and the actual source of this stream in Itasca Lake; 476 on the
American side of the Old Grand Portage, to the Lake of the Woods; 1174
on Red River of the North; 895 on the River St. Croix of the Mississippi;
1376 on the Chippewa River and its tributaries, including the villages of
Lac du Flambeau and Ottawa Lake; 342 on the heads of the Wisconsin
and Monominee rivers; 210 on the northern curve of Green Bay; 274 on
the northwestern shores of Lake Michigan between the entrance of Green
Bay, and the termination of the straits of Michilimackinac, at Point St.
Ignace; and 5,674, within the peninsula of Michigan, so far as the same is
embraced within the limits of the Agency. The latter number covers an
estimate of the Ottawa and Chippewa population indiscriminately.

For the accommodation of these bands, there have been established
thirty-five principal trading posts, exclusive of temporary trading stations,
occupied only in seasons of scarcity. These posts are distributed over six
degrees of latitude, and sixteen degrees of longitude, and embrace a larger
area of square miles, than all the states of central Europe. Much of it is
covered with water, and such are the number and continuity of its lakes,
large and small, that it is probable that this feature, constitutes by far, its
most striking peculiarity. Its productions are fish, wild rice, and game. But
such are the precariousness and dispersion of the supply as to keep the

whole population of men, women, and children, in perpetual vacillation, in its search. The time devoted in these migrations, is out of all proportion, to the results obtained by agriculture, or by any other stated mode of subsistence. And the supply is after all, inadequate. Seasons of scarcity and want are the ordinary occurrences of every year; and a mere subsistence is the best state of things that is looked for.

Traders visit them annually with outfits of goods and provisions, to purchase the furs and peltries, which are gleaned in their periodical migrations. These persons purchase their outfits from capitalists resident on the frontiers, and make their payments during the spring or summer succeeding the purchase. They employ men who are acquainted with the difficulties of the route, and with the character and resources of the people amongst whom they are to reside. These men act as boatmen and canoemen on the outward and inward voyage; they erect the wintering houses, chop wood, fish, cook for the *bourgois,* and are employed on *durwin* [durwaun: portages], or as runners during the hunting season. Much of the success of a trading adventure depends on their efficiency and faithfulness.

In the prosecution of this trade, the laws which have been prescribed by Congress for its regulation, are substantially observed. I am of opinion, however, that more efficiency would be given to the system, if a general revision of all the acts pertaining to this subject, were made. A legislation of thirty years, some of it necessarily of a hasty character, has multiplied the acts, which it is made the duty of Indian Agents to enforce, and the number of clauses which are repealed and modified, leave the original acts mutilated, and they do not, present as a whole, that clearness of intent, which is essential to their due and prompt execution. Some of the provisions have become obsolete; others are defective. A thorough and careful digest of the entire code, including the permanent treaty provisions, would present the opportunity for consolidation and amendment, and while leaving the laws easier of execution, adapt them more exactly to the present condition of the Indians, and to a just supervision of the trade.

The unconditional repeal by Congress, of every former provision relating to the introduction of ardent spirits, is a subject of felicitation to the friends of humanity. Of all the acts which it was in the power of the government to perform, this promises, in my opinion, to produce the most beneficial effects on the moral condition of the northwestern tribes: And its enforcement is an object of the highest moral achievement. My recent visit, as well as former opportunities of remark, has afforded full proofs of the entire uselessness of ardent spirits as an article of traffic with the Indians, and I beg leave to add my voice, to the thousands which are audible on this subject, that the government may put into requisition every practicable means to carry into effect the act.

I have the honor to be, Sir,
very respectfully,
your obedient servant,
HENRY R. SCHOOLCRAFT

Geographical District	Name of the Village or Periodical Encampment	Trading posts established by Indian Dept.	Number of clerks licenced to trade	Number of interpreters, boatmen, &c. employed by the clerks	Total number of white persons engaged in the trade	Amount of goods bonded for, agreeably to duplicates of the invoices on file in the Agency Office
N. W. Coast of L. Huron	Michilimackinac					
	St. Martin's Islands					
	Chenos					
	Drummond Island	1	1	3	4	
St. Mary's River *American side*	Mineeshco River					
	Muscoda Sagi					
	Sugar Island					
	Little Rapids, Kinibitunoong					
	Sault Ste. Marie					
	Misconabies Creek					
	Tacquimenon	1	1	4	5	
	Heart's Blood Lake					
S. Shores of L. Superior	Manistic River					
	White Fish Point	1	3	19	22	
	Shelldrake River, Onzig					
	Two Hearted River					$5,701,59
	Grand Marais					
	Miner's River and Pictured Rocks					
	Grand Island	1	2	8	10	
	Presque Isle and Granite Point					
	Huron Bay					
S. Shores of L. Superior	Keweena Bay	1	3	16	19	
	Ontonagon	1	1	10	11	
	Mouth of Montreal River	1	1	3	4	
	Mauvais River					
	Lapointe or Chegoimegon	1	2	4	6	
	Fond du Lac	1	1			
	Sandy Lake	1	1			
	Pine River and Red Cedar Lake	1	1			
	Pierced Prairie and Noka Seepi	1	1			
	Peckagama Falls, (Mississippi)					
	Lake Winipec	1	2			
Extreme Upper Mississippi	Turtle Lake					
	Cass Lake	1	2			
	Lac Traverse and Itaska Lake					
	Leech Lake, (Mukkundwas.)	1	5	74	88	$13,817,00
	Bear Island of Leech Lake					
	Mille Lac	1	2			
	Rum River					
Old G. Portage to the L. of the Woods *American side*	Old Grand Portage	1	1			
	Rainy Lake	1	3			
	Vermillion Lake	1	1			
	Lake of the Woods	1				
Red River of the North	Red Lake	1	1			
	Pembina	1	1			

Estimated amount vested in boats, or paid in men's wages, &c.	Aggregate amount of capital vested in the trade within the Agency	Estimated amount of returns in furs and peltries on the outfits of 1832, computed at the quoted New-York prices of 1831	Computed distance of the Trading Post from the seat of the Agency	Course of the Post from the Agency	Names of the persons who have received licences to trade, and executed bonds, with sureties, under the several acts of Congress, regulating trade and intercourse with the Indian tribes, during the year ending 30th September, 1832	Total population resident within the Agency in 1832, excluding inhabitants of M. T. at Sault Ste. Marie & Michilimackinac
			Miles			
			12	N.E.		
			40	N.E.		306
						436
			120	N.N.E.	William Johnston / Edward Cadotte / Ecstache Raussain	
			130	N.N.E.	Samuel Ashman / Richardson May / William Johnston	1087
$5,701,59	$11,403,18	$15,204,24				
			180	N.N.W.	Louis Nolin. B. Marvin	
					John Holiday / William Holiday	
			500	N.W.	Jean Bt. Dubay	
			410	N.W.	George Bartlet. J. Brown	
			479	N.W.	Michael Cadotte, jun.	
			500	N.W.	L. M. Warren. M. Cadotte	
			590	N.W.	W. Aitkin. W. Davenport	
			740	N.W.		
			800	W.N.W.	John H. Fairbanks	
			940	W.N.W.	Benjamin F. Baker	
				N.W.	Alfred Aitkin	
				N.W.	Jean Bt. Belonger	
				N.W.	James Ermatinger	
				N.W.		
$13,817,00	$27,634,00	$36,845,33		N.W.	Piere Cota / J. W. Abbott. G. Bungo / Charles Chabattio	
					A. Morrison. Jean Bt. Roy	1870
				N.N.W.	Ambroise Davenport	
					J. Cadotte. S. Lecomble	
				N.N.W.	V. Roy. P. Craphesa	
				N.N.W.	F. Brunet & A. Belonger	481
				N.W.	J. Bt. Dejardin. L. Dufault	
				N.W.	David Aitkin	1250

GEOGRAPHICAL DISTRICT	NAME OF THE VILLAGE OR PERIODICAL ENCAMPMENT	Trading posts established by Indian Dept.	Number of clerks licenced to trade	Number of interpreters, boatmen, &c. employed by the clerks	Total number of white persons engaged in the trade	Amount of goods bonded for, agreeably to duplicates of the invoices on file in the Agency Office
ST. CROIX RIVER OF THE UPPER MISSISSIPPI	Falls of St. Croix					
	Snake River	1	2	8	10	
	Yellow River	1	1	4	5	
	Rice Lake and Lac Vaseux	1	1	2	3	
	Nama Kowagun					
	L. of the Cross of the Namakagun					
	Puckwaewa, (Odabossa's V.)					
CHIPPEWA RIVER OF THE UPPER MISSISSIPPI	Rice Lake of Red Cedar Fork					
	Red Cedar Lake of Lac Chetac	1	1	3	4	
	Lac Courtoreille, (Ottowa L.)	1	2	9	11	
	Red Devil's Band of the Ochasowa					
	Lac du Flambeau	1	1	7	8	
	Trout Lake and Tomahawk Lake					
SOURCES OF THE WISCONSIN & MONOMONEE RIVERS	La Lac or Upper Wisconsin	1	1	4	5	
	Plover Portage and Post Lake					
	Metawonga	1	1	6	7	
	White Clay Portage					
NORTHERN CURVE OF GREEN BAY	Bay de Nocquet					
	Weequaidons					
	White Fish Creek					
N. W. COAST OF L. MICHIGAN	Mouth of Manistic	1	1	4	5	$1000,00
	Mille au Coquin					
	Choiswa					
	Straits of Michigan					
	Point St. Ignace					
PENINSULA OF MICHIGAN	River au Sable (Arenac.)	1				
	Thunder Bay					
	Cheboigon					
	L'Arbre Crosh, Upper and Lower	1				
	Grand Traverse Bay					
	Riviere au Becsie					
	Maskegon	1	1	4	5	$994,00
	Grand River	1	5	14	19	$5000,00
		35	53	206	259	$26,512,59

Estimated amount vested in boats, or paid in men's wages, &c.	Aggregate amount of capital vested in the trade within the Agency	Estimated amount of returns in furs and peltries on the outfits of 1832, computed at the quoted New-York prices of 1831	Computed distance of the Trading Post from the seat of the Agency	Course of the Post from the Agency	Names of the persons who have received licences to trade, and executed bonds, with sureties, under the several acts of Congress, regulating trade and intercourse with the Indian tribes, during the year ending 30th September, 1832	Total population resident within the Agency in 1832, excluding inhabitants of M. T. at Sault Ste. Marie & Michilimackinac
				W.S.W.		
				W.S.W.	Thomas Connor	349
				W.S.W.	Souvraign Dawnee	
				W.S.W.	Louis Ladabouche	387
				W.S.W.		95
				W.S.W.		26
				W.S.W.		53
				W.S.W.		142
				W.S.W.	Louis Corbin	74
				W.S.W.	Benjamin Cadotte	515
				W.S.W.		152
				W.S.W.	Charles H. Oaks	465
				W.S.W.	Paul Grignon	51
				S.W.	G. D. Cameron	125
				S.W.		77
				S.W.		118
				S.W.		34
				S.W.		
				S.W.		
				S.W.		210
$1000,00	$2,000	$2,666,66		S.	Joseph Troque	
				S.		
				S.		239
				S.		
				S.E.		40
				S.E.		
				S.E.		
				S.		
				S.		5,698
				S.		
				S.		
$994,00	$1,988,00	$2,650,66		S.	George Campeau	
$5000,00	$10,000,00	$13,333,33			Rix Robinson	
$26,512,59	$53,025,18	$70,700,22			Joseph Daily	
					Francis Lacroix	
					William Lasley	
						14,279

V. STATISTICAL TABLES of the Indian population, comprised within the boundaries of the consolidated Agency of Sault Ste. Marie and Michilimackinac, in the year 1832, together with the number of Trading Posts established under the act of Congress, of May 26, 1824, and other facts illustrating the condition and operations of the Fur Trade. Prepared under instructions of the War Department of the 3d May, 1832, for visiting the sources of the Mississippi.

NATURE AND GEOGRAPHICAL DISTRIBUTION OF THE POPULATION

Geographical District	Name of the Village or Periodical Encampment	No. of men.	No. of women.	No. of children.	No. of persons of the mixed blood, all ages & sexes.	Population of villages, &c.	Population of geographical districts.
N. W. Coast of Lake Huron	Michilimackinac (See note A.)						
	St. Martin's Islands	18	29	51	140	238 ⎱	
	Chenos [Cheneaux]						
	Drummond Island	16	18	23	7	64 ⎰	302
St. Mary's River, American side	Mineeshco [Munuscong] River (B.)						
	Muscoda Sagi [Charlotte River] (C.)						
	Sugar Island						
	Little Rapids [Mission Rapids]						
	Kinibitunoong (D.)						
	Sault Ste. Marie (E.)	58	73	144	161	436	436
Southern Shores of Lake Superior	Misconabies Creek [Red Carp River?]						
	Tacquimenon [Tahquamenon]						
	Heart's Blood Lake						
	Manistic River						
	White Fish Point (F.)	42	46	98		186	
	Shelldrake River (Onzig)						
	Two Hearted River						
	Grand Marais						
	Miner's River and Pictured Rocks						
	Grand Island	7	6	23	14	50	
	Presque Isle and Granite Point	4	4	12		20	
	Huron Bay	4	6	4		14	
	Keweena[w] Bay (G.)	31	38	43	28	140	
	Ontonagon (H.)	29	32	76	15	152	
	Mouth of Montreal River						
	Mauvais River	32	40	113	28	213	
	Lapointe or Chegoimegon [Chequamegon] (I.)						
	Fond du Lac (K.)	44	46	103	38	231	1006

NATURE AND GEOGRAPHICAL DISTRIBUTION OF THE POPULATION, *Continued.*

Geographical District	Name of the Village, &c.	No. of men.	No. of women.	No. of children.	No. of persons, &c.	Population of villages, &c.	Pop. of geographical districts.
	Sandy Lake	70	83	127	35	315	
	Pine River and Red Cedar Lake	20	19	33	6	78	
	Pierced Prairie and Noka Seepi [Nokaysippi] (*L.*)	22	26	52	12	112	
	Peckagama [Pokegama] Falls (Mississippi.)	4	6	14		24	
	Lake Winnepec [Winnibigoshish] (*M.*)	20	18	41	10	89	
EXTREME UPPER MISSISSIPPI	Turtle Lake	20	21	44	14	99	
	Cass Lake (*N.*)	40	51	66	11	168	
	Lac Traverse [Bemidji] and Itasca Lake (*O.*)						
	Leech Lake Mukkundwas (*P.*)	139	194	373	24	730	
	Bear Island of Leech Lake	26	32	44		102	
	Mille Lac[s] / Rum River (*Q.*)	38	43	57		138	1855
OLD GRAND PORTAGE TO THE L. OF THE WOODS, *American side*	Old Grand Portage (*R.*)	12	11	27		50	
	Rainy Lake	38	40	65	16	159	
	Vermillion Lake	37	40	48	7	132	
	Lake of the Woods	31	34	61	9	135	476
RED RIVER OF THE NORTH	Red Lake	84	74	100	32	290	
	Pembina (*S.*)	142	150	288	304	884	1174
ST. CROIX RIVER OF THE UPPER MISSISSIPPI	Falls of St. Croix / Snake River / Yellow River (*T.*)	80	88	133	38	339	
	Rice Lake and Lac Vaseux [Spooner]	106	114	120	42	382	
	Nama Kowagun [Namekagon]	30	32	33		95	
	Lake of the Cross of the Namakagun	6	6	14		26	
	Puckwaewa (Odabassa's V.)	11	14	28		53	895

NATURE AND GEOGRAPHICAL DISTRIBUTION OF THE POPULATION, *Continued.*

GEOGRAPHICAL DISTRICT	NAME OF THE VILLAGE, &c.	No. of men.	No. of women.	No. of children.	No. of persons, &c.	Population of villages, &c.	Pop. of geographical districts.
CHIPPEWA RIVER OF THE UPPER MISSISSIPPI	Rice Lake of Red Cedar Fork	46	38	58		142	
	Red Cedar Lake of Lac Chetac	19	20	31		70	
	Lac Courtoreille [Court Oreilles] (Ottowa L.)	117	136	195	56	504	1376
	Red Devil's band of the Ochasowa	49	37	66		152	
	Lac du Flambeau	112	127	168	50	457	
	Trout Lake and Tomahawk Lake	15	15	21		51	
	La Lac or Upper Wisconsin (U.)	30	30	60		120	
SOURCES OF THE WISCONSIN AND MONOMONEE RIVERS	Plover Portage and Post Lake	18	23	36		77	
	Metawonga	28	30	43	10	111	342
	White Clay Portage	8	9	14	3	34	
NORTHERN CURVE OF GREEN BAY	Bay de Nocquet [Bay de Noc] Weequaidons	29	34	60	15	138	210
	White Fish Creek	16	18	38		72	
N. W. COAST OF LAKE MICHIGAN	Mouth of Manistic [Manistique] Mille au Coquin [Millecoquins] Choiswa. [Seul Choix] Straits of Michigan Point St. Ignace	46	54	120	14	234	274
PENINSULA OF MICHIGAN	River au Sable (Arenac.) Thunder Bay Cheboigon [Cheboygan] L'Abre Croche, Upper and Lower (V.) Grand Traverse Bay Riviere au Becsie [Betsie] Maskegon [Muskegon] Grand River	1350	1566	2384	374	5674	5674
		3,144	3,571	5,752	1,553	14,020	14,020

EXPLANATORY NOTES

(*A*) Michilimackinac is the seat of justice for Mackinac county, Michigan Territory, is 300 miles NW. of Detroit, has a U. S. circuit court, a population of 1053, by the census of 1830, has a military post, an Indian agency, a collector's office, a flourishing missionary school, &c.

(*B*) This river enters the head of Muddy [Mud] Lake, and is partly the boundary between Michilimackinac and Chippewa counties.

(*C*) This is a tributary of the south branch of the St. Mary's, and is much resorted to by the Indians in their periodical fishing and hunting excursions.

(*D*) Indian gardens at this place, two miles below St. Mary's.

(*E*) This place is the site of Fort Brady, is ten miles below the foot of Lake Superior, and ninety by water NW. of Mackinac. The Indian Agency of Vincennes, Indiana, was removed to this place, in 1822, and consolidated with the agency of Mackinac, in 1832. It is the seat of justice for Chippewa county, M. T. and has a population, by the census of 1830, of 918.

(*F*) The trading post, at this place, is occupied as a fishing station during the autumn, by persons who proceed with boats and nets, from St. Mary's. Bonds are taken by the Indian Office, and licences granted in the usual manner, as a precaution against the introduction of ardent spirits.

(*G*) It is thirty leagues from Keweena Post to Ontonagon, by the most direct water route, but seventy-five leagues around the peninsula.

(*H*) The population enumerated at this post, includes the villages of Ocogib, Lake Vieux Desert, Iron River and Petite Peche Bay.

(*I*) The Chippewas of La Point have their gardens on this river, and reside here periodically. This is a good fishing station. A mission family has recently been located here.

(*K*) This is the most western bay of Lake Superior.

(*L*) Replaces the post of the Isle des Corbeau, which is abolished.

(*M*) The route of Rainy Lake, begins at the post on this lake, which is an expansion of the channel of the Mississippi, about ten miles across. Clear water and yields fish.

(*N*) This lake has been so named in honor of the present Secretary of War, who terminated his exploratory journey there, in 1820.

(*O*) Itasca Lake is the actual source of the Mississippi, as determined by myself, in the expedition, which furnishes occasion for this report.

(*P*) This is a very large expanse of water, clear and pure in its character, and yields fine white fish. It was deemed the head of the Mississippi by Pike, who visited it in the winter of 1806, but it is not even *one* of the sources, as it has several large tributaries.

(*Q*) Named Rum River by Carver, but called *spirit* river by the Indians, not using this word in a physical sense.

(*R*) This route from Old Grand Portage to the Lake of the Woods, is chiefly used by the British traders, and the gentlemen connected with the Hudson's Bay government; but has fallen into comparative disuse, as a grand channel of traders since the introduction of goods direct from England into the Hudson Bay.

(*S*) The estimate of population at Pembina, includes all who are believed to be south of latitude 49 deg. and therefore within the limits of the United States.

(*T*) Embraces all the population of the Fork of St. Croix, connected by a portage with the Brulé River of Lake Superior.

(*U*) The Indians on these streams, rely much on wild rice. Their encampments are temporary. They come into contact with the Winnebagoes and Monomonees, who are their neighbors on the south.

(*V*) The Indian population of the peninsula of Michigan, consists of Ottawas, Chippewas and Pottawatomies, who are not widely separated by language and habits. The Ottawas are however the most agricultural. No Pottawatomies are included in the estimate, and only that portion of Ottawas and Chippewas living north of

Grand River, and northwest of Sagana, as the limits of the Mackinac and St. Mary's joint agency, do not extend south of these places.

☞ The data respecting the fur trade, in the schedules, excludes the business transacted on the Island of Michilimackinac, and the village of Sault Ste. Marie, these places being on lands ceded to the United States, and over which the laws of the Territory of Michigan, operate. They also exclude any amount of trade that may have been carried on, by the white inhabitants of Red River settlement, who may be located south of the national boundary on the north, as this place is too remote to have been heretofore brought under the cognizance of our intercourse laws.

Office of Indian Agency, Sault Ste. Marie,
November 21, 1832.
HENRY R. SCHOOLCRAFT, *Indian Agent*

APPENDIX C

Journal and Letters of Lieutenant James Allen

ON MAY 9, 1832, Major General Alexander Macomb issued orders to the Commandant at Fort Brady to have an officer and ten men detailed to accompany the Schoolcraft expedition. At Schoolcraft's suggestion, Lieutenant James Allen was chosen to lead the military detachment and was directed to keep a detailed journal and provide a map of the route. The Lieutenant was meticulous in carrying out these orders and on November 25, 1833, submitted his report to Major General Macomb. The Journal was so excellent in its coverage that the Secretary of War, Lewis Cass transmitted it to the Speaker of the House of Representatives. It was published as House *Executive Document* No. 323 (23d Cong., 1 Sess., pp. 7-68), and appeared also in the *American State Papers: Military Affairs,* Vol. V, No. 579, pp. 315-44. A long excerpt from the Journal was reprinted in the New York *American,* July 19, 1834 (See Appendix F, No. 6).

Even more significant than the Journal, however, was Allen's map of the route of the expedition which was the first topographical and hydrological delineation of the source of the Mississippi. Its accuracy and detail added much to the knowledge of Wisconsin and Minnesota of that time, as well as giving a day-by-day account of the progress of the trip. The original manuscript map was submitted with the Journal and is now in the records of the Office of Indian Affairs, Record Group No. 77, National Archives. Copies of the map, reduced and drawn by Lieutenant Drayton, accompany the official published Journal. The maps which appeared in Schoolcraft's *Narrative to Itasca* were also taken from Allen's original.

1. The Journal of Lieutenant James Allen, Expedition of 1832. U. S. House *Executive Documents,* No. 323, 23d Cong., 1 Sess., pp. 7-68.

2. James Allen to Alexander Macomb, September 13, 1832. Office of the Adjutant General, Record Group No. 94, National Archives.

3. James Allen to Alexander Macomb, Transmittal of Official Journal, November 25, 1833. *American State Papers: Military Affairs,* Vol. V, No. 579, pp. 313-15.

1. Journal of Lieutenant James Allen

Journal of an "Expedition into the Indian country," to the source of the Mississippi, made under the authority of the War Department, in 1832.

June 7.—The party organized for this expedition consisted of Mr. Schoolcraft, who had the principal conduct of it; Doctor Houghton, the surgeon, to vaccinate the Indians; Mr. George Johnston, interpreter; Mr. Boutwell, a presbyterian missionary; and twenty engagées, or Canadian voyageurs, in the employment of Mr. Schoolcraft, and the military part, consisting of myself and ten soldiers, from the companies at Fort Brady: making an aggregate, of the whole party, of thirty-five souls.

This party may be considered as divided into two parts; that organized by Mr. Schoolcraft, and under his immediate direction and subsistence, and the escort or military part, under my command. I shall therefore designate the former, throughout this journal, as Mr. Schoolcraft's party, or Mr. S. and party, which will be understood to embrace all excepting the escort, the latter being transported and subsisted under my direction.

All our preparations having been completed, we embarked from Saut de Ste. Marie about five o'clock in the afternoon of the 7th of June. Mr. Schoolcraft and party, with their baggage, in one large Mackinac boat and two bark canoes, and the soldiers and myself, with our arms, ammunition, and provisions to last us to Fort Snelling, in a small Mackinac boat. The boats are intended for our journey along Lake Superior, and will be abandoned at Fond du Lac, where, for river navigation, we shall be compelled to use the Indian bark canoes. Our object being, for this day, merely to make a start, we went but six miles, to Point aux Pins, on the Canada side of the St. Mary's river, where we encamped for the night. This is a point of very general encampment for the traders, and is always considered by them, departing from Mackinac, or the Saut de Ste. Marie, as their first point in the Indian country. Here the prices of their goods change, and any article sold at this point, or beyond it, to any of their hands or engagées, is charged at what they denominate the "interior price," which is the same as that placed on their goods at their several trading posts in the Indian country. The St. Mary's river expands greatly above and below this place, and all of it above might be regarded as a bay of Lake Superior, were it not that there is a perceptible current almost to the lake. Point aux Pins is a low, sandy barren, with a few detached pines growing on it. A small stream enters the St. Mary's, a few hundred yards below the extreme point, called Carp river, very remarkable for the great quantities of carp fish[1] it contains, at some seasons of the year. Two hundred yards from its mouth, the stream is eight feet wide, and four or five deep, and, in the spring of the year, is literally filled with these fish. I had visited it on a former occasion, and found them so abundant, that with ten strokes of a spear I killed nine fish, most of them about a foot long, and when the water was so muddy, from their moving in shoals, that I could not see any of them, but judged of their situation only by the motion of the water, occasioned by their moving in such great numbers.

June 8.—Made an early start, and soon passed into Lake Superior between Gros Cap and Point Iroquois, the two points which mark the exit of the lake by the St. Mary's river, which, at this place, is nine miles broad, and seems, from the similarity in appearance of the two capes, at a very remote period, to have forced its way through a continuous mountain that once united them. It has been supposed that an analogy existed between the rock formation of these points; but, on a former occasion, about a year before our present visit, Doctor Houghton and myself made a careful examination of Point Iroquois, of the American side, and could discover no rock whatever: its character, therefore, in this respect, is still conjectural. The name "Iroquois" is given this point, and a small island of the lake near it, from a massacre at this place of Iroquois Indians, by the Chippewas, a long time ago.[2] Gros Cap, immediately opposite, on the Canada side, is a large granitic bluff, rising at first perpendicularly to a height of 150 feet, and afterwards more gradually to a whole height of near 500 feet. It is a remarkable point in the great chain of granite mountains that confine Lake Superior, to the north.

Turning Point Iroquois, the lake extends westwardly, forming a great bay between this and Whitefish point; the distance across being 24 miles, and the depth of the bay from a line joining the two points, 20 miles. This bay receives the Tequamenon [Tahquamenon] and Shelldrake rivers. I made its direct traverse in a direction N. W., by which I reached Whitefish point before the canoes and the other boat, which coasted the bay, but all turned the point near a mile, and encamped together at sunset, on a sandy beach.

Whitefish point is a low, long, narrow tongue of land, running, in an easterly direction, very far into the lake, and dips so gradually under the water as to form a shoal far beyond its extremity. About a mile and a half of the end of the point is composed of shifting sand and gravel, but a few feet elevated above the surface of the lake, and is perfectly barren of vegetation; the part back of this is low and very sandy, but a stinted growth of white and pitch pine, and a few small birch and white cedars, with some shrubs, have rendered the soil more fixed.

On the north side of the point the sand is very fine, (siliceous,) and about a hundred yards from the shore is blown into numerous insulated hillocks, or steep mounds, from 20 to 50 feet high, partially covered with small vegetation, which prevents their being destroyed by the same cause that formed them. The extreme point is made entirely of small pebbles of granite, quartz, hornblende, &c., very round and smooth.

This point is remarkable and important as a fishery of whitefish—as affording more, and a better quality, of that excellent fish, than any other fishery of the southern shore of the lake yet explored. It has been long known as a point where this fish could be taken in gill nets at certain seasons of the year; but no use was made of it, more than is at present of several other fisheries of the lake, where a few Indians, or an individual trader, procure only what is necessary for their immediate subsistence.

But within the last two years, the enterprise of two gentlemen, Mr. [Samuel] Ashman and Mr. [Ecstache] Roussin [Raussain], who had retired from the fur trade of the American Fur Company, has developed many facts, in relation to this fishery, tending to show its importance as a source of business and profitable trade.[3]

These gentlemen commenced the business of fishing at this place, two years ago, without any particular knowledge or experience, with regard to the seasons, localities, or the best means of taking the fish, and, notwithstanding these disadvantages, have made it a source of considerable profit, and are encouraged to continue it more extensively.

The fishery, as at present developed, commences at Shelldrake river, nine miles from the end of the point, on its eastern shore, and extends round the point and along the southern shore of the lake, as far as the Grand Marais, or the commencement of the Grand Sable, a distance of fifty-four miles. The bottom along this part of the coast is sandy, and falls off gradually into deep water, and the shore is a sandy beach—circumstances favorable to the safety and easy working of the nets. The fish occur in equal numbers in every part of its whole extent, but the point is the most desirable locality, from its generally affording, on one or the other side, a lee, and smooth water, where the nets may be used during winds. The fish are taken by means of the gill net alone; the meshes of which are of a size adapted to the fish's head, so as to fasten in the gills when the fish attempts to withdraw its head, after having inserted it in an attempt to force its way in the direction of its movement. The nets are generally eighty fathoms long, and from five to ten feet broad, according to the depth of the water; and are set in a vertical position by leads or sinkers that rest on the bottom, and floats of sufficient buoyancy to support the weight of the net and hold it up. They are tended by fishermen employed for the purpose, two of whom can tend and manage, in fair weather, ten nets; which will yield, every morning, from one to six barrels of fish. The management of nets consists in merely raising them, relieving them of their fish, and dropping in the same place, once each day; which is done by running a canoe along their course, and raising and dropping as the canoe progresses. These nets cost about six dollars each.

The fishing season commences here in the spring, (when the largest and best fish are taken,) about the last of April, and ends about the last of June; and in the fall, occurs in October and part of November; making the whole season a little more than three months. The rest of the year, the whitefish remain in the deep water of the lake. It is remarkable that at no other known fishery of the lake can the whitefish be taken in quantities in the spring; and equally so, that those of this fishery are larger and better than at any of the others. It is also a peculiarity of this fish that they are fatter and better in proportion as they are larger. Some taken here weigh fourteen or fifteen pounds, but the average weight is, in the spring, twenty-five to thirty fish to the barrel of 200 lbs., and, in the fall, thirty to forty. The superior quality of the Lake Superior and Saut de Ste. Marie whitefish, causes them to bring, in Detroit, from one to two dollars per barrel more than any other whitefish of that market. Much of the resources of this fishery, as also the best means of working it, remain to be discovered, and, consequently, no estimate can be formed of its future value to trade. Messrs. Ashman and Roussin have put up at Whitefish point, within the last two years, 559 barrels; others, in the same time, and at the same place, have put up 313 barrels; making the whole proceeds for the above time, 872 barrels, worth in Detroit six dollars per barrel, or 5,234 dollars.

It is probable that there are many other rich whitefish fisheries along the southern shore of the lake, but they are, as yet, unexplored. The northern or Canada shore is said to afford many, as also superior advantages for fishing, from the coast being more serrated by bays, and protected by numerous islands from the effects of winds and seas, that greatly annoy the fishermen on the southern shore.

June 9.—Mr. Schoolcraft's boat, managed by Frenchmen, and carrying most of his provisions and baggage, did not reach our encampment until late last night: this circumstance determined him to strengthen the crew of the boat, by that of Mr. Johnston's canoe, which was accordingly abandoned, and Mr. Johnston placed in charge of the boat, with Mr. Boutwell as passenger, Mr. Schoolcraft and Doctor Houghton occupying the light canoe as before; which, being manned with a full crew, was able to travel at a much speedier rate than either of the boats. We left our encampment after breakfast, at six o'clock, and, following the coast, took a direction nearly due west, which changed in the forenoon to 10° south of west, and in the afternoon to S. 30° W. I got to the Grand Marais at 10 P. M., where Mr. S. and party were already encamped, his boat being now able to precede mine, from the superiority of the boat and crew. The whole of the coast passed to-day, presented a very plain bank of fine sand from twenty to a hundred feet high, and a continued forest of pine, generally small, but sometimes large and beautiful. A picturesque grove of white pine (Pinus strobus) of more than a mile extent along the lake, occurs about ten miles from our encampment. The growth is all large, and unmixed with any other trees, the pines straight, tall, without limb, and thickly set together, on level ground, as far back as we could see.

We passed Twin [Two Hearted] river, twenty-four miles from Whitefish point. It is a small stream, and its mouth is so much filled with sand that it can only be entered by very light craft, and in smooth water. We have travelled to day forty-five miles.

June 10, (Sunday.)—This being the Sabbath, by a rule of Mr. Schoolcraft's, we do not travel, though the weather is fine. The rule however is convenient in observance, as it gives the men time to wash, bake, &c., which they have but little time to do when travelling. We are lying in a beautiful little bay, called the Grand Marais, from its having once been a marsh, which, within the recollection of some old voyageurs, now present, has been washed away to its present state. It is a safe harbor for boats, and is important from its being the only one between Shelldrake river and

Grand island, a distance of near one hundred miles. It is half a mile in depth, opens to the west, and is difficult to enter with a strong west wind and heavy sea, which drive right into it. Traders have met with serious accidents in attempting to run into it under such circumstances. The country about here has nothing peculiar in its appearance—hills are seen to the S. S. W. covered with thick forests of birch and pine.

The Grand Sable, or Great Sand, commences from the west of the entrance to this harbor.

June 11.—Left our encampment at Grand Marais at 2 o'clock in the morning, and passed the Grand Sable before daylight. This is a great deposite of loose, fine, siliceous sand, which forms a plain coast for about nine miles, rising abruptly from the lake at an angle of near 45°, and to a height of about three hundred feet. It is sustained at so great an angle by its moisture; for it is otherwise uncemented, and gives way under the feet, making its ascent almost impracticable. It is deposited in three layers or beds which are distinguishable by a slight difference of color, and rests on a flat rock of variegated sandstone, which is seen a few feet under the surface of the water, near the shore. The summit is in a plain of the same loose drifting sand, which extends back for some miles, and is perfectly barren, containing embedded trunks of trees. In this plain, about a mile and a half back, there is a small lake [Grand Sable Lake], of more than a mile and a half in circumference, of clear, transparent water, and of apparently great depth, enclosed by a beautiful low bank of clear sand, and a beach of small pebbles. This lake is the source of a branch of the Tequamenon river, that empties into Tequamenon bay, between Point Iroquois and Whitefish point, and is remarkable from its occurring in the middle of a sandy plain.

As we progressed, the Grand Sable gradually fell off into a low sandy bank, thirty or forty feet high, covered with a small growth of pine, birch, sugar-maple, and beech, (Fagus ferruginea,) which continues for about twelve miles, and terminates in the grand sandstone formation, called the "Pictured Rocks," which constitutes twelve miles more of the coast to Grand island. This is the most beautiful and picturesque part of the whole southern coast of Lake Superior.

The formation is the "red sandstone," which rises gradually to the height of three hundred feet, in strata nearly horizontal, and from one to eight feet thickness, forming a perpendicular and projecting wall, with but one or two interruptions, from the point where it is first seen, to the entrance of the harbor of Grand island, where it leaves the lake, and, turning to the south, disappears in wooded hills. This wall rises perpendicularly out of the water, which is apparently of great depth immediately at the base; and in places where the falling down of upper portions of the rock has been recent, it is perfectly vertical, with the regularity of masonry from the base to the summit. But generally the rock is projecting, the undermining operations of the water and frost at the base not having progressed far enough to allow the whole entablature above to split, and tumble over from its own weight.

The effect of the long action of the lake on this rock is here curiously exemplified, and can be distinctly observed to a height of more than a hundred and fifty feet above the present level of the water, proving conclusively that at some remote period the water of the lake stood at nearly that height above where it now is. The surface of the rock is not regular, presenting many angular and rounded points and notches, or little coves and bays; and where parts were softer than the general rock, and where water oozed from between the strata near the base, the action of the frost internally, and of the waves externally, has worn out caverns, domes, and arched ways, of great extent and singularity. In some places, water, containing vegetable and mineral matter, has run from the strata near the top, and striped the surface down to the bottom in all varieties of colors. The general surface is almost continuous for about twelve miles, in a direction a little south of west. It is only broken in one or two places by small streams and their little valleys, the largest of which is Miner's river. This stream, which was too small to admit our boat, has its mouth in a little sandy bay, to the east of which the bluff terminates in a remarkable feature, called the "Dorick Rock." This is a large slab or tabular rock, of about fifty feet diameter, and eight feet thickness; supported on the side next to the bay by four columns, the largest of which is about seven feet through, and the smallest about three feet; the other side being supported by the main rock, of which it is a part. This whole structure presents four regular and distinct arches, two of which, being perpendicular to the shore, may be seen from the lake; the other two are radiant to the great arch, and nearly parallel to the shore. The large arch has a span of about thirty-five feet, and a rise of one-fourth the span. Its floor is inclined to the lake, making the height of the soffit at the entrance forty feet, and at the egress eighteen feet, the soffit or interior surface of the arch being horizontal. The lesser arches have a span of from five to eight feet, in the same plane with that of the large arch, but their floors are higher. The columns are round, and have almost the regularity of masonry.[4]

This structure is elevated at its base forty feet, and at its summit one hundred feet above the lake, and is the extreme point of the bluff, which it terminates perpendicularly. The top of the rock is covered with a vegetable soil, and a growth of timber, among which are three pines of from two to three feet diameter.

The Dorick rock is but one of the features of this part of the coast; there are many others equally curious and beautiful, and the whole presents a scenery of grandeur and beauty not surpassed, perhaps, by any other scenery of our country.

From the Pictured rocks we entered the eastern channel to the harbors of Grand island, and, passing round the island, encamped on the southern shore of the western channel, at a trading house.[5] Grand island is a large and elevated island, of about twenty miles circumference, and stands very little out into the lake, beyond the line of the coast, with a broad channel running round it. Back of the island the channel expands into large deep bays, that run into it and the main land, forming commodious and safe harbors for vessels. Next to the lake, it presents high sandstone bluffs, but its other side falls off into a low shore. On a low sandy point of the south side of the island, there is an Indian village, with a present population of fifty-nine souls; thirty-five males and twenty-four females; warriors twelve.

These Indians are well clothed, and look healthy. They derive their subsistence from the fish of the bays of Grand island: herring, trout, and small whitefish, which they take with the spear and in gill nets, and from some game, principally the common red deer, which they kill between this and Lake Michigan; and from their trader, who supplies a part of their provisions in winter. The present trader is Mr. [Louis] Nolan [Nolin[6]], a clerk to Mr. [William] Holiday, of Keewaywenon [Keweenaw] bay. He made last year three packs, worth $900, principally beaver, martens, and muskrats.

Twenty of the Indians now of this village belong rather to Presque Isle, forty miles above, where they live and hunt most of the year. We have travelled to-day forty-three miles. The soil about the trading house is rich and heavily timbered, mostly sugar-maple and birch, and the land is said to be of good quality from here south to Lake Michigan.

June 12.—We were detained at our encampment by a head wind, until 10 o'clock A. M., when, the wind falling, we got out of the western channel, and attempted to make the traverse of a deep bay, twelve miles across in a due west course, but the old sea ran so high that most of my men became sea-sick, and Mr. Schoolcraft, unable to proceed in his canoe, ran into the bay, and made a harbor in the mouth of a small river, where we encamped, having come but about eight miles. This little river has its channel at the mouth through a flat sandstone rock, and is hence called "La Rivière au Galet." It is small, barely admitting our boats. The land here is sandy and poor. Two miles farther, in the bottom of the bay, is the river Aux Trains, and near it an island of the same name.

June 13.—On leaving this bay, we passed a low, rocky shore, four or five miles, and taking a direction due west, which left the shore some distance to our left, we reached Presque Isle [Marquette] at 2 o'clock P. M., a distance of thirty-two miles. I could only see the shore sufficiently to notice its indentations by little bays, and that the land was low, with a sandy beach all the way. Nine miles from the river Aux Trains, we passed Laughingfish river; fifteen miles farther, Chocolate [Chocolay] river; and six miles farther, Dead river, in Presque Isle bay—all small.

Presque Isle is geologically interesting. It is a mass of serpentine rock, about two miles in circumference, rising gradually on all sides, to a height of two hundred feet. The peninsula extends far into the lake, and is connected with the main land by a low, narrow, sandy isthmus, fifty to one hundred yards broad, covered with pine. The rock is the common serpentine, but does not exactly answer to any description of that rock that I have seen, and in some of its characters it resembles chlorite. Its texture is compact, and its grain fine; it is harder than the usual varieties of serpentine, is difficult to cut with a chisel, or to scrape with a knife; its fracture is earthy and uneven, and has a dark dull color, with very small, whitish veins, traversing it in different directions; when polished it exhibits a beautiful, clear, smooth surface, very prettily variegated with different shades of dark green. The mass of the rock is traversed with numerous veins of the precious serpentine, running apparently through it, in different directions, and with different inclinations. These veins may be distinctly traced on the surface, exhibiting the precious serpentine in many varieties of color. They vary from one-fourth to three or four inches in breadth, and each vein is composed throughout of the same variety. Some exhibit it compact, opaque, and almost white, with a light tinge of yellow and green; in others it is seen of a dark, clear, leek green, beautifully translucent. But the finest variety occurs in the broader veins, and in the asbestus form, of a beautiful deep green color, transparent, and polishes well. Its fracture, in the direction of its fibre, exhibits the structure of compact asbestus, and is lustrous, but occasionally shows very small fibres of asbestus; a fracture perpendicular to the fibres shows a very close, compact texture. Another very curious variety was discovered in a small vein; it was of a light green color, opaque, and veined in the manner of the agate.

The great mass of the rock rises gradually from the lake, and on the north side; it was not too steep for us to land on it and walk up its surface, which is generally smooth and regular, and of a very dark, glossy appearance, somewhat resembling hornblende rock. It presents large fissures or openings, however, in one of which I ran my boat three or four times its length, into a little cove with a gravel beach and perpendicular walls around it, where pyrites of iron were found among the pebbles. On the top and north side, the rock is covered with a small growth of trees and bushes; on the east side, for perhaps one hundred feet at the base, it is overlayed with rotten red sandstone, which being broken off perpendicularly toward the lake, shows the line of coincidence of the two rocks as it emerges from the water.

Having procured some specimens of the rock and veins, and made this imperfect examination, which is all that my time would allow, we passed a bay of five miles traverse, in a N. W. course, and touched Granite point,[7] a high bluff peninsula, very like in appearance to Presque Isle, and connected with the shore in a similar manner. The rock however is granite, heaved up in a very irregular and confused mass, presenting numerous irregular fissures, and overlayed with red sandstone for ten or fifteen feet above the surface of the lake, in the same manner as the serpentine rock of Presque Isle. Seven miles farther, in the same direction, brought us across another bay, and to a very rough shore of granite bluffs, where we ran into a small stream which came apparently through a fissure of the rock, and encamped, placing our tents on the rock, sixty feet above our boats, but not more then ten feet from them horizontally.

We have come to-day forty-four miles, and have had high peaked, granitic looking mountains on our left nearly all day. The rock about our encampment shows many large veins of green stone. Mr. Schoolcraft and Dr. Houghton, with the canoe, have their encampment ahead.

June 14.—Leaving our rough harbor, we passed a low sandstone shore of seven or eight miles. A high range of hills was seen off to the south, running N. W. and S. E., probably a part of the chain observed yesterday back of Presque Isle. About ten miles from our encampment, the shore shows a very irregular black rock for two or three miles, which on examination proved to be hornblende rock and hornblende slate. This rock projects into the lake in many points, which present, for some distance from the water, a bare, black, glossy surface. Leaving this, the red sandstone shows itself again, in high, prominent bluff points, embracing deep regular bays, nearly all of which have low sandy shores and beaches in the bottom of their circuit. Six of these bluff points occur nearly in the same N. W. line, in a distance of twenty miles, before we reach Keewaywenon bay; some of them seventy feet high, and all presenting mural precipices to the lake. This sandstone, of which we have seen so much, has a dull, dark red color, occurs in thin strata, and has a very rough, ugly appearance. It contains no organic remains, and is in no way interesting; a thin sandy soil rests upon it, and supports a growth of cedar and pine.

Back of this formation, the chains of granite mountains rise to great heights, and occasionally display the base surfaces of their rugged peaks. They come down to within a mile of the lake, at the entrance of the Keewaywenon bay, where another chain farther back runs off to the south, in the direction of the length of the bay.

From the last of the high sandstone bluff points, described above, the two boats commence the traverse of the great bay Keewaywenon, steering N. 60° W., to a cluster of little rocky islands which are situated in the bay, about eight miles from the shore, and off the mouth of Huron river called the "Huron Islands." These islands, four or five in number, are great masses of granite, grouped near together, of very rugged aspect, and irregular shape. The largest is about a mile in length, one hundred and fifty feet high, and has some little bushes and trees growing in its fissures. The others are bare rock, and served thousands of gulls for nesting places. Some fissures of the large island, on which we landed, are remarkable. One running entirely through the island in a narrow part of it, allows the water to flow through, though at the top, forty or fifty feet above the water, a person may leap over it. South of the Huron islands is the mouth of Huron river, and six miles west of the latter is a long narrow point, called Point Abbaye, which is the western cape of Huron bay, and divides it from Keewaywenon bay. Huron bay opens into Keewaywenon bay between Huron river and Point Abbaye, and runs back to the south and southwest, to a distance of more than twenty miles, almost as far as the great bay of which it is a subordinate branch. It is deep water throughout, but becomes very narrow towards the end, and is used as a fishery by the Indians, affording trout, herring, and whitefish.

Keewaywenon bay is the largest and most remarkable of the whole lake. It is thirty-two miles deep from Point Abbaye, in a southwest direction, and its whole depth, from the extreme point of the peninsula of Keewaywenon, is about seventy miles. This peninsula runs far into the lake, in a northeasterly direction, and seems to approach Granite point in such a

manner as to make the great bay of Keewaywenon to commence properly
between Granite point and the east end of the peninsula. The distance between these two points is between forty and fifty miles. The voyageurs, however, going up the lake, do not consider themselves in Keewaywenon bay
until they get within six or seven miles of Huron river, or the Huron islands.
The breadth of the bay from Huron river is thirty miles, and from the
islands to the nearest point of the peninsula is twenty-two miles; this is the
usual boat traverse in fair weather, and was ours on the present occasion.
We left the islands at 3 o'clock P.M., and crossed the bay in a direction a
little N. of N. W., in five hours and a half, encamping at half past 8, behind
a sandstone bluff point, in a little sandy bay opening to the northeast. All
the traders and voyageurs consider this a dangerous traverse, and boats are
frequently detained for several days on one or the other sides of the bay,
waiting for favorable weather to cross. We were fortunate in having a perfect calm all the way, and crossed without difficulty or apprehension. The
view from the middle of the bay is one of the most beautiful and picturesque of the lake. A high mountain chain that runs along the middle of the
peninsula Keewaywenon, is seen, in front, running far out into the lake,
till its tops seem just emerging above the surface. Behind, to the S. and
S. E. the granite mountains that come down to the lake at Huron river,
show their base surfaces and tops; and the more distant chain which runs
off to the south, gives, in the blue distance, a distinct outline of innumerable high peaks, connected by curves made regular, and well defined by the
distance. To the right and left, in the direction of the length of the bay,
nothing is to be seen but the beautiful expanse of clear water.

Mr. Schoolcraft, in his canoe, left the boats near the Huron islands, and
took the usual canoe route down the bay, intending to visit Mr. [William]
Holiday's trading house, and an Indian village, near the bottom of the bay,
and then make the traverse to Portage river, in a narrow part, and cross the
great peninsula by a portage to the lake on the other side, where he was to
remain encamped till the boats made the tour round. The usual route for
canoes that make the portage, is, from Point Abbaye down the southeastern shore about nine miles, and thence across, in an oblique direction,
about twelve miles, to the mouth of Portage river; up this river six miles,
to a lake twelve miles long and two or three broad, and through this lake
[Portage] to a little river at its head, which is ascended six miles to its
source in a wet savanna; from which, by a portage of one mile, they reach
the lake on the north side of the peninsula, which here, and by this route,
is twenty-five miles broad.

A distance of ninety miles round the point Keewaywenon is saved by
this route across by the portage. Boats, however, must always coast round
the point, and, from the great prevalence of winds and seas so far out in
the lake, this part of the route is frequently tedious, difficult, and dangerous.

The number of Indians about Huron and Keewaywenon bays is one
hundred and thirty, about half of them males, and about twenty-five of
these warriors. They subsist in summer principally on fish, which they take

in sufficient quantities in the bays by gill nets and the spear. Whitefish, herring, and trout are abundant in these bays. In winter they hunt the marten, otter, muskrat, and beaver, and during their hunts are mainly subsisted by their trader, with provisions taken from Mackinac. In this season they depend much on him for their subsistence, and it is questionable if they could now, in the present state of their country, live without the partial supply that he annually distributes to them. Their country is exhausted of the game, deer, bears, &c., that once furnished them food; their fisheries are impracticable at times, from the rigors of winter, and many of them would undoubtedly suffer from starvation were it not for the relief alluded to, which is given them for their furs. They get provisions and goods from their trader, when he first returns from Mackinac, in the fall, and disperse to their several hunting grounds for the winter; from which the men frequently return to bring in their furs, and get fresh supplies. The present trader at this post is Mr. Holiday, of the American Fur Company, who makes this his head quarters for two other posts, at which he has subordinate traders or clerks; one [Louis Nolin] at Grand island, and one [Jean Bt. Dubay] at the mouth of the Ontonagon river. This gentleman has lived and traded at this post for about twenty-four years, only coming out every summer to Mackinac to sell his furs, and get new goods. The Indians of his district now depend on him for their annual supply of clothing, ammunition, &c., for which he usually gets all their furs; but the exhausted condition of their country, requiring, in addition to the usual wants of Indians, a great quantity of provisions, the trade of late years has not been profitable, and his whole returns in furs in the spring seldom exceed by more than one thousand dollars the expenses of his three posts. More than half of his annual stock in trade is provisions. He makes usually at Grand island, three packs; at his own post, on the bay, ten packs; and at the Ontonagon river, two packs; in all, fifteen packs, worth $300 a pack, or $4,500. The furs are principally beaver, martens, rats, otters, and a few bears.

Mr. Holiday is frequently opposed at his several posts by other traders, not of the American Fur Company, but generally with loss to those opposing; for his superior influence over the Indians, acquired from a long residence among them, secures for him all the furs.

June 15.—Started at half past 3 A.M., and commenced the coasting of the peninsula, along its southern shore, in a general direction a little east of northeast, eight miles took us across a sandy bay of no great depth, and to the mouth of a small river, supposed to be "Tobacco river." It runs out in a mouth about ten yards broad, and eighteen inches deep, with a strong current over a flat, sandstone rock, and has three perpendicular falls over the same rock, all of which can be seen at one view from its mouth. The first, 50 yards from the mouth, is five feet; the second, 20 yards farther, seven feet, and the third, 10 yards farther, eight or nine feet. It is remarkable that so large a river should flow from the peninsula, which is in no part more than thirty or forty miles broad, and has a chain of mountains dividing it in the centre.

A few miles from Tobacco river we met Mr. [Charles H.] Oaks, a trader of the American Fur Company, from Lac du Flambeau, his post. He was on his way to Mackinac, with two Mackinac boats, carrying out the furs of his trade the previous winter. Mr. Oaks is the principal trader for the district or department of Lac du Flambeau, between Lake Superior and Green Bay and the Ouisconsin [Wisconsin] river. He has four posts under his charge, Lac du Flambeau, his head quarters; Lac Sable; Chippewa river, and Ouisconsin river; which yield, severally, about the same quantity of furs, but varying, in different years, between 1,500 and $2,000 for each post, and making his whole trade worth between six and eight thousand dollars a year. The Indians of his department get nearly all their goods and necessaries from him, and subsist on the resources of the country, game and fish. In the fall and winter they kill great numbers of the common red deer, which are very plenty about Chippewa river. In the spring and summer, their subsistence is principally fish and berries, and a few furred animals. They sometimes make excursions against the Sioux, but they are not, at present, at war with any other tribe. They are represented as entertaining, generally, a very unfriendly feeling towards the Government of the United States, and are only restrained by fear from depredations on their traders.

Leaving Mr. Oaks, we crossed a large deep bay [Bete Grise] that ran eight or ten miles inland, with a sandy bank and beach for about half its circuit, where the mountains came abruptly down, and form the northern shore of rugged massive rock. From this bay the shore inclines a little more to the east, and presents numerous rocky points, with little coves and sandy bays between. Near the end of the peninsula, the shore becomes more rocky, rough, and abrupt, and the course is east of northeast till we reach the most easterly point, where it suddenly changes to almost due north, varying but two or three degrees west, for a distance of four miles, when it again suddenly changes to nearly due west, along the north side of the peninsula. That part of the shore that runs north and south is the end of the peninsula Keewaywenon, and the most easterly point of it is called "Point Keewaywenon." There is no projecting or attenuated point, but the peninsula is here abruptly truncated in a north and south direction, presenting a rough rocky end, of near four miles, in this course, with a small island, called "Beaver Island," [Manitou] about five miles directly off it in the lake.

This is a dangerous part of the coast for boat navigation. The peninsula offers no safe harbor for boats on its extremity, or near it, on the south side, and we were anxious to get into a harbor on the north side before dark. My boat, however, was several miles behind Mr. Johnston's, and darkness, a strong head wind, and a thick fog, overtook me soon after I turned the eastern point. I was then obliged to grope my way for several miles along a high rocky shore, of most forbidding aspect, against which I was in continual danger of being dashed to pieces, but which I could not leave farther than the length of the oars, lest I should lose sight of it, and get lost and be blown off into the lake. In this situation I continued to hug the shore, and contend with the wind and sea, though not without great apprehension, until half past nine at night, when I ran the boat into a dark opening in the rock, which proved to be a little cove about fifteen feet broad, formed between the main rock and a projecting crag about thirty feet high, and of sufficient length to conceal the boat and protect it from the wind then blowing. The bottom of the cove had been filled in with pebbles for a distance of twenty feet, and on this I encamped, securing the boat by means of cold chisels driven into the rock, to make fast to. My experience to-night proves the necessity, in coasting this lake, of always having a guide in the boat well acquainted with the coast and the situation of its harbors. The severe winds and sudden storms on Lake Superior are proverbial, and it is never considered safe to encamp over night out of a harbor.

This peninsula is the most marked topographical feature of the southern shore of the lake, and is one of the most interesting in its geology and mineralogy. Estimating its length from the bottom of Keewaywenon bay, it is about eighty miles long. It is four miles broad at its extremity, twenty-five or thirty miles in its middle part, twenty miles at the portage, and between thirty and forty at the base, across from the bottom of the bay. A chain of round topped rocky mountains, from 500 to 800 feet high, rise near the end of the point, and extend back, along its centre, to a distance of near forty miles, occupying, for this distance, nearly the whole breadth of the peninsula, and sometimes coming down, at the bottoms of bays, till their bases are washed by the lake. Wherever these mountains have been examined, they are trap rock, and this is undoubtedly the formation of all of them. Several varieties of trap are seen along the shore, and, in fact, constitute all the rock of the shore from Tobacco river. Basalt, amygdaloid, hornblende, greenstone, and rubblestone are among the varieties. The rock of the extreme point, and of the shore, for seven or eight miles beyond, is a coarse crag. It is composed of pebbles, of a dark brown color, showing the same color in their fracture, varying in size from the smallest to more than one foot in diameter, and united by a calcareous cement, which exhibits calcareous spar, in crystals and little veins, in many parts. It does not seem to extend far from the shore towards the mountains, for in many places, where it is worn out to form little coves, the shore, at the bottom of the cove, shows only sand and pebbles that have been worn from the main rock. From its exposed situation so far out in the lake, this rock is much subjected to abrasion from ice, &c., and presents to the lake an irregular, ugly, dark colored surface, generally vertical, and from eight to thirty feet high. Many large portions are detached, and stand out one or two hundred yards in the lake, in huge shapeless masses.

Travelled this day 45 miles.

June 16.—Left my rough encampment, between the crags, at half past four in the morning, in a dense fog, and coasting along the rock in a direction about west; a mile and a half brought us to the "Little Marais"[8] harbor, where Mr. Johnston had preceded us with his boat, and encamped the previous evening, and was now awaiting for us to come up with him, under some apprehension that we had met with accident during the night. This harbor is much used by the voyageurs of Lake Superior, and is the first secure one that occurs after leaving Tobacco river. It is a little basin one hundred and fifty yards across, nearly circular, with a low sandy beach all round, excepting on the side next to the lake, where it is separated by the crag rock spoken of, which forms the shore. The entrance is a narrow gap in the rock; and this again is locked and protected from the lake by a long mass of the same, fifteen feet high, and twenty or thirty broad, placed directly before the entrance, and extending thirty or forty yards on each side of it, parallel to the main rock, leaving a channel open at both ends, and just broad enough to admit boats without oars. The banks of this harbor are much lower than the rocks in front; and there is a small marsh a short distance back; hence, the name of "Marais" for the harbor. Two miles farther brought us to the "Green Rock," a detached block of the crag rock, eight or nine feet high, and as many through the base, to which the voyageurs have given this name, from the color it has acquired from copper green disseminated through it. It is intersected by a vein of calcareous spar, that is also impregnated with the ore, and lies in the water but a few feet from the main rock of the shore, which also presents traces of copper green and copper black.[9]

From the Green rock, the shore has a general direction southwest; and the same rock continues five or six miles, intersected by numerous veins of calcareous spar, all running perpendicular to the shore. Some of them were two feet broad, and could be traced up the rock, and into the lake, as far as we could see. Numerous rocky islands occur along this part a short distance from the main land: some of them bare, and others covered with vegetation. We landed again, twelve miles from the Green rock, at some *copper veins,* discovered by Mr. George Johnston last year. The crag rock had disappeared some miles back, and we now struck upon the amygdaloid, which formed the whole shore, and the base of mountains that rose gradually back. These veins of copper are four or five in number, very near together, and all run perpendicular to the shore. They can be traced by their color many yards into the water, but they soon disappear on the shore, running under the rock. The largest of the veins is about three inches broad at the surface, but it has been excavated for specimens, about two feet in depth, where it is near six inches broad. All the veins are composed alike of the green carbonate of copper and metallic copper mixed. In excavating for specimens in the largest vein, I took out pieces of metallic copper of several ounces weight; and the men picked several pieces from the smaller veins, that occupied their whole breadth, and projected above the general surface of the rock. It would require much time and labor to make such an examination of these veins as would definitely develop their extent and resources, but the inducements their present appearance offers to such an investigation are certainly very strong and flattering.

The rock here is the amygdaloid variety of trap, and presents, all over its surface, innumerable little geodes of quartz gems, agate, cornelian, chalcedony, &c. I knocked many from it, and picked up others that were loose on the shore. And near the *veins* I discovered a large agatized cornelian of more than ten pounds weight, embedded in the rock about a foot under the water; but its surface, having been long exposed to the action of the frost and waves, was very much fractured, and in splitting the rock to obtain it, it was broken into many pieces, most of which rolled into the deep water and were lost. I, however, brought away large geological specimens of the rock, to which much of it is still attached.

After passing four miles more of the same rock, I crossed a beautifully curved bay [Great Sand Bay], about nine miles across and six deep, with a sandy beach, and sand banks sometimes fifty feet high. Leaving the bay, the shore continued regular and less rocky, presenting, alternately, dark sandy beaches and rocky points; and some little bays, with a beach of white sand, and banks of the same. In one of the latter, I encamped at sunset, having travelled this day thirty-two miles.

One of my men caught a trout to-day of more than forty pounds weight, with a trowling line: these fish may be caught in this way along almost any part of the lake, when the boat is sailing.

June 17, (Sunday.)—The last rocky point of this part of the coast was near our encampment, and on examination proved to be amygdaloid, very compact and hard, resembling massive basalt. It showed on its surface many large crystals of amethystine spar, but with their crystals much injured by attrition, the rock being low and subject to be washed by the waves. From the same rock I got a few specimens of the smoky quartz crystals, a very rare mineral. From this point our course was across a bay of fifteen miles traverse, with high banks of light yellow sand and a gravel beach; the shore gently curved, and of no great depth from the line of traverse, which was in direction S. 35° W. When we had made about twelve miles across the bay, we discovered, on the shore, the tents of Mr. Schoolcraft and party, denoting the end of the portage where Mr. S. had promised to wait for us, on parting, three days before, in Keewaywenon bay. This being Sunday, we stopped here for the rest of the day. Mr. S. had come over the portage, from Mr. Holiday's house, the previous afternoon, and Mr. Johnston, who had left me at the copper veins, had arrived at ten o'clock last night.

We have now made the circuit of this great peninsula of the lake, which is, generally, the most difficult part of the whole coast. Running out as it does to near the middle of the lake, at this part it is greatly exposed to winds and rough seas, insomuch that boats are frequently detained seven or eight days at the end of the point, before they can get a calm and smooth water long enough to get round it.

I have been particular in describing this part of our route, because it is the least known of any part of the lake. Its rocks and minerals are nowhere accurately described, and its topography is falsely represented on all the maps of it that I have seen. The most common error in respect to the latter, is the running of the peninsula out too much to the north, and not enough to the east. The true direction of its length is a little (say 4°) east of northeast; and this, as well as I could determine, is also the direction of the chain of hills or mountains that run along its middle. Another error is, the making of two prominent points at the end of the peninsula, and calling one the "East Point" and the other "West Point." These points are not prominent; the shore between them has scarcely any indentation; and, as the line joining them is nearly due north and south, it were fitter to call one end of it North point and the other South point. Such a distinction, however, is not necessary, for the north point is rounded and indeterminate, and the south point is sufficiently protuberant to retain the name of Point Keewaywenon, which is now given to it by the voyageurs and traders, and which is often applied to the whole peninsula.

The mountains run back from the point near thirty miles, but not so far as the portage, which is over level ground, and dry three-fourths of a mile from the swamp to the north end of it, where we are encamped. These mountains show in a few places a bare surface of rock near their summit, but are mostly covered with vegetation, which looks, from the lake, green, and in some parts tall and heavy; it is principally aspen poplar, (populus tremulordes,) birch, (betula papyracea,) cedar, and pine. The forest on the portage and about our encampment is very heavy and strong: birch, sugar-maple, large pine, and hemlock, (pinus canadensis.) The vegetable soil however is but two or three inches thick, and rests on white sand, nearly pure, which forbids the idea of profitable cultivation.

The bank of the lake, at our encampment, is sixty feet high, with a beach of pebbles drifted half way up it. There is no harbor here against northern winds, and our boats were unloaded and drawn out on the beach.

June 18.—A strong northwest wind, which made the lake very rough, forbade the embarkation of Mr. S.'s canoe, and under the prospect of the canoes being detained a considerable time, Doctor Houghton and myself determined to embark in my boat, and run on, with the wind then blowing, to the Ontonagon river, with a view, if the wind still continued, to make a trip to the "Copper Rock," on that river, before Mr. S. could come up, and without detaining the party for that purpose. I accordingly, about noon, loaded my boat, and launched her from timbers into a heavy sea, without accident; but I had scarcely got out when the wind lulled to a calm; and Mr. Schoolcraft, having embarked his boat and canoe, overtook us in a few hours, and we proceeded to La Rivière à Misère [Misery], and encamped 27 miles from the portage. In this distance we passed several bluff points of sandstone rock, from twenty to fifty feet high, with the shore gently curved between them, into sandy bays, presenting high banks of fine yellow sand, and rich green forests back. We passed, successively, the mouths of Salmon Trout, Graverod's[10] and Elm rivers—distant from the portage nine, fifteen, and twenty-two miles—all small, and much filled with sand at the mouths. Our course was, at first, S. 60° W., but, in the latter part, curved in gently to S. 10° W., forming a gradual indentation, at the bottom of which is the little river of our encampment.

There is a range of hills a mile or two back, parallel to the shore of the lake, the sides of which show forests of pine, birch, and sugar-maple; but the country is exceedingly poor in game; and the river has its name, La

Rivière à Misère, or Misery river, from the circumstance of traders having greatly suffered here, in former times, from starvation. There has not
been a trader here for many years.

The shore, about the mouth of the river, is pure marine sand, with little
ridges of pure iron sand—the paper sand of commerce—running near and
parallel to the edge of the water. When this sand is washed up by a gentle
wave, it arranges itself in little rows or ridges, entirely separate and distinct from the siliceous sand which is held in suspension and brought up by
the same wave. This is explained by the difference of specific gravities of the
two sands, and the magnetic affinity of the particles of the iron sand. The
process of the separation may be witnessed at most of the sandy beaches of
Lake Superior, which afford this sand in great quantities. The best time for
collecting it is immediately after the waves have subsided, when it may be
taken in many places perfectly pure, before wind, or other accident, has
mixed it again with the other sand.

This evening was chilly—42° in the air, and 52° in the water. Fahren-
heit.

June 19.—Left the Rivière à Misère at three o'clock in the morning.
The sandy shore continued for about twelve miles, and terminated in a perpendicular bank of sandstone, eight or ten feet high, which is the southwest
point in the traverse of the great bend of the shore that we had just coasted.
Turning this, our direction changed to S. 35° W.; the shore was slightly
curved, and presented the same bank and beach as the preceding bay, with
the same green forest back. We reached the Ontonagon river at eleven
o'clock A.M., distant from our encampment twenty-four miles. The bank,
for some distance before we reached the river, was very low, and the beach
showed more of the iron sand than we had seen at any other part of the
lake. The water for the same distance was shoal and turbid, and of a dark
brown color, which became more deeply tinted as we approached the
mouth of the river. The river is about seventy yards broad at its mouth,
and nearly on a level with the low banks and plains of barren sand which
extend in an area of fifteen or twenty acres, on each side of the mouth. It
is deep, and has a gentle current, excepting at the very mouth, where it is
discharged into the lake, over a shoal sand bar, in a strong current.

Of all the numerous little streams of the lake, which are, not very
properly, dignified with the name of "rivers," this is the most considerable
of the southern shore, to Fond du Lac river; and yet it is only navigable
for canoes 38 miles, and in that distance has many difficult rapids. It has
been noticed by all the travellers of the lake, from Baron La Hontan's[11] to
the present time, for the remarkable mass of native copper found lying on
its shore about forty miles from its mouth, and for the supposed mines of
copper which this mass seemed to indicate in its vicinity. This mass, or
"copper rock," as it has been called, has been so often visited and described, that it has lost a great part of the interest and curiosity which it at
first excited; and the many unsuccessful searches for copper mines, in its
vicinity, have nearly exploded the theory of their existence, the mass referred to being the only trace of copper that has been discovered on the

river. Doctor Houghton and myself were induced to abandon the project of an excursion to the "rock" at this time, as it would have had the effect of detaining the whole party, at least, two days.[12]

This river is also interesting, and has been frequently noticed for its sturgeon fishery. A band of Chippewa Indians have made it their principal dependence for subsistence, as far back as the observations of travellers have extended, and, probably, for a much longer time. The Indians now here, and who still subsist, principally, on these fish, are about seventy-six in number. Their weir or sturgeon dam is in the same place that [Alexander] Henry found it,[13] about seven miles from the mouth of the river, and is built with poles stuck in the mud of the bottom, so close together as to prevent the sturgeon's passing between them, inclined a little down stream, and kept in place at top by transverse poles, to which they are bound with bark, the transverse poles being supported by forked braces, placed below, and inclined up stream. The Indians stand upon supports attached to the weir, and catch the fish with hooks, fastened to long poles, which they move about in the water, at the base of the weir, till they feel the fish against them, when the fish is hooked up by a sudden jerk of the pole. The weir is placed at the foot of the first rapid, and, when the fish are ascending, has an opening made in it to allow them to go up, but which is closed when the fish are descending, and it is at this season that most of them are taken. The water of the river is turbid and of a dark brown color, which prevents fishermen from seeing the fish, or being seen by them. The fish taken here are from two to four feet in length, and are as abundant now as they ever were: and the Indians rely so exclusively on this fishery, that they hunt but little, and make no effort to cultivate the soil beyond the raising of a few potatoes, which are consumed almost as soon as grown. The river presents narrow alluvial bottoms for some miles up, very rich and favorable for the growing of corn, but they are entirely neglected. When the Indians were asked why they did not raise corn, they replied that they had no seed; but this was only eluding the question, for if they had ever manifested a disposition to cultivate it, their trader would soon have supplied the seed, as its successful cultivation there would save him the transportation of a quantity of it from Mackinac for their subsistence and his own.

These Indians looked strong and healthy, but they had a dirty, greasy appearance, and exhaled a fœtid odor, from the oil of the sturgeon. They had their village at the mouth of the river where Mr. Schoolcraft held a council with them, in his tent, soon after our arrival; gave them some tobacco, and had them all vaccinated. He told them, if they would follow him to La Pointe, where he would open some goods, he would give them presents, but they objected to this mode of receiving them, and thought it more consonant with a proper pride and self-respect to have the presents distributed on their own grounds; seeing, however, their objections of no avail, they sacrificed their pride to their cupidity, and agreed to send a canoe with us, for the promised articles. We also met a chief [Mushcosum or Moose's Tail] here from Lac du Flambeau, to whom Mr. Schoolcraft had given a medal last year, who made a speech to Mr. S. in council, and stated, among other things, that he was then on his way to the Saut de Ste. Marie, to deliver himself up to Mr. S. for a murder that had been committed by one of his band [Waba Annimikee] on a Frenchman [Brunet], and to get advice in the matter from the agent; he expressed great regret that the murder had occurred, and represented the difficulty of governing and restraining his young men. He said the other chiefs would not assist him to take the murderer, and bring him out, and he was unable to do it alone. Mr. S., in reply, represented that the President would be very angry when he should learn of this murder, and advised that every effort should be made to bring the murderer to the Saut, and give him up to the agent; and for the present his best course would be to return to his band, and use his influence and power to secure this murderer, and prevent further aggressions.

This chief, also, consented to follow us to La Pointe to get some presents, and promised to pursue the advice of Mr. Schoolcraft.

The Ontonagon band numbers *twenty warriors*; they are too remote from the frontiers of their tribe to engage in the border warfare of the Chippewas and Sioux, and may be considered as *at peace*. They are supplied by their trader, one of Mr. Holiday's clerks, with blankets, ammunition, &c., and provisions when they hunt. They never get many furs, but had taken more the previous winter than usual; principally otter, martens, muskrats, and beaver. Their principal chief had died a short time before, and was universally regretted. The trading house stood on an eminence on the east side of the river; the trader had gone with his furs to Keewaywenon bay, to Mr. Holiday.

From the Ontonagon, our course, S. 70° W., traversed a deep indentation of the shore, and struck it again at a distance of 18 miles, after passing the mouth of Iron river, 15 miles from the former. We then coasted, in the dark, a low rocky shore of sand rock, for 12 miles more, and reached the mouth of Carp river at 2 o'clock in the morning, where Mr. S. with his canoe had preceded the boats in the evening, and encamped. I could find no harbor in the dark shore, nor a place among the rocks where the boat would have been an instant secure, if a wind should have risen, and was forced to continue travelling till I reached the encampment of Mr. S. But this is not the first time, during the voyage, that I have felt the want of a guide in my boat, whose knowledge of harbors and distances might save such unnecessary exposures.

Carp river is quite a small stream, barely admitting boats in its rocky mouth, and drains a part of the Porcupine mountains that rise a few miles back. We saw the tops of these mountains before we reached the Ontonagon, at a distance of more than 40 miles, when they appeared like a long high point, running far out into the lake. On approaching them, however, the appearance of a projecting point was found to be an illusion, produced by the lowness of the land between us and them, which prevents its being seen at the same time; by their oblique direction to the shore and our course, and, perhaps, by those nearest the lake being higher than those back, which would have the effect, at a distance, of making the range seemingly more perpendicular to the shore than it really is. These mountains are near two thousand feet high, and are granite. The sandstone of the shore rises towards them more and more as we approach their bases, and is the same red sandstone that has been noticed on many parts of the coast that we have passed. They come down to the lake a few miles beyond Carp river, and form several miles of the coast, frequently showing a bare surface, but generally covered with a luxuriant heavy forest, similar to that of the country about their base, which is maple, birch, pine, and aspen poplar. Notwithstanding a detention of three hours at the Ontonagon river, we have travelled to-day a distance of 54 miles.

June 20.—Left Carp river at 6 A.M. and in direction S. 30° W. crossed a little sandy bay, with high banks, to Presque Isle river, a distance of six miles. This is one of the largest rivers of the lake, and has it[s] channel from its mouth in a deep ravine of the Porcupine mountains, which here rise immediately from the lake. I went up the river a mile to see two perpendicular falls that occur in this distance; the first, half a mile from the mouth, is 20 feet, and the other, about half a mile further, is 40 feet. The ravine is very deep and narrow, and the sides of it are so thickly covered with a vegetation of large and small trees and bushes, that I could not without difficulty find a point on the acclivity below the greater fall, from which I could get a distinct view of it; it is exceedingly picturesque; the stream above is much contracted between high ledges of rock, and seems to issue out of the mountain; from which, after running a few feet, it is pitched from a shelving sandstone rock into a deep abyss; the water is there deep, and the current gentle for about one hundred yards below, when it is urged with great violence over successive broken ledges of the same rock, until it reaches the next fall of twenty feet; from which it continues in a rapid current over broken rocks almost to its mouth. The quantity of water discharged over these falls is as great as that of the Trenton falls in [Oneida County,] New York, and the scenery is equally beautiful and interesting. Between the two falls the river has another channel, to the east, now dry, but which discharges a portion of its waters, in time of floods, by another mouth; and hence the name "Presque Isle river."

Six miles from this river is Black river, a small stream that drains the south side of the Porcupine mountains. We passed this river two or three miles to the left of our course, (S. 60° W.) and struck the shore at a distance of ten or twelve miles from Presque Isle river, where the sandstone rock is again seen, seven or eight feet above the surface of the water, and inclined up towards the mountains at angles of 30 or 40 degrees; a bank of sand rests on it, and in a few miles the rock disappears entirely; and the sand bank, attaining an elevation of 80 or 90 feet, encloses the Montreal bay, at the bottom of which is Montreal river, twenty-one miles from Black river. We left the shore at the eastern cape of this bay, and made a traverse of twenty-one or twenty-two miles, in a direction due west, to the island of La Pointe [Madeline]; thus leaving Montreal river and Mauvaise [Bad] river of the same bay very far to the left. Montreal river is one of the largest of the lake, but, from its numerous falls and rapids, its navigation is not practicable, excepting near its source; and the route of the traders of Lac du Flambeau, up this river, starts from its mouth, in a portage of near 50 miles 120 pauses. Seven or eight hundred yards from its mouth, it has a perpendicular fall of 14 feet, below which the Indians have a sturgeon weir, like that at the Ontonagon.

Twelve miles further round the bay is Mauvaise river, navigable for canoes 100 miles, which formed a part of Mr. Schoolcraft's route last year.

We reached La Pointe island at 10 o'clock at night, having travelled to-day a distance of 54 miles by the shore, but which was much shortened by our great traverse of Montreal bay.

June 21.—Mr. Schoolcraft, having some business to transact with the Indians of this place, and those that followed us from the Ontonagon, we did not leave until the afternoon. The island of La Pointe, on which we en-camped, is the first and largest of a group of about twenty others, which extend about thirty miles farther towards Fond du Lac, and nearly lock the coast for this distance, lying at distances between one and five miles from the main land. This island has some three or four names on the maps; as, Montreal, St. Michael's, Middle island, &c., but is called the "Island of La Pointe" by all the traders and voyageurs, and any change from this name would only lead to confusion, and is improper; the name is taken from La Pointe Chegoimegon [Chequamegon], a long point that runs out from the main land, from the south, to within about a mile of the island, the name of which is abbreviated, and called "La Pointe." Point Chegoi-megon separates Chegoimegon bay from Montreal bay, which we crossed to reach the island, the former being a bay of 10 or 12 miles depth, and lying south of the island.

This island was, in former times, a place of rendezvous for the Chippewa tribe, where they held great councils on matters which concerned the whole nation. It was also the residence of a large and powerful band. But a change of national policy, by which the several bands act less in concert, and a general impoverishment of the country in their peculiar means of subsist-ence, has destroyed its importance as a place of general council, and re-duced its particular band to about one hundred and eighty-four souls, who are dispersed about the bays and islands in the vicinity, and subsist almost entirely on fish, excepting at the time of their winter hunts, when their trader furnishes them with corn and flour. They take sturgeon from Mont-real river, and small fish from this and Mauvaise river, and whitefish and trout from the lake, which latter they take in gill nets. They have at pres-ent between thirty and forty warriors, and are *at peace,* the Sioux, their natural enemies, being too remote for their excursions. They are supplied with all the articles of Indian trade, by American traders, who also get all their furs.

Their present trader is Mr. [Lyman M.] Warren, a gentleman of the American Fur Company, who makes this his residence, and the head quar-ters of an extensive department and district, embracing the extent of country S. W. of La Pointe, between Snake and St. Croix rivers, and Lac

Courte Oseille [Oreilles] and Chippewa river. The value of his trade, annually, is as follows: At the post of La Pointe $2,000, or 250 beaver skins, 500 martens, 50 bears, 1,000 to 1,500 rats, and 20 or 30 otters, all of excellent quality. At the posts on the St. Croix, $4,000, principally rats, bears, and otters, with a few martens, raccoons, deer skins, foxes, fishers, and beaver. At Snake river post $1,000, same furs as at St. Croix river. At Lac Courte Oseille and Lac Chetac $1,500, principally bears, otter, martens, rats, fishers, and minks. At Chippewa river and Lac Vassale $2,500, same furs as the last, but more beaver. The furs of Chippewa river and Lac Courte Oseille are of a better quality than those farther towards the Mississippi, as of the St. Croix and Snake rivers. The whole seven posts under Mr. Warren yield annually about eleven thousand dollars worth of furs; but each post requires a clerk and some men, and consequent expense, insomuch that the trade is by no means as profitable as it would at first seem to be.

The Indians of this department, excepting those about Lake Superior, subsist chiefly on wild rice and game, such as deer, bears, &c., and generally also supply their particular trader with these articles of provisions.

Mr. Warren has lived for a number of years at his present residence on the island of La Pointe, and has given to this little spot an appearance of civilization. He has built a large, comfortable dwelling, a storehouse, and eight or ten outhouses, which, with the houses of a Mr. [Michael] Cadotte and family, and those of the subagent, formerly at La Pointe, make almost a village. All the buildings are handsomely situated, on a rise of ground, about two hundred yards from the lake, and immediately back of them are cultivated and enclosed fields, in which oats, peas, beans, potatoes, &c. were growing finely. Wheat would grow here, but the want of means to make it into flour prevents its cultivation. The season is too short, and the soil too light to grow corn with any success. The soil of the island is nearly as good as any that I have seen on the lake, but it is light and sandy, and would be thought poor land in Ohio or Indiana. It, however, produces a good luxuriant grass, (genus alopecurus,) which, I observed, Mr. Warren had appropriated in the raising of horses and cows. The timber is sugar-maple, birch, and pine.

There was a mission established on the island last summer, by the Presbyterian Board of Foreign Missions, and Mr. [Sherman] Hall, the minister then sent out, was here now with his lady. The plan and object of this mission is to convert the Indians to the doctrines of Christianity, by preaching; and to teach a school for their children, at which the latter are to be clothed, and subsisted, and educated, at the expense of the Mission Board and other charities. It is purposed to teach them the rudiments of the English language, and to read and write in their own.

Mr. Hall's progress, however, in the accomplishment of these benevolent ends, has not hitherto been very flattering. The Indians have manifested rather an aversion for his doctrines, and a disposition not to listen to his advice. All that lived on the island left it soon after he arrived, and they had learned his motives; and a fear for their own peculiar institutions, or some other cause, still keeps them in a great measure aloof from him. They refuse to come to church, or to attend divine worship, and the only direct means now left him of operating on their minds to his purpose is to visit them at their villages and in their lodges, where, by making their hospitality subserve, he is kindly received, and listened to with seeming attention, but still with little or no apparent effect; none of the Indians having as yet shown any willingness to embrace his doctrines, excepting one Indian man, who has been for some time laboring under a severe disease of the lungs. Mr. Hall is not however discouraged, but hopes, by means of his school, and other efforts, to effect many beneficial results. His school at present contains twelve scholars, all quite young and mostly half breeds, the Indians having shown also an unwillingness to give him their children to instruct.

This mission at La Pointe, and Mr. [Abel] Bingham's at Saut de Ste. Marie, are the only missions that I know of in the Chippewa country.[14] The former has been established several years. The means and efforts at each have been similar, and like unproductive. And, until more successful methods can be adopted by both to accomplish the benevolent designs of those contributing to their support, the propriety of sustaining them at such great expense may well be questioned.

These northern Indians are generally wild, untamed, and unsubdued; they have none of the arts, institutions, or manners of the whites; and their prejudices in favor of their own peculiar habits and institutions, which have descended to them from their forefathers, are engrafted and rooted in their very nature, insomuch that their removal, by the ordinary means of teaching, preaching, and advice, is rather a speculative theory than a result that experience teaches us to expect. The good and humane motives of the missionaries to these Indians cannot be doubted, but the propriety and efficacy of their *method* of proceeding in their work of conversion may be fairly judged of and estimated by the effects actually produced; and these, so far as my observation and experience extend, are by no means proportionate to the expense and labor employed.

The present condition of most of the Chippewa Indians is deplorable. They are mostly very poor. Their country is becoming every day more exhausted of the means of subsistence hitherto used, and they are making no preparations to provide any others. Something seems necessary to be done by humanity, to prepare them for the approaching condition of their country, and to protect them from its threatened calamities. The first thing that a view of their actual condition suggests is to teach them to *cultivate the soil,* and obtain in this way *a subsistence,* which their impoverished woods and forests must very soon refuse to their increased population. This would lead them gradually from their wild pursuits and precarious mode of living, and lay the foundation for the adoption of other customs of civilized life, and among them perhaps Christianity. The Indians cannot be induced to make a change in their habits and manners, unless the advantage be immediate and tangible, and is made evident to their senses. Their prejudices in favor of their own way of thinking and acting are too strong to be easily eradicated; and to expect to effect an entire change of their opinions and habits, by appeals to their understanding, in the manner of preaching Christianity, is to expect more than a knowledge of Indian character will justify. And as long as the missionaries pursue their present method with the Chippewa Indians, so long will their exertions be, in a measure, useless; and until an entirely new system is adopted and pursued, no extensive or permanent change in this people need be expected.

Near the present mission, on the island of La Pointe, are the traces of an old missionary establishment, occupied by the Jesuit missionaries, at a very early period of the settlement of Canada.[15] Very few vestiges of the principles there taught, however, are now to be discovered in the manners or character of the Indians at present in the vicinity.

Mr. Hall has not yet constructed any buildings for his establishment, but at present occupies houses of Mr. Warren, for a school and dwelling. Notwithstanding their remote situation, he and Mrs. Hall seem contented, cheerful, and happy; although, with regard to Mrs. Hall, there is not a single white woman or female that speaks her language, within hundreds of miles of her. Mr. Boutwell, the reverend gentleman who is travelling with us, is to stop and remain with this mission, on our return.

We left the island at 6 o'clock P.M. The channel between the island and the main land, to the west, is from three to five miles broad. Our course through it was due north, to a point of the main land, ten miles ahead, where the shore begins to bend off to the northwest. But, seeing that I could not reach the main land before dark, I turned a little to the east of the proper course, and encamped on a small island about eight miles from La Pointe. Mr. Schoolcraft, with the other boat, crossed the channel, and encamped on the main land. The island of my encampment is called Spirit island,[16] and is held in sacred veneration by the Indians, insomuch that they never hunt or encamp on it. It is about two miles long; its banks rise steeply from the lake, and it is covered all over with a thick, heavy forest of yellow pine. Doctor Houghton, who had gone in the morning in Mr. Schoolcraft's canoe, to vaccinate the Indians of a village at the bottom of Chegoimegon bay, overtook me about 11 o'clock at night, and went on to Mr. S.

June 22.—Left our encampment at 3 o'clock A.M. and in about six miles came up with Mr. Schoolcraft and party, encamped in a sandy bay that they had reached the night before. In a few miles more, we passed all of the group of islands, called sometimes the Twelve Apostles. They are beautifully situated with respect to each other, are all high, and covered with a luxuriant growth of vegetation, and form the most interesting feature of this part of the lake. Twenty-five miles from La Pointe, we passed a rocky bluff point of sandstone rock, called the Detour, from which the Great Fond du Lac bay may be considered as commencing. Our course here changed to south 80° west, and we could see distinctly the mountains on the opposite side of the bay and lake. Here we met a Mackinac boat, with Mr. [J. W.] Abbott, a trader from Leach lake, who said the returns from that quarter were principally bears this year; and that the Leech Lake

Indians had lately gone on a war excursion against the Sioux. At 1 o'clock
passed Birch Bark point, a flat, prominent point, that is midway between
La Pointe and Fond du Lac river, and hence, frequently, called Middle
point. It has steep, sandy banks, ten or fifteen feet high, resting on sand
rock, and is covered with a small growth of birch, aspen, and some large
dead timber. The whole shore to-day is much serrated, forming deep, sandy
bays, with regularly curved shores and high banks of sand. The prominent
points showed mostly an imperfect red sandstone, sometimes in perpendicular bluffs twenty or thirty feet high. High hills are seen to the left, but
the forest does not present the rich verdure of the mountains round La
Pointe, and of the lake generally. Our course from Birch Bark point was
S. 60° W. and we encamped at sunset, on a beach of dark sandstone gravel,
having come to-day fifty-eight miles. Mr. Schoolcraft and party encamped
ahead. We passed to-day Raspberry river, Cranberry creek, and Sandy
river.

June 23.—Following a plain shore about three miles, I came to an
Indian village, at the mouth of Bois Brulé river, where Mr. Schoolcraft had
encamped the previous evening. From this river the shore is sandy, very
regular, and falls off to the south, but our course to Fond du Lac river was
more to the west, and left the shore many miles. The beach and bank round
the end of the bay are very low and flat, and the entrance to Fond du Lac
river is not discernible a short distance from the shore. I was near missing
the entrance, by being in some degree guided by Farmer's map of Michigan,[17] on which this bay and the entrance, like most of the coast, are very
inaccurately delineated. I had approached very near, and was sailing past
it, when Mr. Schoolcraft, who was there waiting for me, attracted me to it
by making signals with flags. We entered the river about 10 o'clock A.M.
having come from our encampment of last night twenty-four miles; and,
exposed as we have been on the lake, for the last sixteen days, we were
glad to leave it. My boat being slower than the other, and both slower
than Mr. Schoolcraft's canoe, the whole party had seldom travelled together, and as in my boat I had no guide, or even a map of the coast that
I could depend on, I was often, in the course of the trip, exposed to danger
and inconvenience. The difficulties of travelling in the night, after I had
once or twice experienced them, determined me to encamp alone, rather
than attempt to overtake Mr. Schoolcraft after dark; and I have, accordingly, been several nights separated from the rest of the party. There is
very little danger in coasting the south of Lake Superior in boats, if there
is a person to guide who is well acquainted with the shore, and particularly
the position and distances of the harbors. The harbors for boats are numerous and good, and notwithstanding the suddenness of the rising of
storms on the lake, it is easy for a person acquainted with the coast, to make
a harbor before the lake gets too rough for a good boat. An accurate map or
chart of the coast would also subserve an excellent purpose, to avoid accidents and inconvenience, but none such has yet been made. The one I
have with me (Farmer's) is, perhaps, the most so of any yet published,
but is far from being a proper guide, and it would be dangerous to depend

on it for any thing like an accurate delineation of the shore, or the relative positions of the numerous bays that must be known to enable one to travel in security and safety. The heavy fogs of the lake are great annoyances to the voyageur; they are frequently so thick and heavy, as to obscure all objects at a distance of twenty or thirty yards, and in such cases compel the traveller to hug closely all the sinuosities of the shore, which are so numerous, deep, and irregular, as to make the distance more than twice what it would be to cross from point to point. I have often, in a fog, run to all points of the compass in less than an hour, and have sometimes, on the clearing up, found myself so far in a deep bay, that I had twice as far to row, to get out of it, as the distance across it. The fogs, too, are often brought up by a wind so suddenly as to leave a boat in the traverse of a bay, far from land, and without any point to direct the steering. In such cases, if the boat has a compass, the proper direction may be preserved; but, without one, there is danger of going out into the lake. The remedy, then, of the practised voyageur is to observe the direction of the wind that brings the fog with respect to the land, and to steer accordingly; and it is remarkable, that scarcely any of the traders' boats carry a compass, when the inconvenience and danger often resulting from such neglect must be experienced on every trip.

The mouth of Fond du Lac river, or "The Entrance," as it is called by the traders and voyageurs, is about eighty yards broad, but is shallow, and would not admit a vessel of three or four feet draught. It expands immediately into two bays, to the right and left, separated from each other by a small island near and directly in front of the entrance. The mouth seems to be in the very end of the lake, and hence it is properly called *Fond du Lac* river. A river that enters the left bay of The Entrance, is also as aptly called *"La Rivière à Gauche* [Nemadji or Left Hand River]." The bays to the right [Superior Bay] and left [Allouez] lie in their length parallel to the shores of the lake, from which they are only separated by low sandy tongues of land, very much attenuated, and sustaining a few little scattering pines. The point to the right, entering, is near fifty yards broad near the end, but it afterwards narrows, and runs back for about two miles, with a breadth of from twenty to forty yards. Our course was through the right hand bay, N. 60° W. for four miles, to a strait one hundred yards broad, by which, in a distance of two hundred yards, we entered another bay [St. Louis Bay], long and narrow, and which contracted gradually to the very narrow, crooked channel of the river.

There was, formerly, a trading house near the entrance, but it has been abandoned and destroyed, and the present house for all the Fond du Lac country is twenty miles above.

The river for this distance is very crooked and winding, but its general course up is southwest; the channel is of variable breadth, and generally deep; the shore is irregular, and presents alternately, on either hand, marshes, bluff sand banks and hills, and is cut up by numerous channels, or "pockets," from ten to one hundred yards broad, which run out straight and generally perpendicular to the river, frequently extending as far inland as we could see. These are separated by long tongues or promontories, of semi-cylindrical shape, rounded on either side up to the summit, fifty or sixty feet, and covered with a thick growth of small trees, aspen, birch, tamrack, (pinus pendulus,) and other species of pine. Several of these singular promontories occur in many places in succession, parallel to each other, with channels between, and present a formation and appearance altogether peculiar.

We arrived at the trading house at 4 o'clock P.M. The river is here penetrating a chain of mountains, is more regular in its course, and has its channel more confined.[18] The trading house is situated at the base of the mountain, on a narrow piece of bottom, three or four hundred yards broad, which is rich, and excepting the gardens, where the trader raises abundance of potatoes, is covered with a very tall, green, luxuriant grass, (principally poa compressa.) We met here Mr. [William] Aitkin, the chief of the department of the country beyond Fond du Lac, and all his clerks, to the number of fifteen or twenty, and their engagées, all just ready to start for Mackinac on their regular summer trip.

This is called the "Fond du Lac Post," and was formerly the head quarters of an extensive district, called "The Fond du Lac Department." The department is still the same, but Mr. Aitkin, of the American Fur Company, the principal of it, has removed his head quarters to the Mississippi, at Sandy lake, which is more central in respect to his several subordinate posts. This is still, however, a place of rendezvous for all his clerks, preparatory to their embarking in boats, with their annual stock of furs, for Mackinac. Here, too, on their return in the fall, a partial distribution of the goods is made; the boats are left, and the navigation in all directions begins *in bark canoes*. The buildings here consist of a dwelling, three or four stores, a large house for the accommodation of the clerks, and some other buildings for the engagées, or Frenchmen. They are handsomely situated on the bank of the river, and directly in front is an island, of about two miles circuit, of very rich soil, and a forest of large elm, and on which the Indians now assembled have their lodges.

Mr. Aitkin very politely gave me the following information in relation to his trade, the Indians, &c.

His department embraces an extent of country from Fond du Lac, north to the boundary line, west to Red river, and south to near the falls of St. Anthony, on the Mississippi, and contains nine permanent posts, from which returns are made every year, viz. Fond du Lac, Lake Superior, on the north side, at Grand Portage, Rainy lake, Vermillion lake, at the head of Fond du Lac river, Red lake, Pembina settlement on Red river, Red Cedar lake, Leech lake, and Sandy lake, Mr. Aitkin's residence. For facilities of the trade there are several other smaller posts, as at Lake Winnipeg [Winnibigoshish], Lake Travers [Bemidji], mouth of Crow Wing river, and others; but these are subordinate, severally, to some one of the larger posts named, which is considered as making the whole "return" for its particular district.

Mr. Aitkin's returns of this year are less than usual, and are as follows:

From Fond du Lac post $2,000, Grand Portage $1,000, Rainy lake $4,000, Vermillion lake $2,000, Red lake $2,000, Pembina $2,500, Red Cedar lake $1,500, Leech lake $5,000, Sandy lake $5,000. The furs from all the posts are of nearly the same kind, and principally martens, muskrats, beaver, otter, foxes, and bears; the proportion of bear skins this year being very great at most of the posts west of Fond du Lac. The whole value of his furs is $25,000; and his expenses in procuring them have been $31,000, leaving a balance against the trade of $6,000.

The trade of this department is perhaps more precarious than that of any other district of the American Fur Company to the north. Here the country, and, consequently, the "hunts," are most affected by dry and wet seasons; and here the British trader comes in direct competition with the American. All along the lines, at Grand Portage, Rainy lake, Lake of the Woods, and Pembina, the British traders get the greater part of the furs of the American Indians; and it is represented that even in the interior as far as Leech lake, Winnipeg lake, Red lake, and Vermillion lake, they secure a great part of the trade by inducing the Indians to carry their furs to them across the line. This is done by paying more for them than American traders can afford to pay; by a free use of whiskey, which is a most potent article in Indian trade, and which is prohibited to American traders, except in small quantities, at a few frontier posts; and by a skilful fostering and management of a strong feeling of attachment which all the Indian of this district are represented to entertain for the British Government and the Hudson Bay Company.

The Indians at Fond du Lac, Grand Portage, Vermillion lake, and Sandy lake are chiefly subsisted by the traders. At the other posts of this department they have abundance of fish and large animals of the forest, and live comfortably. At Red lake they sell great quantities of corn to their trader, which is sent off to other posts.

The population of the Fond du Lac band is 193, of whom about 45 are warriors. They are, however, at peace, as they are too far from the Sioux to go against them. Their country is very poor in all animals for food, and their particular trader furnishes most of their living; the rest they get from the fish of the lake; whitefish and trout, which they take in gill nets, and from the few furred animals they kill. Since the stoppage of whiskey in the trade, they are increasing very rapidly; there being more children born, and fewer deaths among them, from neglect of drunken mothers. They are miserably poor; and although their country is, in a measure, exhausted, and must soon refuse a supply to their increasing wants, they have not reflection, or foresight, or providence enough to save themselves from starvation, by cultivating the soil; which, in many parts, is rich, and would, with little labor, afford them abundance.

There are about 150 Indians encamped on the island here at present; some of them belong to Sandy lake, and some came with us from Bois Brûlé river. Among the latter is an Indian of some distinction, *Yellow Head* [Oza Windib], from Red Cedar lake, who was on his way to visit the agent at Fort Brady, but is now returning with us.

The Indians of other posts of Mr. Aitkin's department, through which we are to pass, will be more particularly spoken of when we reach them. This being Sunday, Mr. Boutwell preached to the Indians through the interpreter.

June 25.—The Indians assembled early in the morning, and regaled us with their usual dance, after which Mr. Schoolcraft held a council and talk with them, and distributed a few presents. Mr. Aitkin embarked all his furs in seven large Mackinac boats, all well manned, and each under the command of a clerk, and started them down the lake. Many of his Frenchmen have Indian wives and families, who are left here till they return.

Mr. Schoolcraft made an arrangement with Mr. Aitkin for bark canoes for the transportation of our whole party above, which we will receive at the head of the Portage, and, as my men are entirely ignorant of their management, he has employed three Indians to go with me to Sandy lake. We embarked in our boats, and ascended the river, over several rapids, two miles farther, to the foot of the grand portage of Fond du Lac river, the head of boat navigation. From here Mr. S. sent his boat back to the Saut, by Canadians, whom he had brought along for the purpose; and I employed an Indian [Mongozid or Loon's Foot] to take mine back to the mouth of the Bois Brulé river, where we purpose to strike the lake again, returning. Here a new scene commenced. Our baggage and provisions for sixty days were to be transported by carrying over a rough portage of nine miles. This was a familiar business with Mr. Schoolcraft's Canadians, but entirely new to the soldiers; the manner of the carrying being altogether different from any thing they had ever experienced. For this purpose the pork had previously been put up in kegs, containing about 75 lbs. each, and the flour in bags of 80 lbs. The mode of carrying is by a leather strap called a "portage collar," composed of a broad piece that is applied to the forehead, and two long tags, which attach to the piece to be carried. *"A load"* for a Frenchman consists of two "pieces," when the pieces are of convenient shape, as a keg of pork and a bag of flour, (from 160 to 200 lbs.) The first to which the portage collar is fastened, is adjusted to rest on the lumbar vertebrae, or small of the back; and the second when practicable, as in case of the bag, is placed longitudinally, one end resting on the keg, and the other along the back of the head, so that when the body is stooped, in the manner of carrying, the weight of the bag is between the shoulders, near the back of the neck; the second piece is also frequently placed transversely on the shoulders, but always, if practicable, in such a manner as to rest its weight very far up towards the neck; when the load is not so adjusted as to sustain the head against the force of the portage collar to draw it back, it is supported by the hands clasped behind it.

The experience of traders, and observation of the manner of the Indians, have proved this to be the most convenient way of carrying, in this country. It is accordingly practised by all; and every thing to be transported over portages, is put up with a view to this method of the portage collar. All the portage roads, too, are selected with the same view.

The portage was commenced by ascending a hill 100 feet high, with an acclivity of about 45°.[19] No pains have ever been bestowed to make a road up it; and the ascent is by means of little imperfect steps, just large enough for the toes, that wind up the hill without any regularity as to direction or relative position. The Frenchmen commenced with full loads, but the soldiers, excepting one or two, were permitted to carry only half loads, or one piece, and even this was found to be more than some of them were equal to. One of them, a very strong man, fell on the hill with a keg of pork, and was disabled.[20]

The portage road, after the hill, was rough, narrow and crooked—a mere uncut path through bad woods, but we got over three pauses, or a mile and a half of it, and encamped on the bank of the river, at a place called the "Roche Galet," from the flat sandstone rock over which the river here runs. A number of Indians followed us from Fond du Lac house, and encamped with us.

June 26.—We commenced carrying at four o'clock in the morning, and continued it until near sunset, or eight o'clock in the afternoon, and passed over twelve pauses, of near half a mile each. The portage road continued a little, narrow, crooked path, with bushes crowding it on either side, winding round trees, through marshes, over ridges, and across ravines, and presenting all the irregularities and inconveniences of a rude trail through difficult woods. There has been little or no cutting to clear it out, and all the bridging consists of a few small poles, laid in the length of the path, which serve rather to annoy than to assist the passenger. No idea can be formed of the difficulty of this portage without witnessing it. The men, with heavy loads, are sometimes forced to wade through a swamp of half a mile, full of roots and bushes, and over their knees in mire at every step. And where the road is dry, it is generally over a hill, or across a gulley, the steep banks of which are worse to pass than the swamps.

When we stopped at night, my men, and even the Canadians, were literally fagged out. Two of the soldiers had snagged their feet, and were disabled, and all of them were galled in the back, by the kegs, in such a degree as to make their loads very painful; and yet they have carried only half loads all the day; whereas the Frenchmen and some of the Indians have carried full loads each time. It requires an experience of years to habituate men to carrying in this way; and the life and habits of soldiers by no means fit them for such labor.

I had four or five Indian women, and as many Indian men, carrying for me, and without these I would not have made half the distance. The Indian women carry better than the men, being less indolent, and more accustomed to it. I saw a small young Indian woman, at the close of the day, carry a keg of one thousand musket ball cartridges, for a distance of one mile, without resting, and most of the distance through swamp that was frequently over her knees; this too after having carried heavy loads all day, and when, with less exertion than she had made, my strongest men were exhausted.[21]

We encamped on the portage near a creek, which enabled us to wash off a little of the mud of the swamps, which we had carried with us all the day. Doctor Houghton had many cases of strains, bruises, and snagged feet, this evening.

June 27.—Owing to the excessive fatigues of yesterday, we did not recommence the carrying till six o'clock, though the sun rose at four. We had four regular pauses to make yet, to the end of the portage, which, for greater ease, were divided into six; there was more mud and mire on the three first than on those of yesterday; the last, only, was dry and good. We accomplished the whole, and arrived at the end of the portage by twelve o'clock, where we encamped, and employed the rest of the day in getting out our canoes, and making arrangements to travel in them.

The general direction of this portage has been a little west of northwest; leaving the river in some parts four or five miles, and touching it but once, at La Roche Galet, from the commencement. It is on the north side of the river, and the land about it is rich, excepting the swamps. In some places we passed groves of sugar-maple, but the general growth is birch and pine; some of the latter being very large and beautiful, measuring eighteen feet in circumference at the base. The length of the portage is nine miles, which is divided into nineteen pauses; the term "pause" being applied to the distance between two resting places, and hence the *pause* is the unit of measure for all portages. We have passed by, in this distance, many rapids and falls of the river; and a perpendicular fall, said to be thirty feet. The river is still rapid at the head of the portage, and shows in its banks and bed a coarse, hard, argillite rock, in place.

June 28.—The necessary arrangements for travelling in our *bark canoes* having been completed the previous evening, we embarked in them at seven in the morning. I have two canoes, in which I have distributed, equally, my men and their provisions and baggage, with two Indians in one, in the bow and stern, and one Indian in the other, in which I go myself.

The river for three miles, to Portage à Couteaux, is a series of difficult rapids; and my men, totally unaccustomed to canoes, had great difficulty in ascending them, being obliged for this purpose to wade in the rapids, and drag or push them along. The river, in this distance, runs over argillite rock, which rises on both sides of the channel, with strata nearly vertical, in high broken and precipitous banks, presenting a scenery altogether peculiar to this kind of rock. The Portage à Couteaux, or knife portage, commences on the west side of the river, at the foot of a rapid, too strong to be ascended in canoes, and in which the channel of the river is divided by a small island, of the argillite; rising, abruptly, to a height of about 100 feet, from a base of but little greater diameter; which, piled up, as it is, in the utmost confusion and irregularity, with many small cedars and pines, that have taken feeble tenure between the vertical strata of the rock, projecting from its rugged sides, in all directions, is remarkable and picturesque.

The portage begins by a steep ascent of the argillite rock, which is seen bare along the greater part of the path, making it broken and difficult; but, being dry nearly all the way, it is much preferable to any part of the grand portage below. It is but three pauses, or a mile and a half in length, and has been aptly called "Portage à Couteaux," from the knife-like effect of the slates on the shoes and moccasins of the voyageurs. It runs along a ridge, and the land on each side is low, swampy, and good for nothing.

The rapids were strong for two or three miles above the portage, and filled with boulders of hornblende rock which made their ascent, by the method of wading, very difficult, the men frequently slipping from the rocks, and plunging over their heads in the water—in great danger of drowning, but much to the amusement of my Indian guides. After the rapids, was a broad, smooth river of gentle current, and banks of the richest soil, supporting a fine growth of maple, elm, ash, poplar, &c. which denoted the rich character of the country. The Indians gave us to understand that this kind of land extended some distance back, and was a bear hunting ground.

We encamped this night nine and a half miles from Portage à Couteaux at the foot of another series of rapids, having travelled this day about 13 miles.

June 29.—Started at half past four in the morning, and continued in rapids through argillite rock again, for about four miles, which occupied us until 11 o'clock. Mr. Schoolcraft and party got ahead of me very fast, as they were always enabled to do in rapids, by the superior skill of their Canadian voyageurs, who could stand up in the canoes, and pole them along; whereas I, for fear of upsetting, could not allow my men to attempt this method, but continued the comparatively slow and secure one that I at first adopted. My canoes, too, were frequently broken, by the awkwardness of the men, allowing them to drive against the rocks; and delay was thus occasioned in making repairs.

From the narrow rocky channel and steep broken banks of the rapids, the river suddenly expanded to three or four hundred yards breadth, with a gentle current; the rocks entirely disappeared; the banks were twelve or fourteen feet high, and exhibited a character, as to soil and timber, similar to that of the smooth part of the river, passed yesterday, and not unlike that of some of the Western rivers, with their extensive rich bottoms and heavy native forests. It is probable, however, that this land is swampy, back, as indicated by the swarms of moschetoes [mosquitoes] that infested us.

Mr. Schoolcraft and party kept ahead, and I encamped alone, having come about 35 miles.

June 30.—Passed several rapids, and a country much the same as yesterday, (23 miles,) until we reached the mouth of East Savanne river, where our route left Fond du Lac river. Mr. S. had encamped here the previous night, but had gone on without waiting for me.

The East Savanne river is a little, narrow, and very crooked stream, having its source in wet meadows and swamps, about 30 miles from its mouth, and running in a general direction northeast, in a very direct line from Fond du Lac river to Sandy lake, on the Mississippi, where we are going; we accordingly ascended it twenty-four miles to the *Savanne Portage*. The country at first was low and rich, afterwards more elevated, and some pine ridges, and the last ten or twelve miles was through a wet savanne, from a half to two and three miles broad, bordered by tamrack and cedar swamps. The river was from ten to thirty feet broad, and very crooked all the way, but particularly so through the savanne, where canoes might be a mile or more apart in the actual length of the river, and only a few yards, in a direct line. The channel was generally seven or eight feet deep; and part of the savanne was so much overflowed that canoes could pass over it, through the grass. About a mile below the portage the river forks, and the channel, though still deep, is so very narrow and crooked that canoes can scarcely turn the shorter bends. The meadow here is dry, and is grown over with a most beautiful, luxuriant, and heavy growth of grass—a species of carex, or sedge. I landed at the portage near the end of this meadow, at 6 P.M., where I found, by a note left for me by Doctor Houghton, that Mr. S. having preceded me about six hours, had gone through four pauses of the portage to encamp. I got part of the baggage through the first pause, and encamped where we landed, in an atmosphere of moschetoes.—Journey this day 47 miles.

July 1, (Sunday.)—It rained constantly, and in torrents, without a prospect of cessation; but the unpleasant situation of our encampment, and my anxiety to overtake Mr. S., who I knew would not travel to-day, determined me to proceed. At the end of the first pause, which was a perfect mud hole throughout, the swamp had water enough to float our loaded canoes, and we accordingly embarked them in a little canal or channel which had been slightly worn through the swamp by the travelling of the traders, and in which the mud was thin enough to allow the canoes, loaded only with our baggage, to be dragged along without much difficulty, more than that of wading through the mire. But this was at every step over the knees, and in many places up to the waist. We worked our canoes and baggage, in this way, through two pauses, or about a mile, as far as we could, and carried the canoes and baggage one pause farther, the greater part of which was a continuation of the swamp, to Mr. Schoolcraft's encampment, on a dry ridge. It rained on us all the way, and my men were much exhausted, from the difficulty of transporting the baggage in the manner described.

July 2.—The ridge of high land, on which we were encamped, was but little elevated above the swamps, but was rich and dry, sustaining a heavy forest of sugar-maple, birch, and linn. It is the dividing ridge of the waters of Lake Superior and the Mississippi. We crossed it in a southwest direction, perpendicular to its general range; but it was not broad, and, in less than half a mile from our encampment, we met with deep, ugly swamps, almost as troublesome as that we had passed yesterday. We had four miles of the portage before us this morning, and Mr. S. made great efforts to accomplish the whole of it this day; and my men, in emulation of his voyageurs to travel at the same rate, completely exhausted themselves long before night. The route was of the worst character, being mostly through

swamp of tough deep, mud, which it was difficult to walk through unen-
cumbered; and that could scarcely be deemed practicable, with the loads
that the men were obliged to carry. They frequently stuck fast in the mud
until they abandoned their load, or were assisted out; and before night
some of my best and strongest men fell down by the road side, unable to
proceed farther. I collected them and the baggage on a dry spot, half a
mile from the end of the portage, and encamped before sunset. Mr. S. had
his tents taken entirely through, and encamped on the bank of the West
Savanne river; his men encamped back with mine. Our journey to-day was
three and a half miles, and much the most fatiguing of all our journey since
we left home.

July 3.—Although it was late in the morning when the men were required to resume the carrying, they still showed, by a tardy, sluggish manner, that they were poorly recovered from the great fatigues of yesterday.
We however got through the remaining pause of this horrible portage by
twelve o'clock, and embarked in the West Savanne river, near its source,
where it was but a few feet broad, and with only water enough to float our
canoes.

The Savanne portage, that we had now crossed, is six miles in length;
the first two through a swamp, such as I have described, and the remaining
four over land more elevated, and some little hills and ridges, but with
deep, ugly swamps intervening, making this much the most troublesome
and difficult of any part of our route. The highest point crossed by the
portage, is about one hundred and fifty feet above the Savanne rivers.

From the place of our embarkation to Sandy lake was eighteen miles.
The river, in this distance, has a devious course through narrow, low
meadows, of a little valley between pine hills. Its direction is about 20°
west of south, and about a mile from Sandy lake it receives a small river
from the east, after which it is thirty yards broad. We passed through the
length of Sandy lake, which is about five miles, and descended its outlet,
or Sandy lake river, a mile and a half, to its junction with the Mississippi,
at Mr. Aitkin's trading post, where we arrived at 4 P.M. and encamped.
The trading house is situated on a long, narrow tongue or point, which
separates the two rivers just before their junction.

It was purposed to remain here a day or two, to make some repairs and
alterations in our canoes, to change our Indian guides, and make other
necessary arrangements preparatory to our ascending the Mississippi. We
found Mr. [Joseph] Boudoin [Beaudoin], one of Mr. A.'s clerks, in charge,
who received us with great kindness and hospitality, and proffered all the
assistance and information in his power.

This situation has long been regarded as an important one for the Indian
trade. It was occupied by the old Northwest Company, and subsequently
by the American Fur Company to the present time. Mr. Aitkin, the present
agent of the company, makes this his residence, and central depot for the
great district over which he has charge; the posts and trade of which have
been described in another part of this journal. His establishment, at present, consists of a large comfortable dwelling, several storehouses, and

barns, stables, &c.; he raises corn and potatoes in fields near the house, and has a good stock of cattle. The soil about the lake and rivers is rich, but, with the exception of a small portion about the house, is subject to inundation during the early spring freshets, when Sandy lake overflows with the Mississippi, and the great flood covers the country for many miles around. The water was now, however, fifteen feet within the banks of the river and lake; the latter, in its confines, presenting the [a] very irregular figure. The lake is within less than half a mile of the Mississippi, and the length of its outlet, Sandy lake river, is only a mile and a half. Just above the junction, the latter is fifty yards broad, and the Mississippi seventy-five yards. Just below, the Mississippi is one hundred and ten yards. Our journey to-day was twenty-five miles. The moschetoes at night were more numerous than I had ever seen then.

July 4.—We found but few Indians here, those belonging to the post being mostly at their hunting grounds and fisheries. Mr. S. however held a council with those present, and distributed some goods, leaving word for the other Indians of the band to meet him at the mouth of Crow Wing river, three hundred miles below, where we expect to strike the Mississippi, after leaving Leech lake, on our return. I took the opportunity of Mr. Aitkin's workshop and workmen to have four oars put to each of my canoes, which, when the canoes and streams will admit of them, are much better than paddles, particularly for soldiers, who can be much easier taught to use the former. In fact, my men continued very awkward in the use of the paddle; and had it not been for my Indian steersmen, I could not have continued thus far with the expedition. I discharged here the three Indians who had come with me from Fond du Lac, and Mr. S. procured me two others, to go as far as Leech lake.

We embarked in the Mississippi at 6 P.M. and ascended it twenty miles, in which distance it winds, deviously, through a valley of low, rich, alluvial bottom, of the best quality of soil, and beautifully timbered; but all subject to inundation.

July 5.—The river this day was of the same character as the part ascended yesterday, crooking through a low, rich bottom, from one to two miles broad, bordered by pine hills and swamps; the shores covered with a rich vegetation of soft maple, elm, walnut, linn, ash, &c. and a luxuriant grass, which clothed the banks in rich verdure down to the water's edge. The river, though considered high, was generally eight or ten feet within its banks; the current was gentle, about two miles per hour, excepting round the points of bends, where it was frequently quite strong. We encamped on the east bank, above the mouth of Swan river; journey 56 miles. General course a little east of north.

July 6.—The valley of the river was narrower than yesterday, but of the same character. In its turns, the river frequently washed the bases of the pine hills, which there rose in high sand banks. The whole country back was pine, pitch and yellow pine; but in many parts the growth had been killed and destroyed by fire, and scarcely any vegetation was to be seen. We encamped on a burnt pine plain, of apparently great extent, (on the east side,) and 100 feet above the river. Mr. S. encamped ahead. Journey 52 miles.

July 7.—Started at half past 3 A.M., and passing the mouths of Trout and Prairie rivers, reached the falls of Pacagama [Pokegama] at half past 12 M., where we had to make a portage of 250 yards, on the east side of the river. The falls of Pacagama are the most considerable of the Mississippi, from the falls of St. Anthony, 750 miles below. The whole fall is between 20 and 30 feet in a distance of a hundred yards, and is nowhere perpendicular; but the channel is much contracted, and in one place the whole water runs down the surface of a smooth, plain rock for a distance of 40 feet, with a pitch of about 12°. The river here breaks through a low ridge that traverses its course, perpendicularly, in a northeast and southwest direction; and the rock is granular quartz, and the first rock of any kind that we have seen in place on the river. About a mile above the falls, Pacagama river, a small stream, comes in from the west, and from this commence the great swamps and savannes (savannas) or wet meadows, which border the Mississippi, on one or both sides, for a great distance above. We were winding through these until 10 o'clock at night, seeking vainly for a dry spot on which to encamp, when we overtook Mr. S. and party, who had been separated from us all this day and yesterday, encamped on a little dry point of oak woods [Point aux Chenes], a kind of island in the vast marshes that he had found before dark. We were detained to-day repairing canoes, but have travelled fifty miles.

July 8, (Sunday)—We remained encamped, washing, cooking, and repairing canoes.

July 9.—The whole party set off together as soon as it was light, and entered immediately a great grass savanne, of eight or ten miles breadth, through which the Mississippi wound, more crooked than any part we had passed.

Pointe au Chêne, a long dry point of oak land, noted by traders and Indians as a place of encampment, runs prominently into the vast fields of grass, about two miles above our encampment. One Indian family were located on it, and subsisted on ducks, which are remarkably abundant along this part of the river. The channel of the river, through the savanne, was sometimes three hundred yards broad, and again branched into many smaller channels, which ran a short distance and expanded into little lakes, bordered only with grass growing in the water, and from which other little channels, through the tall grass, ran on to unite again with the main one. The whole country seemed covered with water, from one to three feet deep, but the grass rose several feet above the surface in the deepest parts, growing very thick; and possessing a strength so great that in many places, as in short bends, the current washed against it with great velocity and force, it stood as erect, as green, and as healthy, as that remote from the river.

Having an Indian guide, who knew the general course of the river, we were enabled to cut off many of its great bends, by running directly through the peninsulas of grass; but although the water was two or three times more than deep enough to float our canoes, such was the nature and growth of the grass that it required the united strength of the whole crew to force a canoe through it.

The grasses observed were several species of carex, or sedge, the bulrush, the joint rush, and the Indian reed, *(Cinna arundinacea.)* These occurred sometimes separately, in areas of great extent, and sometimes altogether. Where the Indian reed grew alone, it was so tall, and straight, and close, that, although in four feet water, we could not penetrate it with our canoes.

Its great deviation from straightness makes it very annoying to follow the course of the river through one of these savannes; for, after pulling near an hour against a strong current, and turning an abrupt point where it is stronger, the voyageur finds himself at once going directly back for the same length of time. After winding through the savanne in this way for several hours, we left the Mississippi on our left, to take a nearer route to Lake Winnipeg, known to our guide, which is laid down on the map, and runs through a long and narrow, but very deep little lake, Lac La Cross [Ball Club Lake], remarkable as affording large, fine whitefish in abundance. From this we ascended a very small river three or four miles, to another little lake, from which we made a portage of 800 yards, into Little Lake Winnipeg [Little Lake Winnibigoshish], through which the Mississippi runs. By this route we cut off a great bend of the river, where it receives Leech Lake river, and saved thirty or forty miles travelling. A few miles farther brought us to Big Lake Winnipeg, and to the trading house, on the north side of it, where we encamped at 5 P.M., having come to-day fifty miles by our route, and by the Mississippi near ninety miles.

This trading house is occupied by a trader of Mr. Aitkin, Mr. [Jean Bt.] Belonger, now present, who has lived here for several years, without once going below. His dwelling and store were situated four or five hundred yards from the lake on a little rise of ground, where he had a fine large garden, in which were growing beautifully vines, potatoes, and other vegetables, and among them *tobacco,* which was particularly remarkable, this being the most northerly point of all the Mississippi; the plant was now small, but looked well, and Mr. Belonger said it grew large and fine before the time for cutting it. He had also a stock of cows, in the finest order, fattened on the grass which grew in luxuriant abundance all around him. The grass is of the *genus alopecurus,* which, the soil being very rich, grows tall and thick, affording, for the mere labor of cutting it, a plenty of the best of hay. Great herds of cattle might be raised about this lake on the grass alone. The forest here is light, and principally oak. A small river which runs past the house and empties into the lake, has its source in a little lake, not a mile above, in which an excellent quality of whitefish are taken. Lake Winnipeg also affords this fish, and a small fish resembling it, called *tullibee* by the French.

This post is of some importance to the Indian trade, eight packs having been made here last winter, but they were mostly bear skins, and on that account not so valuable as packs are generally. It is but a short portage from here to a river of Rainy lake, and this is the route of our traders to that place, which is distant five days' journey. We obtained from Mr. Belonger much valuable information of the country above, and of our proposed route through it. There were but few Indians here present, but about one hundred trade at this post.

July 10.—Started at 4, A.M., and crossing Lake Winnipeg in the direction of its length, which is about fifteen miles, we again got into the Mississippi, from the south west end of the lake. This lake is nearly round, is without islands, and is deep and clear, excepting near the shores, where, for a great part of its circumference, the grass is grown out one or two hundred yards into the water. Pine hills are seen all round the lake, a short distance back.

From Lake Winnipeg to Cass lake, a distance of twenty miles, the Mississippi is very sensibly diminished in breadth and quantity of water, and runs all the way through a savanne of the same character as that described yesterday, but narrow, from one to three miles broad, and bounded on both sides by high pine ridges and plains, on which, in many places, the pine is large, forming thick heavy forests of yellow and pitch pine. At the entrance to Cass lake, by the site of an old village, we were met by a number of Indians, who fired their usual salute, and conducted us to their village, which is at present situated on the large island of the lake, Grand [Star] island, ten miles from the entrance. We encamped near the village, on a long, narrow point of the island, running out to the north, and elevated about 150 feet above the lake.

Grand island occupies a large part of the southwestern half of this lake; it is about eight miles in its greatest length, and has three long, attenuated points, at nearly equal distances from each other, which give its contour a singular shape; that on which we encamped is the most elevated, and has the richest soil, and is, hence, appropriated for the village and gardens; the remainder of the island being mostly pine ridges, and poor. The top of this point is three hundred yards broad, and is slightly undulated by little hills and valleys, and sinkings, wherein, the soil being the richest, the gardens are planted. The whole quantity under cultivation is about eight acres, producing potatoes, corn, and vines, now growing beautifully; and the great extent and abundance of the crops, in proportion to the number of Indians, conveyed an idea of providence and comfort that had not been excited by like evidences of industry any where else among the Chippewas.

The prospect from this high point was beautiful. The lake is twenty miles in length, and nearly round; and from our elevated situation, near the middle of it, we could see much the greater part of its circumference. The water was remarkably clear, deep, and beautiful; the shore was sandy and high, and showed thick heavy forests of pine on hills and plains, immediately back. The immediate shores of the island were boulders of primitive rock. Five or six miles southeast of this is a little high island called "Red Cedar Island," from which the lake took its former name, "Red Cedar Lake."

The Cass lake band of Indians numbers one hundred and forty-eight, of whom about twenty are warriors. Their country or hunting grounds is rich in large game, deer, and bears, which, with their garden vegetables, and the fish of the lake, afford them a plentiful subsistence. Their trader is one of Mr. Aitkin's clerks [James Ermatinger], who was not now present, to whom they give annually a good quantity of furs, beaver, marten, otter, and bears; and he, in return, seems to supply them well with the usual Indian goods. They are not much at war in the field, but from their vicinity to their natural enemies, the Sioux, it can never be said of them that they are at peace. Some of the young men were now absent, at Leech lake, where they had just returned from an excursion against the Sioux, with the Leech lake Indians, under the Leech lake chiefs. Two or three that went from here, had got home, bringing news of their success, and of the loss in battle of one of the Cass lake Indians, the only Chippewa killed in the excursion. They gave us also information of the whole proceeding of the war party, their battle, &c. The party was one hundred strong, consisting almost entirely of the Leech lake band, and was led by Flat Mouth, their principal chief, by whom it had been raised to chastise the Sioux for numerous aggressions on this band, on their hunting grounds west of Crow Wing river. They met a war party of the Sioux of inferior strength, on these grounds, near their western boundary, and defeated them, killing three, and wounding two or three more, but lost one of their own men, as before stated. The Sioux fled, and the Chippewas returned immediately, but so much elated with their success, that one would have supposed, from their manner of relating the story, and the character of their rejoicing, that they had defeated the whole Sioux tribe, and killed half of them. The party had been got up, after the Indian manner, with so much pomp, preparation, and ceremony, that the whole country had been excited; and in their great anxiety and solicitude for the result of the campaign, a single victory and paltry success, as it was all they had done, was viewed as a monstrous achievement. The party had returned after the first little fight apparently satisfied, and without stopping to inquire what more they could do, or how much they had gained for all their trouble.

A portion of one of the Sioux scalps, now taken, had been brought to Cass lake, and the Indians here regaled us with a *scalp dance,* soon after our arrival. They had two other scalps, taken at former periods, and all were exhibited on this occasion, stretched by means of thongs, in the centre of wooden hoops, a foot in diameter, profusely ornamented with feathers; staves or handles, four or five feet long, were attached to the hoops, and in the dance each was carried above her head by an Indian woman, who sang and danced incessantly. The other Indians around, men, women, and children, all engaged in the singing, and kept time on the Indian drum, and by beating any thing, but the dancing was done entirely by the women who carried the scalps. Two of them were young, but such was their excitement on this occasion, that they seemed to have forgotten the peculiar modesty of Indian women of their age; holding their heads erect, casting fierce and wild glances on all around, and showing an expression of countenance, at times, almost fiendish. A like enthusiasm seemed to animate the aged and the children; and an observer of these ceremonies, when he reflects on their frequent occurrence, will not be at a loss to account for the irreconcilable hatred which exists in the breasts of these Indians for their enemies. They had been dancing here for many days previous to our arrival, and they continued now, without the least cessation, until after twelve at night. They expect during this dance, when strangers are present, to receive presents for the benefit of the widows or families of their warriors who may have perished in battle, and our men and voyageurs were liberal in the observance of this custom.

We were busied, from our arrival till night, in making preparations to continue our journey to the source of the Mississippi; and it was arranged to leave our large canoes and most of our men here, and proceed in small canoes, borrowed from the Indians. Five of these were provided for the five gentlemen of our party, and the provisions and necessaries for the trip, each to carry a passenger, a share of baggage, and two voyageurs; this being a full load for canoes of their very diminutive size. But a *branch* of the river which we were to ascend, was represented to be so very small, as to be only navigated with canoes of this size. Yellow Head, an intelligent Indian, who belongs to this village, and who came with us from Lake Superior, continues as our guide.

July 11.—All proper arrangements for our further journey being completed the previous evening, we made an early start. I left my men and baggage in charge of my corporal, and took one of Mr. Schoolcraft's voyageurs and an Indian to conduct my canoe, as I could not entrust the management of so small and delicate a craft to any of my men. These very small canoes require a care and skill to conduct them safely, only known to those long accustomed to the use of them. They are used by the Indians of this country, because the streams are all small; and because, in many of their routes, there are numerous portages, where it is a great object to make the carrying as light as possible. These reasons have determined us to adopt them on this occasion; for we expect to ascend a small branch of the Mississippi, and to make a long portage from its head to the source of the larger branch.

We entered the Mississippi from a bay on the west side of Cass lake, and passed, in a short distance, through two small lakes and a savanne, above all which we still found a large river forty or fifty yards broad, and from two to six feet deep, which wound its way through a narrow valley of low, alluvial bottom, confined by pine hills, up to Lac Travers, forty miles above Cass lake. In this distance there are many rapids running over boulders of primitive rock, but there is no fall, and no rock is seen in place.

Lac Travers may well be arranged among the sources of the Mississippi. It is a beautiful lake, about ten miles long from north to south, and about half as broad, surrounded by pine woods, which rise into high hills on the north and northwest, forming a part of the chain dividing the waters of the Mississippi from those of Red river. The western shore is much indented with bays, but the east and southeast is beautifully regular and plain, with a sandy bank, and beach of pure white sand. The river empties into the south end of the lake, and runs out at the east side, not far from its entrance, leaving the great body of the lake to the north of our passage through it. There is a trading house on the west bank, near the mouth of the river, which is occupied, in winter, by a clerk of Mr. Aitkin. From Lake Travers we passed by a broad channel one hundred yards long, into another small lake [Irving], and, half a mile above this, came to the forks of the river. The branches are of nearly the same breadth, about forty feet, but the stronger current of the right hand branch denoted it much the larger. We ascended the left or east branch [Schoolcraft River], as we had intended, which soon narrowed to twenty feet breadth, and, in a distance of ten or twelve miles, brought us to Lake Rahbahkanna, or Resting lake [Plantagenette], a pretty little lake, four miles in diameter, and nearly round, with a low beach of smooth pebbles all round it. We encamped a few miles above this lake at 7 P.M., having come this day, by my estimate, fifty-five miles. Our course to Lac Travers was northwest; from the latter, nearly south.

July 12.—This was a rainy, disagreeable day, and the moschetoes were numerous, hungry, and extremely annoying, but we travelled, notwithstanding, at our usual speedy rate. Our course has been south, and the valley of the river was savanne and tamrack and cedar swamp, but generally narrow, about half a mile broad, with low ridges and a miserable growth of pine bordering it on both sides. The river has become very small and somewhat rapid; and we have encamped after making a portage of two miles round a chain of rapids. One of our Indians killed a deer this morning, and we saw many more during the day. This country is so very remote and dreary, that the Indians seldom visit it, and the deer are more abundant than about the river below; ducks are also very numerous in the savannes where there is wild rice. Journey 52 miles.

July 13.—We ascended the river in our canoes ten miles farther, to a little lake, (Usaw-way [Assawa], or Perch lake,) about two miles long and half a mile broad; the river was very narrow and crooked, through a low, narrow meadow, and a little above this lake we left it; *seeing that we had now traced this smaller branch of the Mississippi into the very swamps and meadows, from the drainage of which it takes it rise.*

From here we set off, over land, in a southwest direction, to reach Lac La Biche [Itasca], represented as the source of the larger branch. Our canoes and baggage being very light, all was transported at one load, one man carrying the canoe, and the other the baggage of each of the party. In this way we made a portage of six miles in four hours, and struck the lake, the object of our search, near the end of its southeastern bay. The first mile of the portage was through a tamrack swamp, and the remainder, excepting a little lake of 300 yards diameter, was over pine ridges of the poorest character imaginable. The soil was almost pure sand, and the pine was stinted and mostly of the *scrub* species, (pinus banksianus,) which, hung as it was with lichens, and no other growth, not even a bush or shrub, mixed with it, presented a picture of landscape more dismal and gloomy than any other part of this miserably poor country that we had seen. Not a bird or animal, scarce even a fly, was to be seen in the whole distance of this portage, and it would seem that no kind of animal life was adapted to so gloomy a region.

From these hills, which were seldom more than two or three hundred feet high, we came suddenly down to the lake, and we embarked and passed nearly through it to an island, near its west end, where we remained one or two hours.

We were now sure that we had reached the *true source* of the great river, and a feeling of great satisfaction was manifested by all the party; Mr. Schoolcraft hoisted a flag on a high staff, on the island, and left it flying.

Lac La Biche is about seven miles long, and from one to three broad, but is of an irregular shape, conforming to the bases of pine hills, which, for a great part of its circumference, rise abruptly from its shore. It is deep, and very clear and cold, and seemed to be well stocked with fish. Its shores show some boulders of primitive rock, but no rock in place, and are generally skirted near the water with bushes. The island, the only one of the lake, and which I have called Schoolcraft island, is one hundred and fifty yards long, fifty yards broad, and twenty or thirty feet elevated in its highest part; a little rocky in boulders, and grown over with pine, spruce, wild cherry, and elm.

There can be no doubt but that this is the *true source and fountain of the longest and largest branch of the Mississippi.* All our information that we had been able to collect on the way, from traders and Indians, pointed to it as such; and our principal Indian guide, Yellow Head, who has proved to us his close intelligence of the country, represents the same. He has formerly hunted all around it, and says there is a little creek, too small for even our little canoes to ascend, emptying into the south bay of the lake, and having its source at the base of a chain of high hills, which we could see, not two miles off, and that this is the only stream of any description running into it. In fact, the whole country showed that there was no stream beyond, for the lake was shut in on all sides by pine hills, and the only opening through them was that by which it discharged itself. To the west we could see distinctly a range of almost mountains, covered with pine, which was undoubtedly the chain dividing us from the waters of Red river.

It will be seen, from my map, that Lac La Biche is but little west of *south* from Cass lake, and almost due south from Lac Travers, which is a different position from that assigned to it on published maps, where it is invariably represented north of Cass lake. There is, however, a little stream, Turtle river, entering Cass lake from the north, in the route of traders to Turtle lake and Red lake, but it is a very small and insignificant stream, and is only forty-five miles in length.

We left Lac La Biche, from its northern bay, having coasted nearly its whole circumference, and found the Mississippi, at its very egress from the lake, a respectable stream; its channel being twenty feet broad and two feet deep, and current two miles per hour. Its course was northwest and soon ran through a chain of high pine hills, where the channel contracted very much, and numerous rapids occurred of very great fall over boulders of primitive rock; the river running, for the distance, in a deep ravine. We descended twenty-five miles, and encamped.

July 14.—The course of the river was nearly north all day, passing several miles of rapids in the morning, in one of which my canoe was upset, and I lost my compass, and, with every thing else, my notes were wet and much injured. Mr. Schoolcraft, however, furnished me with another compass, and I proceeded, securing my notes as well as I could until night, when I would have an opportunity to dry them. After the rapids, the river was of gentle current, and ran mostly through savannes of wild rice, and tamrack and cedar swamps, but the valley of the swamps and savannes was generally narrow and bounded by hills of inferior pine, and sometimes a small thick growth of aspen poplar, where the pine had been destroyed by fire.

We travelled very rapidly all day, and, when we stopped at night, had made seventy-five miles. After supper, Mr. Schoolcraft and the other gentlemen continued on, being anxious to reach Cass lake; but I remained encamped till morning, that I might, in daylight, continue the tracing of the river, and my observations of the country.

The moschetoes were thick and very troublesome all day, as has invariably been the case in our route through swamps and savannes.

July 15, (Sunday.)—Left my lonely encampment as soon as I could see to trace the river, and ran down with a gentle current, most of the way through savannes and rice meadows, to Lac Travers, a distance of twenty miles. The junction with the branch we ascended is just above this lake, and the lake and river below are described in our route ascending, (July 11.) I travelled very rapidly in consequence of the numerous rapids below Lac Travers, and reached Cass lake and the encampment at 6 P.M., having travelled this day a distance of sixty-five miles. Mr. Schoolcraft and party had gone all night, and arrived at 9 A.M.

Thus the journey to the source of the Mississippi and back has been accomplished in five days, a distance of 290 miles, it being 125 miles to Lac La Biche, by the route ascended, and 165 by that descended, or by the longer and larger branch, which runs from Lac La Biche; this latter being the true length of the river above Cass lake. This makes the length of the Mississippi, above the falls of St. Anthony, 1,029 miles, or 1,038 miles above the St. Peter's river and Fort Snelling. The true character of the river above Sandy lake is represented on my map, which is also, in a measure, descriptive of this part of the country.

My men, being left here during this trip, have had a very useful and necessary rest from the excessive fatigues of the former part of the journey, and, excepting the man who was hurt on the portage of Fond du Lac river, are well recovered. The Indians are represented to have danced the scalp dance every night of our absence, and they are still dancing.

July 16.—Mr. Schoolcraft held a council with the Indians of this band, and constituted the Indian, Yellow Head, a chief, by presenting him with a large medal, the emblem of his authority. Yellow Head, who had travelled with us, and been our principal guide from Fond du Lac, had proved himself, in the course of our journey, to be industrious and intelligent: he had also character and influence with his band, and it is probable he will make a good chief. He seemed fully aware of the responsibility of the new relation in which this placed him to his band; and when he received the medal, and during the speech and advice of Mr. Schoolcraft to him, he manifested, by his manner and countenance, the strongest interest and concern.

The council, and the distribution of the few presents Mr. Schoolcraft had to give, and the vaccination, kept us till 10 o'clock A.M., when we started for Leech lake, parting here with Mr. [Louis] Dufour [Dufault], the trader who had accompanied us from Fond du Lac, and who was going from here to Red lake, his post. Our direction to Leech lake was south, the route leading from a deep bay of the south of Cass lake over a short portage to a little lake [Moss], and thence over another portage of two miles on a pine plain to another little lake [Shiba], from which, by a very small [Steamboat] river, we entered a western bay of Leech lake, and got to the chief's village at 10 o'clock at night, having, notwithstanding the portages, travelled this day a distance of near forty miles.

July 17.—The village of our encampment was Flat Mouth's, (Aish-ki-bug-i-kozh,) [Gueule Plat] who is the principal chief of his band, and perhaps one of the most powerful and influential men of his whole nation. He is also their principal orator, and on all occasions like the present, when councils are held on their general interests, he is looked up to with great confidence and respect, and depended upon to say and do whatever is necessary for the benefit of the whole. He had heard of our coming by a message sent from Lake Winnipeg, on our way up, and seemed to have prepared himself for the occasion. I visited his house, which is built of squared timber, and like the trader's house, early in the morning, and found it in a neat condition, and the walls hung round with his flags, war clubs, spears, pipes, medals, and wampum; all arranged with a peculiar taste. His medals, wampum, and flags were spotted with red paint, a circumstance which he afterwards explained in his speech in council. He invited Mr. Schoolcraft and the interpreter to breakfast with him, his assumed dignity on this occasion, as we understood it, not allowing him to invite any but the principal of the party.

The Indians of this band, who were living at different parts of the lake, in several villages, began to assemble at the chief's village as soon as they heard of our arrival, and Doctor Houghton commenced vaccinating immediately. Flat Mouth dined with Mr. Schoolcraft by invitation, and in the afternoon the council was held, at which most of the band were present. The few presents which Mr. S. had to give them were soon distributed by two or three of the subordinate chiefs; after which Mr. S. held a "talk," wherein he advised the chiefs and warriors to endeavor to put a stop to their feuds with the Sioux; to cultivate peace, and to take care of their women and children; to hunt their rich forests for game, cultivate the soil, raise corn, and endeavor to procure and enjoy some of the comforts of the whites, and to learn to live like them. He told them they ought not to *make* war with their neighbors, but it was not expected of them to sit still and be "struck;" that they might properly carry on a defensive war, but that they should not *go to war* without cause; that their great father, the President, loved them, and was ever watchful of all their actions, and it was his wish that the Sioux and Chippewas should live happily, and at peace with each other.

Flat Mouth spoke in reply. That he considered Mr. Schoolcraft as appointed and sent to listen to the Indians, and he wished him to listen attentively to what he had to say. He intended to speak fearlessly; his young men and warriors expected him to do so, and would think lightly of him if he did not. He had long listened to the admonitions of his great father to maintain peace with the Sioux; but his great father had not fulfilled the promises of protection made to the Chippewas at the treaties of Prairie du Chien and Fond du Lac; and the unchecked aggressions of the Sioux had now become so intolerable that it was necessary for the Chippewas to punish the Sioux themselves, and it was their fixed determination to do so. That it had been promised them, at these treaties, that the "long arm" of the President should be constantly extended over them to protect them; and if the Sioux made further aggressions upon their territory, the arm of the President would reach them, and draw them back and chastise them. This had not been done. The Sioux had, since that time, made frequent inroads, and had killed great numbers of their young men, and, among them, his own son; but the long arm of the President had not yet reached the aggressors, to inflict the promised punishment. He had, therefore, resolved to listen no longer to advice to keep peace, but to revenge his numerous injuries by fighting and killing his enemies; too many of their warriors and relatives had been murdered, for his people to think of any other course. (Here he gave a bunch of short reeds, about 50, to represent the number of his young men killed by the Sioux, since the treaty of Prairie du Chien.) The blood of so many had stained every thing around him, and must, in some way, be washed away; it covered every thing he had received from the Government, his medals, his flags, the letters of advice which had been sent to him from the agent, through the traders; the wampum sent him by the President, and the very ribbons that now suspended the medals and wampum from his hand; all were dyed deep with the blood of his murdered young men. He wished the Government of the United States to wash it off, and make his medals as bright as when he received them; and until this would be done, he could not consent to remain at peace. If Mr. S. could do this, he wished him to do it now, and at once, for he regarded it as a stain upon the Government, and his tribe; and he now threw down his medals before Mr. S. that he might make them again bright, (throwing them down at Mr. Schoolcraft's feet.) His warriors had but now returned from an excursion against the Sioux, in which they had killed three of their enemies, but they were by no means satisfied; and he had sent messages to different bands, inviting to another campaign, and expected before the snow fell to be again in the field. He deplored the poverty and weakness of his tribe; the very trees of the forest were dropping tears of pity over them, and he thought it a duty of the Government of the United States now to give them assistance to chastise their enemies, as had been promised them. If it did not, he would go beyond the Americans, to men wearing hats, (meaning British,) to seek help. He wished to say a great deal to Mr. Schoolcraft, and if he would wait till the next day, he would be prepared to make a better speech, and to say many things more.

During this speech he was surrounded by most of the warriors of his band, who, by their ready and general response, seemed to be well pleased with it. His manner was bold and vehement, particularly when he spoke of the Sioux; and, from the glow of excitement in the eyes and countenances of his warriors, I could see that they fully entered into his feelings.

Mr. Schoolcraft said a few words in reply to parts of the speech, and the council broke up a little before sunset, when we immediately embarked, and went about three miles down one of the bays of the lake to encamp.

This was altogether the most interesting band that we had met with among all the Chippewas whom we had visited. Their lake is the largest of all the lakes which contribute to the waters of the Mississippi, being more than one hundred miles in circumference, and most curiously formed of deep and narrow bays, which afford abundance of wild rice, while their immediate shores are of a character of soil, very rich, and suitable for their gardens. The Leech lake band is too large to live comfortably in one or two villages, and is therefore dispersed in little villages all around the lake, and on two of its islands. The number of the band is put down, from the most accurate information we could obtain, at 836, 806 of whom live about Leech lake, and 30 on Peckagama river.

Their country abounds in furred animals and game, and the lake affords abundance of fish; whitefish, herring, and tullibee, which they take in gill nets at all seasons. Deer and bears are the principal animals of the forest which are hunted for their meat; and beavers, otters, martens, and musk-rats are the chief furred animals, which are taken in such great numbers as to make this one of the most valuable posts of the north for the American trade. About seven thousand dollars worth of furs are annually sold to American traders, and great quantities are taken from here across the lines to the British trader at Rainy lake, and sold there for whiskey and some British goods. These Indians have a partiality for the British, which they take no pains to conceal, and, as far as is in their power, they obtain their supplies from the British traders. Mr. Aitkin is of opinion that four of five thousand dollars worth of furs are annually traded by this band across the lines to the Hudson Bay Company. From their remoteness from white settlements, they still retain much of their native character. They have not been debased or enfeebled with whiskey, from the difficulty of obtaining it in great quantities; and, unlike most of their tribe, they are strong, athletic, muscular men, of large stature, and fine appearance, looking proud, haughty, and unsubdued; and carrying an independence and fearlessness with their manner, that indicates a full estimate of their own strength. They have sometimes robbed their traders of a part of their goods, and have hence acquired the name of "The Pillagers," or "The Robbers;" but, of late years, they have been less troublesome to their traders, and are not much complained of except for their impudence, and a total disregard of, and disrespect for the power and Government of the United States. They are undoubtedly inimical to our Government, and friendly to the British; and such is their ignorance and arrogance, that they have threatened to drive away the American trader, and bring a British one, whom they would maintain and protect among them.

The strength of the band in warriors may be estimated at about two hundred, which is much greater than that of any other single band of the nation; the Chippewas being, in consequence of the great poverty of their country, divided into numerous bands and villages, and scattered over their vast territory.

The Leech lake band, being nearest to the Sioux, are in a state of continual war with them; and their hatred for this enemy of their tribe is perhaps the strongest feeling of their nature, which has grown and strengthened with them from their very infancy. As Flat Mouth remarked to us, "it was decreed by the Great Spirit that hatred and war should ever exist between the Sioux and themselves; that this decree could never be changed; and the Chippewas must ever act accordingly." In the wars of this band with the Sioux, however, they associate with other bands, as those of Lake Winnipeg, Cass lake, and Red lake, as they had done on their recent excursion, when they had sent out a hundred warriors.

The nature of their country protects them from inroads of their enemies to their villages; and they feel inaccessible and secure from any power whatever, even that of the United States. The traders have, in vain, to threaten with the power of the Government to check their excesses; their reply is, that they have not yet seen that power, and that it cannot reach them.

It is probable, however, that our visiting them with such apparent ease, may have the effect of lowering their ideas of their inaccessible position.

They have several war chiefs who are much superior, in appearance, to Flat Mouth, and who have a much better character for warlike qualities. But the latter is the great chief in council, where his oratory sustains his authority; and he is acknowledged, by all, their principal chief.

The excitement of their recent success against their enemies was still prevailing to a great extent, and it was one object of our leaving their village, to escape from the noise of their dancing.

Mr. S. had engaged, for me, two guides and steersmen, in place of the two from Sandy lake, who now left me to return home; but we started so soon after the council, that they were displeased, and did not join us, at night, at our encampment, as they were requested.

July 18.—We waited for our guides to join us until six in the morning, but they did not come, and we embarked without them. Our route was, now, to the head of Crow Wing river, which we were to descend to the Mississippi, and our only guide was a map or sketch of it, drawn by a Leech lake Indian. We ran several miles down a deep bay, to the south of

the lake, and, after much coasting and searching, found the portage leading from it, which we crossed in a direction a little west of south, over a
pine ridge, to a small lake [May]; and passing through this and four other
small lakes, with sandy shores, and clear, beautiful water, filled with fish,
and connected together by very short and narrow channels, we came to
another portage of 700 yards, to another lake, which, with three more little
lakes, and as many more portages, brought us to *Long* [*Water*] [*Eleventh*]
lake, the source of Crow Wing river. These portages were all short and
over pine ridges, with pine forests of yellow and pitch pine; and the lakes
were deep, clear, and beautiful, with the pine hills coming down to the
water. This whole country is pine, and is filled with hundreds of these little
lakes; all of the same character, and without outlet or inlet; three or four
may be seen from a single point, on an elevated hill. It was night when we
got through the last portage, and we encamped at the end of it on the
shores of Long lake, which, though also small, has an outlet, which is Crow
Wing river, or the great western branch of the Upper Mississippi.

Flat Mouth and another chief had overtaken us, but no guides had yet
come, and I felt apprehensive of danger, in descending the river, without
other steersmen than the soldiers, with whom I had not yet dared to trust
the management of my canoes in rapids; and who in fact were unpractised
and unskilled as steersmen, my having had Indians in that capacity all the
way till now. In consequence of the portages, we made but thirty miles
to-day.

July 19.—We took leave of the old chief, Flat Mouth, and his companion, Major Gaw-bo-way [Maji Gabowi], and, starting early, passed through
Long Lake in its length, which was about four miles. This is the first of a
singular chain of eleven pretty little lakes, from two to five miles in length,
and near together, from which Crow Wing river takes its rise. The channel,
or river connecting them, is at first very narrow, shallow, and crooked, but
increases a little in size in passing through each, until, where it leaves the
last of the series, it is thirty yards broad, from two to five feet deep, and
running three miles per hour. We had no other guide through these lakes
than our rude Indian map, and in one of the last of the chain, being then
three or four miles ahead of the other canoes, I was misled in my search
for the outlet, and ran several miles in a wrong direction, into a bay of the
lake, where I found a small river coming into it, and in the meantime Mr.
Schoolcraft's canoes passed me, unobserved. When I had found the right
way, I did not know if Mr. Schoolcraft were in front or rear, and waited
some time for him to come up, and then proceeded, still ignorant of his
situation, until late in the afternoon, when a tremendous storm and rain
drove me to encamp, at half past four o'clock, on a pine plain.

The country passed to-day has no other novelty than that of its total
destitution of Indian habitations; being too near the borders of their respective territories, to be used by either the Sioux or Chippewas, excepting as a
route for their war parties, and as an occasional hunting ground for some
of the daring young men of the Leech lake band, who are sometimes led
hither to hunt, by a scarcity in their immediate grounds, and by the abun-

dance of this, the game here being abundant, from its not being *much* hunted.

It is here that the Chippewas, and particularly the band at Leech lake, have lost so many of their braves, who, in these daring hunts, have been cut off by lurking Sioux. Hence the bitter complaints of the Chippewas against the Sioux, this land being properly a part of the territory of the former, and valuable for game and furs. Journey to-day fifty miles.

July 20.—Started from my encampment as soon as I could see, and in a short time passed the last [First or Sibley] lake of the eleven sources of the river, and to which the river is merely tangent, running only one or two hundred yards through the wild rice and grass of one end of it.

Ten miles below this lake, I passed the mouth of Leaf river, which comes in from the N. W., and is almost as large at its mouth as Crow Wing river, and is navigable for canoes fifty miles, to its source in Leaf Lake. Ten miles below this river, I passed Mr. Schoolcraft's encampment of the previous night, thirty miles from mine. Supposing me to be ahead of him, he had gone on till late at night, to overtake me, and had consequently got this distance ahead of me. As we were in the hourly expectation of meeting on this river a war party of Sioux, coming out against the Chippewas, I felt anxious to be up with Mr. Schoolcraft, and continued with all possible speed, which was now near ten miles per hour, assisted as we were by a strong current. Passing a willow swamp, through which the river ran, for a distance of twelve or fourteen miles, we came suddenly to a most inter-minable chain of strong rapids, twenty-four of which occurred in a dis-tance of thirty miles, and some of them a mile or more in length. From the ignorance of my men in steering canoes, the passage of these rapids was dangerous, but, by directing the first canoe myself, and requiring the other to follow her closely, and in the same track, we got down the whole with but slight injury. It is the method of Canadians and Indians, in descending rapids in canoes, to allow them to float, and to check them continually, by poles, at the bow and stern, to avoid the rocks; but as my men had not the skill for this, I caused them to row with all their might, and steered the canoes with paddles, by means of their headway over the current. By this means, my speed was so much increased, over that of Mr. Schoolcraft, that I overtook him in the afternoon, about 2 o'clock. Below the rapids, the river attained a breadth of more than one hundred yards, and twenty miles below, Shell river comes in from the west, through an immense willow marsh, and discharges itself in a mouth forty yards broad. This is called a large river by the traders, and is navigable for large canoes sixty miles, to its source in Shell lake.

Below this river, the Crow Wing has much of the character of the Upper Mississippi—broad, shallow, muddy, and sandy bottom, with long sand bars running out from the points; it runs through several willow swamps, but is generally confined by high banks, falling from pine hills and plains. We encamped on an elevated pine plain, after sunset, my distance, travelled to-day, being 120 miles, and Mr. Schoolcraft's 90—both greater than usual, in consequence of the rapidity of the general current, and my increased exertion, in the forepart of the day, to overtake Mr. Schoolcraft.

July 21.—The river continued to increase in breadth to its mouth, where it divides into two channels; but just above which it is between two and three hundred yards broad, but shallow, not more than five or six feet deep. About twenty miles from the mouth, it receives Long Prairie river, from the west, navigable for canoes thirty miles, to a lake which is its source. We reached the Mississippi, 40 miles from our encampment, at 12 o'clock.

The Crow Wing river is discharged by two mouths nearly equal, and near a mile apart, separated by Crow island, in one side of which the Mississippi makes its curve. The island is about three miles in circumference, of rich, alluvial, vegetable soil, supporting a rich heavy forest of elm, ash, linn, walnut, soft maple, &c., but like all the little alluvial bottoms of the Crow Wing and Upper Mississippi rivers, it is inundated every spring. The river has its mouth three hundred miles above the falls of St. Anthony, and three hundred below Sandy lake[22], and is the largest river that empties into the Mississippi above the falls of St. Anthony. It is two hundred and ten miles in length to its source in Long lake, from which its general course is nearly south to the Mississippi. It is navigable for canoes all the way, and for boats, in low stages of water, to the rapids, about 80 miles. In very high stages, the rapids may be passed by Mackinac boats, which might then ascend nearly to its source. It is by far the nearest route by water, from Fort Snelling to Leech lake, and presents no greater difficulties to navigation than the Mississippi does above the falls of St. Anthony. It runs, all its length, through a country of pine plains and gentle hills, so regular, smooth and free from undergrowth, that, as I was informed, a cart might be driven, near its banks, almost to Leech lake. If troops were to be sent against the upper bands of Chippewa Indians at any future time, this would be a proper route for them to take, whether in boats or marching: and from the tone and manner of the Leech lake Indians, observed during our visits, and the unfriendly character given of them by their traders, it is probable that such a measure may become necessary.

The Crow Wing river country, and that of all its tributaries, Prairie, Shell, and Leaf rivers, and two or three little streams coming in from the east, is rich in furs and game, such as beaver, marten, rats, bears, &c., and deer; but much of it is not hunted, because of its border character to the Sioux territory.

The east bank of the Mississippi, opposite Crow island, is near one hundred feet high, and the country back is an immense rolling prairie, which is here poor, the soil being dry and sandy. Here we found the whole of the Sandy lake band of Indians encamped, awaiting our arrival; Mr. Schoolcraft having given notice, as we passed Sandy lake on our way up, that we would meet them here on our return. This band consists of about 280 souls, of whom 60 are warriors. Their principal chief is Gros Gueule, or Big Mouth, who in his youth was a man of energy and influence; but he is now old and imbecile, and his authority has declined with his vigor, until his band are not much prone to take his advice. His policy has been peace; and it is many years since his band have fought the Sioux. But he remarked to Mr. S. that he was fearful this state of things would not continue, as the excitement of the recent successful war excursion of their brethren, the Leech lake Indians, had spread to his band, and he might not be able to restrain his young men from taking part in any other expedition against the Sioux that might be got up. This band, however, is poor, and their country exhausted; and these circumstances will, undoubtedly, restrain them more than the influence and advice of their declining chief.

Their hunting grounds are about Sandy lake, and along both banks of this Mississippi as far as this place; but the game of the country, deer and bears, is scarce, and does not, with the fish they get from Sandy lake, and some other small lakes, afford them a sufficient subsistence; and much of their food, in winter, is supplied by Mr. Aitkin, their trader at Sandy lake. Since the prohibition of whiskey in the Indian trade, these Indians, like those of Fond du Lac, have increased more rapidly than the poor state of the country will admit of: and it is now only their trade in furs that saves many of them from starvation. They were, however, pretty well clothed, and looked healthy and comfortable.

Mr. Schoolcraft held a council with them, in which Gros Gueule complained much of the treachery of the Sioux, who, he said, had often, under the appearance and assurance of friendship, invited some of the Chippewas to their lands and villages, to share the abundance of their forests, and when the latter had gone with this prospect, and to escape the poverty of their own hunting grounds, their entertainers had suddenly risen upon them and murdered them all. He hoped the Government would interpose to check the Sioux, and protect the Chippewas from their aggressions, as was promised at the treaties of Prairie du Chien and Fond du Lac.

After vaccinating them, and giving them some presents and advice, we embarked, and proceeded ten miles below to Mr. [Benjamin F.] Baker's trading house, where we encamped.

July 22, (Sunday.)—We remained at the house of Mr. Baker, who politely gave us much valuable information respecting the country, above and below. I am indebted to him for the topography of the country east and west of the Mississippi, from Sandy lake to St. Peter's; in the character, course, and length of the streams which enter the Crow Wing and Mississippi rivers. The following is also derived from him: The prairie, where he lives, east of the Mississippi, extends from about one hundred miles below Sandy lake down below Prairie du Chien, and back from the river to the pine country intervening the waters of the Mississippi and Lake Superior. Its soil is generally poor, but affords abundance of grass; and, in some places, where the prairie is low and level, as near rivers, it is rich. Timber occurs over it in numerous little groves and clusters and isolated trees, but it is, generally, an inferior species of the oak. Pine grows on some of the highest parts, and near some of the rivers—mostly white pine, (pinus strobus.) Mr. Baker has driven a cart from Fort Snelling to his house, in summer; and he says the prairie is practicable for carts as far as Sandy

lake, excepting a few obstructions of narrow rivers. Beaver, otter, and rats
are taken about the rivers; and deer and bears are tolerably abundant
about Mr. Baker's and below, but above, and more remote from the Sioux
and Chippewa boundary line, they have been so much hunted by the Sandy
lake Indians that they are now scarce.

On the west side, opposite Mr. Baker's, is a thick green forest of oak,
poplar, sugar-maple, and pine, which extends up to the pine plains about
Crow Wing river; down, about a hundred and fifty miles, to where it
terminates in prairie; and back from the river to what is called "The
Plains," a part of the great prairie of the Sioux, where they hunt the buffalo.

The buffalo are frequently driven by severe winters to take refuge in this
forest; and they sometimes penetrate it to the Mississippi in search of water,
in winter; but, in summer, they roam continually over their boundless
prairies, and are nowhere seen near the Mississippi, and east of it they are
not now to be found, any where, at any season of the year. The western
side of the river abounds in deer, elk, and bears, much more at this place
than the eastern.

Mr. Baker's house is prettily situated on a point in a bend of the river,
at the foot of a moderate rapid, just above which the river expands, and
three small islands, heavily wooded, of about equal size, lie parallel to
each other in its breadth, separated from themselves and the main land by
four equal and parallel channels, and presenting from the house a very
pretty view. This is the commencement of the thousands of islands of the
Mississippi, which occur from here to its mouth. Mr. Baker is a trader of
Mr. Aitkin—he has been here only one year, and has made but little improvement; but, the land about him being rich, it is his intention to raise
cattle and hogs, and to make this a permanent trading post. Being near
their lines, he will trade with both Sioux and Chippewas, though there is
no village of either near him at present.

July 23.—I abandoned one of my canoes, which was worn out, and
borrowed one of Mr. Baker, to take me to Fort Snelling. He also gave me
two of his Canadians, whom he was sending to the fort for supplies, to act
as steersmen and pilots over the numerous rapids below. I had now four
oars and two paddles in each of my canoes; which being also light of baggage, and my men fresh after the rest of yesterday, we were enabled to
course the rapid current with incredible speed. At a distance of ten miles
we passed the "Little Falls"—a chute, where the river is contracted from
three hundred yards to fifty yards, and falls about ten feet in sixty, through
a formation of talcous slate rock; the first rock we had seen in place, since
leaving the falls of Pacagama. A little further down we passed Pike's
rapids, and the site of Pike's blockhouse, where Lieut. Pike wintered his
command in 1805-'6[23]; and, a little farther, a chain of rapids called the
"Grand Rapids [near Two Rivers]," where the river runs over an extensive rock formation of granular quartz.

We also passed, during the day, another rapid at the mouth of Elk river,
and the "Big Falls," at the mouth of Sac river [opposite Sauk Rapids]; and,
a short distance above the latter, the mouth of Little Sac or Wattah [Watab]

river, where the boundary line of the Sioux and Chippewas, established by
the treaty of 1825, crosses the Mississippi; Wattah river making, in its
whole length, a part of the line, and entering the Mississippi about one
hundred and twenty miles above the falls of St. Anthony. We encamped at
night near the last of six other rapids, called the "Six Prairie Rapids,"
which occur at nearly equal distances apart, in a distance of fifteen miles,
having travelled, during fourteen hours, a distance of 160 miles.[24]

The river was broad, (three or four hundred yards,) excepting at the
rapids; and islands occurred at the point of every bend. The fall in the
rapids was nowhere so great as in the chute passed in the morning. The
banks were high; sometimes coming down in a gentle slope, which was
covered with luxuriant grass (poa compressa) to the edge of the water;
and sometimes abrupt sand to a height of one hundred feet. Before night
the forest had disappeared on our right, and beautiful green prairies were
seen on both sides.

July 24.—A short distance below our encampment, we passed the
mouth of St. Francis, or Parallel river, a considerable stream, running
parallel to the Mississippi, and navigable for canoes one hundred miles.
And farther down, on the same side, the mouth of Rum river, which is
sixty yards broad at its mouth, and is navigable for canoes one hundred
and fifty miles, to Mil [Mille] lac[s], a lake almost as large as Cass lake,
where the American Fur Company have a trading house, and where there
is a village of one hundred and twenty Indians. Another branch of Rum
river, called Kettle river, has its source near Fond du Lac river, one hundred miles north of Mil lac.

Several smaller tributaries of the Mississippi are delineated, in their appropriate place, on the map of this day's journey.

We arrived at the falls of St. Anthony at 1 P.M., and at Fort Snelling at
3 P.M., a distance of ninety miles[25] from our encampment. The river and
country passed to-day have the same character as yesterday, the country
being uneven prairie on both sides, and the river filled with islands, but becoming wider continually, from its numerous tributaries, until it has a
breadth of four hundred yards. The falls have been described by Mr.
Schoolcraft, and other former travellers, who had more time to observe
them than was allotted to me. I have only to correct an error in the height
of the perpendicular fall. It was estimated by Lieut. Pike sixteen feet, and
by Mr. Schoolcraft forty feet. I was told by an officer at Fort Snelling, that,
by actual measurement, it was eighteen feet precisely. Below the falls there
is a considerable rapid, and the whole descent at this place, including also
the rapid above, may be estimated at eighty feet. Between the falls and
Fort Snelling, a distance of nine miles, the channel is contracted, in a deep
ravine, between bluff rocky banks of great height, and the river runs in a
torrent all the way. The house and mill belonging to the United States at
the falls seemed to be in a good state of preservation, though not used.

On my arrival at Fort Snelling, I reported to the commanding officer,
Capt. [William R.] Jouett, and made requisition for provisions to take my
detachment home; the provisions I had started with, from Fort Brady, being

now nearly exhausted. We expected to hear, at the fort, something definitely of the Sac war, but did not, no news having come from it of any consequence.

July 25.—Was occupied at Fort Snelling in preparing the provisions for transportation, in canoes, and over portages; and in making necessary repairs to my tents, canoes, &c., for the remainder of the journey. Capt. Jouett gave me every assistance in his power, but the kegs for my pork could not be completed this day; and although Mr. Schoolcraft had completed his business with the Indians here in the afternoon, we were obliged to remain over night. I purchased a canoe, to replace the one abandoned at Mr. Baker's, the best I could get, but it was a very bad one. I got another man here also, one who had deserted from Lieut. [Robert E.] Clary the preceding summer, at La Pointe, and was taken by Mr. Warren, the trader at La Pointe, to Fort Snelling, and delivered to the commanding officer. This increased my party to eleven men.

July 26.—I completed the packing of my provisions this morning; the pork in kegs, and the flour in bags, and embarked from Fort Snelling at half past 8 A.M. Mr. Schoolcraft started earlier, but was detained at a Sioux village, Little Crow's, below, and I overtook him at breakfast; after which we all proceeded together until one of my canoes was broken on a snag, and I had to put ashore at a Sioux village, to repair, which detained me half an hour, and, in the mean time, Mr. Schoolcraft's canoes got so far ahead that I could not overtake them.[26] This occasioned me some trouble and perplexity; for our route was to leave the Mississippi, at the St. Croix river, forty or fifty miles below Fort Snelling, and I had neither guide, map, or directions, to enable me to distinguish the mouth of the St. Croix from the hundreds of channels into which the Mississippi is divided by its numerous islands. I was misled by two or three of these channels which came in with every appearance of separate rivers, and was, consequently, detained; but at 5 o'clock I got really into the St. Croix, which I soon recognised after I had entered it, by the long lake near its mouth. I proceeded up this lake fifteen miles, and encamped alone, Mr. Schoolcraft and party being somewhere ahead.

The country about the Mississippi, below the falls, is the same as that above, but the river itself is broader, and its banks are higher, the country having preserved its general level, whilst the river has dropped eighty feet at the falls. The valley is from a half to two miles broad, of a low bottom land, or vegetable deposite, and is cut up by channels into numerous little islands, covered with fine rich land-timber, but all subject to inundation.

The St. Croix enters the Mississippi by a mouth seventy-five yards broad, opposite an island of the latter, and fifty miles below Fort Snelling. Its right bank, at the mouth, is a perpendicular rock, eight or ten feet high, (calcareous sand rock,) and the left is a low, acute point. A few hundred yards from the mouth, it opens into a long, narrow lake, Lake St. Croix, which seems to fill or lie in a valley, the hills rising to form its banks, on each side, in green gentle slopes. Journey to day 65 miles.

July 27.—The Lake St. Croix continued twenty-one miles beyond our encampment, making its whole length thirty-six miles, in a north and south direction. It is clear and deep, and seldom more than three or four miles in breadth. The country on each side is the same prairie that borders the Mississippi. The lake gradually contracts at its upper end, to the breadth of the river, and is filled, at this part, with low, little, willow islands, above which the river has a uniform breadth of about seventy yards, and current of two miles per hour. The immediate shores of the river are skirted with a low, narrow, rich bottom, like the Mississippi, but the land about it is higher, poorer, and more hilly, as we ascend. The canoe I got at Fort Snelling proved to be bad and troublesome, and has detained me much in repairing it; in consequence, I have made but forty miles. I have seen nothing of Mr. Schoolcraft, though his encampment of last night was but seven or eight miles above mine.

My encampment to-night is a few miles above a cedar bluff on the east side of the St. Croix, called by the Indians the Standing Cedars, where the Sioux and Chippewa boundary line crosses the river.

July 28.—At my encampment last night, I met a trader, Mr. [Joseph R.] Brown, of the American Fur Company, who had been trading a year or two on the St. Croix, a few miles above, at a post which he had now abandoned, to establish another at the mouth of the river. He represented the rapids above to be so numerous, and so frightfully bad, that I was almost determined to turn about, and go home by the way of Prairie du Chien and Green Bay. But I learned that Mr. Schoolcraft was only seven or eight miles ahead, and I supposed he would wait at the rapids for me to come up, to render me whatever assistance circumstances might require; and after purchasing a canoe from Mr. Brown, the best he had of three, I abandoned the one I had got at Fort Snelling, now almost a wreck, and proceeded.

A few miles above where I encamped, the river is traversed by a primitive rock, which, for a distance of one or two hundred yards, confines the channel within perpendicular walls, fifty feet high, and rises in a high abrupt little island in the middle of the stream, but occasions no rapid. Above this the banks are high and steep, but not rocky, till within a mile of the falls, when the channel becomes suddenly contracted to from fifteen to thirty yards, by rocks forming mural precipices on each side, fifty and one hundred feet high, between which the river, though very deep, is urged with great velocity. This rock and the narrow channel continues, with a few interruptions of coves and fissures, one mile up, to the *falls,* where the river is but forty feet broad, and rushes with great force and violence down a fall of fifty feet in three hundred yards. The whole of this rock is greenstone trap, and its surface presented to the river in high cliffs is exceedingly rugged and broken, prismatic fragments being continually detached from it and tumbled down.

It had not been possible to teach my men the whole science of canoe management, and I had the greatest difficulty in getting through this rocky, rapid, and difficult pass, to the foot of the falls and portage, my canoes being frequently in the most imminent peril of being driven on the rocks, and dashed to pieces by the force of the current. These falls are twenty-four miles above Lake St. Croix. The portage round them is six hundred yards, which we made, and embarked from the head of it at 3 P.M., having been occupied from early morning till this time, steadily and laboriously, in getting eight miles from our encampment.

Above the falls, the river is a continued rapid for five miles; running, for this distance, in a broad channel, over an entire bed of boulders and fragments of rock. But being generally shallow, it was not so difficult or dangerous to ascend, as the rapids below; and my men, by wading by the side of the canoes, could push them along, and in some measure protect them from the rocks. It, however, required five hours to get over this rapid, and we encamped at the head of it, at 8 P.M. on the west bank of the river, near the site of Mr. Brown's late trading house [St. Croix Falls], having, with the utmost exertion, made this day but 13 miles. The land about our encampment is level and very rich, supporting a heavy luxuriant forest of ash, oak, walnut, sugar-maple, &c., but it is the first really good land that we have seen on the river, and does not appear to be extensive. Mr. Schoolcraft encamped last night at the foot of the falls, but did not wait for me this morning, as I had expected he would, and I have not seen him since we left the Mississippi.

July 29, (Sunday.)—Mr. Schoolcraft had made it a rule not to travel with his party, on this expedition, on Sunday, and, supposing he would observe the same on this day, I confidently expected to overtake him before night. I was particularly anxious to do so, inasmuch as I had now no gum[27] for the repair of my canoes, and I knew he had an abundance; and I wished, moreover, to get, through his means, at the first Indian village, two Indians to steer my canoes; by which my men could be saved from much of the wading and consequent hardship and exposure, of the method of ascending rapids that the want of competent steersmen had forced me to adopt; and by which they were now so much exhausted, and bruised in their feet and legs, as scarce to be equal to the exertions still necessary, and required of them. I accordingly urged forward as much as possible, and got to the site of Mr. Schoolcraft's encampment in the afternoon, where I learned, by a note left for me by Dr. Houghton, that the whole party had left, two and a half hours before, with an intention on the part of Mr. S. not to wait for me any where on the route, but to proceed home with all possible speed, giving as a reason for this measure, that the river was falling, and any delay but increased the difficulty of ascending it. I was dissatisfied with this proceeding of Mr. S., and deemed it unwarrantable by the official relations in which we stood to each other, inasmuch as I was thereby deprived of the services of the surgeon and interpreter, to which I considered myself rightfully entitled within the intention of the department, so far as such services might be necessary for the safety of the detachment, and to enable me to execute my instructions. These gentlemen had been employed for the purposes of the expedition, and as the execution of certain of those purposes had been separately assigned to me, I had a right to expect that the means provided for their execution should not be withheld from me by the power to whom they were entrusted by the department to control; but by this sudden and unadvised withdrawal of those means out of my reach, I was not only embarrassed in the performance of an appropriate duty, but placed in a situation of extreme inconvenience, and even danger, which could not have been anticipated or intended by the department in the project of the expedition. It is not to be supposed that the department would require soldiers to travel through such a country as this, and encounter the extraordinary exposure and danger incident to their transporting themselves, without some provision of medical aid; and still less could it be deemed practicable for a detachment of troops to effect a journey through an unknown, wild, inhospitable Indian country, without guides of any kind to direct, or an interpreter, through whose means to obtain guides or necessary geographical information. But such was my situation now; I had this route to travel, of which I neither knew the length or direction, the quantity or character of its difficulties, or the time and means that would be required to overcome them. For supposing that I was to travel it with Mr. Schoolcraft, who had *guides,* I had not made any useful inquiries respecting it. In this embarrassment, I would have turned back and sought another route home; but, from the number of rapids which I had already ascended, I supposed there could not be many more to the summit of the river; and that, consequently, it was as easy to go forward as back, and particularly as, with my present means, it was less difficult to ascend than descend rapids. Moreover, by the route of Prairie du Chien, I could not now hope to reach Fort Brady for a long time, in which apprehensions, with the commanding officer there, for my safety, as he could not hear of me after the return of Mr. S., might, I supposed, lead to measures which a more speedy return by this route might avert. And again, Dr. Houghton informed me in his note that he would wait for me at La Pointe, in Lake Superior; that we might pursue a previous arrangement, by which he was to travel home with me, that we might make some further examinations along the lake; and, unless I called there for him, he could not, probably, get home this fall. These considerations induced me to continue the route, bad as the prospect was of finding it.

But of Mr. Schoolcraft, it is a subject of just complaint that he has separated himself from me at a time when I most depended on him, and when, knowing, as he did, the unfitness of my men for the sole management of canoes on this difficult route, he must have been fully aware of the great exposure and fatigue which I must encounter in the accomplishment of this journey without *his assistance,* which he had now withdrawn, but which it was in his power and was his duty to afford.

Had Mr. Schoolcraft told me at Fort Snelling that it would be for me to perform the remainder of the trip alone, and on my own resources, I might there have secured sufficient resources, or, being relieved from the escort duty of protection to his party, I might have returned home by another and less difficult route, which I probably would have done. But by a strange interpretation or disregard of his official relation to the escort, he has led it, ignorant of such a contingency, into a situation of difficulty not compatible with its separate means of resistance, and there left it to encounter the difficulty as it best might.[28]

I continued a few miles above Mr. Schoolcraft's encampment, and stopped for the night, having given up all hope and prospect of overtaking him. My men having been in rapids most of this day also, were much worn out and discouraged; and my canoes leaked badly, and could not be repaired for want of gum.

The country passed to-day is hilly and poor, with a scattered growth of pine and scrub oak.

July 30.—The rapids to-day were numerous and bad, and, with the exhausted condition of my men, I made but little progress, not more than 14 or 15 miles, and stopped at night, at an Indian village at the mouth of Snake river, 37 miles above the falls.

About three miles below the village, I met three Indians in a very small canoe, with a note for me from Mr. Schoolcraft, by which it appeared that they were sent to "guide and assist me up the rapids," for which service I was to pay them in provisions. They returned with me to this their village, and signified that they would go no further, this being as far as their father (Mr. Schoolcraft) had asked or employed them to go. I gave them to understand, by signs or whatever means I could, that I wished two of them, at least, to guide me to the source of the river, and that I would reward them liberally with provisions for such service, but none of the village would consent to go, excepting one young Indian, the chief's son, who, taking a fancy for a calico shirt I was wearing, agreed to go two days' journey with me, on condition of my adding this to my former liberal offer of provisions. But I could offer nothing to induce any of the others to accompany me, even for two days, because, perhaps, they were not in need of provisions; and I had little else to give them. Undoubtedly, if I had had some articles of Indian goods, I could have succeeded better.

This village is of the Snake river band, the chief of which is Pe-ghee-kee [Pizhickee], who had been to Washington, as appeared by a paper he showed me, signed by Mr. Calhoun. There were sixty or seventy Indians present, ten or twelve of whom were men. Their trader is Mr. [Lyman M.] Warren, who sends goods to them every winter, from his establishment at La Pointe. Their country affords abundance of deer, bears, and fish, and they seemed to be comfortably clothed. They seldom war with the Sioux, being too near the post of Fort Snelling, and they look skulking and mean, and are thieving, as I experienced.

July 31.—It was 9 o'clock this morning when I had completed the repairing of my canoes. I purchased all the gum I could get of these Indians, for which I paid enormously, but could not procure near so much as I wanted; my canoes consuming much of it for the frequent repairs required on this river. We passed rapids again nearly all day, and made but 17 or 18 miles. The river, losing its tributaries as we ascend, is getting lower continually, making the rapids, where the water is shoal, more destructive to the canoes. The country to-day and yesterday is poor, and pine; none of it fit for cultivation. All the way from the falls, the bed of the river is filled with boulders of primitive rock.

August 1.—The river was less rapid to-day, is filled in this part with sand bars, and skirted with low lands and swamps, with pine hills back. We reached the mouth of Yellow river at 4 P.M., a distance of 30 miles. Here is a large Indian village and a trading house, which Mr. Warren occupies in winter, by one of his clerks. Most of the Indians and their chief, however, were absent.

Yellow river comes into the St. Croix from the southeast, and is one of its principal tributaries; it is navigable for canoes 60 miles to its source, near Ottawa [Court Oreilles] lake, and runs through several little rice lakes. My Indian guide from Snake river refused to go further, and I could not induce any of the Indians here to take his place, but I succeeded in making one of them understand that I wished him to sketch me a map of the river above, which he did, though very badly. We encamped a few miles above the village, where some of the Indians followed us unperceived, and, with a most daring theft, stole the bread which was baking at the fire, before which the men were sleeping.

August 2.—Ten miles above Yellow river, we passed the mouth of the Nam-a-kwa-gon [Namekagon] river, another large branch of the St. Croix, coming in from the east, where we found an Indian encampment of two lodges; and I was again unsuccessful in an application, as well as I could make it, for a guide, but they sold me some gum and birch bark for provisions. The St. Croix above was very sensibly less, and its numerous rapids broke my canoes, and detained me as usual; one of them was repaired in the bottom this afternoon, with about six square feet of bark.

In the course of the day, I met a hungry Indian and his wife descending the river in a good little new canoe, which I purchased for an injured bag of flour, of about 80 lbs. weight. The canoe was worth about ten dollars; but the flour, according to traders' prices for it, was worth twenty dollars; and this would appear cheap to any one who should witness its transportation to this place. By means of this canoe I lightened the other two, and passed the rapids much easier. I met, also, the Indian chief of this country, Keppameppa [Kabamappa] with a note from Mr. Johnston, the enterpreter, enclosing a sketch of the Bois Brulé river, which I was to descend to Lake Superior. Journey to-day 16 miles.

August 3.—The river has become so low that we have to wade over all the rapids, *which seem to be interminable*. Many of them, to-day, were over shelving sandstone rock; the fragments of which, broken and strewed in the channel, have cut up my men's feet, and the bottoms of the canoes, horribly. Made about the same distance as yesterday.

August 4.—Passed a long expansion of the river [Whitefish Lake], grown over with wild rice, on the east side of which is an Indian village, of seven or eight lodges, with gardens of potatoes, squashes, and corn, adjacent. This is Keppameppa's permanent village; but all the Indians were now absent, hunting or fishing. Twelve or fifteen miles above this village, we came to another expansion, or narrow rice lake, five or six miles long, the upper end of which receives Ox river; the St. Croix coming in below Ox river, on the west side. From my ignorance of the route, I was near getting lost at this place, by following up the wrong river. A broad, plain channel, with a current all the way, leads up, through the rice, to the mouth of Ox river; but the St. Croix, which is here the smaller of the two rivers, comes in, as it were, on one side of the rice pond, and has its mouth, in a measure, concealed by the grass growing in it. Each canoe passed in succession to the mouth of the former river, without noticing the latter; but I had remarked, as I passed, an opening in the woods, as though a stream came in; and after entering the mouth of the wrong river, I went back, to be satisfied as to this appearance, and found the stream; but, from its being smaller than the other, I was still in doubt which to take, till I had followed it up a short distance, to a rapid, where I observed, on a rock in the bottom, a little red spot, which, on examination, proved to be red lead paint rubbed from Mr. S.'s canoe, which had touched the rock. This little circumstance determined this to be the proper route, and save me from the error of taking the other; which, if I had done, might have led to further error, and been attended with serious consequences: for, if I had been lost for many days in this poor country, till my provisions were exhausted, starvation would have been almost inevitable.[29]

From here the St. Croix, now very small, crooked a few miles through a tamrack and cedar swamp, and brought us to its source, in a beautiful, clear, deep lake, (Upper Lake St. Croix,) twelve miles long, and from one to three wide, with a pretty little island near its southern end, on which were two Indian lodges, but no Indians.

We passed through the length of the lake, which lies north and south, to the portage, leading from its northern extremity to the Bois Brulé river. It is surrounded by pine hills, at the base of which, on its western side, there is a little good land, where the Indians have gardens. The lake is forty-six miles above the Namakwagon river, and two hundred and one miles from the mouth of the St. Croix.

We have now been nearly ten days ascending this river, though, on leaving Fort Snelling, we expected to reach Lake Superior in eight days; but this has been, for me, a most difficult route, and my progress has consequently been very slow.

Excepting twenty or thirty miles at its head, this river is filled with rapids from its source to the falls; and, in a distance of one hundred and twenty miles, its descent cannot be less than seven hundred feet. Our course up the river was, for the first sixty miles, north; afterwards, northeast, to its source. Above Snake river, the country is poor, showing cedar and pine hills next to the river, and pine hills back; mostly yellow and pitch pine.

The country bordering the St. Croix and its tributaries, is called the "Folle Avoine," or Wild Rice country, from its many rice ponds and lakes. I could not ascertain the number of Indians in this country, but they are not numerous. They subsist on wild rice, fish, and game, of which they have abundance, and to spare to their traders, who depend principally on these Indians for their meat. They furnish, annually, about five thousand dollars worth of furs, composed of otter, martens, rats, bears, raccoons, and deer skins, with some beavers and foxes. They looked meaner, and were more thieving than any of the Chippewas I had met with. They hate the Sioux, but seldom war with them.

The portage, from St. Croix lake, runs over a high pine ridge, of six or seven hundred feet elevation above the lake; from the summit of which, looking to the westward, across the valley of the Bois Brulé, high conical peaks, and regular hills, closely covered with only pine, may be seen rising one above another, as far as the eye can discern. The length of the portage is two miles.

About a mile from the head of the lake, and west of the portage, the Bois Brulé has its source in a large spring or little lake, twenty yards across, of clear, cold water, from which the Bois Brulé runs on one side, and a small stream to the lake on the other; one to Lake Superior, and the other to the Mississippi. But in seasons of floods and high waters, the Bois Brulé runs from the large lake, and through the smaller. Where the portage struck the river, the latter was very small, about eight feet broad, five or six inches deep, of very clear and cold water, running swiftly over a sandy bottom. I got part of the baggage through, and encamped on the portage.

August 5.—The men's feet and legs were so very sore, from the effects of their previous wading in the rapids of the St. Croix, that the carrying on this portage distressed them much; and although the baggage was now comparatively light, it occupied them till twelve o'clock to get over what had been left the previous evening.

We embarked, and descended the river 18 miles to encamp. At first, the stream was very narrow and shoal, barely floating the canoes without the men; but after winding through a wet meadow and a tamrack swamp, in which it received several little streams, in a distance of ten or twelve miles, it had increased to a width of thirty feet, and a depth of one or two feet, with a current of one mile per hour. Its shores were very much clustered with a species of alder, (alnus serrulata,) which in narrow parts interlocked over the stream so thick and close, that it was hard to force the canoes through it.

August 6.—Two or three miles from our encampment brought us to the "Little Falls," where the river, from being thirty yards broad above, is contracted to fifteen *feet,* and falls through a rocky channel, fifteen feet in fifty yards. It may be passed in light canoes, skilfully managed, but I had mine carried over the portage 150 yards, on the west side. Below the falls, the river was mostly rapids, which were of so bad a character, from the shallowness of the water, the strength of the current, and the rocks with which they were *filled,* that, to pass them with any degree of safety, we were obliged again to wade by the side of the canoes, and conduct them down; and even by this means we could not save the canoes from great injury. We had to stop frequently to repair, and before night had exhausted all our gum, after which it required one man to bail constantly in each canoe, to keep her free, and when we stopped at night they were all in a sinking condition. The muskets, boxes, all our baggage, excepting the flour, which was piled above every thing else to save it, was wet thoroughly. But it is our greatest misfortune to be out of gum, for without it the canoes cannot be repaired, and without great repairs my canoes will not be in a condition to carry us much farther. I have procured all the gum I could from all the Indians I have met with on the St. Croix, but my canoes have been so often broken as to have required it all. From the wreck of an old canoe found in the river this evening, we have procured a little, with which we have repaired, as well as we could, for to-morrow.

We have come to-day twenty-two miles, in which distance the river is very crooked, winding through a low, narrow valley, which is bordered by cedar and pine hills of the most forbidding aspect.

I made an attempt to walk down the shore, with three of the men, but, from the numerous ridges, ravines, and swamps, we found it much easier to wade in the bed of the river.

The river is exceedingly cold and clear, and is filled with thousands of the real mountain brook trout.

August 7.—This has been a most disastrous day. For the whole distance that we have come, which is about twelve miles, there is scarcely a part of the river that is not rapid, and much of it of the worst character that it is practicable to descend. On starting this morning, I required all the men, but one disabled, to wade, and lead the canoes with the utmost care; but the rapids were so strong, and the rocks so slippery, that it was not possible for them to keep their feet, or to save the canoes from striking often; and, before 8 o'clock in the morning, all my canoes were leaking badly; they had been so often repaired that their bottoms were nearly gummed over, and every touch on a stone knocked some of it off, and opened a leak. At 8 o'clock, however, I met two Indians, in a very little canoe, whom Mr. Schoolcraft had sent from the mouth of the river, to bring me gum, and to pilot me down. The gum was of great service, in enabling me to proceed with my canoes; but their little canoe was too small to carry any thing of consequence, and neither of the Indians would consent to leave it, to take charge of mine; and their piloting was of no use, for my men had not the skill to follow them, or to steer a canoe as they did, by means of poles. In the afternoon, after I had used up all the gum again, in repairs, my largest canoe had her bottom literally torn off in a rapid, and sunk, and her baggage had to be taken by the others, already loaded too much. A little after I met two canoes, with two Indian families, going up, and after failing in an endeavor to purchase one of them with any thing I could offer, I hired the two men to leave their families here, and with one of their canoes to take a portion of my baggage down to the lake, for which I gave them two soldiers' blankets, provisions, and some other articles; but they refused, for additional compensation, to allow a soldier to take the place of either in their canoes, that the other might steer one of mine; fearful, no doubt, from observing the condition of my canoes, that the skill of a soldier was not a good guaranty for the safety of theirs. After this arrangement, we reached the first portage below the falls, where the baggage was carried over a very ugly road, one mile, and the canoes, lighted, passed by the river, and I encamped at the lower end of it. But when my canoes were taken out, one of them proved to be a wreck, and irreparable, which reduced me to one small Indian canoe of my own, and the two still smaller ones of the Indians. These were insufficient to transport my baggage and men, and there was no resource left but to walk, which, from the nature of the country, seemed to be impracticable without a guide, who could lead by some route over the hills, and far back from the river. One of the Indians whom I had hired above, seemed to know the country, and by offer of liberal compensation I induced him, though not without difficulty, to consent to allow a soldier to take his place in the canoe, while he would guide us though the country to the lake; a distance, as I understood him, of one day's journey. I made my arrangements accordingly: seven of the men and myself were to walk, with the guide, and the remainder, including him who was lame, to go with the canoes.

August 8.—When we rose this morning, my guide and his companion had disappeared. I and my men had slept soundly from the fatigues of the previous day, and the rascals had stolen away with their canoe in the night, unperceived, taking with them the articles they had received for their hire, and a quantity of bread that had been left to bake at the fire. I was not in a situation to pursue them, and as they could ascend the river much faster than me, pursuit was useless. I had now but two little canoes left for all my baggage. The soldier who was lame, and a few articles of loading, all it would safely carry, were embarked in the lesser one of the Indians, and the remainder in the other, giving it in charge to two of my best men, with instructions, as it was overloaded, to wade, wherever they could, and lead it down slowly. The remaining seven of the men and myself set out to make our way over land, taking with us provisions for two days, a few blankets, a musket, and a fowling piece. All set off at 6 A.M. I attempted at first to follow the valley of the river, but it was so thickly grown over with brushwood and cedar, and presented so much swamp, as to be utterly impracticable, and I was forced to leave it, and take to the hills, which presented difficulties but little less forbidding: their ascent being six or seven hundred feet, steep, and covered, all the way up, with a growth of tamrack, cedar, and thick undergrowth, which appeared to be impenetrable. Their summits were generally covered with pine, but were irregular, and made a very bad route, which was often, too, intersected by deep ravines, running to the river, and presenting sides as steep and as closely covered with cedar, &c. as the valley itself. Swamps also occurred in the depths of the ravines, and had to be crossed. By means of a compass, I kept, as well as I could judge of it, the general direction of the river, and during the day descended quite to the river several times, to be sure of not getting lost. The men followed me very badly, their feet and legs being bruised and cut, and much swollen, from the effects of the rapids. Most of them found it troublesome to walk at all, and one was so far overcome by sprained and bruised ankles, as to ask to be left in the woods. But as I had only two days' provisions, and knew neither the distance nor difficulty between me and the lake, I felt a strong necessity to urge them on as fast as they could bear. Towards sunset, however, after we had come about thirty miles, we ascended a high peak of a pine hill, where one of the men ascended a tree and got a view of the lake before us; and descending then to the valley of the river, a few miles more brought us to its mouth, and an Indian village. We had walked about thirty-five miles, over an inconceivably bad route, and were all much fatigued; the distance by the river, to the point we left this morning, is forty miles, and our route over the hills has been almost as devious. The Indian canoe, which had started in the morning, arrived about an hour after us; but the other did not, being too much loaded to keep up with the Indians.

August 9.—My canoe had not arrived at eight this morning, and fearing some accident had befallen it, I borrowed a canoe from Mongarid [Mongozid], the chief of the village, and taking one of my men in the bow, and a supply of gum, I set off to meet it. I had applied myself much, necessarily, to the conduct of my canoes, and could now steer one as well as any of my men. We proceeded up the river eighteen miles, over many rapids, and found the canoe and baggage on the shore; the men in charge of it having come thus far with great trouble, when their gum was exhausted, and the canoe so much injured as to be unfit to proceed farther without repairs. We had met one of the men a few miles below, on his way to the mouth of the river for gum.

I repaired the canoe with nearly all the gum I had, and taking half the loading into mine, I embarked again, but had proceeded only a little way when the broken canoe required further repair. It had been so much thumped on the rocks that its bottom was almost destroyed, and was so loose now, on the distending bars, that every knock it got jarred the whole bottom, and cracked off the gum from every part of it. But I could not dispense with this canoe, as the other would not carry the baggage, and had recourse to another, and novel method to keep it afloat. Finding a tough, marly, red clay, in the bank of the river, I took the canoe out, and had its bottom rubbed all over with it, till it was forced into the seams and leaks, so as to stop them completely. I then embarked the canoe, and urged her on, as fast as possible, till the clay dissolved out, and the leaks again opened, when a similar process, hastily repeated, was alike effectual. In this way, applying the clay about every half hour, I reached the mouth of the river, with both canoes, and all the baggage, about ten o'clock at night.

The journey down the Bois Brulé has thus required five days, and has been a scene of trouble, difficulty, and danger, nearly all the way. The river is ninety-four miles long, and from the Little Falls (twenty-two miles from its source) to its mouth, in a distance of about seventy miles, it has a descent of more than seven hundred feet, without a perpendicular fall of more than eighteen inches or two feet in the whole distance; hence some idea may be formed of the great quantity and strength of rapid which must necessarily occur in this short river.

From the falls, the river winds through a deep ravine, between high pine-topped hills, the sides of which, next to the river, were thickly grown over with cedar, pine, tamrack, and brushwood; near the mouth of the river, the hills rose very steeply, and the growth was mostly cedar, (cupressus thy-

oides,) and in some places the whole forest had slid off, exposing a bare
bank of red clay, of considerable height. Where rock occurs in the bed of
the river, *in place,* it is sandstone; but in most of the rapids the bottom is
sandstone fragments, and primitive boulders. The channel, in some of the
rapids, is broad and shallow; in others narrow, with a very powerful current, or chute. The source and mouth of the river are nearly on the same
meridian, but in its course it curves considerably to the east.

My men have suffered more on this river than on any other part of the
expedition. Their fatigues and exposures have been greater than men ought
to be subjected to without strong necessity; but, under the circumstances,
such fatigue and exposure could not be avoided. For, at Fort Snelling, I
had only estimated for flour to take me to La Pointe, in Lake Superior,
where I had a supply, estimating the probable time till I would reach the
lake, at seven or eight days; but I soon found that a much longer time
would be required to accomplish the journey of the St. Croix and Bois
Brulé rivers, and that, although I had an excess beyond what was necessary for the computed time, I was still in danger of not having enough; and,
particularly, as much of the flour was, unavoidably, injured by the constant
sinking of my canoes. The greatest exertions were, therefore, necessary to
avoid the inconvenience of *falling short of provisions,* and the men were
required to do all they could, from the time of our leaving the Mississippi.
But with all the diligence we could use, this is made the fifteenth instead of
the seventh or eighth day that we have been on the way, and one day more
would have exhausted our flour. Mr. Schoolcraft, anticipating such a contingency, has left a bag of flour here for me, which will take me to La
Pointe.

The distance from the Mississippi to Lake Superior, by the route we
have come, is two hundred and ninety-five miles, and is very direct, but
very bad for canoe navigation—both of the rivers being very rapid, and,
at low stages of water, like the present, almost impracticable. In accomplishing it now, my men have been, some of them, badly injured, and all so
much exhausted and overworn, that they could not have continued much
farther in the same way.

I might, however, have avoided many of the difficulties of this route if
I had previously known its character; for, with a small supply of Indian
goods, I might have purchased several small Indian canoes, on the St.
Croix river, where the river became too small for my larger ones; and by
this arrangement alone, most of the trouble might have been saved. Two
men only can work in a canoe to advantage in ascending rapids, and, consequently, the smaller the canoe is, the more *effectual* will be their exertions; and, in descending, the small canoe is easier turned from the rocks;
and when it does strike, it is with less force than the larger one; and it is,
consequently, less injured, and easier repaired. Very small canoes, however, are objectionable with awkward men, as they are then more liable to
be upset than the larger ones.

But the management of bark canoes, of *any* size, in rapid rivers, is an
art which it takes years to acquire; and, in this country, it is only possessed

by Canadians and Indians, whose habits of life have taught them but little
else. The common soldiers of the army have no experience of this kind,
and, consequently, are not generally competent to transport themselves in
this way; and whenever it is required to transport troops, by means of bark
canoes, two Canadian voyageurs ought to be assigned to each canoe, one
in the bow, and another in the stern: it will then be the safest and most
expeditious method that can be adopted in this country.

Mongarid [Mongozid], the chief of this village, has brought my boat
here from Fond du Lac river, where I gave it to him in charge on my way
up, and has kept it safely; he has also shown more willingness to oblige me,
on this occasion, than any Indian I have met with, though he is aware that
I have nothing wherewith to compensate him.

Mr. Schoolcraft had left the mouth of the Bois Brulé on the morning of
the 6th; he was, therefore, four days ahead of me.

August 10 and 11.—Embarked again in my boat on the lake, early on
the morning of the 10th, and reached La Pointe in the afternoon of the
second day. Here I found Dr. Houghton waiting for me, agreeably to promise, and our arrangement for a better examination of some parts of the lake
shore; and Mr. Boutwell, the missionary gentleman, who had made the
route of the expedition with us, and was now to remain with the mission
here, to pursue his pious efforts for christianizing the Indians. The country
along the lake is described in a former part of this journal, and need not
be spoken of again.

August 12 and 13.—Leaving La Pointe on the 12th, with Dr. Houghton,
we reached the mouth of Ontonagon river on the 13th, at 3 P.M., where we
were much disappointed in not finding Indians, expecting, as we did, to
get some of them to conduct us to the "Copper Rock," on this river, which
it was our purpose to visit. The village which we found here, on our way
up, had been broken up, and the Indians dispersed to their gardens and
hunting grounds in the country back. After some search, however, we
found a little Indian canoe laid away in the bushes, and Dr. Houghton and
myself, with two of my men, set off in it, after I had drawn out my boat,
and set the men to repairing her in my absence; the Doctor, who had made
a hasty visit to the Copper the previous summer, undertaking the office of
guide.

August 14.—We reached the forks of the Ontonagon, 38 miles from the
mouth, at 1 P.M. Here the river branches into two equal streams, both of
which being too rapid to ascend farther, we left our canoe, and followed
the ravine of the right branch two and a half miles, when we ascended a
bare bank of red clay five hundred feet high, which, although very steep,
was of easier ascent than any other part, from its being free of timber.
From the summit of this, our course was west, corresponding with that of
the river, and led for seven or eight miles through a tall, heavy forest, and
over the best land by far that I had any where seen on the lake, or near
it—it being elevated, rolling in parts, well watered with beautiful springs,
and very rich in soil and timber—large sugar-maple, birch, hemlock, oak,
&c.; and in several places I saw little patches of leatherwood (dirca) which

grows only on the richest of land. On a little hill here we found trap rock, in place; from which it may be inferred that this rock forms a part of the Porcupine Mountains, which are seen from the lake, between La Pointe and the Ontonagon, and which have, heretofore, been thought to be entirely granite. We finally, to-day, lost the proper route, and got lost, and struck the river six or eight miles above the Copper, where it was broad and deep, with but little current, and abrupt high cedar hills rising immediately from the water on both sides; and, turning back from this point, we encamped on a high hill, in a forest of heavy pine timber.

August 15.—From the great elevation of our encampment we followed down a deep ravine to the river, and after a few hours of troublesome search found the "Copper Rock," the object of this annoying and difficult journey. It lies in the edge of the river, resting on small boulders of primitive rock, and near the foot of a red clay bank, twenty or thirty feet high: it is bright on the surface, from the washing and abrasion of sand during freshets, which makes it very conspicuous, and easily distinguished from the numerous boulders of primitive and sand rock, which form the bed of the river in this part; but it is also much disfigured by the cutting with cold chisels, by travellers, at different times, for specimens; and in one place is mixed with particles of serpentine rock, which seem to effect the solidity of the mass: the copper, however, is continuous throughout, and a specimen, cut from any part of the mass, will contain twice as much native copper as rock. The mass rings, when struck with a hammer, as though it were solid metal, and it is probable that the imperfection of solidity, observed on its surface, does not extend far into it.

Its early visiters, among whom is [Alexander] Henry, have estimated its weight at about *five tons;* subsequently it has been stated at *one ton.* My estimate is, of its mass or solid content, *twenty cubic feet;* and of its weight, consequently, *between four and five tons.* It is probable there are four tons of pure metal in it, after deducting foreign matter: and this, I believe, makes it *the largest mass of native copper ever found.*

We made an attempt to cut through a part of it four inches thick, to get off a specimen of about thirty pounds weight; but when we had cut in about one inch and a half, further effort only broke our chisels, and we did not succeed. Large specimens might be taken from it by means of saws, but its edges and thinner parts, where chisels were effectual, have already been taken away. We however cut off about twelve pounds in little pieces, from different parts of the mass, and left it at 2 P.M.

It was one of the objects of our visit to ascertain if there were any other native copper, or ores of copper, in the vicinity of this extraordinary mass; and after careful search we did not discover a particle or trace of either.

Returning we followed down the bed of the river, which was filled with large and small boulders, and the water being low and rapid, we could wade it without difficulty. About two miles below the Copper we came to the falls, where the river is contracted, between mural precipices of sandstone rock, from fifty to two hundred feet high, and falls about two hundred feet in two miles. The first and greatest perpendicular fall is fifteen feet, after which the river tumbles over successive strata of the rock, and has several perpendicular descents of from one to three or four feet. We could not pass this part without ascending to the top of the precipice; and the rock, on top, was covered with soil and a growth of timber. The strata of the sandstone dip to the south, rising northerly towards the Porcupine mountains. It is six miles from the Copper to the forks of the river, and, excepting at the falls, we found the channel practicable for walking all the way, and much the best route in low stages of water, but not practicable when the river is high. We encamped fifteen miles below the forks.

August 16.—We reached the lake at 10 A.M. and continued our way home.

August 17.—Met Mr. Aitkin, Mr. Warren, and Mr. Oaks, all with their clerks, voyageurs, boats, and goods, on their way back from Mackinac to their several trading posts.

August 18 to 25.—The observations on the coast of Lake Superior, made on my return, are embodied in the journal of the route up the lake.

We were detained by head winds at several points; one whole day at Grand island, and another at Shelldrake river, thirty miles from Saut de Ste. Marie.

A severe northwest wind overtook us off the Pictured rocks on the morning of the 23d, which soon increased to a gale, and made such a sea by the time we reached the first harbor, the Grand Marais, that we could not enter it; for the same reason we could not, safely, run the boat ashore or beach her, and were forced to run on, with the most tremendous seas of this lake, till we found a lee behind Whitefish point, a little before sunset. We could only keep up a light foresail from the morning, but ran, notwithstanding, a distance of ninety miles before night. But ours being a *small* Mackinac boat, we were in great danger, in the afternoon, of being overwhelmed by the seas.

We reached Fort Brady, safely, on the 25th of August, in the afternoon, having been absent eighty days, and travelled, in that time, a distance of two thousand eight hundred miles.

J. ALLEN, *Lieut. 5th Inf.*

NOTES

1. There is some question as to whether Allen is correct in referring to this fish as the carp. According to some writers the carp was not introduced into Michigan until 1877. Drews and Petersen, "The Carp in Michigan," *Michigan History,* 41 (March, 1957), pp. 91-101. The fish may have been the native sucker which abounds in that region and which is similar in appearance to the carp.

2. According to Neill, the Iroquois Massacre took place about 1660 when a party of a hundred Iroquois, who had come to attack the Ojibway, were discovered encamped about five leagues above the rapids of the St. Mary's River by an Ojibway fisherman. The news spread through Ojibway camps; warriors gathered immediately and during the night surrounded the unsuspecting Iroquois. At daylight they swooped down on the sleeping invaders and massacred all but one, who was sent back to New York with the news

of the Ojibway victory. "History of the Ojibways and Their Connection with Fur Traders," *Minnesota Historical Collections,* Vol. V (1885), pp. 402-403. Alexander Henry placed the date of the massacre at 1662 and estimated the Iroquois party at one thousand strong. Milo Quaife, ed., *Alexander Henry's Travels and Adventures in the Years 1760-1776* (Chicago, 1921), p. 185.

3. By 1830 it was evident that the fur trade was rapidly declining and that the future of the American Fur Company was at stake. After John Jacob Astor sold his interest in the company in 1834, it was reorganized and Ramsey Crooks became president. Under Crooks, the American Fur Company developed fisheries on Lake Superior. Stations were established at Grand Portage, Isle Royal, La Pointe, L'Anse, Montreal River, Whitefish Point, Grand Island, and other places. Whitefish, lake trout, herring, and pike by the hundreds of thousands were taken, salted, barreled, and shipped to ports on the lower lakes. Schooners were built by the American Fur Company to facilitate the trade. Indeed, so many fish were caught that the problem arose of finding a market for them. This problem was never solved, and coupled with the panic and depression of the 1830's and 1840's, the American Fur Company's fishing ventures failed. The year 1842 marked the end of Lake Superior's first commercial fishing. For an account of this story, see Grace L. Nute, "American Fur Company on Lake Superior," *Mississippi Valley Historical Review,* Vol. XII (March, 1926), pp. 483-503.

4. These famous arches were reported on by explorers, fur traders, and missionaries from the days of Pierre Radison in 1660 to the renowned European travelers of the nineteenth century. In 1935 the arches, grottos, and caves were destroyed in a rock fall. See Helen Martin, "The Pictured Rocks Then and Now," *Michigan Conservation,* Vol. XXIII (Nov.-Dec., 1954), pp. 24-26.

5. Some of the original fur traders' cabins on Grand Island are still standing and have been restored through the efforts of Mrs. Carroll Paul, the curator of the Marquette County Historical Society.

6. Louis Nolin was the eldest son of Kitche Nolin, a well-known fur trader of La Pointe and Mackinac Island.

7. Granite Point and Granite Island were named by Schoolcraft on the 1820 expedition. Williams, *Schoolcraft's Narrative Journal* (1820), p. 111.

8. Little Marais Harbor is a few miles east of Eagle Harbor.

9. On my return, Doctor Houghton and myself put a blast in the main rock, at this place, which raised off about two feet thickness of it, and developed a vein of pure copper black, from which we obtained many specimens of the richest quality, containing no impurity whatever. The vein was about six inches broad, and ran vertically into the rock, increasing in breadth as it descended. It is probable that the vein descends into the trap rock, to which it belongs, and that the crag rock has been formed round it, by the deposition and cementation of its pebbles. The copper black is one of the richest ores of copper; and this locality of it is worthy of further investigation, which our time would not permit us to make. [J.A.]

Dr. Houghton made a special report on the copper ore on Lake Superior to Lewis Cass, Secretary of War, after the 1831 expedition. See Houghton to Cass, Nov. 14, 1831, Appendix D.

10. Graverod River was named for a trader who was murdered by Indians there.

11. Louis-Armand LaHontan served as an officer in the French Army in Canada from 1683 to 1689. He wrote an extensive account of his travels in

North America, which was published in 1703 as *New Voyages to North America* (London). Although his book has been discredited because of his fictitious account of the "River Long," it remains one of the definitive books on seventeenth century North America.

12. On our return, Doctor H. and myself made this trip; for an account of which, see my journal from August 13 to August 16. [J. A.] Cass and a number of his party made the trip in 1820 to view the famous boulder, although Cass himself got so fatigued from "clambering up the hills" that he had to return without seeing it. In 1826 Cass and Schoolcraft sent men with blocks and tackle to remove the rock, but the attempt failed. Schoolcraft, *Thirty Years with the Indian Tribes* (1851), p. 243. In 1841 Julius Eldred, a Detroit businessman, successfully removed the boulder to display in Detroit. The War Department intervened, however, confiscated the boulder, and placed it in the Smithsonian Institution, where it is still on display.

13. Henry did not actually mention the sturgeon dam or weir, but he did note that three leagues above the mouth of the Ontonagon River was "a fall, at the foot of which sturgeon were at this season so abundant that a month's subsistence for a regiment could have been taken in a few hours." Milo Quaife, ed., *Alexander Henry's Travels and Adventures*, p. 186.

14. For accounts of the Bingham Mission at Sault Ste. Marie, see: Ann Hulbert and Sophia Buchanan, "Sketches of Life of Rev. Abel Bingham," *Michigan Pioneer Collections*, Vol. II (1877-8), pp. 146-57; Jeremiah Porter, "Sketches of a Pioneer Ministry," *Ibid.*, Vol. IV (1881), pp. 85-86; and Abel Bingham, "The Early Mission at Sault Ste. Marie," *Ibid.*, Vol. XXVIII (1897-8), pp. 520-24.

15. Allen is obviously mistaken in referring to the ruins of an early Jesuit mission on the island. Father Claude Allouez is reported to have built a chapel in 1665, but it was located on the mainland, probably near Vanderventer's Creek. In 1835 Rev. Frederic Baraga arrived at La Pointe and built a chapel, which in 1841 was rebuilt as a church. Allen may have seen the ruins of the old French fort built in 1693 or the fort built in 1718. See: John Davidson, "Missions on Chequamegon Bay," *Wisconsin Historical Collections*, Vol. XII (1892), pp. 434-52; and Hamilton N. Ross, *The Apostle Islands* (Batavia, Ill., printed privately), pp. 4-15.

16. Allen camped either on Hermit or Basswood Island.

17. Allen was probably using John Farmer's "Map of the Territories of Michigan and Ouisconsin," published in 1831. Farmer, a famous mapmaker of the Northwest Territory, published a number of maps of Michigan between 1825 and 1859.

18. The American Fur Company post was located on the Minnesota side of the river, now within the Duluth city area. The Northwest Fur Company post, built in 1792, was on the Wisconsin side of the river on the site of Superior, Wisconsin. For a drawing of the American Fur Company post, see Thomas L. McKenny, *Sketches of a Tour of the Lakes* (Baltimore, 1827), pp. 276-77.

19. The expedition had to pass around two difficult parts of the St. Louis River, known as the Grand Portage. The first led around eight miles of swift, treacherous water which was too dangerous for canoes to maneuver. Four miles beyond came the "Knife Portage," so named because slate on the trail was "thin, perpendicular, and sharp like knives." For an account of this portage, see Ralph H. Brown, *Historical Geography of the United States* (New York, 1948), pp. 298-300.

20. This man, Beemis, was kept in hospital more than a year after his re-turn, in consequence of this fall, and was subsequently discharged, at Fort Dearborn, on a surgeon's certificate of disability. [J.A.]

21. The description of the strength of Indian women is not exaggerated by Allen. Many other travelers made similar observations. Johann S. Kohl, who spent two years living with the Indians of the Lake Superior region, told of the hard, toilsome lives led by Indian women: "Their hands are much harder to touch than those of men, and their entire muscular system is far more developed." Kohl, *Kitchi Gami* (London, 1860), pp. 4-5.

22. According to the estimate of the traders, which is probably too great. [J.A.]

23. Pike's Blockhouse was located on the west bank of the Mississippi, a short distance below the town of Little Falls. A bronze marker was placed on the site in 1919 by the Daughters of the American Revolution. Upham, *Minnesota Geographic Names, Minnesota Historical Collections,* Vol. XVII (1920), p. 358.

24. The "Six Prairie Rapids" were located between Clearwater and Elk Rapids.

25. This diminishes the distance from Crow Wing river to the falls fifty miles beneath the estimate of the traders, who make it 300 miles. My estimate is 250. [J.A.]

26. The location of the two Sioux villages is open to question. According to Allen's manuscript map in the National Archives and the maps in School-craft's and Allen's published accounts of the expedition, Little Crow's village was located on the west side of the Mississippi above Gray Cloud Island. Ac-cording to Upham, Little Crow's village was located on the "upper side of Dayton's Bluff, within the area of St. Paul" from 1820 until 1833 or later. From 1837 to 1862 the village, called Kaposia, was on the site of South Park, a suburb of St. Paul. It is possible that the village had already changed to this location by 1832. *Minnesota Geographic Names, Minnesota Historical Col-lections,* Vol. XVII (1920), p. 120.

The second Sioux village noted on the Allen map, where Allen apparently stopped to repair his canoe, was located on the west side of the Mississippi opposite Pine Bend.

27. A resinous exudation from pine, used in the construction and repair of bark canoes, to close the seams and holes in the birch bark. [J.A.]

28. The uniform and obliging politeness which I experienced with Mr. Schoolcraft during the whole previous journey on this expedition, makes me regret to have to record this exception.

It is also due to him to remark in this place, that he did send three Chippewa Indians from the mouth of Snake river, "to guide and assist me up the rapids," but they met me only three miles below their village, and would not accompany me above it, giving me to understand that this was all Mr. Schoolcraft had required of them. They were consequently of no use to me. He also, subse-quently, when he had reached Lake Superior, sent me two Indians in a canoe, who met me on the Bois Brulé river, (which I was descending,) about 45 miles from its mouth, and were of much service to me from there down to the lake. [J.A.]

29. In response to these allegations by Lt. Allen, Schoolcraft retorted that Allen could have learned the correct route by examining the manuscript map in his possession; and even if he had chosen Ox Creek, "his progress would have been arrested by logs and obstructions peculiar to it." Furthermore,

Schoolcraft contended, "not more than twelve hours detention could have resulted, . . . and such delay was fraught with no serious consequences." *Detroit Journal and Michigan Advertiser,* Sept. 10, 1834, Appendix F, No. 7.

2. James Allen to Alexander Macomb.

FORT BRADY, SAULT DE STE. MARIE, Sept. 13th, 1832
SIR,
    I now take the earliest opportunity to report the return, on the 25 of Aug. of the Detachment sent from this Post, to accompany Mr. School-craft on the late Expedition to the Sources of the Mississippi, in obedience to Gen. Order, dated, Washington, May 9*th* 1832.
    The Detachment consisted of myself and ten men and left this Post in company with Mr. Schoolcraft and Party on the 7*th* of June. The Route of the expedition was up Lake Superior to Fond du Lac—up the St. Louis and Savanne Rivers, and across by the Savanne Portage to Sandy Lake, thence up the Mississippi through Winnipeg [Winnibigoshish] and Cassina [Cass] Lakes to Lac La Biche [Itasca] the extreme source of the River. We reached this Lake on the 13*th* of July.
    Our return Route was by Cassina Lake, Leech Lake, the Crow Wing River and the Mississippi to Fort Snelling, and thence home by the Missis-sippi, St. Croix and Bois Brulé Rivers and Lake Superior. We left Fort Snelling on the 26*th* of July and the same day Mr. Schoolcraft and Party left the Detachment, on the Mississippi about 20 mls. above the mouth of the St. Croix—His canoes were propelled by Frenchmen which enabled him, in the rapid waters of the St. Croix and Bois Brulé, to assume a greater rate of travelling than was practicable for me, as I had only soldiers in my canoes whose practical knowledge of their management was limited to what they had acquired on the present expedition. We were consequently a great distance separated for the remainder of the journey, Mr. S. having reached Lake Superior, five days, and this place eleven days before me. Mr. S. had not given me any intimation of a design to make this separation, and I was not provided for such a contingency. I was totally ignorant of the Geography of the country through which we were to pass, and I had neither Guides to direct me nor an Interpreter through whom to procure guides or obtain information necessary to enable me to follow the route with certainty and safety. Under these circumstances—left unexpectedly to make my way through an unknown, wild, inhospitable, Indian country, and deprived as I was, at once, of many resources upon which I had naturally depended, and left entirely to my own, my situation was one of the most painful anxiety, and I was not able to accomplish the remainder of the journey to the Lake without great difficulty and excessive fatigue to myself and men. We reached the Lake, however, in safety, on the 8*th* and 9*th* of Aug. where finding my boat that I had left in charge of an Indian [Mongozid], on my way up, the journey from there home was made with-out difficulty.
    Considering the Detachment as *a part* of the Expedition, it was, as such,

entitled to the services, so far as necessary, of the Surgeon and Interpreter provided for the Expedition, and I do, respectfully, complain, to the Dept. that Mr. Schoolcraft did, unnecessarily and injuriously, deprive the Detachment of the services of the Surgeon and Interpreter in the manner described.

A detailed Report of the Expedition conforming to your instructions will be made out and transmitted as soon as it can be prepared from my notes. [See Appendix C, No. 1.]

The Act. Asst. Qr. Master at this Post has received instructions from the Qr. Master Gen. not to pay the Detachment for extra services on the Expedn. It will be seen, by reference to your order for the Detachment, that an extra compensation is expressly granted. I have therefore to request, respectfully, that the A. A. Qr. Master be instructed to pay agreeably to your order.

> I have the honor to be,
> Very Respectfully,
> Your Obt. Servt.
> J. ALLEN
> *Lt. 5th Inf.*

[Lt. Allen was quite bitter about the treatment he received from Schoolcraft on the journey from Fort Snelling to La Pointe. Although it is apparent that Schoolcraft did not intentionally leave Allen and his military detachment to the dangers of a perilous journey through hostile Indian territory, it is understandable, after reading Allen's journal, why he was so upset. In a review of the published Journals of Lieutenant Allen and Schoolcraft in the New York *American* of July 19, 1834 (Appendix F, No. 6) the controversial episode was brought to public attention. The reviewer castigated Schoolcraft for his "un-Christianlike" actions in deserting the military force.]

3. James Allen to Alexander Macomb.
   Letter of Transmittal for Offical Report.

FORT DEARBORN, November 25, 1833

SIR: In obedience to the foregoing orders and instructions, I have prepared the accompanying map and journal, which are now most respectfully submitted, as embracing my *report* on the several subjects to which you have directed my attention.

I have been induced to report in this form, because, from the circumstances of my position on the expedition, I was not able to collect sufficient facts on which to base a full and separate report, under each of the various heads mentioned in your instructions; and I have thought this the best method of *combining* the observations which I was enabled to make, so as best to comply with your views, and to acquit myself of a responsible duty; and because, in this way, I could present all my remarks in the most concise shape.

The route of the expedition was up Lake Superior, to Fond du Lac; thence, up the Fond du Lac river, ninety-one miles, to the mouth of the East Savanne river, and across by the latter river, the Savanne portage, and the West Savanne river, to Sandy lake and the Mississippi; thence, up the Mississippi, through Lake Winnipeg, Upper Red Cedar or Cass lake, and Lac Traverse, to *Lac La Biche, or Elk lake, the source of the river;* thence, returning, back to Cass Lake, and across the country, by small lakes and portages, to Leech lake; and thence across again, by little lakes and portages, to the source of Crow Wing river, and down this to the Mississippi again; down the Mississippi, fifty-nine miles below the falls of St. Anthony, to the St. Croix river, up the latter to its source, in upper Lake St. Croix; and thence, down the Bois Brulé river, to Lake Superior; again, twenty miles from Fond du Lac river, by which we had left the lake, on our way up; and thence back to the Saut de Ste. Marie, the point from which we started.

We were absent eighty days, between the 6th of June and 26th of August, and travelled in that time two thousand eight hundred miles.

The facts and observations collected on this route, and herewith presented, are all that my time and means would allow me to collect; and I have endeavored, in the following pages [*Journal,* Appendix C, No. 1], to lay them before you, as they were brought under my notice, by the journey and operations of each day; and wherever they are not as full and satisfactory as your instructions would seem to require, the reasons for the deficiency are to be found in the limitation as to time and means, which necessarily and unavoidably applied from my subordinate situation to the principal and conductor of the expedition, and my duty as commander of the detachment of troops constituting the escort.

The primary objects of the expedition, and consequently of Mr. Schoolcraft, being to vaccinate the Chippewa Indians, our movements between points, for this purpose, were generally rapid, scarcely allowing a mere passenger to make many useful observations on subjects of science, connected with the country; and when, in connexion with this, it is considered that I had solely the charge and care of the transportation and subsistence of a detachment of soldiers, under circumstances of great difficulty, it will, probably, not be expected of my observations on several subjects made at the same time, that they could be very minute and complete. Hence the subject of botany, and one or two others, could receive but little attention, and are not much noticed beyond such remarks as would occur to a hasty observer. To the former subject, Doctor Houghton, the surgeon, devoted much attention, and will probably give the result to the public.

On the subjects of geology and mineralogy, I have been enabled to collect many useful facts, which are communicated, principally, in my description of the route up Lake Superior, and contained in my journal between the 7th and 25th of June. My observations on this part of the route are more full and in detail than on any other, as I was enabled to make them from travelling it twice, going and returning. We saw but little rock formation elsewhere.

From the source of the Mississippi to the rapids below Crow Wing river, rock in place is seen but once, at the falls of Peckagama, 150 miles above Sandy lake, where the river runs through a formation of granular quartz. All the formations that did occur, however, are properly noticed in their appropriate place. The poor pine hills about the source of the Mississippi are broken down, primitive rock, showing numerous fragments and pebbles of the quartz gems, and of hornblende, feldspar, mica, &c.

On the subject of Indians, I have endeavored to comply strictly with your instructions, and have given information derived from the most authentic sources, much of it from the Indians themselves but mostly from their particular traders; in obtaining which, particularly the census of the several bands and villages, I was much assisted by the politeness of Mr. Schoolcraft and Doctor Houghton.

The value of the trade in furs, and facts relating to it, were mostly furnished by Messrs Holiday, Warren, Oakes, and Aitkin, of the American Fur Company, who enjoy most of the trade of the country.

It will be perceived that the condition of the Chippewa Indians is rapidly approaching a crisis, when their increased population and decreased resources must bring upon them great calamities, unless a considerable change is previously effected in their means of subsistence and mode of life. Since the humane measures of the Government for the stoppage of whiskey in the Indian trade, they have increased and are increasing rapidly; but the furred and large animals of the country, upon which is their great dependence for their very existence, have diminished in a converse ratio, and are every day becoming more scarce. And yet these Indians, with a characteristic improvidence and blind fatuity, have not made, nor are making, any other provision for their future wants and contingencies, but, on the contrary, manifest, by a continued adherence to their established and peculiar habits of living, an apathy and indifference to their approaching condition of want and misery, altogether inexplicable and astonishing.

Their vast country, though generally poor, has land enough of the richest quality to afford a subsistence, by cultivation, for ten times their present population. But they have not any where sought a living from agriculture; and in parts where the soil is richest, and the Indians most in need, they have been the least attentive to this means of supplying their wants; although some of them, as those about Fond du Lac, and along the shores of Lake Superior, have already experienced, during two or three severe winters, much suffering from starvation, and many of them must have perished but for a scanty relief furnished by their traders.

All the Chippewas, north and west of Lake Superior, entertain unfriendly feelings to the Government of the United States, and would undoubtedly embrace another occasion, similar to that of the last war with Great Britain, to join and assist an English or other powerful enemy: but their hostility amounts to nothing, for they are too poor and weak to attempt to war themselves, and are restrained, by motives of fear and interest, from depredating much upon their traders. Those at Leech lake, and about the sources of the Mississippi, are the least friendly, as my account of them represents.

About the time of the removal of the British traders from this country, it had commenced the decline in Indian resources, which has gone on steadily ever since, until the country is now poor, compared with what it was in the time of the Northwest Company and British trade; and the Indians, contrasting their present condition wtih their former, and without the judgment to know and assign the true cause of the difference, attribute their present comparative distress and want to the change of Government and traders, effected at the time referred to. And this will account for much of their present hostile feeling to the American Government and traders.

All the Chippewa Indians have a most inveterate and irreconcilable hatred for their border tribe, and natural enemies, the Sioux; which, being duly reciprocated by the latter, keeps them both, near their borders, in a state of constant insecurity and warfare, and leads to endless aggressions on the part of each. The Chippewas, however, from their poverty and weakness, suffer most from this state of things, and are seldom able to pursue an offensive war, or to carry their operations much beyond their own country. Whereas their enemies, from their superior numerical strength, and abundant resources in means of subsistence, are enabled to push their excursions into the Chippewa territory, until they are resisted by the inaccessible nature of the country.

The Chippewas, remote from their lines, as those along Lake Superior, at Fond du Lac, &c., are seldom engaged in these wars, or much affected by them: but their border brethren at Leech lake, Red lake, and along the Mississippi, are never at peace. The Leech lake band particularly, being the largest single band of the tribe, and occupying a place near the lines, and made secure by the fastnesses of their lake, are in a state of constant excitement, either from the depredations of their enemies, or their own, upon them; and they suffer and resent more than any other band. They also possess more of the qualities of savage warriors than any other Indians whom we visited. For a particular account of them, see journal, July 16.

Our route, excepting a small portion of it, on the Mississippi, above and below Fort Snelling, in the Sioux' lands, was entirely in the country of the Chippewas, and we saw no other Indians excepting a few of the Sioux at Fort Snelling, and on the river below.

The accompanying *map* is a "delineation of the route and several points of importance," and is as correct a representation of the country as my means of observation would allow me to make it. The collection of materials for this object received as great care and attention as was necessary to supply a deficiency of proper means for this purpose.

I was not furnished with, nor could I procure at Fort Brady, any instruments by which to fix, from astronomical observations, the true geographical positions of points necessary to be known for the construction of an accurate map; and, to obviate this inconvenience, I had recourse to a method of tracing the whole route between the few points fixed and given by the observations of former travellers. For this purpose, a compass, the only instrument I had, was placed in my canoe, where it was constantly under my eye, and as the canoe proceeded in the line of a river, I carried my observations from the compass to a field book at every bend or change of direction; thus delineating, on a large scale, in my field book, all the bends of the river precisely as they occurred: and by establishing a scale of proportion, in the lengths of the reaches, I was also in this way enabled to lay down and preserve the general course of a river with surprising accuracy, as was tested, afterwards, in constructing on my map the routes of rivers between known points. The distances were estimated with great pains and care, from the combined judgments of all the gentlemen of the party, on our rate of travelling, which was very well determined from our travelling much on known distances. Moreover, many of the distances, as the lengths of rivers and diameters of lakes, were long determined by traders and voyageurs, who could judge of them very well from having travelled them much. The portages were well enough measured by pacing them; and their direction was defined in the same way as that of the rivers.

On the portion of the Mississippi above Cass lake, which was the least known of any part of the river and route, I bestowed on the tracing and computing of distances the most unremitted attention; and as I had by this time acquired a great facility in my method, I feel a confidence that the character, course, and length, as represented, of this interesting part, approaches a great degree of accuracy; and the place which I have thus given to Lac La Biche, the source of the great river, may be regarded as being very near its *true position*. This is on the supposition that Cass lake, to which Lac La Biche is thus relatively fixed, has its true geographical position, from the observations of the astronomer, [David] Thompson.

My observations on this part of the route, given on the map, and in my journal, between the 11th and 16th July, may be viewed as settling definitively the question of the true source of the Mississippi, which has excited some interest and curiosity, and upon which map makers have heretofore been seemingly uninformed; as, on all the published maps that I have seen, the river above Cass lake is incorrectly laid down, and Lac La Biche is placed *north* of Cass lake, instead of *south* of it, as it should be.

I have placed Lac la Biche about in latitude 47° 10', and longitude west of Greenwich 95° 54'. It is 165 miles above Cass lake, and 1,029 above the falls of St. Anthony.

Our route from Leech lake, down the Crow Wing river, has also developed new facts in the topography of the country, in the source, length, and character of that river, which claims an interest from its being the largest branch of the Mississippi above the falls of St. Anthony.

The description of the St. Croix and Bois Brulé rivers, of our route returning from the Mississippi to Lake Superior, is also new.

The country embraced by the map, and which did not come under my immediate observation, is described from Indian maps, drawn by Indians well acquainted with it, and from the maps and descriptions of traders. The number of the rivers, and their length and direction, is not far from truth.

The southern shore of Lake Superior, a part of our route, is omitted in the map, but its topographical features are described in the journal.

In my letter to you of September 13, 1832, I had occasion to mention the separation of Mr. Schoolcraft from the detachment on the St. Croix River. The circumstances of that separation are reported in my journal of the St. Croix, July 29.

I have the honor to be,
With the greatest respect, sir,
Your most obedient servant,
J. ALLEN,
Lieutenant 5th Infantry.

APPENDIX D

Journal, Letters and Reports of Dr. Douglass Houghton

THE JOURNAL of Douglass Houghton was originally made up of eight notebooks. The first, which recorded the trip from Sault Ste. Marie to Fond du Lac, was lost or destroyed, except for its cover. The other seven were turned over to the Michigan Historical Commission prior to 1922. In 1932 these diaries were loaned to the Minnesota Historical Society, where they were copied and collated by Dr. Grace Lee Nute.

For several years after the disastrous state office building fire in Lansing in February, 1951, it was feared that the original diaries were among the valuable documents in the custody of the Historical Commission which were destroyed. The editor discovered in 1954, however, that these diaries had been loaned to a biographer of Houghton before the fire and had never been returned to the Historical Commission. Although the diaries have subsequently been misplaced, it is hoped that they will be located soon and returned to the Commission for permanent preservation.

The Journal printed in this appendix was taken from the copy made by the Minnesota Historical Society. The extensive list of plants found by Houghton on the expedition, which appeared at the end of the third notebook, has been deleted. This list can be found in Houghton's "Localities of Plants Collected in the Northwestern Expeditions of 1831 and 1832," Schoolcraft *Narrative to Itasca*, pp. 160-65. Punctuation has been added to make the Journal more readable, otherwise no basic changes have been made.

Sections of the Houghton Journal have been published before, but never in complete form. An excerpt from one of the notebooks, covering the period from July 10 to July 13 was printed in the Detroit *Post and Tribune* of February 15, 1879. Julius Chambers quoted from this newspaper article in his book, *The Mississippi River and its Wonderful Valley* (New York, 1910), pp. 114-16.

In addition to his Journal, Houghton wrote a great deal about the Expeditions of 1831 and 1832. His letters to his brother, Richard, and Professor John Torrey have been preserved and tell much about the trip. His official reports on the vaccination of Indians and on the copper deposits of the Upper Peninsula of Michigan were published by the federal government as well as Schoolcraft in *Narrative to Itasca*. An exhaustive search of the manuscript depositories of the country would undoubtedly turn up other Houghton papers relating to the Expeditions.

1. Journal of Douglass Houghton.

2. Douglass Houghton to Richard H. Houghton, June 15, 1831. Michigan Historical Collections, University of Michigan.

3. Douglass Houghton to Lewis Cass, November 14, 1831. *Narrative to Itasca*, pp. 287-92.

4. Douglass Houghton to Professor John Torrey, March 20, 1832. Torrey Papers, New York Botanical Garden.

5. Douglass Houghton to Henry Rowe Schoolcraft, April 3, 1832. Schoolcraft Papers, Library of Congress.

6. Douglass Houghton to Henry Rowe Schoolcraft, May 12, 1832. Schoolcraft Papers, Library of Congress.

7. Douglass Houghton to Richard Houghton, June 24, 1832. Michigan Historical Collections, University of Michigan.

8. Douglass Houghton to Henry Rowe Schoolcraft, September 21, 1832. Schoolcraft Papers, Library of Congress.

9. Douglass Houghton to Professor John Torrey, November 24, 1832. Torrey Papers, New York Botanical Garden.

1. The Manuscript Journal of Douglass Houghton, June 23 to August 25, 1832

June 23d to July 7

No. 2

From Fond du Lac to the Mississippi near the falls of Peckagama.

June 23. Saturday. Brought forward from no. 1. The indians fired a salute upon our arrival & soon after came together & I vaccinated at one sitting 241. They have a wonderful dread of the Small Pox.

This post is productive of great numbers of otter & bear. The whole number of packs collected from the whole country west of this under the the direction of Mr. [William] Aitkin is 162 packs—Including beaver, otter, muskrat, mink, martin, fisher, bear. These are put up in packs weighing ninety pounds each. The French voyageur[s] had a dance in the Evening.

June 24. Sunday. Remained encamped at the Fort. Divine service by the Rev. Mr. Boutwell, in the forenoon to the Americans & in the afternoon to the indians.

June 25. Monday. The indians danced before us this morning. A short council was held and present[s] distributed. At 9 o'clock Mr. Aitkins boats being in readiness he dispatched them 7 in number to the mouth of the [St. Louis] Riv. He remains until tomorrow. All things being in readiness our two barges & canoe were dispatched for the rapids two miles above. Indians were procured to assist us in taking our baggage across the portage. Arrived at the Grand portage & made three pauses upon it & encamped. Rock sandstone. Canoe taken two miles above, empty. Found a few plants. The portage commences by a steep ascent of nearly 150 feet.

I here first saw pemina [pemmican] or chopped buffalo meat & tallow.

Curious appearance of the medicine man of the indians.

Allens tooth in bad order.

June 26. Tuesday. Made 12 pauses upon the portage. Rain & thunder during a part of the day. Several of the men injured. Encamped at a small creek at night. As we proceed upon the portage the soil improves & occasional maple groves are seen. In other parts the portage is through a complete marsh. Portage paths rendered extremely muddy in all its parts in consequence of the mud. The men are frequently compelled to wade knee deep in mud. Sky became clear at night & the musquitoes annoyed us much.

June 27th. Wednesday. Did not leave our encampment until late in the morning as our men went back for the canoe about three miles. Made six pauses before breakfast, which was taken at 12 o'clock at the end of the portage. Portage path very muddy. The sandstone which was seen at the commencement of the portage is superceded by the Argillite at the head of the Portage. The sandstone undoubtedly overlays the Argillite which would seem to show that the sandstone is of the 1st Gray wacke Formation.[1] The Argillite is more inclined than is usual & rather softer. The sun shone brightly and our baggage which had been thoroughly wet on the previous day was spread out at the head of the portage to dry & we remained at the encampment during the night. We here selected 4 additional canoes in which to perform our voyage from 22 belonging to Mr. Aitkin, which were here. The men employed most of the afternoon in making paddle poles &c. Some presents were distributed to the indians. Indian dogs extremely annoying. Sewed an indians foot. Indians much astonished at Surg. operation.

June 28th. Thursday. Our canoes being loaded & those of the Indians (with two canoes) who were to accompany us I walked with Messrs. Boutwell & Johnston one mile, above to embark while Mr. S[choolcraft] remained in the canoe. The rapids were severe & much difficulty was found in ascending with the canoes. We embarked & proceeded along the river which flows with a rapid current, until we arrived at an almost perpendicular fall [Knife Falls] of several feet. The rapids above continue impassible for a canoe several miles above. Here is the Commencement of the Portage aux Coteau (or Knife portage in allusion to the sharp argillite, which cuts the feet of the men) one and a half miles in length over a country high & dry & of good soil. The river opposite its commencement makes a picturesque appearance. A rocky island rises above the water 100 feet, while the water at its base is white with foam. The portage path is mostly over a soil high & dry & supporting a fine growth of timber among which the maple predominates. Our baggage & canoes were not at the upper end of the portage until 3 o'clock in the afternoon & the men were suffered to rest one hour. In the mean time I re-vac[c]inated those indians who were with us & who had been vaccinated at Fond du Lac, as a part only had taken the discease. We embarked and passed up an almost continuous series of rapids, for a distance of 9 miles where we encamped for the night at the foot of the Grande Rapide. The country bordering upon the river was mostly quite high & supported a fine growth of timber such as Ash, Pine, Maple, &c however, a part of the distance was a mere tamerack marsh & wholly useless for cultivation.

June 29th. Friday. Embarked at 4 A.M. and immediately commenced ascending the Grand Rapid which is about three miles in length, and is a rapid descent over round boulder rocks. The canoes of Lieut. Allen were so much injured by this that it became necessary for him to land for the purpose of repairing which detained him so long that he did not reach us this evening. We continued ascending the stream which for a long distance above the grand rapids was quite mild. The shore was mostly high & containing a growth [of] pine or hard wood, or a second growth of Aspen. We passed two small rivers one from the right [Floodwood] & one from the left, and at length, just before sun set having arrived at the [East] Savannah Riv. which enters the St. Louis from the left we encamped for the night. The St. Louis Riv. is here 150 yards in width.

The Savannah Riv. is a mere creek. We saw during the day a few ducks & the indians who accompanied us killed one or two.

June 30. Saturday. We had encamped on the previous night upon a piece of ground low & marshy and were much annoyed by the musquitoes. Left our encampment early in the morning and proceeded to ascend the Savannah Riv. The stream at first wound its course through a low, wooded & alluvion country, which at length became an extensive savannah, covered with a dense growth of grass. The stream now became more & more winding and upon it were occasional flocks of ducks and teal. The banks were so low & wet as to prevent our landing for breakfast & we continued our course until we arrived at the portage which leads by a small stream [West Savanne] to Sandy Lake. This was twenty four miles from the encampment at the mouth of the river & we did not arrive at the portage until 12 o'clock. The whole length of the portage is 13 pauses being 6 miles.

The stream near the commencement of the portage became so winding that the canoes would scarcely pass and it became necessary to take part of the lading from them and having forwarded that which remained to return for the other. We walked on near half a mile through mud & water nearly knee deep until we arrived at a small knoll of dry ground which is called the commencement of the portage where we took breakfast.

The voyageurs soon after commenced carrying the goods one pause on the portage. This pause was extremely muddy & the[y] frequently sank with their loads nearly to the hip in mud & water. At the end of this pause the portage passed two pauses through a tamerack swamp of the worst kind. The mud was so deep that the voyageurs could not possibly proceed with their loads & accordingly a few pieces being placed in the canoes they were dragged over the mud while the voyageurs sank nearly to their waists. Having passed over this a short distance farther brought us to dry land timbered chiefly with elm & bass wood where we encamped for the night, our voyageurs being almost complet[e]ly worn out.

Just at evening we heard a gun at the commencement of the portage, which we supposed to have been fired by Lieut. Allen.

Found hordes of musquitoes. General direction of the Savannah Portage South West.

July 1. Sunday. A storm of rain which arose during [the night?] continued during the morning & most of the day. Notwithstanding which Lieut. Allen arrived completely drenched at our encampment at abou[t] 11 o'clock a.m.

The musquitoes were extremely annoying during the whole day & while we remained stationary it became necessary for us to keep our tents closed in order even to endure them. Towards evening the sky became clear & the rain ceased, but the musquitoes still remained innumerable.

July 2d. Monday. At an early hour the voyageurs returned for the canoes which had been left one pause back & carried them five pauses ahead, soon after which they commenced carrying the baggage. We arose at about 7 o'clock when nearly all the baggage had been taken from the encampment. The sky was clear & the sun shone brightly. We passed over three pauses to breakfast. The portage path was almost the whole distance a mere quagmire & the men were almost continually more than half leg deep in mud. I found much difficulty in forwarding myself without a load & could scarcely imagine how those who carried loads could walk. The country appeared to be almost wholly an undergrowth of aspen, bass wood and occasionally tamerack.

Towards the termination of the portage we passed over a series of pine ridges with intermediate marshes until we arrived at a low meadow through which the Savannah Riv. flows. This stream is here (18 miles from Sandy Lake) a mere brook, sufficient to float a canoe. It discharges its waters into Sandy Lake. Our tents were forwarded to the end of the portage and we encamped upon a beautiful grassy hillock in the midst of the low ground. The soldiers & voyageurs encamped two pauses back. A gentle south wind had wafted away the musquitoes but as it died away at evening they attacked us in hordes & almost completely drove away all rest.

July 3d. Wednesday. Our men occupied the morning until 10 o'clock in bringing the baggage & canoes to the river. After which a short time was occupied in gumming canoes and arranging baggage. We embarked and proceeded down the river which wound its way through a low meado[w]y country bounded on either side at a short distance by hills supporting a growth of Norway Pine, or which had been replaced by a secondary growth of aspen.

The winding nature of the stream & its narrowness rendered it difficult for us to proceed & consequently our progress was slow. We passed through a small lake and a part of the baggage was taken around two rapids where by the addition of a stream from the east, the water became sufficiently deep & broad to give somewhat the appearance of a river and our progress was much accelerated.

It was not until after 4 o'clock P.M. that we arrived at Sandy Lake. This is an extremely irregular lake containing many deep & sandy bays whence its name. The Amer. Fur Com. station was formerly on the southern shore of this lake upon a low sandy plain, but it has recently been transferred to the junction of the West Savannah Riv. & the Mississippi.

We passed through Sandy lake to its outlet, a distance of 5 or 6 miles and descended this two miles to its junction with the Mississippi (600 miles above the falls of St. Anthony). Here upon a low point of land, almost surrounded by water is the Amer. Fur Comp. station & the residence of Mr. Aitkin. We found a Mr. [Joseph] Bodwin [Beaudoin] a Frenchman in charge who, immediately upon our arrival invited us to take up our quarters in the house of Mr. Aitkin which we did. We found here five hundred miles above the Falls of St. Anthony a fine, convenient framed house with the interior painted & neatly arranged. He has also 8 or 10 head of horned cattle, 4 horses & several swine. He has large fields under cultivation & they are said to be extremely productive. This is the location of a large band of Chippewa indians but they were now absent on their summer hunt. We here saw the curious method of indian burial above ground. The coffins are supported upon poles elevated 4 to 6 feet.

The Savannah Riv. furnishes a good supply of wild Rice.

A fish closely allied to the white fish [tullibee], carp & bass are usually taken in Sandy lake but no fish are taken here in the Mississippi Riv.

Upon our arrival at the post of the fur com. the indians, what few were present, fired a salute in honor of the arrival of the representative of their great father, Mr. S.

The Mississippi immediately below its junction with Sandy Lak[e] Riv. is 100 yards broad. There are fine fields of grass upon the Savannah Riv.

July 4th. Wednesday. We were severely annoyed by the musquitoes in the evening & could only escape them by getting beneath our musquitoe nets. The forenoon of the day was occupied in distributing presents among the few indians who were here.

Lieut. Allen celebrated this anniversary of our independence by inspecting his soldiers and firing 24 rounds of cartriges. The dread in which the indians hold soldiery is truly astonishing. They consider them as men who have sold themselves to die & are consequently afraid of nothing. I vaccinated 59 indians (men, women & children) and afterwards prescribed to several others, besides extracting teeth &c. At six o'clock P.M. all things being in readiness we embarked & proceeded until 9 o'clock when we encamped in a thick wood of h[e]avy timber for the night. Two families of indians of Cass lake accompany us. An amusing circumstance happened here. Our cook while dipping a tea pot of water from the river fell in & was near drowning. He disposed of his tea pot effectually.

Timber Elm, bass wood, maple & aspen. Soil alluvion & good.

July 5th. Thursday. Embarked at 4 o'clock A.M. and followed the winding course of the river through a low alluvious country supporting a dense growth of timber consisting of swamp & white oak, bass wood, maple & aspen, with tamerack, white cedar, spruce, pine & white cedar. Soil apparently good. Stopped at 10 o'clock for breakfast. Late in the day we passed the mouth of Swan Riv. 15 yards broad which is 60 miles above Sandy Lake. This stream is said to furnish an abundance of fish in consequence of which it is the summer residence of a few families of Sandy Lake indians. The indians accompanying us fired a gun at the mouth of the stream & shouted hoping to attract the attention of the indians above, but they were undoubtedly to[o] far distant to hear the signals.

This stream like all the northern stream[s] discharges water highly coloured. Passed numerous small marshs or ponds which communicated with the Riv.

Encamped at 8 o'clock 12 miles above the mouth of Swan Riv. among the tall [horsetails] eaquisita [Equisetum] which are abundant in this northern country. Severely annoyed by musquitoes during the whole day. Saw numerous grey ducks & Mr. J[ohnston] killed a pheasant.

July 6. Friday. Storm of thunder & rain during the night. Hordes of musquitoes. Embarked at ½ before 6 A.M. A gentle breese during the day served to carry the musquitoes chiefly from the canoe, but notwith-standing this the sun came upon us oppressively warm. The Mississippi winds its way along through a country low in places and covered with a growth of elm, ash, & maple, or high & sandy pine ridges. These pine ridges have bee[n] burned over & the pines are seen to be killed for many miles in extent. Their place is supplied by a small growth of bushes chiefly aspen. The river has a current of 3 or 4 miles per hour and in low water it is said to have many distinct rapids, but the present height of the water renders them invisible. We saw & killed several grey ducks & pigeons.

Encamped at sun set upon a bank elevated 20 or 30 feet from the water & surrounded by pines—two miles below Trout Riv. Lieut. Allen did not arrive but a signal gun which was fired in the evening was answered by a shot which shewed that he was not far distant.

July 7. Saturday. Embarked at ¼ after 5 A.M. and continued to ascend the river through a country much resembling that through which we passed the day before except that the high pine timbered land rather pre-dominated. Two miles above our place of encampment we passed the mouth of Trout riv. a small stream which has its source in a lake [Trout] not far distant and which discharges water, which compared with the water of the Mississippi is comparatively pure.

Nine miles above this we passed the mouth of Pra[i]rie riv. a stream which also enters the Mississippi from the right and which derives its name from the immense tract of low prarie through which it passes. Two or three miles above this we encountered rapids which were extremely dif-ficult to ascend in the canoes, but they were not of great extent. Nine miles above this we arrived at the Falls of Peckagama [Pokegama]. The whole stream here passes in a shute of about 20 feet fall in a distance of about 300 yards to the level below, and affords a complete impediment to naviga-tion. The baggage was here landed & together with the canoes carried over a portage of about 300 yards. The falls are here over the quartz rock which certainly comes in, in a singular manner. No rock had been seen since leaving the Portage au[x] Coteau (which is the argillite) and none appeared during this day above.

It is not seen immediately above or below the falls & the whole that is seen is not more than 300 yards in length. We left the Falls at Peckagama at twelve o'clock, having breakfasted there. The falls derive their name from the division of the channel above the falls & which name, by the Indians has been transferred to the falls themselves. Immediately above the falls the country undergoes an essential change. The stream winds its course through immense savannahs which at this time are covered with several inches of water & present a most uninteresting appearance. Occa-s[i]onal points of land of a Sandy Soil & supporting a growth of Norway Pine or from which this timber has been burned reach the river & upon one of these we encamped near sun set. In our course through the savan-nahs we saw numerous ducks & the indians killed several of them.

Lieut. Allen whom we had not seen since the day before arrived at the encampment late in the evening.

We had occasional showers during the day.
Encamped 30 miles above the falls of Peckagama.

Notes to Diary 2—Distances from Fond du Lac to Sandy Lake
Fur Comp. House to Grand Portage 2
Galla 2
Head of Grand Portage (19 pauses) 7
Portage aux Coteau 6
Head of Portage 1½
Mouth of Savannah R. 56½
Savannah Portage 24
Head of Portage 6
Sandy Lake 18
Fur Comp. House 3
                                                   ———
                                                   126
Sandy Lake to Mississippi 2
                                                   ———
                                                   128

Distances from Sandy River to the Forks of the Mississippi
Sandy Lake to Mississippi 2
Mouth of Sandy Riv. to Swan R. 60
Trout Riv. 66
Prairie Riv. 9
Peckagama Falls 9
Peckagama Riv. 3
Vermillion Riv. 30
Deer Riv. 7
The Forks 15
                                                   ———
                                                   201

Forks to Lake Winnipeg 45
Width of Lake Winnipeg 12
Up[per] Red Cedar [Cass] Lake 45
Length of Up[per] Red Cedar Lake 9
Lac Travers [Bemidji] 45
Width Lac Travers 3
Separation 1¼
Separation 4¼
Portage of the Height of Land 45
                                                   ———
                                                   209½
Fork to Lac Vanse 4½
Leech Lake 40½

Cass Lake (Up. Red Cedar Lake) to Turtle Lake 45
Red Lake 45

Length of Red Lake 48
Width 12

Mouth of the Mississippi to its junction with the Missouri ...1200
St. Anthony's Falls 900
Fort Sandy Lake 600
Cass or Upper Red Cedar Lk. 301
Elk Lk. [Lake Itasca] (the Source of the Mississippi)

Indians vaccinated at Portage aux Coteau June 28th Thursday.

Med[icinal] Facts of the Indians [Diary No. 2]

Polypodium hexagonopterum—the radix is given where the action of the uterus has ceased in the gravid uterus.

Thalictrum divicum—Juice of used to allay the inflam[m]ation of poison from the Rhus toxicodendron.

Heuchera americana & Quercus radix used as an astringent to check bleeding.

Euphorbia corollata—Radix. An emetic.

Batschia immeling—Radix is used as a puccoon paint.

The indians scarify with a flint frequently the whole length of the arm.

Extremely fond of bleeding & in performing the operation they not infrequently wind a thre[a]d around the point of a knife & then drive the knife into the arm until the thread checks its progress. The consequence is that accidents of a serious character frequently occur. Saw one at Fon[d] du Lac where an aneurism was the consequence.

Myrica gale—Used as a yellow dye.

They show some little skill in the treatment of wounds. They not infrequently cut by scarifying and applying a horn from which the air is exhausted by the mouth.

The most prevalent diseases among the indians are those of the lungs. Saw a few cases of scrofula. The children are much affected with worms for which they do not possess any remedi[e]s. This vermicular habit of the children appears to arise from the habit of the parents of excessively feeding the children.

The indians invariably prescribe immense doses of the remedies they possess.

They frequently sear wounds with a red hot iron.

The Angelica (radix) powdered & mixed with oil is used as an anti vulnerary medicine & is much esteemed. It is said to reduce inflamation & to induce a healthy secretion of pus.

The Iris versicolor (radix) powdered is used for the purpose of reducing inflamation & its effect is said to be something similar to a blister.

Rubus parviflorus (radix decoction of) is much esteemed as an astringent in disentary [dysentery].

Batschia immeling (radix pulverized & mixed with tallow) is used in checking the progress of ulcers & in eruptive diseases.

July 8 to 17

No. 3

Mississippi R. near the Falls of Peckagama to Leech Lake.

July 8. Sunday. Remained at our encampment. Rain nearly the whole day & extremely cool. One of our indians returned towards evening with 8 ducks. And reported a lodge of indians above us on the river.

July 9th. [Monday.] Embarked at 4 A.M. The morning was chilly & the dew was falling rapidly but we wrapped ourselves in our cloaks & were tolerable comfortable. The Mississippi here wound through a broad savannah & occasionally nearly returned upon itself; but the height of the water, which was so great as to remain 10 or 12 inches over the whole savannah, [enabled us] to take nearly a straight course until we arrived at a smaller stream which enters the Mississippi from the right, here our guides informed us we would save much time by ascending this fork & making a portage to Little Lk. Winnipeg [Winnibigoshish], instead of following the Miss. which bends far to the west. This measure was determined upon & we left the Missis. and ascending the small stream one or two miles we entered Bogotawa [Ball Club] lake 10 miles by 2 and passing through this breakfasted at its head. Half a mile above this we entered a second small lake & from this passing by a stream so small & winding that the canoes could scarce be dragged through we entered a third lake from which by a portage of one pause 806 yards we reached Little Lk. Winnipeg. These two lakes are separated from each other by a beautiful pine ridge, but near the either [edge?] of the lakes the portage is marshy. In taking this route we did not see the junction of the Leech Lk. Riv. with the Miss. which takes place a few miles above where we left the Mississippi.

We passed through Little Lake Winnipeg, a distance of 3 miles & again entered the Mississippi. Little Lk. Winnipeg is a rice Lk. By the tortuous course of the Mississippi at a distance of ten miles we entered Lk. Winnipeg a lake 12 or 15 miles in length and at the foot of which is a trading post situated near the mouth of a small stream [Turtle Portage River]. We found here a half breed in charge & a few indians. I vaccinated 13. The indians do not reside upon the lake but inhabit the woody country between this & Rainy Lk. They are called Mountaineers.

This post is small. There are only three buildings. A small variety of white fish are taken in Lk. Winnipeg & ducks in abundance.

July 10th. Tuesday. Embarked at half after 4 o'clock A.M. & passed through Lk. Winnipeg. Saw great numbers of leeches. The lake appears thickly wooded upon each side. The lake takes its name from its dirty water. Having left this lake we continued to wind along the stream which passes through a country similar to that below being a wide savannah embraced by ridges of yellow pine. Upon one of these ridges we stopped for breakfast & I attempted to follow the ridges & keep pace with the canoes in a botanical excursion but finding this impossible after travelling more than a mile I again embarked. At one o'clock we overtook the indians accompanying who had gone ahead & they presented us several quarts of fine strawberries. We arrived at the entrance into Cassini [Cass] or Up. Red Cedar lake & found here several indians who fired a salute upon our arrival. The chief of the band [Oza Windib] (Yellow head) is the same who has accompanied us from the Riv. Brule on Lake Superior. He informed that the Ind. village is upon a large (Grand) [Star] Island near the centre of the lake. We immediately repaired to it & found here several lodges of indians. Their gardens looked flourishing but the soil is rather sandy. Up. Red Cedar lake was so called from a few trees of red cedar grow[ing] upon an island in the Lk. It is a beautiful transparent sheet of water & furnishes an abundant supply of white fish. It was from this lake that Gov. Cass turned back in 1820 & hence the name Cassini lake has been applied to it. Pike visited on snow shoes in the winter & found it to be in lat. 47° 40′ 42″. One days travel in a S. westerly direction leads to Leech Lk. where reside one of the most powerful & warlike of the Chippewa bands in the north. We have learned that the warriors from Leech Lk. & those from this lake in all 100 in number had joined in a war party against the Sioux & that while proceeding on their expedition they met a party of Sioux proceeding against themselves. An action insued and resulted in the loss of one Chippewa & 3 Sioux. The Chippewa belonged to this band & his widow was here at the time of our visit. The Scalps of the 3 Sioux had been forwarded to this place & the relatives of the Chippewa killed were dancing the Scalp dance. The 3 scalps each consisting [of] a piece of the scalp to which was the attac[h]ed hair, rather larger than a silver dollar, were fastened to a bow of wood & decked fantastically with the feathers of the war eagle. These were supported like so many flags upon sticks by three girls who continued dancing with all the relatives of the disceased while the other indians & particularly those of our party made them presents as a remuneration for the loss of their relative. This served to test the hatred of the Chippewas to the Sioux and to shew how highly they honored one slain in battle. I even saw one of our indian guides pull off the only pair of leggins he had & present them.

As it had been determined that the main body of our party should remain here while the others visited Elk Lk. the actual N. western source of the Mississippi the afternoon was occupied in making necessary arrangements.

I vaccinated 55 men women & children.

A stream enters on the north side of Cassini Lk. which is the route taken to Red Lk.

The corn in the ind. gardens at Red Cedar Lk. appeared fine.

July 11th. Wednesday. At 5 o'clock Messrs. Schoolcraft, Boutwell, Allen, Johnston & myself embarked on our proposed visit to Elk lake [Itasca]. Each one of us occupied a separate canoe which was paddled by one voyageur & one indian who acted as guides. These small canoes were obtained from the indians. We passed through Cassini Lk. which is more than 10 miles in [breadth?] and entered the Mississippi which had here become quite small. We had scarcely entered the river when it commenced raining & continued until 10 o'clock when we stopped upon a pine ridge for breakfast having already passed several rapids. The musquitoes during the time of the rain were annoying in the extreme. We again continued ascending the river through a pine country with a sandy soil until at a distance of 40 miles from Cass Lk. we reached Lac Travers [Bemidji] a beautiful sheet of water 10 or 12 miles in length & 3 or 4 in width. At its entrance were a few scirpi [bulrushes] but as we advanced it becomes free from them. Upon the northern shore are hills apparently elevated some 150 or 200 feet & heavily timbered. The shores are principly sandy. Just before entering the Mississippi above the lake are seen the remains of a trading house which was formerly occupied. No indians reside permanently upon the shores of this lake. The stream where it enters this lake does not exceed 15 yards in width even at this high state of the water. Not more than half a mile above Lac Travers we passed through a second small lake [Irving] an[d] 3 miles above this reached the forks of the river. One of the forks describes a large curve in a westerly direction & this is known as the Mississippi R., while a smaller fork [Schoolcraft or Yellow Head River] enters from a S. westerly direction & traverses the country (as we were informed by our indian guide) in such a manner that by taking this route we will be enabled to reach Elk lake by a portage of 6 miles, half a day sooner by ascending this fork than if we ascend the true Mississippi R. It was accordingly determined that we should pursue the Smaller fork in the ascent & descend the true Mississippi. Soon after leaving the forks we passed through two small grassy lakes [Marquette and LaSalle] in which were many ducks & several were killed by our party. At a few miles distance above these lakes we entered another of beautifully pure water [Lake Plantagenette] & 6 or 8 miles in length, the shores of which were sandy and supported a dense growth of pine.

My canoe previous to entering this had been much injured & it became necessary for my men to put to the shore for the purpose of gumming it. This occupied some time & the party were a long distance ahead of me, we passed through this & entered the stream, a mere creek which continued its course in a most tortuous manner through an immense savannah bounded on either side by at a distance by ridges of sandy pine land. It was not until dark that I reached our party & I found them encamped at a great distance from the stream having waded in the water of the savannah in order to reach a point of gray Pine which was suffici[e]ntly dry to admit of encamping. Here were hordes of musquitoes & upon unrolling the oil cloths from our blankets we found them completely wetted by the rain which had continued almost constantly during the day, but as it had ceased considerably we were enabled to dry our blankets in peace [?] & pass a tolerably comfortable night.

July 12th. Thursday. The damp and fatigue of yesterday gave us many aches on the morning of this day & it was only by great exertion that we were enabled to embark at 5 o'clock A.M.

Mr. Johnston embarked a short time before the others of the party for the purpose of killing game. We had not continued far before we heard the report of his gun & upon our arrival we found that the indian accompanying him had fired upon & killed a large deer which had come to the stream for the purpose of drinking. It was quite amusing to see the indian cut it to pieces.

The banks of the stream for several miles above our encampment were considerably elevated & supported a growth of gray pine or of aspen but we had not proceeded many miles when this stream wound its way through an immense savannah covered with tall grass & an occasional tamerack swamp. Just before arriving at this my canoe became so much injured as to require gumming & this detained us until the others of the party were far advanced. Having gummed our canoe we proceeded expecting soon to find our party encamped for breakfast; but the savannahs were so wet as to prevent them from landing & it was not until near two o'clock that I found them encamped at some distance from the stream in a forest of gray pines. Having breakfasted we proceeded. A slight rain rendered the afternoon uncomfortable in the extreme & increased the musquitoes almost beyond endurance. We continued to ascend the stream through a savannah until 4 o'clock P.M. when our indian guides informed us that the stream, which was here a mere brook was so crooked & rapid that we would find an advantage in making a portage. We accordingly landed & ascended a high sandy hill covered with gray pine & rich in rare plants from which the portage commenced. The course of the stream had been S. westerly but the portage was here in a westerly direction. The canoes & baggage were taken by the men making each a full load & we proceeded upon this pine ridge for a distance of two miles when we arrived at an insignificant fork of the stream which we had left. Here we encamped at the foot of the pine ridge & were immediately attacked by hordes of musquitoes. The sandy pine land over which we passed was barren in the extreme. The morning which had been cloudy & damp was superceded by a pleasant evening & cl[e]ar sky.

July 13. Friday. The sun had scarcely arisen when we embarked and ascended the winding brook at which we had encamped the evening before 12 or 15 miles when we arrived [at] a small lake [Assawa or Perch] or rather pond one or two miles in length & half a mile in width from which the portage to Elk Lk. or Lac La Beiche [Biche] is made. The head of this lake is 120 miles from the forks. The shores of the pond are marshy and the tameracks covered by a dense growth of Lichen present a picture of desolation. Immediately after landing we followed the portage in a westerly direction through a complete marsh, sinking at each step nearly k[n]ee deep into the mud until at near a quarter of a mile from the lake having arrived a[t] a knoll of dry land we stopped for breakfast. We remained here a short time, during which the indian guides amused themselves in shooting pigeons. Two whipporwills were also killed.

Soon after we resumed our march which continued nearly two miles through a tamerack swamp with many fallen trees & thick brush in addition to our sinking deep in the water, we were attacked by hordes of musquitoes & the men found much difficulty in pursuing their way with the canoes. Having passed over or rather through the marsh we arrived at and passed over a series of sandy ridges sup[p]orting a growth of gray pine covered with lichen & presenting a most desolate appearance. These ridges separate the head waters of the Mississippi & its tributaries from those of Red Riv. Having passed over this pine country near 4 miles making six miles in all we arrived at Elk Lake, near its head.[2] This lake is considered the true source of the Mississippi & our party was the first which had ever reached it. The lake is small & irregular having many bays proportionally deep. It is 8 miles in length & has an average width of ¾ of a mile. The shore rises gradually to a considerable height from the water but the soil is the same barren sandy kind which has already been mentioned & the principal timber is gray & yellow Pine & aspen. Near the foot of the lake is a small island [Schoolcraft] upon which we landed & Mr. S. ordered the American flag to [be] hoisted and it was so secured as to remain a long time. This was the first flag ever hoisted at the head of the Mississippi R. No indians reside permanently upon this lake, but the remains of a few lodges were seen upon the island and we saw near them large fish bones & the shells of several immensely large terrapins. The water of the lake is transparent and our indian guides stated that it abounds in fish. We saw numerous shells upon the bottom & I obtained specimens of both bivalve & unnivalve [univalve] molusci [Mollusca].

We arrived at the lake at about one o'clock P.M. and having coasted through it & made some examinations our sole object, of visiting [the source of the] Mississippi was accomplished and at half after four we commenced descending the outlet of the lake, which is here a mere brook passing rapidly over a sandy bottom with occasional rapids over round stones. It became occasionally necessary to cut away trees which had fallen into the stream & made complete obstructions, but notwithstanding this the rapidity of the current was so great that we passed rapidly along & the uncommon height of the water aided us much. Near evening we arrived at a rapid of nearly perpendicular fall where we walked around while the canoes passed down loaded. These rapids were over bowlders of primitive rocks.

At 9 o'clock we encamped upon a sandy pine ridge elevated nearly 100 feet above the stream having proceeded 35 miles. The course of the stream was here Northwesterly being direc[t]ly opposite to its course below.

Near evening a deer was seen feeding at a distance in the savannah & one of the indian guides went in pursuit & fired upon him but missed him.

July 14th. Saturday. It was near five o'clock before we embarked. Immediately after embarking the course of the stream was between hills of sandy pine land and there were occasional places where the water was white with foam as it passed over the large primitive bowlders forming the bottom of the stream. In passing one of these the canoe occupied by Lieut. Allen, in consequence of some mismanagement of the guides capsiz[e]d and the whole contents were precipitated into the rapids & as the stream had here acquired a tolerable size some of the articles which sank could not be recovered. The stream soon passed from these hills & wound its way in a most tortuous manner through an immense savannah. The canoes were ahead of me. In passing through the savannah I saw a deer within a few rods of me, but as I had no gun he was suffered to remain, for when I hollowed at him he only jumped one or two jumps into the grass & stood with his head elevated above it to examine us.

Proceeded 35 miles & landed for breakfast upon a pine ridge possessing the same barren character as that which had been noticed above. We noticed here an indian lodge & near by it the bones & some of the hair of a moose which our guides stated together with bears were found in abundance here & in consequence of which it was a frequent resort of indians in their summer hunts. But a short distance above where we had stopped for breakfast is a portage of 4 pauses to Folle Avoine R., one of the forks of Red Riv., & which course is som[e]times taken in light canoes in reaching Red Riv. & the great N. western plains. The Yellow Head & Mr. Johnston who had preceeded us in the morning returned soon after we had stopped for breakfast & stated that they had visited a place where the Sioux had intrenched themselves for the purpose of waiting the passing of the Chippewas & from which they had killed one man while ascending the Riv. When we descended to them we stopped a few moments to examine them & afterwards continued our course through a country the greater part of which for a width of several miles was covered one or two inches with water & supported an immense growth of grass & scirpi. The stream was more winding than any I had seen & altogether uninteresting. We saw a few ducks & killed 4 or 5.

Near evening we passed the mouth of Pin-id-i-win [Little Mississippi] Riv. or "the riv. where we were killed," so named in reference to a lodge of Chippewa indians who were killed here by the Sioux. It is a stream half as large as the one we had descended. Its junction is 106 miles below Elk Lk.

My canoe had been considerable injured in dragging it over points of the savannah which was occasionally done to save passing a long distance around & near evening my men stopped to gum it. This having been done I proceeded & it was not until near dark that I reached the others of the party who had lande[d] for supper having determined to continue proceeding during the night. Lieut. Allen be[i]ng anxious to take the courses of the stream & for that purpose determined to remain until morning the others of us having had our beds made in the canoes took our places w[h]ile the guides & men paddled forward.

The moon shone brightly & the hills between which we passed enveloped in their sombre covering of pine & partially illuminated by the rays of the moon presented a most picturesque appearance.

Near twelve o'clock I was aroused by the quick discharge of two guns an[d] rising quickly I saw a deer bounding from the water. The indians supposed him to be wounded but under existing circumstances it was impossible to purs[u]e him. We passed Lac Travers 153 miles below Elk lake in the night.

Saw the forked tailed hawk sailing over our heads & fired at him but missed. A rare sp[e]cies.

July 15th. Sunday. At Sun Rise we were a long distance below Lac

Travers. We continued to proceed an[d] arrived at the [Star] Island at 9 o'clock. Lieut. Allen did not arrive until near evening. Early in the morning while we were descending the river one of the indian guides discovered a crane upon the shore & snapped his gun at him but it flashed & he soon after discovered it to be a young one jumped upon the shore & caught it. We found our party at the island much recruited by rest. In the afternoon Mr. Boutwell collected the indians and gave them scripture instruction.

At sunset Lieut. Allen had inspection & fired a few rounds.

The indians who had arrived since we had left here had erected their lodges directly in the rear of our tents & at evening the[y] commenced singing & dancing & their shouts together with the drum upon which they were constantly tapping were extremely annoying. I had just lain down for rest when the dancing suddenly ceased & soon after an indian came & wished me to go & see a woman who had been taken suddenly ill. I did so & found her in violent pain & with many symptoms of a continued fever. I administered & returned to my tent.

Red Cedar Lk. takes its name from the red cedar which is found upon one of its islands. Our guides who had accompanied us from Sandy Lk. were exchanged for new ones to accompany us to Leech Lk.

July 16th. Monday. Much of the morning was occupied in distributing presents to the indian[s]. Mr. S. in the name of the President, their father, presented Yellow Head a flag & medal, thus constituting him a chief. Mr. S. delivered the indians his message, persuading them to lay down the[i]r arms, & cease hostilities with the Sioux at the same time stating that it was not the wish of their father that they should be still & allow the Sioux to kill them. The whole band is 150 strong. I vaccinated this morning 34 persons, some of whom were Leech Lk. Indians & was happy to find upon examination that of the 55 vaccinated on the 10th of July only one had failed to take. We embarked at 10 o'clock & proceeded 16 miles upon the lake to a portage leading S. Westerly, of one pause 1050 yards to a Small lake [Moss], one mile in length. The portage path passed over a sandy ridge timbered chiefly with the pitch pine & which had rather a barren unpromising aspect. I found several interesting plants upon it & saw numerous places where the deer had been stamping. I also saw many places where the gopher had been digging. Having embarked & crossed the small lake a second portage of 4 pauses two miles in length, we found the path dry and the country similar to that we had passed over in making the other portage. From this we embarked on a small weedy lake [Shiba] scarcely half a mile in length which is the actual source of Leech Lk. Riv. This lake is thirty seven miles above Leech Lk. notwithstanding which although it was near sunset it was determined to reach that place this evening. The [Steamboat] Riv. at its commencement is a mere brook winding it[s] way through immense savannahs of wild rice & scirpi but before having travelled far we passed through two small lakes, (producing immense quantities of wild rice) from which the stream becomes much larger.

We did not arrive at Leech Lk. until near eleven & my canoe, which had fallen in the rear, was only enabled to do so by following a small indian canoe which was found at the portage. Some time before our arrival the arrival of the others of our party was announced by the discharge of a volley of guns by the indians.

Upon my arrival the darkness of the night prevented my gaining any idea of our situation & nothing was seen excepting indians & dogs.

July 17. Tuesday. I was awakened by the continued discharge of guns & separating the door of my tent I saw the smok[e] ascending from an indians lodge near by, where some of the indians had assembled & were firing a salute in honor of our arrival. We arose & looked about us. In the rear of us were two or three buildings which we supposed to belong to the traders, but we afterwards learned that we were at the scite of the old indian village & that the trading post had been removed from this to another part of the lake. Upon the removal of the trading post the buildings here were presented to the chief of the band, Flat Mouth [Gueule Plat].

The congregated band of this lake is larger than any other in the Chippewa nation being more than 800 strong & I had never before seen indians who possessed the manly & decided appearance of these. The young men are without exception warriours & scarce a year passes over their heads without their sending a war party against the Sioux. Their chief Flat Mouth has perhaps more absolute authority than any other of the Chippewa nation. He is a man of dignified commanding appearance, & extremely ceremonious. We had before our arrival heard the traders say much of him; & his independen[ce] & authority is a great annoyance to them. It is said of him that upon one occasion the trader here committed some violation, as it was considered, when the chief ordered him to remain in his house & finally even refused him liberty to go to the lake for water & his orders were strictly enforced by his young men. He resides in one of the houses & at an early hour he sent for M[esse]rs. Schoolcraft & Johnston, whom he had before saw to breakfast with him. They stated upon their return that he had three mats spread upon the middle of the floor & pointing to one for Mr. S. & another for Mr. J. he took the third. A white fish cooked finely & a cake with tea constituted the breakfast. An indian woman, his wife officiated, turning out tea as he ordered. It is related of the chief that having two or three wives he had left one with a child at Pembina & after an absence, having returned he requested the child but the woman appearing loth to part with it he drew his knife & cutting the child in twain threw one part to her telling her to take her half.

At about 10 o'clock I visited his house for the purpose of vaccinating the indians of the band. I found the chief sitting upon a bench & upon my arrival he rose to rec[e]ive me while I was introduced by Mr. J.

The room was decorated with war spears, clubs, flags & medals & the the whole character was that of a warrior. I observed in one corner of the room a bed stead upon which were spread his blankets & they made quite a civilized appearance. I commenced vaccinating those who were in the room at the time of my arrival. They were all young men, warriors & were seated upon the floor completely around the room. I vaccinated during the day more than 400 men, women & children, pulled some 15 or 20 teeth & prescribed to the sick. One who had received a ball wound in the leg at an action with the Sioux only a few days before made application & I dressed his wound.

At 11 o'clock Lieut. Allen held inspection & fired a few rounds of cartriges, the military operations of his men excited great interest among the indians.

The chief was invited to dine with us a[t] two o'clock P.M. & soon after a council was held with the indians, presents of calico, shirting, cloth, k[n]ives, trinkets, tobacco, ammunition &c &c were distributed among them & the object of our visit laid before them. The chief replied that he wished us to remain until the morrow, that he might be fully prepared to answer, but when told that we would depart this evening he replied that he had listened to the advice which had been given him to remain at peace, but that his enemies were constantly murdering those of his band, & last of all they had killed his own son while he was hunting & that the last war party was sent out to retaliate his death. He said he was necessitated to fight in self defence. He then alluded to the treaty of Pra[i]rie du Chien & stated that the Americans had not fulfilled their threat to punish the ag[g]ressor, for they then said that they had a long arm & would stretch it out against the trans[g]ressor &c &c.

The council being closed we procured a guide & embarked. When I came to the shore I saw the chief completely attired [*MS. illegible*]. When we arrived he was blacked & in mourning for his son. But he had requested a white shirt from Mr. S. & stated that since he had come to visit him he would wash away his mourning. He was dressed in a military frock coat & hat & made altogether [an] imposing appearance. He stated that he would see us again on the morrow. The indians of this band have greater resources than any I had before seen, game (bear, deer, elk, moose &c in abundance), fish (white fish) & wild rice. Their village was upon a sandy soil (nearly the same as most of this country) but a field of corn & potatoes planted by the indians were in a flourishing state.

Mr. Boutwell made some remarks to the indians. [At this point Houghton gives a list of plants which are included in Henry R. Schoolcraft, *Narrative of an Expedition Through the Upper Mississippi to Itasca Lake . . . in 1832* (New York, 1834) and so are omitted here.]

Sandy Lake to the Mississippi	2
Mouth of Sandy R. to Swan R.	60
Trout R.	66
Prari R.	9
Falls of Peckagama	9
Peckagama R.	3
Vermillion R.	30
Deer R.	7
The Forks	15
Lake Winnipeg	45
Width of Lk. Winnipeg	15

Cass Lake 30
Length of Cass Lake 14
Lac Travers 40
Width of Lac Travers 3½
Separation 4½
Pin-id-i-win (or Riv. where we were killed) 43
Elk Lake 106
Length of Elk Lk. 6

The Forks to Lac Vanse 4½
Leech Lake 40
Lac Traverse by the Southern Fork to Portage to Elk Lk. 120
Portage 6
Cass Lk. to the mouth of the De[s] Corbeau Portage from Cass Lake to Lake (1 pause)

Mouth of the Mississippi to its junction with the Missouri ...1200
St. Anthonys Falls 900
Fort Sandy Lake 600
Cass Lake 303
Elk Lake 211
Length of Elk Lk. 8

Med[icinal] Facts from the Indians No. 3

Lonicera hirsuta (decoction of the radix) is much esteemed as an effectual remedy in gonorrhea.

Trillium pendulam—Decoction of is used as an anodyne.

Lillium [Lilium] philadelphicum is the prarie potatoe of the Indians & is used as an eadible root.

Cypripedium pubescens (the powdered radix) is used as an anodyne. It is also applied to relieve the excessive pain of an inflamed ulcer.

Prenanthis [Prenanthes] altissima (radix decoction of) is used to induce the secretion of lac when it fails to take place as it should.

Polygala Senega—Radix is used in various disceases, & is very much esteemed. Those mentioned by the indian[s] were sore throat &c.

Geranium dissectum—Radix is also sometimes used but its object is not clear.

July 18 to 25

No. 4

From Leech Lake to Fort Snelling.

July 18th. Wednesday. Leech Lake is a large lake, being the third Lake (not considering Lk. of the Woods) in size. 1st. Red Lake, 2d. Mille Lac[s] (the source of Rum Riv.) 3d. Leech Lk. & 4th. Up. Red Cedar or Cassini Lk.

Leech Lake has many deep & irregular bays & several islands of considerable size. Its waters are transparent & afford an abundance of fish particularly the white fish. The name is translated from the Indian & was undoubtedly given in allusion to the great numbers of those animals which are found in its waters.

The sun had arisen before we had embarked. Proceeded down one of the deep bays until we arrived at a portage leading in the direction of the R. des Corbeau where we landed. Our indian guides who were to join us did not arrive & we proceeded upon the portage. From the sandy shore of Leech lake the portage leads over a sandy pine Ridge 1070 yards to a small lake [May]. The path was well beaten, it being the great war road of the Chippewas & we passed over it without difficulty. We here entered a small lake which is the commencement of a series of 5 which discharge their waters into Leech Lake. The channels connecting them were so narrow that the canoes could only be drawn through with great difficulty. Having passed these & a second portage of 700 yards which lead us over a beautiful dry hill wooded with pine we entered a small lake or pond [Lake of the Island] upon the height of land destitute of an outlet. We had crossed this & just landed when one of my men called me to come & see & upon going I saw a peculiar lizzard darting with great rapidity over the baggage which lay upon the shore & running out its tongue. It appeared like a striped snake with eyes. Its swiftness prevented my taking it. I walked around the pond examining the botany & observing numbers of fish near the shore. I returned for a hook & line & with Lieut. Allen & Mr. Johnston succeeded in taking ten fine yellow bass in a short time. While here the chief of Leech Lk. Flat Mouth and his great medicine man [Maji Gabowi] overtook us & we learned that our guides would not join us as they feared to pass through the country in consequence of its nearness to the Sioux. I had forgotten to mention this medicine man is one deserving, of notice among the Leech Lake Indians. He is a tall lank man of a stern & imposing appearance which have undoubtedly assisted him greatly in gaining the reputation he hold[s] among his band. He has five wives who live with him in the same lodge.

A portage of ¾ of a mile lead us to a second lake destitute of an outlet. The portage path here passes over a hill considerably elevated & hence it is called by the indians the hill [Mountain] portage. Having crossed this portage 1900 yards, we arrived at still another Lk. & having crossed this we entered upon a portage of ½ mile which lead us to Long [Water] Lk. [Eleventh] the source of the R. Des Corbeau. Here upon a beautiful elevation we encamped for the night. Flat Mouth & his medicine man took tea with us & had many circumstances of indian war to relate to us. They also mentioned the disturbance now existing between the Fox & Winnebago indians & the United States.

Of the country passed over a few general remark[s] are sufficient. The soil is sand & barren not unfrequently almost pure sand. The high ridges are timbered with pine or when this has been destroyed by fire, aspen &

the low wet land is chiefly elm ash &c with some soft maple—and occasional tamerack swamps. Thermometer 90° in the shade at 12 o'clock.

July 19th. Thursday. The principal part of our party embarked at ¼ before six o'clock A.M. but I was detained a short time in extracting a tooth from the gread med. man & also from his squaw.

I presented Flat Mouth with a lancet & requested him to vaccinate those of his band in whom the vaccine matter should fail. We passed through long lake about 5 miles in length & a mere brook connecting this with a second lake [Little Vermillion or Tenth] enabled us to pass to a second lake but not until we had cut away many bushes. In the same manner we passed through 9 small lakes connected by streams. The last was not passed until near evening & the stream at its outlet was 40 yds wide.

Saw a deer standing on the shore but did not succeed in taking him. We had heard thunder during nearly the whole day & late in the afternoon the clouds completely overspread the sky & it rained & hailed violently while the peals of thunder were terrific. This did not delay us & we continued our course. 55 miles below Long Lk. we passed Shell Riv. a fork of considerable size which joins the des Corbeau near the S. West & proceeding 5 miles below this we encamped upon a high bank. It [was] after 9 o'clock P.M. when we encamped & the darkness was such that we could scarcely distinguish any object except by the glare of the lightning which was playing around us. The grass & bushes were wet & all things around us were truly uncomfortable. Lieut. Allen did not arrive & we fear he has lost the channel.

The country as we descend the streams partakes more of a prarie character & I find the plants which are peculiar to the praries.

Our course during the day was nearly South. Our men shot two or three large pickerel during the progress of the day.

July 20. Friday. Embarked at 6 o'clock A.M. Sky clear. Sun shines brightly. Descended numerous small rapids at which places the bed of the Riv. is of bowlders of Prim[itive] rocks. Stopped for breakfast at 10 o'clock upon a pine opening, not long after which Lieut. Allen reached us. He mentioned that he had lost his way in a small lk. above. Late in the afternoon, one of Lieut. Allens canoes being much injured he stopped to gum it & we all landed for a short time. The banks were elevated & the soil good being a pine opening with a wet prarie back. The same in character as the soil on the Namakwagon [Namekagon] Riv. The country as we descend the Riv. des Corbeau improves & becomes quite prarie like.

The middle of the day was intensely hot, & exposed in the middle of the stream and intensity of the sun was almost unsupportable.

Near evening & 80 miles below Shell Riv. we passed the mouth of Leaf R. 40 yards in breadth & having descend[ed] the des Corbeau 5 or 6 miles farther we encamped upon an elevated bank being a pine opening having traveled during the day 80 miles.

Saw many pigeons & ducks some of which were killed by our men.

July 21. Saturday. Embarked at 5 o'clock A.M. & at a distance of 15 miles below our encampment passed the mouth of Meadow [Prairie] riv.

a stream which enters the R. des Corbeau by a mouth 10 yards in breadth. Prarie Riv. is one of the great war roads of the Chippewas into the Sioux country. We saw above the Chippewa warpath upon the bank of the river Between this & our encampment were several considerable rapids. Below this river the country becomes of a Prarie character although it is chiefly oak openings & thickly timbered pine land. Sandy in its texture. Saw many flocks of ducks & numerous pigeons. As the morning advanced the sky became overshadowed with clouds & appeared much like rain & for comforts sake we stopped rather early, at nine o'clock for breakfast. The stream here had become large being nearly or quite 130 yards in breadth. We breakfasted & had scarcely proceeded down the river 15 miles when two canoes of indians were seen at some distance below us, this announced to us our near approach to the Mississippi R. We soon after arrived at an island dividing the river into two channels, here the indians whom we had met suddenly stopped & fired their guns, & it was not long before a long line of indian lodges upon an elevated bank announced to us the position of the indians. We reached them and the[y] fired a heavy salute upon our arrival. We found them to be encamped at the immediate junction of R. des Corbeau & the Mississippi.

The island before mentioned which is known as Crow Island lies directly in the mouth of the R. des Corbeau, dividing the channel. The R. des Corbeau near its mouth is a fine stream being 160 yards over. The stream is exceedingly short for one of that size being but about 205 miles in length. The general direction is S. East. In travelling by this route we have saved about two thirds of the distance which would be passed over in travelling by the Mississippi.

We landed near the indian encampment & as our canoes bringing goods from Sandy Lk. had not arrived we expected to remain here over Sunday. Our tents were pitched upon a beautiful elevation. We had not however, been here long when the canoe with the goods arrived & it was immediately determined to hold council with the indians & to proceed to a trading post 18 miles below on the Mississippi R.

The indians, many of whom upon our arrival were absent on hunting excursions soon began to come in & one party of them brought in three bears one old & two young ones. One of the cubs was presented to us & we found it to be delicious. The council was held, presents distributed, & the object of our visit stated by Mr. S. Several speeches were made by the chief & braves in answer.

I vaccinated 236 in all. At about 6 o'clock P.M. all things being in readiness we left here for the trading post. The Mississippi has here a current of 4 or 5 miles per hour. Its banks are elevated, & present a beautiful variety of prarie, oak openings & thickly wooded land. These praries furnish food for hordes of deer & elk. At 8 o'clock we arrived at the trading post which is situated upon a beautifully elevated point of land & within an oak opening, directly in the rear is a large prarie the back part of which is skirted with heavy timber. This post of the Amer. Fur Comp. has not been long established. Mr. [Benjamin] Baker the director was present &

we found him a kind, affable & intelligent man. His gardens were fine & showed that the soil was well adapted to farming purposes. Potatoes, corn & pumpkins were the chief [crops]. The indians at the Isle des Corbeau were from the Sandy Lk. Band.

Mr. Baker mentions that the rock (probably granite) makes its appearance about 20 miles above this in the bed of a small stream near the Mississippi.

July 22. Sunday. Remained at our encampment. Mr. Boutwell gave some scriptural instruction to the indians who had come from Isle des Corbeau. I walked back into the prarie & found several interesting plants. Vaccinated 17 & extracted several teeth.

Near evening the rain commenced falling & it rained nearly the whole night.

July 23. Monday. Embarked at ½ after 5 o'clock A.M. Only a few flying clouds & these breaking away soon after the sun shone brightly. 20 miles below we passed the Grand Rapids a chute of 8 or 10 feet fall in 30 yards. The Rock formation here appears being undoubtedly Talcose slate (the first rock in situ which has been seen since leaving the falls of Peckagama). I at first mistook it (from its mixed character) for mica slate— the layers are nearly vertical. There are occasional rapids for a distance of 35 or 40 miles when there is another chute of a less extent. Rock here also appears in situ but it is the gran, quartz rock & it is seen for a distance of 5 or 6 miles, rising in small knobs from the water or from the adjoining shore.

The current is strong being 5 or 6 miles per hour & we descended rapidly; the country through which we passed is delightful in the extreme. A beautiful variety of prarie, oak openings & thickly wooded land (chiefly oak, elm & maple) the banks are sufficiently elevated to secure them from inundation. The soil is rather sandy, but appears to be well adapted to agricultural purposes. We landed for breakfast upon a beautiful prarie of several miles in extent, almost perfectly level & having the appearance of a lake. Upon it was a small growth of grass & I found several plants of great interest. The grass still being damp I determined to proceed without breakfast for two or three hours until it should dry for the purpose of drying my botanical apparatus. I did so & landed upon a prarie 30 miles below for that purpose. While engaged here the others of the party passed & were nearly half a hour in the advance before I started.

As we descended the stream an occasional deer was seen bounding through the grass of the praries & we saw a few ducks upon the river.

Near evening we passed a lodge of indians upon the river and I saw a deer skin stretched upon sticks & meat drying. 10 miles below this I reached the party at near 9 o'clock having advanced during the day 130 miles.

The Mississippi was here ¼ of a mile wide.

July 24th. Tuesday. Embarked at 5 o'clock A.M. Saw two red squirrils swimming the stream. Passed at 20 or 30 miles below our encampment at the mouth of Crow R., and twelve miles below this the mouth of Rum R.

This last R. is a stream of considerable size. It has its source in Mille Lac[s], a lake next in size to Red L. It is the residence of a small band of indians.

Twenty nine miles below Rum R. is the falls of St. Anthony. The whole stream is here precipitated over a perpendicular descent of about 16 feet. The whole descent of the rapids & falls conjoined will not probably vary far from 40 feet. We did not stop for breakfast before arriving at this place & it was near one o'clock P.M. at the time of our arrival. We passed by a portage of one pause (about 600 yards) around the Falls & embarked below. Upon the opposite shore is a saw mill built for the purpose of sawing lumber for Fort Snelling, situated 9 miles below, at the mouth of the St. Peters [Minnesota] R. There are also two or three other buildings & the officers quarters appear spacious. At the time we passed there were only 4 or 5 soldiers here to guard the mills. The hornblende rock which had been seen 150 miles above the falls disappeared & no rock was seen until within two or three miles of the Falls when at a sudden the sandstone is seen elevated in a bluff of 15 or 20 feet of a snow white appearance & capped by a slaty lime stone. The lime stone I found at the Falls to contain stilastrites, encrinites, mitettites &c and well characterized as the mettaliferous lime Rock. The inclination of the rock is but slight but upon pursuing it for some miles it will be seen to be South westerly, and as a lime rock, sandy & indistinct in its characters appears on the Missi[ssi]ppi some hundred miles below constituting the great lead formation. It appears to me that it is the same lime rock which appears here & which by its dip is seen below & crosses the whole country lying between the Miss. R. & Lk. Michigan, forming the rocky bluff of the S. E. coast of Green Bay & forming the Southern boundary of Lk. Huron. This is have [half?] surmise.

This lime stone at the Falls of St. Anthony is of a silicious character & unfit for burning. The stratum of sand stone which appears here may possibly be embraced by the lime stone & belong to the same formation, of this I am not perfectly determined as yet. Its texture is peculiar being almost loose sand destitute of cement. It is of a snowy white colour & appears much like loaf sugar.

In consequence of the loose texture of the sandstone underlying the lime Rock, it is worn away more rapidly than the lime rock in consequence of which large masses of the latter are lying in complete confusion at the foot of the falls. The river is here divided by an island [Hennepin] which separates the water into two unequal channels the greater part of the water pouring over the western side. The water undoubtedly wears away the sandstone rapidly. The island mentioned by Carver as being in the rapids directly below the falls, does not appear, having been, in all probability worn away. Leaving the falls & embarking we proceeded down the rapids & found Lieut. Allen (who had landed upon the opposite side, & had his canoes and baggage take[n] around the falls by a portage of 5 pauses in a cart) not quite ready to start and we waited a few moment[s] for him when we continued our course.

The falls of St. Anthony here drop the water, as it were into the rock formation & we here passed along, with bluffs upon either side elevated some 2 or 300 feet. Nine miles below the Falls the St. Peters R. joins the Mississippi. It is a broad stream navigable a great distance.

Upon the height of land & elevated 200 feet is Fort Snelling. It is placed at the immediate junction of the St. Peters R. & the Mississippi. The appearance of the fort is truly commanding. Upon the opposite side of the St. Peters is a trading Post.

The day was considerably advanced at the time of our arrival, & our tents were immediately pitched upon a piece of low ground immediately before the fort. Having visited Capt. [William R.] Juett [Jouett] the officer in command, we were politely invited to take up our quarters in the fort but as our business required our attendance below we declined doing so.

July 25th. Wednesday. Fort Snelling is constructed of lime stone & is a beautiful work. It is constructed for the accom[m]odation of a regiment of men but is at present only occupied by three companies. Commander Capt. Juett Officers Lieut. [Ingham] Wood, [Jefferson] Vail, [Edward R.] Williams & [blank in MS.] Assistant Surg. [Robert Wood].

It is in lat. 44° and is said to be healthy in the extreme. The gardens of the officers appear fine. Corn, potatoes, melons &c &c flourish finely. The country back is a beautiful rolling prarie, with occasional groves of oak &c. The rock being limestone the soil is durable & well adapted to agricultural purposes. It would support a dense population. There are numerous small lakes in the vicinity of the fort which furnish an abundance of fish & both the Mississippi at this place & the St. Peters R. are well stocked with fish such as pike, bass, & cat fish. Fine opportunities are offered for sporting with the gun as the surrounding country produces an abundance of grouse, (or prarie hen) rail, wood cock, grey snipe, ortelons, pigeons, &c and by extending the tours into the country a few miles deer and elk may be taken in abundance.

This place has been until now the residence of the Ind. Agt. for the Sioux, Mr. [Major Lawrence] Talliaferro. A council was held with the chiefs of two bands resident on the St. Peters river above at some distance & with Peti[te] Corbeau [Little Crow] whose village is on the Mississippi some miles below here.

The commander of the fort now acts as ind. Agent.

Capt. Juett in accordance with instructions from U. S. seized two boats laden with ind[ian] goods & which contained whiskey that traders were taking up the St. Peters for the purpose of trading with the indians. There were 19 casks of alcohol equal to the same number of barrels of proof spirits.

Upon the opposite side of the St. Peters R. is a trading post which appears to be extensive, as there are many buildings. But I did not visit it.

Sioux language is extremely harsh.

Many cattle kept at the garrison.

Distances from Grand Island of Upper Red Cedar Riv.

to Grand Island to portage to Leech Lk.	16	
1st Portage	1050	yds
Length of Lk.	1	m
2d Portage (4 pauses)	2	m
Leech Lk. 8 village	7	
Portage to Riv. des Corbeau	8	
1st Portage (one pause)	1078	yds
1st Lake	1	m
Channel	100	yds
2d Lake	2	miles
Channel	150	yds
3d Lk.	300	yds
Channel	10	yds
4th Lk.	½	m
Channel	10	yds
5th Lk.	¼	m
Channel	200	yds
Marrais	¼	m
Portage	700	yds
7th Lake	¼	m
Portage	¾	m
8th Lake	1½	m
Portage	1960	yds
9th Lake	1	m
Portage (to Long Lake)	½	
Shell R.	60	
Leaf R.	80	
Meadow R.	20	
Mississippi R.	45	

Isle des Corbeau to Bakers Trading Post	18
Great Rapids	20
Little Rock	40
Rum River	112
Falls of St. Anthony	29
St. Peters River (Fort Snelling)	9
Riv. St. Croix	45

Indian Med[icine] & Treatment No. 4

Tradescantia virginica (Powdered Radix) is much esteemed as an emetic.

Liatris scariosa (Deco[c]tion of Radix) used in Hemoptesis.

Asclepias tuberosa, (the bruised Radix is used as a poultice) Is applied to reduce excessive inflamation particularly the inflamed breasts of females.

Arabis hirsuta & Kyllinga noomocephala [?], (the bruised Radix) are used as an antidote to the bite of the Rattle Snake.

Eryngium (bruised Radix) used as an antidote to the bite of the rattle snake.

Rocks in Place on the Mississippi R.

Gran Quartz—Falls of Peckagama.

mica? ⎫
        ⎬ slate—Grand Rapids
Talcose ⎭

200 miles above the Falls of St. Anthony

Hornblende Rock—Little Rock

150 miles above the Falls of St Anth[ony]

Thirty miles up Rum Riv. is a rapid at which place the Rock is Primative Rock (Lieut. Jameson says granite) is seen in place in Bluff of 50 ft.

July 26 to Aug. 1

No. 5

From Fort Snelling to the St. Croix R. near the
Mouth of the Namakwagon R.

July 26. Thursday. The sun had but just risen when our tents were struck, but we were detained a long time & it was near eight o'clock before we embarked. Lieut Allen did not embark at this time. We proceeded 10 or 12 miles down the R. where we arrived at the Peti[te] Corbeau (a Sioux village). It was situated on a beautiful rise of ground beneath the bluffs which bound either side of the river, and several rude houses which were occupied by the indians displayed more of an attempt at civilization than I had anticipated. We stopped here a short time & Mr. S. held a council but we found much difficulty in interpreting the language as there was only one of our men who understood the Sioux language & he but imperfectly & as he did not understand English it became necessary for him to translate into the Chippewa & Mr. J. from that into English. A bag of flour was presented them. I saw an indian boy come in with his bow and arrow & three red squirrils, which appeared almost like the grey squirril.

We proceeded several miles farther & while breakfasting upon a sandy Point Lieut. Allen overtook us. Forty five miles below the mouth of St. Peters R. the St. Croix R. enters the Mississippi & this which communicates with the Bois Brule of Lk. Superior is to be ascended in our return to the lake superior. The banks of the Miss. between the mouth of the St. Peters R. & the St. Croix R. are much elevated being from 150 to 200 feet above the water and this is the level of the country which in soil is similar to that surrounding Fort Snelling. But a few miles above the mouth of the St. Croix R. is a small band of Sioux upon the Eastern side of the Mississippi. They original[l]y belonged to the band of the Peti Corbeau.

We entered Lake St. Croix which commences almost immediately from the Mississippi & ascended the lake 20 miles in a northerly direction where we encamped for the night. Lk. St. Croix is a beautiful sheet of water, through which the waters of the St. Croix enter the Mississippi. It is thirty

six miles in length and has an average breadth of 1½ miles. The shore
is mostly composed of bluffs of calciferous sandstone which rise quite
abruptly to a height of from 150 to 200 feet. The country above is mostly
prarie & oak opening & is beautiful beyond description.

This day has rendered the geology of the country plain. The general
dip of the Rock formation is seen to be South Westerly. The sandstone
which was seen at the falls of St. Anthony proves to belong to the calciferous Sand Rock formation, both the geodiferous & compact varieties
are seen & these are frequently quartzose opalacious & sparry. The carboniferous formation continues through Galena & constitutes the lead formation there as it also does in Missouri. The same metalliferous lime Rock
which appears at the falls of St. Anthony & which capp the bluffs as we
descend the Mississippi may be supposed to form the Easterly shore of
Green Bay & the Southerly Shore of Lk. Huron.

It may with much propriety be supposed that the lead of Galena as well
as that of Missouri are found in the upper of & sandy part of the calciferous sand rock & not far distant from the mettal. L. rock.

July 27. Friday. Embarked at 5 o'clock A.M. The morning was cloudy
but it soon cleared away & the sun shone brightly. On the last evening I
saw a brilliant A[u]rora borealis. The appearance of the lake & its banks
were much the same to the head of Lake St. Croix. When near its head
we saw an immense flock of Pelicans. The general direction of Lake St.
Croix is north & S. & the river enters it from the north. The river for a distance of 25 or 30 miles above the lake has a most desolate appearance.
On either side are low ground subject to be overflowed in the fall & spring
& at all times marshy. These are covered with a dense growth of underbrush & some large trees of elm, ash & soft maple, back from these the
bluffs rise to a great height. Higher up the river we saw trees of the butternut. Thirty five miles above the lake the calciferous sand rock which
had thus far been a constant attendant disappeared & its place was supplied by perpendicular bluffs, forming the immediate pass of the river, of
Hornblende rock (var. greenstone) elevated some 150 or 200 feet. I
landed & procured specimens. The hornblende rock was tough in the extreme & produces that ringing sound which [when?] struck which is peculiar to it. But a short distance above this rock we met an indian trader
[Joseph R. Brown] with four small canoes who was descending the river.
His post was about 25 miles above on the St. Croix R. at a place called
two rocks. It was this trader whom Peti Corbeau had reque[s]ted might be
removed as he was so near the Chippewa & Sioux lines that he was the
cause of war parties of those tribes coming frequently in contact. Although
he traded in Chippewa territory his licence was taken from the agent at
Prarie du Chien. The trader stated that he did not intend to return to re-
occupy this post. We were here in hearing of the falls of the St. Croix R.
and we were anxious to reach them this evening & accordingly although
near sun-set we proceeded but we had scarce left the landing when the
canoe which I occupied struck upon a small stick which penetrated the
bark of the canoe tearing a large piece from it in consequence of which

the canoe filled with water almost immediately. My men by jumping into the water, although it was near their necks, were enabled to prevent its sinking & to take it to the shore. The other canoes continued their course, but I was compelled to wait until mine could be mended. This occupied considerable time and it was quite dark before I embarked again. We had not proceeded far when we entered a nar[r]ow defile of rocks [Dalles of the St. Croix] elevated perpendicularly 150 or 200 feet through which the river had forced [its] way with great velocity. We had passed nearly two miles through this narrow track which seen only by star light was truly grand when we arrived at a strong rapid, where although the water below could scarcely be seen the white foam raised as it passed over gave us in our egg shell canoe a truly frightful prospect. The roar of the water as it dashed from side to side in the chasm did not subtract from the grandeur of the scene. We attempted to ascend the rapids but the canoe struck upon a rock & commenced leaking badly & as the high rocks by which we were surrounded prevented our landing, we much feared that the canoe would sink before we could retrace our steps. However one man continued bailing while the others paddled the canoe down the stream, with great caution as the darkness prevented our seeing the dangers before us.

Having returned two or three miles, I landed upon a sandy point in the river & remained here during the night. As the tents were in the other canoes I wrapped myself in a blanket & placing a musquito net over me lay down upon the sand for the purpose of gaining repose & I soon sunk into a profound sleep from which I did not awake until on the morning of [the 28th]. Lieut. Allen has not arrived.

July 28. Saturday. Long before sunrise I was awakened, by the hoarse crys of a fish hawk which [was] performing its gyration over my head. I immediately awakened my men who hastened to repair & load the canoe when we embarked upon entering this depth of rocks by day light they looked still frightful. They proved to be hornblende rock precisely analagous to that which was seen below.

Having passed through this defile, we commenced ascending a series of rapids & at length arrived at a chute of 10 feet fall in 300 yards [Taylor Falls, Minn.]. Here I found the party had encamped on the preceeding evening & had not yet embarked from the other end. The goods were taken over the portage 400 yds.

The portage path was rocky. The whole water of the river here passes through a narrow opening in the hornblende rock. I found one or two plants here of interest. It was near seven o'clock, before we embarked from the falls. Almost immediately after embarking a series of rapids [Dobney Rapids] commenced which continues almost uninterrupted for a distance of two miles. We found much difficulty in ascending them & when we had nearly reached the head of the series of rapids (which were over bowlders of Primative Rocks) when my canoe struck upon a rock in consequence of which it received so much injury that it became necessary to land for the purpose of mending it. This occupied nearly two hours, when we again embarked & we had not proceeded more than a mile when we arrived where our party had landed, breakfasted, & embarked.

It was the same place where the trader we met had traded. There were two or three buildings & these were all in flames having been set on fire by Mr. Schoolcraft.

We proceeded on our course & found much difficulty from the low state of the water in the stream which although near 400 yards in width was so shallow that frequently it became necessary for my men to wade & drag the canoe.

The country above the Falls assumed a more arable aspect. I only saw the sand rock at one place & here only a short distance. It was nearly ten o'clock at night when a loud yell from my men announced that they were in sight of the fire of our party. Their yell was immediately answered by their fellows at the encampment, and we soon after reached it. The tents were pitched upon a beautiful open pine ridge. We had travelled during the day 40 miles.

July 29. Sunday. I was awakened this morning by one of the men entering the tent and taking a gun which was standing at my head & I learned from the conversation of the men that a deer stood in the water on the opposite side of the river. The gun was, soon after fired, but the fellow missed him.

The water of the Riv. was found to be falling rapidly & we embarked at 4 o'clock P.M. Lieut. Allen had not yet arrived & we had many fears for him, as we had not spoken [to] him since we left the Mississippi R. although he had been seen some distance in the rear on Lk. St. Croix. I left a letter upon a stick for him.

The rapids of the river which were formed by the passage of the water over primative bowlders were annoying in the extreme & our men waded much of the time lifting the canoes. We had not been long in our canoes when a canoe was seen at a distance above us & a yell announced that it contained an indian. He appeared much frightened, but we soon came up with him & found the canoe to contain an indian, a woman & child. They informed us that we would find many indians encamped at Snake R. We proceeded until it was quite dark when we encamped upon a high bank covered with Yellow Pine, having travelled not more than 13 miles. Our course during this day had been South west which indicated to us that the river here took a great bend.

The sandstone formation was seen during almost the whole of our journey this afternoon & rose in low bluffs from the river.

This circumstance leads me to suppose that the primitive formation at the falls separates the sandstone formation of Lake Superior, from the carb. lime stone formation of the Mississippi R. And that the P[r]im. formation continues across the Red Cedar R. above the Falls & by the way of Lac du Flambau to the Fox R.

July 30th. Monday. I was awakened in the night by some animal which was scratching near the fly of my tent, by [but] our yells frightened him away. We embarked at 5 o'clock & it was near eight when we arrived at the mouth of Snake R. a stream 50 yards wide which enters from the west. We found encamped here a part of a band of Indians which remain upon Snake River. They saluted up upon our arrival by firing. The chief, Buffalo [Pizhickee], met us & stated that our arrival was unexpected. A short council was held with them & I vaccinated them all 63 in number. Two canoes of indians agreed to go immediately and assist Lieut. Allen to reach the portage. Mr. S. wrote him a letter.

The indians at Snake riv. were upon a low point of land betwe[e]n Snake R. & the St. Croix. The soil appeared sandy but I saw hills of corn of last year which appeared to have been tolerably good. There is a trading post one or two days marches up this R. [on Pokegama Lake].

We embarked at 11 o'clock & three miles above Snake R. passed the mouth of Kettle R. a stream 30 yards in width which also enters from the west.

A series of rapids [Kettle River Rapids] had commenced some distance below this and our men had waded near a mile when for the purpose of lightening the canoe I also waded & supposing Kettle R. to be a branch of the St. Croix I followed up it some distance before I discovered my mistake & as the water was of considerable depth, being nearly to my arms I had much difficulty in fording it & being obliged to cut across a point of woods to reach the St. Croix I was nearly devoured by musquitoes. Having embarked in my canoe I found that we were soon at the head of this series of rapids & the water was sufficiently deep to allow us to make some progress. I observed in the low land (which was bounded at a distance upon either side by ridges of yellow pine) that the trees were chiefly elm, bass wood, maple & ash with scattering oak & butternut.

The temperature at noon day was almost insupportable the thermometer standing at 88° in the shade, & this made a striking contrast with the temperature at day light in the morning when the thermometer stood at 32° producing a severe frost. This serves well to illustrate the comparative temperature of morning and evening.

Twenty miles above Kettle R. we passed the mouth of Clam R. 30 yards broad, a stream which enters from the east & derives its name from the immense number of clams which are found in a small lake [Clam] which is its source.

Mr. Johnstons canoe had struck upon a rock & was so much injured that he had put to the shore to repair it, & my canoe had fallen far in the rear. Night came upon us & the shore was unfavorable to forming an encampment when suddenly I was aroused by a distant discharge of guns. I supposed we were near some large indian village as the firing continued. Upon my arrival I found Mr. S. encamped & was surprized to find that the whole firing had been done by four indian boys who had come down from Yellow R. on a fishing excursion. They stated that the village of Yellow R. was not far distant & that they would fish to it by day light.

They had collected a large quantity of birch bark for torches & at about 11 o'clock I saw them set out on their fishing. Pieces of bark were placed in a split stick & fastened to the bow of the canoe something like a fishing jack. By the light of these they speared the fish, chiefly carp.

Saw at Snake Riv. the process of weaving mats from rushes.

July 31. Tuesday. Embarked at 4 o'clock. The morning was excessively cold & misty. We reached Yellow R. at 8 o'clock & found here a few indians who saluted our arrival with a salute the balls of their guns whering [whirring?] by us in rapid succession.

It will be a year to-morrow since we visited this same place having encamped the preceeding evening upon a small island 5 miles above this.

Mr. S. presented the indians some provisions & I vaccinated them 33 in number. We saw here a boy some 12 or 13 years old who appeared quite white & upon inquiring we learned that he was the son of an indian trader Mr. Cadotte who was murdered two years ago by the Sioux. Mr. Schoolcraft requested the mother to send him to the Sault promising to educate him & she agreed to do so, but stated that he was her only support at present & that she would send him next summer. We embarked at Yellow R. at 11 o'clock and were five hours in reaching the Namakwagon R. This was the same part of the St. Croix R. over which we travelled last season. We found the river low beyond all conception & the rapids required our men to wade & lift the canoe. We passed three canoes of Indians who shouted loudly upon our approach but we did not speak with them. At the mouth of the Namakwagon we found two lodges containing several families belonging to the Namakwagon Lk. a small expansion of the St. Croix Riv. about 15 miles above this. We stopped & found the chief Pobawackowa [Kabamappa?³] here & Mr. S. presented them a bag of flour. I vaccinated them 19 in number. We here saw the process of making mats from the inner bark of the bass wood coulered [colored] variously. We did not remain here long, but continued ascending the Riv. The Namakwagon R. is quite as large as the St. Croix above the forks & this taking away of half the water made bad much worse. Almost immediately after leaving the Namakwagon R. a series of rapids commenced of such a nature as to require that a part of the baggage should be taken from the canoes & one party of the men carried this a quarter of a mile ahead while the other part lifted the canoe along over the bowlders of hornblende rock. I waded by the side of my canoe & assisted my men in finding the channel. Having passed this first rapid there was, a short space say half a mile of smooth water where a second series commenced and they continued in this way as far as we proceeded. It had become quite dark & we were unable, from the nature of the shore to find a place to encamp. While in this dilemma several canoes of indians from the Namakwagon R. overtook us & informed us that but a short distance above was a fine place. At the request of the chief [Kabamappa] I went from my own to his canoe which managed by himself & squaw soon reached the encampment, which was about 5 miles above the Namakwagon R.

Mr. S. killed a jumping mouse in the tent.

Aug. 1. Thursday. The night was severely cold. A heavy mist which hung over the rapids prevented our party from embarking until 5 o'clock.

The chief took two or three pieces into his canoe. A series of rapids commencing just above where we were encamped I walked half a mile up the Riv. & embarked. Saw the sandstone in place. The sandstone continued to the foot of the Namakwagon in the bed of the R. and was extremely red. The series of rapids continued during the whole distance with occasional intervals of still water.

The banks of the stream presented a most unpromising aspect being low & supporting a varied growth of fir, spruce, pine, ash, elm, tamerack birch, aspen & alder. Passed several small rice lakes. The rice was just in flower.

At night we arrived at Kabber mappa's [Kabamappa] village on the Namakwagon L. [Whitefish Lake] a small rice pond. There were here several permanent lodges but no indians. They had planted corn, potatoes, & pumpkins but they were all much injured by the late frosts & the pumpkins completely killed.

The soil appeared sandy & not well adapted to agricultural purposes. The indians here subsist chiefly on fish which are taken in the stream in abundance, such as sturgeon, cat fish, pike & carp. Two or three miles below the Ind. village is a fishing weir.

We encamped for the night at the scite of the ind. village having travelled 27 miles during the day.

The canoes were much injured.

Distances from the Mississippi R. to Lake Superior, by the way of the St. Croix & Bois Brule R.

Mississippi to the head of Lk. St. Croix	36
Falls of the St. Croix Riv.	45
Portage around the Falls	400 yds
Snake R.	66
Kettle R.	3
Clam Riv.	20
Yellow R.	25
Namakwagon River	15
Kaba Mappa's village on the Namakwagon	32
St. Peters R. to the St. Croix R.	45

Geology No. 5

At the Falls of St. Anthony the metalliferous Lime rock is seen upon a sandstone which I suppose to belong to the calciferous Sand Rock formation. This continues until we arrive within 8 or 10 miles of the Falls of the St. Croix R. where the hornblende rock is seen to cross the Riv. from east to west. This also [is] seen at the falls. But a few miles above the Falls, the Sandstone formation of Lk. Superior is seen which continues occasional[ly] as far as Snake R. & is also seen.

Are not the bluffs of the Red Cedar R. above the falls which are seen at a distance hornblende rock? & is not this a great prim. formation separating the Lime & Sandstone [?].

Sandstone Rock is seen in place 6 miles above Namakwagon R. & continues forming the bed of the river as far as the Namakwagon Lake & it is of an extremely red character.

Euphorbia (The Radix) is much esteemed as a cathartic by the Indian. By the French of the north it is known as the *medicine* of the Grande Rivere.

Aug. 1. to 16

No. 6.

From near the Namakwagon R. (on the St. Croix) to the Copper
Rock of Ontonagon R.

Aug. 2d. Thursday. Detained a short time in the morning in order to allow time for the men to gum the canoes. Embarked at 5 o'clock A.M. and ascended the Stream in a northerly direction. It had become quite small and wound its way through a marshy country of a most forbidding aspect. There were numerous small openings in the river which were well stored with wild rice in flower.

Fourteen miles above the Namakwagon, we passed the mouth of Clear [Eau Claire] R. a stream some 12 or 15 yards over which enters from an easterly direction. Along this is an indian trail which leads to La Pointe on Lk. Sup. Four miles above this a smaller stream Buffalo [Ox] R. enters from the same direction. Eight miles above this we entered Upper Lk. St. Croix a beautiful sheet of water seven miles in length & having an average breadth of 1½ miles. Near the foot of the lake is a small island considerably elevated which is the scite of an indian village. The chief, Nodin, is a son of Kabamappa. The indians were absent.

From the head of Lk. St. Croix an indian path (portage) of three pauses leads into the Bois Brule R. of Lk. Superior. We passed over the portage (the same which was passed by Capt. [Jonathan] Carver). It is in a northerly direction over a series of sandy ridges, supporting a scanty growth of yellow pine. Scattered among these is a scanty growth of deciduous underbrush. Among them I saw the Comptonia aspenifolia. The portage path being on the ridge separating the waters of the Mississippi from those of Lk. Sup. commands a fine prospect. On the right is seen a small lake destitute of an outlet & on the left an immense tamerack swamp lies at the feet & beyond this the hills covered with pine are seen rising above each other in beautiful succession.

At the foot of one of these ridges & within the tamerack swamp is seen a large spring or rather small lake which is the actual source of both the St. Croix and Bois Brule R. the one running southerly & the other northerly. In this spring the water is seen to boil up as it were with great rapidity & it is perfectly pure & has nearly the coldness of ice water. It was near night before all our baggage had arrived at the end of the portage. Yet we embarked the goods & walked ourselves through the marsh. The Riv. is here a mere brook winding its way through the tamerack swamp which in crossing the portage we had seen upon the left. The water proved not to be sufficient to float the canoes & Mr. Johnston went down the stream near a mile with an oil cloth for the purpose of constructing a dam. This raised the water sufficiently for our canoes to proceed through slowly. It was with great difficulty that I walked through the tall grass, brush & mud as far as the oil cloth dam, having crossed in the route several be[a]ver dams. Having arrived here we found that the dam had given way & as it was nearly dark we presumed that the canoes would not proceed. Mr. Boutwell & myself seated ourselves in the grass anxiously awaiting some signal which should inform us. By and by we heard a shot fired & following in the direction, we reached the party at 9 o'clock & found them encamped in a marsh & surrounded by alders which overhung the stream on either side, soon after which rain commenced falling.

Aug. 3. Friday. But little Rain had fallen during the night yet there was sufficient to render the grass & bushes perfectly wet & to render our walk unpleasant. We set out at 5 o'clock & the men dragged the canoes for a distance of several miles, while we walked upon the shore. The musquitoes were annoying. We were at length enabled, ourselves to embark. The stream wound its way through a low country abounding in tamerack & spruce. While passing along the stream Mr. J. amused himself in taking trout. He caught 50 or 60, I never before saw such quantities as this stream contains. At a distance of 35 miles from the portage a stream of considerable size, Hunting R. enters from the west. The Brule is here quite a river but it soon becomes rapid & the bottom being composed of bowlders of Prim. Rocks the passage is difficult in the extreme our men have frequently to wade to their middles in water. The country has a barren steril[e], rocky aspect, while cedar, spruce & birch, are abundant. Saw a few ducks. We descended 20 miles below Hunting R. & encamped for the night. At about 5 o'clock P.M. we passed an indian & his squaw with two or three children who were ascending the Riv. & he presented us several dried fish & some whortleberries for which he was presented in return some pork & flour.

Aug. 4. Saturday. Some rain during the night. Embarked at ½ after 4. Still cloudy. Musquitoes annoyed us all day. Soon after embarking we passed through several miles of good water with a gentle current but of sufficient depth to float the canoes. Having passed this a series of rapids commenced which continues to Lake Superior a distance of 40 miles in a perfect torrent. I had no idea of the descent of this stream from its head. I[t] cannot be less than 6 or 800 feet. Our men were required to wade & support the canoes during a great part of the day & notwithstanding this the canoes were much injured by the rocks which projected in all directions. We were compelled to make four portages around chuttes, they were of one pause each. The Sandstone Rock appeared in the bed of the R. but this was almost universally covered by immense heaps of bowlders of primitive Rocks. Near night as we passed around the fourth falls we supposed ourselves to be near Lk. Superior & it was determined to reach there this evening if possible. We accordingly made all speed possible. But my canoe was soon after so much injured in passing down the constant succession of rapids that one man was required to bail water from it constantly in consequence of which we fell much in the rear, notwithstanding this we proceeded until nine o'clock at night when we struck a second rock and the canoe had nearly filled with water when we reached the shore. My men struck a fire, and opened a bag of flour & were preparing something to eat, but completely overcome by the fatigue of the day I sunk into a profound sleep from which I did not awake until the next morning.

Aug. 5. Sunday. At the first dawn of day my men proceeded to gum the canoe immediately after which I embarked. Found here several lodges of Fond du Lac indians.

The one [Mongozid] who had charge of Allens boat, had the sails spread for drying upon my arrival. Remained encamped during the day. Our canoes were repaired. Indians presented us some fish & small potatoes. Heavy wind during the day & towards evening it rained violently, accomp[anied] with thunder & lightning.

Aug. 6. Monday. Embarked at ½ after 4 A.M. Morning pleasant. Soon after embarking the wind began to rise & it soon came on to blow a gale. The water came over the gunnel of my canoe but I was determined to continue. Mr. Johnston's canoe being low in the water he was obliged to put to the shore to prevent sinking. Mr. S. his canoe being larger, was enabled to keep far ahead. We landed for breakfast at one o'clock & as the provisions were in the canoe ahead we were compelled to make the best of our situation. My men cooked a piece of pork upon a stick & having mixed some flour with water they baked it in hot sand. Of this I was enabled in consequence of my appetite being somewhat sharp to make a tolerable meal. We continued our course and arrived at La Pointe at 9 o'clock in the evening three hours after Mr. S.

The wind had abated sufficiently to allow Mr. J. to proceed & he arrived at 2 o'clock A.M.

Aug. 7. 1832. Messrs. Schoolcraft & Johnston embarked at 7 o'clock A.M. leaving me (at my request) to join Lieut. Allen upon his arrival & to accompany him to the Sault Ste Marie.

Tuesday Aug. 7 to Sunday Aug. 12. Remained in the mission family at La Pointe. During this time I visited many parts of the Island. Crossed to the old fort. Much of the timber upon the Island is popular, original probably pine. Mr. [Sherman] Hall was harvesting a crop of barley which was fine. The potatoes & grass all appeared in a flourishing state. In the garden were beets, car[r]ots, squashes, cucumbers, turnips, & melons. Soil a red clay but will undoubtedly improve by tillage. Only a few indians here now. Visited Mr. Halls school.

Mr. Boutwell of our party remained here.

Lieut. Allen arrived on Saturday afternoon his men nearly worn out & gave a heart rending picture of his travels from the Mississippi.

His repairs occupied the afternoon.

Indians stole Lieut. Allens canoe blankets &c on the Brule R.

Aug. 12th. Sunday. Embarked with a gentle breeze at 5 o'clock A.M. But the wind soon died away & we were obliged to resort to oars. Took a fine trout with the hook.

Made a great traverse to the shore between Presque Isle & Carp R. where we arrived at 9 o'clock at night having made a traverse of 50 miles. We encamped for the night upon a narrow bank of gravel at the foot of the Porcupine Mts. Behind at a distance of ten feet was a thick forest of aspen pine & maple. Night Pleasant & moon shone brightly.

Aug. 14. Monday. Embarked at 5 o'clock A.M. A plover of a peculiar species hovered around the boat. Gentle breeze in the morning with some rain. Sky clear at 10 o'clock. Passed the Porcupine Mts. & arrived at Ontonagon R. at 3 o'clock P.M. We had hoped to find indians here from whom we could procure a guide & canoe to visit the Copper Rock, but in this we were disappointed as the whole of the indians had left the village & were undoubtedly at their gardens on Lake Okkogib [Gogebic?] at the head of the Ontonagon R. We did not however despair and accordingly landed at the site of their village and upon examining the grass we discovered a small canoe sufficient to be worked by two men in which we immediately determined to perform the expedition. Accordingly having crossed the River & encamped the party Lieut. A. gave them some general instructions and we embarked at 4 o'clock P.M. having provision for three days, our cloaks, hammers, chisels & a gun.

Two men worked the canoe one sitting in the bow & the other in the stern. We ascended the Riv. about 15 miles when the darkness of the night prevented our proceeding & we encamped for the night upon a small gravelly point of the R. The day had been tolerably warm and the night was more so than any I had experienced since arriving at the Lk. Under cover of the night hordes of small sand flies & a few musquitoes sallied forth and nearly devoured us. We wrapped our cloaks around us & lay down upon the gravel, before a fire for rest, but the flies soon rendered it necessary to rise and we were deprived of rest nearly the whole night. As we had been unable to procure a guide I had attempted the task although the course is an intricate one & I have visited it but once.

Aug. 15. Tuesday. Embarked at 4 o'clock A.M. & proceeded up the R. Saw a few ducks. Killed a hawk. Saw marks of the water having been 12 feet above its present level. Arrived at the forks of the R. at one o'clock & having taken our canoe from the water & made the necessary preparations, we were in readiness to proceed on our foot journey at 2 o'clock.

We struck into the woods & soon found the indian trail leading across the country to an immense clay hill which we had ascended the year before. This was about three miles above the fork & we reached it in an hour—the labour of ascending it was great & we were nearly overcome by fatigue when we reached its summit. Here we again followed the indian trail (elevated 2 to 400 feet above the R.) in a westerly direction, through a country of rich soil and well adapted to agricultural pursuits. We at length reached a ravine which I recollected to have crossed on the previous year and stopped to taste of the excellent water which flowed through it. Before reaching it I saw but a short distance from the path the trap Rock (or perhaps the greenstone of the Hornblende Rock) in place rising in several distinct knobs, & in a ridge which stretched in the direction of the Porcupine Mts. and appeared like one of its spurs. Upon leaving the ravine we followed the path with much difficulty as an occasional broken twig was nearly all our guide. We had travelled nearly three miles when we arrived at a small pond where I began to suspect we had lost our way, but we still continued to follow the broken twigs nearly three miles farther when we arrived at the termination of the path upon the banks of the R. and here we had evidence of having mistaken our way. The Riv. was here broad & with a gentle current, which would well admit of canoe navigation. We returned upon the trail but had not proceeded far beyond the pond when night overtook us and we could not find the continuance of the path. Much difficulty was found in striking a fire but it was at length accomplished and overcome by fatigue I wrapped my cloak around me, and sunk into a sound sleep on the ground. The soil over which we had passed was fertile. Trees maple, bass wood, elm, ash, pine & spruce. Saw the leather wood &c.

Aug. 16th. Wednesday. I did not awake until near morning when the severe cold of the night & dampness of ground was such as to prevent my sleeping. As soon as it was sufficiently light to enable us to regain the line of the broken branc[h]es forming the trail we commenced again our return & having retraced our steps near a mile we followed in a direct course at near right angles with the path to the R. which we reached at a distance of nearly three miles. While on our way I was severely stung several times by wasps in consequence of walking over a nest of them. Upon arriving at the river I was nearly convinced that we were below the mass of copper, but in order to decide satisfactorily I left the party & proceeded near half a mile down the R. and arrived at a fall in the R. (over sandstone Rock) of near ten feet, this I knew to be below the copper & returning to the party we proceeded to ascend the river and a[t] the distance of half a mile reached the mass of copper. It[s] position and appearance were not altered since I saw them last year except that there was more of the carbonate upon the Rock.

I should think that from my last examinations the size of the rock is rather greater than I had supposed last year & the proportion of rock greater. Having occupied most of the day until 2 o'clock P.M. in procuring some imperfect specimens our chisels were so much injured that we were unable to do more & we accordingly proceeded on our return & concluded to follow the course of the river to the Forks. We had not proceeded far below the falls when it became necessary for us to proceed upon the wooded banks. The scenery was wild & picturesque in the extreme.

Distances from the Mississippi R. to Lake Superior by the St. Croix & Bois Brulé R.

      Miss. R. to the head of Lk. St. Croix 36
      Falls of the St. Croix R. 45

Portage around the Falls	400	yds
Snake R.	66	
Kettle R.	3	
Clam R.	20	
Yellow R.	25	
Namakwagon R.	15	
Kabba-mappa's village on the Namakagon Lk.	32	
Clear R.	14	
Buffalo R.	4	
Upper Lk. St. Croix	8	
Portage (Length of Lk. St. Croix)	7	
Length of Portage (2 pauses)	2	m
Hunting Riv. (of the Brule)	35	
Little Falls (Portage one pause)	42	
Portage one pause		
Second falls	1	
Portage one pause		
3d Falls	½	
Portage one pause		
4th Falls	22	
Portage one pause		
Lake Superior	14	
Length of the Brule R.	117	
Do St. Croix R.	273	
Portage	2	
	392	

Indian Med[icinal] Facts &c. Diary No. 6

Their sweating lodges are a curios[i]ty, a lodge is constructed of bark & covered over with blankets. In this upon one side are placed several large stones heated to redness. The patient seats himself naked upon cedar boughs on the opposite side of the lodge & with a bunch of feathers or the branch of some evergreen tree he sprinkles the stones with water in which has been placed a small quantity of a decoction of the leaves of several evergreens (Pine, white cedar, spruce & balsam).

The lodge is filled with heated vapour & the patient falls into a profuse perspiration. Having remained a suitable length of time (var[y]ing from a quarter of an hour to two hours) he leaves the lodge & either plunges into cold water, or more frequently being wrapped up warm remaining quiet for two or three hours. The indians suppose this to possess miraculous powers. An indian who has been long on some arduous task is perhaps from his constant fatigue & exposure under the influence of some rheumatick affection. This he avers removes it effectually & as he says, "limbers his joints." It [is] used in almost all affections & often with almost as little knowledge as by the devotees of Thompson.

Indians affected by tooth ache not unfrequently drive the tooth from the head with a nail or some instrument of the kind.

The influence of medicine men among the indians is great & we not unfrequently find them with several wives. Their lodges are usually surrounded with images & manitou poles.

Decoction of the centre of the Iron wood (Ostrya virgin) is much used as a remedy for gonorrhea by the Inds.

Geology [Diary No. 6]

Red Sandstone is seen in the bed of the Brule R. nearly to Lake Superior. A few miles before reaching the lake the marly clay is seen rising in high banks from the river. It is extremely red. At the mouth of the Brule I saw a small piece of tufa, evidently formed from the water which flows from the clay saturated with lime.

A few miles east of the Brule R. the sandstone formation commences & continues in bluffs considerably elevated nearly to La Pointe.

At the foot of the Porcupine Mts. the sandstone is much inclined and is very red.

Trap Rock (Greenstone of the hornblende rock ? ? ? ?) was seen rising in high knobs on our way (while lost) to the copper rock of Ontonagon River. They were probably nearly a mile from the Riv. & having the appearance of being a continuance of one of the spurs of the Porcupine Mts. The rock at the Falls of the Ontonagon Riv. is sandstone variegated and but slightly inclined. It rises in bluffs of 2 or 300 feet.

The sandstone is seen on the lake shore but a few miles east of the mouth of Ontonagon R.

Aug. 16 to [Aug. 25]

No. 7

From the Copper Rock of Ontonagon R. to [Sault Ste. Marie].

The bluffs of sandstone rock rose perpendicularly to a height of 3 or 400 feet & below the River was rushing like a torrent among the immense masses of loose rock which were lying in comple[te] confusion. We followed the stream to the Forks having waded it twice. Passed over the whole of the sandstone formation which was much inclined and arrived at our canoe at 5 o'clock P.M. We embarked immediately & proceeded 15 miles down the R. when it had become so dark as to prevent our descending the rapids in safety and we landed at the foot of a clay bluff for the night. It was cold but although exposed to the open air without even a shelter of trees we were rendered tolerably comfortable by the aid of a large fire.

Aug. 16. Thursday. With the first dawning of day we left our encampment & proceed[ed] down the [river]. It rained slightly. We had not proceeded far when a Red deer was observed swimming the river. As he rose the back [man] aimed at him with a gun but it snapped, but as soon as he had gained the bank I fired upon him. But although he was evidently wounded time would not allow us to follow him. We arrived at the mouth of the R. at 10 [o']clock A.M. Found all things in order & the boat had been caulked & new pitched.

Embarked at 11 o'clock & had not proceeded far when a sail was seen coming towards us (the wind was ahead) it proved to be Mr. [Michael] Cadotte of La Pointe. He had a package of letters for our party & from him we learned that the Asiatic Cholera was raging below. Passed several canoes of Indians. Encamped at dark a few miles above the Rivere aux Miscerie [Misery] upon the open sandy shore.

Aug. 17th. Friday. Embarked at half after 4 o'clock A.M. At 7 o'clock we met eleven boats belonging to the traders which were conveying goods to the different trading posts. Mr. [Lyman] Warren of La Pointe, Mr. [Charles H.] Oaks of Lac de Flambeau, & Mr. [William] Aitkin of the Fonde du Lac & Up. Miss. departments were the directors. From them we learned the news of the country below. We remained with them nearly two hours procured some provisions from them & proceeded on our course. The traders were generous to an extreme. A gentle & fair wind arose & continued until near evening when the lake became perfectly calm. We passed the Keweena portage & just before sunset encamped in a small gravelly bay seventeen miles below. The trap rock is first seen to take the place of the sandstone about two miles back. Found many red raspberries near our encampment.

Aug. 18th. Saturday. Embarked at 4 o'clock A.M. and were carried along by a strong south wind at a rapid rate. We had heard during the night repeated peals of thunder & when we embarked the sky was overcast with clouds & betokened a storm & we had not been long in the boat when it commenced raining violently and continued at intervals during the whole forenoon. In the morning we passed along a long coast of rocky shore (trap rock) & not far from the shore the mountains of Kewa [Keweenaw] Pt. rose quite abruptly to a considerable height, the timber appeared stinted and being much of it spruce & white cedar gave a most desolate appearance. At eight o'clock we stopped to examine the vein of copper green which we had examined the year before & we remained here until near 12 o'clock and obtained fine specimens of the cop green, native copper & rock conta[i]ning specks of cop black. Embarked & proceeded along the rugged coast[4] which soon became crag as far as the green rock (about 8 miles from the extreme end of the point) when we also stopped for the purpose of obtaining specimens. The wind when we arrived here was high & we entered a deep bay directly in the rear of the rock where the sea was perfectly quiet & from this walked to the rock. While in the bay we saw two small hawks give chase to a gull and successively dart upon him. The gull shewed his fear by repeated cries but he nevertheless avoided their attacks for a long time & until overcome by fatigue one of the hawks succeeded in bearing him away in his talons. We obtained by the aid of a blast, from the green rock fine specimens of green & blue carb of copper cop black & calc spar coloured by carb of copper.

Embarked from here at 6 o'clock & proceeded under sail with a strong breeze 6 miles to the Little Marrais where we encamped for the night. We here found the rasp[b]erry (Rubus perviflorus) in fruit.

Aug. 19th. Sunday. As soon as the first dawn of day appeared we embarked and proceeded around the most northerly part of the Keweena Pt. The crag continues nearly to the extreme end of the Point, at which place the trap appears. Again as we proceed into the bay the crag rock is seen forming the immediate coast, but it only contin[u]es a few miles where its place is supplied by the trap rock. Having turned the cape we were enabled to sail with an easterly breeze with great velocity & we arrived within sight of the island [Traverse] from which the traverse of the bay is usually made at two o'clock but a fog prevented our making the traverse as we had intended as the Huron islands were invisible but when we had passed within five or six miles of the little island before mentioned we were enabled to perceive the Huron Islands & struck directly for them (distance 24 miles). The wind increased almost to a gale & we were compelled to strike several miles to the west of the Huron Islands & it was dark when we had reached the coast on the opposite side of Huron River. Upon nearing it we found that the whole shore was composed of high bluffs of rock against which the waves were dashing with great fury. We were near being cast upon them but we were enabled by great exertions with the oars to coast along 3 or 4 miles when a fire was discovered upon the shore and upon approaching it we found it to be at the mouth of Huron R. a small stream which enters the lake directly in the rear of the Huron Isds. We landed but found no one near the fire which was upon the shore. We had not been long encamped when a dog was seen prowling around us and a shot was fired at him but missed. This gave us strong reason to suppose that indians were near & we supposed that they had hid for the purpose of stealing from us. Precautions were taken accordingly and we were in readiness to make a serious attack upon them in case they should be discovered.

We had travelled during the day more than 100 miles.

Aug. 20th. Monday. I arose with the first dawn of day & walked out for the purpose of reconnoitering our situation & had not proceeded far upon the shore of the lake when I saw at a distance an indian who immediately run in the woods. Upon looking close I discovered a lodge among the trees and immediately walked to it. The indian appeared under many apprehensions but as I drew near he recognized me, for I had vaccinated him in the spring and came with his hand to receive me. He pointed up the lake and seemed to be surprized that we came from that direction, but when I explained as well as I was able that the boat contained the soldiers of the expedition, who were returning to the Sault de Ste. Marie, he appeared much satisfied, but after all his fears were not sufficiently quieted for him to visit our boat. Upon returning to our encampment I saw upon the sand marks where he had crept along for the purpose of reconnoitering our encampment. He was undoubtedly much frightened.

We embarked at ½ after four & coasted along the long series of high sandstone bluff Points and Sandy bays lying between Huron R. and the granite formation. The wind blew heavily & in gusts so that the sailing was rather dangerous. He had arrived within 7 or 8 miles of Granite point & had already seen several forms of granite upon which the Sandstone was lying when a dark coloured rock induced me to stop for the purpose of examination. I found it to be a succession of Hornblende Rock with thin strata of granite & mica slate.

Landed a short time at Presque Isle for the purpose of collecting minerals & near dark encamped at Riv. aux Mort [Dead River] upon a plain of sand—having travelled 57 miles.

Aug. 21. Tuesday. A heavy wind which arose during the night blew over two of the tents, but the one in which I was, by timely attention was saved in an upright position. Rain storm during the night. When we arose there was a strong head wind (easterly) but it soon moderated & at half after five we embarked. Coasted around the sandy bays & 10 miles from R. de Mort saw several canoes of indians, but did not speak with them.

The wind blew fresh & at ½ after 2 o'clock P.M. passed behind Grand isld. Saw two tents pitched at the trading post. Arrived at the last encampment on Grand Isd. at ½ after 3 o'clock P.M. and determined to proceed as far as Miners river 10 miles beyond before encamping. We proceeded along the high rocky shore, but the wind which had been tolerably fair during the fore part of the day had now, in consequence of a change of our course come to be nearly ahead & the heavy sea which was rolling prevented our making much progress. We however continued our course until half after 8 o'clock in the Evening and were within a mile of the R. when the wind had increased to such an extent that we were compelled to put back, and as the coast was bounded by perpendicular rocks elevated from one to two hundred feet, no landing could be effected until we reached Grand Island. This was a difficult task. The wind was blowing a perfect gale with a high sea & the darkness of the night was great, but we reached Grand Isd. & encamped at half after eleven o'clock at night.

Aug. 22. Wednesday. The wind continued blowing a perfect gale from the north and we were compelled to remain encamped during the day. Visited by indians who presented us with blue berries & a duck for which Lieut. A. presented them flour. Walked back upon the Island. After having passed through a cedar swamp we found the soil to be good & consist of dry ridges supporting a growth of beech & maple timber. Saw the remains of a trading house upon the Island.

Saw the indians Flambeauing [by torchlight] for fish in the evening.

Aug. 23. Thursday. The wind had changed to the South west & with our sails spread we embarked ½ after 4 o'clock A.M. The wind gradually increased & we passed the Pictured Rock, & Grande Sable & arrived at the

Grande Marrais 39 miles from Grand Island at eleven o'clock, the wind
here was blowing a gale but we concluded to continue our course to
White Fish Pt. The wind continued to increase & the sea had soon become so severe that we sincerely regretted our resolution but as there
was no harbour we were compelled either to continue or to beach upon
the shore. Lieut. A. had at one time nearly determined to run upon the
shore but finally concluded to remain at sea a short time longer. The
sea ran mountains high notwithstanding which we reached White Fish Pt.
and with much difficulty having turned it found a lee from the wind. Here
were Messrs. [J. W.] Abbott & [James] Armatinger [Ermatinger] who
were proceeding to Leech Lake for the purpose of trading with the Indians.

Aug. 24. Friday. Wind still continued a gale but it had veered to the
north. Thermometer at 6 o'clock stood at 46°.

Embarked at ½ after 7 o'clock and proceeded along under the coast
to Shell drake R. which we entered and encamped. The heavy sea compelled us to remain there during the day & night. Saw great numbers of
Shell Drakes & killed several pheasants. Saw remains of Indian Lodges &
of stakes for drying fish nets.

Aug. 25. Saturday. Night intens[e]ly cold. Embarked at 3 o'clock A.M.
and having missed our course coasted deep into Tonquoimenon [Tahqua-
menon] Bay, from which we reached Pt. Iroquois at 1 o'clock P.M. Here
a fair wind struck us & we were soon after at the head of the canal at
the Saut St. Mary. We here found Mr. [William] Holliday encamped &
about to proceed up the lake to his several trading posts. There were also
several citizens.

Our boat with ourselves & all the men & baggage was guided over the
rapids in safety by a Frenchman & we landed at the military wharf at
5 o'clock P.M.

NOTES

1. Gray wacke was a sandstonelike rock of prevailing gray color containing
fragments of other dark colored rocks and minerals and often having an
argillaceous cement.

2. It is of interest to note that only Schoolcraft refers to this lake as "Itasca"
in his journal. Boutwell, Allen, and Houghton call it Elk Lake or Lac La Biche.
In light of this great discovery, one may also wonder why the party remained
at the lake only three and one-half hours.

3. Houghton is probably referring to Chief Kabamappa, whose permanent
village was located on Whitefish Lake near Gordon, Wisconsin. Schoolcraft
noted in his journal that this was the Chief that the party met at the forks of
the St. Croix and the Namekagon.

4. It was along this stretch of coastline west of Eagle River that Houghton
was drowned on the night of October 12, 1845. In spite of many years experience on the lakes, Houghton misjudged the fury of the storm and his boat was
swamped before he could navigate it ashore.

2. Douglass Houghton to Richard H. Houghton.

SAULT STE. MARIE, 15 June, 1831

DEAR BROTHER:

Having arrived at my datour I hasten to fulfill my promise of writing to you before my final departure. My passage from Dunkirk [New York] to Detroit although a stormy one was pleasant; perhaps more so than (judging from the crowded state of the boat) could have been anticipated. At Detroit I spent a few days pleasantly with my friends; and on the evening of the 6th we left that place in the Steam Boat Shelden-Thompson, bound for Green Bay. The boat was much crowded having 190 soldiers (forecastle passengers) and 40 or 50 cabin passengers, on board. It was a matter of surprise to me that the banks of the Detroit & St. Clair Rivers contained the dense population that they apparently do, however, all the settlements are embraced in a narrow strip bounding the river. On the afternoon of the 7th we arrived at Fort Gratiot [at Port Huron] situated at the foot of lake Huron & 70 or 80 miles from Detroit. Here we found a Schr. bound direct to this place & after considering the crowded state of the Steam boat, together with the uncertainty of getting passage from Michilimacinack to the Sault, a distance of nearly 100 miles, we decided (in our own minds) that it would be better for us to leave the Steam boat for the Schr. & we accordingly did so. Mr. [John] Hulburt, Suttler at this post (Fort Brady) and Mr. [Angus] Bathune, Agent of the Hudson Bay Fur Company, also took the same Schr. with us. The passage through Lake Huron was made much sooner than could have been anticipated, & even in passing Saginaw Bay (the terror of Sailors) the sea was not sufficiently heavy to prevent my walking the deck of the Schr. without great exertions. Opposite the Thunder Bay Islands (near the head of the lake) we encountered a head wind with some roughness of the waters but it was only for a short time.—Nothing remarkable was noticed with regard to this lake except the great transparency of the water. The bottom could be plainly distinguished at the depth of 8 or 10 fathoms—The head of the lake is spotted with innumerable islands and particularly that arm of it which is at the mouth of St. Marys River; You will here see them from a single point producing perhaps only a single tree to those which have a length of 15 or 20 miles. The first remarkable isld. at the mouth of the river is Drummonds Island, remarkable as having been the resort of the British army after the surrender of Michilimacinack to the American forces. Here they erected a temporary fortification and quite a number of dwelling houses—most of which are now standing. From the water it has the appearance of a delightful village, but it does not contain a single inhabitant, it having been completely evacuated when it was finally declared to belong to the United States. Seven or eight miles above this, on the St. Joseph Isd. is also the site of a British fortification as well as a trading post. These are also completely evacuated although the island belongs to the British government. The wind being slight when we were near this point we manned a yawl and visited it. Nothing remained of the old Garrison except the chimneys of a few of the wood buildings and the base walls of those which were built of stone. Almost all the islands in the mouth of the river are rocky & barren (at least apparently so). They are covered with dwarf cedar, (both red & white) tamarack, white birch & some of them with maple. As we ascend the river the country appears more favorable but still it has all the marks of a northern climate. The mouth of the river for 30 miles, or more, is so completely filled with Islands that we hardly see the mainland, and these islands occasionally embrace lakes, from 8 to 15 miles in length & having a breadth of 8 or 10 miles—the channel is extremely crooked & this added to the current which is great in some places, considerably impeded our progress; & at length between two high points of land where the current was extremely rapid we were obliged to anchor & I presume the vessel has not yet left that point, for I am informed that they frequently remain there 8 or 10 days waiting for a favorable wind. The place where we were anchored is about fifteen miles below this place, & although in our country we would think nothing of walking that distance through the woods, here it is a [illegible word] impossibility. The bushes are a complete barrier. We remained here about twenty-four hours, and the Captain had nearly consented to send us up in his yawl, when we heard distant singing which gradually became louder & louder. I ascended to the yard arm of our vessel but could see nothing until, on a sudden, a bark canoe containing nine men shot with the rapidity of an arrow from beyond a point of land which before this had screened it. Eight of the men were paddling & the ninth was sitting in the centre of the canoe upon its bottom. One of the voyageurs was singing a french song to which they all beat time with their paddles, & they all joined in singing the chorus, thus giving it peculiar effect. The canoe moved with a velocity which was far beyond anything I had imagined possible. Under the U. S. standard, the canoe passed around us at the same time giving us a salute & at length they came along side of our vessel & the director of the canoe came on board; he immediately made enquiries for me. He then said that an Indian had seen the vessel the day before and that Mr. Schoolcraft supposing that I must be on board had sent the canoe for the purpose of conveying me to the Sault. The offer was gladly accepted & I then entered the same canoe which is to carry me during the summer & paddled by the same men. We landed at the Sault on the evening of Saturday the 11th being only the 5th day from Detroit. This is considered a remarkably quick passage, the distance is 400 miles. Upon my arrival here I learned that a canoe had been sent to Michilimacinack for me as they had supposed I would go to that place in the Steam Boat and that it had returned on the morning of the same day that I arrived here, but as they passed through a different channel of the river they missed us.

The town [Sault Ste. Marie] here is pleasantly situated being considerably elevated, but the soil is poor & the warm season so short that no attempts are made at farming, except at raising potatoes & oats. The lat. N. is as you will see by examination about 47° & consequently our nights are much shorter than with you. There is no difficulty in reading ordinary print at 9 o'clock P.M. The Govt. here consists of a neat Stockaded fort, without embankments, & occupied by two companies of infantry. Most of the inhabitants of respectability are connected with the Army & with American & Huds. B. Fur Comp. but not all. The settlements are upon both sides of river. This place although literally out of the world has been settled nearly 200 years. The early settlement of this place is easily accounted for when its situation is considered. The St. Marys River (the outlet of Lk. Superior) has here a descent of 19 feet in about half a mile which gives it a constant foam & prevents ascent except in canoes. Fish are taken here to almost any extent required & at all times of the year. One of the gentlemen who accompanied us from Detroit, Mr. Bethune, Agent & Partner of the Hudson Bay Fur Company has his establishment upon the opposite (Canada) side of the river where there is quite a village. Mr. B. is an intelligent man & has travelled more in the unexplored country than any man I have ever seen. He stated to me that he has been in this western country 16 years, had crossed to the Pacific twice & been stationed at Astoria two years; also that he was stationed at Lake Winnipeg two years. He stated to me that the only outlet of the Lake of the Woods is into Lake Winnipeg & that there is high land between Lake of the Woods & the sources of Lk. Superior. Since my arrival here I have remained at the house of Mr. Schoolcraft, who lives in a style probably superior to any man in the county of Chautauqua [New York]. Mrs. Schoolcraft's (formerly Miss [Jane] Johns[t]on) mother you are perhaps aware is a woman of the Chippeway tribe of Indians. Yet Mrs. Schoolcraft is a woman of great personal accomplishments & of high literary worth & in my mind the fact of her having been descended from the daughter of a Chippeway chief [Waub Ojeeg] detracts not, but rather adds to, her merit. Mr. [John] Johns[t]on (her father) was an Irish nobleman.—Mrs. Schoolcraft has two [three] sisters [Eliza, Charlotte, and Anna Maria], younger than herself who would be an ornament to any society & should undoubtedly, in our Eastern country attract a crowd of admirers. Many & I may say most of the white inhabitants here have Indian wives. There are no young ladies excepting those which are half Chippeway.

We leave here (as now proposed) on Monday next (June 20) & long before you receive this we will be passing through Lake Superior. Before that time I shall make an excursion to Point Iroquois (Lk. Superior) for the purpose of laying the foundation of a Geological map which I am to project.—The tour will be made—(through the lakes to Green Bay incldg. the whole route) in three Bark canoes capable of carrying 3 or 4 tons per piece.—The soldiers headed by a Lieutenant [Robert Clary] & the Interpirter [George Johnston] will occupy two of the boats & these will carry the provisions.—The other boat will carry Mr. Schoolcraft & myself together with our Secty. Mr. [Melancthon] Woolsey; and it will be manned by eight voygeurs or paddlers. This will give us greater speed than the others & will allow us to make all necessary examinations without detaining the other boats. We will remain a long time on Lake Superior & ascend several

of the rivers in order to make our observations as accurately as possible.—
It is quite possible that we may arrive (by a new arrangement, which is
not fully determined) at Green Bay sooner than anticipated in which
case I shall descend to Illinois Riv. etc. in which case I will write from
that place (perhaps in Sept.) & inform you.—I will probably be able to
write you from Keweena[w] Point & perhaps from Fond du Lac Lk. Sup.
by Indian Traders who leave there some time in July. But this will be
chance rather than otherwise.

I left some specimens of Strontian at home which I wish you would
keep carefully for me.

Tell Tucker I shall celebrate the fourth to him at 10 A.M. Remember me
to all & say to some that my time is so completely occupied as well as my
mind in preparation for our journey that I am not able to write to them.

Farewell for a time.

D. H.

[This letter was edited and published in *Michigan History,* Vol. XXXIX
(December, 1955), pp. 474-80.]

3. Douglass Houghton to Lewis Cass.
   Report on Copper in Lake Superior Region.

FREDONIA, N. Y., November 14, 1831

SIR:

In fulfilment of the duties assigned to me in the late expedition into the
Indian country, under the direction of H. R. Schoolcraft, Esq., Indian
agent, I would beg leave to transmit to you the following observations
relative to the existence of copper in the country bordering on the southern shore of Lake Superior.

It is without doubt true that this subject has long been viewed with an
interest far beyond its actual merit. Each mass of native copper which
this country has produced, however insulated, or however it may have been
separated from its original position, appears to have been considered a
sure indication of the existence of that metal in beds; and hence we
occasionally see, upon maps of that section of our country, particular
portions marked as containing "copper mines," where no copper now
exists. But while it is certain that a combination of circumstances has
served to mislead the public mind with regard to the geological situation
and existing quantity of that metal, it is no less certain that a greater
quantity of insulated native copper has been discovered upon the borders
of Lake Superior, than in any other equal portion of North America.

Among the masses of native copper which have engaged the attention
of travellers in this section of country, one, which from its great size was
early noticed, is situated on the Ontonagon River, a stream which empties
its waters into the southern part of Lake Superior, 331 miles above the
falls of the Ste. Marie. The Ontonagon River is, with some difficulty,
navigable by batteaux 36 miles, at which place by the union of two smaller

streams, one from an easterly, and the other from a westerly direction, the main stream is formed. The mass of copper is situated on the western fork, at a distance of six or eight miles from the junction.

The face of the country through the upper half of the distance from Lake Superior is uneven, and the irregularity is given it by hills of marly clay, which occasionally rise quite abruptly to the height of one or two hundred feet. No rock was observed *in situ,* except in one place, where, for a distance, the red sandstone was observed, forming the bed of the river.

The mass of copper lies partly covered by water, directly at the foot of a clay hill, from which, together with numerous boulders of the primitive rocks, it has undoubtedly been washed by the action of the water of the river. Although it is completely insulated, there is much to interest in its examination. Its largest surface measures three and a half by four feet, and this, which is of malleable copper, is kept bright by the action of the water, and has the usual appearance of that metal when worn. To one surface is attached a small quantity of rock, singularly bound together by threads of copper, which pass through it in all directions. This rock, although many of its distinctive characters are lost, is evidently a dark colored serpentine, with small interspersed masses of milky quartz.

The mass of copper is so situated as to afford but little that would enable us to judge of its original geological position. In examining the eastern fork of the river, I discovered small waterworn masses of tap-rock, in which were specks of imbedded carbonate of copper and copper black; and with them are occasionally associated minute specks of serpentine, in some respects resembling that which is attached to the large mass of copper; and facts would lead us to infer that the trap formation which appears on Lake Superior east of the Ontonagon River, crosses this section of country at or near the source of that river and at length forms one of the spurs of the Porcupine Mountains.

Several smaller masses of insulated native copper have been discovered on the borders of Lake Superior, but that upon Ontonagon River is the only one which is now known to remain.

At as early a period as before the American revolution, an English mining company directed their operations to the country bordering on Lake Superior, and Ontonagon River was one point to which their attention was immediately directed. Traces of a shaft, sunk in the clay hill, near a mass of copper, are still visible, a memento of ignorance and folly.

Operations were also commenced on the southern shore of Lake Superior, near the mouth of a small stream, which, from that circumstance, is called Miners' River. Parts of the names of the miners, carved upon the sandstone rock at the mouth of the river are still visible. What circumstance led to the selection of this spot does not now appear. No mineral traces are at this day perceptible, except occasional discolorations of the sandstone rock by what is apparently a mixture of the carbonate of iron and copper; and this is only to be observed where water, holding in solution an extremely minute portion of these salts, has trickled slowly over those rocks.

It does not, in fact, appear that the red sandstone, which constitutes the principal rock formation of the southern shore of Lake Superior, is in any instance metaliferous in any considerable degree. If this be true, it would require but little reflection to convince one of the inexpediency of conducting mining operations at either of the points selected for that purpose; and it is beyond a doubt true, that the company did not receive the least inducement to continue their labors.

In addition to these masses of native copper, an ore of that metal has long been known to the lake traders as the green rock, in which the characteristic substances are the green and blue carbonate of copper, accompanied by copper black. It is situated upon Keweena Point, 280 miles above the falls of the Ste. Marie. The ore is embraced by what is apparently a recently formed crag; and although it is of a kind, and so situated as to make an imposing appearance, there is little certainty of its existence in large quantities in this formation. The ore forms a thin covering to the pebbles of which the body of the rock is composed, and is rarely observed in masses separate from it. The crag is composed of angular fragments of trap-rock; and the formation is occasionally traversed by broad and continuous belts of calc. spar, here and there tinged with copper. Although the ore was not observed in any considerable quantity, except at one point, it apparently exists in minute specks through a greater part of the crag formation, which extends several miles, forming the shore of the lake.

This examination of the crag threw new interest upon the trap formation, which had been first observed to take the place of the sandstone at the bottom of a deep bay, called Montreal [Bete Grise] Bay, on the easterly side of Keweena Point. The trap-rock continues for a few miles, when the crag before noticed appears to lie directly upon it, and to form the extremity of the point; the crag, in turn, disappears, and the trap-rock is continued for a distance of six or eight miles upon the westerly side of the point, when the sandstone again reappears.

The trap-rock is of a compact granular texture, occasionally running into the amygdaloid and toadstone varieties, and is rich in imbedded minerals, such as amethystine quartz, smoky quartz, cornelian, chalcedony, agate, &c., together with several of the ores of copper. Traces of copper ore in the trap-rock were first noticed on the easterly side of Keweena Point, and near the commencement of the trap formation. This ore, which is an impure copper black, was observed in a vein of variable thickness, but not in any part exceeding 2½ inches; it is sufficiently compact and hard to receive a firm polish, but it is rather disposed to break into small irregular masses. A specimen furnished, upon analysis, 47.5 per cent. of pure copper.

On the western side of Keweena Point, the same ore appears under different circumstances, being disseminated through the body of the trap-rock, in grains varying in size from a pin's head to a pea. Although many of these grains are wholly copper black, they are occasionally only depositions of the mineral upon specks of cornelian, chalcedony, or agate, or are more frequently composed, in part, of what is apparently an imperfect steatite. The ore is so connected with, and so much resembles in colour the rock, of which it may be said to be a constituent part, that they might easily, during a hasty examination, be confounded. A random specimen of the rock furnished, upon analysis, 3.2 per cent. of pure copper. The rock continues combined with that mineral for nearly the space of three miles. Extremely thin veins of copper black were observed to traverse this same rock; and in enlargements of these were discovered several masses of amorphous native copper. The latter mineral appeared in two forms—the one consisting of compact and malleable masses, carrying from 4 to 10 ounces each; and the other, of specks and fasciculi of pure copper, binding together confused masses of copper green, and partially disintegrated trap-rock: the latter was of several pounds' weight. Each variety was closely embraced by the rock, although the action of the water upon the rock had occasionally exposed to view points of the metal. In addition to the accompanying copper green, which was in a disintegrated state, small specks of the oxyd of copper were associated in most of the native specimens.

Circumstances would not permit an examination of any portion of the trap formation, except that bordering directly upon the lake. But facts would lead us to infer that that formation extends from one side of Keweena Point to the other, and that a range of thickly wooded hills, which traverses the point, is based upon, if not formed of, that rock. An Indian information which, particularly upon such a subject, must be adopted with caution, would sanction the opinion that the prominent constituents are the same wherever the rock is observed.

After having duly considered the facts which are presented, I would not hesitate to offer, as an opinion, that the trap-rock formation was the original source of the masses of copper which have been observed in the country bordering on Lake Superior; and that at the present day, examinations for the ores of copper could not be made in that country with hopes of success, except in the trap-rock itself; which rock is not certainly known to exist upon any place upon Lake Superior, other than Keweena Point.

If this opinion be a correct one, the cause of failure of the mining company in this region is rendered plain. Having considered each insulated mass of pure metal as a true indication of the existence of a bed in the vicinity, operations were directed to wrong points; when, having failed to realize their anticipations, the project was abandoned without further actual investigation. We would be induced to infer, that no attempts were made to learn the original source of the metal which was discovered, and thus, while the attention was drawn to insulated masses, the ores, ordinary in appearance, but more important *in situ,* were neglected; and perhaps from the close analogy in appearance to the rock with which they were associated, no distinction was observed.

What quantity of ore the trap-rock of Keweena Point may be capable of producing, can only be determined by minute and laborious examination. The indications which were presented by a hasty investigation are here imbodied, and, with deference, submitted to your consideration.

> I have the honor to be,
> Sir, your obedient servant,
> DOUGLASS HOUGHTON

[Houghton continued his investigations of copper deposits on the Keweenaw Peninsula when he became State Geologist in 1837. His famous copper report of 1841 led to the first mining rush in the United States. Thousands flocked to the Keweenaw Peninsula. Copper-mining companies were organized; some were successful—most were failures.]

4. Douglass Houghton to John Torrey.

FREDONIA, N. Y., March 20th 1832

DEAR SIR,

Some time in November last I received, through the hands of H. R. Schoolcraft Esqr. of the Sault Ste. Marie, notice that you had made some requests respecting the plants which were collected during the expedition of the past summer. He also informed me that he had written you upon the same subject.

In the expedition referred to I acted as naturalist, and have now the entire collection of plants, as well as parts of the other collections in my possession. You are undoubtedly well aware of the numerous difficulties which are presented in preserving and securing plants during a long and tedious canoe voyage. With the utmost care, I was unable to preserve many of my duplicate specimens, & others were entirely lost, or much injured. I send you a catalogue, as it was first taken, embracing many common plants which were preserved, mostly for comparison with our Eastern & more southern plants. The unfortunate loss of my most valuable botanical books, of reference, together with an uncommon pressure of business, has prevented any thing more than a cursory examination of the plants, since my return to this place. At the Sault Ste. Marie, by the aid of Dr. [Edwin] James, of the U. S. Army, I was enabled to solve some of my difficulties, the others I shall not attempt until enabled to procure suitable works to do so, & situated as we are here this is no small task.

During the summers of 1824 & 5 I devoted much of my time to collecting and making a catalogue of the plants of this County (Chautauqua) [New York] together with those of the western parts of Pennsylvania & Ohio, and there were several which were stumbling blocks to me & I had hoped, upon my return (having been absent most of the time since that collection was made) to find them in good keeping; but an accident having befallen them, they were together with the catalogue completely destroyed, and as there is not (to my knowledge) a botanist in this county, it may be long ere an other collection will be made.

I am attached to an expedition for the ensuing summer, in the double capacity of Surgeon & Naturalist, which bids fair to be of far greater interest in a botanical point of view than that of the last summer. Should nothing prevent I shall leave here in two or three weeks for the purpose of joining the others of the party, who are now at Galena, Ill. The country to be explored is chiefly between the Mississippi, a little below the Falls of St. Anthony, and the Missouri, as high as Council Bluffs. I do not doubt but this will be like that of the past summer, a constant botanical feast; and I do not intend to leave any exertions untried which will aid in securing the collections which will be made. Should you have any particular plants of that country in view, of which you would like to have an extra number collected, please inform me at this place.

An anticipated visit to N. York has prevented my writing to you upon this subject before, & the imperfect catalogue which I forward, makes me almost regret to do so now. Mr. Schoolcraft will probably visit New York early in the season.

As this catalogue was taken from my pocket notes it does not contain authorities for the specific names, but as Eaton's Manual 5th Edition was the work which I used in the field, you will easily understand it, by reference. Plants of the following genera, upon which subject I have consulted Dr. James appear to be undescribed in the works which we consulted; viz. Artemisia, Lysimachia, Helonias, Drosera, Commelina, Boerhavia, Bunias, Batschia, Eryngium, & Primula. Supposing it would not be uninteresting I have added localities, in the catalogue; of most of the plants there are duplicates. Most of those generic names which stand alone refer to plants, which were collected when circumstances would not permit a specific examination, or which were not described in the works in my possession.

Will you please inform me at what time you will probably publish your proposed work on Cryptogamous plants. We look for its publication with much interest. In a conversation with Dr. Beck of Albany more than a year ago he informed me that he would probably publish his proposed work on Musci early in the last summer. I have not yet learned whether that work is from the press.

Yours &c
Douglass Houghton

[Appended to this letter was a long list of plants which Houghton collected on the Expedition of 1831. Because it has little historical value, it is omitted here. The information can be found in Houghton's, "Localities of Plants Collected in the Northwestern Expeditions of 1831 and 1832." Schoolcraft, *Narrative to Itasca*, pp. 160-65.]

5. Douglass Houghton to Henry Rowe Schoolcraft.

FREDONIA, N. Y., April 3, 1832

DEAR SIR,

I had been preparing for my departure (to join Mr. [Lucius] Lyon) when Mr. [John] Hulbert arrived here, & delivered a package from you;

& the day following your letter, by mail, dated some 10 or 15 days earlier was received. Your expedition for the coming summer was wholly unexpected to me; the route is an interesting one, and will undoubtedly furnish some rare subjects in Nat. History.

My acceptance of Mr. Lyon's proposals was only on certain conditions, and I do not consider it will be a breach of faith to join you as you propose. My friends have been *hammering* me to remain here, to settle in a "dogs life", aye nothing more nor less than the practice of my profession. But they can but little realize the pleasure of a mental feast upon the hidden treasures of nature.

Should nothing occur to prevent it I will accompany Mr. Hulbert upon his return from N. York to the Sault Ste. Marie, & as I understood from him that he would purchase supplies for the Expedition, I will undoubtedly arrive in good season.

Since my last letter to you I have written to Doct. [John] Torrey, & shall probably forward him a suit of the plants when our merchants leave here for N. York. I will also inform him immediately of my determination to accompany you.

I will endeavour to complete an analysis of the Minerals of Presque Isle before leaving here, & as I look for several new botanical works, in a few days, I will have some enjoyment in burying myself among my plants.

Remember me affectionately to all my friends at the Saut, & to little Jane & Johnstons I send each a kiss.

Yours truly
D. HOUGHTON

P.S. Your Journal from Galena to Ft. Winnebago was very acceptable, & your introductory remarks relieve me from a great task, in completing my journal.

[Schoolcraft and Houghton intended to publish a joint account of the expedition of 1831. Houghton was to prepare the narrative and map, and Schoolcraft planned to supply the preface and an account of the Iowa mine country. Although a separate account of this expedition never appeared, much of the material was published by Schoolcraft in the appendix to his *Narrative to Itasca,* including the journal from "Galena to Ft. Winnebago," referred to above (pp. 294-307).]

6. Douglass Houghton to Henry Rowe Schoolcraft.

FREDONIA N. Y., May 12th. 1832

DEAR SIR,

I have this moment learned that an injunction in a suit of great importance to me, in which I am plaintiff, will render it necessary for me to remain here until the 24th. of this month. I shall leave here for the Sault immediately after that date, & shall hope to see you as soon as the 2d. or third of June.

Gov. Cass wrote me a few days ago. He mentioned that the Agencies of Mackinac & the Sault had been united, and that perhaps the additional business might prevent you from proceeding on your expedition this season; but he said, that need not prevent my proceeding immediately to the Sault, as you would probably employ me in vaccinating the Indians; in accordance with a Bill which has just passed congress. I will procure a fresh supply of vaccine matter to be used for that purpose if it should be deemed expedient.

I will undoubtedly reach you before you will wish to set forth on your expedition. This delay was wholly unexpected to me & I regret that it is so.

Yours truly

D. Houghton

P.S. I have been several days engaged in preparing to secure what plants may be collected from the effects of water. Experience teaches me some lessons. I have heard from Torrey & have sent him a suit of Plants. I write at a moments warning and in great haste, that my letter may take this mail.

D.H.

7. Douglass Houghton to Richard Houghton.

Fond Du Lac, June 24, 1832

My Dear Brother:—

We arrived at this place, which is twenty-four miles beyond the head of Lake Superior, on the St. Louis River, last evening. I was much surprised upon our arrival, at the village-like appearance which it presents. There are several capacious log buildings and these are surrounded by a stockade, and this gives it almost the air of a fort. Directly in the rear of the post, the hills rise almost to mountain heights and upon the opposite side of the river they are seen stretching as far as the eye can reach in either direction. The trading clerks and voyageurs of the American Fur Co. who trade west and north of the head of Lake Superior, about two hundred in number, are now collected here, and in addition to these there are between two and three hundred Indians of the band now situated at this place, now present, and adding our own party we can muster between five and six hundred persons, so that you can well imagine we have lively times. Some of these half-French and half-Indian traders have traversed during the winter most of the country bordering on the upper Mississippi River, while others have been as far west as the Rocky Mountains.

Mr. Ai[t]ken, the director of the company in this section of the country is now here—his headquarters at Sandy Lake. He is European French, I suppose, is affable and intelligent, and has been in the Indian country more than twenty years. I also met here a German physician [Dr. Charles Borup] with whom I was before acquainted, who has engaged in the Indian trade, and passed the last winter at Rainy Lake. All the traders will leave here to-morrow for Mackinac, for the purpose of receiving their annual supplies. This day is Sunday, and we are stationary. To-morrow our baggage will be arranged in packages smaller than is usual, weighing ninety pounds, and will commence passing around the falls of this river upon the [Grand] Portage, which is nine miles in length. The Portage is, in consequence of excessive rains, nearly impassable, and for this reason it is calculated that our voyageurs can only carry two packages each, weighing one hundred and eighty pounds, at a load. Between this and Sandy Lake it will be necessary to make about seventeen miles of portage, which will alone occupy about six days. Our precise route is but just determined. We will proceed from this place by the Grand Portage, St. Louis River, Portage Aux Coteau, Savannah River, Savannah Portage, Sandy Lake and Sandy River, to the Mississippi River. From thence ascend the Mississippi River, pass by Little Lake Winnipeg to Upper Red Cedar Lake, and from thence to Lac La Biche; from thence return by another route to Upper Red Cedar Lake, then proceed by Leach [Leech] River to Leach Lake, thence by a series of portages and small lakes to the source of the River de Corbeau [Crow Wing], the great southwest fork of the Mississippi, thence descend the River de Corbeau to the Mississippi, and the latter stream as far as fifty miles below the Falls of St. Anthony, thence we will proceed by the St. Croix River and River Brule, with only a short portage to Lake Superior, which we will enter from the southern shore about four hundred and sixty miles above the Sault Ste. Marie. We hope to complete this immense journy so as to arrive at the Sault Ste. Marie between the middle and the last of August. You can scarcely imagine the difficulties which we will be obliged to encounter, and they certainly beggar description. Although I am now twelve hundred miles from you, I consider this the place where I in reality commence my journey.

I find the vaccination of the Indians an irksome task, chiefly in consequence of the great numbers. Last evening after our arrival I operated upon two hundred and forty at one sitting, and I shall complete the band to-morrow. As yet I have only found a few who had never heard of vaccination. It is astonishing to learn the fearful dread they have of the small-pox. When I commence operating they crowd around me with their arms ready, and anxiously wait their turn. I keep an accurate list of the number, age and sex of those vaccinated, together with the tribe and band to which they belong.

The season is hardly sufficiently advanced to admit of an extensive collection of plants, but I am doing more than could have been expected. I received another letter from Prof. Torr[e]y, respecting my plants of last year, after my arrival at the Sault Ste. Marie, and I was much gratified to learn that the opinion I had given respecting those which I supposed to be undescribed species was supported by the New York botanist. This will give me fresh courage to push the subject this season. My mineral collection, as yet, has been but small. I wish you to write me at the Sault Ste. Marie, so that it can reach there by the 20th of August. We have good health so far, and while our men have hard times upon the portage I have more leisure to make my scientific examinations than I could under other circumstances. To-morrow morning I expect to take up the brachial artery in a case of advanced aneurism.

Love to all members of the family
Your affectionate brother,
DOUGLASS HOUGHTON

[The location of the original of this letter is not known. A typescript of the letter was given to the Historical Collections of the University of Michigan several years ago, but there was no record as to its source. It may be in the Keweenaw Historical Society's Collection, which is now in storage at Houghton, Michigan.]

8. Douglass Houghton to Henry Rowe Schoolcraft.
   Report of Vaccination of Indians.

SAULT STE. MARIE, Sept. 21, 1832

SIR:

In conformity with your instructions, I take the earliest opportunity to lay before you such facts as I have collected, touching the vaccination of the Chippewa Indians, during the progress of the late expedition into their country: and also "of the prevalence, from time to time, of the small-pox" among them.

The accompanying table will serve to illustrate the "ages, sex, tribe, and local situation" of those Indians who have been vaccinated by me. With the view of illustrating more fully their local situation, I have arranged those bands residing upon the shores of Lake Superior; those residing in the Folle Avoine country (or that section of country lying between the highlands south-west from Lake Superior, and the Mississippi River); and those residing near the sources of the Mississippi River, separately.

Nearly all the Indians noticed in this table were vaccinated at their respective villages: yet I did not fail to vaccinate those whom we chanced to meet in their hunting or other excursions.

I have embraced, with the Indians of the frontier bands, those half-breeds, who, in consequence of having adopted more or less the habits of the Indian, may be identified with him.

But little difficulty has occurred in convincing the Indians of the efficacy of vaccination; and the universal dread in which they hold the appearance of the small pox among them, rendered it an easy task to overcome their prejudices, whatever they chanced to be. The efficacy of the vaccine disease is well appreciated, even by the most interior of the Chippewa Indians, and so universal is this information, that only one instance occurred where the Indian had never heard of the disease.

In nearly every instance the opportunity which was presented for vaccination was embraced with cheerfulness and apparent gratitude; at the same time manifesting great anxiety that, for the safety of the whole, each one of the band should undergo the operation. When objections were made to vaccination, they were not usually made because the Indian doubted the protective power of the disease, but because he supposed (never having seen its progress) that the remedy must nearly equal the disease which it was intended to counteract.

Our situation, while travelling, did not allow me sufficient time to test the result of the vaccination in most instances; but an occasional return to bands where the operation had been performed, enabled me, in those bands, either to note the progress of the disease, or to judge from the cicatrices marking the original situation of the pustules, the cases in which the disease had proved successful.

About one-fourth of the whole number were vaccinated directly from the pustules of patients labouring under the disease; while the remaining three-fourths were vaccinated from crusts, or from virus which had been several days on hand. I did not pass by a single opportunity for securing the crusts and virus from the arms of healthy patients; and to avoid as far as possible the chance of giving rise to a disease of a spurious kind, I invariably made use of those crusts and that virus, for the purposes of vaccination, which had been most recently obtained. To secure, as far as possible, against the chances of escaping the vaccine disease, I invariably vaccinated in each arm.

Of the whole number of Indians vaccinated, I have either watched the progress of the disease, or examined the cicatrices of about seven hundred. An average of one in three of those vaccinated from crusts has failed, while of those vaccinated directly from the arm of a person labouring under the disease, not more than one in twenty has failed to take effect—when the disease did not make its appearance after vaccination, I have invariably, as the cases came under my examination, revaccinated until a favourable result has been obtained.

Of the different bands of Indians vaccinated, a large proportion of the following have, as an actual examination has shown, undergone thoroughly the effects of the disease: viz. Sault Ste. Marie, Keweena Bay, La Pointe, and Cass Lake, being seven hundred and fifty-one in number; while of the remaining thirteen hundred and seventy-eight, of other bands, I think it may safely be calculated that more than three-fourths have passed effectually under the influence of the vaccine disease: and as directions to revaccinate all those in whom the disease failed, together with instructions as to time and manner of vaccination, were given to the chiefs of the different bands, it is more than probable that, where the bands remained together a sufficient length of time, the operation of revaccination has been performed by themselves.

Upon our return to Lake Superior I had reason to suspect, on examining several cicatrices, that two of the crusts furnished by the surgeon-general in consequence of a partial decomposition, gave rise to a spurious disease, and these suspicions were confirmed when revaccinating with genuine vaccine matter, when the true disease was communicated. Nearly all those Indians vaccinated with those two crusts, have been vaccinated, and passed regularly through the vaccine disease.

The answers to my repeated inquiries respecting the introduction, progress, and fatality of the small-pox, would lead me to infer that the disease has made its appearance, at least five times, among the bands of Chippewa Indians noticed in the accompanying table of vaccinations.

The small-pox appears to have been wholly unknown to the Chippewas of Lake Superior until about 1750; when a war-party, of more than one

hundred young men, from the bands resident near the head of the lake, having visited Montreal for the purpose of assisting the French in their then
existing troubles with the English, became infected with the disease, and
but few of the party survived to reach their homes. It does not appear, although they made a precipitate retreat to their own country, that the
disease was at this time communicated to any others of the tribe.

About the year 1770, the disease appeared a second time among the
Chippewas, but unlike that which preceded it, it was communicated to
the more northern bands.

The circumstances connected with its introduction are related nearly
as follows.

Some time in the fall of 1767 or 8, a trader, who had ascended the
Mississippi and established himself near Leech Lake, was robbed of his
goods by the Indians residing at that lake; and, in consequence of his
exertions in defending his property, he died soon after.

These facts became known to the directors of the Fur Company, at
Mackinac, and each successive year after, requests were sent to the Leech
Lake Indians, that they should visit Mackinac, and make reparation for
the goods they had taken, by a payment of furs, at the same time threatening punishment in case of a refusal. In the spring of 1770 the Indians
saw fit to comply with this request; and a deputation from the band
visited Mackinac, with a quantity of furs, which they considered an
equivalent for the goods which had been taken. The deputation was received with politeness by the directors of the company, and the difficulties
readily adjusted. When this was effected, a cask of liquor and a flag closely
rolled were presented to the Indians as a token of friendship. They were
at the same time strictly enjoined neither to break the seal of the cask nor
to unroll the flag, until they had reached the heart of their own country.
This they promised to observe; but while returning, and after having
travelled many days, the chief of the deputation made a feast for the
Indians of the band at Fond du Lac, Lake Superior, upon which occasion
he unsealed the cask and unrolled the flag for the gratification of his
guests. The Indians drank of the liquor, and remained in a state of inebria-
tion during several days. The rioting was over, and they were fast recovering from its effects, when several of the party were seized with violent pain.
This was attributed to the liquor they had drunk; but the pain increasing,
they were induced to drink deeper of the poisonous drug, and in this
inebriated state several of the party died, before the real cause was
suspected. Other like cases occurred; and it was not long before one of
the war-party which had visited Montreal in 1750, and who had narrowly
escaped with his life, recognised the disease as the same which had attacked their party at that time. It proved to be so; and of those Indians
then at Fond du Lac, about three hundred in number, nearly the whole
were swept off by it. Nor did it stop here, for numbers of those at Fond
du Lac, at the time the disease made its appearance, took refuge among
the neighbouring bands, and although it did not extend easterly on Lake
Superior, it is believed that not a single band of Chippewas north or west

from Fond du Lac escaped its ravages. Of a large band then resident
at Cass Lake, near the source of the Mississippi River, only one person,
a child, escaped. The others having been attacked by the disease, died
before any opportunity for dispersing was offered. The Indians at this
day are firmly of the opinion that the small-pox was, at this time, communicated through the articles presented to their brethren, by the agent of the
Fur Company at Mackinac; and that it was done for the purpose of punishing them more severely for their offences.

The most western bands of Chippewas relate a singular allegory of the
introduction of the small-pox into their country by a war-party, returning
from the plains of the Missouri, as nearly as information will enable me
to judge, in the year 1784. It does not appear that, at this time, the disease
extended to the bands east of Fond du Lac; but it is represented to have
been extremely fatal to those bands north and west from there.

In 1802 or 3, the small-pox made its appearance among the Indians
residing at the Sault Ste. Marie, but did not extend to the bands west from
that place. The disease was introduced by a voyager, in the employ of
the North West Fur Company, who had just returned from Montreal; and
although all communication with him was prohibited, an Indian imprudently having made him a visit, was infected with and transmitted the
disease to others of the band. When once communicated, it raged with
great violence, and of a large band scarcely one of those then at the village
survived, and the unburied bones still remain marking the situation they
occupied. From this band the infection was communicated to a band
residing upon St. Joseph's Island, and many died of it; but the surgeon
of the military post then there succeeded, by judicious and early measures,
in checking it, before the infection became general.

In 1824 the small-pox again made its appearance among the Indians
at the Sault Ste. Marie. It was communicated by a voyager to Indians upon
Drummond's Island, Lake Huron; and through them several families at
Sault Ste. Marie became infected. Of those belonging to the latter place,
more than twenty in number, only two escaped. The disease is represented
to have been extremely fatal to the Indians at Drummond's Island.

Since 1824, the small-pox is not known to have appeared among the
Indians at the Sault Ste. Marie, nor among the Chippewas north or west
from that place. But the Indians of these bands still tremble at the bare
name of a disease which (next to the compounds of alcohol) has been
one of the greatest scourges that has ever overtaken them since their
first communication with the whites. The disease, when once communicated to a band of Indians, rages with a violence wholly unknown to the
civilized man. The Indian, guided by present feeling, adopts a course of
treatment (if indeed it deserves that appellation), which not unfrequently
arms the disease with new power. An attack is but a warning to the poor
and helpless patient to prepare for death, which will almost assuredly soon
follow. His situation under these circumstances is truly deplorable; for
while in a state that even, with proper advice, he would of himself recover,
he adds fresh fuel to the flame which is already consuming him, under the

delusive hope of gaining relief. The intoxicating draught (when it is within his reach) is not among the last remedies to which he resorts, to produce a lethargy from which he is never to recover. Were the friends of the sick man, even under these circumstances, enabled to attend him, his sufferings might be, at least, somewhat mitigated; but they too are, perhaps, in a similar situation, and themselves without even a single person to minister to their wants. Death comes to the poor invalid, and perhaps even as a welcome guest, to rid him of his suffering.

By a comparison of the number of Indians vaccinated upon the borders of Lake Superior, with the actual population, it will be seen that the proportion who have passed through the vaccine disease is so great as to secure them against any general prevalence of the small-pox; and perhaps it is sufficient to prevent the introduction of the disease to the bands beyond, through this channel. But in the Folle Avoine country it is not so. Of the large bands of Indians residing in that section of country, only a small fraction have been vaccinated; while of other bands not a single person has passed through the disease.

Their local situation undoubtedly renders it of the first importance that the benefits of vaccination should be extended to them. Their situation may be said to render them a connecting link between the southern and northwestern bands of Chippewas; and while on the south they are liable to receive the virus of the small-pox from the whites and Indians, the passage of the disease through them to their more northern brethren would only be prevented by their remaining, at that time, completely separated. Every motive of humanity towards the suffering Indian, would lead to extend to him this protection against a disease he holds in constant dread, and of which he knows, by sad experience, the fatal effects. The protection he will prize highly, and will give in return the only boon a destitute man is capable of giving; the deep-felt gratitude of an overflowing heart.

I have the honour to be,

Very respectfully, sir,

Your obedient servant,

DOUGLASS HOUGHTON

Chippewa Indians	Bands	Males						Females						Total		
		Under 10	10 to 20	20 to 40	40 to 60	60 to 80	Over 80	Under 10	10 to 20	20 to 40	40 to 60	60 to 80	Over 80	Males	Females	Total
Lake Superior	Sault Ste. Marie	93	22	19	8	2	1	75	28	21	10	3	1	145	138	283
	Grand Island	17	9	7	2			12	5	7				35	24	59
	Keweena [w] Bay	23	11	10	6	1		20	12	17	5	2	1	51	57	108
	Ontonagon River	7	8	10	3			13	5	12	6	1		28	37	65
	La Pointe	37	32	40	6	2	1	38	25	28	12	2	1	118	106	224
	Fond du Lac	50	21	45	10	2		41	18	35	13	6	2	128	115	243
Folle Avoine Country	Lac du Flambeau	6	2	6	1	1		2	3	4	2	2		16	13	29
	Ottowa Lake	11	4	8	1			10	3	7	2			24	22	46
	Yellow River	11	2	6	1			11	3	6	2	1		20	23	43
	Nama Kowagun [Namekagon] of St. Croix River	4	1	2	1			4		3	2			8	9	17
	Snake River	14	3	7	4	1	1	25	3	12	1	1		30	42	72
Sources of the Mississippi River	Sandy Lake	75	21	47	10	2		86	19	48	23	6	2	155	184	339
	Lake Winnipeg	4	4	10	3			1	1	1	2			21	5	26
	Cass or Upper Red Cedar Lake	18	5	11	6		1	18	3	8	5	1	1	41	36	77
	Leech Lake	76	43	73	16	4	1	96	41	61	25	2	1	213	226	439
	Lake Superior	227	103	131	35	7	2	199	93	120	46	14	5	505	477	982
	Folle Avoine Country	46	12	29	8	2	1	52	12	32	9	4		98	109	207
	Sources of the Mississippi	173	73	141	35	6	2	201	64	118	55	9	4	430	451	881
	Total	446	188	301	78	15	5	452	169	270	110	27	9	1033	1037	2070

9. Douglass Houghton to John Torrey.

FREDONIA, N. Y., Nov. 24, 1832

DEAR SIR,

I have but just arrived in this place, and the lateness of my arrival, as well as other circumstances, which I could not foresee, will prevent my visiting New York this winter.

I have an opportunity to forward a small package of plants to Albany, (by Dr. Crosby, one of the Electors) and I doubt not but it will reach you in safety. I have but a short time to prepare them, and a great pressure of business, together with an almost constant chit chat of friends, do not add much to the facilities.

Nearly all the plants are labelled in my collection, but as it was done in great haste and under unfavorable circumstances I would be unwilling to send them without reviewing. Time will not allow me to do this, and to obviate all difficulties I have concluded to send them with the bare localities. I send a few common plants for the purpose of settling difficulties in my own mind.

I will probably leave here for Detroit (to which place you will please direct your communications) in three or four days. I trust that the coming season will allow me an opportunity to investigate the Nat. Hist. of the Peninsula of Michigan, and a part of Indiana, but it is somewhat difficult to determine so far in advance. At present I am most anxious to complete, for publication, a Geological Map of Michigan, N. West, & a part of Missouri Terrs. My collection of Rocks, Minerals, shells &c. which were shipped several weeks ago at the Sault Ste. Marie have not yet arrived, & I almost fear they are lost.

Among my collection of plants of this year I notice from my field notes the following in addition to those which I forward you. Some of them were collected barely for comparison.

Yours &c

DOUGLASS HOUGHTON

[The list of plants has been omitted here. It can be found in Houghton's "Localities of Plants Collected in the Northwestern Expeditions of 1831 and 1832." Schoolcraft, *Narrative to Itasca,* pp. 160-65.]

APPENDIX E

Journal and Letters of the Reverend William Thurston Boutwell

WILLIAM THURSTON BOUTWELL was the fourth member of the expedition who kept a journal, and in many respects his report is the most interesting of them all. Boutwell was a religious zealot and by 1832 had already decided to spend his life as a missionary for the Indians, in fact, among the very tribes he was visiting on this tour. He was harsh in his criticisms of these "pagan" Indians and the "irreligious" voyageurs who failed to observe the Sabbath. Of particular value, are his observations on Indian life and customs, which are the most candid, albeit naive, of all the diarists. Also of great interest is Boutwell's diary from August, 1832, to August, 1837, which describes his life as missionary among various Chippewa tribes of Wisconsin and Minnesota. This part, however, obviously is beyond the scope of this appendix, and must await separate publication.

There is some doubt as to the provenience of Boutwell's Journal. According to Russell Fridley, Director of the Minnesota Historical Society, it was either given or loaned to the Society prior to 1889. Subsequently the diary was lost, although fortunately not before J. Fletcher Williams, the librarian of the Society, had an opportunity to copy it in longhand. The Journal printed here is from the Williams copy of the Journal in the possession of the Minnesota Historical Society.

Sections of the Boutwell Journal have been published before. The Minnesota Historian, Edward D. Neill, quoted extensively from it in his "Memoir of William T. Boutwell," *Macalester College Contributions,* Second Series, No. 1 (St. Paul, 1892). Excerpts from the diary relating to the expedition of 1832 were published in "Schoolcraft's Exploring Tour of 1832," *Minnesota Historical Collections,* Vol. I (St. Paul, 1872), pp. 153-76.

Boutwell left other material relating to the 1832 expedition in addition to his Journal. Several of his letters to the American Board of Foreign Missions written en route were published in the *Missionary Herald* and are reprinted in this appendix.

The letter from Boutwell to Julius Chambers of July 27, 1880, is also included in this section as well as Boutwell's interview with Jacob Brower since they bear upon the controversy of the derivation of the name "Itasca."

1. The Journal of Reverend William Thurston Boutwell, June 7 to August 12, 1832. Minnesota Historical Society.

2. William T. Boutwell to Editor, *Missionary Herald,* June 25, 1832. *Missionary Herald,* Vol. XXVIII (September, 1832), pp. 293-94.

3. William T. Boutwell to Editor, *Missionary Herald,* August 8, 1832. *Ibid.,* p. 404.

4. William T. Boutwell to Julius Chambers, July 27, 1880. Chambers, *The Mississippi River* (New York, 1910), pp. 111-31.

5. Interview, William T. Boutwell by Jacob Brower [1890?]. Brower, *The Mississippi River and Its Source, Minnesota Historical Collections,* Vol. VII (Minneapolis, 1893), pp. 148-49.

1. Journal of the Reverend William Boutwell

Sault Ste. Marie, June 5th, 1832. Left Mackinaw 1:30 o'clock, Monday morning, for this place, where we arrived in about 36 hours, a distance of 70 miles.

June 7, 1832. Embarked at the head of the Portage at 6 o'clock, p.m. and proceeded to Point aux Pines [Pins], 6 miles, where we passed the night. Rose at 4 o'clock and embarked. Passed Point des Chiens on our right, 3 miles distant. Soil sandy, producing pine thinly interspersed with oak and white birch.

The expedition from the Sault embarked in two barges [Mackinaw boats] and two canoes, Lt. Allen, of the U.S. Army, in command of the escort, which numbers 10. The provisions and Indian presents for the expedition are to be conveyed to Fon[d] du Lac in a barge.

Mr. Schoolcraft and myself embarked in our canoe, with 8 men. Mr. Johns[t]on the interpreter and Doctor Houghton, the surgeon, embarked in the other, with 6 men, 34 in all. Leaving Point aux Chien, we next came to Point Iroquois, on our left, and Gros Cap on our right. These opposite points are by many travellers considered the entrance in to the Superior.

Iroquois Point is so called from the following circumstance. This nation and the Ojibways were at war, when a party of the former came from a place near Montreal, called Lake of the Two Mountains [in 1662]. They encamped on this point, and spent the night in a war dance. The Ojibways assembled at Great [Gros] Cap in great numbers, on the Canada side. Next morn, when the Iroquois had ceased from their dance, and fallen asleep, the Ojibways crossed in canoes, part of them above, and a part below the point. They came upon them from both sides, and murdered all save one old man and woman, whom they spared to carry the intelligence back to their nation. The Indian name of the point is Nadoueuigoning, composed of the word Nadoue (Iroquois) and Okon, a bone.

Mr. Johnston, who came to this country in the year [1792] observed to me that the point was still strewed with bones and human skulls.

Passing this place, we put into a deep bay [Whitefish] on our left, hoping to find some Indians. Here we breakfasted, during which I was not a little amused with a specimen of French habits. Our voyageurs had occasion to wash their linen, instead of hanging which on the bushes, they spread them on the dry sand. Here we found an Indian Grave, supposed to be that of a Menominee. His totem bore the mark of the Eagle.

Re-embarked, and reached White Fish Point, where we passed the night.

Saturday, June 9. Breakfasted on a piece of red deer. Embarked at 8 in the barge, with our own supplies, being under the necessity of abandoning one of our canoes, in order to furnish a Capt. for the boat. Mr. J. and myself embarked. He lashed our canoe mast to that of the boat, and hoisted a fine top sail. This much accelerated our canoe. Soon came up with Mr. S.'s canoe and at length passed Lieut. Allen with the escort.

At 2 o'clock p.m. passed the River du Coeux [Two Hearted] 60 miles from Saint Marie's and 24 from White Fish Point, where we passed the night.

In the p.m. for the first time, saw an eagle's nest. It appeared to be nearly the size of a bushel basket. It was composed of dry sticks. Next came to Point Maline, turning which, we entered the Grand Marais, a beautiful and safe harbor for boats. There we intend to pass the Sabbath. The Lord make it a good day to us.

Monday, June 11th. Passed the Sabbath at Grand Marais. A fine harbor. Preached at 10 and at 5. Few of our party manifested a disposition to hear the word of life. One reason, however, may be the fact that but few understood English.

At half past one, resumed our Journey. Passed the Grand Sable or sand banks and came to the Pictured Rocks. These exceed in grandeur and picturesque scenery, even the Falls of Niagara. They extend from 10 to 12 miles, varying in height and interest. For this distance there are but two places where boats can with any safety put to the shore in a gale. Saw two beautiful otters this morning. Disembarked at the Mine[r]s River, as it is called, but with more propriety a stream, and examined a few rocks &c. where they had chiseled the initials of their names. The wind was very boisterous, in passing the Pictured Rocks. Ice still remains in large bodies on the rocks.

At 5 o'clock reached the Indian village on Grand Island. We were welcomed with the discharge of a few muskets in testimony of kind feeling. Read the commandments and made a few remarks. Dr. H. vaccinated men, women, and children, to the number of 46.[1] Seven hunters on the Island.

From Grand Island, we made for the main land, on our left, ¾ of a mile. There is a small trading post belonging to Mr. [William] Holiday, under the care of a clerk, Mr. Louis Nolin, a half breed; but the miserable condition of the buildings, if buildings they can be called, and the bushes and weeds infesting his door yard and its neighborhood, indicate a want of energy.[2] He has a half-breed woman.

June 12. Were detained until 11 o'clock this morning, by head winds, when they abated and we embarked, but had not proceeded far, when we were obliged to put into the first harbor we could find. The sea ran mountain high, and not a little frightened our oarsmen when our boat dipped, as it occasionally did. We made into a deep bay [Au Train], where we found a fine stream, which afforded a safe anchorage for our boat. There we found Mr. S. who was in advance of us.

The Frenchmen here found a turtle, which they esteem as one of their luxuries. They were unsuccessful for a long time in getting its head from under its shell in order to kill it, when one of them put its tail to the fire, a second ready with two sticks, seized its head as it thrust it from under its covering, and a third cut it off. So much for French wit.

June 13. Re-embarked at half past four. So cold, I was obliged to put on two overcoats. At 10 A.M. so warm, I was obliged to change my dress

of overcoats for a shooting jacket. Head winds during the day. Much
thunder at a distance.

Saw a fine red deer (nanashkish). He came to the lake shore for to
drink. It is but a few years since this species of deer have been taken so
far north. In appearance, it resembled a calf four weeks old, though more
slender in body and with longer legs.

Disembarked at Presque Isle and collected a few specimens of minerals,
the precious serpentine, pyrites of iron, &c. At a short distance, passed
Granite Point, about 12 miles from which we slept. A heavy thunder
storm during the night.

The banks, or shore, from Grand Isle to Huron Isles, are high, abounding with red sand stone. The growth of wood from the Grand Sable to
Grand Island, is mostly beach and maple, interspersed with a few pines,
spruce and hemlock. Where the shore is bluff and the red sand stone, the
growth is hard wood for the greater part.

June 14. Embarked at half past 4, and came to Yellow Dog River, Mr.
S.'s encampment, and there breakfasted. Cold, and so foggy, that we could
not see an object 100 rods. About 10, the fog disappeared, and it was
quite mild. Reached Huron Islands at 2 o'clock. These islands are the
habitation of immense numbers of gulls. We carried away about two dozen
eggs. They build their nests in the crevices of rocks. The bird is one-third
smaller than the domestic hen, but its egg is one-third larger, and of a dark
brown color, with spots.

From Huron Isles, we made a traverse of 20 or more miles, across the
Anse Kiwina [Keweenaw Bay]. At the bottom of this bay, Mr. [William]
Holiday resides.

We were from 3 o'clock till half past 8, in crossing this traverse—5½
hours.

Mr. J. estimates this day's march at 63 miles. Mr. Schoolcraft tells me
that Mr. Holiday has planted 70 bushels potatoes and sowed 6 bags of peas,
probably 7 bushels.

June 15th. Re-embarked this morning at the bay near the Traverse
Island in the Anse Kiwina, at a quarter before 4. Came to a small river
called Tobacco River and breakfasted. The river abounds with Red Carp.
Our oarsmen killed several with poles. Leaving this river, which has several little falls near its mouth, we soon discovered two boats. They proved
to be Messrs. [Charles] Oaks and [Bazile or Paul] Beaulieu on their way to
Mackinac. The former of whom tells me that the Lac du Flambeau Indians
are preparing for a war excursion against the Sioux. Mr. O. had some
wampum, which these Indians were sending to Mr. Schoolcraft, Indian
Agent, to inform him of their intention.

Head winds and foggy this morning. The coast exhibits a sterile soil, the
banks are low, sandy shore. The projecting points exhibit the red sandstone. The growth is mostly small white birch, spruce, and hemlock—some
cedar. The extreme point of Kiwininon exhibits a most desolate spectacle.
Shore is lined with the trap rock. The beach presents nothing but a growth

of small white birch. Everything exhibits the appearance of a fire having been through the region and which must have destroyed all before it, leaving neither root nor branch. Large pines are yet standing, decayed.

At 8 in the evening, reached the Petit Marais and encamped. This is the finest harbor for small craft that I ever saw. Its entrance is safely guarded on each side by an immense mass of rock forming a perfect canal for several rods. For safety, strength and beauty, nature has so far excelled all that art could have invented.

June 16, 1832. Struck our tent at half past 6, and proceeded to the Big [Grand] Marais, a distance of 3 or 4 miles, and breakfasted. Here we obtained some specimens of the Copper Rock, calx spar. The shore is very bold, lined with trap rock. Immense masses occasionally separated from the main shore, stands a few yards out in the lake, over which a heavy sea breaks. The fog this morning is very unpleasant, obscuring every object unless within a few yards. The sea is smooth and calm. Two overcoats I found quite comfortable again this morning. Pursued our way till we had passed a cluster of islands ½ or ¾ of a mile south of which we went ashore and obtained a few more specimens of copper, also a few of agate.

Mr. J. observed to me, that Mr. S., himself, and the party spent a day in search of a copper rock in this vicinity, discovered by an Indian, now dead. A daughter of the Indian could not be prevailed on to direct them to it, lest she should die.[3]

Fog dispersed about 12 and at 9 in the evening reached what is called Kiweninon [Keweenaw] Portage, 310 miles from the Sault and 400 from Mackinaw. There we found our friends Schoolcraft, and Dr. Houghton, who visited Mr. Holiday's post in the bottom of Kiweninon Bay and then followed the Tobacco River and made the portage.

June 17, 1832. Kiweninon Portage. Here we passed the second Sabbath after leaving the Sault. Lt. Allen reached us at 11, after having spent the night previous in Camden's Bay, 12 or 14 miles in our rear. Preached about half past 3, in English. About one third of our party attended. At 5 collected most of the men and Mr. Johnston read a portion of scripture in French and the tract entitled, "Les deux Chemins." The men listened with apparent interest. But I soon witnessed that all my preaching was of no avail. Some of the men soon returned to their sport. Never was I before so sensible of the laxity of Catholic principles. The Sabbath with these men is a mere holy day. The major part of the men have passed the day in throwing the quoit.[4] The whole day with them has been one of recreation.

Our tents are pitched on a bluff from 20 to 30 feet above the water level. A few steps to the north, a small cross marks the place where a child has been buried, on which has been written, "Alex. Cadote."[5] The whole is enclosed with a few logs scored at the ends and put together in such a manner as to raise a sort of wall. The water has, at some former time, washed the beach within a few yards of the grave. A human skull lay in the sand and other human bones. The skull was entire, except on one side, a fracture twice as large as a dollar. Mr. J. tells me that an Indian was killed here 20 years ago in a drunken frolic by a blow from an ax. A pipe, pewter basin, and kettle, were found in the sand. Mr. J. tells me that it is the custom to deposit in the grave of a warrior, a pipe, ax, gun, war-club, and often his medicine bag. And in the grave of a female, a bag containing needles, an awl, sinews, and thread, a hatchet, kettle, portage collar, and whatever trinkets they manifested a fondness for.

Monday, June 18. Kiwina or Kiwinina Portage. We calculated on an early march this morning, but are yet detained by high winds; though fair, yet too boisterous for a canoe. Lieut. Allen and Dr. Houghton embarked at 11 in a barge for the Antinagon [Ontonagon], 51 miles from this place. The wind abated and at 2 o'clock embarked in the canoe with Mr. Schoolcraft. Leaving this portage, the banks for several miles are very bold, presenting a most picturesque scene; high bluffs of red sand stone which the constant action of the water has wrought into every variety of shape, forming the most beautiful arches and basins and occasionally an almost perfect pyramid. Little cascades which presented themselves every few miles gave additional beauty to the scenery. The banks were heavily wooded with a fine growth of beech, oak, pine and maple, interspersed with hemlock and birch.

From the portage, 10 miles, or so, we passed Salmon trout river, so called from the fish which is taken.

Passed Granrods [Graverod] River next, so denominated for the circumstances of a trader by this name who was murdered by one of his men, who had beguiled his wife, said to be distinguished for her beauty. This is not the first instance in which a man has lost his life for having a handsome wife.

Passed Lieut. Allen and encamped at the river Misery, so appellated from the fact that one or two traders nearly famished here.

The cold was excessive for June; was obliged to put on an overcoat to be comfortable before a good fire.

Soon after leaving Kewinan Portage, the Porcupine Mountains hove in sight, estimated by some 1600 feet higher than the lake.

Tues., June 19, 1832. Embarked with Mr. S. at half past 3. Leaving Misery river, passed a deep bay, where the Indians take many fish, from which it derives the name of Fish Bay. The coast is low and sandy, growth indicates a sterile soil. Breakfasted just after we left Hunting [Flint Steel] River on our left 9 miles from the Antinagon, which is, as some suppose, receives its name from a Chief who seems to have received his name from On-a-gon, a bowl.[6]

Just before entering this river, we spied two beautiful young deer on the beach. Thirty miles from its mouth, is the celebrated virgin copper rock, weighing, as Mr. Schoolcraft estimates it, one ton.

Approaching the Antinagon, a flag was waving in the air, and soon we were saluted by the discharge of muskets. Thus did the red man remind me that I was free born and dwell in freedom's happy land.

Our tent was no sooner pitched than the principal Chief, followed by his men, young and old, came to extend the friendly hand, each bearing in the other the emblem of peace and friendship, the pipe, and (goshkipitagon) tobacco pouch. The Chief was followed by a young man of 20, leading a little boy of not more than 5 years. This was the son of a chief who had died last week. On his neck hung his deceased father's medal and a plate of silver in the shape of a half moon, an ornament which is frequently seen among the Indians.

The old chief, Kondi Kondi, was seated at the head of the tent, at the right of Mr. S., and the lad at his right, till a complete circle was formed and the entrance occupied promiscuously.

No sooner than all were seated, the Chief expressed his satisfaction and that of his young men, in receiving a visit from Mr. S. as they were in much need of some of his Tobacco, and it would afford them a pleasure to smoke with him. The Tobacco was distributed, and the Chief and the little lad receiving a double portion, and commenced business.

Two other chiefs from different bands were present on the occasion, Moso Jid [Mozojeed] (anus of the Moose) from Ottawa Lake and Mosh-Koshwon [Mushcosum or Moose's Tail] from Lac du Flambeau.

The former began his speech, after expressing his pleasure in meeting us, by saying that he was on his way to the Sault to make a surrender of himself to Mr. Schoolcraft, in the place of an Indian of his band [Waba Annimikee], who had murdered a half-breed [Brunet], and who had escaped from himself and others who undertook to bring him to the Sault. He expressed his regret that any of his young men should act so foolish and intimated that he thought it was done in part to show the individuals contempt and disregard to the chief, himself, but that he would follow any advice which might be given. Still, he could not see a great distance among the thick trees, intimating that he could not see and prevent evils at a distance. He finally gave his word that every means should be taken to bring the murderer to the Sault next year. He made his escape by night through the aid of his mother.

By and by, a small bundle, or rags rolled up in a blanket, was brought into the tent and placed next to the chief. This was for a remembrance of the deceased chief. In one end was stuck two or three feathers. Several poles were raised on which were hung strips of old cloth to appease the angry spirits or for a sacrifice.

Mr. Schoolcraft now told them who I was and that as their friend and his friend, he had invited me to accompany him on his visit to them. He spoke to them on the importance of learning the arts of cultivating their lands and having schools for their children.

I then read to them some portions of Scripture, and remarked to them what was doing for their people by the Christian public. And that they would ere long send them someone to teach their children and tell them about God, Jesus Christ, and heaven, if they desired it. The Chief replied that he must first call his band together and talk with them, before he could speak for them, saying also, that he had no children, himself.

I then called P[eter] Quinn (interpreter) to tell him what God is doing for their kindred at the Sault. All listened with deep interest to him.

Mr. Schoolcraft invited several Chiefs to accompany us to La Pointe, where he should open his bales of clothing, cooking utensils &c. when he would make them some presents. He supplied them with Tobacco and made them a handsome present in provisions. At a late hour in the p.m., we took our leave and marched until 10 in the evening. About midnight the barges came up.

June 20, 1832. La Pointe. Passed the night at Carp River and embarked this morning at 6 o'clock and came to Presque Isle river and breakfasted 60 miles from Magdalen [Madeline] Island. On leaving this river, met Mr. [Lyman M.] Warren, Mr. [Frederick] Ayer and Mrs. [John] Campbell on their way to Mackinaw. Three boats in all, two belonging to Mr. W. and the other to Mr. [Michael] Cadotte and the Mission of La Pointe. The morning quite warm and the sea calm and delightful. The coast from Antinagon, 30 miles to river La Carp, is almost continuous iron bound. From River Presque Isle onward, it is still the same with now and then a short distance intervening, occasionally, which is red clay, approximating the red sand stone. Generally, the beach is but little elevated. The growth is white birch, maple, poplar, interspersed occasionally with spruce.

Passed the Montreal River, 20 miles, and Mauvais [Bad], 9 miles, from this Island. The wind breezed up and afforded us a fine sail. Disembarked at half past 7 and was happy to meet Brother and Sister Hall in fine health and spirits.

Our tour from the Sault to this place has been performed in 10 days of travel. Two days we rested in obedience to the Divine Command. In honoring God, we have been prospered on our way. Mr. Johnston and Lt. Allen arrived this evening with the boats. It is now 3 o'clock. Daylight appears and the cocks are crowing.

June 21, Magdalen Island. The weather is pleasant and a real New England June day. Mr. [Sherman] Hall and myself have just taken a walk over Mr. Warren's farm. Potatoes are out of the ground and peas also, both of which look well. About ⅛th of an acre of corn Mr. W. has planted, as an experiment, I am satisfied that the soil will, if manured, yield good corn, if the season is of sufficient length. It is a mixture of clay and sand, naturally wet. The grass, where it had sufficient moisture, looked fine. On the whole, I am highly gratified with the appearance of the outdoor concerns. Peas and potatoes Mr. W. has heretofore raised—peas, 100 bushels last year and with a favorable season, he calculates on a yield this year from his seed of 200. With industry and economy, a man may live and support a family. There is much land in N.E., cultivated which is far inferior in quality.

The Indians are absent at the Mauvaise, working their gardens and doing more than usual in this way, the present year. The school, and in short the whole concern, is embarrassed at present for want of a teacher and interpreter. Still, I am happy to say that the prospect and encouragement for doing Indians good, is more favorable than I anticipated.

In the course of the day a few Indians returned to the Island among whom was Goguagani. He is the second Chief. The old Bizhiki [Pizhickee] being on a journey to the Sault. Then Mr. S. distributed some of his presents among the Indians and made some valuable presents to the Mission family and school. Goguani in reply said he should have been under the necessity of hunting a whole year to have purchased the articles presented.

Re-embarked at 6, passed Point du fret [Froid?] and Spirit Island, came to the Dr[?] Gam[?] and encamped.[7] About 12 Dr. Houghton came up with us, who went to the Mauvais to vaccinate, and 12 men and 4 boys. The tobacco was distributed when all compassed the fire and began their smoke. Mr. S. here distributed presents to the Indians. I addressed them on the subject of attending to the instructions of the Missionaries. Poguoch enini remains with Mr. Hall, who is alone, Mr. W[arren] being on his journey to Mackinac for his annual supplies and to make his returns.

Passed a small bay on our right at the foot of which I am told are still to be seen traces of the old fort[8] once occupied by the Jesuits and which I learn was abandoned about 1760 when the English took possession of the Canadas.

Came next to Point au Froid [on Madeline Island] and from thence to Spirit Island.[9] I am told the Indians never encamp on this Island. They imagine it to be the residence of some evil spirit and also to be infested by rattle snake.

Lieut. Allen, not being aware of these superstitions, put ashore and made his encampment for the night. I heard no complaint from him the next day, save from the musketoes.

June 22, 1832. Re-embarked at half past 5, and came to River aux Sables [Sandy River] and breakfasted. Soon left the cluster of islands in our rear, which Lieut. Bayfield of the Royal Navy, estimates at 36.[10] This gentleman surveyed the coasts of Lake Superior and Huron, a few years since, under the direction of the Royal Navy. His observations and results have not been given to the public. Mr. Cadotte makes the cluster to consist of 24. He has not noticed such as are very small or destitute of wood.

Left River aux Sables with a fair wind and came to Bois Brule River and encamped for the night. This river, Mr. S. expects to return by, after leaving the St. Croix. The land just back from the beach is evidently rich, and susceptible of cultivation. There is a small Indian garden of potatoes, a few yards square, which are up and look well. Musketoes in abundance. The coast is very similar in quality and appearance to which I have already passed and noticed.

River Brule is 69 miles from La Pointe, and 21 from the mouth of the St. Louis; 90 miles, therefore, from La Pointe to the mouth of the St. Louis.

Here we met two Indians and their families from Red Cedar Lake. They inform us that the Pillagers, 100 in number, are on a war excursion against the Sioux.

March 16.[11] I learnt from Mr. Cadotte this morning, that Lieut. Bayfield made the number of islands, 22, in his survey.

June 23, 1832. Left the Brule at 4 this morning, and at 9 entered the mouth of the Saint Louis. The wind from the east is strong. The weather rainy and cold. Quite ill with a cold and severe pain in the head. Pitched our tent, waited for the boats and here breakfasted. Embarked at 11 o'clock, in the midst of a heavy shower of rain, and reached Mr. [William] Aitkin's fort at 4 p.m.

The Saint Louis, from its mouth thus far is exceedingly winding in its course, 24 miles, and 114 from La Pointe.

I was much surprised on reaching this trading post, in finding so large a number of souls on the ground—400 or upwards, in the opinion of Mr. Aitkin. Nor was I less surprised in witnessing the scene which presented itself, yelling of Indians, barking of dogs, crying of children, running and shouting of the multitude, and flourish of flags, all combined to make me feel that I was no longer among civilized beings. Mr. A., his brother [David Aitkin], Dr. [Charles W.] Borup,[12] and several other gentlemen in the employ of Mr. A., as clerks, met us on the shore and invited us to accept of accommodations such as they had, and which were comfortable and good for this country to afford. Mr. S. and myself accepted the kind offer of Mr. A. to whom we felt much indebted for his attention and hospitality. Mr. A.'s buildings consist of two small comfortable dwelling houses, made of logs, a small out house for a sort of storage building, and a fourth building from 40 to 60 feet in length, covered with elm bark. Mr. A. himself now winters in the vicinty of Leech Lake, 170 miles distant, and leaves this establishment in charge of a clerk.

After recovering from my surprise and finding myself surrounded by this large number of souls, the major part of whom had never so much as heard of the name of Jesus, or the way of salvation, it occurred to me that I was the only one on whom devolved the duty of preaching Christ and his Cross to them. But when I remembered that they neither understood my language, nor I theirs, my spirit shrank from the task. But the Lord opened a wide and effective door and gave me attendance.

Though Mr. A. was ready to embark as soon as the rain subsided, yet he remained with his clerks and opened his doors, and invited me to preach.

June 24. Sabbath. At 10 o'clock, we repaired to the mess room, where I preached to 30 or 40 souls, French, half-breeds, Americans, and a few Indians, who came in through curiosity. This was the first sermon, Mr. A. told me, that had been preached at this place. Mr. A. ordered his men to attend, which order was obeyed.

At 4 p.m. I met the Indians, half-breeds, and French, in the same place. More than twice the number assembled that were present in the morning. On my right sat Mr. Johnston, my interpreter, while my left was occupied by one of the Chiefs. Around and before me on the floor, sat his men, women and children, for the first time to listen to the words of life. They listened with attention and apparent interest. A greasy blanket and a breech-clout, with a pair of leggins composed their dress. Some of the Children were as naked as when they were born, save a breech-clout. All were painted with every variety of figure imaginable, save here and there one that was blacked with charcoal. All with pipes and tobacco pouches.

Read to them the 10 commandments and a portion from Math. XXV., and remarked, after which Mr. J. read a tract in French. They seemed much pleased with the singing.

There is no Sabbath with these Indians. To them, every day is alike. Three times during the day, the Chief Mangozia [Mongozid] came to Mr. S. for permission to dance, but followed his advice with the promise of indulgence in the morning.

From 5 p.m. till midnight, my ears were filled with the monotonous sound of their drum, which was the first thing heard in the morning.

There is no Sabbath with the Indians, nor is there any with the French half-breed voyageurs. Saturday evening, the viol and the dance were their amusement. This was the last thing Saturday evening, and the first thing Sabbath morning. More from Mr. Aitkin's influence than anything else, the viol was still during the day, which was spent in playing cards; but the evening was spent again with the viol and in the dance. These men are more hopeless than the Indians, even, whose example before, and influence upon them, is most pernicious. There are few exceptions, where they are not as degraded, in intellect, and as disgusting with filth, as the Indians themselves.

One of Mr. Aitkin's clerks tells me these men paid $2 a piece for common candles to dance by. This same clerk also assures me he once sold a barrel of shrub[13] at this place for $1288.

Fond du Lac, June 25. Almost the first thing I saw this morning was a column of 30 or more Indians, with the chief at their head, approaching our door. The beat of the drum and hor[r]id yells at short intervals and their naked, painted bodies were enough to awaken fear in a mind not accustomed to the like. As they approached, every man held his musket in a presented position, and which they discharged when they came before the door. The first sight of their naked bodies, save the breech-cloth, the uncouth gestures, raising their whole body and settling their whole weight, was comical in the extreme. Two flags were borne on the right of their column. After they reached the yard, and fired their guns as a salute, the pipe was then and first presented to Mr. Schoolcraft, myself, and Mr. Johnston, and finally went the rounds. Their musicians were seated, two drums, and a few squaws accompanied with their voices.

There was much ceremony in leading the young men on to the ground. All being ready, the drums beat, and the dancers began their perpendicular motion, up and down, up and down, holding their muskets in their hands at the same time. Their muskets, paints, feathers, bells, war-clubs, knives, &c. looked more like what I can imagine a war dance than a dance of respect. Their bodies were rubbed with charcoal, with streaks of red, white, and green. The head was ornamented with the feathers of an eagle. After some length of time, one of the warriors began a sort of philippic to the young men, recounting his deeds of valor, in which he was careful to mention the number of enemies he had killed. A bag of flour and some tobacco was carried into their midst, when their yell became so loud as to astound a man. All sat down, and a pipe was lit and borne around by the master of ceremonies, of which every Indian must smoke a little.

One character which attracted particular attention was the Moshkiki-simini, medicine man. Two long fox-tail plumes in the form of a pair of horns, were fastened on his head, and projected forward. He was rolled in a fine buffalo robe and leggined. His dress was so cumbersome as to prevent his joining in the dance, except occasionally he would become so animated as to hop up a little. He seemed to be rather a gent, a looker-on, a man of consequence.

Two pouches were hung to many for tobacco. A skunk skin tied to the ankle is a mark of courage with them. Little bells hung to the knee, or in a belt, gave variety to the noise. Their flag staffs were set in the ground near which they arrived. A large number of men, women and children sat around and seemed to enjoy the scene much.

Early this morning, Mr. Aitkin's barges, five in number, left for Mackinac.

At half past 12, took our leave of Mr. Aitkin, to whom we felt much indebted for his attention and hospitality. Mr. D[avid] Aitkin and Dr. Borup, also showed us much attention, to the former of which I am particularly indebted for facts relative to the settlement on Red River, or, as it is sometimes called, Selkirk's Settlement.

From Mr. A.'s post to the Grand Portage, it is two miles, or thereabouts, where our barge with supplies, and our canoe, was unloaded. Barges proceed no higher up the river, which is very rapid. Canoes, however, can be forced with poles nearly two miles farther, when they are obliged to land, and from which they are carried across on the back.

We were an hour and a half in reaching the portage landing, so strong is the current. From this place we sent back our boat and five men who accompanied us from the Sault. We have procured Indians to make good their place. Two are to accompany us to Leech Lake, as bow men in Lieut. Allen's canoes, from 15 to 20 are aiding us in making the portage.

To begin our portage at this end, we ascend the bank from the river, from 60 to 80 feet, in an angle of 45°. To the soldiers, this was a new business. The first attempt they made to ascend but few were successful. It was amusing to see the foot of the ascent literally strewed with men and baggage, flour bags, port kegs and knapsacks. This portage, which is 9 miles in length, is divided into 19 "poses" [pauses] or resting places. We made 3 and rested for the night at the canoe landing.

June 24 [26]. At 4 in the morning, the men began their day's work, and made 12 "poses," through mud and water in many places to their knees. A rain during the day has rendered the path much worse than it otherwise would have been. Yet the men take their keg of port, 70 lbs. and a bag of flour, 80 lbs. and in some instances, two bags, and a keg, 230 lbs. and carry it half a mile before they rest. In a few instances, men have taken 3 bags—240 lbs.

But what has surprised, and not a little amused me, is to see some of the squaws with a bag of flour, 80 lbs., a small trunk, and a soldier's knapsack on her back, wading through mud and water to her knees. Often she is seen with a bag of flour, knapsack, and a child, on top of all.

Grand Portage, St. Louis River. Breakfasted this morning at 8 o'clock, during which a shower fell, sufficient to moisten our hard bread and cheese.

At 12, another shower, till the portage path was filled with water. Musketoes here are *savage* in the extreme, and not wanting in numbers. Our
men this evening all look, to say nothing how they feel, like crest-fallen
fowls. Even the Indians are not ashamed to say—nindaick uz. Often during the day they would sing out, Manatot, Keget manatot, (bad, very bad).
My oilcloth coat served as an excellent protection against the rain and
wet from the bushes.

Mr. Aitkin estimates the size of the upper lakes, as follows: 1. Red
Lake. 2. Mille Lacs, probably in reference to its islands, so called. 3.
Leech Lake. 4. Upper Red Cedar Lake.

June 27, 1832. Commenced our march this morning at six o'clock. The
men were refreshed with rest, but some of them were quite lame, one or
two so much so as to be disabled for carrying. Road quite bad, wet and
muddy, though the weather is fair. At 11, cloudy; a prospect of more rain.
One of the soldiers who is disabled, asked for tracts. Burke, a Catholic, is
a very profane man.

Quite well myself this morning, notwithstanding the fatigue and rain of
yesterday. Some of the Indians complain of lame backs and sore feet.

Selfishness is a prominent characteristic of the squaws. You may give
and continue to give, and they are not satisfied. They will eat from morn
till night and still ask for more. An old squaw is one of the most selfish
and capricious of beings. Some of the young squaws carry a load both
ways. The sucking child and cradle must ride back and come again on a
bag of flour, and when tired, sit down. But to rise again requires all their
strength. The squaw is often seen with rolls of bark which make the lodge
where they spend the night, traps, kettles, blankets, axes, and on top of all,
the cradle, with a nursing child, while the Indian takes only his gun. The
squaws are horribly filthy in their persons, as well as Sluttish in their habits.

Arrived at the end of the portage at one. Our men and the Indians were
all much worn with fatigue. The weather is exceedingly warm. Our party
now consists of 33 in all, 15 voyageurs, Mr. Schoolcraft, Dr. Houghton, Mr.
Johnston, our interpreter, Lt. Allen, 10 soldiers, and two Indians for bow-
men in his canoes; Mr. [Louis] Du Fois [Dufault], who pilots us to the
head of the Mississippi; and myself.

June 27. End of Grand Portage. Here Mr. S. obtained four canoes from
the American Fur Co. which in addition to ours, makes us five in all. To
transport a canoe across this portage is immense labor, owing not so much,
however, to the distance, as to the winding and muddy path. Mr. A. always
leaves his at this place.

Mr. Schoolcraft here distributed presents, mostly to such as aided in
making the portage, 17 in No. The Indians seemed highly gratified with
their presents, such as tobacco, a shirt, ammunition, lead, flints and steel,
fish-hooks, ribbons, mirrors, &c. The women, 10 of whom aided, received
a piece of calico, thread, tobacco, awls, needles, ribbons, handkerchiefs, &c.
Flour and Indian meal were issued to them, which they received in the
usual manner, in one corner of a dirty blanket, or an old unwashed shirt.

It is perhaps difficult to determine which are the most squalid in their habits, the Indians, or some of the French voyageurs, who, as often as any way, receive their rations in their pocket-handkerchief, or hat.

The Saint Louis, at this end of the portage, is also very rapid, and Mr. Cote [Piere Cota?], one of Mr. Aitkin's Clerks, tells me they were obliged to draw the canoe up the stream by ropes just before reaching the next portage, 9 miles distant.

The evening is dark and cloudy. A strong wind from the east and a prospect of rain.

June 28, 1832. Grand Portage, St. Louis. We have been detained here 3 or 4 hours this morning, by a heavy fog, which is a common occurence, I am informed, in the vicinity of the rapids. The expected rain has not come, though the sun has not shown itself through the fog. Seven o'clock in the a.m., and all are now busy in loading our canoes, 5 in number, besides two Indian families with each a canoe and who take a few pieces of our baggage.

The canoes found much difficulty in ascending the rapids, one or two so much so, that they were obliged to cordell[e] them by hand. The water is chocolate colored and covered with foam in the eddies, from the falls and rapids.

Reaching Knife Portage, at 11, so called from the slate rock standing edgewise which renders it very unsafe for moccasins and feet; one or two of the men wounded themselves badly. Here we breakfasted. Our Indian friends followed us, dogs and all; each canoe brings one or more. The scenery here is picturesque indeed. Directly opposite to our landing is a small island, rising in the middle of the stream nearly 100 feet, thinly covered with pines, spruces, and cedar. Were the rock in the vicinity of our populous cities, it w[oul]d doubtless be valuable for tyling.

Knife Portage is but 9 miles from Grand Portage, but in getting here, we were obliged to walk half the way. It is three poses in length, when we came again to the same river, S[t] Louis.

There I saw more of the habits of Indian neatness. To see them eat is enough to disgust forever even a hungry man. All get around the kettle, or soup dish, and each uses his fingers or the whole hand even, to the best advantage. Children, entirely naked, except a strip of cloth two inches in width, tied in a knot before, and which served for a breech-cloth, these I could endure, but to see a squaw lick a kettle cover, both in diameter and circumference, is a little too much.

As to discipline, they have none. A child offended an old woman, upon which she took up a fire brand and threw it at him.[14] The Indians are fond of attention. Nothing pleases them more than for a white man to notice them, ask the name of everything, and try to speak a few words of Indian.

Made the portage and after gumming and repairing our canoes, embarked at 4, and came to the Grand Rapids, about 10 miles, where we are comfortably encamped for the night.

In reaching this place, we ascended no less than four or five rapids, one or two of which required all the skill and strength of the men. In ascending one of them, which flowed like a mill tide, the current broke over and wet me considerably. Often the men are obliged to spring in the water and lighten the canoe, which they at the same time steady by hand. No one can form the least idea of the difficulty of ascending these rapids till he undertakes it himself.

The scenery thus far has been delightful. The maple, elm and oak grow here in perfection. The cedars are larger than I ever saw before. If I am not greatly mistaken, we passed many beautiful white oaks, Beech and Aspen and Iron-wood is abundant. The banks are generally low and apparently often overflow. If Mr. Du Fois, our guide, is correct, the river must rise at least 30 or more feet. We have advanced 12 or 14 miles today.

River St. Louis, June 29, 1832. Embarked this morning at half passed four, and commenced our ascent of the Grand Rapids, 3 miles, or thereabouts in length. At some of the ascents, we were under the necessity of bridling our canoes, or dragging them by the bow. At another, unload a part and make a small portage. Canoes ascend those rapids by inches, often dragged for rods, while you feel the bottom rubbing on stones. Some of our men have harnessed themselves Indian fashion, with a breech cloth. They are often obliged to get overboard in the middle of the rapids in order to lighten it.

The musketoes here are voracious, long billed and dyspeptic. They gore me until the blood runs. Landed at 9 and breakfasted in their midst.

Continued to ascent rapid after rapid, till we reached what are called the lowlands, where we found comparative smooth water, and sufficiently deep for a steamboat. The banks are from 8 to 10 feet high, an alluvial deposit, covered with blue joint, and a thrifty growth of oak, bass wood, elm, ash, and maple. Pine and cedar are frequent, also, the white birch, and aspen, some spruce and cedar.

An old Indian in Company with us, left his offering of tobacco on a large stone.

Reached the river Savannah [East] at half past 7 and encamped amid musketoes, ten thousand times ten thousand. Quite ill in the morning, but much better this evening. Showery this morning, with some thunder. Here we leave the St. Louis.

River Savannah, June 30, 1832. Commenced our march this morning, at half past 4, amid musketoes that were very annoying. This river is deep, but the channel is quite narrow and exceedingly winding. Its banks are low and covered with blue joint, and a species of cut grass. The growth of wood and timber near its mouth is indifferent, till you proceed a few miles, when it becomes valuable in size and quantity. White birch, elm, maple, pine, oak and ash. Ducks in abundance.

About 10 a.m. we came to the swamps in which we rode nearly two hours. The stream is infinitely more winding here in its course, than in the forest. These swamps extend for miles, and are covered with blue joint and cut grass of the finest quality.

Reached the portage at 12 o'clock and here breakfasted. To describe the difficulties of this portage would puzzle a Scott, or a Knickerbocker, even. Neither language nor pencil can paint them. After making about half a pose, our baggage was landed on a wharf made of poles. A dyke was then made and our canoes brought up through mud and water knee deep, and landed in the portage path. A few pieces were put on board, and one at the bow and another at the stern, the latter pushing and the former drawing in mud and water to their middle, made their way in this manner for half a mile, and unloaded on a second wharf. When all was up, a second dyke was made, which raised the water sufficient just to swim the canoes, which were loaded a second time, and carried all to another pose. Some of the gentlemen were carried across in the canoes with the baggage. Others, with myself, forced their way on foot, through mud and water. The musketoes came in hordes and threatened to carry away a man alive, or devour him ere they could get him away. Made three poses and reached a maple ridge where we encamped, and spent the Sabbath.

July 1, 1832. Savannah Portage. About 10 this morning, Lieut. Allen came up in the midst of a torrent of rain. He was detained at the Grand Rapids, to mend his canoes, which he broke three times in ascending them. He encamped at the head of the portage Saturday eve, three poses distant. Saturday night, very rainy. Sabbath morning and during a part of the day, came down in torrents. The rain and the musketoes prevented our having any service. Most of the day all of us were obliged to house ourselves as well as we could. The men at one moment would be singing an Indian hymn, at the next a dancing tune, when perhaps an Indian would begin to drum and sing, that he might not fail to make his part of the noise and to render the scene of confusion more perfect.

This day has passed without either profit or pleasure to myself, though the reading of the word and a few pages of [John Bunyan's] Pilgrim's Progress, might be excepted, had not my attention been so oft interrupted and discomposed by every strange and before unheard of noise. Some of our Indian friends still follow us.

July 2, 1832. Rose at 6. Pleasant sun this morning, but the musketoes are smoke and fire proof. Was almost devoured while attempting to mend my pantaloons, which suffered a sorry rent in the mud on Saturday. Much bickering and dissatisfaction among the soldiers this morning about carrying their baggage. Not a little profanity.

The rain Saturday evening and the Sabbath, has rendered the portage almost impassable for man or beast. The mud, for the greater part of the way, will average ankle deep, and from that, upwards. In spots, it is difficult to find bottom—a perfect quagmire. Our men look like renegades, covered with mud from head to foot, some have lost one leg of the pantaloons, others both. Their shirts and moccasins are of a piece, full of rents and mud. Face, hands and necks, look like men scarred with the smallpox.

About six p.m. I reached the end of the portage, to which Mr. Schoolcraft had forwarded my baggage, and here I found both him and the Dr. The men have come through with our light baggage, but remain one pose behind, with the remainder, till morn. Mangled toes and bruised legs were brought forward to the Dr. which I venture to say will long fix in mind the fatigues of this portage.

The stream [West Savanne] into which we now put our canoes is very small, rising in some bog or fen, like to what we have been passing, and flowing 18 or 20 miles, empties into Sandy Lake.

To all the other severities of this portage, is yet to be added, that of being half devoured by musketoes. They exceed all description for being voracious, as if they never saw a human being, and were fully determined he should not escape till they had made a meal off him, at least. They are, if possible, more numerous than frogs, locusts or lice of Egypt, rising in clouds from the grass and underbrush.

Within a half mile of this end of the portage, we cross a pine ridge which seems to have escaped the ravages of fire which in past time seems to have destroyed the first growth of timber and fell into a swamp of fine grass. The men have made 9 poses with the baggage &c.

July 3, 1832. End of Savannah Portage. Morning cloudy. Our baggage was all brought up by 9 o'clock. Our canoes are now preparing and we soon leave for Sandy Lake, 18 miles. I now sit in what is called the Valley of the Mississippi. Yesterday I put my foot into one of its tributaries, but hope today to see this grand river, itself.

Bruised skins, sore toes and legs are gathered in good numbers around the Doctor's tent this morning. Every one will carry some mark in remembrance of this portage. Struck our tents and embarked at 11 o'clock in the West Savannah. This is just sufficient in width and depth to receive our canoes. Its course is northwest and passes through a low land bounded on either side by small pine ridges at the distance of 30 to 100 rods. Its banks are covered with the blue joint and sedge of a most luxuriant growth. The grass on this, as on the East Savannah, furnishes forage sufficient for immense numbers of cattle, but it rots on the ground.

About 4 p.m. reached Sandy Lake, which was grateful, indeed, after the endless windings of the Savannah.

We were welcomed under a salute of musquetry, from the few Indians that remained, the main body of whom were absent, some fishing up the river, and others hunting, down it. We were cordially entertained by Mr. [Joseph] Beaudoin (or Bodwoin) a clerk, in Mr. Aitkin's employ, Mr. A. himself being absent, on his journey to Mackinac. The weather being extremely warm, we suffered to a great degree from musketoes, night and day. At night the atmosphere was alive, and the noise resembled that of a swarm of bees. Mr. Aitkin has a large establishment here, a two-story dwelling house, from 40 to 48 feet by 30, I should judge: a store house still larger, besides a small house for his men. One or two other small out houses, besides stables for 30 head of cattle, 3 or 4 horses, and 15 swine. He raised 600 or 700 bushels of potatoes last year. He has from 12 to 15 acres under improvement, cultivates barley, peas, and potatoes to a considerable extent, but no corn. Still, I am persuaded it would grow here. His potatoes look exceedingly well. His barley has been overflowed by the Savannah and mostly destroyed.

July 4, 1832. Mr. Aitkin's post, Sandy Lake. The morning again cloudy but excessively warm. And the musketoes in the house even worse than out of doors. The country around is low and flooded at this time. Mr. A.'s post is located on a point of land where the Savannah unites with the Mississippi. It faces the former on the east, and the latter on the west, elevated 15 or 20 feet above either, and perhaps 3 to 5 [feet] rods from each. Lieut. Allen measured the Mississippi at the mouth of the Savannah and found it 110⅓ yards across.[15] The Savannah River communicates with Sandy Lake, a short distance in a direct line, but from one to two miles in its circuitous winding. The lake is small, but very irregular in form, full of bays and islands. Mr. S. today called together what Indians were on the ground and issued to them presents, leaving a string of wampum and some tobacco for the principal chief, with a request that himself and people meet us on our return at the mouth of the Des Corbeau. Mr. S. then made a few remarks to them, touching the object of my visit and commending myself to their friendship as I was a friend of his. I then made a few remarks, and presented the principal chief[16] with a small tract in Indian, as a memento of myself. At 11 Lieut. Allen inspected his men and reminded us of its being the Fourth of July by a salute in honor of each independent state.

On arriving at this post, the first thing that caught the eye, was a flag. Here, as at other places, we were welcomed by a salute from the Indians. The mode of burial here is something peculiar, such as I never before witnessed; four posts are set in the ground, united by slats, upon which, 8 or 10 feet high, the coffin is suspended in the air. A chief, Peskinanib, died about 10 days ago and is buried in this way, with his flag-staff planted at the head of his coffin. Left at 5 p.m. and marched till 9. The heat and musketoes completely did me up and I went to bed sick.

July 5, 1832. River Mississippi. Struck our tent and marched at 4. Rained heavily and got drenched from head to foot. This day has passed heavily. It has been fight, fight, till I am tired, and almost sick of such existence. The Mississippi is deep, with low banks covered with luxuriant elms, maple and cedar. The shore is a rich deposit from the bed of the stream. Passed Swan river, 60 miles from Mr. A.'s post, about 6 this eve. The musketoes this evening came in clouds from the grass and bushes where we are encamped. Comfort is a term that a man is a stranger to on such a tour as this, it is fatigue, heat, rain and musketoes. We have marched from four this morning till half past 8 this evening for 16 hours. I have not been out of the canoe but once, for my breakfast, feet and legs to my knees, wet the greater part of the time. The river, as yet, does not diminish in width. Here and there little bays of stagnant water. The river has been very winding, a strong current and angles are frequent, from due west to due north west. Ash is abundant and occasional ridges of pine are seen. One of the soldiers, Burke, is quite ill this eve. Mr. J. and Lieut. A. did not come up until nearly half past 9. One canoe of Lt. A.'s came near sinking. All are tired and worn down with fatigue and fighting, myself not among the least. Thunder this evening and prospects of more rain. Half past 11 o'clock.

July 6, 1832. Ascending the Mississippi. This is the 30th day since we left the Sault. Rose at 5:30. The weather quite hazy and a prospect of more rain. Marched at 6; halted for breakfast at 11. The sun has come out quite warm, and a fine breeze takes the musketoes high and dry; thus a man gets a little comfort. The banks are quite low this morning, exhibiting a marshy appearance. A pine ridge has been on our right or left for several miles, which the river seems to cross at short intervals. The country here is not so interesting as what we passed yesterday, more subject to be overflowed. The edge of the water is often lined with small grey willows, infested with musketoes, which sally out in clouds, when approached. This afternoon, the banks have been occasionally high on one hand, but the reverse on the other. For a long distance, dry dead pines have caught the eye on either hand, which the fire at some former time has destroyed. Hardly one remains alive. A very miserable growth of weeds and small white birch have sprung up, with whortleberry bushes. Clay is here and there seen in these sand banks. This eve we encamped on a high bluff in the midst of dead pines, hoping to avoid musketoes, but after the wind fell, which has disabled them from annoying us through the day, they came upon us in clouds. Killed two or three ducks, upon which we supped. A fine red squirrel, in attempting to cross the stream, came in contact with a paddle, and was taken on board. He road two or three miles, the men supposing he would die, but ere they were aware, he ran up the body of one of the men, and leaped into the stream and swam ashore.

Lieut. A. has not come up this eve, but answered our report, from which we concluded he is not far in the rear.

The river is so high that when in low water, there are several rapids, there is now only a strong current.

July 7, 1832. Pikigimi banwitig. Struck our tent at 5 a.m.[17] and arrived here at 10 p.m. The country exhibits all the marks of stirility I noticed yesterday, sand-banks, dead pines, birch bushes, willows, &c. The water being high the Kokabikance [Falls of Pokegama], or fall of water over stones, presents a beautiful prospect to the eye. The greatest fall of perhaps 5 feet, making in all a descent of 15 feet or more perpendicular. A mile below, we ascended a considerable rapid. Twice our canoe was carried down stream in spite of paddles, the poles not being of sufficient length to reach bottom. The whole width of the main falls is not more than 20 yards. The change in the atmosphere is great since yesterday. Cloaks are quite comfortable this morning, but yesterday it was like a torrid zone, with my shooting jacket on. Here we are obliged to make a short portage, perhaps 200 yards.

Left these falls at 12 and entered on a real Savannah, the end of which I almost despair of ever seeing, more serpentine than can be imagined. The borders of the stream are lined with wild rice, sedge, rushes, the tall-leaved Indian rush, sweet flag and common flags. The white pond lily is seen here and there. White and yellow pines bound the prospects, no less than 3 or 4 of which lie recently shattered by the lightning. One we passed which the lightning had marked in the manner of a screw; 5 times it surrounded it.

We have marched against both wind and current this p.m. the former of which has been very strong. For variety this p.m. we had quite a shower. We are comfortably encamped this evening, on a pine ridge, which occasionally bounds the stream. Here we spend the Sabbath. The Manomin, or Wild Rice, first made its appearance just below the Falls.

July 8. Miss. River, 30 miles from the Falls. The morning indicates a rainy day. Confusion and profanity among the soldiers. I all but wish I had the command, I would still their noise, if I could not put them in humor with each other. Never was I more rejoiced than when Lt. A. came out and silenced them.

It is holy day again with the Catholic Frenchmen. I have a practical demonstration of the influence of the Catholic religion. It allows wicked men to live as they list and trample upon one of the sacred institutions of God, the holy Sabbath. To their profanity, also, there is no length or breadth.

Sabbath eve: 7 p.m. It has been showery during the day and prevented our regular service in English. Read a few hymns and portions of the scripture to a few Indians who travel in company with us, to which they listened attentively. Gave an Indian tract to Vezanindibea [Oza Windib], (Yellow Head) which he received very gratefully. Called the Indians and French together at 4 p.m. Read, sang, and prayed with them. A shower interrupted me while addressing them. A keg was all that served as a desk and seat for me. Mr. Johnston is of great service to me in giving them religious instruction, as he speaks English, French and Ojibway. I felt exceedingly depressed and annoyed by the conduct of some of the men, but found some relief in reading the word of God and in retirement.

No one can appreciate the blessings of the Sabbath and the privilege of Christian worship, till in a land where he finds neither. How often do I think of the House of God, where I once worshipped with those who love the courts of the Lord. While I write, my ears are annoyed with the jingle of the coppers where the Catholics are gambling.

A Frenchman in Mr. Aitkin's employ [La Plante], has just arrived from Leech Lake, who informs us of the return of the Pillagers from their war excursion. They met the Sioux and had an engagement, in wh[ich] they lost one man and killed three, whose scalps they brought home. He also states that the Sioux came to the Pembina Settlement, where they scalped a child and fled. The Ojibwas pursued them for revenge, and overtook them and killed four of their party. How long will it be when these savages shall learn war no more! It is now an eye for an eye, a tooth for a tooth. Eschke-bag-a-kosh [Aishkibugikozh or Flat Mouth] is the name of the Chief who led the war party from Leech Lake.

July 9, 1832. Great Winnipeg Lake (Winnibogoshish). Embarked at 4:30 this a.m. The recent rains had so raised the Mississippi that we made our way in an almost straight course across the marsh, through the sedge, Indian rush, and grass as high as a man's waist. Duck, gulls and black birds were seen in almost every direction, the former of which we killed in abundance and robbed one nest of its eggs.

Reached Point aux Chiens where we left the winding Mississippi to our left and entered Pagataunon River, which took us into a small lake 10 miles in length, bearing the same name [Ball Club Lake[18]], from the circumstances of the Indians playing ball on it in the winter, as Mr. Johnston supposes. Leaving this Lake, we entered the mouth of a small river, where we disembarked and breakfasted. Passed up this stream about 200 yards, and entered another small lake, leaving which, entered a still smaller stream, which we followed from 2 to 3 miles, and came to a larger one, which we crossed, and made a portage of 806 paces. Then the aspect of the soil began to change for the better, luxuriant yellow pines, ash and maple. Our canoes were now put into the waters of the Smaller Winnipeg [Little Winnibigoshish], 2 miles, perhaps, in width, and 4 in length. Entered the Mississippi again, on crossing this from E. to W. and in about two hours were in the large Winnipeg. This is a beautful body of water, extending to the W. as far as the eye can reach. The E. shore is covered with a luxuriant growth of oak, maple, &c. The trading post is on the north shore at the mouth of a small river. It is under care of Mr. Aitkin, who has a French-man here by the name of Belazhe [Jean Bt. Belonger]. He states the no. of men here at 25—probably 100 or more in all. He has not met with much opposition from the Hudson Bay Company at Rainy Lake, 5 days' journey from this. They are supplied with liquors and he has none. They sent other Indians with goods to get furs from his Indians, who reported on their re-turn that they had 60 kegs. These are mixed with 3 parts of water, thus making 4 kegs of one. A keg they sell at 5 "plues." One beaver, otter, or bear, or 3 martins, is a "plus."

The name Winnipeg seems to be derived from Winot, dirty, and nibi, water.[19] I counted 12 dogs.

July 9. Big Winnipeg [Winnibigoshish] Lake. Mr. Blonzha [Belonger] has eight head of cattle, has been here two years, in which time he has cleared 2 to 4 acres, which he has under cultivation. Last year he raised 160 bushels of potatoes. This year he has planted 30 kegs and calculates, provided the season is favorable, on a crop of 300 bushels. They look well now, as also do his peas. This is the first year he has tried peas and corn. Pumpkins look fine—also his tobacco. He raised some last year quite good, he says. The soil is easy to work, a rich loam, approximating to the sand. The growth of wood is fine. This garden suffered this season, from being overflowed. He has a log house, with deer-skin windows, which, when well oiled, admit sufficient light. The chimney is topped out with clay and straw. He has a small store house and a stable for his cattle, made of logs. He is also building a house which is part finished. The chimney to the upper floor is round stones bedded in clay, mud, above is topped out with straw and mud, as the other.

The few Indians present requested permission to dance this evening, as they wished for some tobacco. Two men and boys, with muskets in their hands, performed, while two men drummed, one on a paddle, handle, as they had but one drum. It was so dark that I could not well examine their dress, except one had a skunk's tail hung on each side, and a head dress which extended behind, covering nearly all his otherwise naked back. They were much animated when the tobacco was thrown in to their midst on the ground.

July 10. [Upper] Red Cedar or Cass Lake. Embarked this morning at 5 and crossing the lake from E. to W. entered the Mississippi once more. All the characteristics before mentioned as to ducks, gulls, black birds, rush, horse-tail, sedge, flag, and angles, still remain. The banks are ridges of pines sparsely mixed with oaks, much more, however, than before mentioned. At 2 p.m. reached the entrance of Red Cedar Lake or Cassena Lake. The two families who accompanied us from Fond du Lac, fired a few guns, and collected five other families of their friends, and as we came up, all gave us a salute. We made a traverse to Grand [Star] Island, of 10 miles, and encamped. On approaching this isle, to my great surprise, on a bluff 60 or more feet high, I saw corn and potatoes. The latter, also pumpkins, looked very fine and luxuriant. The former of which they have cultivated from time immemorial, and which was first obtained from Red River. Last year they raised 100 bags, which will average 3 pecks to a bushel, and 200 bags of potatoes. The soil is light and easy to work, sandy on the hills and the ravines, which wash. An application has been made for some beans to plant. Just beyond our tent are two graves. At the head of one stands a pole, with a scalp hung on it. These graves are about 15 feet apart and the grass is worn entirely from between them, by dancing.

There, I witnessed the first scalp dance. Some of the young men from this place accompanied the Pillagers against the Sioux, and the scalps taken are sent here for them to participate in the rejoicing. The Indian, also, who was killed, belonged to this place. To his widow, a scalp has been sent on from Red River, also, and these have been the cause of rejoicing this evening. The widow, I saw this evening. She had been out for wood in her canoe, which we have obtained for our route to Lac la Biche [Itasca].

The sensation was indescribable while looking at these scalps and witnessing their shouting and dancing. I have a lock of hair from one of them. A piece of wood is turned in the form of an ox bow. In this, the scalp is stretched, the hair hanging down full length. This hair is trimmed with feathers of divers colors, and suspended at the top to a stick three feet long. This seems as a handle to shake it in the air. Three young women, each holding one of them in the air, led the dance this evening, while men, women and children accompanied the drum with their voices. Our voyageurs each procured some tobacco, and after the dance began, all ran, shouting, and presented their tobacco, which goes to the widow.

I visited their lodges before the dance began, and read the 10 commandments, and sang a few hymns, with two of our men. All listened with astonishment, never before having heard them. As I had no interpreter, I could not address them.

Arrangements are now made to leave our heavy canoes, our baggage, and all our men, save 8, to take us to the head waters of the Mississippi, with the aid of 3 Indians, in their small canoes.

July 11. Kamiskuanakakag [Gamisquawakokagag]. (upper Red Cedar Lake) Latitude 47° 40′, Mr. Schoolcraft thinks. Embarked this morning at 5. Traversed Lake Cassena, in a course South by West, and made a portage across a point of land, 200 yards. Traversed a small [Allen's] bay, and made another portage of the same length across a point, and fell into the Mississippi. At 7 o'clock it began to rain and continued to come down in a torrent for three or four hours, when it partially abated. All were drenched, from head to foot. Ascended then considerable [Metoswa] rapids, in one of which the men were obliged to get out and raise the canoe, by walking. Breakfast at 11, in the midst of a heavy rain, and re-embarked at 12:30. Reached Lake Travers [Bemidji], 45 miles from the Upper Cedar, or Cassena Lake, at 2:30 p.m. after a march of 8 hours. Traversed this Lake in an hour or a little more, and passed a small log house on the W. shore, where the American Fur Company send some traders to winter. This is a fine country for red deer, bear, moose &c. Ducks are abundant, which we have killed in numbers. The country changes in its appearance, at Cassena Lake. The change is a happy one. Elm, maple, and some oak, and yellow pine, appear on banks not high but moderately elevated. The Indian in the bow of my canoe has pointed out to me traces of the bear, and the deer, as we passed, which escape the eye of a white man. Leaving Lake Travers, we crossed two small lakes [Marquette and La Salle], and at 6 p.m. entered another, 8 or 10 miles in length, which the Indians call Kobekonon Sakaigon [Kubbakunna], i.e. Landing Lake [Plantagenette]. This we also traversed, and entered the Mississippi, in a course S.W. At about 8:30 encamped, having made a march of about 60 miles, as it is estimated. I ought perhaps to mention, that Dr. Houghton filled his canoe half full of water in ascending the rapids, and only escaped trying the depth of the river by getting ashore as soon as possible.

Musketoes and wet feet are my constant companions this evening. All our beds are wet. Found my oil cloth pantaloons were beneficial.

July 12. Passed a comfortable night, musketoes and wet, notwithstanding, and embarked this morning at 5:30. Since leaving Kabikonon Lake, the country has lost every pleasing effect, and assumed one of the most worthless, I ever saw. There is no variety. All before you a ridge of pine or a cedar swamp on either hand; the stream more circuitous, zigzag, and winding, than it is possible to imagine. Sometimes its course is in the midst of a marshy musketoe swamp, sometimes shooting to the extreme edge of these ridges, or these impenetrable swamps. Its banks are lined with willows of three or four species, dogwood, sedge, Indian rush, black alder, &c. all contributing in a high degree to the propagation of musketoes. We had not proceeded far this morning, when one of our Indians killed a fine deer. For the first time, I witnessed a specimen of Indian dexterity, in using the knife. Not more than 20 minutes elapsed, we had the skin off and the meat dissected, and we were under way. Mr. Johnston tells me it is the custom to give to the first person who comes. He being the first on the ground, received the four quarters of meat. The skin and other parts were given to another. Not an iota was left—even the clotted blood being saved.

Reached the forks of the river, one leading South, West [Schoolcraft or Yellow Head River], and the other, which we pursue, West. Made a portage of a mile and a half, on account of rapids, and encamped. Some rain today, and musketoes by the 10,000 lbs. Wet and tired, yet in tolerable health. Saw frequent vestiges of the bear and deer today. I might notice, perhaps, that the udder of the deer was roasted and eaten. The intestines were given to one of the voyageurs. The feet were roasted and eaten, the oil put on their hair and muskets. I should go hungry some time before I made a hearty meal from their cooking. Particulars, I pass by. Marched 40 miles today.

Friday, July 13. Omoshkos [Omoshkozo] Sagaiigun (Elk Lake). Embarked at six and marched until 9, when we reached the point in the stream where we make another portage, one of six miles. Breakfasted at 9, and at 11, took all our effects on our backs, and entered a swamp to begin with. Nearly all this distance is over a pine ridge, or rather highland, the soil, the most worthless, if the growth may determine it—hardly anything but small gray pine, here and there a large pitch pine. Occasionally a low place, so low, a man only finds bottom when he finds himself to his middle in mud.

At the end of 4 miles, we find ourselves at Lac la Biche. This Lake is from 6 to 9 miles in length, and from 100 to 800 yards in breadth.[20] Its shore is wooded with pine, white birch, basswood, elm, and maple. There is but one island [Schoolcraft] in it, and this is small, on which we raised a flag, and left it. This Lake abounds with turtle; many large shells are seen on the island, where the Indians have encamped. The lake is very irregular in shape and from this reason, the Indians gave it the name, Moshkos, an Elk.

Left the lake at 5 p.m., and entered a small stream on the north, which is the outlet. The current is very strong, and channel deep, but narrow. The growth for 15 or 20 miles indicates a good soil, when we fall upon savannahs of the most devious windings. We marched until 10 in the evening, and then encamped. The deer and bear frequent this region, several of the former of which we have seen. The stream which forms the outlet of this Lake, abounds with fish. The Indian in the bow of my canoe, exhibited great dexterity in the use of the spear, sometimes throwing it for some distance, at his prey, and making it fast. Saw a fine doe in the open savannah just before dark. The Indian fired upon her, but was at such a distance, he missed. Elk were formerly taken in large numbers at this Lake.

July 14. Embarked at half past 5, and descended two or three very strong and difficult rapids, where my Indians both got out and walked down in the stream, steadying the canoe. They manifested much skill in managing a canoe in rapids, and amongst stones. She shipped water but twice in three times.

In descending these rapids, Lieut. Allen was upset and all his effects with him, in the stream. A keg of pork came bouncing over rock after rock, till one head was stove in. One of my Indians caught it as it was passing, and with his spear took in a loaf of bread also. All was found, save the compass. The men in Mr. Schoolcraft's canoe, had their breakfast swept off. The fall is 10 or 15 feet in the space of 100 yards. Nothing can exceed the grandeur of the scene in descending a large stream in a small canoe when the water is smooth. The canoe is not only borne with all the rapidity of the stream, but its speed is made, if possible, to exceed that of a race horse, when impelled by the paddles.

Passed the embankment of the Sioux, on the border of the stream where they dug two large cavities, sufficient to receive 30 men. It just overlooks the stream and afforded them a fine opportunity of effecting their purpose, which they did. It is not known how many Ojibways were killed. Just at eve we came to the Lake which is known by the name "where they killed us," [Piniddiwin] from the circumstance of a whole family being murdered there, by the Sioux.

Marched until eve, when we halted and took our tea, and concluded to reimbark and march all night, in order to reach the Upper Red Cedar, or Cassena Lake, before the Sabbath, where we left our baggage and men. Our beds were spread, and our passage more pleasant and comfortable even than could have been supposed.

At half past 9, all re-embarked, save Lt. A. who remained for day light, in order to better take the bearings and the course of the river. A beautiful moon, and a clear sky gave a new aspect to the scenery, which surpassed the painting of a Scott. The quacking of the ducks, disturbed by nightly visitants, gave an additional variety to the passing scene. No sooner had I fallen into a fine drowse, my slumbers were broken by the discharge of two muskets almost at the same instant. On awaking, I found that the Indians had espied a fine deer by moonlight, I was not so buried myself in sleep, but that I distinctly heard its jump. The high grass and deep water, and imperfect light of the moon, prevented them from finding it. Passing a short distance, and we started another.

I soon fell asleep and on awaking found myself descending rapids, head foremost. The Indians and men had become sleepy, and in order to give the steersman an opportunity to take a nap, the bow man had turned himself and the canoe so that she literally descended stern foremost. Thus they managed to refresh each other. At 7 o'clock, when we halted for supper, our march was estimated at 90 miles.

July 15. Grand Isle, Upper Red Cedar Lake. Arrived here at 9 this morning, having marched all night, and after an absence of 4 days, found all well, and our men much recruited. As our party were so much fatigued by our excursion, it was thought best to omit our English service, and that I direct what time and strength I had, to the Indians.

Retired with the pious soldiers and spent a pleasant interview in prayer and conversation. Found that they were in a depressed state of mind. They were, however, aware of the cause, and seemed rather disposed to feel that they had mistaken duty in volunteering on the excursion. Their fellow soldiers had been very censorious and contentious during Lieut. Allen's absence. Read to some of the Indians, who came to our tent, and in the P.M. collected 70, who listened with much apparent interest and fixed attention to the words of life, some for the first time. Our meeting was near the graves before mentioned, and on the ground where their horrible dances are often exhibited. One important qualification in a missionary to the Indians, is, that he is able to sing. When we assembled, 5 or 6 men were

seated on the ground at the game of platter, which was laid aside. I seldom
have witnessed a more still and interesting audience. Mr. J. read to them
the account of the Creation, and the flood, after which I read the ten commandments, and remarked on them, and the object of my visit. The principal chief is absent. The greater number present were young. The inquiry
was put to the principal man present, "would you like to have a missionary
come and instruct your children, &c." to which he replied, that neither
himself nor any present, could answer it, as the old men were absent, and
many of the young men are very vicious.

Have just visited a lodge this evening where was a woman very sick,
affected with epileptic fits. The lodge was filled with smoke and crowded
with Indians, smoking over a little fire, while the sick person lay in one
corner on some hay, and her groans so loud as to be distinctly heard to our
tent, several rods distant. Dr. Houghton got up and visited her. She fainted
while I was in. The Dr. bled her and gave her some medicine, which seemed
to relieve her.

Immediately after our meeting, their scalp dance began and continued
without cessation, till 11 o'clock. I learned from the men who remained,
that the Indians have danced night and day since we have been gone.

Three canoes passed here, Mr. [Louis] Default [Dufault] tells, from
Leech Lake, to Red Lake. The object of their visit is to carry wampum and
tobacco to invite that band to join them in another war excursion, to revenge the death of the man who was recently killed and whose brother
resides at Red Lake. One Indian asked for some salt and brought us in return, some fine potatoes which were a luxury, not to say a matter of interest in this distant region.

One of our men caught a young sand hill crane this morning, as we
descended the river. Its bill is at least 10 inches long, and its wings, from
tip to tip, 5 feet at least, and its neck 18 or 20 inches.

Mr. Schoolcraft estimates the route by which we returned from Lac la
Biche, at 180 miles.

July 16. The Indians were assembled this morning and Mr. S. addressed
them and made them presents of ammunition, lead, knives, tobacco, calico,
cloth, beads, thread, needles, beads, feathers, ribbons, awls, flints. A medal
and flag were presented to Ozonshtiguan [Oza Windib], Yellow Head. The
chief's compliment of tobacco was next presented to him, which he distributed equally to the last mite.

Tobacco and wampum Mr. S. sent to the Red Lake chiefs, acknowledg-
ing the receipt of his pipe.

At 10 a.m. we embarked for Leech Lake, where we arrived about 10 in
the evening, a distance of about 40 miles. We made two portages, one of
about half a mile, the other of nearly two miles, both of them across sandy
ridges, mostly pine. After passing a winding stream, in which we were
about one hour, we entered a beautiful stream [Steamboat River] sufficiently wide and deep to swim a vessel of several tons. This stream enters
the Lake, one of its branches taking its rise in the small lake where we
embarked, after making the second portage.

Mr. Schoolcraft's visit to Upper Red Cedar Lake or Cassena band, has evidently been attended with a happy influence. They now must feel that our government is exercising paternal care for their interests. Their presents will long keep awake the kind feelings which they have called into exercise, and which they received with marked expressions of gratitude.

I much regretted that I could not see the chief, as it must, after all, depend on him and his principal men whether a door is ever to be opened to send them the bread of life. And unless the chief is kindly disposed, all would be in vain, for without him, the others will not encourage the introduction of the gospel. This band is free from Catholic influence, so far as I could learn. Nor is there any distinguished medicine man whose influence is much to be feared.

July 17. Leech Lake. Was not a little surprised, this morning, in finding a plot of potatoes and corn at the head of our tent. The Indians raise corn and potatoes as well as at Upper Red Cedar Lake, or Cassina and Red Lake.

A message came this morning from the chief [Flat Mouth], to Mr. Schoolcraft, to breakfast with him, which he did. The table was a mat spread in the middle of the floor, around which Mr. S. and the chief were seated, while his wife waited on the table. She took her breakfast by herself, in one corner. Their table was served with fish and tea, and something in a dish in the form of butter, which he did not taste. His house is of logs, about 20 feet each way, with a stone chimney. Dr. H. and myself were introduced by Mr. J. His room was hung at one end with an American flag and an English flag, 4 or 5 medals, several war clubs, spears, tomahawks, and other implements of war. The walls of his room were completely lined with warriors. The chief was painted black in mourning for his son. Several were painted in like manner. Others were painted red, and the head ornamented with feathers. Some with a skunk skin round the head and heels, and one tipt with 12 feathers, indicating that he had killed that number of warriors. Their countenances were full of wildness such as I never saw before. They look, some of them, as fierce as the tiger, and bold as the lion, and may be well denominated "Pillagers," if the report be true that they hesitate not to take the trader's kettle from the fire and eat without his permission, and yet he dares not resent or resist it. Mr. Aitkin has threatened to desert them. They in fact kept the trader in his house a few years ago, forbidding him to leave it.

The old chief made many complaints today, of their hard usage, especially against Mr. Aitkin. Here Mr. Schoolcraft issued presents to a large amount and addressed them. The chief rose, giving his hand to each, and then remarked, that he wished Mr. S. to remain until the morrow, as he had many things to say, and which required time for reflection. Mr. S. then requested me to speak, when I addressed them on the subject of my visit. They listened attentively while I related to them what the Christian people are doing for the Ojibways in Canada, at the Sault & La Pointe. Also what they are doing for the Senecas, Oneidas, and Stockbridge Indians, at Green Bay and what is doing at the Sandwich Islands, and as-

sured them of the interests felt for them as a tribe, and what they were
ready to do for them in the way of instruction, if they wished. The Chief
then announced to the Indians that he would speak a few words, as we
should be displeased if he did not. He commenced as follows: that he was
sorry that Mr. S. considered them as children, and not as men. He lamented
that their condition was what (it) was, since even the trees wept over it.
And when he heard that Mr. S. was on his way to visit them, he hoped the
day would dawn, but he felt that the cloud still hung over them. He felt at
first inclined to go and meet him, when he heard of his coming, in hopes
that he would send his people relief, and if he refused to do it, he thought
of going farther, to the British government, for that aid which the government had so often promised, and in particular, at Fond du Lac, and the
prairie. The promise was, when they smoked the pipe with the Sioux, that
the first one who crossed the line, should be flogged. This proved they had
not fulfilled; that their Great Father, the President of the United States,
had not stretched out the long arm which he had promised. And when his
own son was killed, he determined not to lay down arms as long as he saw
the light of the sun. He did not think that the Almighty ever made them to
sit still and see their people killed. And this, his young men would never
do. Since they had listened to the advice of the Long Knives, not a year
had passed without some of their people being killed, giving to Mr. S. a
bundle of sticks, and intimating at the same time that the number was 43.

The medals of each chief, and a string of wampum was then brought forward, all painted with vermillion. He laid them at Mr. Schoolcraft's feet,
saying that these and all his letters were stained with blood, and he wished
to leave them for him to wipe off. The words of the Long Knives had
passed through the forests as a rushing wind, but they had only shaken the
trees, and it had not stopped even to break them down, nor to smooth over
the rough places. It was not that they wished to be at war with the Sioux,
but when the latter came into their country, and killed their young men,
then we [they] are obliged to revenge their death. Nor would he conceal
from Mr. S. the fact, that he had already sent tobacco and pipe stems to
their neighbors, to come to their relief. And he expected that this year
would not end before others among his young men would fall, and that
the blood which had begun to run would not soon cease to flow. And although they had been successful in the late excursion, yet they did not feel
that they had taken sufficient revenge. He himself was inclined to believe
that the agent at S[t.] Peters, [Lawrence] Taliaferro, encouraged the Sioux
to fight, for he even told him he might come with his young men and made
[a raid] on the Sioux during his [Taliaferro's] absence at S[t.] Louis.
Another man, also a trader among the Sioux, [Joseph] Ravile [Renville],
he expected had encouraged the Sioux to make war on them, and whom he
believed was the cause of his son's death.

The old man sat with as much dignity as if he was king of an empire, on
his bed or trunk, while his wife sat crouched down by the side of the bed
on the floor, as if the most menial servant. He requested a white shirt of
Mr. S., that he might lay aside his mourning. Mr. S. gave him one, and to

our surprise, the old man came out as we were leaving, in his regimentals, ruffle shirt, gloves, fur hat, pantaloons and shoes. I did not know him till he spoke, so entirely altered was his appearance.

Guitche Asaie [Nesia], (Elder Brother) is the second, and Machi Gabo [Maji Gabowi] (Stirring Man) is the third Chief. (Feb. 1835. This man I do not find acknowledged here as a chief. He is chief only in doing evil. This is the only prominence he can at present claim.)

On our way here we met Muchi Gabo, the great medicine man of Leech Lake, who has 5 wives as it is said. He is more than six feet in stature, and large-boned and muscular. This is the man who scalped Governor Semple of the Red River settlement, in 1816 or '17 when the North West and Hudson Bay Companies were at strife. The Governor prohibited the North West Co.'s people to pass the fort with pemmican when they left the river, and attempted to convey it by carts over land. The Gov. took a body of men and went out and commanded firing upon them, whence a skirmish ensued, in which the Governor was shot from his horse, though probably not mortally wounded. While sitting on the ground, this Indian came up, and, tho' the Gov. begged for life, yet he shot and scalped him. There is much of the cunning in his countenance. His influence is considerable, and to be suspected, should a mission be established here.

One man applied to Dr. H., who was wounded in the leg, just above the knee, by a ball in the late battle. The ball was lodged in the leg. One man I saw here, with 12 feathers on his head, and a wreath of skunk skin round the head and heel.

Corn, potatoes, I believe beans or peas, they have raised for many years in considerable quantities. The soil is sandy, but the black sand, which is productive. The growth in the vicinity is mostly the yellow pine, thickly interspersed wth oak. Muchi Gabo related to Mr. Johnston, that they had 8 places of living during the year.

July 18. Embarked this morning about 6 a.m. and as our expected guides from the village did not arrive, found some difficulty in finding the portage path, after traversing a bay of about 3 miles. First part, eight miles from the village. Our way, this morning, lies through a series almost infinite, of small lakes and over short portages. The first portage is one "pause," 1078 yards. The whole number of portages today, is five, the longest four pauses, of 1900 yards, nearly 2 miles, and the shortest of one pause. The whole number of small lakes passed today is nine, several of which are connected by narrow channel, some of which are not more than 10 yards. The country is almost wholly yellow pine, some as beautiful timber as I ever saw. The old Chief, Esh-ke-bug-e-kosh, and Muchi Gabo, overtook us in the afternoon, with their wives. The guides have not come, for what reason, I know not, unless it be through fear of the Sioux, or because we did not wait for them, from whence they concluded we did not wish them. The old chief and Mucha Gabo supped with us.

July 19. Embarked at 6 a.m. and crossed a long lake [Long Water] a branch of the Des Corbeaux, about 6 miles, and entered a narrow and extremely winding channel of one mile, in which we were detained an hour and a half. From this, we entered [Little] Vermillion Lake, perhaps 3 miles in length. A channel of 800 yds. led us into Birch Lake, one mile. Channel of 50 yards, and we came to Lake Plé, 3 miles long. A channel of 3½ miles led us to a lake with no name [Ossowa], of 2 miles in length, and 40 yards wide, shells in great numbers here. Next we enter Catas Le [Lac Vieux Desert], or the old wintering grove, 4 miles in length, a channel of 20 yards, and we entered an anonymous lake [Summit] of 3 miles, leaving which, a channel wide and beautiful, of 8 miles bro[ugh]t us into Long Rice Lake. In all, we have crossed today 8 or 9 small lakes, and all connected by small channels. Were overtaken this p.m. by a most severe storm of wind and rain, while on a Lake. The thunder and lightning were truly appalling, yet the latter the most sublime spectacle, one I have seldom seen. Our canoe was driven ashore by the violence of the wind, though no one suffered injury, nor did we disembark. At 6 p.m. after a march of 2 days from Leech Lake, we reached the forks of the Des Corbeaux. It is a grand stream even here, 70 or more yards wide. We had not descended far, before we were overtaken by another storm of wind, rain, thunder and lightning, accompanied by hail. Marched till about 7 in the evening, in hopes to overtake Lt. Allen, but did not. The country is pine, cedar, tamarack, aspen, high ridges, bordering the lakes, and the channels, with a little marsh intervening between the water and the ridge. A barren, worthless soil. The distance from Long Lake, the source of this fork, to its junction with the other, may be 35 or 40 miles. An Indian canoe would find it an easy day's march. Came down the stream 14 miles, and encamped.

Friday, July 20. Crow Wing, or Des Corbeaux, River. Embarked this morning at 6. A strong current and several rapids. Small islands occasionally, in the middle of the stream, some of which are covered with wood, others with grass. The banks are yellow pine, entirely, for 50 miles from the forks, when here and there an elm may be seen. An evident and striking change for the better in soil and particularly in the growth of timber, is seen as we descend. Elm, oak, maple, and ash, of the most luxuriant growth, appear on an alluvial bank of one or two feet in height, extend back, varying in width, to the pine ridges in the rear. Prairies of beautiful meadows in one instance when we landed, I discovered. Wild rice in considerable abundance in the stream. Have passed several old canoes today, which are supposed to have been abandoned by the late war party. Encamped at 8 o'clock about 14 miles below what we suppose is Leaf River, 85 or 95 miles from the forks.

July 21. Mr. [Benjamin F.] Baker's post, 18 miles from mouth of Des Corbeaux. Embarked at 5 a.m. marched 4 hours, when we breakfasted just below the mouth of the Prairie River, about 140 miles below the Forks. The rice disappears as we descend the river. White pines and high banks also take the place occasionally of an alluvial bank. At 12 o'clock, after a march of about 50 miles, reached the mouth of the Crow Wing River, which swells to an exceeding river, after receiving the waters of these tributaries, Leaf, Prairie and Gull Rivers, the latter of which is 12 or 15 miles only, from its mouth. Mr. Baker informs us that the voyageurs follow Gull River in the winter, in going from here to Leech Lake, and walk the distance in three days. The small lakes are numberless through this region. A man may voyage in any direction by water, if he will make short portages. The country is sandy and mostly wooded with pine, which the fire has cleared of brush. We have been 3½ days from Leech Lake to the mo. of the Des Corbeaux River, a distance of nearly 230 miles.

At the mouth of this river, we met the Sandy Lake Indians, who were absent when we passed. They were expecting us and had sent two canoes up the river to meet us and give them the signal of our approach. All were encamped on the banks of the Mississippi, which for several rods were lined with canoes and lodges, near which 4 or 5 flags were raised. When we approached, all collected on the bank of the river, and commenced their discharge of muskets and yells of congratulation. Encamped with a view of spending the Sabbath here, but as our goods soon arrived, from Sandy Lake, concluded to distribute the presents and descend the river 18 miles to Mr. Baker's post.

The old chief [Grosse Gueule or Big Mouth], after expressing the pleasure of seeing us, made some complaints against Mr. Aitkin. He does not supply them with ammunition in the summer during his absence. This leads them to go to Saint Peter's for it and they meet the Sioux, and are often killed. Mr. A. does not tell the truth, &c. He waits for Government to fulfill their promise at Fond du Lac, in 1826, at Prairie du Chien, in 1825. He don't know how he should act, if a war party came along, nor have, nor how if stems are sent.

The women and children were gone, many of them, for berries, and some of the hunters for game, two of whom returned, ere we left, with three bears. The presents were distributed, and we left immediately. One or two young men, with medals given to their fathers, now deceased, made speeches. One, the White Fisher, began thus.

Though, I am only a little dog without hair, yet I will say a word. I can do right with one hand, but evil with the other. He reminded us once more of the pledge at the Fond du Lac, and Prairie du Chien treaties. They presented us with some bears' meat as we left. It was very finely flavored, similar to veal. The bear is generally coarse, but this was, I presume, one of the cubs. As it was impracticable for me to present the object of my visit, Mr. Johnston invited the Indians to come to Mr. Baker's post, where we should pass the Sabbath. We embarked at 6 p.m. and reached the post at 8, a distance of 18 miles. Mr. B. wintered in 1831 at Leech Lake. He gives these Indians the same name with all others who have spoken of them. He says a man could not keep a cow, or a horse even, to draw his wood; the Indians would kill it. If the trader does not give them credits to the amount they wish, they threaten to break open his store. They are impudent and care not for their trader, but regard him as their servant. Mr. [William] Stitt also made much the same remarks to me. He also has wintered with them.

The old chief wishes the lines to be run and they will keep their side and ask no more of the Sioux than this.

The Indians have a game of platter—play for tobacco, traps, and everything. "Hide the moccasin," also. Girls shuffle a bundle of sticks and then "odd or even" them.[21]

July 22. Mr. Baker's post. Early this morning, canoe after canoe came, agreeable to Mr. S.'s request. I took my little tract and sat down among several of the men smoking and began to read, when all ears seemed to listen with the deepest interest and much curiosity. Mr. Johnston then gave them some account of the Indians at the Sault, and vicinity, to which they listened with interest and said all was good. The old chief remarked that he could not give me an answer to what I should say relative to a school among his people, as some of his chiefs were absent, to whom he must consult. This is a characteristic. If one acts or advises, all the others are jealous and he does not do or say what he often would.

At 4 p.m. we collected about, we collected about [sic] 40 men, women and children, and Mr. J. read to them the account of the creation, flood, &c. I then read to them the Ten Commandments and addressed them, after which Mr. J. addressed them. All listened with much interest and were evidently pleased to hear the things spoken.

Mr. Baker speaks well of these Indians and feels desirous that a school should be established near him. He thinks it possesses many advantages over Sandy Lake, both in point of communication with the Leech Lake Indians and the civilized world. It is but two days march from S[t.] Peter's in a canoe, or by land in the winter. He drove a cart from there to his post. It is 2 or 3 days march from Sandy Lake and Leech Lake in the winter. From Mr. Baker's post to Leech Lake, with a pack, 4 days' march, and from there to Red Lake, three days.

July 23. Descending the Mississippi. Embarked at Mr. B.'s, where we passed the Sabbath, at 6 o'clock; descended two small rapids and came, at 8 o'clock to the Little Falls. In half an hour reached another considerable one. At 10, halted for breakfast, having descended seven considerable rapids. The stream is higher than it has been known for many years. There are many small islands in it, well wooded. The banks are generally high, with a bold shore, here and there for miles there is an alluvial bottom on one side. Post oak, elm, white walnut, are the most numerous. Mr. B. is situated on a point of land apparently as you approach it, forming a dam in the stream with three small islands parallel to each other and the banks on either side. The country around is prairie, with post oak. The whole country is the most inviting to emigrants and interesting of any part of the United States that I have even seen. If there is any thing that can meet the wishes, and fill the soul of man with gratitude, it is here. What would require the labor of years in Vermont and New Hampshire, to live, is all prepared here to his hand. As far as the eye can reach is one continuous field of grass and lands exhibiting the appearance of a country that has been cultivated for centuries and now deserted by its inhabitants. Gentle, but not large swells are seen here and there, which give variety and beauty to the scene. The soil is easy to cultivate and rich as black earth approximating to a sand. The clumps of oak on the prairies seen at a distance, resemble an orchard; and the leaves rustling in the wind and showing their under side give them the beauty of blossoms. Nothing can be more picturesque and grand, than the high banks which rise before you at a distance as you ascend. The Islands also, are the richest in soil, which is alluvial, covered with high grass, walnut, maple, elm, butternut, &c. and in some places so thick that it is almost as if a man should throw a handful of beans in a stream and each should become an island. We have marched today 13½ hours. Our rate will average 10 miles per hour or more. When we put ashore for breakfast, Mr. Baker, who accompanies us to Saint Peter's observed that we had come a distance which it requires days to ascend. Have passed several streams on our right, which come in as tributaries, among which is the Watab, forming the line settled in 1825, at the Treaty of Prairie du Chien, as dividing the Ojibways and the Sioux. The next considerable stream is the Sauk, just at the head of the rapids of the same name. We have passed only two Indian Lodges during the day, and from both obtained venison. The latter made a cache this morning and deposited an elk. We are now quietly encamped within the Sioux dominion. We have as yet seen none. The country here presents the appearance of having once been cultivated, but long since forsaken of its occupants. The gentle swells and beautiful ravines, give the whole an appearance of a spacious field waving with grass.

July 24. Fort Snelling—S[t.] Peters. Embarked this morning at 5, and marched till 12, when we reached the Falls of S[aint] Anthony, where we breakfasted. About 20 miles above these Falls, we passed the river which communicates with Mille Lacs. This and the Saint Francis river, are the two principal, on our left in descending the Mississippi from the mouth of the Des Corbeaux. And these are not difficult in crossing with a horse or cart by land to Mr. B.'s post. The Falls of Saint Anthony are beautiful, but nothing which inspires one with awe. The waters are divided in nearly the middle of the stream by a clump of trees on a bluff of rock. The perpendicular fall is perhaps 20 feet, just at the foot of wh[ich] is a chute of 10 or 15 feet more in descent. Here we made a portage of one pause and embarked in the rapids below. These falls are 9 or 10 miles from the junction of the Saint Peter's [Minnesota] River with the Mississippi, at which point the Fort is located on a bluff 200 feet high overlooking the junction of the two streams. This is almost delightful country for agriculture. The fort has a saw and grist mill and a farm at the falls. They are now getting hay. We were a few minutes over an hour in coming from the falls. Mr. B. calls it 200 miles from here to his post. We make it 214 by our calculation.

The foot is so elevated that it overlooks the surrounding country for miles. The Saint Peters is a most delightful stream, winding its way through prairies with the most delightful swells, and ravines with a carpet of the most delightful green. The gardens attached to the fort present all the variety of vegetables found in a North east garden—corn, peas, potatoes, onions, beats, squashes, &c.

July 25. The officers at this post at present are Capt. [William R.] Jewett [Jouett], Lieuts. [Jefferson] Vail, [Jonas K.] Greenough, [Edward

R.] Williams, and [Ingham] Wood. Surgeon, Dr. [Robert] Wood. Mrs.
W. is the only lady in the garrison. This fort was built to convene one bat-
talion, 6 or 8 companies, but at present there are but three here and those
not full. The walls and most of the buildings are of stone. It is the most
spacious fort I have seen. The tower commands an extensive view of the
adjacent country and the Mississippi and S[t.] Peter's Rivers.

The American Fur Company have an establishment within a mile situated at the junction of the two rivers. Mr. [Alexis] Bailey is in charge of
the establishment. He has a stock of cattle, horses, swine and a few sheep.
Corn, potatoes and grass, together with garden vegetables, grow here
luxuriant.

The fur traders in this vicinity have been in the habit of bringing in
whiskey with the permission of the Indian Agent, Mr. Taliaferro, who is
now absent. The agency is filled by Capt. Jewett, who is an efficient man
and a friend to the cause of temperance. He has arrested two men who
were smuggling whiskey into the country. Mr. Hazen Mooers, we found
him, whom he had arrested and from whom he had taken his whiskey.
But he allows him to pass without seizing his goods as the Indians would
suffer. He trades at the head waters of the Saint Peter's River, and on the
waters of Red River. At dusk, Lt. Greenough arrived with another trader,
having seized his whiskey. He also, the same evening, dispatched his canoe
off again under Lieut. W. to intercept others, who are in the habit of carrying it from the Mississippi across by land, to the S[t.] Peters, while they
come up by the Fort with their goods. Capt. J. is a Kentuckian, a great
talker, but truly deserving of much credit for the firm course he is pursuing in relation to the article.

Capt. Jewett sent for the Indians and gave Mr. Schoolcraft an opportunity of counciling with them. Three chiefs were present, Black Dog, Little Crow, and the Man who floats on the Water. Mr. S. stated to them,
the object of his tour among the Ojibways, and their complaints against
the Sioux in making war on them, also, their wishes to have the line run,
that each may know their appropriate ground.

Little Crow then arose and shook hands with each, and by expressing
his satisfaction in seeing us. He recollected the Treaty at Prairie du Chien,
in 1825, when they smoked the pipe with the Ojibways, and agreed all to eat
and drink from the same dish. He denied that they were in league with the
Foxes and Sauks, as had been represented and hoped Government would
punish them for their conduct. With regard to the line, it was very near his
people, and he wished, as did all present, that it should be run and immediately, the sooner the better. He then alluded to the late war party from
the Ojibways, who had killed two of his nephews and taken their scalps.
Yet he did not complain, nor would he retaliate. Twenty or 30 of his men
were present. Little Crow is considered the most influential man among
the Sioux, also a good Indian. He was much disaffected with having a post
near their lines, which bring the Ojibways and Sioux together.

July 26. Embarked this morning. Made a call at Little Crow's village, 9
miles down the river. About 20 men were present: gave them some tobacco

and a bag of flour. The old chief gave me a pipe. They have 5 or 6 quite comfortable bark houses at this village, and farther down the river they have another village, nearly as large. Their houses are much preferable to any among the Ojibways, that I have seen, except that of Esch ke buge-cosh [Aishkibugikozh or Flat Mouth]. They raise corn, potatoes, &c. Leaving the garrison, the character of the country and the banks of the river are altogether changed. The banks are high bluffs for the most part, thinly wooded with elm, maple, cotton-wood and ash.

Reached river S[aint] Croix at almost 3,—45 miles from Fort Snelling. A short and wide stream passed, and we are in the Lake of the same name, which is surrounded by the most beautiful scenery. The banks are high and guarded by rocks in many places, in the crevices of which the red cedar groves are abundant. The tops of the hills are destitute of wood almost entirely. The shrubbery is the small prairie oak: We have passed the Lake, 30 miles, and encamped—75 miles, we estimate our march today.

The shore here is limestone, upon strata of sand stone. The first appearance at the Falls of St. Anthony and still continuous.

Friday, July 27. Saint Croix River. Embarked this morning at 5, and in 2½ hours entered the Saint Croix River at the head of the Lake. It is characterized by innumerable small islands, which, in high water are overflowed. High bluffs covered with shrubbery appear at some distance, and we loose sight of prairies entirely. Saw a large squad of pelicans this morning. They are a large white bird with a mandible similar to the goose, just behind which, on the under side, is a large pouch. We estimate the Lake at 12 leagues, or 40 miles, in length, and one broad, but in many places not more than a half mile. It abounds with fish, which are seen leaping out of the water for flies. Mr. J. calls them sturgeon. Many of them have a snout or sword 3 or 4 inches long.

The shores of this Lake are the most picturesque of any lake of the size I have witnessed. A dozen or 20 mounds rising in a sugar loaf or pyramid form, may be seen at one glance, covered with the most beautiful carpet of green, with hardly a shrub. The river banks are alluvial and covered with a rich growth of maple, elm, walnut ash, iron-wood, and butternut, prevail. Many rivulets come in on the east, but one considerable stream [Apple River] on the right. White pine appears this p.m. and occasional small prairies. Sand and stony bottom alternate in the stream. Our march today has been 35 or 40 miles. Saw wild geese, tracks of deer and bear, also.

July 31. River S[t.] Croix, above the Forks. Down came the tent this morning, over my head, while wrapped in a sound sleep. Embarked at 5, and in about 3 hours, reached Yellow River, 12 or 15 miles, communicating with Ottoway [Court Oreilles] Lake. Mr. [Daniel] Dingley was formerly located on this river, a short distance from its mouth. Here we found a few Indians, who received us with a salute. Breakfasted here. Here, for the first time saw new potatoes. An old squaw brought us a bowl of them and a pan of pulverized venison. The Indians here raise corn and pumpkins to a considerable extent. The soil is light and sandy, but capable of cultivation. Dry pines, which the fire has killed, characterize both banks at a small distance from the water. The forks are 15 miles from Yellow River, one of which is denominated the Namikagon [Namekagon], and this, the St. Croix. At the forks, found two or three families of Indians, among whom was the old chief [Kabamappa] of Pokuena village.

Leaving the forks, we were obliged to disembark in the stream and lighten our canoe, by carrying up the river. Ascended two or three considerable rapids, and while looking for an encampment, the old chief and two other small canoes overtook us and conducted us to the foot of the "portage des femmes," or women's portage, as it is termed.

As we ascend, the banks are low, inundated in high water, but covered with the most luxuriant grass, blue-joint, and a species of the red top.

My teeth chatter with my great coat on this morning. Have made a march of about 30 miles.

Pikogonagon [Pokonokuning] (Yellow River) is called the hip-bone from a ridge on its borders.

Aug. 1. The fog this morning prevented our embarking till 6. Ascended rapid after rapid till 11, and made but about 8 miles from our encampment. Water very low, and the Indians say they never saw it more so. For miles, our men were obliged to wade, and in many places lift the canoe over stones which in the rapids stand high out of the water, hardly leaving a possibility of ascending the channel.

Rice looks more interesting as we ascend the stream, than I have witnessed on any other river. It hardly appears below the forks. This is the principal support of the Indians, many of whom are now assembled at Rice Lake for preparing it for harvesting, by tying it in small bunches before it ripens. Deer are taken here.

The country above the forks presents few if any inducements to the agriculturist to locate here. The stream is skirted by a narrow strip of maple, elm, ash, white birch, aspen, cedar and spruce, in the rear of which the growth of pine is luxuriant.

The old chief, Kahi Mahi [Kabamappa] has accompanied us today and been of much aid to us. His village is about 32 miles from the forks, 26 of which we have travelled today. We find corn, potatoes, pumpkins here, the latter of which, the frost has injured. This is rare, the old man says.

Aug. 2. Head of the Brule. Embarked this morning at 5, reached the portage at one. Leaving Kahi Mahi's village, we found good water, 4 hours. The St. Croix here is skirted by savannahs, which yield monsmiu [rice] in abundance. Passing Clear Water [Eau Claire] River in 4 or 5 miles, came to Buffalo [Ox] River, both coming in on our right as we ascend. Leaving the latter, the stream is very winding, the channel rocky and exceeding[ly] difficult to pass for two miles, when we entered Lake St. Croix, which is the source of this fork. The river also has a lake of the same name at its junction with the Mississippi.

The lake at the source has a small island nearly in its center, on which are the relics of two or three old lodges. The length of the lake, which is rather oblong in form, is from 7 to 9 miles. From Kahi Mahi's village to the portage, 30 or 35 miles. The portage is 1850 [3,350] yards, or about 2 miles, over a pitch pine ridge, which the fire has almost leveled of all its growth.

Embarked near the head of the Brule, which rises near the foot of the pine ridge in a boiling spring, whose waters divide, a part entering the Saint Croix Lake, and the other forming this stream. The water is as fine as any well water I ever drank.

Embarked at half past six, and at 8 found ourselves half a mile or so. The water was so low, we formed a dam with our oilcloth, which was of much service. [Houghton and] I wandered down the Savannah nearly a mile and a half, and waited until nearly 9, for the canoes, when the signal was given for me [us] to return. The musketoes were not a little annoying in the high grass, weeds, and bushes. Our march today may be estimated at 35 miles.

Aug. 3. Descending the Brule. Struck our tent this morning, at 5:30, and instead of embarking, sent the men with the red canoe ahead, when they were obliged to make a portage in order to get it into the stream, which is extremely winding. Started on foot again to try the Savannah. Walked a mile or more through wet grass, weeds and bushes to my head, musketoes all the time annoying me. Embarked with Mr. S. in our empty canoe, and soon found the stream widening and deepening so much that 3 miles from its source it is in many places 5 feet in depth. Tributaries from the Savannah supply it. Never was I in a much worse hole than here —the alders on each bank met interlocked in the middle of the stream, through which we were obliged to force our way. But what is a matter of no little surprise to me, is, that this is the highway to two or three posts, and yet you would hardly suppose a rat even, could pass. It must have been much better than now when Carver passed, if not, I trust he has a faint recollection of it. Our canoe was well filled with sticks, leaves, bugs, worms and spiders of every kind. Nothing but black alder and tamarack meets the eye for miles. When the latter assumes the entire ascendancy, here and there a solitary white pine and spruce. Cedar then comes in. Of all the streams I have seen, this is the most dismal, for 10 or 15 miles at its head. At the first rapids, 25 or 30 miles from its head, the stream is rocky, which continued most of the day, very full of rapids, and strong current. The timber improves as we descend. Elm prevails; here and there a pine ridge. The stream abounds with trout.

Aug. 4. Mouth of the Brule. We are two days from the head of the Brule, 10 from Saint Peter's, including the sabbath, during which we rested. Embarked this morning, 20 minutes before 5, marched two hours, and came to the head of the second series of rapids. Arrived at the mouth of the river at 10 in the evening, after a pause of 3 hours. Made 4 portages in ascending the second series of rapids, of one pause each. Two-thirds the length of this river is a continual series of rapids, some of which are very formidable. Between the two series, there is a tract of land that is interesting, and highly susceptible of cultivation. But at the head of the second series, there is an instantaneous change in the growth, leaving beautiful elms, pine, spruces, cedar, linn, and aspen, occupy their places.

We have been one month in making our tour to the head of the Mississippi and in our return, and since we left Sandy Lake. Never was I more rejoiced to see an old friend, than I am this eve, to see the lake, after the fatigues attending our ascending the S[t.] Louis, and descending the Brule. We have been on the march 14 hours today, some of the time we have dragged our canoes over stones like sleighing on bare ground. Our men have waded more than three-fourths the distance.

Sabbath, Aug. 5. Mouth of the Brule. The Sabbath! O how does it remind me of Christian privileges and Christian friends, with whom I have worshipped in the house of God. I almost fancied that I heard the Church going bell. But Oh, how soon did the Indian Drum dissipate all my pleasant thoughts, and tell me, here is the home of the red man and the savage.

Entered a lodge today, and found them at a game of platter. I began to read to one who sat near me, when the game ceased, and all listened. Read and sang, till one or two at length joined in the hymn of praise. They seemed to be delighted and surprised to hear reading or singing, in their language.

A heavy shower this morning. The elements are at this moment raging as if striving with each other for the mastery. A heavy shower is near, and the Indians have begun their yells and beating of drums, as if to render confusion more confounded or in order to appease the anger of their imaginary spirits.

Monday, Aug. 6. La Pointe. Embarked at the Brule this morning at 4:30, and were favored with a fine wind, which brought us to Sandy River at 12, where we had breakfast. On putting out again, we found that the wind had ceased, and we were obliged to make our way by the paddle alone.

Reached the post at La Pointe about 6 p.m. and were happy to find Bro. Hall and family in health. Were not a little disappointed in find[ing] that no boat or canoe had arrived from Mackinac, from where we hoped to have heard something respecting the progress and result of the War. If I ever felt the exercise of gratitude, it was to find myself safely returned in comparative health, after a fatiguing tour of 6 weeks.

Lieut. Allen, whom we have not seen since the morning after we left Saint Peter's, I fear will find much difficulty in coming through and regret that he is left in our rear, how many days, time only can determine.

Aug. 7. Messrs. Schoolcraft and Johnston left us about 7 o'clock, having exchanged two small canoes for one that will ride on the lake. They man them 14, besides Paguash enimi, who wishes to return.

Aug. 11. About 10 this morning, we espied a sail at a distance, which proved to be Lt. Allen. We were happy, indeed, to greet him once more, and much amused at the history of his adventures from the mouth of the St. Croix River.

Aug. 12. Lieut. Allen and Dr. Houghton, who had tarried with us for Lt. A., left this morning for the Sault, intending to visit the copper rock, 30 miles from the mouth of the Ontonagon River, as they passed.

Have employed myself in writing my friends and the Board, as this opportunity may be the last till after the close of navigation.

The Indians were very treacherous. They stole off in the night with a canoe which Lt. Allen had purchased of them for two blankets and other small articles. Stole provisions also.

About 11 o'clock a.m. Bro. Hall and myself repaired to the school room, where 25 or 30 Indians and French collected. We spent an hour or more in singing, reading and praying with them. No one can realize the embarassment under which we labor, without an interpreter. It is painful, indeed, to see those fellow beings sunk in ignorance and yet to be unable to communicate with them, so as to remove it, by declaring to them the simple truth of God.

NOTES

1. The journalists do not agree on the number of Indians on the island. Boutwell noted that Dr. Houghton vaccinated forty-six; Allen recorded fifty-nine "souls": or thirty-five males and twenty-four females; whereas Schoolcraft's official count was fifty.

2. The trading post was located on the western shore of Munising Bay, on the location of what later became the village of Onota. It was near the site of the famous Bay Blast Furnace.

3. The attitude of this girl can easily be explained. Indians believed that strangely shaped rocks were dwelling places for powerful spirits. Frequently they avoided these places altogether, but if they did happen to go near them they would leave tobacco or some other gift to win the favor of the powerful spirit. Schoolcraft often observed this superstitution among the Indians. *Summary Narrative* (1855), p. 99.

4. In quoits, a game similar to horseshoes, opposing players attempt to pitch the quoit, a flattened ring of iron, over stakes or hobs driven into the ground a short distance apart.

5. The Cadot or Cadotte family played a prominent part in the early history of the Lake Superior region. Jean Baptiste Cadotte spent his life in the western fur trade with his headquarters at Sault Ste. Marie. His mother was a Chippewa, as was his wife. In the 1760's he entered a partnership with Alexander Henry, the famous English fur trader and adventurer, to mine copper in the Ontonagon region. After this project failed, Jean devoted all his energy to the fur trade until 1796 when he turned his property over to his sons, Jean Baptiste, Jr., and Michael, both of whom became prominent in the Minnesota and Wisconsin fur trade. Michael lived at La Pointe. His daughters married Truman and Lyman Warren, the latter of whom was met by the expedition while he was on his way to Mackinac. The child, "Alex," was connected with this family.

6. Several meanings for Ontonagon have been presented. The Reverend William Gagnieur, an authority on Indian place names, maintains it is derived from the Indian word Nintonaganing, meaning "the place of my dish." Other writers have presented the meanings "fishing place," "place of the wooden bowl," and "place where game is shot by guess." "Indian Place Names in the Upper Peninsula and Their Interpretation," *Michigan History,* (July, 1918), Vol. II, pp. 544-45.

7. The editor is unable to explain the meaning of "Dr. Gam." It was apparently a reference to the sandy bay in which the party encamped.

8. Boutwell and Allen were in error in stating that the Jesuits occupied the fort on Madeline Island. Father Allouez and Father Marquette were located on the southwestern shore of Chequamegon Bay, possibly at the mouth of Vanderventer's Creek.

The "Old Fort" site was located at the southwestern extremity of Madeline Island, on present-day Grant's Point. The French adventurer, Pierre Le Sueur, had built the fort in 1693 and, according to legend, French fur traders dismantled the fort in 1761, after learning of the horrible murder of a fur trader and his family there by a voyageur. The new fort, built by the American Fur Company in 1718, was located a few miles north, on the west shore of the island. The Protestant mission was located between the two forts. Reuben G. Thwaites, "The Story of Chequamegon Bay," *Wisconsin Historical Collections,* Vol. XIII, pp. 408-14.

9. Lt. Allen and Boutwell may have been in error in calling this Spirit Island. Judging from Lt. Allen's description of his eight-mile journey from La Pointe he must have encamped on either Basswood or Hermit Island. It was probably the latter, which is, as he estimated, two miles long. Manitou Island was called "Devils" or "Spirit Island" by the Indians, but it is located over fifteen miles from La Pointe. Devil's Island, located about ten miles north of Manitou, was called "Evil Spirit Island," but it too, was too far from La Pointe to fit Allen's description. It is possible, of course, that Hermit Island was then called Spirit Island.

10. Lt. Henry Wolsey Bayfield of the Royal Navy surveyed the Canadian coastlines of the Great Lakes and the entire shore line of Lake Superior. His manuscript map of Lake Superior was outstanding in detail and remains today a document of great historical value. The town of Bayfield, Wisconsin, was named after him.

11. Boutwell apparently made the correction in his journal at a later year.

12. Dr. Charles William Wulff Borup played an interesting part in the development of Minnesota. Born in Copenhagen, Denmark, in 1808, he studied medicine and came to America in 1828, whereupon he became a clerk in the Indian trade. He served as clerk at Yellow River, Watab, and at other posts and ultimately succeeded Lyman Warren as representative of the American Fur Company at La Pointe. He later was prominent in financial circles in St. Paul. He died in 1859.

13. A liquor composed of fruit acid with spirit to preserve it.

14. This treatment of children was not typical of the Indian parents in general. They were very indulgent with their children and seldom beat or whipped them.

15. This was done by stretching a line across the river. All the diarists recorded the correct distance, except Dr. Houghton who reported that the river was "100 yards broad."

16. Grosse Gueule, or Big Mouth, was the principal chief at Sandy Lake and, according to Schoolcraft, was absent hunting and fishing when the expedition arrived. Boutwell was probably referring to a lesser chief, possibly Inineervi, or the "Manly Man."

17. The journalists do not agree on the time of departure for July 7. Allen reported that they started at 3:30 A.M. and Houghton at 5:15 A.M. Nor is there agreement as to the name of the place of encampment. Schoolcraft recorded that they stayed at Point aux Chenes, whereas Allen wrote that this point was

two miles above their encampment. Boutwell also noted that they reached Point aux Chenes later.

18. There are a variety of spellings for the name of this lake. Schoolcraft spelled it Bogottowa; Houghton, Bogotowa; and Boutwell, Pagataunon. J. A. Gilfillan, an authority on Minnesota geographical names, gives the Indian name as Pagautowan. The lake resembled the instrument the Indians used in playing the game of lacrosse. It is now called Ball Club Lake. J. A. Gilfillan, "Minnesota Geographical Names Derived from the Chippewa Language," *The Geological and Natural History Survey of Minnesota,* Fifteenth Annual Report, 1886 (St. Paul, 1887), p. 459.

19. According to Gilfillan the name meant "miserable-wretched-dirty-water" from the Indian *Winni:* filthy; *bi:* water; *osh:* bad, an expression of contempt; *ish:* an additional expression of contempt. *Ibid.,* p. 459.

20. Itasca is made up of three arms of water projecting one to the north, one to the southwest and the other to the southeast. Lt. Allen reported that the lake was seven miles long and one to three miles broad; Houghton thought it was eight miles long and had an average width of three fourths of a mile, whereas Schoolcraft estimated its length at seven to eight miles. It is apparent, from an examination of the map of Itasca accompanying Schoolcraft's *Narrative* (p. 56), that Schoolcraft and the others were measuring the distance of the southeast arm of the lake, since the southwest arm is shown as much shorter. Actually the distance from the outlet of Itasca to the extreme southeast point of the lake is 22,639 feet—or a little over four miles whereas the distance to the southwest point is 17,926 feet or about three and four tenths miles. Jacob Brower, *Itasca State Park* in *Minnesota Historical Collections,* (1904), Vol. XI, pp. 96-98.

21. "Hide the Moccasin" was a common guessing game of northern Indian tribes. Four moccasins were commonly used, and a ball was hidden under one of them. The opposing side attempted to guess the location of the ball. The stick game was played with four marked sticks of two different sizes which were hidden under a basket, the object being to guess their relative positions. See Smithsonian Institution, Bureau of American Ethnology, *Handbook of American Indians,* Frederick W. Hodge, ed., Bulletin 30, Part 1 (Washington, D. C., 1912), pp. 484-86.

2. William T. Boutwell to Editor, *Missionary Herald.*

Fond du Lac, June 25, 1832

I write in the midst of confusion; all is hurry and bustle to make ready for our departure from this place, where we arrived on June 2d. We passed the Sabbath with Mr. Aitkin, who was on the point of embarking for Mackinaw, but who remained with his clerks and men till this morning.

On arriving here I was not a little surprised to find nearly 400 souls. French half breed, Indians and white men. The scene at our landing was such as I never before witnessed, and enough to fill one, unaccustomed to the like as myself, with wonder, if not with fear. The yelling of Indians, barking of dogs, crying of children, running of the multitude, discharge of musketry and flourish of flags, was noise in the extreme.

But my feelings were indescribable, when I came to my senses and felt

that on myself devolved the duty of preaching to this motl[e]y group, the
only salvation by Jesus Christ. And what depressed me more than all, the
majority neither understood my language, nor I theirs, sufficiently to address them, except through an interpreter.

The Lord, however, opened a wide and effectual door, and gave me ut-
terance. At ten o'clock I preached to about 40 in English, the first sermon
ever preached here—and at four, P.M., I addressed, through Mr. Johnston, more than twice that number—French, half breeds and Indians.
Many of the latter of whom, for the first time, listened to the word of life.
All listened with attention and interest.

My interpreter sat on my right, while a chief occupied a seat at my left,
around and before me, on the floor, sat his men, women and children, in a
state of almost entire nudity, many of whom had no more than a cloth
about the loins and blanket, but some of the children not even a blanket.

All with their pipes and tobacco pouches, painted with all the variety of
figures that can be imagined. The chief came to Mr. Schoolcraft three
times, during the day, for permission to dance, but followed his advice,
with the promise of the privilege in the morning. From five o'clock till
twelve at night, my ears were filled with the monotonous beat of the Indian drum.

This morning, the drum was the first thing heard; and at eight, 30 or
more, who joined in the dance, headed by their chief, came before our
door, where they exhibited for an hour. Their approach was the most
comical—a half hop, timed by the beat of two drums, accompanied with
a monotonous sound of the human voice—each holding his musket in a
presented position, which, as they came near, was discharged—two American flags were borne, at the right of their column.

The pipe was now lit, and first presented to Mr. S. and next to myself,
then to Mr. Johnston, and finally went the rounds, when they commenced
their dance, accompanied with the monotonous drum and the voices of a
few squaws. At short intervals all united in a yell.

The bodies of the principal part of the men were naked, except the cloth
about the loins and leggins, and painted in a manner to exhibit the most
hideous spectacle possible. Their heads and the bodies of many were
ornamented with the feathers of the eagle. One character, in particular,
attracted my attention—this was their medicine man. He was superbly
painted, leggined and rolled in a fine Buffalo robe, which being too cumbersome to join in the dance, he stood by as a looker on.

The pipe and dance with them are the highest marks of respect, and on
which occasions they always expect presents. After the dance had proceeded a short time, one of the warriors began a sort of Philippic to the
young men, recounting his exploits, in which he was careful to tell them
how many of the Sioux he had killed.

And here too I must acknowledge the kindness of my friend, Mr. S.,
who, immediately on receiving his instructions from the war department,
dispatched a canoe for me to Mackinaw, and has been assiduous in every
possible way, of making my tour pleasant and profitable. I trust I shall

be able to furnish the public and the Board with facts of the most interesting character.

Passed 24 hours at La Point, with brother H., who is in health, and I am happy to say, laboring not without the prospect of doing good. I left Mackinaw on the 4th and St. Maies [Mary's] on the 7th of June. Met Mr. Warren, Ayer and Mrs. Campbell, one day's march from the Point.

Mr. Oaks informed us of a war party, forming at Lac Du Flambeau, by the chief, called the White Crow, to go against the Sioux. Mr. O. had some wampum from this chief to Mr. S., expressive of his intention. Reaching the Point, we met an Indian directly from that band, saying the chief had abandoned the excursion in consequence of the death of a child.

3. William T. Boutwell to Editor, *Missionary Herald.*

LA POINTE, Aug. 8, 1832

Since I last wrote you from Fon[d] Du Lac, a kind Providence has enabled me to make the tour to the head waters of the Mississippi, and safely returned me to this place; where I arrived on the 6th instant.

Leaving Fon Du Lac, we continued our route up the St. Louis, till we reached one of its tributaries, the Savannah. This we pursued to its very source; when we made a portage, and reached a tributary of the Mississippi—the western Savannah, which first empties into Sandy lake.

Leaving this lake, we embarked on the 4th of July, and from this point commenced our ascent up the Mississippi—now become our high way. We arrived at Cassena or Upper Red Cedar lake on the 10th. Here our baggage, our large canoes, and our men, save seven or eight, were left, when Mr. S. procured two Indians as guides, and five Indian canoes in which we embarked and made our ascent to Elk lake, where we arrived on the 13th.

We returned to Cassena lake by a different fork from that by which we ascended, and next visited Leech lake. From thence we directed our course to the Des Corbeau, which we descended to its juncture with the Mississippi, and thence down this to the St. Anthony's and St. Peter's to the mouth of the St. Croix, which we ascended to its source, and by a portage reached the head of the Brule. This we descended, and once more found ourselves on the shores of Lake Superior.

Our tour from the Saut to Elk lake, and from thence to this place by the Des Corbeau, we estimate at nearly 2,400 miles, which we travelled in sixty days. We were enabled to make the tour in a much shorter time than was anticipated, on account of the waters being favorable on the Upper Mississippi. The Indians spoke of their being much higher than they ever before saw them at this season of the year.

The Ojibeways in this part of the Mississippi, in particular at Leech lake, we found in a state far from being favorable for receiving instruction at present. They are evidently much disaffected toward our government, and disposed to make war upon their neighbors the Sioux. The cause of their disaffection is grounded on the promise made to them at the treaty of Prairie du Chien in 1825, which, as they say, was this, that their great father would punish the first individual, or party of individuals, who should violate the treaty. They feel, and say, that the Sioux have violated the compact made when they smoked the pipe of peace and mutually agreed to burn the implements of death. They say, that the Sioux enter their country, murder their young men, women, and children; and our government sit and look on, while they neither punish them, nor are willing that they should rise and do it themselves. This treaty was referred to by almost every chief on the Upper Mississippi, who made a speech; but by no one more feelingly than by the old chief at Leech lake, who had just returned from an excursion against the Sioux which he led himself, and in which he had taken three scalps and lost but one man. He justified himself in the course he had pursued by saying, that it was not so bad for them to kill Sioux, as for the Sacs and Foxes to kill white men. His speech with two or three incidents accompanying it, I shall give you hereafter, in which he was so frank as to say, pipe stems and wampum had already been sent to invite the different bands in that section to join in forming another party, which though he would not lead them himself, yet he might not be the last man to follow. It is more than probable, that the Indians at Cassena and Red lakes cherish the same sentiments and feelings which were developed here, from the fact that they are in the immediate vicinity; the former being but a few hours, and the latter but two or three days march, which in this country is hardly a matter of reckoning. But all seemed desirous of peace, and particularly, that the line should be definitely marked, each party pledging that if this was done, they would keep their own side of it. The major part of the Indians, but especially some of the chiefs, seemed highly to appreciate the appropriation of government, ($12,000 if I mistake not,) for the purpose of vaccinating the tribes on our frontiers.

Dr. Houghton, who accompanied the expedition as surgeon and naturalist, had on his vaccinating list when he left here on his return, nearly 2,000 belonging to the Ojibewa tribe.

I am waiting the return of the traders, who are daily expected, when we shall consult with Messrs. Warren and Oaks, relative to one of us visiting the Lake Du Flambeau region this fall. Till their return I shall take charge of the school, and relieve Mr. Hall, who has been much embarrassed with the care of this and other concerns. We are all in usual health, though I suffered somewhat during the tour from rheumatism, exposed as I was to rains by day, and wet blankets by night.

Every Sabbath, with but two or three exceptions, brought me in contact with more or less Indians, whom I addressed through our interpreter.

4. William T. Boutwell to Julius Chambers

STILLWATER, [MINNESOTA], July 27, 1880

DEAR MR. CHAMBERS:

As you say, it was in 1872 that inquiry was raised regarding the origin of the word "Itasca." The Secretary of the Minnesota Historical Society, knowing I had accompanied the Schoolcraft expedition, addressed a note to me with the request that if I had any knowledge regarding the origin of the name I would favour him with a reply. I gave to him the time, place, and circumstances under which I first heard the word uttered by Mr. Schoolcraft. Here are the facts:

As we were coasting along the south shore of Lake Superior one beautiful morning, the lake as calm and smooth as a mirror, Mr. Schoolcraft turned to me with this question: "Mr. Boutwell, can you give to me a word in Greek or Latin that will express 'true head' or 'source'?"

After a moment's reflection, I replied, "I cannot; but I can give you two words." I gave to him "veritas caput." He wrote out the two words and, shortly after, turning to me, said, with animation:

"I have it!" Then and there, I first heard the word "I-tas-ca."

With much esteem, yours,

W. T. BOUTWELL

5. Interview of William Boutwell by Jacob Brower [1890?]

"Mr. Schoolcraft and myself were personal friends and at his instance I became a member of his party in 1832. We proceeded on our westward journey along the south shore of Superior in the same canoe, as companions. I think it was at a point west of the Pictured Rocks, while we were voyaging in our canoe, that Mr. Schoolcraft suddenly turned to me one day and asked the question, 'what is the Greek and Latin definition of the headwaters or true source of a river?' After much thought I could not rally my memory of Greek sufficiently to designate the name; but in Latin, I selected the strongest and most pointed expressions. The first words given by me were *Verum Caput*. But I told Mr. Schoolcraft, if he wanted stronger words, he could take *Veritas Caput,* which meant, 'Truth' 'Head.' I wrote the words on a slip of paper and Mr. Schoolcraft told me he should strike out the first and last letters of *Veritas, Caput,* and that 'Itasca shall be the name.' "

This interview was a very interesting one, had at Mr. Boutwell's home, during which he related many circumstances concerning the voyage of 1832. He said no religious ceremonies were held at Itasca lake at that time. Being a missionary he was known among the Indians as "The Black Coat."

APPENDIX F

Newspaper Reports of Expedition of 1832

THE EXPEDITION of 1832 attracted considerable attention in the newspapers. Dr. Douglass Houghton wrote reports for the *Detroit Journal and Michigan Advertiser* from various points along the route, and these accounts were published as they were received. Other papers quoted from these news stories.

Some of the newspaper articles contain information about the expedition which is not found in other sources. Conclusive evidence that Schoolcraft derived the name "Itasca" from the Latin words "Veritas Caput" appears in news articles in the *Democratic Free Press and Michigan Intelligencer* of October 25, 1832, and the *Detroit Journal and Michigan Advertiser* of September 26, 1832. Although Schoolcraft later implied that the name was derived from Indian mythology, the news accounts prove otherwise.

The controversy between Lieutenant James Allen and Schoolcraft also found its way into newsprint. In 1834 the New York *American* reviewed the published accounts of the two men and aired the dispute. Schoolcraft was severely criticized for the "unaccountable and inhumane desertion" of the Lieutenant and his military force in hostile "enemy country." Schoolcraft answered these charges in a masterful letter, which was published in the *Detroit Journal and Michigan Advertiser*. These two news stories help clarify the points of the controversy.

1. *Detroit Journal and Michigan Advertiser,* May 30, 1832.
2. *Detroit Journal and Michigan Advertiser,* July 18, 1832.
3. *Detroit Journal and Michigan Advertiser,* August 8, 1832.
4. *Detroit Journal and Michigan Advertiser,* September 26, 1832.
5. *Democratic Free Press and Michigan Intelligencer,* October 25, 1832.
6. New York *American,* July 19, 1834.
7. *Detroit Journal and Michigan Advertiser,* September 10, 1834.
8. *Detroit Journal and Michigan Advertiser,* October 8, 1834.
9. *Detroit Journal and Michigan Advertiser,* October 8, 1834.

1. *Detroit Journal and Michigan Advertiser,* May 30, 1832.

EXPEDITION TO THE NORTH-WEST.—Dr. Houghton who accompanied Mr. Schoolcraft, on his expedition to the North-west last summer, is about to leave this place for Sault Ste. Marie—from which point, the expedition under the immediate direction of the latter gentleman will proceed, early in June next, on its destined tour. The party which is to proceed from Sault Ste. Marie, will consist of some thirty or forty persons. The original plan of this expedition which was in part carried into effect during the last season, is this season to be completed. By Doct. Houghton who accompanies this expedition as U. S. Surgeon and naturalist, we have been politely furnished with the following summary, which will show some of the objects, for the accomplishment of which, this expedition has been instituted, and the proposed route through the country.

The expedition will proceed north of the most northern point visited by Governor Cass in 1820—visit the most northern sources of the Mississippi—pass north of them to Red Lake, and descend its outlet to the forks of Red river of lake Winnipec. From this point the party will probably ascend Red river to the outlet of Ottertail lake, and having passed through this lake, will, by a portage, enter the river Des Corbeaux; the great south west fork of the Mississippi, which remains unexplored. From the mouth of this stream the Mississippi will be descended to the mouth of the Chippewa river (below the Falls of St. Anthony); and the latter stream will be ascended into the country of Lac du Flambeau, and the sources of the Wisconsin river.

It is mostly new ground for observation and research. It separates, very nearly, the territory of the Chippewa from that of the Crees and Assinaboines, on the north and north west; from the Sioux and Winnebagoes on the west and south west; and from the Menomonies on the south and east.

The object of the expedition upon the part of the U. S. is to effect, or rather to re-establish a peace between the Chippewa and Sioux Indians. Justice and humanity to the Indians form the basis of the measure, which is of a character purely persuasive.

2. *Detroit Journal and Michigan Advertiser,* July 18, 1832.

We have been favored with a letter from Dr. Houghton, dated at La Pointe, Lake Superior, June 21, 1832. The following extracts will interest our readers.

Dear sir,—After a somewhat tedious voyage we arrived at this place last evening, and we intend to remain here during the greater part of this day.

In passing thus far through Lake Superior, we have seen numerous small parties of Indians, from the bands resident far in the interior, and have been enabled, through time, to gain a tolerably accurate knowledge of the general state of the Indians.

From the information we have gained respecting the Chippewa Indians of the lake, I would be lead [led] to infer that they are in an uncommonly restless state. A war party, headed by the Chief White Crow, left Lac des Flambeaux several days ago, & is now descending the Chippewa river, against the Sioux Indians. As we have not learned what other bands they may have prevailed upon to join them, it is impossible to form an opinion of the probable result. It also appears that two war parties of the Sioux have proceeded against the Chippewas of Red Cedar river, this spring; but is more than probable that they have returned unsuccessful.

Difficulties of a different kind exist upon the northern shore of the Lake. During the past winter, a band of Mush-ke-gons, or mountaineers, speaking a dialect of the Chippewa language, fell upon a trading post, situated on the Nipagon river, belonging to the Hudson's Bay Fur Company, and murdered, indiscriminately, all the traders occupying the post. This induced the company to collect their forces from different posts, and to send them against the band of Indians. An action took place in which 20 traders, and 40 Indians were killed. The difficulties still remain unsettled.

An express which arrived at Michipocoten, (one of the posts of the Hudson's Bay Fur Company), brings information that the annual supply ship of the Company has been crushed by the ice, and the ship and cargo completely lost.

In accordance with instructions, the Indian Agent at the Sault Ste. Marie, Mr. Schoolcraft, made great efforts during the last season to prevent the introduction of ardent spirits into the Indian trade upon this lake, & we have reason to believe that none was taken into the lake country by American traders; but notwithstanding all this caution on the part of the Indian Agent, we regret to learn that whiskey has been taken to several of the trading posts, one or two hundred miles south of Lake Superior, and the lake traders complain that it influenced the Indians to go in that direction to exchange their furs; and in consequence of which, they are this spring in a more miserably destitute situation than usual. The whiskey was, as we are informed, taken into the country from the Mississippi river; and, in all probability, it was done without the knowledge of the Indian Agent at Prairie des Chiens, or at St. Peter's.

3. *Detroit Journal and Michigan Advertiser,* August 8, 1832.

Extract of a letter from a gentleman [Dr. Houghton?] accompanying the expedition to the North-west, dated at La Pointe, June 27.

"It gave us much pleasure, on our arrival at this island, to find the Rev. Mr. [Sherman] Hall, who came here last season as a missionary, actively engaged in his work of good. Mrs. Hall, a truly amiable and accomplished woman, may emphatically be said to have taken up the cross. She is undoubtedly the first white female who has passed thus far through Lake Superior, and she is now separated more than four hundred miles from any associate of her own sex. The Rev. Mr. Boutwell, who is to join Mr. Hall in his missionary labors, came with us from the Sault Ste. Marie, and he will still remain with the party until our return to the St. Peter's river, from which place he will cross the country to his original place of destination.

"The mission upon this island (as the island may be said to be the centre of Chippewa influence) cannot fail to exert a most powerful influence upon the whole tribe of Chippewa Indians. But as the band situated upon the island find it necessary to disperse during a great part of the year, in order to procure food, efficient means will be required to carry the measure into full effect, as it will in consequence, probably, be found necessary to adopt the children, to be educated, into the mission family. This measure, as far as means would permit, has already been adopted. In addition to this, the extreme poverty of the lake Indians, renders it impossible for them, often to furnish even suitable clothing for those children, who, under other circumstances, would attend the school, and it will probably be found of the first importance that assistance of that kind be furnished to a certain extent.

"Separated as the missionaries are from the whole civilized world and with an opportunity to communicate with it but once in a year, and particularly in this inhospitable climate, the utmost precaution is necessary to provide for actual want; and with all the precautions which can be taken they must suffer many, very many inconveniences which are wholly unknown to those who reside where the necessaries of life can be daily procured.

"A box of clothing, directed to the mission by a Society of Ladies at Lowville, N. Y. has been received, and will be productive of much good. It is to be hoped that others will follow their praiseworthy example.

"We shall probably leave here this evening, and proceed by Fond du Lac, St. Louis river, and Sandy Lake to the Mississippi river, which we hope to reach as soon as the 3d or 4th of July, and by the sources of the latter stream, we will in all probability, pass into Nelson's river."

4. *Detroit Journal and Michigan Advertiser,* September 26, 1832.

Mr. Schoolcraft arrived in our city on Saturday last, having recently returned from a tour to the north west. He describes the country visited by him as highly interesting in its geographical features.—From an interesting conversation with him, and from such notes as he has been kind enough to furnish us, we are enabled to give the annexed details. From the valuable aids which this gentleman has already given to the cause of science, we anticipate much additional light relative to the topographical and geological features of the country he has so lately explored. Assisted as he has been, by Dr. Houghton and Lieut. Allen, we have no doubt that when their joint observations are submitted to the public, they will afford a mass of information highly desirable to the lovers of science. In the mean time we give the following outline of the tour.

From the head of Lake Superior they passed, by the route of the St. Louis and Sewanne [Savanne] portage, to the Upper Mississippi. They found the waters in a fine state for ascending, being so high in some places that large tracts of prairie land were passed over in canoes, which, in the expedition of 1820, displayed intricate and circuitous channels. Several days journey were saved in this way. They reached [upper] Red Cedar or Cass Lake on the tenth of July, being eleven days earlier in the season that the light canoes of Gov. Cass, reached this Lake in 1820. The waters being favorable for tracing this stream to its source, the principal part of the party, including the detachment of fifth infantry, under command of Lt. Allen, were here encamped. Indian guides and the smallest class of Indian canoes were procured—such as would contain but one person with his bed, beside the two men who are required to navigate it.—With these they proceeded through a channel sometimes expanding into lakes, about fifty miles. Here the Mississippi has its ultimate forks. Their guide [Oza Windib] led them up the left or western branch, through a number of lakes and a stream, continually lessening in size, to the source of the fork in Usawa [Assawa] lake.—From this a portage of about six miles was made, in a north course, into La Biche or Elk Lake, the absolute source of the principal, or northwestern fork of the Mississippi. This is a pleasant sheet of clear water, of irregular shape, about seven miles long.—They named it Itasca Lake, being an elision of the expression—*veritas caput*. It has an island, upon which they landed, caused some trees to be felled, cut some canes, and hoisted the American flag; they secured the flag staff with braces, and left the flag flying. In descending, they found the stream very rapid, often compressed and narrow, then widening out into savannas. They computed the distance back to Cass Lake, about 180 miles. Courses and distances were accurately kept; and a map is in preparation which will exhibit the true character of the source of this stream. From Cass Lake they pursued a series of portages and lakes, to Leech Lake; and from the latter, another series of portages and lakes, into the head of the river De Corbeau [Crow Wing], which they followed to its junction with the Mississippi, about 240 miles above the Falls of St. Anthony. They reached St. Peters the last week in July, and returned through the rivers St. Croix and Broule [Brule], into Lake Superior.

At every Indian village councils were held with the Indians; & the objects of the Government explained. They were vaccinated under the recent act of Congress. Much statistical and geographical information has been obtained; and interesting facts respecting the natural history. The party were received with respect, and a friendly feeling manifested to the Government. No evidences of connexion with the Black Hawk party were discovered, and the political influence of the visit is believed to have been beneficial. Reports in detail, &c., will be made to the Governmert. All the party returned in health—no accident of a serious character having befallen a single individual.

5. *Democratic Free Press and Michigan Intelligencer,* October 25, 1832. [From the *Galenian* of Galena, Illinois, of August 22, 1832.]

ST. PETERS, July 25, 1832

DR. ADDISON PHILLEO.

Dear Sir—I arrived at this place yesterday, from an expedition through the Chippewa country on the sources of the Mississippi, accompanied by a detachment of troops under command of Lieut. Allen of the 5th Infantry.

A commanding influence has been exercised, in former years, over some parts of this extensive region by the Northwest Company, and, since its fall, by the Hudson's Bay Company, who oppose our traders strenuously on the lines, and supply their Clerks with highwines, to attract the Indian population to their posts. Political and commercial power go together, and the former is made subservient to the latter. Medals and flags are, I am informed, distributed by them to Indians living within the boundaries of the United States. Old prejudices are kept alive, and new ones are excited. The strife for furs merges every thing else. And, if it is not marked by the sanguinary acts, which characterised the last years of the rivalry for the fur trade, carried on among themselves, it is not less ardently, recklessly, and successfully pursued, with respect to American traders.

Many of the Chippewas on Lake Superior, and in the region of *Lac du Flambeau* still visit the British posts in Upper Canada, to procure the presents which are annually distributed there. We met a large party, in canoes, who were destined for the British post at Penetanguishine. And these men would pass Fort Brady, on their outward, and inward route.

To counteract the *political* influence thus exerted, has been among the objects of the expedition, and to keep them at peace with the government, and with *each other*. The latter, has been a task of difficulty, as the state of hostile feeling, among the Chippewas and Sioux, has acquired the inveteracy of a hereditary feud. War parties are continually trespassing upon the territorial boundaries of each other. And fresh scalps have been danced, after the Indian manner, at Red Lake, at Cass Lake, and at Leech Lake, during the time of my passing through the country. War has been the engrossing theme, and it has not been an easy task, to declare pacific maxims, and enforce them with arguments which a savage people could appreciate, while the war drum, and the scalp yell were sent forth from other parts of the premises.

We found the waters of the Mississippi in a good state for ascending, and I availed myself of this circumstance to carry into effect, the desire of visiting its actual sources,—a point which has continued to be problematical in our geography. Pike placed it at Leech Lake in 1806. Gov. Cass carried it much further north, and left it at [upper] Red Cedar Lake in 1820. But it was then ascertained that its sources were considerably north and west of that lake. I encamped the expedition (with the troops and heavy baggage) at this last named lake, and proceeded up the river in five small birch canoes, capable of containing one man and his bed, in addition to the Indian and Canadian who conducted it.

The Mississippi, above this point, expands into several lakes, the largest of which is called *Traverse* [Bemidji]. A few miles above this, it is formed by the junction of a southwest, and northwest branch. We ascended the former, through a number of lakes, to its source, in a small creek, being an inlet into a lake. From thence we made a portage of six miles, with our canoes, into *La Biche* or Ibasca [Itasca] lake,—(the latter being a derivative from *veritas caput,*) which is the true source of this celebrated stream, being at the same time its most western, and most northern head.

This lake is about seven miles long, having somewhat the shape of the letter Y [inverted]. It has clear water, and pleasant woody shores. It has a single island, upon which I landed, caused some trees to be felled, and hoisted the national flag. We left this flag flying, and proceeded down the Northwest or main fork. A descent of about 180 miles brought us back to our party at Red Cedar, or Cass Lake.

Very respectfully, dear sir,
Your friend and obedient servant.
HENRY R. SCHOOLCRAFT
U. S. Indian Agent

6. New York *American,* July 19, 1834.

REVIEW OF THE WEEK.

Narrative of an Expedition through the Upper Mississippi to the Itasca Lake, the actual source of this river: by Henry R. Schoolcraft. New York: Harpers.

Letter from the Secretary of War, transmitting Lieut. Allen's Report of his visit with H. R. Schoolcraft, to the Northwest Indians, in 1832. Washington: [Pub. Doc. 323.]

Reader, did you ever look upon the Mississippi? Not the turbid big sewer of the Southwest, with its dirty current and swampy shores—the lengthened channel of the muddy Missouri that has been so grievously mis-named!—but the broad and limpid tide, that, swollen with the pure snows of the North, comes rolling from a thousand crystal lakes, through rocky bluffs that lift their battlemented turrets like the towers of by-gone days along its waters, or lead off their grey walls so far into the prairie that miles of meadow intervene between their base and the flower-kissed current. Have you ever stood upon those frowning battlements, and looked down into the clear depths beneath you—there where a hundred green islands, like the floating gardens of Montezuma, seem dropt upon the sunny surface —or glancing from their shadowy copses, have you watched the salient points of the bold bluffs opposite assume a thousand changes as the gorgeous clouds of sunset would drift over the pearly sky above you? If so, you are to be envied for having seen one of the most beautiful rivers of the world, at a season when it wears its loveliest aspect—though, under whatever sky it may be viewed, no one will ever forget his glorious impressions when he first beheld the Upper Mississippi. And this is the stream, so grand and beautiful, whose very tide alone, did it but flow in a contrary direction, would steal one away from the vulgar haunts of men, and lure him on unconsciously into the wilderness, whose sources have been but now explored. The barbarous waters of the Nile and the Niger have had hundreds of victims; and the savage fountains of the Missouri and the Oregon have been long since tasted;—but it is only now, when the commerce of an Empire is floating upon its bosom, that we know where the Father of Rivers takes his rise.

The discovery, we do not hesitate to say, is primarily due to Mr. Secretary Cass, as the institutor of the present expedition; and next to him, the persevering Mr. Schoolcraft, and the accomplished young officer, Lieutenant James Allen, of Ohio, must divide the honor between them. Mr. Schoolcraft was, indeed, the head of the expedition; but, as we shall show hereafter, its difficulties and its dangers were more than equally shared by his military companion; while we apprehend that modesty alone, and not want of ability, has prevented Mr. A. from giving the result of his observations in a form to attract equal attention with the valuable work of Mr. Schoolcraft. Of the two accounts of the expedition, drawn up by these gentlemen, the unpretending and succinct official statement of the young officer, we do not hesitate to say, is the best written of the two; but the more ample and satisfactory publication of Mr. S. embodies a variety of information in relation to the general condition of the country, and the various Indian tribes through which the exploring party passed, that will make it sought with avidity, and will amply repay perusal. Indeed, next to Governor Cass, we can recollect no one to whom the public are more indebted for a laudable research, and industry displayed in illustrating Indian subjects, and unfolding the resources of our northern frontier, than to Mr. Schoolcraft. The former gentleman, (Governor Cass,) however, has been by no means generous in giving the results of his own observations to the public; and we could wish that some would arise, who, to the zeal of the latter, would only add as much literary, as he possesses scientific, qualification. Such we know there are, among the accomplished young officers upon our frontier posts: but—whether from want of ambition, from mistaken modesty, or from lack of leisure, we are unable to determine: they have hitherto contributed so little to the small stock of national literature, that we almost despair of their ever being stirred up to a sense of what they are capable of doing, of what they owe to themselves, to the army, and to the country. There is not a post upon the frontier, but what numbers among its officers men whose talents and cleverness would make them an acquisition to literary circles, however, exacting; and it is not to be longer borne, that, with the amplest and freshest materials among them for their exercise,

they should still be squandered in obscurity. We take the official report of
Lieutenant Allen to the Secretary of War, as a bond for his actual appearance hereafter in the court of literature, and dismiss him for the present.

The expedition of Mr. Schoolcraft, which was nominally undertaken by
virtue of an act of Congress to vaccinate the Northwestern Indians within
our territories, is the third national attempt that has been made to arrive at
the true sources of the Mississippi. Gen. Pike's being the first, and a movement in that direction by Governer Cass, with an exploring party, the
second. A ridiculous Italian, of whom a hundred laughable stories are told
on the frontier, has in the meantime most absurdly claimed, in a book published abroad, to be the true discoverer of the fountain head. Lac La Biche,
or Itasca Lake, as Mr. Schoolcraft more euphoniously calls it, has been
long known to the Indian traders, but its position has always been laid
down erroneously upon the map; and it is now found that the Mississippi
after long running to the north till it reaches a high latitude, and diffuses
itself in a hundred swamps and lakes, becomes again a distinct stream, and
taking a sudden dip to the South, hides its head at last in a lake of clear
water somewhere about the latitude of Fond du Lac, on Lake Superior.
The discovery, approach to and examination of this important geographical
point, is so interesting, that our readers will not blame us for giving here,
the impressions of both the discoverers. The limits within which Mr. Allen
was restricted, by the nature of an official report, prevented him of course
from expatiating upon the scene; but his rapid glance at its general features must not be lost, and we therefore quote his journal. [The news
article continues with a lengthy reprint of Lieutenant Allen's Journal including the section in which Schoolcraft left the military escort to return
alone on the St. Croix River.]

We do not know what excuse Mr. Schoolcraft proposes to himself for
this unaccountable and inhumane desertion which is mentioned with so
much mildness by his forgiving companion, but we do know that the rigid
observance of the Sabbath among his men, which he takes so much pains
to parade in his pages, does not weigh a feather with us when balanced
against an act so un-Christianlike: an act which, even in that country,
where life is certainly held a cheaper commodity than it is here, was regarded with indignation and dismay. The escape of Mr. Allen was almost
a miracle: for he had not only, with the most inadequate means, to contend with the well-known difficulties of his situation—but unknown wholly
to themselves—his little band were travelling through an enemy's country,
and liable to be cut off at any moment. The Sauk and Fox war had broken
out while the party were far in the wilderness, and scalps were in high request in their present neighborhood. Our view of this matter, however, will
not prevent us from doing justice to some most valuable additions to our
knowledge of Indian life in Mr. Schoolcraft's book when we again return
to it, which we propose more than once to do.

[Schoolcraft's reply appeared in the *Detroit Journal and Michigan Advertiser,* of September 10, 1834.]

7. *Detroit Journal and Michigan Advertiser,* September 10, 1834.

MICHILIMACKINAC, August 19th, 1834

SIR.—It is not without reluctance that I am induced to call the attention of your readers a few moments to a notice of my narrative of the ascent to the source of the Mississippi in 1832, which is given in the New York American of the 19th of July. Satisfied that the public should settle its measures of literary approval or disapproval in its own way, I should deem it unbecoming to offer any thing, in the nature of dissent, or extenuation, were it not to shield myself from the imputation of having injured a member of the party.

I am charged in the article referred to, with lapses of duty in regard to Lt. Allen, who accompanied me in command of the escort, and whose skill and assiduity were alone relied on, for topographical observations, delineations and maps. And I am, in consequence, visited with rebuke and reprobation. The circumstance of this officer's falling behind the party, a few days, on the home route through the St. Croix, is imputed to no other cause than an intention on my part to desert him, and leave him to pursue his way, without adequate means, and all this, as the writer asserts, while travelling "through an enemy's country and liable to be cut off at every moment."

To those who are acquainted with the geographical features of the country, it will not be necessary to say a word about its being *an enemy's country.* It is occupied exclusively by the Chippewas, who were quite friendly, received us every where with cordiality, and freely gave us every aid in their power. It is true, Mr. Allen encamped at lower points in the valley for several of the last days of our ascent of the river, but he was as safe as I was, and neither he nor myself felt any apprehension from Indian hostility. Our parting was, in its nature, accidental, and arose from the difference of the duties which devolved upon us. We had frequently been separated at other points of the route, where there was more cause for apprehension. I supposed he would come up, during the delays caused by official transactions with the several bands, and had I found any reason for apprehension among them, I should immediately have stopped and awaited his arrival, or gone back with him to St. Peters. But there was neither danger, nor thought of danger, from Indian hostility, although it was known that the Sauc war had broken out, in a skirmish between a party of militia under Major Stillman and some Indians in the northern skirts of Illinois. But the country was so far south of us, and the disturbance seemed of so local a character, that it was only conversed of, as some thing occurring at a distance. And whatever precautions might have been deemed necessary, had we determined to descend *south* to Prairie du Chien, none were required in going *eastward* into the territories of a friendly nation. Not only were the Chippewas friendly, but they were, and *are* separated from the territories of the Saucs and Foxes by a large part of the Sioux nation. The hostile Indians never came nearer than about 500 miles. But there was still a wider space between us, at the time of

our entering the St. Croix. The Black Hawk and his adherents were then
in the area between the Rock river and Wisconsin, and when this chieftain reached the banks of the Mississippi, in his flight westward on the
7th of August, it was at a point more than two hundred miles below the
mouth of the St. Croix. At that time, the last canoes of the expedition, in
command of Mr. Allen, had left the St. Croix altogether, and were, on
their *third days' march* descending the Brulé, and within a short distance
of the banks of Lake Superior.

It is unnecessary to dwell on this subject. Had there been any apprehension of danger from an Indian foe, when at St. Peters, it would have
evinced gross temerity to have proceeded on the journey without a competent escort. And if a request to this effect, had been made to Capt.
Jouett, the commanding officer at Fort Snelling, there is no doubt he
would have promptly furnished it. As a proof that there was no apprehension on his part, it may be mentioned that he, at the time of our visit, kept a
canoe, with a subaltern and a few men plying between the fort and Lake
Pepin, to intercept the illicit introduction of ardent spirits into the Indian
country. My impression is, that Lieut. Allen left one, out of two kegs of
ball-cartridge at the fort. The inference is obvious, that *he* entertained no
apprehensions, of the nature suggested. There were no fire-arms in my
party, except a couple of shot guns.

I have remarked that the separation from Mr. Allen was unpremeditated.
It arose from circumstances which could not be calculated or foreseen,
such as the points at which the Indians could be met in council, how long
a time would be necessary to assemble them, &c. After getting above the
falls of the St. Croix, I waited a number of hours for the ascent of the
military at the place called the Two Rocks. I then proceeded up the river
several leagues and encamped, and waited here the next day till evening.
Some conversation then took place in the party as to our vicinity to Snake
river, when it was considered better to proceed a few miles further that
evening, to ensure our arrival there the next morning. We supposed Mr.
Allen would certainly come up, during the council, and the delay caused
by vaccinating the Indians. I immediately, however, despatched three Indians to aid him up, and to serve as guides, for his canoes, to the head of
the river. There was no purpose of abandonment or the withdrawal of any
aid whatever. There was, however, a strong purpose, formed by the double
motives of friendship and duty, to make every arrangement to facilitate
his passage through the country, and to aid him in the execution of his
duties, as I had always done at previous stages of the journey. The Indians
of that quarter, being within my agency, were personally known to me, and
confided in. Most of them had received their medals and flags from my
hands, and all had motives of interest (if nothing beyond it,) to yield a
compliance with my requests. I had every reason, therefore, to believe
that they would faithfully give Mr. Allen and his party the aid I wished.
To put his mind at ease as to the route, I directed a map to be forwarded
to him from the Forks by the hands of an Indian, which might guide him
safely to the spot of debarkation at the head of the river. New guides were

provided for his canoes on the Brulé, and provisions deposited at several points to meet any extra demands, which the exigencies of the route might have produced. At Yellow river, at the junction of the Namakagon, and at the Fish Dam on the main fork of the St. Croix, these objects were distinctly attended to, and the Indians prepared for his arrival, and furtherance on the voyage. And again on the second day's descent of the Brulé, & at the mouth of that river where Mongazed [Mongozid] and his party faithfully remained to await him with his boat, and at Lapoint[e], where Dr. Houghton, the surgeon, was left to accompany his party down to the lake. It was not forgotten that Mr. Allen had no interpreter on the St. Croix, but as he spoke the French language, and Canadians resided in the capacity of trading clerks at the principal villages it was thought that he would be able through their instrumentality and some knowledge of the Indians existing in his party, to get along very well. The only point where doubt arose as to the route, was at the mouth of Ox [Buffalo] creek, near the source of the river, and the question was which of the branches should be taken. A reference to the manuscript map, might easily have decided this, as the *left hand* fork terminated in lake St. Croix, the actual source and point of landing. Had Ox creek been followed up, his progress would have been arrested in a very short distance by logs and obstructions peculiar to it. The whole length is not over half a day's march, but it is not navigable far. Not more than twelve hours detention could have resulted, at any rate, and such a delay was fraught with no serious consequences.

I will now direct a moment's attention to the organization of the party. This expedition was undertaken by me, not for the purpose of vaccinating the Indians, but, of tracing the Mississippi to its source. This object was connected with an effort to restore peace among the Chippewas and Sioux, and to induce them to adhere to the terms of the general treaty of peace and limits concluded with the various tribes, under the auspices of Gen. [William] Clark and Gov. Cass at Prairie du Chien in 1825. The summer of 1831 had been devoted to these objects among the bands south of St. Anthony's falls, and it was determined to go north of that point the next year, as far as we could get means to carry an exploring party. A project for this purpose was revived late in the fall, but contingent altogether upon the legislation of Congress. In addition to the ordinary appropriations of the year, applicable under the several heads of expenditure in the Indian Department, an act was passed granting a specific sum to arrest the prevalence of the small pox among the western Indians, a small part of which was assigned to the projected expedition. A surgeon and physician was engaged who was also competent to make observations in botany and geology. Mr. Allen received command of the military escort, but at so late a time, that no instruments were provided for astronomical observations. There was no sextant or quadrant to be had in the country, and whatever was done to enable him to indicate and preserve facts important in the civil or military geography of the country was the result of personal arrangements between that gentleman and myself. How well he has acquitted himself, of the task is only known to those who have examined his combined map, of which the sketch published at Washington, with his report furnishes but an imperfect conception. All the delineations, and the octavo maps in my narrative, were furnished by him, except the first, which was copied from his delineations by Dr. Houghton.

Two or three remarks may be added respecting the time applicable to this expedition. Having received instructions to effect definite objects, with a definite sum of money, the first question to be arranged was a pecuniary one. It was requisite to employ men, and order every other expense with strict reference to this result. It was therefore a question of time, as well as money. And after accomplishing all that the government actually required, the following out the Mississippi to its source, was left very much to opportunity and personal inclination. Much depended upon diligent travelling, and the state of the waters after reaching a comparatively high northern latitude. And not an hour was therefore consumed in useless delay. We were in motion, during the greater part of the time, seventeen to eighteen hours out of the twenty four, and we averaged 40 miles per day, during the whole time out, including all stops and portages and days of councilling, and of rest—which amounted to about two-sevenths of the time. We travelled slower on the St. Croix than any other part of the route, owing to the depressed state of its channel.

The area of the former explorations under Gov. Cass was passed over with rapidity. On getting to Cass lake, the waters were found in a good state for going higher. But the soldiers in command of Mr. Allen, could be pushed no farther. It was no time to stand upon points. I procured each gentleman of the party a hunting canoe and two men, and setting out early, reached *the source* the third day. The accomplishment of this end, was to me, the attainment of the great object. Our return was very rapid. We were back at Cass lake in two days. This was the principal theatre of geographical discovery. All who were with me, were actively and meritoriously engaged in the objects constituting their departments of labor and observation.

To avoid retracing our route down the Mississippi, we went over an Indian trail, from Cass to Leech lake. Finding it was practicable from that point to follow a series of portages and lakes, to Crow wing river—an unexplored main branch of the upper Mississippi, we adopted that route, and safely descended that stream to its mouth, which we reached on the 21st July. At this point my narrative closes. About 250 miles below, the Mississippi has its greatest falls, (St. Anthony's) eight or nine miles south of which is the Post of St. Peters. Here the men all enjoyed about two days rest, and the main objects of the expedition here terminated. The only object of interest now was the home route through the St. Croix, for which the requisite arrangements were made. Lieut. Allen resupplied his command, discarded all that could be considered superfluous from his baggage, and took an additional soldier. I promised to supply him with provisions on Lake Superior (which I punctually did) that he might be relieved from its transportation. He requested no further aid, nor did he indicate that he expected me to provide him gum, (an article in daily use on the voyage) or any other article essential in the management of canoes. Indeed, in my opinion, (and I think also in his) he started from fort Snelling under better auspices than I recollect to have observed at other points. His men had now been accustomed to paddling canoes, crossing portages, and the peculiar labor of ascending & descending rapids, during the season. We had passed through the only portions of the route, where danger from Indian hostilities could have been at all apprehended, namely the *line of country between Leech lake and the mouth of the Crow Wing* river and perhaps, the *trip to the source,* and also, the place of *crossing the Sioux boundary.* We were about to pass thro' a section of the Chippewa country, of a character decidedly friendly, and there were no associations connected with the accomplishment of the route, but those of an exhilarating character. It was thought, by traders, that we could accomplish the route in 7 days. The party were in reality nine. Lieut. Allen required thirteen owing to the bad quality of one of his canoes, and the impediments which he has described. It is to be observed that we did not uniformly encamp together, during any stage of the route, except at those points of it, connecting important positions, where the Indians were to be met. It was deemed sufficient to be present at those points, and at all others, to keep as much as possible within supporting distance. His absence, therefore, at the first two or three encampments on the St. Croix, was not unusual. And I attributed it to a desire to execute a perfect delineation of the river, as he had previously remarked to me, the difficulty he found in making observations either very early, or very late, on account of the obscurity at those hours. The falls and rapids were not as formidable in number and velocity, as those of the St. Louis, which he had previously mastered, and I had every reason to consider the Indian guides, which I had despatched from the first point where their services could be obtained, as competent and faithful, as I had found them at other points. I have since learned that their defection, was caused by the amount of labor the soldiers expected them to perform, and to some difficulties respecting the quantity of provisions they consumed. Mr. Allen was the disbursing officer of his command, he provided his own supplies (sometimes by request thro' me) and made his own arrangements as to encampment, mode of travelling &c. If any of these arrangements were therefore defective, I hope they are not justly chargeable to me. And if I have failed, at any point, to afford *any and every* aid, which my official relation to the party, rendered due to any integral part or member of it, it has been wholly unintentional, and is the result of wants or wishes which were unknown to me.

In the observations which I have made respecting the services and merits of Lieut. Allen, as an adjuncant in my recent tour, I have not been unmindful of the tone of his remarks in his journal. But as these remarks, first seen by me in his printed journal (and the first indication to me, of his dissatisfaction,) may have been considered by him necessarily explanatory of the cause of his delay, and as I regarded them rather as the record of first impressions, in moments of excitement under the difficulties and hardships he was obliged to encounter, than as intended to be seriously accusatory, I do not deem it proper to make them the subject of comment.

I should have been pleased if, in the relation of friendship in which we lived, and travelled and parted, he had thought proper to apprise me of the existence of feelings which the journal indicates.

On the subject of the literary criticism in the American, I have not a word to say. I am too sensible of deficiencies in these particulars, to doubt that many defects must present themselves to the reader. And I can with candour say, that the reflection and experience of later years, has impressed with a renewed sense of the indulgence extended towards me by men of cultivated and exalted minds.

In these remarks, names, dates and places have been introduced as necessary to precision. No person is designed to be injuriously referred to. Justice is meant to be rendered to each of the members of the party, who are endeared to me by many associations, and I should feel mortified, if on a review of what has been written, it is found to have been withheld, in aught, from Mr. Allen, who performed an arduous and meritorious service. So far as localities are specified, their introduction is intended for those at a distance, who must often judge of things of this nature, in the hurry of perusing a newspaper notice. But of this class of readers, it will not be deemed harsh to remark, that they are often compelled (in the imperfect state of northwestern geography) to rely on the dicta of such notices, the writers of which are apt in the truth of general and prominent conceptions, to annihilate whole areas of country, and bring together people and places the most widely separated.

Respectfully,
HENRY R. SCHOOLCRAFT

P.S. The editor of the New York American is requested to insert the above.

[A draft of this letter addressed to George L. Whitney, Editor, dated August 19, 1834 is in the Schoolcraft Papers, Library of Congress.]

8. *Detroit Journal and Michigan Advertiser,* October 8, 1834.

LAKE SUPERIOR.—The investigations made at Keweena[w] Point by Mr. Schoolcraft and Doctor Houghton on their late expedition to the sources of the Mississippi, though only superficial, warrant inferences that copper ore will be found there in such abundance as to invite and reward future exertions. The mineral associations are there all of a promising character, and the specimens brought back are rich in variety and beauty. The determination of such an important fact is highly to be estimated. It may have a mark'd influence on the coming prosperity of Lake Superior. It is known that arrangements are now in progress by the great Fur company of the north west, to extend its establishment at *La Pointe* so as greatly to enlarge the business on those waters; much of that which has been heretofore transacted on the lower Lake, at Mackinac, will hereafter be done at that more remote place. A schooner will be constructed at the

Sault St. Marie this winter, to be launched the ensuing season. Such a craft will at once open new facilities for the advancement of science as well as commerce, and we may anticipate that Lake Superior will in the course of a few years more be nearly or quite as well known as its sister Lakes below; and that its mineral wealth, its picturesque and often sublime scenery, will have other witnesses and admirers than the rare few who have the enterprize of Mr. Schoolcraft and his associates.

[This reporter showed great acumen as a prognosticator. After Houghton's extensive report in 1841 on copper deposits in the Upper Peninsula, thousands flocked into the area to mine the valuable metal. The millions of tons mined on the Keweenaw Peninsula brought prosperity to this section of Michigan.]

9. *Detroit Journal and Michigan Advertiser,* October 8, 1834.

Narrative of an Expedition through the Upper Mississippi to Itasca Lake, the actual source of this river &c. under the direction of HENRY R. SCHOOLCRAFT.

The appearance of a work so intimately connected with the vast Interior of which Detroit is one of the principal outlets, would seem to have demanded an earlier notice.—We have not, however, been as remiss in reading as in reviewing the book. Well knowing that it would form a consummation of Mr. S.' travels in the upper Mississippi region, we felt a strong desire to see it forthcoming. We felt anxious to be satisfied that the "actual source" of the Mississippi had at length been discovered. Notwithstanding our confidence in the enterprize and veracity of Mr. S. we still thought there were grounds for distrust. What had eluded the research of so many previous travellers, we feared might still elude that of Mr. S. Lt. Pike did not pretend to have drunk at the fountain of the river; but he believed, and the public likewise believed, that he had not fallen far short of that ultimatum, and had left little for subsequent enterprize to accomplish. Mr. [Giacomo] Beltrami, the demi-Munchausen Italian, was ready to make oath that he was the Bruce of the American Nile, and Gov. Cass' party (of which Mr. S. was one) of 1820, although stopping somewhat short of the initial spring, believed it had established an index, by which its successors, having more time, or more of the travelling season, before them, would be able to reach it without mistake. Had Major Douglass' map then been protracted, no doubt Lake La Biche would have been laid down fifty or sixty miles due north, or northerly, of Cass Lake, as the true source. The party of 1820 collected at that Lake such information, as led to a supposition that such was the direction of that part of the river remaining to be explored. It seemed to be taken for granted that the descent of the river must be down on the map; and that it would be contrary to hydrographic rule to look for it in a different direction. So reasoned the framers of the treaty of '83, who had no doubt the Mississippi had something like a perpendicular current due south from the 49th deg.

It is a somewhat singular coincidence, that the mouth of the Niger and the source of the Mississippi should have been determined within nearly the same period of time. Both these noble streams were struck by their first discoverers about midway, leaving enterprize to work on either hand, in order to complete the development. That of the Mississippi is now complete; while, scarcely retarded by disaster and death, that of the Niger may be expected in a few years.

The plan of this last work of Mr. S. is highly to be commended. He begins where he had previously left off, and goes over no ground which had been trod before, excepting in a few preliminary observations, which are a convenient and almost indispensable help to those who may not have the previous volume at hand, to mark the connexion between the two expeditions.

Mr. S. was accompanied in the expedition by Lt. Allen of the U. S. A. whose maps are appended to the work. These maps are all valuable improvements on our geography. They will serve to correct many gross errors, and render certain what has heretofore been only conjectural.

Mr. S. was also accompanied by Doctor Houghton, a scientific gentleman every way capable of seizing all the advantages presented by the route for investigations in the departments of botany and mineralogy. The little leasure which his professional engagements left him previous to the publication of this volume, enabled him to prepare only a mere list of the plants which were deposited in his herbarium. But we trust the public will yet be favored with the result of his investigations in both the departments of which he had the more especial charge. The mineral resources of Lake Superior had been but cursorily examined during the previous expeditions.

The necessity of a rapid passage up and down the Lake, in order to leave the major part of the season for the performance of the ulterior journey, urged the expedition along its shores with too much haste for any thing more than the most desultory observations. A like necessity rendered the examinations, in this respect, of even the last expedition only comparatively satisfactory. Enough however was seen to direct future enquiry with much advantage. The region around the celebrated "copper rock" was so far examined as to determine, with some degree of certainty, that no searches for copper ore in that vicinity afford any promise of success. Their are no traces of those rock formations which are now believed to be almost invariably found associated with this metal. Had science guided the labors of those early speculators who sunk the shaft on the Ontonagon, the result would not probably have been, as it now is, only a proof of their ignorance or folly.

We have no room for extracts, or for remarks on the literary character of the work. The appendix embraces some dissertations on the structure of the Indian languages, which will be highly appreciated by all who have engaged in that interesting study. Mr. Schoolcraft enjoys some peculiar advantages in his pursuit of it. He has daily intercourse with those who, combined with a liberal knowledge of our own language have a most thorough knowledge of some of the aboriginal languages. This is especially the case with that of the Chippewa. Under such favoring circumstances, he has traced out words and phrases in all their varieties and combinations. Those innumerable and delicate shades of meaning, dependent on certain slight changes of form and association, which could be developed only by an intelligent person, equally well versed in both tongues, are here exhibited with striking distinctness. These dissertations or lectures are only a part of the investigations which appear to have been made by Mr. S. of this subject. It is to be hoped that they will all be given to the public, as contributions to the stock of aboriginal philology which are much needed and desired. Where the basis of speculations has unavoidably been so unsubstantial and conjectural, it is important that all materials which are likely to give it solidity should be thrown in without unnecessary delay.

BIBLIOGRAPHY

PRIMARY SOURCES

Manuscripts
William L. Clements Library, University of Michigan:
  Lewis Cass Papers
Detroit Public Library, Burton Historical Collection:
  George Johnston Papers
  Henry R. Schoolcraft Papers
Library of Congress:
  Henry R. Schoolcraft Papers
Michigan Historical Collections, University of Michigan:
  Douglass Houghton Papers
  Henry R. Schoolcraft Papers
  Chase S. Osborn Papers
Michigan Historical Commission:
  Territory of Michigan Papers
Marquette County (Michigan) Historical Society:
  Henry R. Schoolcraft Papers
Minnesota Historical Society:
  Lawrence Taliaferro Papers
  William T. Boutwell Papers
The National Archives:
  Department of War Records
  Office of Indian Affairs
Sault Ste. Marie Carnegie Library:
  Johnston Family Papers
  Henry R. Schoolcraft Papers

Printed Sources
Allen, James, *Schoolcraft and Allen—Expedition to Northwest Indians*. United States *House Executive Document* No. 323, Twenty-third Congress, First Session, 1833-34.
American State Papers, Documents Legislative and Executive of the United States. Indian Affairs, Vol. II. Washington, D.C.: Gales and Seaton, 1834.
American State Papers, Documents Legislative and Executive of the United States. Military Affairs, Vols. IV and V. Washington, D.C.: Gales and Seaton, 1860.
Boutwell, William T., "Schoolcraft's Exploring Tour of 1832," *Minnesota Historical Society Collections*, Vol. I (1872), pp. 153-76.
"Calendar of American Fur Company's Papers," *Annual Report of American Historical Association for Year 1944*. Washington, D.C.: United States Government Printing Office, 1945. Three volumes.
Carter, Clarence E. (ed.), *The Territorial Papers of the United States*. Vols. X, XI, and XII. Washington, D.C.: United States Government Printing Office, 1942-45.

Eastman, Mary, *American Aboriginal Portfolio*. Philadelphia: Lippincott, Grambo & Co., 1853.

Kappler, Charles J. (ed.), *Indian Affairs: Laws and Treaties*. Washington, D.C.: United States Government Printing Office, 1904. Two volumes.

Pike, Zebulon M., *Exploratory Travels Through Western Territories of North America*. London: Paternoster-Row, 1811.

Schoolcraft, Henry R., "Expedition into Indian Country," United States *House Executive Document* No. 152, Twenty-second Congress, First Session.

———, *Historical and Statistical Information Respecting the History, Condition, and Prospects of the Indian Tribes of the United States*. Philadelphia: Lippincott, Grambo & Co., 1851-57. Six volumes.

———, "A Memoir on the History and Physical Geography of Minnesota," *Minnesota Historical Society Collections*, Vol. I (1872), pp. 108-32.

———, *Narrative of an Expedition Through the Upper Mississippi to Itasca Lake*. New York: Harper & Brothers, 1834.

———, *Personal Memoirs of a Residence of Thirty Years with the Indian Tribes on the American Frontier*. Philadelphia: Lippincott, Grambo & Co., 1851.

———, "Report on Expedition among the Northwestern Indians," United States *House Executive Document* No. 125, Twenty-second Congress, Second Session.

———, "Report on the Fur Trade," United States *Senate Document* No. 90, Twenty-second Congress, First Session.

———, "Sketches of Lake Superior: From Letters Written by Melancthon L. Woolsey to Jane Johnston Schoolcraft," *Southern Literary Messenger*, Vol. II (February, 1836), pp. 166-71.

———, *Summary Narrative of an Exploratory Expedition to the Source of the Mississippi River in 1820: Resumed and Completed by the Discovery of its Origin in Itasca Lake in 1832*. Philadelphia: Lippincott, Grambo & Co., 1855.

Newspapers
Detroit Courier, 1832
Detroit Democratic Free Press and Michigan Intelligenser, 1831-35
Detroit Journal and Michigan Advertiser, 1830-34.
New York American, 1834

Periodicals
American Journal of Science, 1830-35
American Philosophical Society, *Proceedings*, Vol. I, 1744-1838
American Philosophical Society, *Transactions*, 1830-35
Michigan History Magazine
Michigan Pioneer and Historical Collections
Minnesota History
Minnesota Historical Society Collections
Missionary Herald, 1830-1835
Wisconsin Historical Collections

SECONDARY SOURCES

Baker, James H., "Lake Superior," *Minnesota Historical Society Collections*, Vol. III (1880), pp. 333-55.

————, "The Sources of the Mississippi, Their Discoveries, Real and Pretended," *Minnesota Historical Society Collections,* Vol. VI (1894), pp. 1-28.

Bald, F. Clever, *Michigan in Four Centuries.* New York: Harper & Brothers, 1954.

Blakely, Russell, "History of the Discovery of the Mississippi River and the Advent of Commerce in Minnesota," *Minnesota Historical Society Collections,* Vol. VIII (1898), pp. 303-418.

Blegen, Theodore C., *The Land Lies Open.* Minneapolis: University of Minnesota Press, 1949.

Bradish, Alvah, *Memoir of Douglass Houghton, First State Geologist of Michigan.* Detroit: Raynor & Taylor, 1889.

Brower, Jacob V., *Itasca State Park, Minnesota Historical Collections,* Vol. XI. St. Paul: McGill Warner Co., 1904.

————, *The Mississippi River and its Source. Minnesota Historical Collections,* Vol. VII. Minneapolis: Harrison & Smith, 1893.

Brown, Ralph, *Historical Geography of the United States.* New York: Harcourt, Brace, & Co., 1948.

Chambers, Julius, *The Mississippi River and Its Wonderful Valley.* New York: G. P. Putnam's Sons, 1910.

Chittenden, Hiram M., *The American Fur Trade of the Far West.* New York: F. P. Harper, 1902.

Clapp, Alice, "George Johnston, Indian Interpreter," *Michigan History,* Vol. XXXIII (Autumn, 1939), pp. 350-66.

Davidson, John N., "Missions of Chequamegon Bay," *Wisconsin Historical Collections,* Vol. XII (1892), pp. 397-425.

Federal Writers Project of Works Progress Administration, *Minnesota.* New York: Hastings House, 1947.

Folsom, W. H. C., *Fifty Years in the Northwest.* St. Paul: Pioneer Press, 1888.

Folwell, William W., *A History of Minnesota.* St. Paul: Minnesota Historical Society, 1921. Four volumes.

Gale, Edward C., "The Legend of Lake Itasca," *Minnesota History,* Vol. XII (September, 1931), pp. 215-25.

Gilfillan, Joseph A., "The Ojibways in Minnesota," *Minnesota Historical Society Collections,* Vol. IX (April, 1901), pp. 55-128.

————, "Minnesota Geographical Names Derived from the Chippewa Language," *The Geological and Natural History Survey of Minnesota. The Fifteenth Annual Report of the State Geologist.* St. Paul: Pioneer Press, 1887, pp. 451-77.

Glazier, Willard, *Headwaters of the Mississippi.* New York: Rand, McNally Co., 1894.

Goodykoontz, Colin B., *Home Missions on the American Frontier.* Caldwell, Idaho: Caxton Printers, 1939.

Hart, Irving H., "The Origin and Meaning of the Name, 'Itasca'," *Minnesota History,* Vol. XII (September, 1931), pp. 225-29.

Hodge, Frederick W. (ed.), *Handbook of American Indians.* Smithsonian Institution, Bureau of American Ethnology, *Bulletin No. 30.* Washington, D.C.: United States Government Printing Office, 1912.

Johnson, Ida M., *The Michigan Fur Trade.* Lansing: Michigan Historical Commission, 1919.

Kohl, Johann, *Kitchi Gami.* London: Chipman & Hall, 1860.

Kuhm, Herbert W., "Indian Place Names in Wisconsin," *Wisconsin Archeologist,* Vol. XXXIII (March-June, 1952), pp. 1-157.

Neill, Edward D., *The History of Minnesota*. Philadelphia: J. B. Lippincott, 1858.

———, "History of the Ojibways, and Their Connection with Fur Traders," *Minnesota Historical Society Collections*, Vol. V (1885), pp. 395-510.

———, *History of the Upper Mississippi Valley*. Minneapolis: Minnesota Historical Commission, 1881.

———, "Memoirs of William Thurston Boutwell," Macalester College *Contributions*, Second Series, No. 1.

Nute, Grace Lee, "The American Fur Company's Fishing Enterprises on Lake Superior," *Mississippi Valley Historical Review*, Vol. XII (1926), pp. 483-503.

———, *Lake Superior*. New York: Bobbs-Merrill, 1944.

———, "Posts in the Minnesota Fur-Trading Area," *Minnesota History*, Vol. XI (December, 1930), pp. 353-86.

———, *The Voyageur*. New York: D. Appleton & Co., 1931.

———, *The Voyageur's Highway*. St. Paul: Minnesota Historical Society, 1947.

Osborn, Chase and Stellanova, *Schoolcraft—Longfellow—and Hiawatha*. Lancaster, Pa.: Jacques Cattell Press, 1943.

Quaife, Milo (ed.), *Alexander Henry's Travels and Adventures in the Years 1760-1776*. Chicago: R. R. Donnelley & Sons, 1921.

Raney, William F., *Wisconsin, A Story of Progress*. New York: Prentice-Hall, Inc., 1940.

Riggs, Stephen R., "Protestant Missions in the Northwest," *Minnesota Historical Society Collections*, Vol. VI (1894), pp. 117-88.

Rintala, Edsel K., *Douglass Houghton, Michigan's Pioneer Geologist*. Detroit: Wayne University Press, 1954.

Roddis, Louis H., *The Indian Wars of Minnesota*. Cedar Rapids, Iowa: The Torch Press, 1956.

Ross, Alexander, *Red River Settlement*. London: Smith, Elder & Co., 1856.

Ross, Hamilton N., *The Apostle Islands*. Batavia, Ill.: Batavia Herald Co., 1951.

Thwaites, Reuben G., "The Story of Chequamegon Bay," *Wisconsin Historical Collections*, Vol. XIII (1895), pp. 408-14.

Upham, Warren, *Minnesota Geographic Names*. Minnesota Historical Society *Collections*, Vol. XVII (1920).

Warren, William W., "History of Ojibways Based upon Traditions and Oral Statements," *Minnesota Historical Society Collections*, Vol. V (1885), pp. 21-395.

Williams, Mentor L., *Schoolcraft's Indian Legends from Algic Researches, the Myth of Hiawatha, Onéota, the Red Race in America, and Historical and Statistical Information Respecting . . . the Indian Tribes of the United States*. East Lansing: Michigan State University Press, 1956.

———, (ed.), *Schoolcraft's Narrative Journal of Travels . . . to the Sources of the Mississippi River in the Year 1820*. East Lansing: Michigan State University Press, 1953.

Winchell, N. H., *The Geology of Minnesota*. Vol. VI of the Final Report. St. Paul: Pioneer Press, 1901.

INDEX

Abbott, James W., 155, 187, 286
Aishkibugikozh: *see* Gueule Plat
Aissippi River: *see* Clam River
Aitken, Alfred, 99 n. 28, 155
Aitken, David, 154-55, 316, 318
Aitken, William A., 99 n. 20, 155, 190-
    192, 197-98, 231, 244, 283, 297
    complaints against, 337
    residence at Sandy Lake, 323-24, 347
    trading house of, 12
Aitken County, Minn., 99 n. 20
Akeek River: *see* Kettle River
Algic Researches, by Henry R. School-
    craft, xiv
Algic Research Society, xiii
Algonquins, 59, 60, 93
Allen, Lt. James, 23, 63, 135, 143
    biographical sketch of, xviii
    controversy with Schoolcraft, 104 n.
        87, 219-21, 234 n. 28, 235-36, 352,
        360, 361-66
    journal of expedition, 164-235
    letter to Alexander Macomb, 236-41
    map of expedition, 100 n. 30, 150,
        163, 206, 234 n. 26
    orders from War Dept., xviii
    records kept by, 37
    report of expedition, 235-66, 358-60
    views on missionary work, 97 n. 17
Allen Lake: *see* Third Lake
Allen's Bay, 46, 101 n. 54, 328
    named by Schoolcraft, xxvi
Allouez, Fr. Claude, 233 n. 15, 346 n. 8
Allouez Bay, 189
American Board of Foreign Missions,
    xvii, xix, xxvii, 9, 131, 133, 135-36,
    137, 185
American Fur Company, xx, xxv, 100 n.
    32 and 35, 104 n. 83, 346 n. 12
    established, 22
    facts respecting fur trade, 154-57
    fisheries of, 161 n. F, 165-67, 232 n. 3
    posts of, 99 n. 20, 173-74, 182, 184-85,
        190-92, 197-98, 200, 204, 209-10,
        214, 218, 233 n. 18, 247-48, 259,
        264, 267, 270, 273, 309, 316, 329,
        337-38, 340, 345 n. 2, 346 n. 8, 352
    value of trade in 1832, 191

American Philosophical Society, 151
Andrus Creek: *see* La Salle River
Andrusia Lake, Minn., xxvi, 28, 100 n. 37
Apostle Island, 115, 184, 187
Apple River, Wis., 341
Arkansas River, 38
Ashman, Samuel, 155, 166, 167
Assawa Lake, 33, 100 n. 46, 204
Astor, John Jacob, 22, 232 n. 3
Athabasca fur post, 57, 102 n. 65
Atkinson, Gen. Henry, 80
Au Sable River, Mich., 156-57, 160
Au Train Bay (Lake Superior), 309
Au Train Island (Lake Superior), 170
Au Train River, Mich., 170
Ayer, Rev. Frederick, xix, xxvii, 98 n.
    14 and 16, 99 n. 20, 314

Babisikundadi, 74
Bad River, Wis., 87, 115, 183, 314
    description of travel on, 6
    fur trade on, 154-55
    Indian village on, 158
Bailey, Alexis, 340
Baker, Benjamin F., 155, 336-38
    trading post of, 74, 103 n. 78, 214-15,
        264-65
Balize, La., 37
Ball Club Lake (Bogottowa, Lac La
    Cross), 99 n. 26, 200, 252, 326-27
    description of, 18-19
    origin of name, 347 n. 18
Balsam of Fur Lake: *see* Sapin Lake
Baraga, Fr. Frederic, 233 n. 15
Bart, Lavoire, 149
Bartlett, George, 155
Basswood Island (Lake Superior), 233 n.
    16, 346 n. 9
Bathune, Angus, 282, 284, 287, 289
Bay de Noc, 156-57, 160
Bayfield, Lt. Henry W., 315, 346 n. 10
Bayfield, Wis., 346 n. 10
Bear Island (Leech Lake), 49, 154-55,
    159
Beaudoin, Joseph, 197, 247, 323
Beaulieu, Bazile or Paul, 310
"Beaver Island": *see* Manitou Island
Beemis, Private, 143, 234 n. 20

375

Ox (Buffalo) River, Wis., 89, 223, 276, 342, 363
Oza Windib (Yellow Head), xxii, 32, 33, 34, 41, 45, 191
 as leader of expedition to Itasca, 25
 presents given to, 46, 258, 326, 332
 speech of, 206-207
 village of, on Star Island, 20-21
Ozhaw-Guscoday-Wayquay, xiii, 103 n. 70

Pacific Ocean, xi
Painted Rock, Minn., 148
Painted Rock Falls: see Little Falls
Pami-tascodiac: see Wolf Lake
Pamitchi Gumaug Lake: see Bemidji
Parallel River, Minn., 215
Paul, Mrs. Carroll, 232 n. 5
Peace Rock, xxvii
Pecatonica River, Wis., 7
Pembina, N. Dak., 27, 101 n. 55, 152
 fur trade at, 154-55
 Indian village at, 18, 159
 population of, 161 n. S
Pemidjegumaug: see Bemidji
Penetanguishine, Ontario, 22, 149
Pepin Lake, Minn., 37, 117, 147
Perault, Jean B., 12-16, 57, 99 n. 21, 102 n. 67
Perch Lake, Minn.: see Assawa Lake
Peskinanib, 324
Petit Corbeau: see Little Crow
Petite Peche Bay (Lake Superior), 161 n. H
Pic, fur post at, 57, 102 n. 66
Picquette, Joseph, xx
Picquette, Louis, xx
Pictured Rocks, 168-69, 231, 232 n. 4, 285-86, 309
 fur trade at, 154-55
 Indian village at, 158
Pike, Lt. Zebulon M., xii, 22, 46, 54, 56, 216
 accounts of, 97 n. 1 and 2
 exploration of Mississippi River, xi-xii, 3
Pike's Bay (Cass Lake), 47
Pike's Blockhouse, at Little Falls, 215, 234 n. 23
Pillagers (Leech Lake Chippewas), xxvii, 15, 49, 51-62, 71
 fur trade of, 57
 fur traders, hostility toward, 333, 337
 missionaries, attitude toward, 349
 origin of name, 57-58, 101 n. 58, 210, 301-302
 presents given to, 54

Pillagers—Continued
 Sioux, hostilities with, 49-50
 war party of, 18, 26
Pine Bend (Sioux village), 234 n. 26
Pine Lake, Minn., 67
Pine River, Minn., 12, 15, 17, 154-55, 159
Piniddiwin River: see Little Mississippi River
Pizhickee (Chi Waishki or The Buffalo), 11, 12, 85, 98 n. 18, 118-19, 227, 273, 314
Place of the Hip Bone: see Pokonokuning
Plaie Lake, Minn., 34
Plantagenette Lake (Kubbakunna or The Rest in the Path), 204, 254, 329
 description of, 29, 31
 named by Schoolcraft, xxvi
 origin of name, 100 n. 45
Plant life, 26, 199-200
 collected by Houghton, 305
 of Lake Superior, 179
 of St. Louis River Valley, 245
 of Upper Mississippi River, 255, 348-49
Plover Portage, Wis., 116, 156-57, 160
Point Abbaye, 172
Point aux Chenes, Minn., 17, 99 n. 24, 199, 326, 346-47 n. 17
Point aux Pins, Ontario, 164, 308
Point des Chiens, Mich., 308
Point du Froid (Madeline Island), 315
Point Iroquois, 10, 165, 286, 289
Point Maline, Mich., 309
Point Prescott, Minn., battle at, xiv
Pokegama Falls, Minn., 38, 99 n. 23, 199
 Cass expedition at, 4
 description of, 325, 349
 fur trade at, 154-55
 Indian village at, 159
Pokegama Lake, Minn., xxvii, 85, 273
Pokegama River, Minn., 199
Pokonokuning (Place of the Hip Bone), 86, 120, 342
Polyganum Lake, Wis., 115
Pontiac's War, 22
Popinoshees, 59
Porcupine Mountains, 181-83, 279-80, 312
Portage, Wis., 7
Portage à Couteaux: see Knife Portage
Portage des Rats, 27
Portage Lake, Mich., 173
Portage River, Mich., 173-74
Porter, Gov. George B., 129, 147
Porter, Rev. Jeremiah, 133, 134
Post Lake, Wis., 156-57, 160

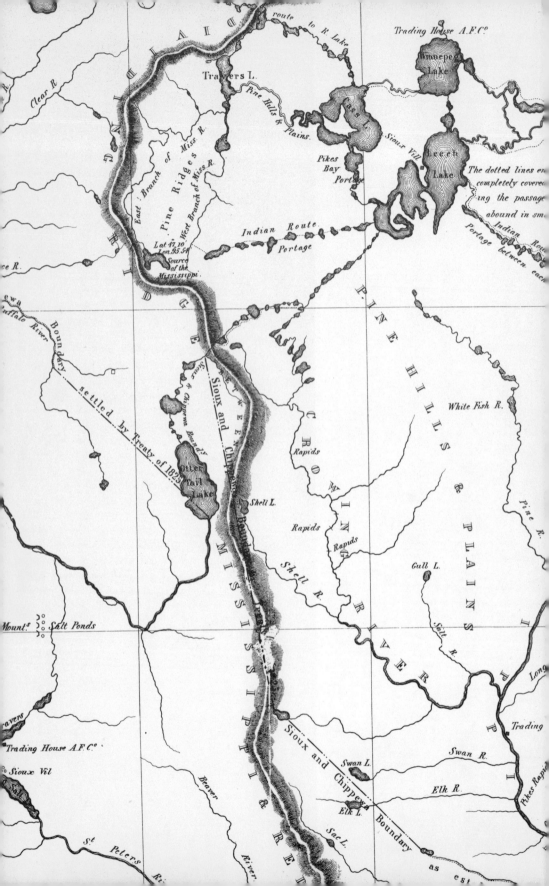

route to R. Lake

Trading House A.F.Cº

Winnepec Lake

Travers L.

Pine Hills & Plains

East Branch of Miss. R.

Pine Ridges

West Branch of Miss. R.

Clear R.

Pikes Bay Portage

Sioux Vill

Leech Lake

The dotted lines en
completely covere
ing the passage
abound in sm

Indian Route. Portage

Lat 47.10
Lon 95.54

Source of the Mississippi.

Indian Route

Portage between each

ce R.

PINE HILLS & PLAINS

Buffalo River

Boundary

settled by Treaty of 1825

Sioux and Chippewa Boundry

Sioux and Chippewa Boundary

White Fish R.

Pine R.

Rapids

CROW WING RIVER

Otter Tail Lake

Shell L.

Rapids

Rapids

Gull L.

BETWEEN

Shell R.

Mounts Salt Ponds

Salt R.

MISSISSIPPI & RET

Travers

Trading House A.F.Cº

Sioux Vil

Beaver

Sioux and Chippewa Boundary

Swan L.

Swan R.

Trading

Elk R.

Elk L.

Long

Pikes Rapi

Sac L.

St. Peters R.

River